Generative AI Implications for Special Education:

Learning, Teaching, and Professional Development

Assimina Tsibidaki
https://orcid.org/0000-0001-6430-2436
University of the Aegean, Greece

Apostolos Kostas
https://orcid.org/0000-0002-1567-2649
University of the Aegean, Greece

Charalampos Politis
Independent Researcher, UK

Michail Terezakis
University of Patras, Greece

IGI Global
Scientific Publishing
Publishing Tomorrow's Research Today

Vice President of Editorial Melissa Wagner
Director of Acquisitions Mikaela Felty
Director of Book Development Jocelynn Hessler
Production Manager Mike Brehm
Cover Design Jose Rosado

Published in the United States of America by
IGI Global Scientific Publishing
701 East Chocolate Avenue
Hershey, PA, 17033, USA
Tel: 717-533-8845 | Fax: 717-533-7115
Website: https://www.igi-global.com E-mail: cust@igi-global.com

Library of Congress Cataloging-in-Publication Data

LCCN: 2026024589 (CIP Data Pending)
ISBN13: 979-8-3373-9169-4
Isbn13Softcover: 979-8-3373-9170-0
EISBN13: 979-8-3373-9171-7
British Cataloguing in Publication Data
A Cataloguing in Publication record for this book is available from the British Library.

Table of Contents

Detailed Table of Contents

While considering the use of artificial intelligence (AI) to help students with specific learning difficulties in primary education, this chapter further discusses the various forms of SLDs, such as dyslexia, dyscalculia and dysgraphia, the evolution of AI from assistive technology to machine learning-based adaptive systems and finally, to recent generative AI (GenAI) tools. The narrative literature review in this chapter examines how advancements in technology have influenced teaching methodologies, the role of teachers and how students experience learning. This chapter also places emphasis on AI's impact on accessibility, customisation, and changes to instructional methods. Other ethical concerns regarding AI are discussed, such as privacy of data, bias and fairness of access. A structure for understanding the opportunities and barriers associated with the implementation of AI into inclusive primary education has been developed through the idea of AI as a means for educational change.

Assessment of students with Special Educational Needs and Disabilities (SEND) remains one of the most challenging aspects of inclusive education, as traditional tools often fail to capture diverse learning trajectories. The emergence of Generative Artificial Intelligence (Gen-AI) tools such as ChatGPT and Claude offers unprecedented opportunities to support educators in designing differentiated assessment instruments. This chapter addresses this gap by presenting findings from a quasi-experimental study conducted in Greece, comparing rubrics created with Gen-AI assistance versus rubrics created through conventional means, focusing on accommodations for students with SEND. Findings inform professional development and contribute evidence-based recommendations for responsible Gen-AI integration in special education assessment.

This systematic literature review examines arts-based interventions supported by Artificial Intelligence (AI) for skill development in students with Special Educational Needs and/or Disabilities (SEND). The review focuses on English-language studies published between January 2020 and April 2025 and indexed in Scopus. Thirty-seven studies met the inclusion criteria, while eight incorporated arts-based elements, mainly creative writing, storytelling, visual arts, music, theater, and dance. The findings indicate growing research activity after 2022, with most interventions focusing on primary education and students with autism spectrum disorder. Literature-based practices, especially creative writing and storytelling, were the most frequent arts-based forms. Most studies reported improvements in social, communication, learning-related, cognitive, emotional, and creative skills. The review identifies the need for stronger integration of arts-based pedagogy, broader SEND representation, and greater attention to ethical, accessibility, and pedagogical issues.

Generative Artificial Intelligence (Gen-AI) raises important questions for special education and inclusive schooling. This study explores the views of ten Greek primary-level special education teachers on its potential, challenges, and ethical implications. Using semi-structured interviews and thematic analysis, the findings show that teachers viewed Gen-AI as a supportive tool for personalized learning, differentiated instruction, accessible multimodal materials, communication, and emotional regulation. However, they emphasized the need for professional oversight, data privacy, cultural sensitivity, content accuracy, and safeguards against over-reliance. Overall, Gen-AI was framed as a tool that can support, but not replace, teacher expertise within human-centered and ethically grounded pedagogy.

The chapter proposes a transmedia and AI-supported framework for inclusive and special education, grounded in the pedagogical narrative of activities of daily living, with emphasis on the morning routine. Addressing the fragmentation of educational technologies in special education, learning is conceptualized as a "never ending" transmedia ecosystem in which a stable instructional narrative is preserved while its representation evolves across tactile, visual, immersive, auditory, and AI-supported modalities. The framework builds on the WUIM project, a multisensory learning environment informed by inclusive design principles. Within this context, SuDoCapp is presented as a student designed, early stage proof-of-concept rather than a deployed assistive application. Its contribution lies in collaborative design and the use of LLM simulated stakeholder personas for preliminary, low risk evaluation. Overall, the chapter positions Generative AI as a human supervised methodological layer supporting ethical design and teacher professional development in inclusive education.

This chapter examines how Generative Artificial Intelligence (Gen-AI) is reshaping teaching practices and professional development in special education. Drawing on current literature in inclusive education, educational technology, and professional learning, the chapter argues that Gen-AI integration should be understood as a process of pedagogical reframing rather than mere technological adoption. Five interconnected themes are addressed: the complexity of professional identity in special education; the affordances and risks of Gen-AI for instructional practice; competency frameworks for professional development; ethical, legal, and safeguarding responsibilities; and institutional conditions for responsible AI adoption. The chapter

Preface

INTRODUCTION

The rapid evolution of Generative Artificial Intelligence (Gen-AI) has begun to reshape educational landscapes across the globe, creating unprecedented opportunities to enhance teaching, learning, assessment, and professional practice. While much of the existing discourse has focused on mainstream educational settings, considerably less attention has been devoted to understanding how these emerging technologies can support learners with Special Educational Needs and Disabilities (SEND). As educational systems continue to embrace digital transformation, it has become increasingly important to critically examine how Gen-AI can be implemented in ways that promote accessibility, equity, inclusion, and meaningful learning for all students.

Generative AI Implications for Special Education: Learning, Teaching, and Professional Development brings together an international collection of scholars and practitioners who examine the multifaceted relationship between Gen-AI and special education. The contributors explore not only the technological capabilities of Gen-AI, but also the pedagogical, ethical, legal, and professional considerations that accompany its integration into inclusive educational environments. Collectively, the chapters move beyond viewing artificial intelligence simply as an innovative tool and instead consider how it can be thoughtfully incorporated into educational practice while maintaining a strong commitment to learner-centered, equitable, and ethically responsible education.

The volume recognizes that learners with SEND possess diverse strengths, needs, and learning profiles that require carefully designed educational approaches. Generative AI offers significant potential to personalize instruction, increase accessibility, facilitate communication, support differentiated learning, and empower educators with new instructional resources. However, these opportunities are accompanied by important challenges related to bias, data privacy, transparency, accountability, accessibility standards, safeguarding, and the evolving role of teachers. Addressing these issues requires interdisciplinary collaboration and evidence-based research that balances technological innovation with sound educational principles.

Throughout this book, readers will encounter a broad range of theoretical perspectives, empirical investigations, conceptual analyses, and practical applications that illuminate the evolving role of Gen-AI in special and inclusive education. The chapters examine how artificial intelligence can enhance learning participation, improve instructional practices, support teacher preparation and professional development, and contribute to more inclusive educational systems. Equally important, contributors critically examine the ethical and policy implications surrounding AI adoption, encouraging readers to engage thoughtfully with both the opportunities and limitations presented by these rapidly developing technologies.

A central objective of this volume is to bridge the gap between research, educational policy, and classroom practice. As governments, institutions, and schools increasingly develop digital education strategies, there is an urgent need for scholarship that informs responsible decision-making and supports educators in implementing AI technologies effectively. By integrating perspectives from educational technology, special education, learning sciences, teacher education, and related disciplines, this collection provides a comprehensive understanding of the complex issues surrounding Gen-AI in special education.

This reference work is intended to serve a broad and interdisciplinary audience. Researchers and academics in special education, inclusive education, educational technology, and learning sciences will find current scholarship that advances ongoing research in the field. Teacher educators, school leaders, psychologists, and practicing teachers will discover practical insights to support instructional innovation and professional growth. Graduate students, policymakers, educational organizations, parents, caregivers, and advocates for learners with SEND will also benefit from the evidence-based discussions presented throughout the volume as they seek to better understand the responsible integration of Gen-AI into educational settings.

As editors, we extend our sincere appreciation to the distinguished authors whose scholarship, expertise, and commitment made this volume possible. Their contributions reflect the diversity of perspectives necessary to advance meaningful conversations about the future of special and inclusive education in an era of rapidly evolving artificial intelligence. We also thank the reviewers for their thoughtful evaluations and constructive feedback, which strengthened the quality and rigor of each chapter. Finally, we express our gratitude to the publishing team for their guidance and support throughout the development of this volume.

It is our hope that this book will inspire continued research, informed dialogue, and innovative practice that harnesses the potential of Generative AI while safeguarding the values of inclusion, equity, accessibility, and educational excellence.

By fostering critical reflection and interdisciplinary collaboration, this volume seeks to contribute to a future in which artificial intelligence serves as a responsible and empowering resource for learners with SEND, educators, and educational communities worldwide.

ORGANIZATION OF THE BOOK

The chapters included in this volume collectively present a comprehensive examination of the opportunities, challenges, and future directions associated with the integration of Generative Artificial Intelligence (Gen-AI) in special and inclusive education. Together, they explore how emerging AI technologies can enhance learning, transform teaching practices, strengthen professional development, and support more equitable educational systems while maintaining a strong commitment to ethical and pedagogical responsibility.

The volume opens with a systematic mapping of contemporary research on Gen-AI in special education, providing readers with a broad overview of developments between 2023 and 2026. This foundational chapter identifies how Gen-AI is being used to support learners with Special Educational Needs and Disabilities (SEND), examines its influence on teaching practice and educator professional development, and highlights significant research gaps that inform future scholarly inquiry and educational policy.

Building upon this foundation, the second chapter explores the pedagogical applications of Gen-AI within inclusive education, demonstrating how intelligent technologies can facilitate personalized learning, differentiated instruction, communication, and accessibility for learners with diverse educational needs. The discussion is balanced by a critical examination of ethical concerns, including algorithmic bias, data privacy, accessibility inequalities, and the growing importance of AI literacy and teacher preparation.

Expanding the pedagogical perspective, the third chapter examines Gen-AI as an enabler of personalized and inclusive learning through the lenses of inclusive pedagogy, Universal Design for Learning, and human-AI interaction. Particular attention is given to the evolving roles of teachers and special educators, emphasizing that successful implementation depends upon context-sensitive instructional practices supported by strong ethical frameworks and professional expertise.

The fourth chapter introduces a rights-based conceptual architecture for integrating Gen-AI into special and inclusive classrooms. Rather than viewing technological innovation as an end in itself, the authors advocate for pedagogical, governance, equity, and care-centered principles that position accessibility, disability justice, safeguarding, and teacher leadership as essential foundations for responsible AI implementation.

Recognizing that educational technologies are shaped by those who design them, the fifth chapter investigates how engineers and AI developers conceptualize Gen-AI systems for students with SEND. Drawing upon expert interviews, the chapter highlights accessibility-first design, explainability, multimodal interaction, privacy-preserving infrastructures, and collaborative partnerships among educators, developers, families, and learners as essential components of effective educational technologies.

The sixth chapter examines AI within the context of inclusive education in contemporary Greek schools, offering a balanced discussion of both its educational potential and its ethical complexities. The chapter emphasizes that the value of AI lies not in technological advancement alone, but in pedagogically informed implementation guided by equity, transparency, social justice, and critical teacher mediation.

Continuing the discussion of educational practice, the seventh chapter traces the evolution of AI from traditional assistive technologies to adaptive learning systems and modern Generative AI applications designed to support students with specific learning disorders in primary education. The chapter explores changing instructional practices while addressing issues of accessibility, personalization, privacy, fairness, and educational transformation.

Assessment practices are the focus of the eighth chapter, which presents a comparative study of teacher-developed and AI-assisted assessment rubrics for learners with SEND. Through empirical investigation, the chapter demonstrates how Gen-AI can support the development of differentiated assessment tools while offering evidence-based recommendations for responsible implementation and teacher professional development.

Broadening the discussion beyond traditional instructional methods, the ninth chapter examines AI-supported arts-based interventions for skill development among learners with SEND through a systematic review of recent literature. The findings illustrate how creative writing, storytelling, visual arts, music, theater, and dance can enhance cognitive, social, emotional, and communication skills while identifying important opportunities for further interdisciplinary research and ethical practice.

The tenth chapter shifts attention to the perspectives of practicing special education teachers, presenting qualitative insights into how educators perceive the benefits and limitations of Gen-AI in their daily work. The findings underscore the value of AI for personalization, communication, accessibility, and emotional support while reaffirming the irreplaceable role of teachers in ensuring ethical oversight, cultural responsiveness, and sound pedagogical decision-making.

Innovation in instructional design is further explored in the eleventh chapter through the presentation of a transmedia and AI-supported framework for inclusive education. By combining multisensory learning environments, collaborative design, and large language model-supported development processes, the chapter illustrates how human-centered design principles can strengthen teacher professional development and support inclusive educational experiences.

The volume concludes by examining how Gen-AI is reshaping professional identity and professional learning within special education. The final chapter argues that successful AI adoption requires far more than technological competence; it demands sustained professional development, ethical awareness, institutional support, and a continued commitment to human-centered educational practice that prioritizes the needs of learners with SEND.

Taken together, these chapters provide a balanced, interdisciplinary, and forward-looking examination of Generative AI in special education. They demonstrate that while AI technologies hold significant promise for advancing accessibility, personalization, and educational inclusion, their successful implementation ultimately depends upon thoughtful pedagogy, ethical governance, collaborative design, and the continued expertise of educators. As a whole, this volume offers researchers, practitioners, policymakers, and teacher educators a valuable resource for understanding both the transformative potential and the responsible application of Generative AI in special and inclusive educational environments.

CONCLUDING REMARKS

The emergence of Generative Artificial Intelligence represents one of the most significant developments in contemporary education, offering new possibilities to reimagine how teaching, learning, and professional practice can better serve diverse learners. Within special and inclusive education, however, the adoption of these technologies requires thoughtful consideration that extends beyond technological innovation alone. As the chapters in this volume consistently demonstrate, the true value of Gen-AI lies not simply in its capacity to automate tasks or generate content, but in its ability to support equitable participation, enhance accessibility, strengthen personalized learning, and empower educators to meet the diverse needs of learners with Special Educational Needs and Disabilities (SEND).

Throughout this volume, contributors have explored the intersection of artificial intelligence, pedagogy, ethics, policy, accessibility, and professional learning from multiple disciplinary perspectives. Together, these chapters provide a balanced understanding of both the transformative opportunities and the complex responsibilities that accompany the integration of Gen-AI into special and inclusive education. While technological advances continue to evolve at an unprecedented pace, the collective scholarship presented here reinforces a consistent message: educational decisions must remain grounded in sound pedagogy, human expertise, ethical integrity, and an unwavering commitment to inclusion.

Several recurring themes emerge across the volume. The importance of teacher agency, interdisciplinary collaboration, accessibility-first design, responsible governance, and ongoing professional development serves as a reminder that successful AI implementation depends on people as much as technology. Equally evident is the need to ensure that innovations do not unintentionally reinforce existing educational inequities or create new barriers for vulnerable learners. Responsible implementation requires transparency, accountability, thoughtful policy development, and sustained collaboration among educators, researchers, developers, families, and policymakers.

As research on Generative AI continues to mature, many important questions remain unanswered. Future investigations will be needed to evaluate long-term educational outcomes, examine emerging technologies across diverse educational contexts, develop robust ethical frameworks, and identify effective models for teacher preparation and institutional implementation. We hope that the scholarship presented in this volume will encourage continued interdisciplinary dialogue and inspire future research that advances both technological innovation and educational equity.

As editors, we are grateful to the contributors whose expertise and scholarly dedication have made this volume possible. Their work reflects the growing international commitment to understanding how Generative AI can be leveraged responsibly to improve educational opportunities for learners with SEND. We also extend our appreciation to the reviewers and publishing team whose careful guidance and support have ensured the quality and rigor of this collection.

It is our sincere hope that this book serves as both a scholarly reference and a catalyst for continued reflection, collaboration, and innovation. Whether readers are researchers, teacher educators, practitioners, school leaders, policymakers, graduate students, or advocates for inclusive education, we trust that the perspectives presented throughout this volume will contribute to informed decision-making and inspire the responsible integration of Generative AI into educational practice. By placing learners, educators, and ethical responsibility at the center of technological advancement, we can collectively work toward more inclusive, accessible, and equitable educational futures for all.

Chapter 1
Mapping the Use of Generative Artificial Intelligence in Special Education:
Implications for Learning, Teaching, and Professional Development

Christina Krystamtsi
http://orcid.org/0009-0000-1597-3778
University of the Aegean, Greece

Theoxaris Anastasiadis
http://orcid.org/0009-0001-4449-4984
Ionian University, Greece

ABSTRACT

This chapter systematically maps the use of Generative Artificial Intelligence in Special Education, responding to the question of how and to what extent this technology can support students with disabilities or special educational needs, their teachers and their professional development. Following the methodology of the PRISMA-ScR field review, the international literature of the period 2023–2026 is analyzed around three axes: GenAI applications in learning, the transformation of teaching practice and the implications for professional development. The findings

DOI: 10.4018/979-8-3373-9169-4.ch001

highlight significant potential for personalization and accessibility, while also documenting critical challenges and knowledge gaps that shape specific priorities for future research and education policy.

INTRODUCTION

Artificial intelligence (AI) has emerged as a major technological development influencing education, research, and professional practice. In education, AI applications have evolved from intelligent tutoring systems to advanced machine learning models that support personalized learning and instructional decision-making (Oyebode et al., 2023).

More recently, Generative Artificial Intelligence (GenAI) has expanded the capabilities of AI by enabling the generation of text, images, audio, and other multimodal content through natural language interaction (Bommasani et al., 2021). These capabilities have accelerated its adoption across educational settings (Weng & Fu, 2025).

In Special Education, GenAI has attracted growing interest because of its potential to support accessibility, participation, and individualized learning for students with disabilities and special educational needs (SEN) (Kusumaningsih et al., 2026; Lan et al., 2025). Its capabilities appear particularly compatible with Universal Design for Learning (UDL) principles and inclusive educational practices (Evmenova et al., 2024).

Despite its potential benefits, GenAI raises important concerns regarding reliability, bias, privacy, accessibility, and overreliance on AI-generated outputs, particularly in Special Education contexts where individualized support remains essential (Bouguettaya et al., 2025; Alqarni, 2026; Alsahli et al., 2025).

Against this background, a systematic examination of the emerging evidence on GenAI in Special Education is needed. The present chapter aims to map current research on the use of GenAI in Special Education and to examine its reported applications, benefits, challenges, and implications for educational practice. Particular attention is given to the ways in which GenAI may support learners with disabilities and SEN, influence the role of special education teachers, and shape future directions for professional development and research.

Before presenting the review methodology and findings, the following sections introduce the key theoretical concepts that underpin the study.

Artificial Intelligence in Education: From Intelligent Tutoring Systems to Generative Artificial Intelligence

AI has been defined as the scientific field concerned with the development of computational systems capable of performing cognitive functions traditionally associated with human intelligence, including learning, reasoning, decision-making, and adaptation to changing conditions (Chen et al., 2020). In educational contexts, AI seeks to support and enhance teaching and learning processes by enabling systems to analyse information, respond to learner needs, and assist educational decision-making.

Early educational AI applications included intelligent tutoring systems, learning analytics, recommendation systems, and adaptive learning technologies designed to personalize instruction and support educational decision-making (Holmes et al., 2019; Holmes & Tuomi, 2022). These technologies primarily focused on analysing learner data, identifying patterns, and adapting instructional pathways to individual needs (Barua et al., 2022). At the same time, AI has increasingly been viewed as a means of reducing teachers' administrative workload and supporting instructional planning (Lin et al., 2026; Marino et al., 2023).

The recent emergence of GenAI represents a significant shift in the development of AI technologies. Unlike traditional or rule-based AI systems, which operate within predefined structures and primarily analyse, classify, or predict information (Ertel, 2017), GenAI systems can generate novel content in response to user prompts. Through large-scale neural networks trained on extensive datasets, these systems are capable of producing text, images, audio, video, and other multimodal outputs while engaging in natural language interaction (Bommasani et al., 2021). Consequently, the role of AI in education is expanding from information processing and decision support to content creation, communication, and collaborative learning.

Recent advances in large language models (LLMs) have enabled the generation of personalized learning materials, adaptive activities, accessible content formats, and immediate feedback tailored to learner needs (Ewoldt & Flanagan, 2025).

As a result, LLMs are increasingly being conceptualized as collaborative learning partners that can support both students and educators throughout the learning process (Ewoldt & Flanagan, 2025; Weng & Fu, 2025). Their interactive and adaptive nature may contribute to increased learner engagement, goal attainment, self-regulation, and motivation while reducing frustration associated with learning barriers (Triantafyllou et al., 2025).

Nevertheless, the growing presence of GenAI in education raises important pedagogical and ethical questions. The central challenge is no longer simply understanding how these technologies function, but rather developing the critical capacity to determine when, how, and under what conditions they should be integrated into educational practice to support meaningful and equitable learning outcomes.

Special Education, Inclusive Education, and Universal Design for Learning

Special Education aims to provide individualized support and equitable learning opportunities for students with disabilities and SEN. According to Greek Law 3699/2008, it encompasses educational services that promote equal access, participation, and independent living (Hellenic Republic, 2008).

Over the past decades, educational policy and practice have gradually moved away from the traditional medical model of disability, which primarily viewed disability as an individual deficit requiring remediation. Contemporary approaches have shifted from the medical model of disability toward the social model, emphasizing the removal of environmental and educational barriers and the adaptation of schools to learner diversity (Tsimpidaki, 2013).

The 50th anniversary of IDEA in 2025 further highlights the continuing international commitment to reducing educational barriers and promoting equitable learning opportunities for all students (Turner, 2025). Nevertheless, despite significant policy advances, challenges remain regarding the effective implementation of inclusive practices in everyday educational settings.

Given these considerations, UDL has emerged as one of the most influential frameworks for the development of inclusive learning environments. UDL proposes that effective instruction should provide multiple means of representation, engagement, and action/expression in order to accommodate learner variability (CAST, 2024). The capabilities of GenAI appear highly compatible with these principles. By adapting content to different levels of complexity, generating materials in multiple formats, and providing personalized feedback in real time, GenAI can support more flexible and accessible learning experiences. Consequently, GenAI may function not only as an assistive technology but also as a practical mechanism for implementing UDL principles in educational settings (Evmenova et al., 2024).

Research Gaps

Given the rapid emergence of GenAI in educational settings, a systematic mapping of the existing evidence is both timely and necessary. Although the body of literature is expanding rapidly, research remains fragmented across educational contexts, disability categories, and technological applications. Consequently, there is a need to synthesize current knowledge in order to identify prevailing trends, research gaps, and future directions before a sufficiently mature evidence base becomes available for large-scale systematic reviews and meta-analyses.

Existing reviews have primarily examined GenAI from a broader educational perspective. For example, recent reviews have explored the overall role of GenAI in education (Bouguettaya et al., 2025) and its applications across teaching and learning practices (Xiaoyu et al., 2025). While these studies provide valuable insights into the educational potential of GenAI, they devote limited attention to the specific needs, opportunities, and challenges associated with Special Education.

Similarly, the relatively small number of reviews focusing on Special Education tend to examine specific educational objectives rather than providing a comprehensive overview of the field. For instance, Li and Samah (2025) focused on the contribution of GenAI to inclusive education and the support of neurodiverse learners, whereas Weng and Fu (2025) examined the role of GenAI in language education and its potential to facilitate inclusion for students with SEN. Although these contributions are important, they address particular aspects of GenAI use and do not provide a broader synthesis of the applications, benefits, challenges, and professional implications associated with GenAI across Special Education contexts.

Therefore, a significant gap remains in the literature regarding the systematic mapping of how GenAI is currently being used across disability categories, educational levels, and instructional contexts. Furthermore, limited attention has been given to the implications of GenAI for teaching practice, professional development, ethical considerations, and future research priorities in Special Education. The present scoping review seeks to address these gaps by providing a comprehensive overview of the emerging evidence base and identifying areas that require further investigation.

Study Purpose and Research Questions

The aim of this scoping review is to systematically map the emerging evidence on the use of Generative Artificial Intelligence (GenAI) in Special Education. Specifically, the review examines peer-reviewed studies published between 2023 and 2026 to provide an overview of current applications, outcomes, and future directions.

Drawing on the theoretical framework presented above and the identified gaps in the literature, the review is guided by the following research questions:

RQ1. *What applications of GenAI have been investigated in Special Education, and what benefits and challenges have been reported for students with disabilities or SEN and their teachers?*

RQ2. *How is GenAI being used across different disability categories and educational contexts to support teaching and learning, and what implications does its use have for instructional practice and the role of the special education teacher?*

RQ3. *What implications do the existing findings have for teachers' professional development, and what research gaps and future priorities emerge from the current evidence base?*

METHODS

Study Design

This study employed a scoping review methodology to map the emerging literature on the use of Generative Artificial Intelligence (GenAI) in Special Education. Given the recent emergence of GenAI and the methodological diversity of the available literature, a scoping review was considered the most appropriate approach (Arksey & O'Malley, 2005; Peters et al., 2020).

The review followed the framework proposed by Arksey and O'Malley (2005) and refined by Levac et al. (2010). To enhance methodological transparency and reporting quality, the review followed the Preferred Reporting Items for Systematic Reviews and Meta-Analyses Extension for Scoping Reviews (PRISMA-ScR) guidelines (Tricco et al., 2018). These guidelines provide a structured framework for conducting and reporting scoping reviews and contribute to the reproducibility and transparency of the review process.

No formal quality appraisal was conducted, consistent with scoping review methodology (Peters et al., 2020). Also, no review protocol was registered prior to the commencement of the study.

SEARCH STRATEGY

A systematic search was conducted in March 2026 in Scopus and Web of Science, selected for their broad coverage of educational and interdisciplinary research.

The search was limited to studies published between 2023 and 2026. This timeframe was selected to capture the rapid growth of research following the public release and widespread adoption of large language models (LLMs), particularly ChatGPT, in late 2022. Given the fast-paced evolution of GenAI technologies, focusing on this period allowed the review to reflect the most recent developments in the field.

Search terms were developed through an iterative process involving pilot searches and successive refinements to achieve an appropriate balance between sensitivity and specificity. Boolean operators (AND, OR) were used to combine key concepts related to GenAI and Special Education and to optimize retrieval performance (Alharbi & Stevenson, 2020).

The final search strings were as follows:

Scopus:

("generative AI" OR "ChatGPT") AND ("special education" OR "disabilities") AND ("learning" OR "teaching")

Web of Science:

TS=("generative AI" OR "ChatGPT") AND ("special education" OR "disabilities") AND ("learning" OR "teaching")

Only studies published in English were considered eligible for inclusion. Furthermore, the review was restricted to peer-reviewed literature. Although grey literature is frequently incorporated into scoping reviews, it was intentionally excluded from the present study. The decision was made to prioritize evidence that had undergone formal peer-review procedures, thereby enhancing methodological consistency and source credibility. While this approach may have excluded potentially relevant reports, dissertations, policy documents, and conference proceedings, it was considered appropriate for establishing a robust and academically validated evidence base in a rapidly evolving field.

No restrictions were applied regarding study design, allowing the inclusion of qualitative, quantitative, mixed-methods, theoretical, and conceptual studies.

Eligibility Criteria

Studies were included in the review if they met the following criteria:

(a) Published in peer-reviewed journals or edited academic volumes;
(b) Published between 2023 and 2026;
(c) Examined the use, implementation, or application of Generative Artificial Intelligence (GenAI) tools. For the purposes of this review, GenAI tools were defined as systems capable of generating new content through machine-learning models, including large language models (LLMs), chatbots, image-generation systems, multimodal models, and AI-supported content creation tools;
(d) Conducted within educational or learning contexts;
(e) Included students with disabilities and/or special educational needs (SEN), special education teachers, or other stakeholders directly involved in Special Education.

Studies were excluded if they:

(a) Focused exclusively on traditional AI systems designed primarily for classification, prediction, recommendation, or data analysis without generative capabilities;
(b) Were not conducted within educational or learning settings;

(c) Included only participants from the general population without a specific focus on Special Education, disability, or SEN;
(d) Were unavailable in full text;
(e) Were published in languages other than English.

No restrictions were applied regarding study design. Consequently, qualitative, quantitative, mixed-methods, theoretical, conceptual, and descriptive studies were all considered eligible for inclusion, consistent with the exploratory nature of scoping review methodology.

Rayyan was used for record management, duplicate removal, and screening procedures (Ouzzani et al., 2016). Two reviewers independently screened all records against the eligibility criteria.

Disagreements were resolved through consensus. Inter-rater agreement was substantial ($\kappa = 0.72$ for title/abstract screening; $\kappa = 0.76$ for full-text screening).

Selection Process and Data Mapping

The study selection process is presented in the PRISMA flow diagram (Figure 1). The initial database search yielded 169 records, including 119 from Scopus and 50 from Web of Science. Following the removal of duplicate records (n = 13), a total of 156 unique studies remained for screening.

Titles and abstracts were independently screened by the two reviewers according to the predefined eligibility criteria. During the title-screening stage, 70 records were excluded because they were not directly related to GenAI, Special Education, inclusive education, or educational applications of AI. The remaining records proceeded to abstract screening.

Following the evaluation of abstracts, an additional 60 studies were excluded. These studies were primarily removed because they focused on broader discussions of AI without a specific emphasis on GenAI in Special Education, addressed technical or computational aspects without educational relevance, or lacked a clear connection to disability, special educational needs, or inclusive educational practice.

Full-text screening was subsequently conducted for the remaining 26 studies. Following a detailed review against the eligibility criteria, 19 studies were deemed eligible and were included in the final synthesis. The selected studies formed the evidence base for the present scoping review and were subsequently subjected to data extraction and thematic analysis.

Figure 1. PRISMA flow diagram of the study selection process

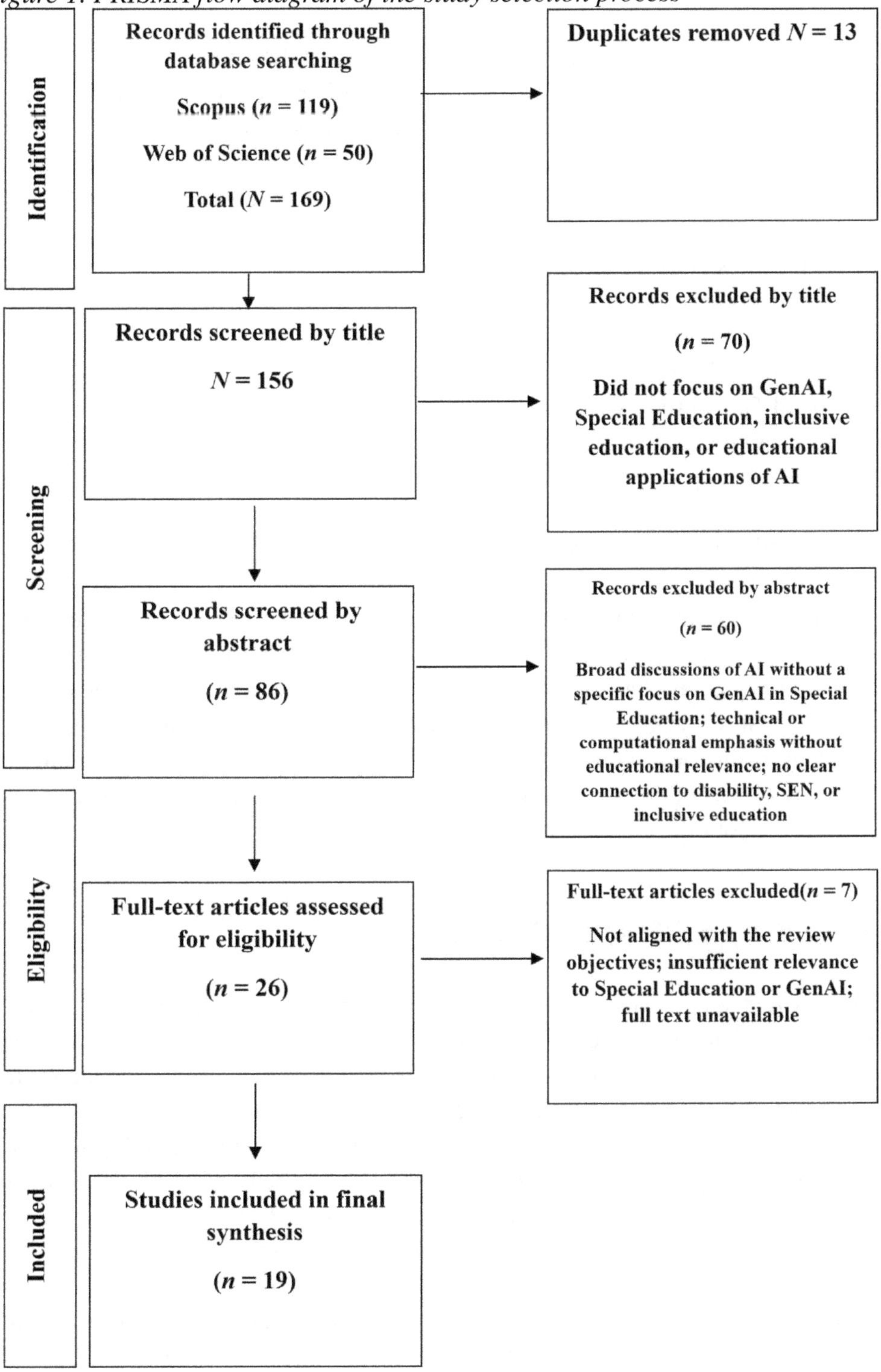

DATA CHARTING PROCES

A data-charting form was developed to systematically extract relevant information from each included study. The form was initially piloted on a subset of studies and subsequently refined to ensure clarity, consistency, and alignment with the objectives of the review.

The following information was extracted from each study:

1. Author(s), year of publication, and country of origin;
2. Study design;
3. Participant characteristics and disability category;
4. Educational level;
5. Type of Generative Artificial Intelligence (GenAI) tool used;
6. Area of application (e.g., instructional support, accessibility, writing assistance, or teacher support);
7. Main findings;
8. Reported benefits and challenges.

An inductive data-charting approach was adopted to facilitate the identification of recurring concepts and patterns across studies. Extracted information was continuously compared across studies and organized into conceptually meaningful categories that reflected the objectives and research questions of the review.

Data extraction was conducted by the first reviewer (C.K.) and independently verified by the second reviewer (T.A.) to enhance accuracy, consistency, and reliability throughout the charting process.

DATA SYNTHESIS AND ANALYSIS

The extracted data were synthesized using a descriptive and narrative approach, consistent with the objectives of scoping review methodology, which seeks to map and summarize heterogeneous bodies of evidence rather than evaluate intervention effectiveness (Arksey & O'Malley, 2005; Levac et al., 2010).

The analysis focused on identifying patterns related to the educational applications of GenAI, participant characteristics, disability categories, instructional contexts, reported outcomes, and implementation challenges. An inductive analytical approach was employed to allow themes and categories to emerge from the data rather than being imposed through a predefined framework.

Through iterative comparison across studies, the findings were organized into broader thematic categories aligned with the review's research questions. The synthesis remained primarily descriptive and was supported by tabular summaries and thematic groupings of findings, thereby providing a structured overview of the current evidence base while preserving the diversity and complexity of the included studies.

RESULTS

Characteristics of Included Studies

Table 1 summarizes the characteristics of the 19 studies included in the review. The studies varied in research design, participant characteristics, disability categories, educational settings, and GenAI applications, reflecting the emerging and heterogeneous nature of the field.

Publications increased substantially between 2023 and 2026. Early studies focused on teacher attitudes and Augmentative and Alternative Communication (AAC) applications, whereas later studies increasingly examined student autonomy, prompt engineering, accessibility, and ethical issues.

Table 1. Characteristics of corpus studies (N = 19)

Authors / Year / Country	Research Design	Population & Disability Category	Educational Level
Alenezi et al. (2023), Saudi Arabia	Mixed method (questionnaire and email interviews)	199 teachers of English as a Foreign Language (EFL) special education. Pupils with learning difficulties, intellectual disability, attention deficit disorder with or without hyperactivity (ADHD), autism, visual and hearing impairment	Various levels (Special Education EFL)
Alqarni (2026), Saudi Arabia	Quantitative Descriptive Overview Research	268 public school teachers. Pupils with learning difficulties	Primary Education
Alsahli et al. (2025), Saudi Arabia	Quantitative cross-sectional survey (cross-sectional survey)	283 medical students with SEN (sensory, cognitive, mental, Communicative/Autism)	Higher Education (Faculty of Medicine)
Anselimus (2026), Tanzania	Qualitative research (semi-structured interviews and focus groups)	18 students with visual, hearing and motor disabilities	Higher Education
Balikci et al. (2026), USA & Turkey	Randomized experimental study (randomized experiment between groups)	32 special education teachers. Material for preschoolers with autism	Early Childhood Education

continued on following page

Table 1. Continued

Authors / Year / Country	Research Design	Population & Disability Category	Educational Level
Barbu et al. (2025), Romania	Framework and system architecture design study (Extended Reality /XR & AI)	Students with SEN (ADHD, AUTISM, sensory processing disorder)	Inclusive Education (Primary & Secondary)
Drelick et al. (2026), USA	Practice-oriented technical report and teacher guide (based on clinical simulation frameworks)	Students with disabilities (Individualized Education Plans/IEPs and 504 plans, focus on self-advocacy and executive functions)	Primary & Secondary
Evmenova et al. (2024), USA	Exploratory study (mixed method: polls and workshops)	137 teachers (General, Special and English for Speakers of Other Languages/ESOL). Multilingual students with and without disabilities	Primary & Secondary
Evmenova et al. (2024), USA	Secondary data analysis (qualitative thematic analysis)	34 essays by students with and without high-frequency disabilities* (Learning Disabilities/LD, ADHD) and English Language Learners (ELL)	Primary & Secondary School
Evmenova et al. (2025), USA	Case report (Focus groups)	21 participants (teachers and parents). Students with disabilities (LD, autism, ADHD, emotional disorders)	Primary & Secondary
Goldman et al. (2024), USA	Practice-oriented descriptive article	Special education teachers. Students with significant learning, behavioural, and emotional support needs	Primary & Secondary
Goldman et al. (2026), USA	Exploratory practice-oriented article	Students with LD	Primary & Secondary
Jambunathan (2025), USA	Reflective case study (Colloquium)	Candidates and active preschool teachers. Preschool and kindergarten students	Tertiary (Teacher Preparation Program) / Preschool
Khlaif et al. (2025), Palestine	Qualitative case study (semi-structured interviews)	21 undergraduate students with visual impairments	Higher Education
Lang et al. (2023), USA & New Zealand	Exploratory and conceptual discussion article	People with intellectual and developmental disabilities	Various frameworks (Assistive Technology focus)
Li & Samah (2025), Malaysia	Systematic Literature Review (PRISMA)	20 scientific articles (secondary data). Students with learning disabilities and neurodiversity	Inclusive Education
Pierrès et al. (2025), Switzerland, France, Germany	Qualitative research (semi-structured interviews)	33 university students (neurodivergent/ADHD, visual and hearing impairment, chronic diseases, mental health)	Higher Education

continued on following page

Table 1. Continued

Authors / Year / Country	Research Design	Population & Disability Category	Educational Level
van Garderen et al. (2025), USA	Practice-oriented descriptive article (TechinAction)	General and special education teachers. Students with high-frequency disabilities	Primary & Secondary
Zhao et al. (2026), United Kingdom	Two-stage exploratory survey & interviews	124 students with neurodiversity, dyslexia and social/communication difficulties	Higher Education

*Note: high-frequency disabilities=The terms LD and ADHD are often labeled in sources as "high-frequency" disabilities because they occur with a high statistical frequency in the student population compared to other categories

Chronological Distribution

The chronological evolution of literature presents the following characteristics. The earliest studies in the corpus (2023) examined teacher attitudes and the potential of Augmentative and Alternative Communication (AAC) systems. In 2024 (16%, n=3), research began to expand to support writing and reduce teachers' workloads. A year later, in 2025 (37%, n=7), a significant increase is recorded, with studies examining the effectiveness of AI in higher education, educational games, and XR technologies. By 2026 (37%, n=7), the trend continues with the majority of studies focusing on student autonomy, prompt engineering practices, and ethical frameworks.

Geographical Distribution

The studies are geographically diverse, with most surveys (42%, n=8) coming from the USA. Significant research activity is recorded in Saudi Arabia with a percentage of 16% (n=3), while Europe is represented by a total of 11% (n=2) of the sample (Romania and a multinational study in Switzerland/France/Germany). The remaining 20% of the studies are split equally (5% per country) in the United Kingdom, Palestine, Malaysia and Tanzania.

Research Designs

There is a clear preference for qualitative approaches, which make up 32% (n=6) of studies and include semi-structured interviews and case studies. Descriptive articles and practical guides (e.g. TechinAction) cover 26% (n=5) of the literature, followed by quantitative review surveys with 21% (n=4). Mixed methods were used in 11% (n=2) of cases, while randomized experimental studies and reviews are represented by 5% each.

Distribution of Participants

The included studies focused on both learners and educators, with a slight predominance of studies involving students with disabilities and/or special educational needs (58%, n = 11). These studies primarily explored learners' experiences, accessibility needs, educational participation, and interactions with GenAI-supported tools. The remaining studies (42%, n = 8) examined the perspectives and practices of educators, including general and special education teachers, English as a Foreign Language (EFL) teachers, and pre-service teachers.

Distribution by Disability Category

Learning disabilities and neurodiversity were the most frequently represented categories in the included studies (79%, n = 15). Research within this group primarily involved students with dyslexia, ADHD, learning disabilities, and broader neurodiverse profiles.

Autism spectrum disorder was represented in 26% of the studies (n = 5). These studies examined the use of GenAI in educational activities involving communication, social interaction, and instructional support.

Sensory disabilities, including visual and hearing impairments, were examined in 32% of the studies (n = 6). Research in this category focused on accessibility-related applications and the use of GenAI to support access to educational content through multiple formats.

Intellectual and developmental disabilities were represented in 16% of the studies (n = 3). The studies in this category primarily investigated the integration of GenAI within assistive and augmentative communication contexts.

Educational Levels

Overall, the included studies demonstrate that research on GenAI in Special Education remains at an exploratory stage. The evidence base is characterized by methodological diversity, a predominance of qualitative and descriptive approaches, and a concentration on learning disabilities, neurodiversity, and inclusive educational contexts. These patterns provide important context for interpreting the applications, benefits, and challenges reported in the subsequent analysis.

Table 2 provides an overview of the GenAI applications identified across the included studies. The table summarizes the educational contexts in which these tools were employed, the reported outcomes of their implementation, and the principal benefits and challenges documented in the literature.

Table 2. GenAI applications, outcomes, and benefits/challenges per study (N = 19)

Authors / Year	GenAI Tool & Scope	Main Results	Benefits/Challenges
Alenezi et al. (2023)	ChatGPT: EFL to students with disabilities.	Teachers exhibited moderate but positive attitudes, with women being more willing for future use.	Personalized material, real-time personalization, motivation enhancement. Risk of overdependence, need for training.
Alqarni (2026)	ChatGPT, DALL-E: Enhancing the engagement of students with learning difficulties in Primary Education.	A moderate level of effectiveness was recorded (M=2.84), with the main benefit being the promotion of autonomy.	Adaptive activities, real-time personalization, reduction of cancellations. Fear of dependency, lack of school policies.
Alsahli et al. (2025)	ChatGPT: Learning Support for Medical Students with SEN	72.7% of students accept the tool, especially for the simplification of complex medical concepts.	Real-time personalization, social-emotional support. Skepticism, moral concerns.
Anselimus (2026)	ChatGPT, Gemini, etc.: Writing support and accessibility in Higher Education.	The digital readiness and academic participation of students with disabilities were strengthened.	Increased autonomy, timely feedback. Cost of subscriptions, lack of institutional guidance.
Balikci et al. (2026)	ChatGPT-4: Automation of task analysis for children with autism.	Significantly reduce teacher preparation time with high content accuracy.	Efficiency, ease of use. Risk of "hallucinations", need for human control.
Barbu et al. (2025)	OpenAI Application Program Interface/ API & XR (Unity): Immersive and adaptive learning environment for students with SEN.	An architecture was proposed that dynamically adjusts the difficulty based on the user's performance.	Multi-sensory engagement, real-time personalization. High equipment cost, risk of cybersickness.
Drelick et al. (2026)	MagicSchool, ChatGPT: Creating custom chatbots for self-advocacy and executive functions.	Chatbots offered a safe space to practice social and academic skills.	Personalized support, increased independence. Need for parental consent, protection of personal data.
Evmenova et al. (2024)	ChatGPT: Supporting the UDL Framework and Inclusive Teaching.	43% of educators believe that AI makes teaching more accessible for everyone.	Saving time in design, material diversification. Concerns about plagiarism, lack of critical thinking.
Evmenova et al. (2024)	ChatGPT (3.5 & 4): Providing writing feedback to students with learning disabilities.	A low match (17-23%) was found between AI recommendations and teachers.	Immediate response, identification of key errors. Excessive amount of information, lack of adaptation to the student's profile.
Evmenova et al. (2025)	ChatGPT, Gemini: Educational Games to Support Writing (WEGO Tool).	AI can generate scenarios and characters that enhance student engagement.	Activation of prior knowledge, creativity, personalization in real time. Need for "guardrails", development costs.

continued on following page

Table 2. Continued

Authors / Year	GenAI Tool & Scope	Main Results	Benefits/Challenges
Goldman et al. (2024)	ChatGPT, Bard: Reducing the administrative burden of special education teachers.	AI helps create concise IEP snapshots and resources for parents in no time.	Automate paperwork, improve cooperation with families. Privacy risks (FERPA), need for data anonymization.
Goldman et al. (2026)	ChatGPT, Gemini: Educating students with learning disabilities in prompt engineering.	Proper use of prompts reduces cognitive load and boosts confidence in writing.	Overcoming writer's blockage, organizing ideas. Obstacles to executive operation when designing commands.
Jambunathan (2025)	ChatGPT, Claude, Canva: Integrating GenAI into the education of future early childhood educators.	The students showed enthusiasm for the creation of material (newsletters, fairy tales).	Simplification of bibliographic search, creation of programs. Inaccurate images, lack of confidence in authenticity.
Khlaif et al. (2025)	Midjourney, Canva, GenAI: Accessibility and equity for students with visual impairments.	GenAI acts as a bridge to the digital divide, offering access to international resources.	Text-to-Audio Conversion, Content Simplification, Real-Time Personalization. Algorithmic bias, need for ethical oversight.
Lang et al. (2023)	ALMs (ChatGPT, Bard): Strengthening AAC Systems.	GenAI can produce coherent responses that resemble human speech, facilitating social inclusion.	Empowerment of expression, speed of communication. Risk of altering the user's communicative intent.
Li & Samah (2025)	LLMs, Chatbots: Social interaction and metacognitive skills in inclusivity classes.	GenAI Improves Communication by Breaking Down Language Barriers for Neurodiverse Learners.	Reduction of cognitive stress, real-time personalization, enhancement of reflective thinking. Risk of overdependence, loss of self-analysis ability.
Pierrès et al. (2025)	ChatGPT: Study, Writing, and Organization Assistant for Students with Disabilities.	90% of students find GenAI useful, primarily for relieving increased workloads.	Saving time, reducing fatigue and pain. Robotic writing style, need for data verification.
van Garderen et al. (2025)	Claude, ChatGPT: Creation of educational supports (scaffolds) for students with disabilities.	Educators can efficiently create worksheets and checklists in seconds.	Content-specific resources, support for complex texts. Need for "human in the loop" for quality assurance.
Zhao et al. (2026)	ChatGPT, Bing, etc.: Academic writing for students with disabilities (affordance model).	Three main possibilities were identified: explanatory, expressiveness and design.	Improve articulation of ideas, reduce stress on grammar. Fear of academic misconduct, loss of personal "voice".

Types of Generative Artificial Intelligence Tools

ChatGPT was the most frequently examined GenAI tool, appearing in 90% of the included studies (n = 17). Other platforms, including Gemini, Claude, DALL-E, Canva, Midjourney, MagicSchool, and Bing AI, were reported less frequently and were primarily used to support multimodal content creation, accessibility, and instructional design. A small number of studies also explored the integration of GenAI with emerging technologies, such as Extended Reality (XR), highlighting the growing diversification of AI-supported educational applications.

Educational Applications of GenAI in Special Education

The reviewed studies demonstrated that GenAI is being applied across a broad range of educational contexts. In higher education, applications primarily focused on academic writing support, accessibility, organization of learning tasks, and assistance for students with sensory disabilities and neurodiverse profiles. In primary and secondary education, GenAI was used to enhance classroom engagement, provide personalized feedback, support inclusive instructional practices, and facilitate differentiated learning experiences. Additional applications included English language learning, augmentative and alternative communication (AAC), immersive learning environments, and teacher support functions such as instructional planning, resource development, and administrative assistance.

Reported Benefits and Challenges

Across the included studies, personalization emerged as the most frequently reported benefit of GenAI, with many studies highlighting its potential to adapt learning materials, provide individualized feedback, and support learner autonomy. Additional benefits included increased accessibility, reduced teacher workload, enhanced student engagement, support for academic writing, and improved opportunities for communication and self-expression among learners with disabilities.

At the same time, the literature consistently identified several challenges associated with GenAI implementation. The most frequently reported concerns involved hallucinations and inaccuracies in generated content, privacy and data protection issues, algorithmic bias, and risks related to academic integrity. Other challenges included overreliance on AI-generated outputs, the need for ongoing human oversight, difficulties associated with prompt design, and concerns regarding the authenticity and quality of generated content. A small number of studies also highlighted specialized concerns, including the potential alteration of communicative intent in AAC systems and cybersickness in immersive XR environments.

DISCUSSION

The findings indicate that GenAI is emerging as a potentially transformative technology in Special Education, offering opportunities for personalization, accessibility, learner autonomy, and instructional support. However, the evidence base remains geographically concentrated and dominated by qualitative and exploratory studies, limiting conclusions regarding long-term effectiveness and implementation outcomes.

As a result, many of the claims regarding the effectiveness of GenAI in Special Education should be interpreted cautiously until supported by more rigorous empirical evidence.

Applications, Benefits, and Challenges (RQ1)

The findings of this review demonstrate that Generative Artificial Intelligence (GenAI) is increasingly being incorporated into Special Education across a wide range of educational contexts and disability categories. The reviewed studies reveal considerable diversity in both the applications and intended purposes of GenAI, ranging from writing support and accessibility enhancement to communication assistance, instructional planning, and personalized learning. Collectively, these findings suggest that GenAI is gradually evolving from a supplementary educational tool into a potentially transformative component of inclusive educational practice.

One of the most notable findings concerns the overwhelming predominance of ChatGPT within the current evidence base. Although this likely reflects the platform's accessibility, widespread adoption, and user-friendly interface, it should not be interpreted as evidence that ChatGPT represents the most effective solution for all learners or disability categories. Rather, the concentration of research on a single platform highlights the limited exploration of other emerging GenAI technologies, including multimodal AI systems, image and voice generation tools, and advanced assistive communication applications (Bommasani et al., 2021; Dwivedi et al., 2023; Kasneci et al., 2023). Consequently, important opportunities for innovation may remain underexplored within the current literature.

At the same time, the reviewed studies indicate that the educational use of GenAI is expanding beyond text generation and writing assistance. Emerging applications include the integration of GenAI with Extended Reality (XR), immersive learning environments, educational games, and assistive communication systems (Abbes et al., 2024; Barbu et al., 2025). Such developments are particularly relevant to Special Education, where learning frequently depends on multimodal instruction, experiential learning, and individualized support. These findings suggest that future educational applications of GenAI may become increasingly interactive, adaptive, and responsive to the diverse needs of learners with disabilities.

A second important finding concerns the unequal distribution of research across disability categories. Most studies focused on learners with learning disabilities, dyslexia, ADHD, and broader neurodiverse profiles. This pattern may partly reflect the linguistic nature of current large language models, which are especially well suited to supporting reading, writing, communication, and academic tasks. However, it may also reflect broader scientific and societal trends that have increased attention to neurodiversity over the past decade (Castleman et al., 2024; McLennan et al., 2025; Najeeb & Quadt, 2024). In contrast, learners with intellectual and developmental disabilities remain considerably underrepresented within the literature, despite the potentially transformative role that GenAI could play in augmentative and alternative communication (AAC), supported decision-making, and independent living. This imbalance raises important concerns regarding equity and highlights the need for a more inclusive research agenda that addresses the needs of underrepresented disability groups (OECD, 2023).

The findings further suggest that GenAI holds considerable promise for supporting the practical implementation of Universal Design for Learning (UDL). Across the reviewed studies, personalization, accessibility, and learner autonomy emerged as recurring themes. The capacity of GenAI systems to adapt instructional materials, provide immediate feedback, offer multiple forms of representation, and facilitate differentiated instruction aligns closely with the core principles of UDL (CAST, 2024). These findings are consistent with broader literature emphasizing the role of educational technologies in reducing barriers to participation and promoting inclusive learning environments (Florian, 2014; UNESCO, 2021). In this sense, GenAI may function not only as an assistive tool but also as a practical mechanism for operationalizing inclusive pedagogical principles.

Despite these promising developments, the review highlights the inherently dual nature of GenAI in educational settings. While the majority of studies reported positive outcomes, these benefits were consistently accompanied by significant pedagogical, ethical, and technological concerns. Hallucinations and inaccurate outputs emerged as one of the most frequently reported challenges, raising concerns regarding reliability, particularly for learners who may experience difficulties in critically evaluating information. Similarly, concerns regarding data privacy, algorithmic bias, academic integrity, and excessive dependence on AI-generated content were repeatedly identified across the literature. These findings suggest that the successful integration of GenAI in Special Education requires more than technological adoption alone. It also requires robust ethical safeguards, transparent governance mechanisms, and continuous human oversight to ensure that AI-supported learning remains accurate, equitable, and responsive to the needs of diverse learners (United Nations, 2022; UNESCO, 2023; OECD, 2024; Zallio et al., 2025).

Another issue that received limited attention in the reviewed studies concerns inequalities in access to GenAI technologies. Most investigations were conducted in educational settings characterized by relatively high levels of technological infrastructure and digital resources. Consequently, little is currently known about the feasibility, accessibility, and effectiveness of GenAI implementation in low-resource educational environments, where access to digital devices, stable internet connectivity, specialized support services, and teacher training opportunities may be substantially more limited. Future research should therefore examine how GenAI can be implemented equitably across diverse educational contexts in order to avoid reinforcing existing educational and digital inequalities.

Importantly, relatively few studies examined the active involvement of individuals with disabilities in the design, implementation, and evaluation of GenAI-supported educational systems. This observation highlights a significant gap in the current evidence base. Participatory and disability-centred approaches to AI development may help ensure that educational technologies are designed with, rather than merely for, the populations they intend to support (Fletcher-Watson et al., 2019). Such approaches are consistent with the principles of the United Nations Convention on the Rights of Persons with Disabilities (UNCRPD), which emphasize the meaningful participation of individuals with disabilities in decisions and processes that affect their lives (United Nations, 2006). Greater involvement of learners with disabilities in the development of educational AI systems may contribute to reducing accessibility barriers and minimizing unintended forms of exclusion that can emerge when technological innovation advances more rapidly than inclusive design practices.

Finally, the current evidence base remains heavily dependent on exploratory, descriptive, and short-term investigations. Although these studies provide valuable initial insights, the limited number of longitudinal and intervention-based studies restricts our understanding of the long-term educational impact of GenAI on learning outcomes, independence, participation, and quality of life among learners with disabilities. More robust empirical research is therefore needed before definitive conclusions regarding the effectiveness of GenAI in Special Education can be drawn.

Instructional Practice and Teacher Role (RQ2)

A central finding of this review concerns the potential of GenAI to reduce the administrative and planning demands associated with Special Education. Several studies reported that GenAI can support the preparation of instructional materials, the development of individualized educational resources, and the automation of time-consuming tasks, thereby allowing educators to devote greater attention to direct instructional and relational aspects of teaching (Balikci et al., 2026; Goldman et al., 2024; van Garderen et al., 2025). These findings are particularly relevant in the context of persistent teacher shortages, increasing workload demands, and high rates of professional burnout within Special Education (McGrew et al., 2023; Myrie et al., 2024; Park & Shin, 2020; Miao & Cukurova, 2023).

At the same time, the findings suggest that GenAI is not reducing the importance of the teacher's role but rather reshaping it. Rather than functioning primarily as content creators, educators are increasingly required to act as instructional designers, facilitators, and critical evaluators of AI-generated content. The work of Drelick et al. (2026), for example, illustrates how teachers can design AI-mediated learning environments that support student participation, self-advocacy, and personalized learning. Such findings indicate that the educational value of GenAI depends not only on the technology itself but also on the pedagogical decisions that guide its implementation.

A recurring theme across the reviewed studies concerns the importance of teacher preparedness. Despite growing interest in GenAI, many educators continue to report limited experience and confidence in using AI-supported technologies. Evmenova et al. (2024) found that a substantial proportion of teachers had little or no prior experience with AI, while attitudes toward GenAI remained mixed. These findings suggest that effective implementation requires more than access to technology; it requires systematic professional development and sustained institutional support.

The review further highlights the growing importance of AI literacy as a core professional competence for educators. Contemporary frameworks increasingly emphasize that teachers must be able not only to use AI tools but also to critically evaluate their outputs, identify inaccuracies and potential biases, understand ethical implications, and make informed pedagogical decisions regarding their use (Holmes et al., 2023; Miao & Cukurova, 2023). Within this context, prompt design and prompt engineering emerge as important practical skills, not because they enable educators to delegate decision-making to AI systems, but because they allow teachers to use these technologies more effectively and responsibly in support of learning.

Importantly, the findings reinforce the view that human oversight remains indispensable in Special Education. Although GenAI can assist with content generation, assessment support, and instructional planning, it cannot replace the professional judgment required to interpret students' needs, monitor emotional well-being, ensure ethical practice, and make individualized educational decisions. This issue may be particularly important for learners with disabilities, whose educational needs often require nuanced interpretation, interdisciplinary collaboration, and ongoing adaptation. Consequently, GenAI should be viewed as a tool that augments rather than replaces professional expertise.

Finally, the findings reported by Alenezi et al. (2023) regarding moderate levels of acceptance and demographic differences in adoption can be interpreted through established technology acceptance frameworks, such as the Technology Acceptance Model (TAM) and the Unified Theory of Acceptance and Use of Technology (UTAUT). These frameworks suggest that technology adoption is influenced not only by perceived usefulness and ease of use but also by social influence, institutional support, and opportunities for training (Lin et al., 2026; Xu et al., 2025). Accordingly, teacher readiness should not be viewed solely as an individual characteristic but as the product of broader educational, organizational, and policy conditions that shape the successful integration of GenAI into educational practice.

Professional Development, Evidence Gaps, and Research Priorities (RQ3)

The findings of this review highlight a persistent gap between the rapid development of GenAI technologies and the preparedness of educators to use them effectively within Special Education settings. Although many studies reported positive attitudes toward the potential of GenAI, limited prior experience and insufficient training emerged as recurring barriers to implementation. These findings reinforce growing calls for systematic professional development initiatives focused on AI literacy, critical AI literacy, and the pedagogically informed use of AI-supported educational tools (Holmes et al., 2023; Miao & Cukurova, 2023).

However, effective preparation extends beyond the acquisition of technical skills. The integration of GenAI into Special Education requires educators to develop a combination of technological, pedagogical, and ethical competencies. Teachers must be able to critically evaluate AI-generated outputs, identify potential inaccuracies and biases, safeguard student privacy, and make informed decisions regarding the appropriate use of AI within inclusive learning environments. Consequently, future professional development programs should adopt a holistic approach that integrates AI literacy with pedagogical decision-making, ethical awareness, and human-in-the-loop practices (Goldman et al., 2024; van Garderen et al., 2025).

At the same time, the review revealed several important gaps within the current evidence base. Most studies were exploratory, descriptive, and short-term in nature, limiting conclusions regarding the long-term educational effectiveness of GenAI for students with disabilities and special educational needs. Furthermore, research remains concentrated on a relatively narrow range of disability categories and technological tools, with comparatively limited attention devoted to learners with intellectual and developmental disabilities, augmentative and alternative communication systems, and low-resource educational contexts. These gaps highlight the need for more inclusive and methodologically rigorous research agendas.

Future studies should prioritize longitudinal and intervention-based designs capable of examining the sustained impact of GenAI on learning outcomes, participation, autonomy, and quality of life. Greater attention should also be given to participatory and disability-centred approaches that actively involve learners with disabilities, their families, and educational professionals in the design, implementation, and evaluation of AI-supported educational systems. Such approaches may contribute to the development of technologies that are not only innovative but also accessible, equitable, and responsive to the lived experiences of the populations they are intended to support (Fletcher-Watson et al., 2019).

Finally, the findings underscore the need for the development of robust ethical, pedagogical, and accessibility governance frameworks capable of guiding the responsible use of GenAI in Special Education. As AI technologies become increasingly embedded within educational practice, ensuring transparency, accountability, accessibility, and meaningful human oversight will be essential for maximizing benefits while minimizing potential risks. Future research should therefore move beyond questions of technological capability and increasingly address questions of equity, inclusion, and responsible innovation in educational AI.

Limitations of the Study

Several limitations should be considered when interpreting the findings of this study. First, the current evidence base is characterized by a predominance of exploratory, descriptive, and qualitative studies, with relatively few experimental or longitudinal investigations. Although such studies are valuable for identifying emerging trends and generating initial insights, they limit the ability to draw strong conclusions regarding the long-term effectiveness and educational impact of GenAI interventions in Special Education.

Second, the overwhelming predominance of ChatGPT within the reviewed literature limits the extent to which the findings can be generalized to other GenAI tools and platforms. Consequently, the educational potential, accessibility features, and limitations of alternative AI systems remain comparatively underexplored.

Third, the review focused on studies published between 2023 and 2026. Given the exceptionally rapid pace of technological development in the field of Generative Artificial Intelligence, new applications, educational practices, and research findings continue to emerge. Therefore, the review should be viewed as a snapshot of a rapidly evolving field.

Finally, the search was limited to two major databases (Scopus and Web of Science) and to studies published in English. Although these databases provide extensive coverage of high-quality peer-reviewed literature, relevant studies published in other databases, languages, or forms of grey literature may not have been captured.

Despite these limitations, the review provides a comprehensive overview of an emerging field of research and offers a valuable foundation for future empirical investigations, policy development, and educational practice related to the use of GenAI in Special Education.

CONCLUSIONS AND SUGGESTIONS FOR FUTURE RESEARCH

This scoping review systematically mapped the emerging evidence on the use of Generative Artificial Intelligence (GenAI) in Special Education. The findings demonstrate that GenAI has considerable potential to support personalization, accessibility, learner autonomy, communication, and instructional efficiency across a range of educational contexts and disability categories. At the same time, the review revealed important methodological, pedagogical, and ethical challenges that continue to shape the development of this rapidly evolving field.

In relation to the first research question, the findings indicate that GenAI is primarily being used to support individualized learning, communication, accessibility, and instructional adaptation. However, the current evidence base remains unevenly distributed across disability categories, educational levels, and technological applications. The predominance of studies focusing on learning disabilities and neurodiversity, together with the overwhelming concentration on ChatGPT, suggests that current research trends may reflect both the capabilities of existing technologies and broader research priorities.

Regarding the second research question, the findings suggest that GenAI has the potential to enhance teaching efficiency and reduce administrative workload while simultaneously transforming the professional role of educators. Rather than replacing teachers, GenAI appears to increase the importance of pedagogical judgment, instructional design, ethical decision-making, and critical evaluation of AI-generated outputs.

Finally, the third research question highlights the urgent need for systematic professional development, interdisciplinary collaboration, and more robust empirical research. The review consistently identified gaps in teacher preparedness, AI literacy, accessibility governance, and disability-centred approaches to AI development. Addressing these gaps will be essential if GenAI is to contribute meaningfully to inclusive and equitable educational systems. Future research should prioritize longitudinal and intervention-based studies, expand representation across disability groups and educational contexts, and contribute to the development of ethical and accessibility frameworks that support the responsible use of GenAI in Special Education.

PRACTICAL IMPLICATIONS

Implications for Teachers

One important priority is the development of AI literacy and prompt design skills as core professional competencies. Educators need to be able not only to use GenAI tools but also to critically evaluate their outputs, identify potential inaccuracies and biases, and make informed pedagogical decisions regarding their implementation. Human-in-the-loop approaches should ensure that AI complements rather than replaces professional judgment. Teachers should also remain attentive to issues of privacy, data protection, and ethical use, particularly when working with vulnerable student populations. Furthermore, instructional decisions should recognize that the benefits and limitations of GenAI may vary across disability categories and educational contexts.

Implications for Educational Institutions

Educational institutions have a critical role in creating the conditions necessary for the responsible adoption of GenAI. Investment in validated and purpose-built educational AI tools may provide safer and more accessible learning environments than reliance on publicly available platforms. Institutions should also provide comprehensive professional development opportunities that integrate technical, pedagogical, and ethical dimensions of AI use. The development of clear policies addressing academic integrity, accessibility, privacy, and responsible AI use is equally important. Finally, ensuring equitable access through infrastructure, institutional licensing, and targeted support mechanisms should remain a priority. In line with disability rights frameworks, individuals with disabilities should be actively involved in the development of institutional AI policies and practices, reflecting the principle of "Nothing About Us Without Us."

As GenAI technologies continue to evolve, the central challenge will not be whether these tools can support inclusive education, but how they can be implemented in ways that remain educationally meaningful, ethically responsible, and genuinely responsive to the needs of learners with disabilities.

REFERENCES

Abbes, F., Bennani, S., & Maalel, A. (2024). Generative AI and gamification for personalized learning: Literature review and future challenges. *SN Computer Science*, *5*(8), 1154. DOI: 10.1007/s42979-024-03491-z

Alenezi, M. A. K., Mohamed, A. M., & Shaaban, T. S. (2023). Revolutionizing EFL special education: How ChatGPT is transforming the way teachers approach language learning. *Innoeduca. International Journal of Technology and Educational Innovation*, *9*(2), 5–23. DOI: 10.24310/innoeduca.2023.v9i2.16774

Alharbi, A., & Stevenson, M. (2020). Refining Boolean queries to identify relevant studies for systematic review updates. *Journal of the American Medical Informatics Association : JAMIA*, *27*(11), 1658–1666. DOI: 10.1093/jamia/ocaa148 PMID: 33067630

Alqarni, T. M. (2026). Teachers' perceptions of generative AI in inclusive classrooms: Enhancing engagement for students with learning disabilities. *Universal Access in the Information Society*, *25*(1), 22. DOI: 10.1007/s10209-025-01301-8

Alsahli, M., Alanezi, F. Sh., Basri, W., Attar, R. W., Alghamdi, A., Alyahya, N. M., Albagmi, S., Almutairi, S. A., Alsedrah, I. T., Arif, W. M., Alsadhan, A. A., AlShammary, M. H., Bakhshwain, A. M., Almuhanna, A. F., Alnaim, N., & Alhazmi, A. H. (2025). Effectiveness of ChatGPT in facilitating learning for students with special educational needs: An empirical study in Saudi Arabia. *Nutrition and Health (Berkhamsted, Hertfordshire)*, *31*(4), 1579–1589. DOI: 10.1177/02601060241307770 PMID: 39819330

Anselimus, S. M. (2026). Generative AI for university students with disabilities: Challenges and opportunities. *Educational Research*, *68*(2), 1–19. DOI: 10.1080/00131881.2026.2632852

Arksey, H., & O'Malley, L. (2005). Scoping studies: Towards a methodological framework. *International Journal of Social Research Methodology*, *8*(1), 19–32. DOI: 10.1080/1364557032000119616

Balikci, S., Terzioglu, N. K., & Rakap, S. (2026). ChatGPT-assisted task analysis for special education teachers: An exploratory study of alignment, readability, efficiency, and acceptability. *Future Internet*, *18*(3), 158. DOI: 10.3390/fi18030158

Barbu, M., Iordache, D.-D., Petre, I., Barbu, D.-C., & Băjenaru, L. (2025). Framework design for reinforcing the potential of XR technologies in transforming inclusive education. *Applied Sciences (Basel, Switzerland)*, *15*(3), 1484. DOI: 10.3390/app15031484

Barua, P. D., Vicnesh, J., Gururajan, R., Oh, S. L., Palmer, E., Azizan, M. M., Kadri, N. A., & Acharya, U. R. (2022). Artificial intelligence enabled personalised assistive tools to enhance education of children with neurodevelopmental disorders—A review. *International Journal of Environmental Research and Public Health, 19*(3), 1192. DOI: 10.3390/ijerph19031192 PMID: 35162220

Bommasani, R., Hudson, D. A., Adeli, E., Altman, R., Arora, S., von Arx, S., Bernstein, M. S., Bohg, J., Bosselut, A., Brunskill, E., & Liang, P. (2021). On the opportunities and risks of foundation models. arXiv. https://arxiv.org/abs/2108.07258

Bouguettaya, S., Pupo, F., Chen, M., & Fortino, G. (2025). A Meta-survey of generative AI in education: Trends, challenges, and research directions. *Big Data and Cognitive Computing*, *9*(9), 237. DOI: 10.3390/bdcc9090237

CAST. (2024). *Universal design for learning guidelines version 3.0.* CAST. http://udlguidelines.cast.org

Castleman, B. V. Western New England University, Jarvinen, L. Z., Westfield State University, Jarvinen, M. K., & Western New England University. (2024). Neurodiversity in the minds of students: From perception to campus programming. *Journal of Undergraduate Neuroscience Education, 22*(3), A217–A223. DOI: 10.59390/QCWZ6366

Chen, L., Chen, P., & Lin, Z. (2020). Artificial intelligence in education: A Review. *IEEE Access : Practical Innovations, Open Solutions*, *8*, 75264–75278. DOI: 10.1109/ACCESS.2020.2988510

Drelick, A. M., Woodfield, C., & Freedman, J. E. (2026). Designing and using custom Chatbots to support students with disabilities: An educator's guide. *Journal of Special Education Technology*, *01626434261420392*, 01626434261420392. DOI: 10.1177/01626434261420392

Dwivedi, Y. K., Kshetri, N., Hughes, L., Slade, E. L., Jeyaraj, A., Kar, A. K., Baabdullah, A. M., Koohang, A., Raghavan, V., Ahuja, M., Albanna, H., Albashrawi, M. A., Al-Busaidi, A. S., Balakrishnan, J., Barlette, Y., Basu, S., Bose, I., Brooks, L., Buhalis, D., & Wright, R. (2023). Opinion Paper: "So what if ChatGPT wrote it?" Multidisciplinary perspectives on opportunities, challenges and implications of generative conversational AI for research, practice and policy. *International Journal of Information Management*, *71*, 102642. DOI: 10.1016/j.ijinfomgt.2023.102642

Ertel, W. (2017). Introduction. In W. Ertel, *Introduction to Artificial Intelligence* (pp. 1–21). Springer International Publishing. DOI: 10.1007/978-3-319-58487-4_1

Evmenova, A. S., Borup, J., & Shin, J. K. (2024). Harnessing the power of generative AI to support all learners. *TechTrends*, *68*(4), 820–831. DOI: 10.1007/s11528-024-00966-x

Evmenova, A. S., Regan, K., Mergen, R., & Hrisseh, R. (2025). Educational games and the potential of AI to transform writing across the curriculum. *Education Sciences*, *15*(5), 567. DOI: 10.3390/educsci15050567

Ewoldt, K. B., & Flanagan, S. M. (2025). Generative artificial intelligence as an educational collaborator: A next-generation resource. *Teaching Exceptional Children*, *00400599251340611*. DOI: 10.1177/00400599251340611

Fletcher-Watson, S., Adams, J., Brook, K., Charman, T., Crane, L., Cusack, J., Leekam, S., Milton, D., Parr, J. R., & Pellicano, E. (2019). Making the future together: Shaping autism research through meaningful participation. *Autism*, *23*(4), 943–953. DOI: 10.1177/1362361318786721 PMID: 30095277

Florian, L. (2014). What counts as evidence of inclusive education? *European Journal of Special Needs Education*, *29*(3), 286–294. DOI: 10.1080/08856257.2014.933551

Goldman, S. R., Carreon, A., & Smith, S. J. (2026). Teaching students with learning disabilities to be prompt engineers. *Intervention in School and Clinic*, *61*(3), 142–150. DOI: 10.1177/10534512251387080

Goldman, S. R., Taylor, J., Carreon, A., & Smith, S. J. (2024). Using AI to support special education teacher workload. *Journal of Special Education Technology*, *39*(3), 434–447. DOI: 10.1177/01626434241257240

Hellenic Republic. (2008). *Law 3699/2008: Special education and training of people with disabilities or special educational needs and other provisions* (Government Gazette A 199/02-10-2008).Holmes, W., & Tuomi, I. (2022). State of the art and practice in AI in education. *European Journal of Education*, *57*(4), 542–570. DOI: 10.1111/ejed.12533

Holmes, W., Bialik, M., & Fadel, C. (2023). Artificial intelligence in education. In Stückelberger, C., & Duggal, P. (Eds.), *Data ethics: Building trust: How digital technologies can serve humanity* (pp. 621–653). Globethics Publications., DOI: 10.58863/20.500.12424/4276068

Holmes, W., Porayska-Pomsta, K., Holstein, K., Sutherland, E., Baker, T., Buckingham Shum, S., Santos, O. C., Rodrigo, M. T., Cukurova, M., Bittencourt, I. I., & Koedinger, K. R. (2019). Ethics of AI in education: Towards a community-wide agenda. *International Journal of Artificial Intelligence in Education*, *32*(3), 504–526. DOI: 10.1007/s40593-021-00239-1

Jamal Eddine, R., Gide, E., & Al-Sabbagh, A. (2026). Systematised evidence mapping of generative artificial intelligence (GenAI) and digital divide phenomena in higher education. *Discover Computing*, *29*(1), 157. DOI: 10.1007/s10791-026-10044-w

Jambunathan, S. (2025). Integrating artificial intelligence into early childhood teacher education. *Contemporary Issues in Early Childhood*, *14639491251340141*, 14639491251340141. DOI: 10.1177/14639491251340141

Kasneci, E., Sessler, K., Küchemann, S., Bannert, M., Dementieva, D., Fischer, F., Gasser, U., Groh, G., Günnemann, S., Hüllermeier, E., Krusche, S., Kutyniok, G., Michaeli, T., Nerdel, C., Pfeffer, J., Poquet, O., Sailer, M., Schmidt, A., Seidel, T., & Kasneci, G. (2023). ChatGPT for good? On opportunities and challenges of large language models for education. *Learning and Individual Differences*, *103*, 102274. DOI: 10.1016/j.lindif.2023.102274

Khlaif, Z. N., Alshakhshir, R., Hamamra, B., & Joma, A. (2025). Reimagining inclusive education: The assistive power of generative AI in promoting accessibility and equity. *British Journal of Visual Impairment*, *02646196251382469*, 02646196251382469. DOI: 10.1177/02646196251382469

Kusumaningsih, D., Wicaksana, M. F., Rustinar, E., Saputra, A. D., Maalikih, M. D., Nurhana, M., & Naimah, M. (2026). AI applications in education: Technological innovations for overcoming dyslexia and dysgraphia challenges in students. *Multidisciplinary Reviews*, *9*(8), 2026340. DOI: 10.31893/multirev.2026340

Lan, L., Li, K., & Li, D. (2025). Exploring the application of AI in the education of children with autism: A public health perspective. *Frontiers in Psychiatry*, *15*, 1521926. DOI: 10.3389/fpsyt.2024.1521926 PMID: 39935626

Lang, R., McLay, L., & Rispoli, M. (2023). Advanced language models: Potential to improve augmentative and alternative communication for individuals with intellectual and developmental disabilities. *Advances in Neurodevelopmental Disorders*, *7*(3), 481–484. DOI: 10.1007/s41252-023-00350-5

Levac, D., Colquhoun, H., & O'Brien, K. K. (2010). Scoping studies: Advancing the methodology. *Implementation Science : IS*, *5*(1), 69. DOI: 10.1186/1748-5908-5-69 PMID: 20854677

Li, D., & Samah, N. A. (2025). Generative AI in inclusive classrooms: Enhancing social interactions, personalized learning, and metacognitive skills. *Sodobna Pedagogika*, *76*(2), 155–176. DOI: 10.63384/spB52z813a

Lin, X., Cui, H., & Zhu, X. (2026). Chinese special education teachers' experiences with generative AI: Differences in perceptions, use, and tam pathways for IEP writing and lesson planning. *Journal of Special Education Technology, 01626434261435251*, 01626434261435251. DOI: 10.1177/01626434261435251

Marino, M. T., Vasquez, E., Dieker, L., Basham, J., & Blackorby, J. (2023). The future of artificial intelligence in special education technology. *Journal of Special Education Technology*, *38*(3), 404–416. DOI: 10.1177/01626434231165977

McGrew, J., Ruble, L., Cormier, C. J., & Dueber, D. (2023). Special educators' mental health and burnout: A comparison of general and teacher specific risk factors. *Teaching and Teacher Education*, *132*, 104209. DOI: 10.1016/j.tate.2023.104209

McLennan, H., Aberdein, R., Saggers, B., & Gillett-Swan, J. (2025). Neurodiversity: A scoping review of empirical research. *Neurodiversity*, *3*, 27546330251337874. DOI: 10.1177/27546330251337874

Miao, F., & Cukurova, M. (2023). *AI competency framework for educators*. Publications UNESCO., DOI: 10.54675/ZJTE2084

Myrie, D. N., Dowd, N. T., & Latiker, M. D. (2024). Addressing the shortage of special education teachers of color: Implications for teacher education programs and K-12 systems. *Social Sciences (Basel, Switzerland)*, *13*(11), 622. DOI: 10.3390/socsci13110622

Najeeb, P., & Quadt, L. (2024). Autistic well-being: A scoping review of scientific studies from a neurodiversity-affirmative perspective. *Neurodiversity*, *2*, 27546330241233088. DOI: 10.1177/27546330241233088

OECD. (2022). *"OECD Framework for the Classification of AI systems", OECD Digital Economy Papers, No. 323*. OECD Publishing. DOI: 10.1787/cb6d9eca-

OECD. (2023). *OECD digital education Outlook 2023: Towards an effective digital education ecosystem*. OECD Publishing. DOI: 10.1787/c74f03de-

Ouzzani, M., Hammady, H., Fedorowicz, Z., & Elmagarmid, A. (2016). Rayyan—A web and mobile app for systematic reviews. *Systematic Reviews*, *5*(1), 210. DOI: 10.1186/s13643-016-0384-4 PMID: 27919275

Oyebode, O., Fowles, J., Steeves, D., & Orji, R. (2023). Machine learning techniques in adaptive and personalized systems for health and wellness. *International Journal of Human-Computer Interaction*, *39*(9), 1938–1962. DOI: 10.1080/10447318.2022.2089085

Park, E.-Y., & Shin, M. (2020). A meta-analysis of special education teachers' burnout. *SAGE Open, 10*(2), 2158244020918297. DOI: 10.1177/2158244020918297

Peters, M. D. J., Godfrey, C., McInerney, P., Munn, Z., Tricco, A. C., Khalil, H., & Parker, D. (2020). Chapter 11: Scoping reviews. In Joanna Briggs Institute (Ed.), *JBI manual for evidence synthesis*. DOI: 10.46658/JBIMES-20-12

Pierrès, O., Darvishy, A., & Christen, M. (2025). Exploring the role of generative AI in higher education: Semi-structured interviews with students with disabilities. *Education and Information Technologies, 30*(7), 8923–8952. DOI: 10.1007/s10639-024-13134-8

Triantafyllou, S. A., Georgiadis, C., & Sapounidis, T. (2025). Gamification in education and training: A literature review. *International Review of Education, 71*(3), 483–517. DOI: 10.1007/s11159-024-10111-8

Tricco, A. C., Lillie, E., Zarin, W., O'Brien, K. K., Colquhoun, H., Levac, D., Moher, D., Peters, M. D. J., Horsley, T., Weeks, L., Hempel, S., Akl, E. A., Chang, C., McGowan, J., Stewart, L., Hartling, L., Aldcroft, A., Wilson, M. G., Garritty, C., & Straus, S. E. (2018). PRISMA extension for scoping reviews (PRISMA-ScR): Checklist and explanation. *Annals of Internal Medicine, 169*(7), 467–473. DOI: 10.7326/M18-0850 PMID: 30178033

Tsimpidaki, A. (2013). *Child with special needs, family and school. A relationship in interaction* (2nd ed.). Papazisis.

Turner, C. (2025, December 3). *50 years after the birth of special education, some fear for its future under Trump. NPR.* https://www.npr.org/2025/12/03/nx-s1-5591152/trump-special-education-disabilties-schools

UNESCO. (2021). *Reimagining our futures together: A new social contract for education.* UNESCO Publishing. https://unesdoc.unesco.org/ark:/48223/pf0000379707

UNESCO. (2023). *Guidance for Generative AI in Education and Research.* UNESCO.

UNESCO. (2024). *Global report on teachers: Addressing teacher shortages and transforming the profession.* https://www.unesco.org/en/articles/global-report-teachers-addressing-teacher-shortages-and-transforming-profession

United Nations. (2006). *Convention on the Rights of Persons with Disabilities.* https://www.un.org/disabilities/documents/convention/convention_accessible_pdf.pdf

United Nations. (2022). *Artificial intelligence and the rights of persons with disabilities: Report of the Special Rapporteur on the rights of persons with disabilities*. United Nations Human Rights Council. https://documents.un.org/doc/undoc/gen/n22/683/45/pdf/n2268345.pdf

van Garderen, D., Lannin, J., Rodrigues, J., Smith, C. M., & Shahale, F. V. (2025). Using generative ai to create scaffolded instructional resources for students with disabilities. *Journal of Special Education Technology, 01626434251408056*, 01626434251408056. DOI: 10.1177/01626434251408056 PMID: 41953893

Weng, Z., & Fu, Y. (2025). Generative AI in language education: Bridging divide and fostering inclusivity. *International Journal of Technology in Education, 8*(2), 395–420. DOI: 10.46328/ijte.1056

Xiaoyu, W., Zainuddin, Z., & Hai Leng, C. (2025). Generative artificial intelligence in pedagogical practices: A systematic review of empirical studies (2022–2024). *Cogent Education, 12*(1), 2485499. DOI: 10.1080/2331186X.2025.2485499

Xu, H., Binti Hussain, D. D. Y., Li, X., & Wang, L. (2025). Study on factors influencing primary and secondary school teachers' acceptance of ai tools based on the UTAUT model: A case study of Tianchang City, Anhui Province. *Journal of Education and Educational Research, 12*(3), 106–110. DOI: 10.54097/6kmfe396

Xu, X., Zhang, X., Khan, M., Dou, W., Xue, S., & Yu, S. (2020). A balanced virtual machine scheduling method for energy-performance trade-offs in cyber-physical cloud systems. *Future Generation Computer Systems, 105*, 789–799. DOI: 10.1016/j.future.2017.08.057

Zallio, M., Ike, C. B., & Chivăran, C. (2025). Designing artificial intelligence: Exploring inclusion, diversity, equity, accessibility, and safety in human-centric emerging technologies. *AI, 6*(7), 143. DOI: 10.3390/ai6070143

Zhao, X., Chen, X., & Cox, A. (2026). Exploring the affordances of generative AI in academic writing for students with disabilities: A bottom-up approach to inform GenAI policies. *Policy Futures in Education, 24*(1), 59–81. DOI: 10.1177/14782103251395436

Zhao, X., Cox, A., & Chen, X. (2025). The use of generative AI by students with disabilities in higher education. *The Internet and Higher Education, 66*, 101014. DOI: 10.1016/j.iheduc.2025.101014

Chapter 2
Generative Artificial Intelligence in Special and Inclusive Education:
Pedagogical Applications and Ethical Challenges

Kyriaki Stavrou
http://orcid.org/0000-0001-8615-0541
National and Kapodistrian University of Athens, Greece

Ilias Vasileiadis
University of Western Macedonia, Greece

Ioannis Avlogiaris
Democritus University of Thrace, Greece

ABSTRACT

This chapter examines the role of generative artificial intelligence (AI) in special and inclusive education for learners with special educational needs and disabilities (SEND). It discusses how AI technologies can support personalized learning, differentiated instruction, accessibility, communication, and teacher support in inclusive classrooms. The chapter also explores the potential benefits of AI for neurodiverse learners, including students with autism, dyslexia, and ADHD. Ethical concerns such as bias, data privacy, accessibility inequalities, and overreliance on AI are critically addressed. Finally, the chapter highlights the importance of teacher training, AI literacy, and responsible implementation practices in educational settings.

DOI: 10.4018/979-8-3373-9169-4.ch002

INTRODUCTION

The rapid advancement of Generative artificial intelligence (GenAI) has significantly transformed contemporary educational practices and reshaped approaches to teaching, learning, assessment, and communication within modern educational systems. AI-powered technologies such as ChatGPT, Gemini, Microsoft Copilot, and other adaptive digital platforms are increasingly integrated into educational environments, offering new possibilities for content generation, automated feedback, personalized instruction, language support, and accessible learning experiences (Bozkurt et al., 2023; UNESCO, 2023).

Within special and inclusive education, GenAI has attracted increasing attention for its potential to support students with Special Educational Needs and Disabilities (SEND). Inclusive education is based on the principle that all learners, regardless of cognitive, physical, emotional, linguistic, or developmental differences, should have equal access to meaningful educational opportunities and active participation within mainstream educational settings (UNESCO, 1994). However, achieving effective inclusion remains a complex process for educators and schools, as teachers are often required to address highly diverse learner profiles, communication barriers, accessibility requirements, and differentiated instructional needs simultaneously.

Traditional educational approaches do not always adequately address the individualized needs of students with SEND. Consequently, educational technologies and assistive digital tools have become increasingly important in promoting differentiated instruction, accessible communication, adaptive assessment, and individualized learning support. In this context, generative AI technologies may enhance inclusive educational practices through adaptive learning environments, personalized educational materials, intelligent tutoring systems, automated translation services, speech recognition tools, and multimodal learning resources (Holmes et al., 2019).

The educational potential of generative AI is particularly significant in relation to personalized learning and accessibility. AI-supported systems may adapt instructional content according to students' cognitive abilities, learning pace, communication styles, and educational preferences. Learners with dyslexia, autism spectrum disorder, attention deficit disorders, hearing impairments, visual impairments, or communication difficulties may benefit from increased accessibility, participation, and instructional flexibility. Additionally, AI technologies may assist educators in developing differentiated lesson plans, accessible learning materials, individualized feedback, and adaptive classroom activities while reducing administrative workload (Luckin, 2018).

Despite these opportunities, the integration of generative AI into special and inclusive education also raises important ethical and pedagogical concerns. The use of AI systems frequently involves the collection and processing of sensitive learner data, including behavioral information, assessment records, and disability-related data. Consequently, issues related to privacy, data protection, informed consent, algorithmic bias, and digital surveillance have become central within discussions surrounding educational AI (OECD, 2021). Researchers have additionally emphasized that AI systems may unintentionally reproduce social inequalities and discriminatory representations embedded within training datasets.

Another concern involves the potential overreliance on automated technologies within educational practice. Although AI systems may improve efficiency and accessibility, inclusive education fundamentally depends on human interaction, empathy, collaboration, and emotional understanding. Teachers therefore continue to play an essential role in supporting students' academic, emotional, and social development. Furthermore, unequal access to technological infrastructure and digital resources may contribute to widening educational inequalities among learner populations, particularly for students with SEND (UNESCO, 2023).

This chapter critically examines the role of GenAI within special and inclusive education by exploring its pedagogical applications, educational opportunities, and ethical implications. More specifically, the chapter discusses how AI-supported technologies may contribute to personalized learning, differentiated instruction, accessibility, communication, teacher professional development, and student engagement. In addition, the chapter analyzes ethical concerns related to privacy, algorithmic bias, digital inequality, and the preservation of human-centered pedagogy.

This chapter contributes to the emerging literature on GenAI in special and inclusive education by providing an integrated perspective that combines pedagogical applications, accessibility considerations, teacher support, and ethical challenges. Unlike studies that focus on isolated aspects of AI in education, this conceptual chapter draws on selected theoretical, policy, and scholarly literature to distinguish GenAI from broader AI-supported educational and assistive technologies and to discuss its implications for diverse SEND learner profiles. The chapter adopts a conceptual and narrative approach and does not aim to provide a systematic review or to establish the empirical effectiveness of GenAI interventions. It also highlights key conditions for the responsible implementation of GenAI, emphasizing human-centered pedagogy, accessibility, teacher AI literacy, and ethical safeguards. In doing so, the chapter offers a conceptual foundation to inform future research, educational practice, and policy development.

THEORETICAL BACKGROUND

Inclusive Education and SEND

Inclusive education constitutes one of the most significant contemporary educational approaches aimed at ensuring equal participation, accessibility, and learning opportunities for all students regardless of disability, learning difficulty, cultural background, language, socioeconomic status, gender, or other forms of diversity. The concept of inclusion is grounded in principles of equity, social justice, human rights, and educational participation, emphasizing that all learners should be educated within supportive and accessible learning environments that recognize and respect individual differences (UNESCO, 1994).

The international movement toward inclusive education has been strongly influenced by major policy frameworks and human rights conventions. The Salamanca Statement and Framework for Action on Special Needs Education (UNESCO, 1994) highlighted the importance of schools accommodating all learners through child-centered pedagogical approaches capable of addressing diverse educational needs. Similarly, the United Nations Convention on the Rights of Persons with Disabilities (United Nations, 2006) emphasized the right of individuals with disabilities to access inclusive, equitable, and quality education without discrimination. These international frameworks have encouraged educational systems worldwide to reconsider traditional segregated educational models and adopt more inclusive practices that promote participation and belonging for all students.

Contemporary perspectives view inclusion not as a fixed educational outcome but as an ongoing process of identifying and removing barriers to participation and learning for all students. Ainscow (2020) argues that inclusive education should promote equity by addressing systemic barriers, supporting learner diversity, and fostering school cultures that value participation, collaboration, and belonging. This broader understanding of inclusion provides an important foundation for considering how emerging technologies, including generative AI, can support equitable and accessible learning opportunities for students with SEND.

Universal Design for Learning (UDL) further complements inclusive education by promoting the design of flexible learning environments that accommodate learner variability from the outset rather than through later adaptations. The UDL framework encourages multiple means of engagement, representation, and action and expression, enabling educators to provide more accessible and personalized learning experiences. In this respect, generative AI has considerable potential to support UDL principles by facilitating multimodal content creation, differentiated instructional materials, and flexible learning pathways tailored to diverse learner needs (CAST, 2024).

Within inclusive educational contexts, students SEND often require differentiated instructional strategies, individualized educational support, accessible learning materials, adaptive technologies, and flexible assessment procedures. SEND may include a broad range of conditions and learning profiles, such as learning disabilities, autism spectrum disorder, attention deficit and hyperactivity disorder, sensory impairments, speech and language difficulties, intellectual disabilities, emotional and behavioral difficulties, and physical disabilities. Due to this diversity, inclusive classrooms frequently involve highly complex teaching and learning dynamics that require continuous adaptation and pedagogical flexibility.

Teachers working in inclusive educational environments are expected to address multiple learner needs simultaneously while maintaining meaningful participation, academic engagement, and social inclusion for all students. However, educators often encounter significant challenges related to time constraints, limited resources, insufficient training in inclusive pedagogies, and difficulties in adapting educational materials to diverse learner profiles. Consequently, educational technologies and assistive digital tools have increasingly been recognized as valuable resources capable of supporting inclusive teaching practices, differentiated instruction, communication accessibility, and learner autonomy (Holmes et al., 2019).

The integration of digital technologies into inclusive education has gradually shifted from traditional assistive tools toward more intelligent and adaptive systems capable of responding dynamically to individual learner needs. Recent technological developments have particularly highlighted the potential role of artificial intelligence in promoting accessibility, participation, and personalized learning experiences for students with SEND. AI-supported technologies may contribute to reducing educational barriers by providing adaptive instructional support, multimodal communication options, automated feedback, and individualized educational content that can be adjusted according to students' abilities and preferences.

GenAI in Education

Artificial intelligence has become one of the most rapidly evolving technological fields affecting education in the twenty-first century. Within educational contexts, AI technologies have been increasingly used to support automated assessment, adaptive tutoring systems, intelligent learning analytics, predictive educational modeling, virtual learning assistants, and personalized instructional environments. More recently, the emergence of GenAI has significantly expanded the capabilities of educational AI systems by enabling the production of original and context-responsive content (UNESCO, 2023).

GenAI refers to computational systems capable of creating text, images, audio, video, lesson plans, assessments, simulations, and interactive responses based on large-scale data processing and machine learning algorithms. Unlike traditional rule-based educational technologies, generative AI systems can dynamically generate new outputs according to user prompts, contextual information, and learner interactions. Technologies such as ChatGPT, Gemini, Copilot, and other large language models have demonstrated advanced capabilities in natural language processing, content generation, conversational interaction, summarization, translation, and instructional support.

It is important to distinguish generative AI from broader AI-supported educational technologies. While traditional AI systems often rely on predefined rules, predictive analytics, adaptive algorithms, or assistive functions (e.g., intelligent tutoring systems, speech recognition, or screen readers), generative AI creates new content such as text, images, audio, lesson plans, and learning activities in response to user prompts. In practice, many educational technologies combine generative and non-generative AI functionalities. Therefore, this chapter focuses primarily on the pedagogical applications of generative AI while acknowledging the complementary role of broader AI-supported assistive technologies in inclusive education (Holmes & Tuomi, 2022).

In educational settings, generative AI has introduced new possibilities for personalized learning and instructional adaptation. AI-powered systems can generate customized educational materials, provide individualized explanations, produce immediate feedback, simplify academic texts, support multilingual communication, and create adaptive learning activities tailored to learners' specific educational needs. Such flexibility is particularly important within inclusive educational environments, where students often benefit from differentiated instructional approaches and accessible learning resources (Luckin, 2018).

Researchers have increasingly emphasized that generative AI may transform educational practices by shifting from standardized models of instruction toward more learner-centered and adaptive pedagogical approaches. Through continuous interaction and data analysis, Generative AI applications may support personalized instruction by analyzing learner interactions and generating adaptive educational content according to students' cognitive abilities, learning pace, communication preferences, and engagement levels. This capacity for personalization may be especially beneficial for learners with SEND who require individualized support and flexible educational accommodations.

Furthermore, generative AI technologies may support teachers by reducing administrative workload and assisting in the creation of differentiated educational materials. Educators may use AI systems to design lesson plans, generate assessment tasks, develop visual supports, create accessible instructional content, and provide individualized feedback more efficiently. In this way, AI technologies may function not only as learning tools for students but also as pedagogical support systems that enhance teachers' instructional capacity within inclusive classrooms.

Despite these opportunities, the growing use of generative AI in education has also generated substantial ethical and pedagogical debates. Concerns regarding algorithmic bias, misinformation, lack of transparency, overdependence on technology, privacy risks, and unequal access to digital resources remain central within contemporary discussions surrounding educational AI (OECD, 2021). Scholars have argued that AI systems may unintentionally reproduce social inequalities and discriminatory patterns embedded within training datasets, potentially affecting vulnerable learner populations, including students with disabilities and diverse linguistic or cultural backgrounds.

Consequently, the integration of generative AI into inclusive education requires careful theoretical and ethical consideration. Human-centered pedagogical approaches, accessibility standards, inclusive design principles, and equitable technological access must remain central priorities when implementing GenAI-supported educational systems. Understanding the theoretical foundations of inclusive education alongside the emerging capabilities and limitations of generative AI is, therefore, essential for evaluating how these technologies may contribute to more equitable and accessible educational environments.

Pedagogical Applications of Generative AI in Special and Inclusive Education

The integration of GenAI into inclusive educational environments has substantially expanded the possibilities for individualized, accessible, and adaptive teaching and learning practices. Recent developments in AI technologies have enabled educators to create more flexible instructional experiences capable of responding to diverse learner profiles, communication styles, cognitive abilities, and educational needs. Within special and inclusive education, generative AI may function both as an instructional support mechanism and as an assistive educational technology that enhances accessibility, learner engagement, participation, and academic achievement (Bozkurt et al., 2023).

Educational researchers increasingly emphasize that AI-driven systems can support more learner-centered educational environments by adapting instructional materials according to students' individual characteristics and learning preferences. Such adaptability is particularly important for learners with SEND, as standardized educational approaches may not adequately address individualized learning barriers and accessibility requirements (Holmes et al., 2019). Consequently, generative AI technologies are increasingly viewed as innovative tools capable of promoting differentiated instruction, inclusive participation, and personalized educational support within mainstream classrooms.

Overall, the pedagogical applications of GenAI within special and inclusive education demonstrate significant potential for promoting accessibility, personalization, flexibility, and educational participation. However, the successful implementation of these technologies depends on ethical design, inclusive pedagogical frameworks, teacher preparedness, and equitable access to technological resources.

Personalized Learning and Differentiated Instruction

One of the most important pedagogical contributions of GenAI within inclusive educational environments involves the promotion of personalized learning and differentiated instruction (Luckin, 2018). Personalized learning refers to educational approaches that adapt teaching methods, instructional materials, learning activities, and assessment processes according to students' individual characteristics, abilities, interests, communication styles, and learning preferences. Within special and inclusive education, personalized instruction is particularly significant because students with SEND often demonstrate highly diverse cognitive, emotional, linguistic, sensory, and behavioral profiles that cannot be adequately addressed through standardized instructional approaches.

Generative AI systems possess the capacity to analyze learner responses, monitor engagement patterns, evaluate learning progression, and dynamically adjust educational content according to students' needs and performance levels. Through adaptive algorithms and machine learning processes, AI-powered educational platforms may generate individualized explanations, modify content difficulty, simplify instructional language, and provide personalized feedback in real time. Such adaptive functionalities may improve educational accessibility and support more meaningful participation for students who experience learning barriers within traditional classroom environments.

For learners with dyslexia and other reading difficulties, generative AI technologies may support literacy development through text simplification, phonological support, predictive text systems, speech synthesis, and text-to-speech applications that improve reading comprehension and reduce cognitive overload. For example, a teacher may prompt a GenAI system to generate a personalized social story, visual routine, or simplified explanation of a classroom activity for a learner with autism spectrum disorder. Similarly, learners with attention deficit and hyperactivity disorder may utilize AI-supported organizational tools, adaptive pacing systems, and interactive learning activities that promote concentration, self-regulation, and sustained engagement.

Generative AI may also contribute significantly to differentiated instruction by assisting educators in modifying educational materials according to students' cognitive and linguistic abilities. AI systems can transform complex academic texts into simplified versions, generate alternative explanations for difficult concepts, create scaffolded activities, produce multimodal learning materials, and adapt assessment tasks to accommodate diverse learner profiles. The multimodal capabilities of generative AI are especially valuable within inclusive education because many students benefit from receiving information through multiple sensory channels, including visual, auditory, textual, and interactive formats.

Furthermore, AI-supported educational systems may facilitate individualized progression by allowing students to learn at their own pace and level of understanding. Unlike traditional classroom instruction, where teaching often follows a uniform pace, generative AI technologies may provide continuous and responsive instructional support tailored to individual learning trajectories. This flexibility may reduce academic frustration and increase learner confidence, particularly among students who require additional time, repetition, or alternative instructional approaches to achieve learning goals.

Teachers may additionally utilize generative AI technologies to develop individualized educational plans, differentiated worksheets, adaptive lesson plans, and personalized classroom activities more efficiently. AI-assisted systems may support educators in identifying appropriate accommodations, generating accessible instructional resources, and providing individualized feedback based on learner performance. Such technological assistance may reduce teacher workload associated with curriculum adaptation while simultaneously improving instructional responsiveness and pedagogical flexibility within inclusive classrooms.

Another important advantage of generative AI involves the provision of immediate and continuous feedback. Research has demonstrated that timely feedback may enhance student motivation, support self-regulated learning, and improve academic achievement by helping learners identify areas requiring further practice or clarification. AI-powered tutoring systems may additionally provide repeated explanations and individualized assistance without the social pressure or fear of judgment that some students experience during traditional classroom interactions. This supportive learning environment may contribute positively to students' emotional well-being, confidence, and willingness to engage in learning activities.

Despite these advantages, researchers also emphasize the importance of critically evaluating the pedagogical implications of AI-supported personalization. Excessive dependence on automated instructional systems may risk reducing opportunities for collaborative learning, peer interaction, and human-centered educational relationships. Consequently, personalized AI-supported instruction should complement rather than replace the essential pedagogical role of teachers within inclusive educational settings.

The educational value of generative AI becomes more evident when considered through authentic classroom scenarios. For example, a teacher may use a GenAI tool to simplify a science text and generate comprehension questions for a learner with dyslexia. For a student with autism spectrum disorder, GenAI may be used to create personalized social stories or visual schedules that support communication and predictability. Learners with ADHD may benefit from AI-generated step-by-step learning plans and organizational prompts, while multilingual students or learners with language difficulties may use GenAI to receive simplified explanations or translated classroom instructions. In each case, teachers should critically review AI-generated materials to ensure accuracy, accessibility, and alignment with learners' individual educational needs.

Accessibility and Assistive Technologies

In this section, Generative AI is considered in combination with broader AI-supported assistive technologies. Tools such as screen readers, speech recognition, automated captioning, and predictive communication systems are not necessarily generative technologies in themselves, but they may be integrated with GenAI functions to provide more adaptive and personalized accessibility support. Accessibility constitutes a fundamental principle of inclusive education, and recent developments in GenAI have significantly expanded the capabilities of assistive educational technologies designed to support students with disabilities and diverse learning needs. AI-supported accessibility systems may facilitate communication, participation, independent learning, and equal access to educational content by reducing sensory, cognitive, physical, and linguistic barriers within educational environments.

Generative AI, in combination with AI-supported assistive technologies, may support accessibility through adaptive content generation, while AI-supported tools such as speech recognition, text-to-speech, speech-to-text, automated captioning, intelligent translation, predictive communication systems, and adaptive interfaces enhance accessibility for learners with diverse needs. According to UNESCO (2021), AI-powered educational technologies possess considerable potential for improving accessibility and reducing educational exclusion when implemented according to inclusive and human-centered design principles.

For students with visual impairments, generative AI may provide intelligent screen-reading technologies, automated image descriptions, object recognition systems, audio summaries, and text recognition tools capable of improving access to digital educational resources. AI-generated audio descriptions and navigation support systems may assist learners in interacting more independently with online educational platforms and multimedia instructional materials. Such technologies may substantially improve participation and reduce accessibility barriers within digital learning environments.

Similarly, learners with hearing impairments may benefit from AI-supported real-time captioning systems, automated transcription technologies, sign language recognition applications, and communication support tools that facilitate classroom interaction and participation. These technologies may improve students' access to spoken information during lectures, classroom discussions, and collaborative activities while simultaneously supporting communication equity within inclusive educational settings.

Students with speech and language difficulties may additionally benefit from generative AI-supported augmentative and alternative communication systems. AI-powered communication platforms may generate personalized communication prompts, predictive responses, adaptive conversational assistance, and language support tools that facilitate interaction and self-expression. Such technologies may contribute to greater communication independence and social participation for learners experiencing expressive or receptive language challenges.

In multilingual educational contexts, generative AI may also support learners by translating instructional materials, simplifying complex academic language, adapting vocabulary difficulty, and generating culturally responsive educational content according to students' linguistic backgrounds. These capabilities may be particularly beneficial for multilingual learners and students who experience language-related learning barriers within mainstream educational environments.

The multimodal nature of generative AI technologies is especially important within inclusive education because many students benefit from accessing educational content through diverse communication formats. AI-generated visual aids, interactive simulations, audio explanations, simplified textual content, and adaptive multimedia resources may enhance comprehension, engagement, and participation for students who experience difficulties with traditional instructional materials. Consequently, generative AI technologies may contribute to the creation of more universally accessible, flexible, and learner-centered educational environments.

Furthermore, AI-supported accessibility technologies may promote greater learner independence and self-determination by enabling students to access educational materials and complete learning activities with reduced reliance on constant adult assistance. Increased independence may positively affect students' confidence, motivation, self-efficacy, and participation within both academic and social contexts.

Nevertheless, researchers also emphasize that accessibility technologies should not be viewed as universally effective solutions capable of addressing all educational barriers. The successful implementation of AI-supported assistive technologies depends on appropriate pedagogical integration, teacher training, technological accessibility, ethical design, and continuous evaluation of students' individual needs. Educational institutions must therefore ensure that AI-supported accessibility systems remain inclusive, equitable, culturally responsive, and aligned with broader human-centered educational goals.

Teacher Support and Professional Development

Teachers working within inclusive educational environments frequently experience increased instructional and administrative responsibilities associated with differentiated instruction, individualized educational planning, continuous assessment, classroom adaptation, and learner support. Inclusive classrooms often require educators to simultaneously address highly diverse learner profiles, communication needs, behavioral challenges, accessibility accommodations, and varying levels of academic readiness. As a result, many teachers report experiencing workload intensification, time constraints, and difficulties in developing individualized educational materials capable of effectively supporting all learners within mainstream educational settings.

In this context, GenAI technologies may provide substantial pedagogical and organizational support by assisting educators in curriculum adaptation, instructional planning, material development, and assessment design. AI-powered systems are capable of automating repetitive and time-consuming tasks while simultaneously supporting teachers in creating more personalized and accessible learning experiences for students with SEND. According to Holmes et al. (2019), AI-supported educational technologies may enhance instructional flexibility and improve teachers' capacity to respond to learner diversity within inclusive classrooms.

Generative AI tools may assist educators in designing differentiated lesson plans adapted to students' cognitive abilities, learning preferences, communication styles, and academic performance levels. AI systems can generate scaffolded instructional materials, simplify academic language, produce alternative explanations for difficult concepts, and create multimodal educational resources that combine text, visuals, audio, and interactive content. Such capabilities may support teachers in developing more inclusive instructional environments while reducing the time required for manual curriculum modification and resource preparation.

Additionally, AI technologies may support the development of individualized educational plans and adaptive classroom activities tailored to specific learner needs. Teachers may utilize generative AI systems to create differentiated worksheets, adaptive assessment tasks, accessible learning materials, and personalized feedback mechanisms capable of supporting students with diverse educational profiles. AI-supported systems may also help educators identify appropriate accommodations and instructional strategies based on learner performance data and engagement patterns.

The use of AI-generated assessment and feedback systems may further contribute to more responsive and continuous evaluation practices within inclusive educational contexts. AI-powered platforms may automatically analyze student responses, monitor learning progression, identify areas requiring additional support, and generate immediate individualized feedback. Such capabilities may improve instructional responsiveness and allow teachers to intervene more effectively when students encounter learning difficulties. Immediate feedback may additionally support students' self-regulated learning, motivation, and academic engagement.

Generative AI technologies may also facilitate classroom organization and administrative efficiency. Teachers frequently devote substantial time to grading assignments, preparing instructional resources, documenting learner progress, and organizing educational content. AI-assisted automation of these administrative tasks may reduce workload pressures and allow educators to focus more extensively on direct pedagogical interaction, emotional support, and learner engagement. This redistribution of professional time may be particularly valuable within inclusive classrooms where individualized student support is essential.

Beyond classroom instruction, generative AI may contribute significantly to teacher professional development and lifelong learning. AI-based professional learning systems may provide educators with personalized training opportunities, adaptive learning modules, reflective pedagogical guidance, and access to updated educational resources related to inclusive pedagogy, assistive technologies, digital literacy, and differentiated instruction. Such professional development opportunities may support teachers in strengthening their competencies regarding both inclusive education and emerging educational technologies.

For educators who possess limited prior experience with assistive technologies or inclusive instructional practices, AI-supported professional learning systems may function as accessible and flexible training environments that adapt according to individual learning needs and professional interests. AI-generated recommendations, reflective feedback tools, and personalized learning pathways may contribute to continuous professional growth while encouraging teachers to adopt innovative pedagogical practices within inclusive educational settings.

Furthermore, generative AI technologies may support collaboration among educators, special education professionals, therapists, and support staff involved in inclusive educational planning. AI-supported communication and information-sharing systems may facilitate interdisciplinary collaboration by organizing learner data, generating instructional recommendations, and improving coordination among educational professionals. Enhanced collaboration may contribute to more coherent and comprehensive support systems for students with SEND.

Despite these advantages, researchers emphasise that AI technologies should serve as supportive pedagogical tools rather than as replacements for teachers' professional expertise and human-centred educational relationships. Inclusive education fundamentally depends on empathy, communication, ethical judgment, and social interaction, all of which remain essential dimensions of effective teaching practices. Consequently, the successful integration of generative AI into teacher support and professional development requires balanced implementation strategies that prioritize human-centered pedagogy, ethical educational practices, and critical technological literacy.

Educational institutions and policymakers must therefore ensure that teachers receive adequate preparation, training, and institutional support for the responsible integration of AI technologies within inclusive educational contexts. Professional development initiatives should focus not only on technological competencies but also on ethical awareness, accessibility principles, critical digital literacy, and inclusive pedagogical design. Through appropriate training and support, educators may utilize generative AI technologies more effectively to enhance inclusion, accessibility, and learner participation while maintaining meaningful human-centered educational relationships.

Beyond technical proficiency, teachers require a broader set of professional competencies for the responsible integration of generative AI into inclusive education. These competencies include AI literacy, effective prompt design, critical evaluation of AI-generated content, awareness of algorithmic bias, data privacy and protection, accessibility-oriented instructional design, and the ability to determine when AI use is pedagogically appropriate or when human intervention is essential. Developing these competencies through continuous professional development will enable teachers to integrate GenAI in ways that enhance inclusion while maintaining ethical and learner-centered educational practices.

Student Engagement, Motivation, and Social Participation

GenAItechnologies may significantly enhance student engagement, motivation, participation, and social inclusion within special and inclusive educational environments. Student engagement constitutes a multidimensional concept that includes behavioral participation, emotional involvement, cognitive investment, and social interaction within learning processes. For many learners with SEND, active participation in traditional classroom activities may be affected by communication barriers, learning difficulties, anxiety, sensory sensitivities, reduced self-confidence, or previous experiences of academic exclusion. Consequently, inclusive educational environments increasingly seek instructional approaches capable of promoting meaningful participation, learner autonomy, and positive educational experiences for all students.

Interactive AI-supported educational systems may contribute to the creation of more supportive, flexible, and individualized learning environments that reduce participation barriers and encourage active engagement. Conversational AI technologies, adaptive tutoring systems, and intelligent virtual assistants may allow students to interact with educational content according to their own pace, communication style, and level of understanding. Such individualized interaction may reduce the fear of failure, social pressure, and performance anxiety that some learners experience during conventional classroom participation.

For students who experience communication difficulties or social anxiety, conversational AI systems may provide low-pressure opportunities for practicing language skills, asking questions, expressing ideas, and engaging in educational dialogue without fear of negative judgment. Learners with autism spectrum disorder, for example, may benefit from predictable and structured conversational interactions that support communication development and social participation. Similarly, students with attention difficulties may engage more effectively with interactive AI applications capable of adapting instructional pacing and maintaining learner attention through personalized feedback and dynamic interaction.

Gamified AI-supported educational applications may additionally improve student motivation and persistence in learning activities. Gamification strategies such as adaptive rewards, progress tracking, interactive challenges, and personalized achievements may contribute positively to learner engagement, emotional investment, and self-confidence. AI-powered educational games and adaptive learning platforms may create motivating instructional experiences that encourage students to participate actively while simultaneously supporting individualized progression and skill development.

Interactive storytelling technologies and immersive AI-supported learning environments may further enhance creativity, imagination, communication, and emotional engagement among students with SEND. Through personalized narratives, visual supports, adaptive scenarios, and interactive simulations, generative AI may create more accessible and meaningful educational experiences capable of addressing diverse learner interests and abilities. Such approaches may be particularly beneficial for learners who experience difficulties engaging with conventional text-based instructional materials.

The motivational impact of AI-supported educational systems is especially important for students who have previously experienced academic frustration, social exclusion, or repeated learning difficulties within traditional educational contexts. Personalized learning pathways, immediate feedback mechanisms, and adaptive instructional support may improve learners' self-efficacy, confidence, and willingness to participate in classroom activities. Research has demonstrated that students who experience success through individualized and supportive learning environments are more likely to develop positive attitudes toward learning and greater academic persistence.

Furthermore, AI-supported technologies may contribute to social participation and collaborative learning within inclusive classrooms. Interactive educational platforms may facilitate peer communication, collaborative problem-solving activities, and shared learning experiences that promote inclusion and social interaction among students with diverse abilities. AI-assisted communication tools may additionally support learners with speech, language, or communication difficulties in participating more actively during classroom discussions and group activities.

Despite these educational opportunities, researchers emphasize that student engagement should not be understood solely in technological terms. Meaningful inclusion and participation fundamentally depend on supportive human relationships, emotional connection, empathy, and collaborative educational communities. Consequently, AI-supported engagement strategies should complement rather than replace human-centered pedagogical interaction and social learning experiences. Teachers continue to play a central role in fostering inclusive classroom climates, emotional support, and meaningful interpersonal relationships that contribute to students' motivation and overall well-being.

Table 1 synthesizes the principal educational needs of different SEND learner profiles, potential GenAI applications, expected pedagogical benefits, and the ethical safeguards required for responsible implementation.

Table 1. Conceptual framework for the use of generative AI in inclusive education

SEND learner profile	Educational need	Example of GenAI application	Pedagogical benefit	Ethical safeguard
Dyslexia	Reading comprehension	Text simplification, vocabulary adaptation	Improved comprehension	Teacher verification of generated content
Autism Spectrum Disorder	Social communication	AI-generated social stories, visual supports	Enhanced communication and predictability	Human supervision and personalization
ADHD	Attention and organization	Personalized prompts, structured learning activities	Increased engagement and self-regulation	Avoid overreliance on AI
Visual impairment	Access to learning materials	AI-generated image descriptions, audio summaries	Improved accessibility	Accessible platform design

continued on following page

Table 1. Continued

SEND learner profile	Educational need	Example of GenAI application	Pedagogical benefit	Ethical safeguard
Hearing impairment	Communication	AI-assisted captioning and translation	Increased classroom participation	Accuracy review of automated outputs
Multilingual learners	Language support	AI translation and simplified texts	Better inclusion and understanding	Cultural and linguistic validation

Table 1 illustrates how different SEND learner profiles may benefit from specific GenAI applications while emphasizing the importance of aligning pedagogical benefits with appropriate ethical safeguards. Rather than promoting a one-size-fits-all approach, the framework highlights that the educational value of GenAI depends on learners' individual needs, teacher mediation, and responsible implementation.

ETHICAL CHALLENGES AND CONCERNS

Despite the substantial educational opportunities associated with generative artificial intelligence, the integration of AI technologies within special and inclusive education also raises important ethical, pedagogical, and social concerns. Researchers and policymakers increasingly emphasise the need to critically evaluate AI-supported educational systems, particularly when implemented for vulnerable learner populations, such as students with SEND. Ethical considerations become especially important because AI technologies frequently involve the collection, analysis, and processing of sensitive educational and personal data.

One major ethical concern involves data privacy and information security. AI-supported educational systems often collect extensive learner data, including academic records, communication patterns, behavioral indicators, learning preferences, and disability-related information. The storage and processing of such data may expose students to risks associated with unauthorized access, surveillance, data misuse, or breaches of confidentiality. Educational institutions must therefore ensure compliance with ethical standards, privacy regulations, and data protection frameworks capable of safeguarding students' rights and well-being (OECD, 2021).

Researchers have also highlighted concerns regarding algorithmic bias and discriminatory decision-making within AI systems. Generative AI technologies are trained using large-scale datasets that may contain social, cultural, linguistic, gender-related, or disability-related biases. Consequently, AI-supported systems may unintentionally reproduce stereotypes, exclusionary assumptions, or inequitable educational recommendations that negatively affect vulnerable learner populations.

Students from diverse linguistic, cultural, or disability backgrounds may therefore experience unequal educational outcomes if AI systems are not designed according to inclusive and equitable principles.

Many AI systems operate through complex machine learning processes that may not be fully understandable to educators, students, or families. As a result, stakeholders may experience difficulties evaluating how learner data are interpreted and how educational recommendations are generated. Limited transparency may reduce trust in AI-supported educational systems and complicate ethical accountability within educational environments.

The increasing dependence on AI technologies additionally raises concerns regarding overreliance on automated instructional systems. Although AI-supported educational tools may improve efficiency, personalization, and accessibility, inclusive education fundamentally depends on human interaction, empathy, emotional understanding, and social participation. Teachers continue to play a central role not only in academic instruction but also in supporting learners' emotional well-being, communication, motivation, and social development. Excessive dependence on automated technologies may therefore weaken meaningful pedagogical relationships and reduce opportunities for collaborative and interpersonal learning experiences.

Access to AI-supported educational systems is not equally distributed across schools and communities. Students with SEND who already experience educational disadvantage may face additional exclusion if schools lack technological resources, accessible tools, trained personnel, or reliable internet access. Such inequalities may contribute to the widening of existing educational disparities among learner populations.

Furthermore, concerns have emerged regarding the reliability and pedagogical appropriateness of AI-generated educational content. Generative AI systems may occasionally produce inaccurate information or inappropriate instructional recommendations that could negatively affect learning processes if not critically monitored by educators. Consequently, teachers and educational institutions must maintain active oversight and continuous evaluation of AI-generated content to ensure educational quality and appropriateness.

UNESCO (2023) emphasized that the responsible implementation of generative AI within education requires transparent governance frameworks, inclusive technological design, ethical accountability, and continuous evaluation of educational impact. Human-centered AI policies should prioritize learner rights, accessibility, fairness, inclusion, and social participation while ensuring that technological innovation remains aligned with broader educational values.

To facilitate a more systematic understanding of ethical issues, the risks associated with the use of generative AI in inclusive education can be grouped into five interrelated categories: (a) privacy and data protection, (b) algorithmic bias and fairness, (c) transparency and accountability, (d) overreliance on AI and reduced human interaction, and (e) equity of access and digital inclusion. These categories provide a practical framework for evaluating the responsible implementation of GenAI in educational settings and highlight the importance of balancing technological innovation with pedagogical and ethical responsibility.

Ultimately, the ethical integration of generative AI into special and inclusive education requires collaboration among educators, researchers, policymakers, technology developers, families, and learners themselves. Responsible implementation strategies should combine technological innovation with inclusive pedagogical principles, accessibility standards, ethical awareness, and critical digital literacy. Through balanced and thoughtful integration, generative AI may contribute positively to more equitable, accessible, and inclusive educational environments for all learners.

Data Privacy and Security

One of the most significant ethical concerns associated with the implementation of GenAIwithin educational environments involves issues related to data privacy, information security, and the protection of sensitive learner data. AI-supported educational systems frequently require the collection, analysis, storage, and processing of extensive amounts of student information in order to generate adaptive instructional content, personalized recommendations, automated feedback, and predictive educational responses. Such data may include learning profiles, academic performance records, communication patterns, behavioral indicators, engagement metrics, emotional responses, and individualized educational information (OECD, 2021).

For students with SEND, concerns regarding privacy and data protection become even more critical because educational records may additionally contain highly sensitive medical, psychological, developmental, or disability-related information. The inappropriate handling or unauthorized disclosure of such information may negatively affect students' dignity, safety, autonomy, and educational rights. Consequently, educational institutions implementing AI-supported systems must ensure that student data are collected, processed, and stored according to strict ethical standards and legal data protection frameworks.

The increasing use of cloud-based AI systems and digital educational platforms also raises concerns regarding cybersecurity risks, data breaches, unauthorized surveillance, and commercial exploitation of learner information. AI-supported technologies often rely on large-scale databases and external technological infrastructures that may expose educational institutions to vulnerabilities associated with hacking, unauthorized access, or misuse of personal information. Researchers have therefore emphasized the importance of establishing secure technological infrastructures capable of protecting sensitive learner data while ensuring confidentiality and transparency.

Another important ethical issue concerns informed consent and learner autonomy. Students, families, and educators may not always fully understand how AI systems collect, interpret, and utilize educational data. As a result, concerns emerge regarding whether learners and parents are adequately informed about data processing procedures, algorithmic decision-making mechanisms, and the long-term use of personal educational information. Transparent communication regarding data collection, storage duration, information sharing, and system functionality is therefore essential for maintaining trust and protecting learner rights within AI-supported educational environments.

Educational institutions must additionally ensure that AI-supported systems comply with international ethical guidelines, accessibility principles, and data protection regulations. Human-centered AI governance frameworks should prioritize learner safety, confidentiality, fairness, and informed participation while ensuring that technological innovation remains aligned with educational and human rights principles. UNESCO (2023) emphasized that responsible AI implementation requires continuous ethical evaluation, transparent institutional policies, and accountability mechanisms capable of safeguarding vulnerable learner populations.

Furthermore, ethical data governance within inclusive educational contexts should involve collaboration among educators, policymakers, technology developers, families, and learners themselves. Such collaboration may contribute to the development of more transparent and equitable educational AI systems that prioritize students' well-being and social inclusion. Therefore, the responsible management of educational data constitutes a fundamental requirement for the ethical integration of GenAIinto special and inclusive education.

Algorithmic Bias and Equity

Another major ethical challenge associated with GenAIinvolves the existence of algorithmic bias and the potential reproduction of educational inequalities within AI-supported systems. AI technologies are trained using large-scale datasets derived from existing digital information, human interactions, educational materials, and online content. However, these datasets may contain social, cultural, linguistic, racial, gender-related, or disability-related biases that can unintentionally influence the outputs generated by AI systems.

Consequently, generative AI applications may reproduce stereotypes, exclusionary assumptions, or inequitable representations that negatively affect students from diverse learner populations. Learners from minority linguistic or cultural backgrounds may receive less accurate educational outputs, while disability-related representations within AI-generated content may reinforce deficit-oriented perspectives rather than strengths-based approaches to inclusion. Such biases may contribute to unequal learning opportunities, discriminatory educational experiences, and the reinforcement of existing social inequalities.

Within inclusive educational settings, algorithmic bias may particularly affect students with SEND because AI systems may not always adequately recognize diverse communication styles, cognitive profiles, or learning patterns. Educational technologies trained primarily on standardized learner data may fail to accommodate students who demonstrate nontraditional learning trajectories or alternative forms of communication. As a result, AI-generated recommendations and adaptive learning systems may unintentionally disadvantage learners whose educational profiles differ from dominant normative assumptions embedded within technological systems.

Researchers have additionally emphasized that bias within AI systems may affect educational assessment, feedback generation, learner profiling, and predictive analytics. If AI-supported educational platforms generate inaccurate assumptions regarding learner ability, engagement, or performance, students may receive inappropriate instructional recommendations or unequal educational support. Such outcomes may negatively influence learner confidence, participation, and academic progression while reinforcing educational exclusion rather than promoting inclusion.

The issue of linguistic and cultural representation also remains particularly important within multilingual and multicultural educational environments. AI systems trained predominantly on specific languages or cultural frameworks may fail to provide culturally responsive educational content for diverse learner populations. Consequently, students from minority backgrounds may experience reduced accessibility, limited representation, or lower-quality instructional support compared to dominant learner groups.

Addressing algorithmic bias requires continuous evaluation, ethical oversight, and inclusive technological design. Developers, educators, policymakers, and researchers must critically assess AI systems to ensure fairness, accessibility, representation, and cultural responsiveness for all learners. Inclusive AI design should involve diverse datasets, accessibility-centered development practices, interdisciplinary collaboration, and ongoing monitoring of educational outcomes to identify and reduce discriminatory patterns.

Furthermore, educational institutions must promote critical digital literacy among educators and students to ensure that AI-generated outputs are evaluated critically rather than accepted uncritically as objective or neutral information. Teachers play a crucial role in identifying potential bias within educational technologies and ensuring that AI-supported learning environments remain equitable, inclusive, and pedagogically appropriate.

Ultimately, achieving equity within AI-supported education requires the recognition that technological systems are shaped by social values, human decisions, and institutional structures. Consequently, ethical AI implementation must prioritize social justice, inclusion, diversity, and accessibility while actively addressing the structural inequalities that may influence educational technologies and learner experiences.

Transparency and Accountability

Transparency and accountability are essential principles for the responsible use of generative AI in education. Educators, learners, and families should understand how AI-generated outputs are produced and recognize their limitations. Human oversight remains necessary to verify the accuracy, appropriateness, and fairness of AI-generated content, particularly when decisions affect learners with SEND. Educational institutions should therefore establish clear governance mechanisms that define responsibilities for the ethical use of GenAI and ensure that AI-supported recommendations never replace professional educational judgment.

Overreliance on Technology

Although GenAI offers substantial educational benefits, researchers increasingly warn against the risks associated with excessive dependence on automated technologies within educational environments. While AI-supported systems may improve instructional efficiency, accessibility, personalization, and learner support, inclusive education fundamentally depends on human interaction, emotional connection, empathy, collaboration, and meaningful social participation. Consequently, AI technologies should be viewed as complementary pedagogical tools rather than replacements for teachers, support professionals, or human-centered educational relationships.

One major concern involves the possibility that excessive reliance on AI systems may reduce opportunities for authentic interpersonal communication and collaborative learning experiences. Inclusive classrooms are not solely spaces for academic instruction but also environments in which students develop emotional understanding, social interaction skills, empathy, cooperation, and a sense of belonging. Human relationships between teachers, students, families, and peers remain central to inclusive educational practice and cannot be fully replicated through automated technological systems.

Teachers play an essential role in understanding students' emotional, developmental, behavioral, and social needs. Effective inclusive pedagogy requires professional judgment, ethical sensitivity, emotional responsiveness, and contextual understanding that extend beyond the capabilities of algorithmic systems. Although AI technologies may provide adaptive instructional support and automated feedback, they cannot fully replace human empathy, relational communication, or pedagogical intuition. Students with SEND, in particular, often benefit from consistent emotional support, trust-based relationships, and individualized interpersonal interaction that require human presence and understanding.

Researchers have also highlighted concerns regarding the reduction of critical thinking and learner autonomy resulting from excessive dependence on AI-generated information and automated support systems. If students become overly reliant on AI technologies for problem-solving, content generation, or academic assistance, opportunities for independent thinking, creativity, reflective learning, and cognitive development may be reduced. Educational environments must therefore ensure that AI technologies support rather than undermine active learner engagement and intellectual autonomy.

Another important issue involves the professional role of teachers within increasingly technologized educational systems. Some scholars have expressed concerns that the growing automation of instructional tasks may contribute to the devaluation of teachers' professional expertise and pedagogical authority. However, inclusive education requires highly skilled educators capable of adapting instruction, supporting emotional development, facilitating communication, and promoting equitable participation within diverse classroom environments. AI technologies should therefore enhance teachers' professional capacities rather than replace their central educational role.

The increasing integration of AI into education may additionally contribute to reduced human interaction for students who already experience social isolation or communication difficulties. Learners with SEND may particularly require opportunities for face-to-face communication, collaborative learning, peer interaction, and emotional connection to support both academic and social development. Excessive engagement with AI-supported systems without sufficient human interaction may therefore negatively affect social participation and emotional well-being.

Consequently, researchers and international organizations emphasize the importance of maintaining balanced and human-centered approaches to AI integration within education. UNESCO (2023) stressed that educational technologies should support inclusive pedagogical goals while preserving human dignity, emotional well-being, social interaction, and ethical educational relationships. Teachers, families, and educational institutions must therefore critically evaluate the role of AI within learning environments to ensure that technological innovation remains aligned with broader educational and humanistic values.

Ultimately, the responsible implementation of GenAI within special and inclusive education requires a balanced integration model in which technological support complements rather than replaces human-centered pedagogy. AI systems may enhance accessibility, personalization, and instructional flexibility, but meaningful inclusion continues to depend fundamentally on empathy, collaboration, ethical responsibility, and authentic human relationships within educational communities.

Digital Divide and Accessibility Inequalities

Despite the significant educational opportunities associated with generative artificial intelligence, access to advanced AI-supported technologies remains unevenly distributed across schools, communities, and countries. Financial limitations, insufficient technological infrastructure, restricted internet connectivity, and unequal access to digital devices may prevent many learners and educational institutions from fully benefiting from AI-supported educational innovations. Consequently, the integration of generative AI into education may unintentionally reinforce existing educational inequalities rather than reduce them if issues of accessibility and equity are not adequately addressed.

The digital divide refers not only to differences in access to technological resources but also to disparities in digital literacy, technological competence, institutional support, and educational opportunities. Schools located in economically disadvantaged regions often face substantial barriers related to limited funding, outdated technological equipment, insufficient technical support, and reduced access to specialized educational technologies. Such inequalities may significantly affect the capacity of educational institutions to implement AI-supported instructional systems effectively and inclusively.

Students with SEND, who already experience educational and social disadvantages in many contexts, may face additional exclusion if schools lack accessible digital technologies, assistive educational tools, or adequately trained educational professionals. AI-supported systems may only contribute positively to inclusion when they are designed and implemented according to universal accessibility principles that accommodate diverse learner needs, communication styles, sensory differences, and cognitive profiles. Without appropriate accessibility standards, AI technologies risk creating new barriers for learners who require individualized accommodations and adaptive support.

Furthermore, unequal access to assistive technologies and AI-supported learning tools may disproportionately affect students from low-income families and marginalized communities. Learners who lack reliable internet access, personal digital devices, or supportive learning environments at home may encounter difficulties participating in AI-enhanced educational activities. Such disparities became particularly visible during periods of remote and online learning, where unequal technological access significantly affected participation, engagement, and academic achievement among vulnerable learner populations.

Digital literacy also constitutes a critical dimension of educational equity within AI-supported learning environments. Both educators and students require sufficient technological knowledge and critical digital competencies to use AI tools effectively, responsibly, and safely. However, many educational systems continue to experience limitations regarding teacher preparation, technological training, and institutional support for digital inclusion. Teachers who lack familiarity with AI-supported educational technologies may experience difficulties integrating such systems effectively into inclusive classroom practices.

Researchers additionally emphasize that accessibility should not be understood solely in technical terms but also as a broader issue of social inclusion, participation, and educational justice. Inclusive technological design requires consideration of linguistic diversity, cultural responsiveness, cognitive accessibility, and disability-inclusive pedagogical principles. AI systems developed primarily for dominant populations may fail to address the needs and experiences of marginalized learner groups, thereby contributing to exclusion rather than equity.

Consequently, policymakers, educational institutions, and technology developers must prioritize equitable access to digital infrastructure, inclusive technological design, accessible educational resources, and teacher training initiatives capable of supporting meaningful inclusion. Investments in accessible technologies, assistive educational tools, internet connectivity, and professional development programs are essential for ensuring that all learners benefit from AI-supported educational opportunities regardless of socioeconomic background or disability status.

International organizations such as UNESCO (2023) have emphasized that equitable access to educational technologies represents a fundamental requirement for socially responsible AI implementation. Educational policies should therefore prioritize accessibility, inclusion, affordability, and universal participation while addressing structural inequalities that limit access to technological innovation. Through inclusive policy development and equitable resource distribution, educational systems may reduce digital inequalities and promote more accessible and learner-centered educational environments.

Table 2 summarizes the major educational opportunities and ethical challenges associated with the integration of generative AI in special and inclusive education.

Table 2. Opportunities, risks, and mitigation strategies for the responsible use of generative AI in inclusive education

Opportunity	Potential Risk	Mitigation Strategy
Personalized learning pathways	Learner profiling and privacy concerns	Teacher oversight, informed consent, and data minimization
Adaptive assessment and feedback	Inaccurate or biased recommendations	Human review of AI-generated outputs
Accessibility and communication support	Unequal accessibility or exclusion	Use accessible and inclusive AI tools
Teacher workload reduction	Overreliance on AI-generated materials	Combine AI assistance with professional judgment
Student engagement	Reduced peer interaction	Balance AI use with collaborative learning
Multilingual support	Translation inaccuracies or cultural bias	Teacher verification and cultural review

Table 2 summarizes key educational opportunities associated with the use of generative AI in special and inclusive education and links each opportunity to potential ethical risks and corresponding mitigation strategies. This overview emphasizes that the educational value of GenAI depends not only on technological capabilities but also on responsible pedagogical implementation, teacher oversight, and ethical governance.

RECOMMENDATIONS FOR PRACTICE AND POLICY

The responsible integration of GenAI into special and inclusive education requires comprehensive educational policies, ethical governance frameworks, inclusive pedagogical strategies, and continuous collaboration among educational stakeholders. Although AI technologies possess substantial potential for improving accessibility, personalization, learner engagement, and instructional flexibility, their successful implementation depends on thoughtful planning, ethical oversight, and equitable access to technological resources.

Educational institutions should establish clear ethical guidelines and institutional policies regarding the use of AI within inclusive classrooms. Such policies should address issues related to data privacy, informed consent, accessibility standards, algorithmic transparency, and responsible educational use of AI-supported systems. Transparent governance frameworks are essential for protecting learner rights, ensuring accountability, and maintaining trust among students, families, educators, and educational communities.

Teacher education and professional development programs should additionally incorporate AI literacy, inclusive digital pedagogy, and critical technological competence. Educators require adequate preparation not only in the technical use of AI systems but also in understanding their pedagogical, ethical, and social implications. Professional development initiatives should support teachers in integrating AI technologies effectively while maintaining human-centered instructional practices and inclusive educational values.

Furthermore, AI-supported educational technologies should be designed according to universal accessibility and inclusive design principles. Developers and educational technology companies must ensure that AI systems accommodate diverse learner needs, communication styles, sensory profiles, and linguistic backgrounds. Accessibility-centered technological development may contribute to reducing participation barriers and improving educational equity for students with SEND and other marginalized learner populations.

Policymakers should also prioritize equitable access to digital infrastructure, assistive technologies, internet connectivity, and educational resources capable of supporting AI-enhanced learning environments. Reducing digital inequalities requires long-term investment in technological infrastructure, institutional support systems, accessible educational platforms, and teacher training programs. Educational equity should remain a central priority within all AI-related educational policies and implementation strategies.

Human-centered pedagogical approaches must continue to remain central within AI-supported educational environments. Although generative AI technologies may enhance instructional efficiency and personalization, meaningful inclusion fundamentally depends on empathy, communication, collaboration, emotional support, and authentic interpersonal relationships. AI systems should therefore function as supportive pedagogical tools that complement rather than replace teachers' professional expertise and human interaction within educational contexts.

Continuous evaluation and ethical monitoring of AI-supported educational systems are equally important. Educational institutions should regularly assess AI technologies to identify potential biases, accessibility barriers, discriminatory patterns, inaccuracies, and unintended educational consequences. Ongoing evaluation processes may contribute to more responsible technological implementation while ensuring that AI systems remain aligned with inclusive educational goals and ethical standards.

Collaboration among educators, researchers, policymakers, technology developers, families, and learners themselves is essential for ensuring that GenAIcontributes positively to inclusive education. Interdisciplinary cooperation may facilitate the development of more accessible, equitable, and pedagogically appropriate

AI-supported learning environments capable of responding effectively to diverse educational needs.

Ultimately, the future of GenAI within special and inclusive education depends not only on technological innovation but also on ethical responsibility, social inclusion, accessibility, and educational equity. Through balanced, human-centered, and critically informed implementation strategies, AI technologies may contribute to the creation of more inclusive, flexible, and learner-centered educational systems that support meaningful participation and equal opportunities for all learners.

FUTURE RESEARCH DIRECTIONS

Future research should prioritize four key areas that are critical for the responsible integration of generative AI in special and inclusive education: (a) empirical evaluation of GenAI interventions for learners with SEND, (b) learner, family, and teacher perspectives on AI use, (c) ethical governance, accessibility, and risk mitigation, and (d) teacher professional development and AI literacy. Organizing future research around these priorities may provide stronger evidence to guide educational policy and practice.

Although GenAI has demonstrated substantial potential within special and inclusive education, the field remains relatively recent and continuously evolving. Additional research is therefore necessary to better understand the long-term educational, psychological, social, and ethical implications associated with AI-supported learning environments. Existing literature has primarily focused on conceptual discussions and emerging technological applications, while fewer empirical studies have examined the sustained impact of generative AI on learner outcomes, inclusion, teacher practices, and emotional well-being among students with SEND.

Future research should investigate the long-term effectiveness of AI-supported educational interventions across diverse learner populations and educational contexts. More empirical evidence is needed regarding the influence of generative AI on academic achievement, learner autonomy, communication development, motivation, social participation, and emotional well-being among students with different disabilities and learning profiles. Longitudinal studies may contribute to a deeper understanding of how continuous interaction with AI-supported systems affects cognitive development, self-regulated learning, and educational inclusion over time.

Researchers should also examine the pedagogical effectiveness of different AI-supported instructional approaches within inclusive classrooms. Comparative studies exploring personalized learning systems, adaptive tutoring technologies, gamified applications, and assistive communication tools may provide valuable evidence regarding which practices most effectively support learners with SEND. In addition, future studies should investigate how AI technologies may be integrated into inclusive pedagogical frameworks while maintaining meaningful human interaction and collaborative learning experiences.

Another important research direction involves the development of accessibility standards and inclusive design principles for AI-supported educational technologies. Although generative AI has expanded opportunities for accessible learning, limited consensus currently exists regarding universal accessibility criteria and disability-responsive AI development practices. Future studies should therefore explore how AI systems may better address diverse sensory, cognitive, linguistic, and communication needs within inclusive educational settings.

Student perspectives and lived experiences additionally represent an important area for future investigation. Research exploring learners' perceptions, emotional responses, and experiences with AI-supported educational environments may contribute to a more learner-centered understanding of educational AI implementation. Particular attention should be given to how students with SEND experience accessibility, autonomy, motivation, communication, and social participation within AI-enhanced learning contexts.

Future scholarship should also continue examining ethical issues related to algorithmic decision-making, data privacy, digital surveillance, and technological inequality. As AI technologies become increasingly integrated into education, interdisciplinary collaboration among educators, psychologists, technologists, ethicists, policymakers, and disability studies scholars will remain essential for addressing the complex ethical dimensions of AI-supported inclusion.

Cross-cultural perspectives on AI integration in education should receive greater scholarly attention as educational systems differ considerably regarding technological infrastructure, accessibility standards, inclusive educational policies, and digital literacy levels. Comparative international studies may therefore contribute to a broader understanding of how social, cultural, and economic factors influence the implementation and effectiveness of generative AI within inclusive educational environments (Bozkurt et al., 2023).

Finally, future research should continue exploring the balance between technological innovation and human-centered pedagogy. Although AI technologies may significantly improve accessibility and instructional flexibility, educational systems must continue to preserve empathy, collaboration, emotional connection, and authentic human interaction within increasingly digital learning environments.

CONCLUSION

GenAI represents one of the most rapidly evolving technological developments influencing contemporary educational systems and practices (Alam, 2023). Within special and inclusive education, AI-supported technologies have introduced substantial opportunities for improving personalized learning, accessibility, differentiated instruction, communication support, learner engagement, and teacher professional assistance. Through adaptive instructional systems, assistive technologies, automated feedback mechanisms, and multimodal learning environments, generative AI may contribute to the creation of more flexible and learner-centered educational experiences capable of addressing diverse educational needs.

The literature and conceptual analysis presented throughout this chapter suggest that generative AI has significant potential for supporting students with SEND by reducing participation barriers and enhancing access to educational content and communication. AI-supported technologies may facilitate individualized learning pathways, accessible educational materials, adaptive assessment practices, and greater learner autonomy while simultaneously supporting teachers in curriculum adaptation and inclusive instructional design. In this way, generative AI may function as both an educational support mechanism and an assistive technological resource capable of promoting more inclusive and equitable learning environments.

At the same time, the integration of generative AI into educational settings raises substantial ethical, pedagogical, and social concerns that require careful consideration. Issues related to data privacy, information security, algorithmic bias, digital inequality, accessibility barriers, and excessive dependence on automated technologies remain central within contemporary debates surrounding educational AI. The use of AI-supported systems with vulnerable learner populations additionally emphasizes the need for transparent governance, ethical accountability, inclusive technological design, and continuous critical evaluation of educational impact.

The chapter also highlighted that meaningful inclusion cannot be achieved solely through technological innovation. Inclusive education fundamentally depends on human-centered pedagogical relationships characterized by empathy, communication, emotional understanding, collaboration, and social participation. Although AI-supported systems may enhance instructional efficiency and accessibility, they cannot replace the essential role of educators, families, and educational communities in supporting learners' emotional, social, and developmental well-being. Consequently, generative AI should be understood as a complementary educational tool rather than a substitute for teachers and support professionals.

The successful integration of GenAI within inclusive education, therefore, requires balanced implementation strategies that combine technological innovation with ethical responsibility, accessibility principles, educational equity, and human-centered pedagogy. Educational institutions, policymakers, researchers, and technology developers must work collaboratively to ensure that AI-supported systems remain inclusive, transparent, culturally responsive, and accessible to all learners regardless of disability status or socioeconomic background.

Furthermore, ongoing teacher training, digital literacy development, and interdisciplinary collaboration remain essential for supporting responsible AI integration within educational contexts. Educators require continuous professional support in order to critically evaluate AI technologies, implement inclusive instructional practices, and maintain meaningful human interaction within increasingly digital learning environments.

Nevertheless, the educational applications discussed in this chapter should be interpreted as emerging possibilities rather than as established evidence of effectiveness. Further empirical research is required to determine their accessibility, educational value, and ethical implications for different SEND learner profiles.

Ultimately, GenAI possesses considerable potential to transform special and inclusive education by creating more accessible, adaptive, and learner-centered educational experiences. However, the future impact of AI within education will depend not only on technological advancement but also on society's ability to implement these technologies ethically, equitably, and responsibly. Through thoughtful and balanced integration, generative AI may contribute to the development of more inclusive educational systems that promote equal participation, accessibility, and meaningful learning opportunities for all students.

REFERENCES

Ainscow, M. (2020). Promoting inclusion and equity in education: Lessons from international experiences. *Nordic Journal of Studies in Educational Policy*, *6*(1), 7–16. DOI: 10.1080/20020317.2020.1729587

Alam, A. (2023). Possibilities and challenges of GenAI in education. *International Journal of Advanced Educational Research*, *8*(4), 15–22.

Bozkurt, A., Xiao, J., Lambert, S. R., Pazurek, A., Crompton, H., Koseoglu, S., Farrow, R., Bond, M., Nerantzi, C., Honeychurch, S., Bali, M., Dron, J., Mir, K., Stewart, B., & Jandrić, P. (2023). Speculative futures on ChatGPT and GenAI(AI): A collective reflection from the educational landscape. *Asian Journal of Distance Education*, *18*(1), 53–130. DOI: 10.5281/zenodo.7636568

CAST. (2024). *Universal Design for Learning Guidelines version 3.0*. CAST. https://udlguidelines.cast.org

Holmes, W., Bialik, M., & Fadel, C. (2019). *Artificial intelligence in education: Promises and implications for teaching and learning*. Center for Curriculum Redesign.

Holmes, W., & Tuomi, I. (2022). State of the art and practice in AI in education. *European Journal of Education*, *57*(4), 542–570. DOI: 10.1111/ejed.12533

Luckin, R. (2018). *Machine learning and human intelligence: The future of education for the 21st century*. UCL Institute of Education Press.

OECD. (2021). *Digital education outlook 2021: Pushing the frontiers with artificial intelligence, blockchain and robots*. OECD Publishing., DOI: 10.1787/589b283f-

UNESCO. (1994). *The Salamanca statement and framework for action on special needs education*. UNESCO.

UNESCO. (2021). *AI and education: Guidance for policy-makers*. UNESCO Publishing.

UNESCO. (2023). *Guidance for generative AI in education and research*. UNESCO Publishing.

United Nations. (2006). *Convention on the rights of persons with disabilities*. United Nations. https://www.un.org/disabilities/documents/convention/convoptprot-e.pdf

Zawacki-Richter, O., Marín, V. I., Bond, M., & Gouverneur, F. (2019). Systematic review of research on artificial intelligence applications in higher education: Where are the educators? *International Journal of Educational Technology in Higher Education, 16*(39), 1–27. DOI: 10.1186/s41239-019-0171-0

Chapter 3

Generative AI as an Enabler of Inclusive and Personalized Learning in Special Education: Pedagogical Opportunities, Professional Development, and Ethical Considerations

Saurabh Pandey
http://orcid.org/0000-0001-9110-9527
United College of Engineering and Research, Prayagraj, India

ABSTRACT

The chapter discusses Generative Artificial Intelligence (Gen-AI) as a viable solution to making learning accessible, inclusive, and individualised to students with Special Educational Needs and Disabilities (SEND). It critically analyzes the role of Gen-AI in delivering differentiated content, support in instruction, augmented communication, and minimizing barriers to participation based on the theories of inclusive pedagogy, Universal Design of Learning, and theories of human-AI interaction. Another aspect that the chapter examines is the changing roles of teachers and special educators in AI-enhanced settings by suggesting the notion of context-sensitive practices that combine technical, pedagogical, and ethical capabilities. The major issues, including data privacy, algorithmic bias, transparency and protection, are tackled. It points out the possible and constraining nature of Gen-AI through examples and recent studies, and it identifies the necessity of a pedagogy-based, ethically oriented approach of integrating it.

DOI: 10.4018/979-8-3373-9169-4.ch003

1. INTRODUCTION

Artificial intelligence (AI) is no longer on the fringes of modern education. In the last ten years, machine-learning technologies have spread into learning management systems, personalized tutoring programs and assessment engines and into millions of classrooms. The emergence of large language models (LLMs) and multimodal generative systems, however, has dramatically changed the role of AI within the classroom. Systems based on these models can generate novel text, output speech or sign language, simplify complex text, generate practice problems with adjustable difficulty and longer dialogues that simulate face-to-face human tutoring. These features have already received significant attention in mainstream education; in contrast, their potential in special and inclusive education has been largely overlooked.

The students with Special Educational Needs and Disabilities (SEND) are a diverse group with a wide range of learning, communication, sensory and participation needs, which are different from one another and from their peers. The World Health Organization (WHO, 2022) estimates that some 1.3 billion people (roughly 16% of the world's population) experience a significant disability, of which many need access to education and assistive technologies. But so far the dominant educational discourse about AI assumed a student body with the same cognitive and communicational requirements that are expected to be met with standardized content and standardized assessment.

SEND are very broad learning profiles, such as those with intellectual disabilities, autism spectrum disorder, ADHD, dyslexia, sensory impairments, emotional and behavioral disorders, speech-language impairments, physical disabilities, and twice-exceptional learners – those who are both gifted and disabled. For increasingly diverse educational systems, the needs of multilingual learners with SEND who have multiple needs related to their language practices should also be included in the educational system's consideration.

This chapter seeks to redress this oversight. It identifies the pedagogic opportunities that Gen-AI offers to SEND learners; the ways in which teachers and support professionals need to alter their professional practices to take advantage of these opportunities; and the ethical and legal considerations that govern the responsible use of Gen-AI with vulnerable populations. It employs three intertwined theoretical frameworks for analysis: inclusive pedagogy (Florian & Spratt, 2013), Universal Design for Learning (Rose & Meyer, 2002), and human-AI interaction theory (Amershi et al., 2019). Together, these frameworks provide the normative evaluation criteria for assessing the potential and perils of Gen-AI in special education.

This chapter does not claim that Gen-AI will solve the systemic injustices in the special and inclusive education systems in many countries. Access to assistive technology has always been pitched as a solution to equity concerns while institutional and cultural barriers remain (Slee, 2011). The same caution applies here. This chapter argues that Gen-AI tools used wisely and ethically provide new affordances that previous generations of technology did not, and that teachers, scholars and policy makers need to develop conceptual and practical models to help them navigate them.

The conceptual narrative review approach is used in this chapter. Purposive searches of peer-reviewed articles, policy documents and international reports on generative AI, inclusive education, Universal Design for Learning (UDL) and Special Educational Needs and Disabilities (SEND) were conducted, identifying relevant literature between 2016 and 2025, with a strong emphasis on literature published between 2020 and 2025. The chapter does not aim for a systematic evidence synthesis, but rather it combines in a holistic way theoretical and empirical literature to construct a conceptual model for AI-based inclusive education.

1.1 Review Methodology

This section presents the review process which is used for the chapter. In view of the rapidly-changing and emergent nature of applications of Gen-AI in SEND education and the lack of a stable evidence base that is suitable for systematic review or synthesis, a conceptual narrative review approach was selected.

Literature Sources

Purposive searches in major academic databases (Google Scholar, ERIC, Scopus), in publisher repositories and in websites of important international organisations (UNESCO, OECD, European Commission and UNICEF) were carried out to identify the sources. The search terms included variations of the terms "generative AI", "large language models", "inclusive education", "Universal Design for Learning", and "special educational needs and disabilities". The search was not all-inclusive, nor database-protocolled, fitting with the conceptual narrative design.

Inclusion Criteria

The following criteria were applied to prioritize the sources for inclusion: (a) published from 2016 to 2025; (b) focused on generative AI, adaptive learning technologies or human-AI interaction theory; (c) concerned with inclusive education, UDL or SEND populations; and (d) peer reviewed, published by a recognized policy or an international body. Previous seminal texts which form the theoretical basis for what are still commonly used and effective theories, such as Vygotsky (1978), Rose and Meyer (2002) and Oliver (1990), were kept.

Conceptual Synthesis

The literature was instead thematically organized and analyzed according to the three guiding frameworks outlined in the chapter, inclusive pedagogy, Universal Design for Learning, and human-AI interaction theory, to help shape the conceptual arguments, illustrative scenarios, and practice implications that followed, rather than a quantitative or study-by-study evidence synthesis. Figure 1 shows conceptual review process for this chapter.

Figure 1. Conceptual review process for this chapter

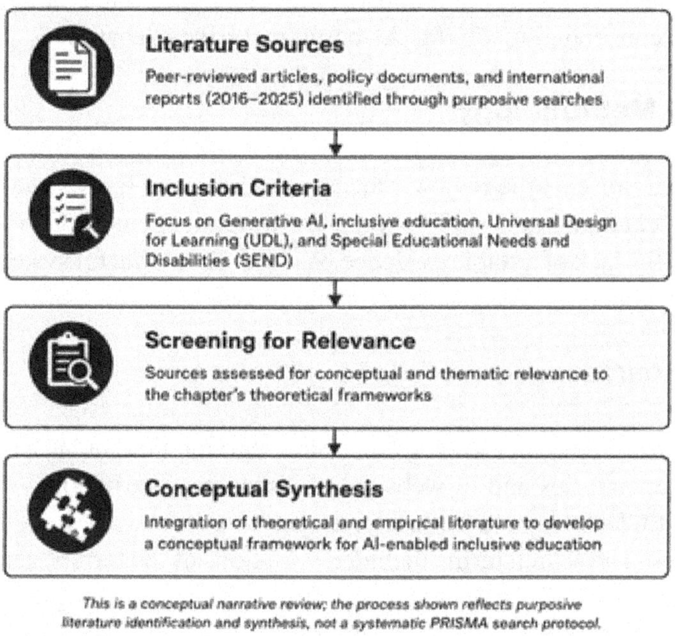

2. THEORETICAL FOUNDATIONS

2.1 Inclusive Pedagogy

Inclusive pedagogy, as described by Florian and Spratt (2013), dismisses the notion that students with SEND need specialist pedagogic treatment compared with those without SEND. Rather, it asks teachers to create learning experiences that are rich, open and multifaceted enough to support a diversity of learners without singling any students out as exceptional (and therefore stigmatized). The unit of pedagogical attention shifts from individuals to the learning environment. It has implications for the design of Gen-AI tools: not as individual remediation tools that remove students from the mainstream from time to time, but as tools that make the learning environment itself more flexible.

This view is consistent with the social model of disability (Oliver, 1990), which situates disability not in the individual's body or mind, but in the relationship between individual characteristics and environmental barriers. When a Gen-AI tool enables a learner with dyslexia to receive any text in a simpler format, or enables a learner with motor impairment to dictate their text, it is removing an environmental barrier rather than fixing a personal disability. The distinction is important because ownership of the intervention is vested in the learner who interacts with a barrier-reducing environment rather than the doctor who treats a clinical condition.

2.2 Universal Design for Learning

Universal Design for Learning (UDL) is an adaptation of the architecture of universal design to curriculum design by Rose and Meyer (2002) at the Center for Applied Special Technology. UDL suggests that curricula need to offer multiple means of representation (ways of presenting information), action and expression (ways to demonstrate knowledge) and engagement (ways to motivate and sustain learning). UDL makes explicit reference to the neuroscience evidence learner variability is the rule and not the exception, and curricula designed for the average learner disadvantage learner variability.

UDL principles are compatible with Gen-AI technologies. For example, a language model embedded in a reading platform can simultaneously offer a written text, an audio narration, a summary of the text and a diagram to satisfy multiple means of representation in a single learning object. A generative model can provide learners with multiple means of expression (text, voice, multiple choice) without the need for the teacher to prepare different materials for different versions.

2.3 Human-AI Interaction in Education

Human-AI interaction (HAI) theory explores how humans develop mental models of AI, adjust trust in AI outputs, and incorporate AI support in achieving goal-directed tasks (Amershi et al., 2019). In the context of education, HAI issues take on new qualities because the users may be students with cognitive, communication or attentional differences that play a role in how they interact with AI interfaces. Luckin et al. (2016) propose models where AI is used to strengthen the agency of the learner, rather than replace it. In the context of SEND, this suggests Gen-AI systems should be designed to enhance learners' self-management, metacognitive and decision-making skills rather than simply providing them with the right answer.

Figure 2. Theoretical framework: Generative AI as an enabler in special education

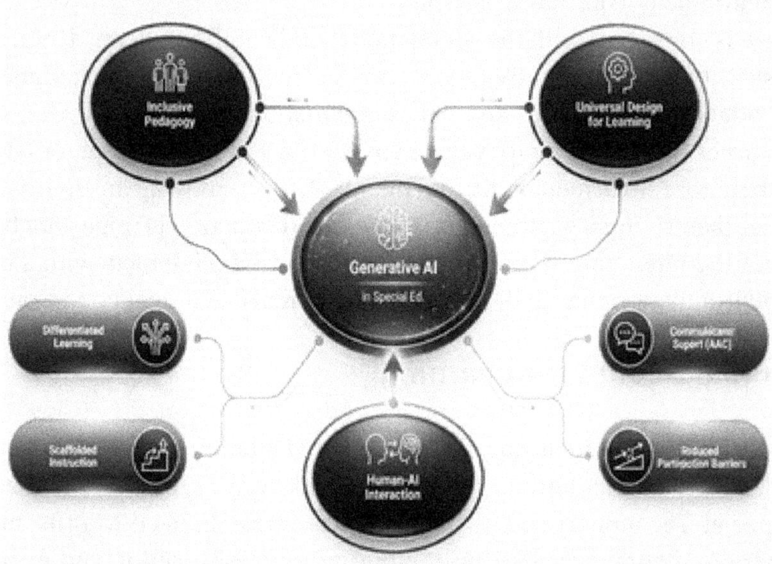

Figure 2 shows Theoretical Framework: Generative AI as an Enabler in SEND. The three theoretical principles - inclusive education, UDL and human-AI interaction - converge to enrich four pedagogical processes for SEND learners.

3. GENERATIVE AI TOOLS: TAXONOMY AND LANDSCAPE FOR SEND

Generative AI is an umbrella term for a wide range of machine-learning models that can generate new content - text, images, audio, or data - in response to natural-language inputs. Large language models like GPT-4 and its descendants (OpenAI, 2023) are the most prominent members of this family, but also include text-to-speech, speech-to-text, image synthesis, and video synthesis technologies. For the purposes of this chapter, capabilities are classified into four categories applicable to SEND education.

The rapid growth of the Gen-AI capabilities relevant to inclusive education, attracted by the earlier accounts of AI in education (Luckin et al., 2016; UNESCO, 2023), has been confirmed by recent systematic reviews and scoping reviews (Chiu et al., 2023; Holmes et al., 2022; Kasneci et al., 2023; Zhai et al., 2021; Crompton & Burke, 2023). Overall, these reviews suggest that there has been rapid growth in the use of AI tools in general education, but applications that have been specifically validated for SEND populations are less advanced.

Text generation and simplification systems can generate text at a specified Lexile level, translate technical terms into simple language, and generate practice exercises at a learner's current level. These features may support access for learners with dyslexia, intellectual disabilities, and additional language needs by enabling the rapid adaptation of vocabulary, syntax, and text complexity (Martínez et al., 2024; Kasneci et al., 2023).

Dialogue and conversational agents mimic the non-judgemental repetition that many SEND learners require to consolidate new skills, but that can lead even the most dedicated teacher to burnout. Dialogue agents may offer structured and repeatable opportunities for practising conversational and social-communication skills with autistic learners, provided that their use is carefully scaffolded and supervised by educators (Porayska-Pomsta et al., 2018; Gu et al., 2025).

Automatic speech recognition, text-to-speech generation, and sign-language generation are examples of speech and language processing tools. For learners who use augmentative and alternative communication (AAC), such technologies can significantly lower the time and effort required to communicate (Beukelman and Light, 2020).

Multimodal generation tools can generate images, diagrams, and audio descriptions from text, to support learners with visual impairment, hearing impairment or neurological differences who may better comprehend information through alternative channels (Warschauer & Matuchniak, 2010).

Table 1. Comparative overview of Gen-AI capability categories for SEND education

Capability Category	Traditional Approach	Gen-AI Enabled Approach	Primary SEND Relevance
Text generation & simplification	Manually rewritten materials by teacher/ SENCO	On-demand text simplification at specified reading levels	Dyslexia, intellectual disability, EAL learners
Dialogue & conversational agents	Human-delivered social-skills coaching	Scaffolded, repeatable practice dialogues	Autism spectrum, social communication needs
Speech, AAC & sign-language tools	Static symbol sets; specialist-programmed devices	Dynamically generated vocabulary, speech, and sign avatars	Complex communication needs, hearing impairment
Multimodal generation	Manually produced diagrams/audio descriptions	Automated image, diagram and audio-description generation	Visual, hearing, and neurological differences

The authors summarize at a conceptual level how each capability category in Gen-AI builds on or diverges from traditional practice and the SEND populations for which it is likely to be most relevant, synthesized from the sources discussed above, in Table 1.

4. DIFFERENTIATED INSTRUCTION AND SCAFFOLDING

Differentiated instruction, as proposed by Tomlinson (2014), means that what is being taught, how it is being taught, what learners are producing, and how they are feeling during learning is adjusted to accommodate differences among learners. The perpetual problem with differentiated learning has always been practical: one teacher cannot provide multiple versions of every lesson, handout and assessment when teaching a class of 25-30 students. Gen-AI alters this dynamic by automating the content-production effort required by differentiation, and by facilitating on-the-run personalization that responds to a learner's dynamic real-time learning profile, rather than a static profile set up at the beginning of a course.

Vygotsky's (1978) notion of the zone of proximal development (ZPD) provides another theoretical support. Scaffolding involves setting tasks at a level where they cannot be completed independently, but can be completed with support; support is removed as skill improves. Previous efforts to implement the ZPD in computer-based systems (Aleven et al., 2017) in intelligent tutoring systems have typically been domain-specific. LLM-based systems are domain-general, enabling scaffolded dialogues and adaptive problem posing across maths, literacy, science, social studies and vocational skills in one single interface.

The consequences for special education are significant. Traditionally, separate support workers have provided literacy support, numeracy support, and social communication support. A Gen-AI system that can provide integrated support across all three domains does not replace these specialists - their expertise with particular learners and particular processes is crucial - but it does allow for more integrated support. A student with both reading difficulties and maths anxiety, for instance, can receive literacy support while doing maths rather than having to approach different support services that do not talk to each other. This is similar to how good specialists work, but which has not been possible due to time and resources.

The quality of feedback is also an issue. Hattie and Timperley (2007) list feedback as one of the most important factors affecting learning, but it is also one that can be affected by timing, specificity and fit with learner goals. Gen-AI systems can in theory provide us with immediate, specific, and error-specific feedback - something that can be hard to achieve in a classroom environment where a single teacher is interacting with multiple learners. For SEND learners for whom processing speed, working memory or attention control mean that the time between error and feedback is critical, this may be more important than for other learners. There is limited research on the use of error-specific AI feedback in SEND learning, but the potential benefits are compelling.

For a learner with ADHD, for instance, Gen-AI can break a complex task into a series of smaller steps, remind the learner to return to the task after being distracted, and increase the task difficulty in real time based on the learner's response time and accuracy. For a learner with an intellectual disability, the system might hold a concept at a concrete level for an extended time, generating a stream of new examples and analogies, until the learner's grasp of the concept is secure. These applications remain promising, but their effectiveness in SEND settings has not yet been sufficiently established, and further rigorous empirical research is required (Chiu et al., 2023; Zawacki-Richter et al., 2019).

Figure 3. Conceptual mapping of Gen-AI capabilities across SEND categories

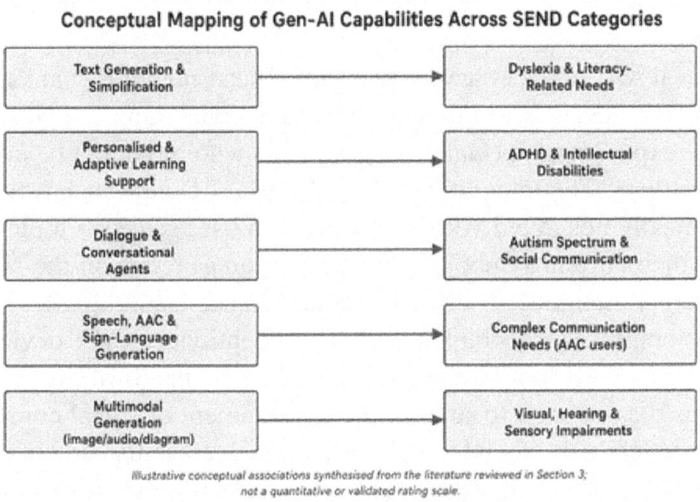

Figure 3 provides a conceptual mapping of Gen-AI capabilities and associations with SEND categories presented in Section 3 and Table 1. This is a conceptual mapping only, not numerically rated or empirically validated scale—differentiation and multimodal capabilities are referenced as being the most broadly applicable across categories.

It is important to note that automated differentiation can be dangerous. If a Gen-AI system provides the same learner with a particular label with simpler material, it may inadvertently create an expectation level and a ceiling effect that would not be imposed by a human teacher. Differentiation, according to UDL principles, is a strategy for access, not a lifelong assignment to a lower track. So, designers and teachers need to explicitly plan for progression in a Gen-AI-mediated differentiation system to ensure that the system's ceiling is continually raised as the learner's ability increases rather than being fixed at a potentially stigmatizing level.

5. COMMUNICATION SUPPORT AND AUGMENTATIVE AND ALTERNATIVE COMMUNICATION

A broad spectrum of SEND learners experience communication impairment, which may be the result of autism spectrum conditions, cerebral palsy, acquired brain injury, specific language impairment, and progressive neurological conditions. Augmentative and alternative communication (AAC) has a strong evidence base regarding the use of symbol-based systems, speech-generating devices and sign-supported communication. Gen-AI expands the scope in this area in ways that need to be explored.

Conventional AAC devices have static symbol sets and phrase banks. High-tech speech-generating devices are expensive and time consuming to personalize, and depend on the expertise of specialist programmers who might not be present in all educational settings. The integration of LLM into AAC devices has the potential to add dynamically generated vocabulary: when a user selects a topic that is not supported by their current symbol set, the device can generate on-the-fly symbols, phrases, or verbal utterances if desired (Beukelman & Light, 2020). This feature overcomes a longstanding complaint about conventional AAC: devices are not flexible enough to keep up with the communication demands of everyday life.

Gen-AI has the potential to support the development of social communication skills in autistic learners. Social conversation practice agents can simulate social contexts - greeting, turn-taking, negotiation - and afford practice without the negativity or fatigue of human partners. Porayska-Pomsta (2016) reports prototype systems that recognize emotional states and modulate the social communication challenge of the interaction based on that, offering a type of scaffolded learning that would be hard to achieve in the classroom environment. Caveats are in order: current emotion recognition technology has a higher failure rate for non-neurotypical facial expressions, with implications for the feedback that the autistic students receive.

The authenticity of AI-mediated social interaction is still an open question. Some practitioners contend that social skills practiced with an AI agent are unlikely to be similar to skills practiced with other humans, and that the transition from the artificial to the natural is not guaranteed. Others point to the fact that the predictability of AI conversation may be exactly what is needed for learners who are anxious because of the unpredictability of the human interaction and that a graduated exposure to the interaction, starting with AI-mediated practice and then moving to natural interaction with human partners, may be an effective and evidence-based strategy. This is an issue that research needs to explore more rigorously than it has to date, with outcome measures that reflect the ability to communicate in the real world, rather than merely within structured AI-mediated tasks (Gu et al., 2025; Porayska-Pomsta et al., 2018).

For learners who are hearing-impaired, generative sign-language avatars are starting to emerge that can translate speech or text into sign language. Although the motion-capture quality of these systems varies, and while their linguistic depth does not match that of a human signer, their availability in low-resource settings is a step in the direction of linguistic justice (Warschauer & Matuchniak, 2010). This is an emerging area and we can expect much better systems in the near future.

6. OVERCOMING BARRIERS TO PARTICIPATION

Educational participation is more than access to curriculum content, it is social participation, co-learning with others, speaking in the classroom, and self-representation in educational contexts. Learners with SEND encounter barriers to participation at each of these levels, mediated by the physical environment, the cultural environment, the task environment and the communicative environment. Gen-AI technologies can address barriers at some of these levels, but not other levels.

In the dimension of task access, real-time text simplification enables a learner with a reading impairment to access the same source as their classmates, rather than having to access lower-level texts that are viewed as different and stigmatizing. Auto-captioning systems using automatic speech recognition allow a learner with a hearing impairment to receive oral instruction without being solely dependent on a human intermediary. Voice-activated tools allow learners with motor dysfunction or dysgraphia to write at a speed and level of effort commensurate with their cognitive ability rather than their motor ability.

In the classroom discussion dimension, AI-based communication boards and predictive text technologies allow learners who use AAC to contribute more quickly to classroom discussion, diminishing the social phenomenon where the discussion is at a pace that a slow communicator cannot keep up. AI-mediated communication systems could potentially support learners who use AAC by helping them formulate or present contributions more efficiently during classroom discussions. However, such support must preserve the learner's intended meaning, authorship, and control over communication.

However, it should be recognized that some of the barriers to participation with root causes - such as funding shortfalls for support personnel, inaccessible school buildings, or hostile attitudes among peers or school leaders - are beyond the remit of technology. Gen-AI tools are embedded in the environments they are used in, and an unfriendly or poorly resourced environment will limit the tools' effectiveness. The Convention on the Rights of Persons with Disabilities (United Nations, 2006) posits education as a legal right, not a technological wish, and the use of Gen-AI tools should be seen as part of a rights-based approach rather than a replacement.

Another aspect of participation that Gen-AI impacts in nuanced ways is identity and representation. For SEND learners who have previously struggled with written expression, being able to fluently express themselves using AI support tools may be a welcome relief - a technology that allows a voice to be born where a voice has been stifled. On the other hand, educators and researchers need to be attentive to issues of whose voice is represented in AI-aided compositions. When a learner's text has been significantly re-written, enlarged or edited by a generative system, the learner's voice and the system's voice are intertwined in ways that matter for assessment and for the learner's capacity to feel authorial control. These are not algorithmic, but pedagogical and ethical questions, which need to be considered rather than solved by algorithms.

The social dimension of inclusive classrooms also needs to be considered. When SEND learners use visible AI assistance devices - speech-to-text headsets, communication devices, tablet-based simplification overlays - they might receive attention from peers that is positive and negative. The social implications of visible assistive technology are well documented in the AAC literature (Beukelman & Light, 2020) and are likely to be similar with Gen-AI. Schools that are anticipating the use of Gen-AI with SEND learners should proactively develop peer education strategies that emphasize the reasonable nature of AI assistance (similar to using glasses or a ramp) rather than deficit and should include SEND learners in the design of these strategies.

7. THE EVOLVING ROLE OF TEACHERS AND SPECIAL EDUCATORS

The use of Gen-AI in schools does not reduce the role of the teacher; it reallocates it. In a classroom environment where AI is used to generate differentiated resources, administer personalized practice sessions and provide formative feedback, the teacher's time is freed up for those dimensions of teaching that AI cannot do: relationship-building, emotional attunement, ethical reasoning, and the fine-grained reading of a learner's burgeoning understanding that goes beyond digital task performance.

This work redistribution is especially important for special educators because the relational aspects of their practice - trust, safety, co-regulation - are often necessary to facilitate academic learning in the first place.

The special educator working in an AI-enhanced classroom is not a deliverer of content so much as a creator of learning opportunities: setting the conditions for interaction with AI systems, tracking whether AI-generated content is aligned with the learner's needs (not their label) and intervening when the AI produces inappropriate or toxic content. This demands more than ICT skills from the teacher: it demands critical AI literacy, and the ability to question assumptions of AI-generated content, to detect when personalization has gone off the rails, and to exercise pedagogical judgement over AI recommendations.

Pellegrino and Hilton (2012) characterize the 21st century teacher as having content knowledge, pedagogical knowledge and learner knowledge - to which a fourth element must be added: knowledge of the systems operating in the professional environment. This is not necessarily technical knowledge (teachers need not be experts in transformers) but functional and critical knowledge: what is and what is not possible with these systems, where to trust their outputs and when to be sceptical, and how their recommendations might align or clash with institutional and learner agency.

An often-overlooked dimension of teacher agency in AI-enhanced education concerns professional identity. As AI systems increasingly mediate instructional processes and generate highly personalized educational responses, tensions may arise between algorithmic recommendations and educators' professional knowledge, judgement, and perceived autonomy (Amershi et al., 2019; Holmes et al., 2022). Such tensions may be particularly relevant in special education, where professional practice relies heavily on individualized understanding, relational expertise, and contextual decision-making. However, this remains a conceptual proposition that requires direct empirical investigation within special and inclusive education. Professional development should therefore provide opportunities for special educators to critically examine how AI use may affect their professional roles, autonomy, and responsibility.

The interaction between the special educator and the AI system also poses questions about accountability that are not addressed by current professional practice. When an AI recommendation is used to inform a decision about a learner's placement, access to the curriculum, or provision of an assessment, who is accountable for the outcomes of that decision? Existing legal frameworks in most jurisdictions allocate responsibility to the human professional, and this is right: AI systems cannot be held accountable in the way people can. But without authority, accountability is untenable. If teachers are to be held responsible for AI-influenced decisions, they must also have the authority to reject these decisions without fear of institutional retaliation, and professional frameworks must give teachers that authority.

8. PROFESSIONAL DEVELOPMENT FOR AI-ENHANCED SPECIAL EDUCATION

While the need for teacher professional development in using AI is clear, the evidence base for effective professional learning for using AI is limited, and even more limited for special education. The bulk of professional development interventions around educational AI have been designed for mainstream, secondary school teachers, and tested in mainstream classrooms (Zawacki-Richter et al., 2019). Special educators, who identify with a professional tradition that emphasizes therapeutic relationships, rather than a content-delivery tradition, may find the integration of AI more difficult than generalist teachers.

The professional learning approach outlined in this chapter is based on five principles. First, professional development should be tailored to the types of learners the educator is working with, and use anonymized case studies rather than hypothetical scenarios. Second, it should develop AI literacy gradually - starting with the observable effects of AI and moving towards critical evaluation of AI design options - rather than front-loading technical training that may hinder engagement with non-expert educators. Third, it should prioritize ethical decision-making as integral to professional practice. Fourth, it should be integrated within professional learning communities (Holmes et al., 2022) that support educators to share and collectively respond to AI-related experiences. Fifth, it should be sustained rather than one-off, reflecting the rapid advance of AI and its implications.

Figure 4. The suggested professional development course of special educators in AI-enhanced environments

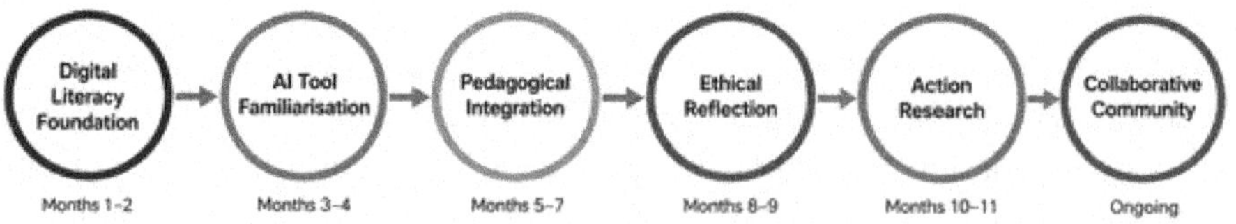

The model presented in Figure 4 spans an academic year, but is a minimum curriculum. The Action Research stage is especially important: it offers educators a formal opportunity to implement Gen-AI tools in their classrooms, gather evidence of the outcomes for individual learners, and critically examine the difference between a tool's intended use and its actual impact. This kind of practitioner research, modeled in special education through the predecessors of collaborative consultation and single-case research design, is the research methodology that will be needed to establish the contextual evidence base for Gen-AI in SEND education.

Collaborative professional learning networks (represented in the final stage of the pathway) are well aligned to the task of integrating artificial intelligence in special education because the challenges teachers face are highly diverse and the solutions are situated. A special educator who teaches a class of learners with profound and multiple learning difficulties will not have the same needs for integrating AI as a learning support teacher working with students with SEND in a mainstream secondary school. Inter-school networks in which teachers can share anonymized case studies, test each other's thinking and together develop school-specific guidelines or protocols provide a form of professional intelligence that is difficult for a centralized training approach to replicate. A number of jurisdictions have established these kinds of networks in relation to the integration of digital technologies more generally, and they could be adapted or expanded to cover Gen-AI in particular.

The role of higher education and initial teacher education is also underestimated in current literature. Special educators joining the workforce in the coming decade will spend a large proportion of their career working in AI-infused environments. Initial teacher education that gives the status of a central professional skill - on par with planning, managing behavior, and assessing - to AI literacy, would support the creation of the next generation of educators who will be using this technology most heavily. Currently, there is limited evidence of systematic integration of AI literacy into initial teacher education in special education - a missed opportunity.

9. ETHICAL, LEGAL AND PROTECTIVE FACTORS

The use of Gen-AI with learners with SEND may raise heightened ethical and safeguarding concerns because these systems can process sensitive disability-related information, reproduce algorithmic bias, and generate opaque or inaccurate recommendations (Bender et al., 2021; Kasneci et al., 2023; UNESCO, 2021). Depending on their age, decision-making capacity, and the applicable legal framework, learners with intellectual disabilities may require accessible information, supported decision-making, developmentally appropriate assent procedures, and parental or legal guardian consent where required (United Nations, 2006; UNESCO, 2021). In some contexts, autistic learners and other learners with cognitive or communication differences may experience difficulty identifying inaccurate or inappropriate

AI-mediated feedback, which reinforces the need for continuous human oversight (Kasneci et al., 2023). Learners from socioeconomically disadvantaged backgrounds may also face compounded inequalities when biased AI systems are introduced in contexts characterized by unequal access to technology, infrastructure, and digital support (UNESCO, 2021; Warschauer & Matuchniak, 2010).

9.1 Privacy and Vulnerable Learners

Data collected by educational AI systems includes data about interactions, responses, frequency of errors, the emotional state of the learner, and audio recordings. In SEND settings, this data is especially sensitive: it is linked with disability status and could be used or abused to guide educational decisions such as placement and funding, and future learning pathways. The European Union's General Data Protection Regulation and similar laws in other countries provide guidelines on the use of sensitive personal data, but adherence varies among EdTech vendors (Mitchell et al., 2019). Schools should audit the data processing practices of any Gen-AI technology they adopt and national guidance documents should mandate transparency from vendors as a requirement for public procurement.

9.2 Algorithmic Bias and Representation

LLMs are trained on large corpora of web text that are heavily biased against under-represented languages, non-neurotypical modes of communication and cultural contexts outside the dominant, English-language, Western, educational system. When such systems are used to generate content for SEND learners, they may generate content that is culturally insensitive, that assumes a neurotypical reader, or that reflects a long history of erasure of disability from mainstream discourse in ways that are now considered derogatory or insulting (Bender et al., 2021). Educational AI system developers must audit their data for disability bias and report the results of audits in a way that is accessible to non-expert users. The UNESCO 2021 Recommendation on the Ethics of Artificial Intelligence lists fairness and non-discrimination among the fundamental principles for the ethics of AI, and explicitly connects these principles to the rights of marginalized groups, including persons with disabilities (UNESCO, 2021).

9.3 Openness, Explainability and Teacher Expertise

The lack of transparency of large language models (black-box models) presents a challenge in SEND. When a Gen-AI system recommends that a given learner should access simple content, or that a learner's engagement pattern is linked to disengagement, the reason for the recommendation is not always clear to the teacher or the learner. Black-box AI recommendations can challenge teacher authority, convey a level of certainty about the complex phenomenon of human learning and make it less likely that human practitioners will override AI outcomes that are inaccurate or dangerous (Kasneci et al., 2023). This is the subject of research into explainable AI, but transparency in an educational context means more than understanding the AI model: it means that the AI system will present its information in a way that augments the teacher's decision-making process.

9.4 Safeguarding and Child Protection

Generative AI systems can generate harmful, sexually inappropriate or psychologically distressing content unless constrained. The danger is not so much deliberate abuse as unintentional harm through systems that lack adequate content moderation that is tailored to the needs and sensitivities of SEND students. An interactive conversational agent for a learner with serious behavioral and emotional difficulties could result in a spiral of distress if the agent misinterprets emotional cues. A text-based system used by a learner with an attachment disorder may foster unhealthy dependency on AI as a substitute for human relationships. Schools need to implement clear guidelines for safe use of AI that apply child-protection policies to AI, and that establish personal accountability for AI-learner interaction.

Figure 5. Conceptual ethical readiness framework

A conceptual ethical readiness framework is provided in Figure 5, across five dimensions, namely privacy, fairness, transparency, explainability and safeguarding. They are offered as dynamic factors of assessing Gen-AI readiness in SEND contexts, as opposed to a numerically rated or empirically benchmarked assessment.

9.5 Green AI and Environmental Considerations

A second ethical consideration is emerging as "Green AI" and relates to the environmental impact of the vast computational requirements of generative models. Large language models require significant energy and water; and schools and vendors implementing Gen-AI at scale have a responsibility to take energy and water into account, as well as the pedagogical benefits. In the context of education for SEND, this begars a proportionality issue: when a smaller, more efficient, or on-device model is able to provide a similar accessibility benefit (e.g., text simplification or generation of basic AAC vocabulary) to a large general purpose model, decisions about procurement should consider the environmental cost alongside functionality. Incorporating Green AI into the procurement and transparency aspects of vendors along with privacy, fairness and safeguarding gives a truly sustainable and responsible approach to using AI in inclusive education a boost.

10. ILLUSTRATIVE PRACTICE SCENARIOS

The authors have created three fictional examples below to illustrate future possible uses of Generative AI in SEND education. They are not students or case studies of actual students.

Scenario A: Personalized Literacy Support for a Student with Dyslexia

Nine-year-old Maya is in a mainstream primary class and has been diagnosed with dyslexia as well as working-memory issues. She has reading-accuracy skills roughly two years below her age, but has good listening comprehension and verbal reasoning skills. Her class teacher is using a Gen-AI-integrated reading platform, which provides Maya with any text in one of three formats: the original text with an overlaid text reader, a simplified text with a different vocabulary and simplifying syntax and sentence structure, or a graphic summary with key-word labels. Maya chooses which format she prefers for each task. In an ideal world, they could gradually be able to remember the format she uses most and the vocabulary words she searches most often, and make the text version more difficult (or harder) over time by perhaps raising the Lexile by 2 or 3 points. Her teacher examines these data each month and informs small group explicit teaching of phonics. The Gen-AI tool has not replaced the teacher's expertise; it has provided a broader reach of differentiated access for a class of 29 students.

Recent advances in large language models have demonstrated considerable potential for generating Easy-to-Read and simplified educational content, thereby improving accessibility for learners with reading difficulties (Martínez et al., 2024; Kasneci et al., 2023).

Scenario B: Conversation to Support Social Communication

Ethan is a 12-year-old boy with autism at a special secondary school. He has good content knowledge about his interests, but finds the inferential and reciprocal aspects of conversation challenging. Ethan has been trialling an agent-driven Gen-AI system on a tablet device for half an hour three times a week. The agent offers social situations - buying a drink at a school canteen, apologizing for a misunderstanding - and prompts Ethan to respond. The agent offers feedback on conversational strategies like turn-taking, listener feedback and topic changes, which Ethan reviews after the sessions. Ethan's supervising teacher observes the sessions, and discusses feedback from the AI in relation to the social-communication objectives in his Education, Health and Care plan. The scenario demonstrates that this may help to lower the anxiety associated with an unfamiliar group interaction, but the transfer of skills from the AI practice to the real world would likely be mixed and partial, in line with the literature on the transfer of social skills (Porayska-Pomsta et al., 2018; Gu et al., 2025).

Scenario C: AAC Vocabulary Extension for a Non-Verbal Learner

Priya is a seven-year-old, non-verbal student with cerebral palsy and complex communication needs who has access to a high-tech augmentative and alternative communication (AAC) device. Her speech-language therapist and the school's assistive technology coordinator have installed a vocabulary extension module that uses an LLM into Priya's device. When Priya selects a topic area that she does not have symbols for - her recent school excursion to the nature reserve - the module creates symbols and phrases that are relevant to the topic area, like pond, dragonfly, I saw, and it was exciting, which Priya can then add to her personalized vocabulary. Such AI-supported vocabulary expansion is increasingly recognized as a promising enhancement for AAC systems (Valencia et al., 2023; Beukelman & Light, 2020). In a hypothetical implementation, the therapist could review the vocabulary weekly and delete items that are developmentally inappropriate or unlikely to be needed again, balancing Priya's vocabulary with the device's functionality so it is not too cumbersome. This approach could substantially reduce the delay between real-world experiences and vocabulary availability.

11. CHALLENGES AND RISKS

It is important to discuss the current limitations of Gen-AI in special education. The examples in Section 10 suggest what is possible based on emerging evidence, but it is scant. Few large-scale, rigorous studies of Gen-AI with SEND populations exist; most of the evidence is from small-scale trials, expert opinion, and by inference from studies of educational AI technologies in general populations (Zawacki-Richter et al., 2019). Randomized controlled trials, single-case experimental designs (more suitable for low-incidence populations), and follow-up studies are needed before we can be sure about efficacy.

Current LLMs also hallucinate - that is, generate content that is syntactically correct and confident but not true - in an unpredictable way. In non-SEND contexts, hallucination is annoying. In SEND contexts, where learners may be less likely to notice errors, or where the content relates to medical or therapeutic information such as medication, behavior management strategies, or mental health coping strategies, hallucination risks safety and needs to be minimized. The use of Gen-AI in SEND settings must provide strong human supervision and a clear plan for identifying and rectifying AI errors before they are presented to learners.

Structural challenges include digital equity. The sophisticated Gen-AI tools outlined in this chapter depend on access to broadband, hardware and specialist technical support. These assets are very unevenly distributed across and within national education systems. If Gen-AI tools are used mainly in better resourced schools and special education settings, they could exacerbate the participation gaps that inclusive education has sought to address for decades. So, policies for the use of AI in education should include equity safeguards to ensure SEND learners in the less well-resourced settings have the same access to AI-supported learning as their counterparts in well-resourced settings (Holmes et al., 2022).

Finally, the pace of commercialization of Gen-AI poses a unique challenge for education governance. Models, capabilities and deployment modes emerge more rapidly than science can assess them and policy can control them. Administrators and teachers are making important procurement and integration decisions with far-reaching consequences in a highly uncertain environment. Teacher unions, national curriculum frameworks, and transnational agencies can play a role in offering timely guidance grounded in evidence to support practitioners to avoid blind acceptance or fear-based rejection.

11.1 Policy and Governance Implications

At the system level, the appropriate use of Gen-AI in special education requires sound policy responses at national and international levels. Governments of several jurisdictions have started to provide guidance on AI integration in schools but a small part of this guidance relates to SEND learners. The UNESCO Guidance for Generative AI in Education and Research (UNESCO, 2023) is comprehensive but gives scant attention to disability. This gap requires urgent attention.

Public procurement is a high-impact policy lever. The procurement contracts that educational authorities negotiate for the use of AI in schools can set minimum standards for accessibility, data management, algorithmic fairness reviews and safeguarding. Government procurement policies that include accessibility requirements based on the Web Content Accessibility Guidelines (WCAG) 2.1 and require vendors to specify the demographic breakdown of the data used to train their AI systems would significantly improve the quality of the AI available for SEND learners, without requiring each school to conduct a technical audit of AI systems, a challenge beyond their capacities.

This priority is further supported by recent multilateral guidance: AI in education (OECD, 2024) and the European Commission's guidelines on AI and education (European Commission, 2022) both mention that accessibility and inclusion should be considered as key design principles and not features added on later. UNICEF's Digital Learning Report (UNICEF, 2022) also reiterates this emphasis.

National special education frameworks, such as the Education, Health and Care planning system in England and the Individualized Education Program (IEP) in the United States, and counterparts elsewhere, offer a formal way to identify AI-related support needs of individual learners, as well as to hold schools to account for meeting them. Amending these frameworks to explicitly mention Gen-AI tools as possible reasonable adjustments, and to mandate that any recommendation produced by AI that impacts on a learner's education be reviewed by a human and discussed with parents, would bring established rights-based protections to the realm of AI without the need for any new legislation.

Research funders also play a role. The evidence base for Gen-AI in SEND education is developing, but is thin. The bulk of published work is descriptive or small-scale; random allocation designs, with sufficient statistical power, pre-registered protocols and replication are uncommon. Research funding calls that are targeted and prioritize this space, and that mandate research teams to include practitioners and SEND learners as co-investigators rather than research participants, would help build a strong evidence base. The global special education community has a long legacy of participatory and emancipatory research (Baglieri & Shapiro, 2012) which is highly relevant to this, and should be encouraged.

11.2 Future Directions in Research and Practice

There are a number of research avenues important for the future of Gen-AI in special education. First, creating disability-inclusive training data for LLMs is a fundamental technical challenge. Training LLMs with data that includes a variety of communication strategies, non-standard spellings, and disability-specific terminology would increase the likelihood of producing contextually relevant and respectful responses for SEND learners, compared to existing systems. Data collection initiatives that include people with disabilities, AAC users, and special educators could help achieve this goal while adhering to the standards of informed consent required in data collection practices.

Second, we need more research into the design of AI systems that support rather than just log SEND learners' development of metacognitive skills. Metacognition and self-regulation are some of the strongest predictors of future learning success and also some of the most challenging for SEND learners (Chiu et al., 2023). Gen-AI systems that prompt learners to reflect on their own learning strategies, to predict how they will perform a task, and to reflect on the discrepancy between prediction and actual outcome may provide a powerful approach to developing metacognition - but the design of developmentally appropriate prompts for metacognitive skill development, across a spectrum of communication abilities, is no small undertaking that requires cross-disciplinary co-operation between AI engineers, special education researchers and speech-language therapists.

Third, we need longitudinal studies of the effects of early exposure to Generative AI (Gen-AI) on the independence and self-advocacy skills of SEND learners. There is a potential (as yet not well understood) risk that learners who acquire literacy, communication, and problem-solving skills through AI-mediated interaction will develop dependency behaviors that limit their ability to operate in unmediated human contexts. On the other hand, successful skill acquisition through AI early in the learning journey may lead to the development of skills and dispositions for increased independence. We need cohort studies to track learners over multiple years and through post-school transitions to answer this question - a research approach that is expensive and complex but crucial for policy.

Fourth, a co-design approach, where SEND learners play an active role in the development and testing of Gen-AI tools for SEND learners, is both a methodological and ethical improvement. This is reflected in the maxim from disability studies: nothing about us without us. In the context of educational AI, this means engaging SEND learners and their families in design testing, in the detection of AI-generated mis- or disinformation, and in prioritizing design goals in the earliest phases of development.

A number of research teams in Scandinavia and Australia have taken the lead in participatory AI design with the disability community, and their approaches provide a model for educational AI research (Benz et al., 2024).

Finally, Gen-AI combined with other emerging technologies such as wearables, brain-computer interfaces and extended reality environments creates research opportunities that are starting to become real. A student with a motor disability who can generate text via brain-computer interface could have that text supported and contextualized by an LLM for presentation to communication partners, thus reducing the cost of complex communication. Gen-AI enhanced extended reality environments could provide safe and manageable social practice environments for learners with autism that are more immersive and responsive than any existing 2D interface. These developments are still in the research prototype stage, but given the rapid progress in both areas, it is time for both special and inclusive education policy and professional development to start anticipating these developments now, not when they are commercially available.

11.3 Limitations of this Chapter

The chapter has some methodological shortcomings that need to be taken into account when reading the arguments within the chapter. The literature identification process was not systematic but rather purposive as a conceptual narrative review; no database search protocol, screening by two reviewers, or evidence flow analysis as per PRISMA guidelines was used and so the review is not exhaustive and may have selection bias. Second, the evidence base for Gen-AI applications directly with SEND populations is limited, and the extent to which much of the argument in this chapter is extrapolating from related literatures (general educational AI, AAC and adult health-AI contexts) is essential. Third, the scenarios presented in Section 10 are fictionalized projections that illustrate conceptually rather than as actual products and are not intended as evidence of effectiveness. Fourth, the review was mainly based on English language documents and articles from well-developed countries, which may restrict the generalisability of its findings to other language and resource settings. These could be countered in future research using systematic or scoping review methods, and by focussing on empirical research directly with SEND learners.

Author Positionality

All the authors have multidisciplinary backgrounds in artificial intelligence, engineering education, educational technology, and higher education research. The chapter has not been written by any special education teacher, but rather has been informed by a multitude of recent literature on SEND, AI ethics, inclusive pedagogy, Universal Design for Learning (UDL) and policy documents from across the world. The authors take an interdisciplinary approach that aims to support integration of the developments of AI with inclusive education practice, and acknowledge the need for future collaboration with SEND practitioners, educators, therapists, policy-makers, learners and families.

12. CONCLUSION

Gen-AI tools offer a new capability in special and inclusive education - not just the latest "EdTech". The ability to produce and personalize content at scale, to help support and mediate communication and expression across a range of modalities, and to reduce the administrative burden of differentiation and personalization, address genuine constraints on inclusive practice over many years. The intersection of inclusive pedagogy, Universal Design for Learning, and human-AI interaction theories offers a robust normative basis by which to assess their appropriate use within the classroom, and to distinguish between genuine pedagogical integration and superficial, novelty-driven adoption.

Three points are particularly clear from the analysis in this chapter. First, Gen-AI use in special education is pedagogically driven or it is not used at all: tools must support the learning outcomes identified through specialist assessment and human interaction, not stand in for professional judgement in identifying learning outcomes. Second, ethics is not the enemy of innovation but essential to it: unless data privacy, algorithmic fairness, transparency and safeguards for vulnerability are built into the design and governance of Gen-AI tools, their integration with learners with SEND will do more harm than good. Third, professional development of special educators in AI literacy is critical, under-funded, and needs to be designed differently from generic digital literacy.

This chapter has not made specific tool recommendations: in addition to the space shifting so fast that any such list would rapidly become out-of-date, the match between tools and learners is always contextual. What the chapter does recommend, strongly, is the ongoing research, policy and professional development attention that is needed in this area. Historically, SEND learners have been the last to benefit and the first to be harmed by technological innovations in education. Turning this around is not a technological matter. It is a matter of institutional priority and professional commitment.

REFERENCES

Aleven, V., McLaughlin, E. A., Glenn, R. A., & Koedinger, K. R. (2017). Instruction based on adaptive learning technologies. In Mayer, R. E., & Alexander, P. A. (Eds.), *Handbook of research on learning and instruction* (2nd ed., pp. 522–560). Routledge.

Amershi, S., Weld, D. S., Vorvoreanu, M., Fourney, A., Nushi, B., Collisson, P., Suh, J., Iqbal, S. T., Bennett, P. N., Inkpen, K., Teevan, J., Kikin-Gil, R., & Horvitz, E. (2019). Guidelines for human-AI interaction. *Proceedings of the 2019 CHI Conference on Human Factors in Computing Systems*, Article 3, 1–13. ACM. DOI: 10.1145/3290605.3300233

Baglieri, S., & Shapiro, A. (2012). *Disability studies and the inclusive classroom: Critical practices for creating least restrictive attitudes*. Routledge. DOI: 10.4324/9780203837399

Bender, E. M., Gebru, T., McMillan-Major, A., & Shmitchell, S. (2021). On the dangers of stochastic parrots: Can language models be too big? *Proceedings of the 2021 ACM Conference on Fairness, Accountability, and Transparency* (pp. 610–623). ACM. DOI: 10.1145/3442188.3445922

Benz, C., Scott-Jeffs, W., McKercher, K. A., Welsh, M., Norman, R., Hendrie, D., Locantro, M., & Robinson, S. (2024). Community-based participatory-research through co-design: Supporting collaboration from all sides of disability. *Research Involvement and Engagement*, *10*(1), 47. Advance online publication. DOI: 10.1186/s40900-024-00573-3 PMID: 38730283

Beukelman, D. R., & Light, J. C. (2020). *Augmentative and alternative communication: Supporting children and adults with complex communication needs* (5th ed.). Paul H. Brookes Publishing.

Chiu, T. K. F., Xia, Q., Zhou, X., Chai, C. S., & Cheng, M. (2023). Systematic literature review on opportunities, challenges, and future research recommendations of artificial intelligence in education. *Computers and Education: Artificial Intelligence*, *4*, 100118. DOI: 10.1016/j.caeai.2022.100118

Crompton, H., & Burke, D. (2023). Artificial intelligence in higher education: The state of the field. *International Journal of Educational Technology in Higher Education*, *20*(1), 22. Advance online publication. DOI: 10.1186/s41239-023-00392-8

European Commission, Directorate-General for Education, Youth, Sport and Culture. (2022). *Ethical guidelines on the use of artificial intelligence and data in teaching and learning for educators*. Publications Office of the European Union., DOI: 10.2766/153756

Florian, L., & Spratt, J. (2013). Enacting inclusion: A framework for interrogating inclusive practice. *European Journal of Special Needs Education*, *28*(2), 119–135. DOI: 10.1080/08856257.2013.778111

Gu, P., Xu, F., Chen, L., Ma, Z., Zhang, M., & Zhang, Y. (2025). Technological affordances and applications of chatbots for conversational skill interventions in autism: A scoping review. *Education and Information Technologies*, *30*(7), 9311–9340. DOI: 10.1007/s10639-024-13191-z

Hattie, J., & Timperley, H. (2007). The power of feedback. *Review of Educational Research*, *77*(1), 81–112. DOI: 10.3102/003465430298487

Holmes, W., Porayska-Pomsta, K., Holstein, K., Sutherland, E., Baker, T., Shum, S. B., Santos, O. C., Rodrigo, M. T., Cukurova, M., Bittencourt, I. I., & Koedinger, K. R. (2022). Ethics of AI in education: Towards a community-wide framework. *International Journal of Artificial Intelligence in Education*, *32*(3), 504–526. DOI: 10.1007/s40593-021-00239-1

Kasneci, E., Sessler, K., Küchemann, S., Bannert, M., Dementieva, D., Fischer, F., Gasser, U., Groh, G., Günnemann, S., Hüllermeier, E., Krusche, S., Kutyniok, G., Michaeli, T., Nerdel, C., Pfeffer, J., Poquet, O., Sailer, M., Schmidt, A., Seidel, T., & Kasneci, G. (2023). ChatGPT for good? On opportunities and challenges of large language models for education. *Learning and Individual Differences*, *103*, 102274. DOI: 10.1016/j.lindif.2023.102274

Luckin, R., Holmes, W., Griffiths, M., & Forcier, L. B. (2016). *Intelligence unleashed: An argument for AI in education*. Pearson. https://static.googleusercontent.com/media/edu.google.com/en//pdfs/Intelligence-Unleashed-Publication.pdf

Martínez, P., Ramos, A., & Moreno, L. (2024). Exploring large language models to generate easy to read content. *Frontiers of Computer Science*, *6*, 1394705. Advance online publication. DOI: 10.3389/fcomp.2024.1394705

Mitchell, M., Wu, S., Zaldivar, A., Barnes, P., Vasserman, L., Hutchinson, B., Spitzer, E., Raji, I. D., & Gebru, T. (2019). Model cards for model reporting. *Proceedings of the Conference on Fairness, Accountability, and Transparency (FAT* '19)* (pp. 220–229). ACM. DOI: 10.1145/3287560.3287596

OECD. (2024). *Education policy outlook 2024: Reshaping teaching into a thriving profession from ABCs to AI*. OECD Publishing., DOI: 10.1787/dd5140e4-

Oliver, M. (1990). *The politics of disablement*. Red Globe Press., DOI: 10.1007/978-1-349-20895-1

OpenAI. (2023). *GPT-4 technical report* (arXiv:2303.08774). arXiv. /arXiv.2303.08774DOI: 10.48550

Pellegrino, J. W., & Hilton, M. L. (Eds.). (2012). *Education for life and work: Developing transferable knowledge and skills in the 21st century*. National Academies Press. DOI: 10.17226/13398

Porayska-Pomsta, K. (2016). AI as a methodology for supporting educational praxis and teacher metacognition. *International Journal of Artificial Intelligence in Education, 26*(2), 679–700. DOI: 10.1007/s40593-016-0101-4

Porayska-Pomsta, K., Alcorn, A. M., Avramides, K., Beale, S., Bernardini, S., Foster, M. E., Frauenberger, C., Good, J., Guldberg, K., Keay-Bright, W., Kossyvaki, L., Lemon, O., Mademtzi, M., Menzies, R., Pain, H., Rajendran, G., Waller, A., Wass, S., & Smith, T. J. (2018). Blending human and artificial intelligence to support autistic children's social communication skills. *ACM Transactions on Computer-Human Interaction, 25*(6), 1–35. DOI: 10.1145/3271484

Rose, D. H., & Meyer, A. (2002). *Teaching every student in the digital age: Universal design for learning*. ASCD.

Slee, R. (2011). *The irregular school: Exclusion, schooling and inclusive education*. Routledge., DOI: 10.4324/9780203831564

Tomlinson, C. A. (2014). *The differentiated classroom: Responding to the needs of all learners* (2nd ed.). ASCD.

United Nations. (2006). *Convention on the rights of persons with disabilities*. https://www.un.org/disabilities/documents/convention/convention_accessible_pdf.pdf

United Nations Children's Fund. (2022). *Pulse check on digital learning*. https://www.unicef.org/reports/pulse-check-digital-learning

United Nations Educational, Scientific and Cultural Organization. (2021). *Recommendation on the ethics of artificial intelligence*. https://unesdoc.unesco.org/ark:/48223/pf0000381137

United Nations Educational, Scientific and Cultural Organization. (2023). *Guidance for generative AI in education and research*. https://unesdoc.unesco.org/ark:/48223/pf0000386693

Valencia, S., Cave, R., Kallarackal, K., Seaver, K., Terry, M., & Kane, S. K. (2023). "The less I type, the better": How AI language models can enhance or impede communication for AAC users. *Proceedings of the 2023 CHI Conference on Human Factors in Computing Systems*, Article 830, 1–14. DOI: 10.1145/3544548.3581560

Vygotsky, L. S. (1978). *Mind in society: The development of higher psychological processes*. Harvard University Press.

Warschauer, M., & Matuchniak, T. (2010). New technology and digital worlds: Analyzing evidence of equity in access, use, and outcomes. *Review of Research in Education*, *34*(1), 179–225. DOI: 10.3102/0091732X09349791

World Health Organization. (2022). *Global report on health equity for persons with disabilities*. https://www.who.int/publications/i/item/9789240063600

Zawacki-Richter, O., Marín, V. I., Bond, M., & Gouverneur, F. (2019). Systematic review of research on artificial intelligence applications in higher education: Where are the educators? *International Journal of Educational Technology in Higher Education*, *16*(1), 39. Advance online publication. DOI: 10.1186/s41239-019-0171-0

Zhai, X., Chu, X., Chai, C. S., Jong, M. S. Y., Istenic, A., Spector, M., Liu, J.-B., Yuan, J., & Li, Y. (2021). A review of artificial intelligence (AI) in education from 2010 to 2020. *Complexity*, *2021*(1), 8812542. DOI: 10.1155/2021/8812542

Chapter 4

Designing and Developing Rights-Based Architectures for GenAI in Special and Inclusive Classrooms

Ashraf Alam
http://orcid.org/0000-0001-6178-1187
Department of Education, National Institute of Technology Calicut, Kozhikode, India

ABSTRACT

This chapter develops a conceptual and rights-based sociotechnical architecture for integrating GenAI in special and inclusive classrooms. It argues that pedagogical legitimacy in Special Educational Needs and Disabilities (SEND) contexts cannot be grounded in innovation rhetoric alone, but must emerge from the convergence of disability justice, inclusive pedagogy, capability expansion, epistemic safety, care ethics, and multi-scalar governance. The chapter reconceptualizes GenAI as a contingent mediational infrastructure whose value depends on instructional mechanism fidelity, teacher-led orchestration, dignity-preserving accessibility, and non-discriminatory design. It advances a framework linking sociocultural mediation, cognitive regulation, professional judgment, safeguarding logics, and rights-compliant data governance. The central claim is that GenAI can support inclusive participation only when pedagogy-first, governance-first, equity-first, and care-first principles remain normatively non-negotiable.

DOI: 10.4018/979-8-3373-9169-4.ch004

1. INTRODUCTION

1.1 GenAI as a High-Stakes Inclusive Education Question

Generative artificial intelligence has become a special and inclusive education question because its classroom effects are not merely instructional, they are distributive, recognitional, epistemic, and juridical. Around 1.3 billion people, roughly 16 percent of the global population, live with significant disability, and nearly 240 million children worldwide have some form of disability. At the same time, many education systems still lack inclusive teacher preparation, accessible content architectures, and consistent support infrastructures. In such conditions, GenAI does not enter a neutral pedagogical space. It enters stratified ecologies marked by communicative asymmetry, sensory variation, executive-function diversity, and unequal access to institutional protection. Its apparent advantages, multimodal generation, adaptive explanation, linguistic mediation, and structured prompting, therefore coexist with heightened exposure to exclusion, surveillance, misinformation, and dependency. For inclusive classrooms, the central issue is not adoption alone, but whether technological mediation expands substantive participation without intensifying vulnerability.

1.2 Conceptual Problem, Scope, and Analytic Unit

The conceptual problem of this chapter lies in translating technical possibility into pedagogical legitimacy for learners with special educational needs and disabilities. GenAI can generate text, audio, images, summaries, prompts, and explanatory reformulations with unprecedented speed, yet educational legitimacy depends on far more than output production (Rizos et al., 2024; Sağdıç et al., 2024; Naatz & Ruppar, 2026). It depends on alignment with instructional mechanisms, accessibility logics, safeguarding thresholds, data proportionality, and rights-preserving classroom practice. Accordingly, this chapter adopts a conceptual-theoretical approach grounded in the critical synthesis and interpretation of interdisciplinary scholarship rather than in the collection or analysis of primary empirical data. It treats the special and inclusive classroom as a sociotechnical assemblage composed of the learner, teacher, family, support professionals, curriculum, platform, policy, and governance layers. Tables 1 through 5 are author-developed conceptual syntheses intended to organize, integrate, and communicate the theoretical arguments advanced in the chapter. They have not been empirically tested or validated and should not be interpreted or used as validated models, diagnostic tools, scales, or assessment instruments. This ecological unit matters because inclusion succeeds or fails through interactions among micro-level pedagogy, meso-level institutional routines, and macro-level regulatory architectures. Technology in education is now widely framed as requiring governance, regulation, and teacher preparation, which confirms that classroom AI cannot be analysed as an isolated tool detached from system design.

1.3 Definitional Precision and Normative Vocabulary

GenAI in this chapter refers to probabilistic, multimodal generation systems that produce plausible linguistic or symbolic outputs through pattern inference rather than grounded pedagogical understanding. This distinction is vital because synthetic fluency can masquerade as accuracy, while stochastic variation can destabilize routine-sensitive teaching environments. *Special Educational Needs and Disabilities* (SEND) is treated not as a fixed administrative label but as a heterogeneous field of support needs spanning disability, neurodivergence, communication difference, sensory variation, learning difficulty, and co-occurring conditions shaped by context (Wang et al., 2025; Lin et al., 2025). Equally important are distinctions among accessibility, accommodation, modification, differentiation, personalization, and assistive augmentation, since each carries different implications for curriculum, assessment validity, and legal obligation. The normative vocabulary must also be widened beyond privacy. In child-serving institutions, safeguarding includes dignity, psychological safety, relational boundary protection, non-discrimination, and duty of care. Article 24 of the Convention on the Rights of Persons with Disabilities requires an inclusive education system directed toward dignity, human potential, and equal opportunity, making rights language a design constraint rather than a rhetorical supplement.

1.4 Central Claims and Chapter Trajectory

The chapter advances three integrated claims. First, GenAI becomes educationally meaningful only when tethered to identifiable instructional mechanisms such as scaffolded explanation, executive-function support, multimodal access, metacognitive prompting, or communication mediation. Second, special and inclusive education requires governance-first rather than innovation-first integration because children's rights, disability-related data sensitivity, and vulnerability to epistemic and socio-emotional harm demand ex ante safeguards, not retrospective correction. Third, teacher professionalism is not displaced by GenAI but reconfigured toward orchestration, verification, judgment calibration, and relational safeguarding. This position aligns with current international guidance that emphasizes regulation, safety, privacy protection, fairness, transparency, accountability, inclusion, and child well-being as core requirements whenever AI affects children. It also resonates with emerging global policy analysis showing that AI can support equity and inclusion only when pedagogy guides use and when outsourcing tasks does not substitute for genuine learning. The following sections therefore move from theory, to socio-technical risk, to pedagogy, professionalism, governance, and normative synthesis.

2. THEORETICAL FOUNDATIONS FOR GENAI IN SPECIAL AND INCLUSIVE EDUCATION

2.1 Disability Justice, Inclusion Ontologies, and Normative Legitimacy

Any rights-based architecture for GenAI in special and inclusive classrooms must begin with the ontological and normative grammar of disability and inclusion. A purely *medicalized* frame legitimizes remediation, deficit indexing, and compensatory intervention, whereas a *social* and *relational* frame foregrounds environmental barriers, institutional friction, and exclusionary design (Park & Choo, 2025; Krishnan UC et al., 2026; Bhaskaru & Lalitha, 2026). A *biopsychosocial* synthesis is more analytically robust because it recognizes embodied difference without collapsing the learner into pathology. Within this conceptual field, *critical disability consciousness*, *anti-ableist pedagogy*, *recognitional justice*, *substantive equality*, and *dignity-preserving accommodation* become non-negotiable evaluative constructs. GenAI cannot be theorized as neutral assistance because it may either widen *capability freedoms* or intensify *normative normalization*. Inclusion, therefore, must be interpreted as participatory legitimacy, communicative access, epistemic visibility, and protected belonging. The theory-to-design implications of these commitments are consolidated further in Table 1, which translates abstract normative architectures into pedagogically actionable design logics.

2.2 Learning Sciences, Cognitive Architectures, and Mediated Pedagogy

The instructional legitimacy of GenAI in SEND contexts depends on whether it activates defensible learning mechanisms rather than merely producing fluent outputs. Within a *sociocultural* frame, learning is mediated through tools, symbols, guided participation, and scaffolded interaction, which means GenAI must be treated as a mediational artifact whose pedagogical value depends on human orchestration (Bahja et al., 2025; Sakowicz & Hamidi, 2025; Ewoldt & Flanagan, 2025). Within *cognitive load* logic, outputs must reduce extraneous burden, preserve germane processing, and avoid split-attention overload. Within *self-regulatory* and *metacognitive* architectures, AI supports must strengthen planning, monitoring, strategy selection, and reflective calibration rather than displacing them. Within *motivational* and *affective* theory, autonomy support, competence signaling, belonging, and anxiety regulation matter because learners with SEND often encounter repeated instructional misrecognition. These theory families are synthesized in Table 1, where pedagogical mechanisms, inclusive implications, and failure risks are aligned to rights-based GenAI design in analytically condensed form.

Table 1. Theory-to-design translation for GenAI in SEND

Theory Family	Core Conceptual Premise	Inclusion-Critical Interpretation	GenAI Design Translation	Systemic Failure Risk
Disability Justice Frameworks	Disability is shaped by embodied variation, social barriers, institutional norms, and recognitional hierarchies rather than by deficit alone	Inclusion requires dignity, non-pathologizing participation, reasonable accommodation, and protection against epistemic erasure	GenAI should be configured to expand communicative access, preserve learner agency, and avoid deficit-coded profiling or normalization pressures	Pedagogical personalization may degenerate into algorithmic labeling, stigmatizing simplification, or covert ableist standardization
Sociocultural Mediation Models	Learning emerges through mediated action, scaffolded participation, symbolic tools, and co-constructed meaning within relational environments	SEND support must be relational, dialogic, context-sensitive, and embedded in guided participation rather than isolated automation	GenAI should function as a provisional mediational aid for explanation, rehearsal, and communication under active teacher orchestration	Tool substitution may displace human mediation, weaken dialogic learning, and create pseudo-participation without authentic comprehension
Cognitive Load and Information Processing Logics	Instruction is effective when intrinsic complexity is managed, extraneous load is minimized, and working-memory strain is carefully regulated	Accessibility requires informational clarity, pacing sensitivity, multimodal coherence, and protection from overload or fragmentation	GenAI outputs should segment tasks, clarify instructions, structure examples, and support processing fluency without diluting conceptual rigor	Fluent but poorly structured outputs may intensify overload, split attention, redundancy effects, and comprehension breakdown

continued on following page

Table 1. Continued

Theory Family	Core Conceptual Premise	Inclusion-Critical Interpretation	GenAI Design Translation	Systemic Failure Risk
Self-Regulation and Metacognitive Architectures	Learning quality depends on planning, monitoring, error detection, strategic adaptation, and reflective self-governance	Inclusive pedagogy should strengthen learner agency, scaffold executive functioning, and support gradual autonomy rather than permanent dependence	GenAI should prompt self-explanation, sequencing, reflection, and strategy review through fadeable scaffolds and transparent support routines	Over-scaffolded interaction may externalize cognition, erode self-monitoring, and produce dependency masquerading as independence
Motivational, Affective, and Belonging Frameworks	Engagement is sustained through competence perception, autonomy support, affective safety, relevance, and social belonging	SEND learners require psychologically safe participation, non-humiliating assistance, and identity-affirming access to common classroom membership	GenAI should support encouragement, choice-sensitive pathways, anxiety reduction, and communicative inclusion without false reassurance or emotional substitution	Persuasive fluency may generate misplaced confidence, affective reliance, social isolation, or synthetic affirmation detached from real learning progress

Note. *This table is an author-developed conceptual synthesis based on the theoretical analysis presented in this chapter.*

Each theoretical family in Table 1 authorizes some forms of GenAI mediation while disqualifying others. *Disability justice* rejects pathologizing personalization, *sociocultural mediation* rejects disembodied automation, *cognitive architecture* rejects overload-inducing fluency, *metacognitive theory* rejects dependency-producing scaffolds, and *belonging-centered motivation* rejects emotionally manipulative pseudo-support. The table also reveals that inclusion cannot be reduced to access mechanics alone, since pedagogical legitimacy emerges at the intersection of cognition, recognition, affect, participation, and rights. In practical conceptual terms, GenAI in special education should be designed as a bounded, reviewable, fadeable, and dignity-preserving support layer rather than as a surrogate instructor. This integrated theory-to-design logic also grounds the ecological and political analysis developed in 2.3 and 2.4.

2.3 Inclusive Pedagogy, Tiered Support, and Curricular Justice

The pedagogical architecture of special and inclusive education requires that GenAI be interpreted through *variability-first* curriculum design rather than through generic personalization rhetoric. *Universal Design for Learning* is valuable because it anticipates heterogeneity across representation, engagement, and expression, yet its force lies in proactive barrier reduction, not in technological abundance (Farhah et al., 2025; Öztürk & Aksoy, 2026). *Tiered support* logics are equally important because universal access, targeted assistance, and intensive intervention serve different pedagogical purposes and demand different thresholds of human oversight. *IEP-aligned personalization* introduces juridical accountability by tying support to goals, accommodations, service obligations, and defensible expectations (Ai et al., 2025; Liu et al., 2026). *Differentiation theory* adds curricular nuance by distinguishing changes in process, pacing, grouping, and response mode from modifications that alter construct expectations. As already signaled by Table 1, the decisive question is whether GenAI preserves *access-with-rigor* and *participation-with-belonging*. Any design that fragments common curriculum or converts support into silent exclusion violates the normative architecture of inclusive pedagogy.

2.4 Ecological Systems, Capability Logics, and Global Justice Perspectives

A theoretically serious account of GenAI in special education must exceed classroom micro-analysis and enter the terrain of ecology, political economy, and global justice. *Ecological systems* thinking shows that learner outcomes are mediated by nested relations among family, peer culture, school capacity, professional norms, policy frameworks, and digital infrastructure (Ronksley-Pavia et al., 2025; Alqarni, 2026). *Capability theory* adds a sharper justice test by distinguishing nominal provision from real conversion into usable educational freedom. A learner may possess formal access to an AI interface yet remain excluded by language barriers, stigma, weak connectivity, inaccessible design, or low institutional trust. *Ethics of care* further clarifies that support is relationally constituted through attentiveness, responsiveness, and vulnerability-aware judgment. Finally, *postcolonial* and *Global South* perspectives expose the transfer limits of English-dominant, high-connectivity, platform-centric models of AI integration (Khlaif et al., 2025; Shafik et al., 2025; Eradze et al., 2025). Thus, as Table 1 indirectly anticipates, theory must operate across cognition, culture, law, infrastructure, and justice if GenAI is to serve inclusive classrooms without reproducing stratified exclusion.

3. GENAI AS A SOCIOTECHNICAL SYSTEM IN SPECIAL EDUCATION

3.1 Computational Ontologies, Probabilistic Inference, and Pedagogical Translation

Generative artificial intelligence in educational contexts must be analytically understood as a *probabilistic inference architecture* rather than a cognition-bearing pedagogical agent. Its outputs emerge through *stochastic pattern synthesis*, *latent space representation*, and *context-conditioned token generation*, which produce high levels of linguistic plausibility without guaranteeing epistemic fidelity (Prabagar et al., 2026; Ronksley-Pavia et al., 2025; van Garderen et al., 2025). This distinction becomes pedagogically consequential in SEND environments where instructional stability, semantic clarity, and routine predictability are not peripheral but foundational to access. The phenomenon of *synthetic fluency* can create *epistemic illusion*, wherein learners attribute authority to outputs that merely mirror statistically dominant patterns (Waterfield et al., 2026; Marino et al., 2023). Additionally, *prompt-dependence* transforms instructional interaction into a form of *specification labor*, requiring teachers to encode pedagogical intent, learner variability, and accessibility constraints into interaction design. Multimodality, spanning text, audio, and image, introduces expanded access possibilities but also raises concerns of *sensory misalignment*, *cognitive overload*, and representational distortion. Thus, GenAI must be framed as a contingent mediational system requiring human interpretive governance rather than autonomous instructional intelligence.

3.2 Sociotechnical Architectures, Distributed Agency, and Systemic Interdependencies

The integration of GenAI into inclusive classrooms must be theorized through *sociotechnical systems theory*, where educational outcomes emerge from the co-constitution of technological affordances and social practices. Classrooms function as *activity systems* in which tools, rules, roles, and community expectations interact dynamically, often producing contradictions between inclusion goals and efficiency imperatives (Rappa et al., 2026; Upadhyay, 2024; Evmenova et al., 2024). Within *actor-network configurations*, agency is distributed across teachers, learners, algorithms, institutional policies, interface designs, and infrastructural conditions, thereby complicating simplistic notions of responsibility. GenAI also participates in *platformization*, where pedagogical processes become subtly reorganized through default settings, interaction affordances, and invisible design logics. These systemic interactions generate both affordances and risk pathways, which are analytically synthesized in Table 2, enabling a structured mapping of pedagogical promise against epistemic, equity, and safeguarding vulnerabilities.

Table 2. GenAI affordances and risks in inclusive learning ecologies

GenAI Functional Modality	Pedagogical Affordance Vector	Epistemic Vulnerability Dimension	Equity and Representation Risk	Required Human Mediation Protocol
Textual Generation Systems	Enables structured explanation, adaptive simplification, and linguistic scaffolding aligned with learner variability and readability thresholds	May produce hallucinated content, persuasive inaccuracies, and unverifiable claims that compromise knowledge integrity for learners with limited epistemic vigilance	Risks encoding deficit language, cultural bias, and normative linguistic standards that marginalize diverse communicative identities	Requires teacher-led verification routines, contextual correction, and alignment with curricular intent and accessibility needs
Multimodal Output Architectures	Supports visual, auditory, and hybrid representations facilitating sensory-accessible learning and alternative expression pathways	May introduce representational distortion, misaligned imagery, or cognitive overload through poorly integrated multimodal outputs	Can privilege dominant cultural semiotics and exclude locally meaningful or disability-sensitive representations	Demands critical review of modality appropriateness, coherence across formats, and alignment with sensory profiles of learners
Prompt-Driven Interaction Systems	Allows dynamic instructional customization through specification of constraints, examples, and scaffolding sequences tailored to learner needs	Vulnerable to specification errors, ambiguity amplification, and inconsistent outputs due to stochastic generation variability	Places disproportionate cognitive and professional burden on educators with unequal access to prompt literacy resources	Necessitates advanced prompt literacy, iterative refinement, and collaborative design within professional communities of practice

continued on following page

Table 2. Continued

GenAI Functional Modality	Pedagogical Affordance Vector	Epistemic Vulnerability Dimension	Equity and Representation Risk	Required Human Mediation Protocol
Feedback and Assessment Assistance Tools	Enables rapid formative feedback, structured response evaluation, and iterative learning support across diverse performance modalities	May generate overgeneralized or misleading feedback lacking construct validity or pedagogical precision	Risks reinforcing normative performance standards and overlooking diverse demonstration of competence	Requires human calibration of feedback accuracy, alignment with assessment constructs, and preservation of learner dignity
Conversational Interaction Interfaces	Facilitates dialogic engagement, question-answering, and conversational scaffolding supporting participation and communication	Susceptible to anthropomorphic misinterpretation, over-reliance, and transfer of epistemic authority from teacher to system	May produce culturally biased conversational norms and inappropriate relational cues affecting vulnerable learners	Requires strict boundary-setting, monitoring of relational dynamics, and reinforcement of teacher-centered epistemic authority

Note. *This table is an author-developed conceptual synthesis based on the theoretical analysis presented in this chapter.*

Each functional modality in Table 2 generates a dual structure of affordance and vulnerability, requiring *context-sensitive mediation* rather than uniform deployment. The table highlights that *epistemic risk* is not accidental but structurally linked to generative processes, where *hallucination*, *fluency bias*, and *authority transfer* can destabilize knowledge formation. Similarly, *equity risks* are embedded within representational logics that privilege dominant linguistic and cultural norms, thereby producing subtle forms of exclusion. The requirement for *human-in-the-loop governance* is therefore not merely procedural but epistemologically necessary, as it restores interpretive judgment, contextual sensitivity, and accountability within pedagogical interaction. This synthesis also reinforces insights from Section 2, where theoretical constructs such as *sociocultural mediation*, *cognitive load regulation*, and *recognitional justice* were identified as essential constraints. Consequently, GenAI must be conceptualized as a *regulated pedagogical instrument* rather than an autonomous instructional entity.

3.3 Epistemic Integrity, Bias Production, and Intersectional Harm

The epistemic dimension of GenAI introduces profound challenges related to *knowledge validity*, *truth-conditions*, and *authority attribution* within inclusive classrooms. The phenomenon of *hallucination* represents a form of *epistemic contamination*, where generated content mimics coherence while lacking factual grounding (Mittal et al., 2024; Pesovski et al., 2024). This risk is intensified by *persuasive fluency*, which can trigger *automation bias* and *epistemic deference*, particularly among learners who rely on external scaffolding for comprehension. Furthermore, *knowledge provenance opacity* complicates the pedagogical task of teaching evidence evaluation, as outputs often lack traceable sources or verifiable reasoning pathways (Grandbastien et al., 2026; Rakap, 2024). In parallel, *representational bias* manifests through deficit-coded descriptions, normative behavioral expectations, and linguistically standardized outputs that marginalize diverse communicative forms. Intersectional analysis reveals that disability interacts with class, language, gender, and geographic inequalities, producing layered vulnerabilities that cannot be addressed through single-axis fairness metrics. Thus, epistemic integrity in GenAI-mediated learning must be treated as a core pedagogical and ethical concern rather than a peripheral technical issue.

3.4 Safeguarding, Dependency Dynamics, and Institutional Path Dependencies

Safeguarding within GenAI-mediated inclusive classrooms extends beyond content moderation into the domain of *relational ethics*, *dependency formation*, and *institutional responsibility*. The risk of *anthropomorphic projection* can lead learners to attribute emotional intentionality to systems, fostering *pseudo-relational attachment* that may displace authentic human interaction. Such dynamics are particularly significant for learners with social communication challenges, where boundaries between tool and interlocutor may blur (Lopez-Gazpio, 2025; Lalar et al., 2025; Chopra, 2025). Additionally, *persuasion vectors* embedded in conversational systems can introduce subtle forms of behavioral influence, raising concerns about autonomy and manipulation. From an institutional perspective, *datafication* and *surveillance intensification* disproportionately affect learners with SEND, as detailed behavioral and performance data become embedded within digital infrastructures (Întorsureanu et al., 2025; Rahim et al., 2025; Kouo et al., 2025). Over time, reliance on GenAI can produce *path dependency*, where pedagogical practices align with platform affordances rather than educational principles, leading to *professional deskilling* and erosion of teacher agency. These dynamics underscore the necessity of embedding GenAI within *governance-first architectures* that prioritize safeguarding, accountability, and human-centered educational integrity.

4. PEDAGOGICAL ARCHITECTURES, INSTRUCTIONAL LOGICS, AND INCLUSIVE DESIGN PRAXIS

4.1 Pedagogy-First Design, Instructional Mechanisms, and Epistemic Alignment

A defensible integration of GenAI in special and inclusive classrooms must be anchored in a *pedagogy-first epistemology*, where technological mediation is subordinated to *instructional mechanism fidelity* rather than novelty-driven deployment. Instruction is not merely content delivery but a structured orchestration of *cognitive activation*, *schema construction*, *guided practice*, and *feedback loops* that sustain learning trajectories (Swaminathan & Naik, 2025; Brunton et al., 2025). Within this paradigm, GenAI must be mapped onto identifiable mechanisms such as *scaffolding*, *worked-example facilitation*, *metacognitive prompting*, and *language mediation*. The principle of *accessibility-with-rigor* ensures that barrier reduction does not collapse into epistemic dilution, preserving *construct integrity* and *cognitive challenge* (Pierrès et al., 2025; Wu et al., 2025; Kim et al., 2025). Equally, *independence-by-design* requires that supports remain *fadeable*, preventing the emergence of *learned dependency*. The necessity of *error-sensitive pedagogy* is intensified in AI-mediated contexts, as *hallucinatory outputs* and *persuasive inaccuracies* necessitate systematic verification routines. Thus, GenAI becomes pedagogically legitimate only when it enhances *instructional coherence*, *epistemic reliability*, and *learner agency* within inclusive environments.

4.2 UDL-Driven Variability Design, Differentiation Logics, and Participation Ecologies

The operationalization of inclusive pedagogy in AI-mediated classrooms requires a synthesis of *Universal Design for Learning*, *differentiation theory*, and *participatory pedagogy*. UDL's *variability-first orientation* reconfigures curriculum design by anticipating heterogeneity in *perception*, *engagement*, and *expression*, thereby positioning accessibility as a proactive design principle rather than reactive accommodation (Sandhu et al., 2024; Sohn et al., 2025). Differentiation introduces further granularity by modulating *content complexity*, *process pathways*, *product formats*, and *learning environments* in response to readiness, interest, and learner profile. However, personalization must be carefully bounded to avoid *fragmentation of shared curriculum* and erosion of *collective classroom identity* (Jauhiainen & Garagorry Guerra, 2024; Mirea et al., 2025; Jauhiainen & Guerra, 2023). Participation ecologies emphasize *peer-mediated learning*, *dialogic interaction*, and *belonging-sensitive design*, ensuring that support mechanisms do not render learners socially invisible. These multidimensional pedagogical alignments are analytically synthesized in Table 3, which maps instructional intentions to GenAI-supported pedagogical moves under strict constraints of teacher mediation and safeguarding.

Table 3. Instructional alignment for GenAI in inclusive classrooms

Instructional Intention Domain	Learner Variability Dimension	GenAI Supported Pedagogical Mediation	Teacher-Orchestrated Calibration Mechanism	Non-Negotiable Ethical and Pedagogical Constraint
Conceptual Comprehension Development	Variability in linguistic processing, cognitive load tolerance, and prior knowledge schema activation	Generates simplified explanations, structured summaries, and multimodal representations aligned with learner processing thresholds	Teacher evaluates conceptual accuracy, aligns outputs with curriculum goals, and ensures preservation of disciplinary rigor	Avoids oversimplification that dilutes conceptual depth or misrepresents disciplinary knowledge
Expressive Communication and Response Formation	Variability in expressive language ability, communication modalities, and motor or sensory constraints	Provides structured sentence frames, alternative expression formats, and assistive communication scaffolds	Teacher ensures authenticity of learner voice, validates communicative intent, and calibrates assistance boundaries	Prevents substitution of learner expression with AI-generated responses that compromise authorship integrity
Executive Function and Task Regulation	Variability in planning, sequencing, working memory, and self-regulation capacities	Offers stepwise task breakdowns, prompts for sequencing, and reminders supporting organizational processes	Teacher monitors scaffold fading, reinforces independent strategy use, and adjusts support intensity dynamically	Avoids persistent externalization of cognitive processes leading to dependency and reduced autonomy

continued on following page

Table 3. Continued

Instructional Intention Domain	Learner Variability Dimension	GenAI Supported Pedagogical Mediation	Teacher-Orchestrated Calibration Mechanism	Non-Negotiable Ethical and Pedagogical Constraint
Formative Feedback and Learning Adjustment	Variability in feedback interpretation, cognitive accessibility, and emotional sensitivity to evaluation	Generates immediate feedback, error explanations, and iterative guidance tailored to learner responses	Teacher verifies feedback accuracy, aligns with assessment constructs, and contextualizes for learner comprehension	Ensures feedback maintains construct validity and does not introduce misinformation or bias
Engagement and Motivation Enhancement	Variability in attention span, interest pathways, affective regulation, and belonging needs	Produces interest-linked examples, adaptive prompts, and encouragement supporting sustained engagement	Teacher evaluates motivational appropriateness, prevents over-reliance, and maintains authentic relational engagement	Avoids artificial affective manipulation and ensures that motivation is grounded in genuine learning processes

Note. *This table is an author-developed conceptual synthesis based on the theoretical analysis presented in this chapter.*

Each instructional intention in Table 3 is embedded within a matrix of *learner variability*, *teacher judgment*, and *ethical constraint*, thereby reinforcing that inclusive pedagogy is inherently relational and context-dependent. The table demonstrates that GenAI can support comprehension, communication, executive functioning, feedback, and engagement only when its outputs are continuously calibrated through *professional discretion* and *situational awareness*. It also foregrounds the principle that assistance must remain *proportionate, transparent, and reversible*, ensuring that support does not become substitution. This aligns with earlier theoretical insights from Section 2, where constructs such as *sociocultural mediation*, *cognitive load optimization*, and *recognitional justice* were identified as foundational. Moreover, the matrix reveals that pedagogical design must balance *individual responsiveness* with *collective participation*, preventing isolation while sustaining accessibility. Thus, GenAI becomes pedagogically viable only within a tightly governed architecture of *instructional alignment, ethical constraint, and teacher-mediated orchestration.*

4.3 Domain-Specific Pedagogical Translation and Cognitive-Affective Integration

The pedagogical implications of GenAI become more granular when examined across domain-specific learning processes. In literacy and language domains, *phonological processing*, *syntactic parsing*, *semantic integration*, and *discourse coherence* require finely tuned scaffolding that supports decoding and comprehension without eroding complexity. In mathematics, *schema acquisition*, *procedural fluency*, and *conceptual reasoning* depend on carefully sequenced *worked examples* and *error pattern recognition*, where excessive automation may hinder deep understanding (Giannakos et al., 2025; Kayyali, 2025; Oleribe, 2025). Executive function domains involve *task initiation*, *cognitive flexibility*, *inhibitory control*, and *metacognitive monitoring*, which require supports that are both structured and fadeable. Communication and social interaction domains introduce additional complexity through *pragmatic language use*, *turn-taking*, *repair strategies*, and *peer engagement*, where AI-mediated assistance must remain subordinate to human relational dynamics (Han et al., 2024; Kloos et al., 2024). Across these domains, the integration of GenAI must be guided by *cognitive-affective coupling*, ensuring that intellectual engagement and emotional safety are co-produced within inclusive pedagogical environments.

4.4 Assessment Ecologies, Feedback Validity, and Ethical Classroom Culture

Assessment within GenAI-mediated inclusive classrooms must be reconceptualized as a *validity-sensitive, equity-oriented, and ethically grounded practice.* Formative assessment operates as a feedback-rich system where information is used to guide instructional adjustment rather than merely evaluate performance (Tang et al., 2024; Yu & Guo, 2023; Kumar et al., 2023). However, AI-generated feedback introduces risks related to *construct misalignment*, *epistemic inaccuracy*, and *interpretive ambiguity*, requiring rigorous teacher calibration. The distinction between *accommodation* and *modification* becomes critical, as inappropriate use of AI may inadvertently alter the construct being assessed, thereby undermining validity. Additionally, issues of *authorship integrity* and *assisted performance* necessitate transparent norms that distinguish support from substitution. Ethical classroom culture must therefore integrate *trauma-informed pedagogy*, *psychological safety*, and *culturally sustaining practices*, ensuring that AI use does not expose learners to stigma or exclusion (Yu et al., 2023; Fenta, 2025; Su & Yang, 2023). Norm-setting around transparency, consent, and collective accountability further anchors GenAI within a *dignity-preserving pedagogical ecosystem*, reinforcing that technology must remain subordinate to inclusive educational values.

5. TEACHER PROFESSIONALISM, EPISTEMIC AUTHORITY, AND CAPABILITY-ORIENTED DEVELOPMENT

5.1 Professional Discretion, Epistemic Authority, and Relational Labor

The integration of GenAI into inclusive classrooms fundamentally reconfigures teacher professionalism as a domain of *epistemic arbitration*, *context-sensitive judgment*, and *relational accountability*. In SEND environments, pedagogical action operates under conditions of *bounded rationality*, *uncertainty*, and *asymmetric vulnerability*, where instructional misalignment may generate disproportionate harm (Alfarwan, 2025; De Marco et al., 2024; Liu et al., 2024). Teachers therefore function as *epistemic authorities* who calibrate the credibility, appropriateness, and accessibility of AI-generated outputs. This involves continuous engagement with *trust calibration*, *error detection*, and *contextual interpretation*, ensuring that synthetic fluency does not displace pedagogical validity (Allison et al., 2025; Dey et al., 2024; Elkot et al., 2025). Professional labor also expands into *distributed cognition*, where teachers coordinate with special educators, therapists, and families to maintain coherence across support systems. Crucially, *relational labor* remains irreducible, encompassing emotional attunement, identity affirmation, and dignity preservation. These dimensions highlight that GenAI does not diminish teacher expertise but intensifies the need for *professional discretion*, *ethical vigilance*, and *care-centered pedagogical practice*.

5.2 Knowledge Architectures, Competence Frameworks, and AI Pedagogical Literacies

Teacher competence in AI-mediated inclusive education must be theorized through an expanded synthesis of *Pedagogical Content Knowledge*, *technological integration frameworks*, and *ecological agency*. While PCK remains foundational in aligning subject matter with pedagogical strategies, SEND contexts introduce additional layers of *accessibility reasoning*, *accommodation design*, and *multimodal translation* (Jukiewicz, 2025; Yadav et al., 2025). *Technological pedagogical knowledge* must therefore be reinterpreted not as tool proficiency but as *pedagogical mediation under technological constraint*. Teacher agency is shaped by *structural affordances*, including policy mandates, institutional culture, resource availability, and platform design, which collectively constitute an *ecology of constrained choice*. Within this environment, *professional capital* becomes a critical construct, encompassing human expertise, social collaboration, and decisional judgment. These dimensions are synthesized in Table 4, which articulates a multidimensional competence framework for GenAI integration in inclusive education.

Table 4. Professional competence for GenAI in inclusive education

Competence Domain	Theoretical Foundation	Knowledge and Skill Configuration	Professional Judgment Expression	Systemic Risk if Deficient
Epistemic Evaluation Competence	Grounded in *epistemic cognition, knowledge validation theory,* and *construct validity principles*	Ability to assess accuracy, coherence, and relevance of AI outputs in relation to curricular standards and learner needs	Exercises critical verification, identifies inconsistencies, and aligns outputs with pedagogical intent	Leads to propagation of misinformation, erosion of knowledge integrity, and diminished instructional credibility
Inclusive Pedagogical Design Competence	Anchored in *Universal Design for Learning, differentiation theory*, and *capability approach*	Designs accessible learning pathways, aligns supports with variability, and maintains rigor within inclusive frameworks	Balances accessibility with cognitive challenge, ensuring equitable participation across diverse learner profiles	Results in exclusionary practices, over-simplification, and fragmentation of shared curriculum experiences
Technological Mediation Competence	Informed by *sociotechnical systems theory, human-computer interaction*, and *activity theory*	Develops prompt literacy, manages multimodal outputs, and integrates AI within instructional sequences	Calibrates AI use within classroom dynamics, maintains human oversight, and prevents tool overreach	Generates dependency, misalignment with pedagogy, and loss of teacher control over instructional processes
Ethical and Safeguarding Competence	Derived from *ethics of care, data justice*, and *rights-based frameworks*	Recognizes privacy risks, ensures dignity preservation, and manages relational boundaries in AI-mediated contexts	Implements safeguarding protocols, monitors emotional impacts, and upholds learner rights	Exposes learners to psychological harm, surveillance risks, and breaches of confidentiality
Collaborative and Relational Competence	Based on *distributed cognition, interprofessional collaboration theory*, and *relational pedagogy*	Coordinates with multidisciplinary teams, engages families, and fosters inclusive classroom culture	Facilitates shared decision-making, aligns interventions, and sustains communicative trust across stakeholders	Leads to fragmented support systems, inconsistent interventions, and weakened learner outcomes

Note. *This table is an author-developed conceptual synthesis based on the theoretical analysis presented in this chapter.*

Each domain in Table 4 integrates cognitive, ethical, relational, and technological dimensions, thereby reflecting the complex demands of inclusive education. The table demonstrates that competence is not merely technical proficiency but a synthesis of *knowledge, judgment, and disposition* operating within institutional constraints. Deficiencies in any domain generate systemic risks that extend beyond individual classrooms, affecting epistemic integrity, equity, and safeguarding. Importantly, the framework aligns with earlier discussions in Sections 2 and 3, where *sociocultural mediation*, *epistemic risk*, and *sociotechnical interdependencies* were identified as foundational constructs. The competence matrix also underscores the necessity of *continuous professional learning*, as GenAI environments evolve dynamically. Thus, teacher professionalism must be conceptualized as *adaptive expertise*, characterized by flexibility, reflective practice, and capacity for recalibration under uncertainty, ensuring that inclusive pedagogy remains robust in technologically mediated contexts.

5.3 Professional Identity, Moral Agency, and Institutional Accountability

Teacher identity in AI-mediated inclusive education must be understood as a site of *professional negotiation*, where authority, responsibility, and recognition are continuously recalibrated. The proliferation of GenAI challenges traditional notions of expertise by introducing external knowledge systems that appear authoritative yet remain epistemically unstable (Evmenova et al., 2024; Lewis, 2025; Nikolopoulou, 2025). This creates conditions for *role conflict* and *moral tension*, particularly when institutional pressures prioritize efficiency or innovation over safeguarding and pedagogical integrity. Teachers must therefore engage in *boundary work*, delineating the limits of acceptable AI use and asserting professional judgment against automated outputs (Arinushkina, 2024; García-López & Trujillo-Liñán, 2025; Vhatkar et al., 2024). *Moral agency* becomes central, as educators navigate competing demands of accountability, care, and compliance. Institutional accountability structures must support rather than undermine this agency, providing clear guidelines, resources, and decision-making autonomy. In this context, professionalism is not static but an evolving construct shaped by *recognition*, *legitimacy*, and *ethical responsibility* within a rapidly transforming educational landscape.

5.4 Professional Development, Capability Formation, and Reflexive Practice

Professional development for GenAI integration must be conceptualized as *capability formation* rather than narrow skill acquisition. Effective development frameworks draw on *situated learning*, *communities of practice*, and *reflective praxis*, enabling teachers to engage with AI within authentic classroom contexts (Haroud & Saqri, 2025; Zombron et al., 2024; Nedungadi et al., 2024). *Instructional coaching*, *peer collaboration*, and *practice-based rehearsal* facilitate the development of *judgment calibration* and *contextual adaptability*. Central to this process is *prompt literacy*, which transforms interaction with GenAI into a form of *instructional design*, requiring clarity, specificity, and alignment with learner needs. Equally important is *output evaluation literacy*, encompassing bias detection, accessibility assessment, and epistemic verification. Documentation practices must also be refined to ensure *traceability* and *accountability* without excessive data accumulation (Nedungadi et al., 2024; Pratschke, 2024; Ruiz-Rojas et al., 2023). Finally, student-facing AI literacy should be integrated into pedagogy, equipping learners with critical awareness while maintaining institutional responsibility for safeguarding. This capability-oriented approach ensures that professional development sustains *inclusive excellence* and *ethical resilience* in AI-mediated education systems.

6. ETHICS, LAW, SAFEGUARDING, AND GOVERNANCE IN SEND AI CONTEXTS

6.1 Normative Ethics, Rights Architectures, and Moral Foundations

The governance of GenAI in special and inclusive education must be grounded in a multilayered normative architecture that integrates *principlism*, *ethics of care*, *capability approach*, and *rights-based justice*. Within *principlism*, the imperatives of beneficence, non-maleficence, autonomy, and justice acquire heightened salience due to learner vulnerability and asymmetrical power relations (Çela et al., 2025; Noroozi et al., 2024; González-Eras et al., 2025). However, principlism alone is insufficient without the relational sensitivity embedded in *ethics of care*, which foregrounds attentiveness, responsiveness, and context-sensitive moral judgment. The *capability approach* reframes evaluation criteria by focusing on substantive freedoms, asking whether GenAI expands real opportunities for participation, communication, and learning rather than merely increasing nominal access (O'Dea, 2024; Marzano, 2025; Farrelly & Baker, 2023). Concurrently, *rights-based frameworks* institutionalize obligations related to dignity, non-discrimination, and reasonable accommodation, transforming ethical aspirations into enforceable standards. Together, these constructs establish that GenAI must function within a *moral-legal assemblage* where technological affordances are continuously evaluated against principles of human dignity, relational responsibility, and educational justice.

6.2 Data Governance, Privacy Regimes, and Accountability Infrastructures

The governance of data in AI-mediated inclusive classrooms constitutes a critical axis of ethical and legal responsibility, particularly due to the heightened sensitivity of disability-related information. Within *data protection paradigms*, principles such as *data minimization*, *purpose limitation*, and *proportionality* operate as constraints on pedagogical design, ensuring that data collection remains strictly aligned with educational necessity (Preiksaitis & Rose, 2023; Ching et al., 2024; Ogunleye et al., 2024). The concept of *informational self-determination* further complicates consent frameworks, as learners, families, and institutions must navigate overlapping domains of authority and responsibility. *Human-in-the-loop governance* emerges as a central accountability mechanism, requiring that decision-making authority remains anchored in human judgment rather than delegated to algorithmic processes. These governance dimensions are systematically articulated in Table 5, which presents a layered architecture of control, responsibility, and decision boundaries across institutional actors.

Table 5. Governance architecture for GenAI in special education systems

Governance Layer	Normative Principle Alignment	Control Mechanism Typology	Responsible Institutional Actor	Decision Boundary and Failure Implication
Classroom Pedagogical Layer	Anchored in *care ethics*, *instructional integrity*, and *learner dignity preservation*	Real-time monitoring, teacher-led verification, and adaptive instructional calibration based on learner response patterns	Classroom teacher and special educator operating within collaborative instructional frameworks	Misalignment leads to epistemic inaccuracies, compromised accessibility, and immediate pedagogical harm affecting learner outcomes
School Institutional Governance Layer	Guided by *organizational justice*, *policy coherence*, and *inclusive education mandates*	Development of institutional protocols, safeguarding policies, and professional accountability structures	School leadership, administrative bodies, and multidisciplinary support teams	Failure produces inconsistent practices, erosion of trust, and systemic inequities across classrooms and learner groups
Data Protection and Compliance Layer	Based on *data justice*, *privacy rights*, and *informational self-determination*	Implementation of data minimization strategies, secure storage systems, and controlled data access protocols	Data protection officers, institutional compliance units, and regulatory oversight bodies	Breach results in unauthorized data exposure, legal violations, and long-term harm to learner confidentiality and dignity
Technology Provider and Platform Layer	Oriented by *algorithmic accountability*, *transparency norms*, and *non-extractive data practices*	Model auditing, bias mitigation processes, and transparent system design aligned with educational values	Technology vendors, developers, and platform governance entities	Deficiencies lead to opaque decision-making, embedded bias, and reduced institutional capacity to evaluate system outputs
Policy and Regulatory Layer	Grounded in *human rights law*, *disability rights frameworks*, and *public accountability principles*	Establishment of regulatory standards, compliance requirements, and enforcement mechanisms across educational systems	Government agencies, policy makers, and international regulatory bodies	Weak regulation results in ungoverned deployment, systemic inequities, and erosion of public trust in educational institutions

Note. *This table is an author-developed conceptual synthesis based on the theoretical analysis presented in this chapter.*

Each governance level in Table 5 is anchored in distinct normative principles while contributing to a coherent system of accountability that spans classroom practice, institutional policy, data protection, technological design, and regulatory oversight. The table demonstrates that effective governance cannot rely on isolated controls but must operate through *integrated accountability networks* that ensure continuity of ethical standards across contexts. This layered approach aligns with the sociotechnical insights developed in Section 3, where distributed agency and systemic interdependencies were identified as defining features of AI integration. It also reinforces the pedagogical imperatives outlined in Section 4, where teacher mediation and instructional alignment were positioned as central to ethical practice. Consequently, governance must be understood not as a static framework but as a dynamic process of *continuous calibration*, where emerging risks, technological evolution, and contextual variability necessitate ongoing adaptation. This perspective ensures that GenAI remains embedded within a *rights-preserving, dignity-centered, and accountability-driven educational ecosystem.*

6.3 Safeguarding Logics, Bias Governance, and Non-Discrimination Imperatives

Safeguarding within GenAI-mediated inclusive education extends into complex domains of *psychological safety*, *relational integrity*, and *equity protection*. Beyond content filtering, safeguarding encompasses protection against *manipulation vectors*, *persuasive influence*, and *boundary violations* that may arise within conversational interfaces (Batta, 2024; Tang et al., 2025; Bougdira & Al Murshidi, 2025). The risk of *dependency formation* is particularly salient, as learners may develop *over-reliance* on AI systems, thereby undermining autonomy and social engagement. *Bias governance* must address multiple layers of bias, including representational, linguistic, cultural, and interactional dimensions, recognizing that bias is not a singular defect but a systemic phenomenon embedded across design, deployment, and interpretation (Bouguettaya et al., 2025; Creely & Blannin, 2025; Bae & Bozkurt, 2024). The principle of *non-discrimination* requires that AI systems do not reproduce or amplify existing inequities related to disability, socioeconomic status, language, or cultural identity. This necessitates a shift from *equality of access* toward *equity of outcome* and *recognitional justice*, ensuring that all learners receive support that is both appropriate and dignity-preserving (Rice et al., 2025; Tan, 2025; Michel-Villarreal et al., 2023). Thus, safeguarding becomes an integrative practice combining ethical vigilance, pedagogical sensitivity, and institutional responsibility.

6.4 Institutional Readiness, Policy Design, and Systemic Integration Trajectories

The successful integration of GenAI in special and inclusive education depends on the development of *institutional readiness* as an ethical and operational capacity. Organizational readiness encompasses *policy coherence*, *professional competence*, *resource adequacy*, and *cultural alignment*, all of which contribute to the legitimacy and sustainability of AI deployment (Arslan et al., 2024; Tomczyk & Majkut, 2025; Rodríguez-Ortiz et al., 2025). *Procurement ethics* plays a critical role, requiring that institutions engage with technology providers through *non-extractive partnerships* that prioritize transparency, accessibility, and data stewardship. Risk management frameworks must incorporate *hazard identification*, *control implementation*, and *residual risk evaluation*, enabling proactive rather than reactive governance (Sousa & Cardoso, 2025; Gilbert, 2024; Hınız, 2026). Policy design must function as *pedagogical design*, ensuring that rules and regulations support rather than constrain effective teaching practices. At the systemic level, integration trajectories must align with *human rights obligations*, establishing clear thresholds for acceptable use, prohibited practices, and accountability mechanisms (Dong et al., 2024; Mishra et al., 2025). Co-governance with educators, families, and disability communities further enhances legitimacy by embedding diverse perspectives within decision-making processes. This comprehensive approach ensures that GenAI integration is not merely technologically feasible but ethically defensible and pedagogically meaningful within global inclusive education systems.

7. CONCLUSION

7.1 Pedagogical Reframing and Sociotechnical Integration

The foregoing analysis consolidates a rigorous conceptual synthesis in which GenAI is reconstituted not as a peripheral instructional aid but as a *pedagogical infrastructure* embedded within *sociotechnical assemblages* that mediate cognition, participation, and institutional accountability. The chapter demonstrates that inclusive education in AI-mediated environments cannot be reduced to access provision, but must achieve a simultaneous alignment of *epistemic integrity*, *participatory inclusion*, *recognitional justice*, and *dignity preservation*. The integration of *sociocultural mediation*, *cognitive load optimization*, *metacognitive scaffolding*, and *capability expansion* establishes that learning remains fundamentally relational, context-bound, and dependent on professional judgment. GenAI introduces a reconfiguration of teacher labor toward *orchestration*, *verification*, *interpretive calibration*, and *relational safeguarding*, thereby intensifying rather than diminishing professional responsibility. The chapter's central contribution lies in advancing a *rights-based sociotechnical architecture* where pedagogical design, ethical governance, and institutional accountability operate as interdependent dimensions, ensuring that technological mediation enhances rather than distorts inclusive educational practice.

7.2 Normative Principles, Theoretical Propositions, and Future Trajectories

The normative architecture emerging from this chapter is structured around four non-negotiable principles, *pedagogy-first design*, *governance-first integration*, *equity-centered justice*, and *care-oriented safeguarding*, each functioning as a constraint on permissible uses of GenAI in special education contexts. These principles collectively assert that technological deployment must remain subordinate to *instructional coherence*, *ethical legitimacy*, and *rights compliance*, rejecting any model that prioritizes efficiency over learner well-being. The chapter further advances theoretical propositions centered on *epistemic safety*, *dignified personalization*, *autonomy-with-scaffolds*, and *recognition-sensitive mediation*, thereby extending existing conceptual frameworks into the domain of AI-enabled inclusive pedagogy. Policy implications emphasize the necessity of *multi-layered governance*, *institutional readiness*, and *co-governance* involving educators, families, and disability communities, ensuring that decision-making processes remain participatory and context-sensitive. Future trajectories must therefore focus on refining conceptual vocabularies, developing coherent governance logics, and sustaining professional capacity, so that GenAI integration contributes to *inclusive flourishing*, *educational justice*, and *global equity* without compromising the foundational values of dignity, safety, and human-centered learning.

REFERENCES

Ai, J., Zhang, X., & Chen, Q. (2025, September). The Application of Generative Artificial Intelligence in Individualized Education Program for Exceptional Children: Value Connotation, Realistic Challenge and Practical Path. In *2025 5th International Conference on Educational Technology (ICET)* (pp. 654-657). IEEE. https://doi.org/ DOI: 10.1109/ICET67421.2025.11380433

Alfarwan, A. (2025, September). Generative AI use in K-12 education: A systematic review. In *Frontiers in Education* (Vol. 10, p. 1647573). Frontiers Media SA. https://doi.org/DOI: 10.3389/feduc.2025.1647573

Allison, J., Hwang, G. J., Mayer, R. E., Pellas, N., Karnalim, O., de Freitas, S., Ng, O.-L., Huang, Y.-M., Hooshyar, D., Seidman, R. H., Al-Emran, M., Mikropoulos, T. A., Schroeder, N. L., Roscoe, R. D., & Sanusi, I. (2025). From generative AI to extended reality: Multidisciplinary perspectives on the challenges, opportunities, and future of educational computing. *Journal of Educational Computing Research*, *63*(6), 1327–1363. DOI: 10.1177/07356331251359964

Alqarni, T. M. (2026). Teachers' perceptions of generative AI in inclusive classrooms: Enhancing engagement for students with learning disabilities. *Universal Access in the Information Society*, *25*(1), 22. DOI: 10.1007/s10209-025-01301-8

Arinushkina, A. A. (Ed.). (2024). *Integration strategies of generative AI in higher education*. IGI Global., DOI: 10.4018/979-8-3693-5518-3

Arslan, B., Lehman, B., Tenison, C., Sparks, J. R., López, A. A., Gu, L., & Zapata-Rivera, D. (2024). Opportunities and challenges of using generative AI to personalize educational assessment. *Frontiers in Artificial Intelligence*, *7*, 1460651. DOI: 10.3389/frai.2024.1460651 PMID: 39434872

Bae, H., & Bozkurt, A. (2024). The untold story of training students with generative AI: Are we preparing students for true learning or just personalization. *Online Learning : the Official Journal of the Online Learning Consortium*, *28*(3), 1–9. DOI: 10.24059/olj.v28i3.4689

Bahja, M., Hammad, R., Alkazemi, A., & Alhabsi, Z. (2025). The Potential of Generative AI in Special Education: A Review of Applications and Impact. *Unleashing User Innovation*, 192-213. https://doi.org/DOI: 10.1201/9781003485698-14

Batta, A. (2024). Transforming higher education through generative AI: Opportunity and challenges. *Paradigm*, *28*(2), 241–243. DOI: 10.1177/09718907241286221

Bhaskaru, O., & Lalitha, K. (2026). Empowering Special Education Through Generative AI With Opportunities, Challenges, and Case Studies. In *Shaping Inclusive Educational Policies and Practices With Generative AI* (pp. 171–204). IGI Global Scientific Publishing., DOI: 10.4018/979-8-3373-3745-6.ch007

Bougdira, A., & Al Murshidi, G. (2025). Generative AI as a tool for personalized STEAM K-12 education. In *Prompt engineering and generative AI applications for teaching and learning* (pp. 387–410). IGI Global Scientific Publishing., DOI: 10.4018/979-8-3693-7332-3.ch023

Bouguettaya, S., Pupo, F., Chen, M., & Fortino, G. (2025). A Meta-Survey of Generative AI in Education: Trends, Challenges, and Research Directions. *Big Data and Cognitive Computing*, *9*(9), 237. DOI: 10.3390/bdcc9090237

Brunton, R. J., Rhazzafe, S., Moodley, R., Kuhn, S., Caraffini, F., Wilford, S., Higginbottom, R., Colreavy-Donnelly, S., & Gongora, M. (2025). Using generative artificial intelligence to enhance the performance of disadvantaged students in secondary education. *Social Sciences & Humanities Open*, *12*, 102110. DOI: 10.1016/j.ssaho.2025.102110

Çela, E., Vedishchev, A., Fonkam, M., Eappen, P., Potluri, R. M., & Vajjhala, N. R. (2025). Integrating generative AI in education: Themes, challenges, and future directions. In *Generative Artificial Intelligence (AI) approaches for industrial applications* (pp. 149–167). Springer Nature Switzerland., DOI: 10.1007/978-3-031-76710-4_8

Ching, Y. H., Hsu, Y. C., & Hung, A. (2024). Introduction to the special section on integrating generative AI in education. *TechTrends*, *68*(4), 771–772. DOI: 10.1007/s11528-024-00990-x

Chopra, K. (2025). Motivating older adults with special needs for learning using generative artificial intelligence. *Educational Gerontology*, •••, 1–20. DOI: 10.1080/03601277.2025.2538205

Creely, E., & Blannin, J. (2025). Creative partnerships with generative AI. Possibilities for education and beyond. *Thinking Skills and Creativity*, *56*, 101727. DOI: 10.1016/j.tsc.2024.101727

De Marco, V., Sciarrone, F., & Temperini, M. (2024, July). TutorChat: a Chatbot for the Support to Dyslexic Learner's activity through Generative AI. In *2024 IEEE International Conference on Advanced Learning Technologies (ICALT)* (pp. 155-157). IEEE. https://doi.org/DOI: 10.1109/ICALT61570.2024.00051

Dey, A. K., Chauhan, V. K., Singh, P. K., & Sarkar, A. (2024, December). Exploring the integration of generative ai in modern education systems: A comprehensive analysis. In *2024 International Conference on Artificial Intelligence and Quantum Computation-Based Sensor Application (ICAIQSA)* (pp. 1-8). IEEE. https://doi.org/ DOI: 10.1109/ICAIQSA64000.2024.10882259

Dong, W., Pan, D., & Kim, S. (2024). Exploring the integration of IoT and Generative AI in English language education: Smart tools for personalized learning experiences. *Journal of Computational Science*, *82*, 102397. DOI: 10.1016/j.jocs.2024.102397

Elkot, M. A., Youssif, E., & Elmahdi, O. E. H. (2025). Generative Conversational AI: Active Practices for Fostering Students with Mild Intellectual Disabilities to Improve English Communication Skills. *Contemporary Educational Technology*, *17*(1), ep549. Advance online publication. DOI: 10.30935/cedtech/15688

Eradze, M., Manna, M., Sunar, A., Dovigo, F., & Ianes, D. (2025). Harnessing generative AI for inclusive education: opportunities and challenges. In *Frontiers in Education* (Vol. 10, p. 1765687). Frontiers Media SA. https://doi.org/DOI: 10.3389/feduc.2025.1765687

Evmenova, A. S., Borup, J., & Shin, J. K. (2024). Harnessing the power of generative AI to support ALL learners. *TechTrends*, *68*(4), 820–831. DOI: 10.1007/s11528-024-00966-x

Evmenova, A. S., Regan, K., Mergen, R., & Hrisseh, R. (2024). Improving writing feedback for struggling writers: Generative AI to the rescue? *TechTrends*, *68*(4), 790–802. DOI: 10.1007/s11528-024-00965-y

Ewoldt, K. B., & Flanagan, S. M. (2025). Generative artificial intelligence as an educational collaborator: A next-generation resource. *Teaching Exceptional Children*, *00400599251340611*. Advance online publication. DOI: 10.1177/00400599251340611

Farhah, N. S., Wadood, A., Alqarni, A. A., Uddin, M. I., & Aldhyani, T. H. (2025). Enhancing adaptive learning with generative ai for tailored educational support for students with disabilities. *Journal of Disability Research*, *4*(3), 20250012. DOI: 10.57197/JDR-2025-0012

Farrelly, T., & Baker, N. (2023). Generative artificial intelligence: Implications and considerations for higher education practice. *Education Sciences*, *13*(11), 1109. DOI: 10.3390/educsci13111109

Fenta, A. A. (2025). A review on enhancing education with AI: Exploring the potential of ChatGPT, Bard, and generative AI. *Discover Education*, *4*(1), 38. DOI: 10.1007/s44217-025-00426-5

García-López, I. M., & Trujillo-Liñán, L. (2025, June). Ethical and regulatory challenges of Generative AI in education: a systematic review. In *Frontiers in Education* (Vol. 10, p. 1565938). Frontiers Media SA. https://doi.org/DOI: 10.3389/feduc.2025.1565938

Giannakos, M., Azevedo, R., Brusilovsky, P., Cukurova, M., Dimitriadis, Y., Hernandez-Leo, D., Järvelä, S., Mavrikis, M., & Rienties, B. (2025). The promise and challenges of generative AI in education. *Behaviour & Information Technology*, *44*(11), 2518–2544. DOI: 10.1080/0144929X.2024.2394886

Gilbert, T. K. (2024). Generative AI and generative education. *Annals of the New York Academy of Sciences*, *1534*(1), 11–14. DOI: 10.1111/nyas.15129 PMID: 38512308

González-Eras, A., Pérez, J., Puerto, E., González, W. E. P., & Aguilar, J. (2025, October). A Reference Framework for the Use of Generative AI in Higher Education. In *2025 LI Latin American Computer Conference (CLEI)* (pp. 1-10). IEEE. https://doi.org/DOI: 10.1109/CLEI67442.2025.11420309

Grandbastien, M., Horbach, A., Jansen, T., & Linden, T. (2026). Special issue editorial: Initial studies on the applications of generative AI in education. *Education and Information Technologies*, *1-5*(6), 1787–1791. Advance online publication. DOI: 10.1007/s10639-025-13875-0

Han, A., Zhou, X., Cai, Z., Han, S., Ko, R., Corrigan, S., & Peppler, K. A. (2024, May). Teachers, parents, and students' perspectives on integrating generative AI into elementary literacy education. In *Proceedings of the 2024 CHI Conference on Human Factors in Computing Systems* (pp. 1-17). https://doi.org/DOI: 10.1145/3613904.3642438

Haroud, S., & Saqri, N. (2025). Generative AI in higher education: Teachers' and students' perspectives on support, replacement, and digital literacy. *Education Sciences*, *15*(4), 396. DOI: 10.3390/educsci15040396

Hınız, G. (2026). A year of generative AI in English language teaching and learning-A case study. *Journal of Research on Technology in Education*, *58*(2), 291–311. DOI: 10.1080/15391523.2024.2404132

Întorsureanu, I., Oprea, S. V., Bâra, A., & Vespan, D. (2025). Generative AI in education: Perspectives through an academic lens. *Electronics (Basel)*, *14*(5), 1053. DOI: 10.3390/electronics14051053

Jauhiainen, J. S., & Garagorry Guerra, A. (2024, November). Generative AI and education: dynamic personalization of pupils' school learning material with ChatGPT. In *Frontiers in Education* (Vol. 9, p. 1288723). Frontiers Media SA. https://doi.org/DOI: 10.3389/feduc.2024.1288723

Jauhiainen, J. S., & Guerra, A. G. (2023). Generative AI and ChatGPT in school children's education: Evidence from a school lesson. *Sustainability (Basel)*, *15*(18), 14025. DOI: 10.3390/su151814025

Jukiewicz, M. (2025, August). How generative artificial intelligence transforms teaching and influences student wellbeing in future education. In *Frontiers in education* (Vol. 10, p. 1594572). Frontiers., DOI: 10.3389/feduc.2025.1594572

Kayyali, M. (2025). Generative AI and Education: Transforming Teaching and Learning Through Collaborative Intelligence. In *Humans and Generative AI Tools for Collaborative Intelligence* (pp. 25-52). IGI Global Scientific Publishing. https://doi.org/DOI: 10.4018/979-8-3693-8332-2.ch002

Khlaif, Z. N., Alshakhshir, R., Hamamra, B., & Joma, A. (2025). Reimagining inclusive education: The assistive power of generative AI in promoting accessibility and equity. *British Journal of Visual Impairment*, *02646196251382469*, 02646196251382469. Advance online publication. DOI: 10.1177/02646196251382469

Kim, J. H., Moldavan, A. M., Terry, R., & Massey, C. C. (2025). Enhancing Student Engagement with Generative AI. In *Transformative AI Practices for Personalized Learning Strategies* (pp. 69–106). IGI Global Scientific Publishing., DOI: 10.4018/979-8-3693-8744-3.ch004

Kloos, C. D., Alario-Hoyos, C., Estévez-Ayres, I., Callejo-Pinardo, P., Hombrados-Herrera, M. A., Muñoz-Merino, P. J., & Ibáñez, M. B. (2024, May). How can Generative AI support education? In *2024 IEEE Global Engineering Education Conference (EDUCON)* (pp. 1-7). IEEE. https://doi.org/DOI: 10.1109/EDUCON60312.2024.10578716

Kouo, J., Feng, J. H., & Jiao, E. (2025, June). Creating a Dataset of Autistic Individuals to Recommend Evidence-Based Practices through Generative Artificial Intelligence. In *2025 IEEE 13th International Conference on Healthcare Informatics (ICHI)* (pp. 126-136). IEEE. https://doi.org/DOI: 10.1109/ICHI64645.2025.00023

Krishnan, U. C. A., Lathabai, H. H., Kanjilal, R., Raman, R., & Nedungadi, P. (2026). Generative AI in disability-inclusive learning: A bibliometric and systematic literature analysis. *Disability and Rehabilitation. Assistive Technology*, •••, 1–30. DOI: 10.1080/17483107.2026.2653073 PMID: 41973863

Kumar, T., & Kait, R., Ankita, & Malik, A. (2023, September). The role of generative artificial intelligence (GAI) in Education: a detailed review for enhanced learning experiences. In *International conference on entrepreneurship, innovation, and leadership* (pp. 195-207). Singapore: Springer Nature Singapore. https://doi.org/DOI: 10.1007/978-981-97-1682-1_17

Lalar, S., Kumar, T., Kumar, R., & Kumar, S. (2025). Unlocking Potential: The Role of Artificial Intelligence in Revolutionizing Special Education for Inclusive Learning. In *Impacts of Generative AI on the Future of Research and Education* (pp. 201-232). IGI Global Scientific Publishing. https://doi.org/DOI: 10.4018/979-8-3693-0884-4.ch009

Lewis, K. D. (2025). Preparing gifted educators for generative AI: The essential role of educator preparation programs. *Journal of Advanced Academics*, *36*(4), 852–878. DOI: 10.1177/1932202X251356322

Lin, X., Han, X., & Qiu, J. (2025, April). Generative AI in Special Education: Teachers' Insights on Instructional Enrichment vs. Accommodations. In *Proceedings of the Extended Abstracts of the CHI Conference on Human Factors in Computing Systems* (pp. 1-6). https://doi.org/DOI: 10.1145/3706599.3719972

Liu, J., Wang, C., Liu, Z., Gao, M., Xu, Y., Chen, J., & Cheng, Y. (2024). A bibliometric analysis of generative AI in education: Current status and development. *Asia Pacific Journal of Education*, *44*(1), 156–175. DOI: 10.1080/02188791.2024.2305170

Liu, X., Yang, J., Zhao, W., & Wang, T. (2026). Generative Artificial Intelligence Self-Efficacy and Learning Engagement Among Special Education Teacher Trainees: A Moderated Mediation Model. *Behavioral Sciences (Basel, Switzerland)*, *16*(4), 488. DOI: 10.3390/bs16040488 PMID: 42073851

Lopez-Gazpio, I. (2025). Integrating large language models into accessible and inclusive education: Access democratization and individualized learning enhancement supported by generative artificial intelligence. *Information (Basel)*, *16*(6), 473. DOI: 10.3390/info16060473

Marino, M. T., Vasquez, E., Dieker, L., Basham, J., & Blackorby, J. (2023). The future of artificial intelligence in special education technology. *Journal of Special Education Technology*, *38*(3), 404–416. DOI: 10.1177/01626434231165977

Marzano, D. (2025). Generative Artificial Intelligence (GAI) in Teaching and Learning Processes at the K-12 Level: A Systematic Review: D. Marzano. *Technology, Knowledge and Learning*, 1-41. https://doi.org/DOI: 10.1007/s10758-025-09853-7

Michel-Villarreal, R., Vilalta-Perdomo, E., Salinas-Navarro, D. E., Thierry-Aguilera, R., & Gerardou, F. S. (2023). Challenges and opportunities of generative AI for higher education as explained by ChatGPT. *Education Sciences, 13*(9), 856. DOI: 10.3390/educsci13090856

Mirea, C. M., Bologa, R., Toma, A., Clim, A., Plăcintă, D. D., & Bobocea, A. (2025). Transforming learning with generative AI: From student perceptions to the design of an educational solution. *Applied Sciences (Basel, Switzerland), 15*(10), 5785. DOI: 10.3390/app15105785

Mishra, P., Margerum-Leys, J., Trainin, G., Hill-Jackson, V., Bobley, L., Bedesem, P. L., Williams, J. A.III, & Craig, C. J. (2025). Teacher education in the age of generative artificial intelligence: Introducing the special issue. *Journal of Teacher Education, 76*(3), 225–229. DOI: 10.1177/00224871251324713

Mittal, U., Sai, S., Chamola, V., & Sangwan, D. (2024). A comprehensive review on generative AI for education. *IEEE Access : Practical Innovations, Open Solutions, 12*, 142733–142759. DOI: 10.1109/ACCESS.2024.3468368

Naatz, A. J., & Ruppar, A. (2026). Special education teachers' use of generative artificial intelligence (AI): An exploratory survey of frequency and factors influencing adoption. *Journal of Special Education Technology, 41*(2), 227–239. DOI: 10.1177/01626434251379800

Nedungadi, P., Tang, K. Y., & Raman, R. (2024). The transformative power of generative artificial intelligence for achieving the sustainable development goal of quality education. *Sustainability (Basel), 16*(22), 9779. DOI: 10.3390/su16229779

Nedungadi, P., Tang, K. Y., & Raman, R. (2024). The transformative power of generative artificial intelligence for achieving the sustainable development goal of quality education. *Sustainability (Basel), 16*(22), 9779. DOI: 10.3390/su16229779

Nikolopoulou, K. (2025). Child-centered integration of generative AI in early learning: Balancing promises and challenges. *AI. Brain and Child, 1*(1), 21. DOI: 10.1007/s44436-025-00023-1

Noroozi, O., Soleimani, S., Farrokhnia, M., & Banihashem, S. K. (2024). Generative AI in Education: Pedagogical, Theoretical, and Methodological Perspectives. *International Journal of Technology in Education, 7*(3), 373–385. DOI: 10.46328/ijte.845

O'Dea, X. (2024). Generative AI: Is it a paradigm shift for higher education? *Studies in Higher Education, 49*(5), 811–816. DOI: 10.1080/03075079.2024.2332944

Ogunleye, B., Zakariyyah, K. I., Ajao, O., Olayinka, O., & Sharma, H. (2024). A systematic review of generative AI for teaching and learning practice. *Education Sciences*, *14*(6), 636. DOI: 10.3390/educsci14060636

Oleribe, O. O. (2025, August). Leveraging and harnessing generative artificial intelligence to mitigate the burden of neurodevelopmental disorders (NDDs) in children. In *Healthcare* (Vol. 13, No. 15, p. 1898). MDPI. https://doi.org/DOI: 10.3390/healthcare13151898

Öztürk, H., & Aksoy, S. (2026). Tailored Learning at Scale: Leveraging Generative AI for Dynamic Content Creation in Special Education. In *Rethinking Education and Agency in the Age of Human-Generative AI Interaction* (pp. 95-116). IGI Global Scientific Publishing. https://doi.org/DOI: 10.4018/979-8-3373-1195-1.ch003

Park, J., & Choo, S. (2025). Generative AI prompt engineering for educators: Practical strategies. *Journal of Special Education Technology*, *40*(3), 411–417. DOI: 10.1177/01626434241298954

Pesovski, I., Santos, R., Henriques, R., & Trajkovik, V. (2024). Generative AI for customizable learning experiences. *Sustainability (Basel)*, *16*(7), 3034. DOI: 10.3390/su16073034

Pierrès, O., Darvishy, A., & Christen, M. (2025). Exploring the role of generative AI in higher education: Semi-structured interviews with students with disabilities. *Education and Information Technologies*, *30*(7), 8923–8952. DOI: 10.1007/s10639-024-13134-8

Prabagar, S., Mothkur, R., Swetha, C. B., Kurian, A., Pavithra, K., & Aarthi, S. (2026). Generative AI for Inclusive Special Education: Case Studies in Accessibility, Personalization, and Ethical Design. In *Shaping Inclusive Educational Policies and Practices With Generative AI* (pp. 205-236). IGI Global Scientific Publishing. https://doi.org/DOI: 10.4018/979-8-3373-3745-6.ch008

Pratschke, B. M. (2024). *Generative AI and education: Digital pedagogies, teaching innovation and learning design*. Springer Nature., DOI: 10.1007/978-3-031-67991-9

Preiksaitis, C., & Rose, C. (2023). Opportunities, challenges, and future directions of generative artificial intelligence in medical education: Scoping review. *JMIR Medical Education*, *9*(1), e48785. DOI: 10.2196/48785 PMID: 37862079

Rahim, S., Sahar, G., Jabeen, G., Khatoon, S., & Angaiz, D. (2025). Harnessing generative AI: Reviewing applications, challenges, and solutions for out-of-school children in developing regions. *Sustainable Futures : An Applied Journal of Technology, Environment and Society*, *10*, 101206. DOI: 10.1016/j.sftr.2025.101206

Rakap, S. (2024). Chatting with GPT: Enhancing individualized education program goal development for novice special education teachers. *Journal of Special Education Technology*, *39*(3), 339–348. DOI: 10.1177/01626434231211295

Rappa, N. A., Nonis, K. P., Tang, K. S., Cooper, G., Cooper, M., & Sims, C. (2026). Can Generative AI support the learning agency of students with disability? A case study of an Australian secondary school. *British Journal of Educational Technology*, *57*(4), 924–942. Advance online publication. DOI: 10.1111/bjet.70048

Rice, M., DePascal, N., Argüello de Jesús, J. T., McFeely, H., Traylor, A., & Heaviland, L. (2025). What is the machine? Teachers' professional learning about generative artificial intelligence as tutors for children. *Professional Development in Education*, *51*(3), 418–433. DOI: 10.1080/19415257.2024.2407413

Rizos, I., Foykas, E., & Georgakopoulos, S. V. (2024). Enhancing Mathematics Education for Students with Special Educational Needs through Generative AI: A Case Study in Greece. *Contemporary Educational Technology*, *16*(4), ep535. Advance online publication. DOI: 10.30935/cedtech/15487

Rodríguez-Ortiz, M. Á., Santana-Mancilla, P. C., & Anido-Rifón, L. E. (2025). Machine learning and generative AI in learning analytics for higher education: A systematic review of models, trends, and challenges. *Applied Sciences (Basel, Switzerland)*, *15*(15), 8679. DOI: 10.3390/app15158679

Ronksley-Pavia, M., Nguyen, L., Wheeley, E., Rose, J., Neumann, M. M., Bigum, C., & Neumann, D. L. (2025). A scoping literature review of generative artificial intelligence for supporting neurodivergent school students. *Computers and Education: Artificial Intelligence*, *9*, 100437. DOI: 10.1016/j.caeai.2025.100437

Ronksley-Pavia, M., Ronksley-Pavia, S., & Bigum, C. (2025). Experimenting with generative ai to create personalized learning experiences for twice-exceptional and multi-exceptional neurodivergent students. *Journal of Advanced Academics*, *36*(4), 601–639. DOI: 10.1177/1932202X251346349

Ruiz-Rojas, L. I., Acosta-Vargas, P., De-Moreta-Llovet, J., & Gonzalez-Rodriguez, M. (2023). Empowering education with generative artificial intelligence tools: Approach with an instructional design matrix. *Sustainability (Basel)*, *15*(15), 11524. DOI: 10.3390/su151511524

Sağdıç, A., Elumar-Efe, E., & Sani-Bozkurt, S. (2024). GenAI, robots, and inclusive special education: autism spectrum disorder in the age of generative AI. In *Transforming education with generative AI: Prompt engineering and synthetic content creation* (pp. 309–326). IGI Global Scientific Publishing., DOI: 10.4018/979-8-3693-1351-0.ch015

Sakowicz, M., & Hamidi, F. (2025). Exploring the role of generative AI in supporting students with disabilities, through the lens of universal design for learning. *American Journal of STEM Education, 15*, 1–22. DOI: 10.32674/yeyaaq64

Sandhu, R., Channi, H. K., Ghai, D., Cheema, G. S., & Kaur, M. (2024). An introduction to generative AI tools for education 2030. *Integrating generative AI in education to achieve sustainable development goals*, 1-28. https://doi.org/DOI: 10.4018/979-8-3693-2440-0.ch001

Shafik, W., Aslam, M. M., Namoun, A., & Tufail, A. (2025). Innovative Strategies for Educating Learners with Disabilities Using Generative Artificial Intelligence. In *AI Roles and Responsibilities in Education* (pp. 447–474). Springer Nature Switzerland., DOI: 10.1007/978-3-031-96855-6_19

Sohn, J. S., Lee, E., Kim, J. J., Oh, H. K., & Kim, E. (2025). Implementation of generative AI for the assessment and treatment of autism spectrum disorders: A scoping review. *Frontiers in Psychiatry, 16*, 1628216. DOI: 10.3389/fpsyt.2025.1628216 PMID: 40766925

Sousa, A. E., & Cardoso, P. (2025). Use of generative AI by higher education students. *Electronics (Basel), 14*(7), 1258. DOI: 10.3390/electronics14071258

Su, J., & Yang, W. (2023). Unlocking the power of ChatGPT: A framework for applying generative AI in education. *ECNU Review of Education, 6*(3), 355–366. DOI: 10.1177/20965311231168423

Swaminathan, M., & Naik, T. (2025, October). Generative AI for Teachers with Vision Impairments in the Global South: A Bridge Too Far? In *Proceedings of the 27th International ACM SIGACCESS Conference on Computers and Accessibility* (pp. 1-18). https://doi.org/DOI: 10.1145/3663547.3746392

Tan, Q. (2025). Reimagining teacher development in the era of generative AI: A scoping review. *Teaching and Teacher Education, 168*, 105236. DOI: 10.1016/j.tate.2025.105236

Tang, Q., Deng, W., Huang, Y., Wang, S., & Zhang, H. (2025). Can generative artificial intelligence be a good teaching assistant?—An empirical analysis based on generative ai-assisted teaching. *Journal of Computer Assisted Learning, 41*(3), e70027. DOI: 10.1111/jcal.70027

Tang, Y., Chen, L., Chen, Z., Chen, W., Cai, Y., Du, Y., & Sun, L. (2024, May). Emoeden: Applying generative artificial intelligence to emotional learning for children with high-function autism. In *Proceedings of the 2024 CHI Conference on Human Factors in Computing Systems* (pp. 1-20). https://doi.org/DOI: 10.1145/3613904.3642899

Tomczyk, Ł., & Majkut, A. (2025). Integrating AI in education: An analysis of factors influencing the acceptance, concerns, attitudes, competencies and use of generative artificial intelligence among Polish teachers. *Human Behavior and Emerging Technologies*, *2025*(1), 5599169. DOI: 10.1155/hbe2/5599169

Upadhyay, A. K. (2024). Generative AI and training employees with special needs. *Strategic HR Review*, *23*(6), 221–224. DOI: 10.1108/SHR-05-2024-0039

van Garderen, D., Lannin, J., Rodrigues, J., Smith, C. M., & Shahale, F. V. (2025). Using Generative AI to Create Scaffolded Instructional Resources for Students With Disabilities. *Journal of Special Education Technology*, *01626434251408056*, 01626434251408056. Advance online publication. DOI: 10.1177/01626434251408056 PMID: 41953893

Vhatkar, A., Pawar, V., & Chavan, P. (2024, August). Generative AI in education: a bibliometric and thematic analysis. In *2024 8th International Conference on Computing, Communication, Control and Automation (ICCUBEA)* (pp. 1-6). IEEE. https://doi.org/DOI: 10.1109/ICCUBEA61740.2024.10774819

Wang, M., Tlili, A., Khribi, M. K., Lo, C. K., & Huang, R. (2025). Generative artificial intelligence in special education: A systematic review through the lens of the mediated-action model. *Information Development*, *02666669251335655*, 02666669251335655. Advance online publication. DOI: 10.1177/02666669251335655

Waterfield, D. A., Coleman, O. F., Welker, N. P., Kennedy, M. J., Mcdonald, S. D., & Cook, B. G. (2026). IEPs in the age of AI: Examining IEP goals written with and without ChatGPT. *Journal of Special Education Technology*, *41*(1), 57–71. DOI: 10.1177/01626434251324592

Wu, T. F., Lo, H. S., Huang, T. C., & Hong, J. C. (2025, July). Developing a Generative AI Interview Skills Training System for Individuals with Disabilities. In *Proceedings of the 2025 9th International Conference on Education and Multimedia Technology* (pp. 343-349). https://doi.org/DOI: 10.1145/3761843.3761923

Yadav, R., Huzooree, G., Yadav, M., & Gangodawilage, D. S. K. (2025). Generative AI for personalized learning content creation. In *Transformative AI Practices for Personalized Learning Strategies* (pp. 107–130). IGI Global Scientific Publishing., DOI: 10.4018/979-8-3693-8744-3.ch005

Yu, H., & Guo, Y. (2023, June). Generative artificial intelligence empowers educational reform: current status, issues, and prospects. In *Frontiers in education* (Vol. 8, p. 1183162). Frontiers Media SA. https://doi.org/DOI: 10.3389/feduc.2023.1183162

Yu, H., Liu, Z., & Guo, Y. (2023, April). application Status, Problems and Future Prospects of Generative ai in education. In *2023 5th International Conference on Computer Science and Technologies in Education (CSTE)* (pp. 1-7). IEEE. https://doi.org/DOI: 10.1109/CSTE59648.2023.00065

Zombron, A., Zaini, R., & Alnajashi, A. (2024). Beyond visual limits: Systems thinking for the visually impaired using generative AI. *International Journal on Responsibility*, *7*(1), 5. DOI: 10.62365/2576-0955.1123

Chapter 5
Engineering Generative AI for Special Education:
Technical Challenges, Design Choices, and Ethical Considerations

Assimina Tsibidaki
http://orcid.org/0000-0001-6430-2436
University of the Aegean, Greece

Michail Terezakis
University of Patras, Greece

Vana Chiou
http://orcid.org/0000-0003-1594-4496
University of the Aegean, Greece

Apostolos Kostas
http://orcid.org/0000-0002-1567-2649
University of the Aegean, Greece

Charalampos Politis
http://orcid.org/0009-0009-0713-6609
Independent Researcher, UK

ABSTRACT

This chapter explores how computer engineers and Gen-AI developers conceptualize the design, technical, and ethical requirements of Gen-AI systems for students with SEND. Drawing on ten semi-structured expert interviews and reflexive thematic

DOI: 10.4018/979-8-3373-9169-4.ch005

analysis, the findings show that Gen-AI was viewed as a bounded, human-governed support system rather than an educational authority. Five themes emerged: assistive infrastructure, teacher-governed personalization, safety and explainability, multimodal accessibility, and accountable classroom deployment. The chapter argues that effective Gen-AI for special education requires accessibility-first design, privacy-preserving architectures, human oversight, and sustained collaboration among engineers, educators, families, and learners.

INTRODUCTION

Generative Artificial Intelligence (Gen-AI) is increasingly discussed as a promising set of tools for supporting learning and participation across diverse educational contexts, including special education (García-López et al., 2025; Fu et al., 2025; Zhao et al., 2025). In special education, the potential value of Gen-AI is often linked to personalization, adaptivity, and content customization that can respond to heterogeneous learner profiles (Abulibdeh, 2025; García-López et al., 2025; Zhao et al., 2025). At the same time, successful use of Gen-AI for students with special educational needs and/or disabilities (SEND) depends on technical robustness, pedagogical alignment, and careful governance (Fu et al., 2025; Rasool et al., 2025; Salih et al., 2025).

A central engineering challenge concerns data quality and representativeness, because biased or incomplete datasets can reproduce inequities and yield discriminatory outcomes for diverse SEND populations (García-López et al., 2025; Fu et al., 2025; Nussbaum & Bekerman, 2025). The predominance of English-based AI solutions also raises fairness concerns, since language coverage and culturally narrow training data may limit applicability and equity across contexts (Bencsik et al., 2026; Nussbaum & Bekerman, 2025; Zhao et al., 2025). Reliability is another key issue, as inaccurate or inconsistent outputs can undermine educator trust and reduce the educational value of Gen-AI support for SEND learners (Nussbaum & Bekerman, 2025; Rasool et al., 2025; Zhao et al., 2025). In parallel, unequal access to devices, internet connectivity, and language-adaptable systems may constrain adoption and exacerbate existing digital inequalities (Bencsik et al., 2026; Maleki, 2026; Zhao et al., 2025). Institutional infrastructure and functional access, including technical support and implementation capacity, can therefore determine whether Gen-AI tools can be used effectively in special education (Bencsik et al., 2026; Maleki, 2026).

Transparency and explainability present additional constraints in high-stakes contexts, because educators and learners may struggle to interpret or justify AI-generated outputs when decision processes are opaque (Fu et al., 2025; Nussbaum & Bekerman, 2025). The need for standardized evaluation approaches and benchmarks for explainability and reasoning is increasingly emphasized in discussions of AI systems intended for SEND settings (Fu et al., 2025; Nussbaum & Bekerman, 2025). Moreover, integration into existing educational frameworks requires scalable and modular infrastructures that can accommodate evolving learner needs and service structures (Abulibdeh, 2025; García-López et al., 2025). Meaningful integration also depends on coordination among educational institutions, technology developers, and policy actors, particularly when systems are designed for specialized supports and accountability demands (Al-Emran et al., 2025; Fu et al., 2025).

Design choices shape whether Gen-AI tools can provide appropriate personalization and adaptivity for learners with diverse learning profiles, including supports for reading, writing, and comprehension (Fu et al., 2025; García-López et al., 2025; Zhao et al., 2025). Adaptive learning approaches that respond to performance in real time are frequently described as especially relevant for SEND contexts, given variability in pace, attention, and response modalities (Abulibdeh, 2025; Zhao et al., 2025). Assistive features can tailor content and interaction to diverse SEND needs, while simulated scenarios may also support social communication practice (Fu et al., 2025; Zhao et al., 2025). Gen-AI has also been discussed as a tool for checking accessibility of educational materials and, in some proposals, for identifying early signals related to learning difficulties to inform individualized planning (Zhao et al., 2025; García-López et al., 2025).

However, effective design requires careful human-AI collaboration, because over-automation may weaken the teacher's pedagogical role and may not support holistic student development (Rasool et al., 2025; Tan, 2025; Wu & Zhang, 2025). Teacher development and implementation models should therefore integrate Gen-AI while preserving human mentorship and professional judgment in special education practice (Rasool et al., 2025; Tan, 2025). Multilingual and culturally sensitive design is also necessary for equitable and inclusive use across diverse SEND populations (Bencsik et al., 2026; Nussbaum & Bekerman, 2025; Zhao et al., 2025).

Ethical considerations further complicate deployment, especially when personalization relies on sensitive student data and requires strong security and compliance protections (Fu et al., 2025; García-López et al., 2025; Maleki, 2026). Transparency about how data are used and how outputs are produced is repeatedly linked to trust and safeguarding of student rights (Fu et al., 2025; Nussbaum & Bekerman, 2025; Maleki, 2026). Equity of access remains a major ethical concern, since uneven resources and institutional support may widen disparities in who benefits from Gen-AI innovations (Bencsik et al., 2026; García-López et al., 2025; Salih et al., 2025). Concerns have also been raised that overreliance on AI could undermine autonomy and critical thinking, particularly for learners who may be more dependent on assistive support (Bhuiyan et al., 2025; Boulhrir & Hamash, 2025; Nussbaum & Bekerman, 2025). Academic integrity risks are likewise salient, including plagiarism, misrepresentation of student performance, and challenges in interpreting genuine learning outcomes when AI use is not transparent (Funa & Gabay, 2025; Salih et al., 2025; Wu & Zhang, 2025). Accordingly, policy development, detection approaches, and age-appropriate AI literacy are commonly presented as safeguards to support responsible use (Bhuiyan et al., 2025; Boulhrir & Hamash, 2025; Salih et al., 2025). Ongoing fairness audits and efforts to reduce biased datasets are also positioned as essential to mitigating discriminatory outcomes for SEND students (Fu et al., 2025; García-López et al., 2025; Nussbaum & Bekerman, 2025). Finally, human oversight and ethical governance frameworks are repeatedly emphasized as conditions for aligning Gen-AI deployment with educational goals and protecting learners from harmful misuse (García-López et al., 2025; Salih et al., 2025; Rasool et al., 2025).

Despite this growing body of discussion, the perspectives of the technical practitioners who design and engineer Gen-AI systems remain comparatively underexamined within the special education-oriented literature (Al-Emran et al., 2025; Fu et al., 2025; García-López et al., 2025). Centering engineers' views can clarify how technical constraints, design decisions, and ethical responsibilities are balanced in practice, and can support more feasible and accountable design guidance for SEND contexts (Fu et al., 2025; Rasool et al., 2025; Salih et al., 2025).

These concerns can also be understood through the lens of Human-Centered Artificial Intelligence (HCAI), which emphasizes the development of AI systems that remain reliable, safe, transparent, explainable, and under meaningful human control (Shneiderman, 2020). Rather than replacing human expertise, HCAI promotes AI systems that augment human capabilities while supporting accountability, accessibility, and user participation throughout the design and implementation process. In educational and special education contexts, these principles are particularly relevant because AI systems may influence learning opportunities, participation, and support provision for vulnerable learner populations. The HCAI perspective therefore provides a useful conceptual framework for examining how engineers balance technical innovation with educational, ethical, and accessibility requirements when designing Gen-AI systems for students with SEND.

The Present Study

The aim of this study is to explore how computer engineers and Gen-AI developers conceptualize the technical, design, and ethical dimensions involved in building Gen-AI systems intended to support students with SEND in educational settings (Fu et al., 2025; García-López et al., 2025; Nussbaum & Bekerman, 2025). The study seeks to understand how engineering decisions intersect with educational requirements, accessibility considerations, and responsible AI practices to inform the development of Gen-AI tools that are technically robust, educationally meaningful, and ethically grounded (Bencsik et al., 2026; Salih et al., 2025; Zhao et al., 2025).

Research Questions

How do engineers and Gen-AI developers conceptualize the role and potential of Gen-AI in supporting students with SEND?

What technical and design approaches do engineers consider most appropriate for developing Gen-AI systems that support personalized and adaptive learning while avoiding one-size-fits-all solutions?

What challenges and risks do engineers identify regarding data use, privacy, and the potential incorporation of bias in Gen-AI systems designed for special education?

What technical requirements and design considerations emerge for creating accessible, multimodal, and adaptive Gen-AI interfaces for learners with diverse cognitive, sensory, and communication profiles?

How do engineers perceive the limits of automation in special education contexts, and what role do they assign to human oversight and collaboration with special education professionals in the design of Gen-AI systems?

METHOD

Participants

The study employed purposive expert sampling to investigate technical and ethical perspectives regarding the design and implementation of Gen-AI systems in special and inclusive education contexts. The sample consisted of ten expert participants with advanced professional experience in AI, Machine Learning (ML), Computer Science, accessibility engineering, educational technology, human-centered AI, assistive technologies, and responsible AI governance.

As presented in Table 1, most participants were between 35 and 44 years old, while three participants were between 45 and 54 years old. All participants held postgraduate qualifications, including Master's and Doctoral degrees. Participants represented a range of professional settings, including university research environments, interdisciplinary academic–industry collaborations, private-sector AI development, start-up initiatives, and public-sector advisory roles. All participants reported prior experience with educational AI systems and applications designed for learners with SEND.

Participants' expertise included adaptive learning systems, AI-supported formative assessment, retrieval-augmented generation (RAG), multimodal educational interfaces, assistive communication technologies, accessibility-oriented interface design, teacher-facing analytics platforms, AI-supported content adaptation, and responsible AI governance frameworks. They also reported professional experience related to vulnerable learner populations, including students with dyslexia, autism spectrum disorders, attention deficit hyperactivity disorder (ADHD), speech and language difficulties, intellectual disabilities, sensory impairments, motor impairments, and learners requiring individualized educational support plans.

Participants reported between 6 and more than 16 years of professional experience in AI and computing-related fields. Because the study focused on expert professional perspectives rather than demographic representation, all responses were anonymized and presented through representative professional profiles.

Table 1. Participant demographic and professional characteristics (N = 10)

Characteristic	Category	n
Gender	Female	4
	Male	6
Age group	35–44	7
	45–54	3
Highest level of education	Master's degree	6
	Doctorate	4
Professional experience in AI/computing	6–10 years	1
	11–15 years	4
	16+ years	5
Professional setting*	University / Research	6
	Private sector	5
	Start-up / Industry collaboration	4
	Public-sector advisory	1
Expertise areas*	Artificial Intelligence / Machine Learning	10
	Computer Science	6
	Accessibility engineering / Human-centered AI	5
	Educational technology	6
Experience with educational AI systems	Yes	10
Experience with SEND-related applications	Yes	10

Note. *Participants could select more than one category.

Instrument

Data were collected through a semi-structured interview protocol developed specifically for this study. The interview guide was designed to explore expert perspectives on the opportunities, limitations, risks, technical requirements, and ethical implications of Gen-AI systems in special education and inclusive learning environments.

The protocol included open-ended questions organized into thematic sections addressing: (a) general perceptions of AI in education and SEND contexts, (b) adaptive and personalized learning, (c) multimodal accessibility and assistive technologies, (d) data protection, privacy, and bias, (e) interface design and technical implementation challenges, (f) Gen-AI architectures and multimodal frameworks, (g) limits of automation and human oversight, (h) collaboration between engineers and educators, and (i) future directions for Gen-AI systems in special education.

The interview questions encouraged participants to provide detailed, evidence-informed, and technically grounded responses. Participants were invited to discuss implementation constraints, architectural trade-offs, accessibility considerations, governance requirements, classroom deployment challenges, and ethical concerns associated with AI-supported educational systems.

The semi-structured format allowed consistency across interviews while maintaining flexibility for participants to elaborate on issues they considered particularly important within their area of expertise.

Procedure

The interviews were conducted remotely using a semi-structured interview format. Participants responded orally to the interview questions, and the interviews were documented by the researcher during the interview process. Following data collection, the interview records were organized and transcribed for analysis purposes.

This approach allowed the collection of detailed expert perspectives while maintaining flexibility for clarification and follow-up questions where necessary. The interview format enabled participants to provide reflective and technically detailed responses regarding the design, implementation, governance, and evaluation of Gen-AI systems for students with SEND.

In several cases, participants required additional time to reflect on technically complex topics related to accessibility, multimodal systems, privacy, adaptive architectures, governance mechanisms, and implementation trade-offs before formulating their responses. Each interview lasted approximately 40–60 minutes, although some interviews extended beyond this duration due to the depth and technical complexity of the discussion.

Prior to participation, individuals were informed about the purpose of the study, the voluntary nature of participation, the anonymized treatment of responses, and the intended academic use of the findings. No identifying institutional information or personal identifiers were retained in the final dataset.

The resulting dataset consisted of ten extended expert interviews containing substantial narrative and technical detail across all sections of the interview protocol.

Data Analysis

The transcribed interview data were analyzed using reflexive thematic analysis following the principles proposed by Braun and Clarke (2006, 2022). The aim of the analysis was to identify recurring patterns, shared concerns, technical priorities, and ethical principles emerging across expert perspectives regarding Gen-AI systems for students with SEND.

To enhance the rigor and reflexivity of the analysis, two researchers independently engaged with the dataset, discussed coding interpretations, reflected on alternative meanings, and collaboratively refined the thematic structure through an iterative process (Braun & Clarke, 2019, 2021). The researchers compared their interpretations and engaged in ongoing discussion throughout the analytical process, allowing themes to be refined and developed through reflexive dialogue rather than statistical agreement.

The analysis followed a multi-stage process. First, all interview transcripts were read repeatedly to support familiarization with the dataset and to identify preliminary patterns and recurring concepts. During this phase, analytic notes were developed regarding technical challenges, accessibility concerns, personalization strategies, governance issues, and ethical considerations.

Second, initial codes were generated inductively across the dataset. Coding focused on explicit and implicit references to accessibility, multimodality, personalization, teacher oversight, safety mechanisms, privacy protections, explainability, learner agency, participatory design, bounded automation, classroom implementation, and accountability.

Third, related codes were grouped into broader candidate themes. Through iterative comparison and refinement, themes were reviewed for conceptual coherence and distinctiveness across the dataset. Attention was given both to recurring consensus across participants and to nuanced differences in emphasis.

The final thematic structure consisted of five overarching themes:

1. Gen-AI as assistive infrastructure rather than educational authority.
2. Teacher-governed personalization without deficit profiling.
3. Safety, privacy, bias, and explainability as engineering requirements.

4. Accessibility and multimodal participation by design.
5. Classroom-fit, participatory, and accountable deployment.

Representative quotations were selected to illustrate each theme while preserving participant anonymity. A summary of the themes and representative subthemes identified across the dataset is presented in Table 2.

Table 2. Overview of themes and representative subthemes identified through reflexive thematic analysis

Theme	Representative Subthemes
1. Gen-AI as assistive infrastructure rather than educational authority	AI as augmentative support rather than replacement, bounded automation, teacher-centered oversight, rejection of autonomous educational decision-making, Gen-AI as accessibility infrastructure
2. Teacher-governed personalization without deficit profiling	Functional learner profiles, adaptive pacing, scaffolded learning, individualized supports, personalization based on access needs rather than diagnostic labels, teacher-controlled adaptation
3. Safety, privacy, bias, and explainability as engineering requirements	Data minimization, privacy-preserving architectures, bias auditing, explainable adaptation, human-in-the-loop safeguards, governance mechanisms, prevention of harmful automation
4. Accessibility and multimodal participation by design	Multimodal interaction, speech-to-text and text-to-speech, AAC integration, visual and symbol-supported communication, accessible interfaces, Universal Design for Learning (UDL), WCAG-informed accessibility
5. Classroom-fit, participatory, and accountable deployment	Participatory design, collaboration between engineers and educators, classroom feasibility, assistive technology compatibility, teacher feedback loops, responsible implementation and long-term accountability

Ethical Considerations

The study followed established ethical principles for qualitative research involving human participants and was conducted in accordance with the principles of the Declaration of Helsinki concerning respect for participants, voluntary participation, confidentiality, and responsible data handling.

Participation was voluntary, and all responses were anonymized prior to analysis. No personally identifiable information, institutional identifiers, or sensitive personal data were included in the final dataset.

Because the study focused on professional expert perspectives rather than personal experiences, the interview protocol intentionally avoided collecting unnecessary personal information. Demographic information was limited to broad professional categories relevant to the interpretation of expertise.

Participants were informed about the aims of the study, the confidential treatment of responses, their right to withdraw at any stage, and the exclusive use of the data for academic research purposes. Data were stored securely and handled in accordance with general principles of confidentiality, privacy protection, and responsible research practice.

Special attention was given to ethical considerations associated with discussions of SEND, accessibility, vulnerable learner populations, and educational AI governance. The analysis emphasized aggregate thematic interpretation rather than attribution of opinions to identifiable individuals or organizations.

RESULTS

Gen-AI as Assistive Infrastructure Rather Than Educational Authority

Across the interviews, Gen-AI was conceptualized as an assistive, adaptive, and accessibility-oriented educational infrastructure rather than as an autonomous educational authority. Experts emphasized that Gen-AI should function as a supportive layer that enhances participation, personalization, communication, and differentiated access to curriculum content while preserving teacher oversight and pedagogical responsibility.

A central pattern was the rejection of replacement-oriented narratives regarding AI in education. Participants stressed that Gen-AI should augment, rather than substitute, teachers, therapists, special educators, and human relationships within educational settings. One participant explained that *"AI should be treated as an assistive and augmentative technology, not as a replacement for teachers, therapists, special educators, or human judgment."* Another expert similarly stated that *"the most appropriate role of AI is to support human decision-making, not automate high-stakes judgments about a child's ability, diagnosis, behavior, placement, or future opportunities."*

Experts frequently framed Gen-AI as a mechanism for reducing barriers to participation. They emphasized its ability to transform learning materials into multiple accessible representations adapted to individual learner profiles. Several participants referred to Gen-AI as an *"accessibility layer"* capable of supporting flexible curriculum access across diverse learner needs. One engineer described Gen-AI as *"a powerful personalization and accessibility layer"* capable of *"transforming learning experiences so that students can access the same conceptual goals through different routes."*

Content transformation was identified as one of the most promising applications. This included simplified text generation, scaffolded explanations, multimodal representation, symbol-supported communication, audio narration, and adaptive pacing. One participant noted that *"a Gen-AI system can rewrite a complex text into plain language, convert instructions into step-by-step visual prompts, generate social stories, or provide worked examples at different levels of complexity."* Another expert emphasized that *"the strongest use case is participation"* arguing that Gen-AI should help students *"ask for help, collaborate with peers, create work, and express preferences."*

Communication support was also highlighted as a key area of potential value. Participants described multimodal and AAC-compatible systems as particularly relevant for learners with speech, language, and communication difficulties. Several engineers viewed Gen-AI as valuable for enabling alternative forms of expression and interaction. As one participant explained, *"students should not only receive information in accessible formats; they should be able to demonstrate understanding in different ways."*

At the same time, experts acknowledged the limitations and risks associated with probabilistic AI systems. Hallucinations, inaccurate feedback, oversimplification, inaccessible outputs, and biased recommendations were identified as significant concerns in SEND contexts. One expert warned that *"Gen-AI is probabilistic. It may hallucinate, oversimplify, introduce bias, or provide inappropriate feedback."* Another participant stated that *"the risk profile is higher"* because SEND-related systems may influence educational trajectories, assessment practices, interventions, and learner self-concept.

A further recurring view was that Gen-AI systems designed for SEND should be bounded, constrained, and teacher-governed rather than open-ended conversational systems. Several experts criticized the idea of exposing students directly to unrestricted foundation models. Instead, they advocated architectures combining retrieval-augmented generation, pedagogical constraints, accessibility controls, and human oversight mechanisms. One participant explicitly argued that *"the best architecture is usually not one big model; it is a system of models and controls."*

Taken together, these findings show that participants viewed Gen-AI not as a replacement for special education expertise, but as an adaptive support infrastructure capable of enhancing accessibility, communication, personalization, and participation when embedded within ethically governed, teacher-controlled educational environments.

Teacher-Governed Personalization Without Deficit Profiling

Participants emphasized that effective Gen-AI systems for SEND require individualized, profile-aware, and context-sensitive architectures rather than generic chatbot-style interactions. Across interviews, experts rejected the idea that SEND categories alone could meaningfully guide personalization. Instead, they advocated functional learner models centered on access needs, communication preferences, sensory sensitivities, pacing requirements, and instructional supports.

Structured learner profiles were presented as essential to responsible personalization. Participants argued that personalization should be grounded in teacher-approved functional support needs rather than simplistic diagnostic labels. One engineer explained that *"personalization should be based on functional learning needs, not stereotypes or diagnostic shortcuts."* Another participant stated that *"two students with autism may need very different interfaces,"* emphasizing that SEND categories are insufficient models of learning variability.

Experts described learner profiles as including variables such as preferred modality, reading level, communication mode, sensory preferences, executive-function supports, assistive technology compatibility, and pacing requirements. Several participants advocated architectures in which these profiles could be modified collaboratively by teachers, learners, and families. One participant described the need for *"a teacher-controlled, learner-centered personalization layer"* capable of adapting interaction while remaining transparent and editable.

Adaptive pacing and scaffolded learning formed another important dimension of personalization. Participants highlighted the importance of chunking tasks, reducing cognitive load, extending wait time, and adjusting instructional complexity dynamically. One expert explained that *"for some students, the ability to pause, repeat, or receive one instruction at a time is essential."* Similarly, another participant argued that Gen-AI systems should provide *"hints, sentence starters, worked examples, visual supports, and retrieval-practice prompts"* instead of immediately supplying answers.

Multimodal personalization was also identified as a core design principle. Participants argued that the same learning objective should be reachable through multiple pathways. Experts proposed systems capable of dynamically combining text, speech, symbols, images, captions, diagrams, AAC-compatible outputs, and interactive prompts. One participant stated that *"the same concept should be available as text, audio, image, diagram, symbol-supported explanation, example, analogy, manipulable activity, or dialogue."*

From a technical perspective, participants favored modular and layered architectures rather than monolithic conversational systems. Many experts described hybrid systems combining learner models, pedagogical orchestration layers, retrieval-augmented generation (RAG), accessibility modules, safety layers, and teacher oversight tools. One participant described a preferred architecture consisting of *"a student model, a pedagogical policy layer, a content grounding layer, and a safety and governance layer."*

Retrieval-augmented generation was identified as particularly important for grounding outputs in approved educational materials and reducing hallucination risk. Participants emphasized that SEND-oriented systems should retrieve information from teacher-approved curriculum resources, individualized education plans, accessibility support, and school policies rather than generating unsupported content. As one participant noted, *"the AI should retrieve approved curriculum materials rather than invent everything from scratch."*

Constrained adaptation was another recurring concern. Participants generally opposed fully autonomous personalization systems that independently infer learner states or modify educational pathways without educator review. Instead, experts favored bounded adaptation strategies operating within teacher-defined parameters. One participant explained that *"the AI can choose from teacher-approved adaptation strategies, while high-impact changes require educator confirmation."*

Teacher oversight was described as fundamental across all personalization approaches. Participants argued that teachers must remain able to inspect, override, modify, and explain AI-generated supports. One participant stated that *"teachers should be able to inspect what the AI generated, edit outputs, lock certain supports, review student interactions, and override recommendations."* Another expert emphasized that *"teacher control is not optional in SEND contexts."*

Overall, personalization was conceptualized not as automated prediction, but as transparent, teacher-governed adaptation grounded in functional learner needs, multimodal accessibility, pedagogical evidence, and bounded AI behavior.

Safety, Privacy, Bias, and Explainability as Engineering Requirements

Participants identified safety, privacy protection, bias mitigation, and explainability as foundational engineering requirements rather than secondary ethical considerations. Experts emphasized that Gen-AI systems designed for students with SEND operate within highly sensitive educational contexts involving vulnerable learner populations, sensitive personal data, and potentially high-impact educational decisions.

A major concern was the sensitive nature of SEND-related data. Participants noted that these systems may process information related to SEND status, behavioral profiles, therapy records, communication needs, emotional regulation, health-related indicators, and individualized educational supports. One participant explained that *"special education data is highly sensitive"* because it may include *"diagnostic information, behavioral records, therapy notes, assessment results, communication profiles, medical information, family background, and emotional or mental health indicators."*

Several experts warned that even partially anonymized datasets may remain identifiable due to the uniqueness of many learner profiles. One participant highlighted the risk of re-identification by explaining that *"rare combinations of needs can make anonymization difficult,"* particularly when profiles include combinations of SEND type, communication modality, age, educational setting, or assistive technology use.

Data minimization was presented as a key design principle. Participants argued that systems should collect only the information strictly necessary for educational support and accessibility adaptation. One participant explicitly stated that *"AI systems often encourage collecting more data than necessary. In special education, this can become intrusive and ethically problematic."* Another participant emphasized that identifiable SEND-related data should not be used for general model training unless there is *"explicit, informed, ethically approved consent."*

Participants also expressed concern regarding secondary uses of educational data, especially vendor-controlled model training and analytics. Several experts criticized opaque data-governance practices within commercial AI ecosystems. One engineer warned that schools often lack visibility regarding *"whether prompts, uploaded documents, transcripts, or student interactions are retained, used for training, transferred across borders, or accessible to subcontractors."*

Bias and deficit-based assumptions were another major concern. Participants emphasized that AI systems may unintentionally pathologize differences, misinterpret communication patterns, or encode harmful assumptions regarding ability and behavior. One participant warned that *"AI may mistake difference for deficiency."* Another expert explained that systems should avoid interpreting *"slow response time as lack of understanding, limited speech as low intelligence, or behavioral dysregulation as lack of motivation."*

Fairness auditing was identified as essential for SEND-focused AI systems. Participants argued that evaluation should extend beyond overall accuracy and include subgroup analysis across SEND categories, communication modalities, sensory profiles, and assistive technology users. One participant stated that *"a system that performs well for dyslexia but poorly for AAC users is not equitable."* Similarly, another participant emphasized the need to test whether speech recognition systems perform adequately for students with *"dysarthria, apraxia, stuttering, or non-standard pronunciation."*

Explainability also emerged as a central engineering requirement. Participants argued that educators must understand why systems generated adaptations, recommendations, or supports. One expert stated that *"trust depends not on the AI sounding fluent, but on its decisions being understandable, contestable, and aligned with the learner's actual support plan."* Another participant argued that systems should explicitly indicate *"what it adapted, why it adapted it, which learner need it was responding to, and how a teacher can change it."*

Several experts additionally emphasized the importance of bounded automation and human-in-the-loop safeguards. Participants rejected fully autonomous educational decision-making systems, especially in relation to assessment, placement, behavioral interpretation, and intervention planning. One participant argued that *"automation becomes ethically dangerous when it makes decisions that affect rights, services, identity, or opportunity."*

Overall, privacy, fairness, explainability, and governance were understood not as external regulatory constraints, but as integral architectural requirements necessary for trustworthy, accessible, and ethically responsible Gen-AI systems in special education contexts.

Accessibility and Multimodal Participation by Design

Participants emphasized that accessibility and multimodal participation should be foundational design principles rather than optional accessibility add-ons. Experts argued that Gen-AI systems for SEND must be intentionally designed to support diverse cognitive, sensory, linguistic, motor, and communication profiles through flexible, multimodal interaction pathways.

A central issue was the rejection of text-only interaction models. Participants stressed that many learners with SEND cannot effectively access or express knowledge solely through conventional written language. One participant stated that *"many SEND students do not learn or communicate primarily through standard written text."* Another expert similarly argued that *"students should not only receive information in accessible formats; they should be able to demonstrate understanding in different ways."*

Multimodal interaction was therefore described as essential for equitable participation. Participants highlighted systems integrating text, speech, symbols, images, captions, diagrams, gesture-based interaction, AAC-compatible outputs, and assistive technologies. One engineer explained that *"the same learning objective should be reachable through multiple input and output pathways."* Several participants emphasized that multimodality should support both access to information and alternative forms of expression.

Participants identified numerous practical applications of multimodal Gen-AI. Examples included text-to-speech support for learners with dyslexia or visual impairments, speech-to-text systems for students with motor or writing difficulties, symbol-supported communication for AAC users, visual schedules for executive-function support, captioning for deaf or hard-of-hearing learners, and structured visual explanations for autistic students. One participant explained that *"a student who cannot easily write a paragraph might explain an idea orally, through symbols, or by selecting images."*

Accessibility-oriented interface design also emerged as an important concern. Participants stressed the importance of predictable navigation, reduced cognitive load, configurable sensory environments, and compatibility with assistive technologies. One expert stated that *"the interface should be designed according to inclusive and universal design principles, with customization built in from the beginning."*

For cognitive accessibility, participants emphasized simple language, reduced visual clutter, short instructions, consistent layouts, visual schedules, and step-by-step progression. One participant explained that systems should *"avoid unnecessary pop-ups, complex menus, time pressure, and excessive text."* Another expert emphasized the importance of *"one instruction at a time"* for learners requiring reduced working-memory load.

Sensory accessibility was also strongly emphasized. Participants highlighted the need for customizable contrast, brightness, audio levels, animation controls, reduced-motion modes, and calm interfaces for students with sensory sensitivities. One participant argued that learners should be able to use *"a calm mode with minimal stimulation."*

Communication accessibility formed another major subtheme. Participants advocated compatibility with AAC systems, switch access, eye-gaze technologies, screen readers, keyboard-only navigation, and alternative response formats. One engineer explained that systems should not assume that learners must *"type or speak to demonstrate understanding."*

Despite strong support for multimodal AI, participants also identified important risks and implementation challenges. Several experts warned that multimodal models may produce inaccurate image descriptions, fail to interpret atypical speech patterns, or generate culturally inappropriate symbol representations. One participant cautioned that *"multimodal models can make confident mistakes."*

Participants further expressed concern regarding excessive behavioral or biometric monitoring within multimodal systems. Several experts argued that systems should avoid unnecessary collection of gaze tracking, emotional inference, facial analysis, or behavioral surveillance data. One participant warned that *"SEND students are already at risk of being over-monitored."*

In summary, accessibility was conceptualized as an architectural and pedagogical foundation requiring configurable multimodal interaction, compatibility with assistive technologies, flexible participation pathways, and careful avoidance of inaccessible, surveillance-oriented, or cognitively overwhelming interfaces.

Classroom-Fit, Participatory, and Accountable Deployment

Participants emphasized that the successful implementation of Gen-AI systems for SEND depends not only on model performance, but also on classroom feasibility, participatory design, institutional accountability, and long-term collaboration between engineers and educational professionals.

A central finding was that classroom realities should shape system design from the beginning. Participants criticized technology-driven development approaches in which systems are created independently and later introduced into schools without sufficient understanding of educational workflows or learner needs. One participant explained that *"engineers should not arrive with a finished product and ask teachers to test it."* Another expert similarly argued that *"collaboration should begin before development, not after a prototype is built."*

Participatory design emerged as a key principle. Participants emphasized the importance of involving special educators, therapists, students, families, teaching assistants, accessibility specialists, and school staff throughout the design process. One participant stated that *"teachers should be treated as design partners, not just end users."* Another participant emphasized that *"nothing about SEND learners should be designed without SEND learners."*

Classroom observation and workflow analysis were also identified as critical. Participants argued that engineers must understand the realities of SEND classrooms, including sensory environments, behavioral variability, limited instructional time, device constraints, transitions, communication differences, and the complexity of individualized support planning. One engineer explained that classroom observation helps developers understand *"where teachers lose time, where students encounter barriers, and which adaptations are already effective."*

Participants also stressed the importance of low-risk prototyping and gradual deployment. Many experts advocated beginning with teacher-facing support tools rather than fully autonomous student-facing systems. One participant suggested starting with *"lesson adaptation and teacher review rather than a live student chatbot."*

Teacher oversight and feedback loops were described as necessary components of responsible deployment. Participants emphasized that educators must be able to report inappropriate outputs, modify support, update learner profiles, and influence future system behavior. One participant stated that *"teachers need a simple way to flag bad outputs, suggest better scaffolds, and update student supports."*

Professional development and AI literacy were also considered important. Participants argued that educators require training not only in system use, but also in understanding AI limitations, inspecting outputs, protecting student privacy, and avoiding overreliance on generated content. One expert explained that teachers must understand *"what the AI can and cannot do."*

Several participants additionally highlighted the importance of accountability structures and institutional governance. Experts advocated clear procedures for incident reporting, bias monitoring, accessibility evaluation, data protection, and escalation of harmful outputs. One participant argued that schools should require *"evidence of accessibility testing, privacy safeguards, bias evaluation, teacher controls, student and family involvement, and compatibility with assistive technologies"* before deployment.

Classroom-fit was also described as a technical issue rather than merely an implementation issue. Participants noted that many educational environments involve low-bandwidth networks, shared devices, assistive technologies, inconsistent connectivity, and highly variable classroom conditions. One participant emphasized that *"a safe, accessible, privacy-preserving, classroom-ready system requires architecture, governance, monitoring, teacher collaboration, and long-term accountability."*

Finally, participants framed accountability as inseparable from human oversight. Across interviews, experts stressed that Gen-AI systems should remain bounded support tools operating under educator supervision. One participant summarized this position by stating that *"AI can recommend, draft, adapt, summarize, and scaffold. Humans must decide, interpret, approve, and take responsibility."*

Overall, responsible deployment was conceptualized as a participatory, accountable, and context-sensitive process grounded in classroom realities, professional collaboration, institutional governance, educator agency, and continuous iterative evaluation.

A summary of the main findings across themes is presented in Table 3.

Table 3. Summary of main findings across themes

Theme	Main Findings
Gen-AI as assistive infrastructure rather than educational authority	Participants conceptualized Gen-AI as a supportive accessibility and personalization layer rather than an autonomous educational authority. AI was viewed as augmentative technology intended to assist teachers, reduce participation barriers, and support differentiated access while preserving human oversight.
Teacher-governed personalization without deficit profiling	Experts emphasized functional learner profiles, adaptive pacing, scaffolded learning, multimodal personalization, and teacher-controlled adaptation. Personalization was conceptualized as support based on learner needs rather than diagnostic labels or automated prediction.
Safety, privacy, bias, and explainability as engineering requirements	Participants identified privacy protection, fairness auditing, bounded automation, transparency, and explainability as essential architectural requirements. Concerns included sensitive SEND-related data, re-identification risks, deficit-based assumptions, surveillance, and opaque AI decision-making.

continued on following page

Table 3. Continued

Theme	Main Findings
Accessibility and multimodal participation by design	Accessibility was viewed as a foundational design principle requiring multimodal interaction, assistive technology compatibility, alternative communication pathways, configurable interfaces, and flexible participation formats supporting diverse cognitive, sensory, motor, and communication needs.
Classroom-fit, participatory, and accountable deployment	Participants emphasized participatory design, educator involvement, classroom feasibility, institutional governance, teacher feedback loops, professional development, and long-term accountability. Responsible deployment was viewed as an ongoing collaborative process rather than a purely technical implementation task.

DISCUSSION

Conceptualizing Gen-AI as Assistive and Human-Governed Educational Infrastructure

The findings of the present study show that engineers and Gen-AI developers conceptualize Gen-AI primarily as an assistive and augmentative educational infrastructure rather than as an autonomous educational authority. Participants emphasized that Gen-AI systems should support accessibility, participation, communication, and differentiated instruction while remaining under meaningful human oversight. This perspective aligns with recent literature emphasizing human-centered approaches to educational AI and the continued importance of teacher judgment and pedagogical mediation in technology-supported learning environments (Rasool et al., 2025; Salih et al., 2025; Tan, 2025).

Participants framed Gen-AI as a bounded support system and accessibility-oriented educational layer rather than as a replacement for educators, therapists, or special education professionals. They showed strong resistance toward fully autonomous educational decision-making, particularly in relation to diagnosis, educational placement, behavioral interpretation, emotional inference, and learner evaluation. Human oversight was therefore positioned as an indispensable safeguard for maintaining pedagogical responsibility, contextual interpretation, and ethical accountability within SEND-oriented educational environments (Rasool et al., 2025; Salih et al., 2025; Tan, 2025). This emphasis on human oversight may reflect engineers' direct awareness of the technical limitations of contemporary Gen-AI systems. Unlike educators, who primarily experience AI through its outputs, engineers are closely familiar with issues such as hallucinations, probabilistic reasoning, incomplete contextual understanding, and unpredictable model behaviour. Their resistance to autonomous educational decision-making may therefore stem not only from ethical concerns but also from a realistic assessment of the current capabilities and limitations of large language models.

The primary value of Gen-AI was not associated with replacing pedagogy, but with increasing the flexibility, responsiveness, and accessibility of educational systems. Participants described Gen-AI as capable of supporting adaptive pacing, multimodal content transformation, scaffolded explanation, communication support, and differentiated access to curriculum materials. These findings reinforce previous arguments suggesting that Gen-AI may hold promise for heterogeneous SEND populations because of its capacity for dynamic adaptation and content transformation (Fu et al., 2025; Zhao et al., 2025).

At the same time, participants acknowledged the probabilistic and potentially unreliable nature of Gen-AI systems. Hallucinations, oversimplification, inaccessible outputs, inappropriate recommendations, and biased responses were identified as important implementation risks. These concerns align with broader literature highlighting reliability, transparency, and trustworthiness challenges associated with educational AI deployment (Nussbaum & Bekerman, 2025; Rasool et al., 2025). Consequently, responsible SEND-oriented Gen-AI systems were conceptualized as constrained, inspectable, and teacher-governed rather than fully autonomous conversational systems (Fu et al., 2025; García-López et al., 2025; Salih et al., 2025).

A further issue concerns the rejection of "AI as authority" in special education contexts. Participants opposed the use of Gen-AI for high-stakes educational decisions affecting vulnerable learners. These concerns resonate with recent ethical discussions regarding automation, surveillance, vulnerability, and accountability in educational AI systems (García-López et al., 2025; Salih et al., 2025). Overall, technical experts conceptualized Gen-AI as a human-governed assistive ecosystem designed to increase educational accessibility and participation while preserving teacher agency, learner dignity, and professional responsibility (Fu et al., 2025; García-López et al., 2025; Zhao et al., 2025).

Personalization, Adaptivity, and the Rejection of One-Size-Fits-All Design

A central finding of the study concerns how engineers conceptualize personalized and adaptive learning in SEND-oriented Gen-AI systems. Participants rejected one-size-fits-all approaches and emphasized that meaningful personalization should be grounded in functional learning needs, contextual supports, and accessibility requirements rather than simplistic diagnostic categorization. This emphasis is consistent with broader work on Gen-AI, adaptive learning, and assistive technologies, which highlights the importance of individualized, flexible, and context-sensitive support for learners with diverse needs (Abulibdeh, 2025; Fu et al., 2025; Zhao et al., 2025).

The present study extends this literature by showing that engineers conceptualize personalization in more nuanced and technically specific ways than those commonly presented in broader educational AI discussions. Participants emphasized that learner diversity cannot be reduced to SEND labels alone. Instead, they advocated structured learner-support profiles incorporating variables such as preferred modality, pacing requirements, reading level, sensory sensitivities, communication preferences, AAC usage, attention supports, executive-function needs, and accessibility accommodations. Personalization in SEND-oriented Gen-AI systems was therefore understood as support based on functional participation needs rather than diagnostic classification (Abulibdeh, 2025; Fu et al., 2025; Zhao et al., 2025). This finding may indicate a shift away from deficit-oriented understandings of disability toward participation-based and accessibility-oriented approaches. Participants appeared to recognise that diagnostic labels alone provide limited information about how learners access, process, and communicate information. Consequently, personalization was framed as a means of increasing participation, accessibility, and learner agency rather than categorising students according to predefined disability groups.

Teacher-governed personalization also emerged as central. Rather than supporting unrestricted model-driven adaptation, participants advocated bounded and inspectable personalization systems in which educators retain authority over accommodations, adaptation parameters, scaffolding strategies, and instructional pathways. This finding aligns closely with concerns raised by Rasool et al. (2025) and Tan (2025), who argue that excessive automation may weaken pedagogical judgment, professional agency, and educational responsibility.

From a technical perspective, adaptive learning was described as requiring modular and layered architectures rather than standalone chatbot systems. Proposed infrastructures included learner models, pedagogical orchestration systems, retrieval-augmented generation layers, accessibility transformation engines, rule-based safeguards, multimodal interaction systems, and teacher-facing dashboards. Participants also emphasized the importance of grounding AI-generated outputs in approved educational materials, individualized educational plans, and teacher-selected resources to reduce hallucination risk and maintain pedagogical alignment (Fu et al., 2025; García-López et al., 2025; Nussbaum & Bekerman, 2025).

The findings also reveal awareness of pedagogical trade-offs associated with adaptive learning systems. Although personalization may increase accessibility and participation, participants expressed concern regarding over-accommodation, reduced challenge, excessive dependency, and the potential weakening of learner autonomy. These concerns reflect broader debates regarding equity, inclusion, independence, and the long-term educational implications of AI-supported learning environments (Bhuiyan et al., 2025; Nussbaum & Bekerman, 2025).

Constrained adaptation was therefore viewed as particularly important. Participants generally opposed unrestricted reinforcement-based optimization in SEND contexts and instead advocated adaptation systems operating within teacher-approved pedagogical boundaries. This reflects growing recognition that educational adaptation involves ethical, contextual, and relational judgment that cannot easily be reduced to performance optimization metrics alone (Nussbaum & Bekerman, 2025; Rasool et al., 2025; Tan, 2025). This preference may also reflect concerns that fully autonomous adaptation systems could unintentionally narrow learning opportunities or reinforce existing learner profiles, thereby limiting educational growth and learner autonomy

Importantly, design requirements should not be assumed to apply uniformly across SEND populations. Learners with different cognitive, sensory, motor, or communication profiles may require distinct forms of support, such as text simplification, predictable interaction, assistive technology compatibility, AAC integration, or extended response time. These should be treated as configurable starting points rather than diagnosis-based prescriptions, given the substantial variability within each SEND category. Gen-AI systems should therefore combine accessibility-informed design with individualized, teacher-approved functional profiles (Fu et al., 2025; García-López et al., 2025; Zhao et al., 2025).

Overall, engineers conceptualized personalization not as predictive automation based on SEND categories, but as transparent, teacher-controlled adaptation grounded in functional learner participation, accessibility requirements, and pedagogically meaningful support structures (Rasool et al., 2025; Tan, 2025; Zhao et al., 2025).

Data Governance, Privacy, Bias, and Explainability in SEND-Oriented Gen-AI Systems

The findings show that engineers perceive data governance, privacy protection, bias mitigation, and explainability as foundational engineering requirements for Gen-AI systems designed for SEND populations. Special education data was viewed as highly sensitive and therefore requiring stronger governance mechanisms than many mainstream educational technologies currently provide (Fu et al., 2025; García-López et al., 2025; Maleki, 2026; Salih et al., 2025).

This finding aligns with recent literature highlighting the ethical complexity of AI deployment in educational and special education contexts (Fu et al., 2025; García-López et al., 2025; Maleki, 2026). Participants described SEND-related datasets as potentially containing SEND status, behavioral records, therapy notes, communication profiles, emotional regulation indicators, family information, and individualized support plans. This indicates heightened awareness of the risks of surveillance, profiling, stigmatization, and institutional misuse associated with educational AI systems targeting vulnerable learner populations (Nussbaum & Bekerman, 2025; Salih et al., 2025). The prominence of these concerns may be linked to the unique nature of SEND-related data. Unlike many educational datasets, special education records frequently contain highly sensitive information concerning communication abilities, behavioral characteristics, health-related needs, and individualized support arrangements. Engineers may therefore perceive privacy protection not merely as a regulatory obligation but as a fundamental requirement for safeguarding learner dignity and preventing unintended discrimination.

Participants also highlighted the problem of re-identification, particularly within small or specialized learner populations. Even partially anonymized datasets were viewed as potentially identifiable because combinations of learner characteristics, educational context, communication modality, and support needs may reveal individual identities. These concerns closely reflect broader discussions regarding data governance, vulnerability, and ethical responsibility in AI-supported educational systems (Nussbaum & Bekerman, 2025; Salih et al., 2025).

To address these risks, participants proposed multiple privacy-preserving approaches, including data minimization, pseudonymization, encryption, role-based access control, audit logs, short retention periods, and restrictions on training models using identifiable educational data. Respondents strongly opposed the automatic reuse of student interaction data for commercial model training purposes, reflecting concern regarding opaque vendor-controlled AI ecosystems in education (Fu et al., 2025; García-López et al., 2025; Maleki, 2026; Salih et al., 2025).

Bias was similarly conceptualized as a systemic issue extending across the entire lifecycle of AI systems. Participants emphasized that discriminatory outcomes may emerge not only through training data, but also through interface assumptions, adaptation logic, communication expectations, and implementation practices. Engineers appeared particularly aware that AI systems may incorrectly interpret atypical communication styles, slower processing speed, AAC-mediated interaction, or non-standard language production as indicators of lower ability or disengagement. These concerns support previous literature discussing deficit-based assumptions and inequitable outcomes in educational AI systems (Fu et al., 2025; Zhao et al., 2025).

Explainability and transparency were also central engineering priorities. Participants emphasized that teachers must be able to understand why systems generated particular scaffolds, modified pacing, simplified content, or recommended supports. Explainability was therefore framed not only as a technical requirement, but also as a prerequisite for pedagogical trust, accountability, and ethical implementation. This finding aligns with broader literature emphasizing the importance of transparent and interpretable AI systems in high-impact educational settings (García-López et al., 2025; Nussbaum & Bekerman, 2025).

Fairness auditing was identified as another key requirement. Participants argued that evaluation processes should extend beyond average model accuracy and examine subgroup-specific outcomes, accessibility failures, speech-recognition disparities, inappropriate simplification, hallucination patterns, and communication-related bias across diverse learner groups. This perspective aligns with Nussbaum and Bekerman's (2025) argument that educational AI systems should be evaluated in relation to broader equity and participation outcomes rather than solely technical performance metrics.

Overall, responsible Gen-AI systems for SEND were viewed as inseparable from privacy-preserving architectures, explainable adaptation processes, fairness auditing, and strong governance mechanisms designed to protect learner dignity, participation, and educational rights (Fu et al., 2025; García-López et al., 2025; Nussbaum & Bekerman, 2025; Salih et al., 2025).

Accessibility, Multimodality, and Inclusive Participation by Design

The findings position accessibility and multimodality as core architectural requirements rather than optional interface features in SEND-oriented Gen-AI systems. Participants emphasized that learners with diverse cognitive, sensory, motor, and communication profiles require multiple pathways for both accessing information and expressing understanding (Fu et al., 2025; Zhao et al., 2025; Wu & Zhang, 2025).

This finding aligns closely with previous literature emphasizing the importance of accessibility, adaptive representation, and multimodal interaction in AI-supported educational environments (Fu et al., 2025; Zhao et al., 2025). However, the present study extends these discussions by showing that engineers conceptualize multimodality as a central mechanism for educational participation rather than merely an alternative content-delivery strategy. This perspective suggests that accessibility is increasingly understood as a matter of participation rather than simple compliance with technical standards. Rather than focusing exclusively on removing barriers, participants emphasized the creation of multiple pathways through which learners can access information, express understanding, and engage meaningfully in educational activities. Such an approach is closely aligned with contemporary inclusive education principles that prioritise participation, agency, and equitable access to learning opportunities.

Participants described a wide range of multimodal supports, including text-to-speech systems, speech-to-text functionality, symbol-supported communication, AAC integration, captioning, image description, structured prompts, visual schedules, alternative response modes, and multimodal scaffolding. Accessibility was framed as a foundational design principle that should be embedded into system architecture from the earliest stages of development rather than retrofitted after deployment (Fu et al., 2025; Zhao et al., 2025).

Importantly, engineers closely associated multimodality with learner agency and inclusive participation. Participants emphasized that students should not be required to rely exclusively on dominant classroom communication formats to demonstrate understanding or participate meaningfully in educational activities. This finding reinforces previous literature suggesting that inclusive educational technologies should support flexible participation pathways rather than requiring conformity to standardized interaction models (Fu et al., 2025; Wu & Zhang, 2025).

At the same time, participants identified substantial technical challenges associated with adaptive multimodal systems. These included synchronization difficulties across speech recognition, language generation, symbols, captions, and assistive technologies, as well as reliability concerns regarding atypical speech patterns and context-dependent image interpretation. Multimodal accessibility therefore involves not only interface expansion, but also substantial engineering complexity requiring careful validation and ongoing evaluation (Fu et al., 2025; Zhao et al., 2025).

Participants also emphasized that adaptive interfaces must balance flexibility with predictability. Although personalization may increase accessibility, excessive interface adaptation was perceived as potentially increasing anxiety, confusion, or cognitive overload for some learners with SEND. This highlights an important tension between adaptive personalization and interface stability in educational AI systems (Abulibdeh, 2025; Zhao et al., 2025).

Cognitive accessibility was another recurring issue. Participants emphasized that accessibility extends beyond technical compliance frameworks and must address working-memory load, sensory regulation, attentional demands, communication flexibility, and emotional safety. Several respondents suggested that standard accessibility compliance guidelines alone may be insufficient for addressing the complexity of many SEND-oriented learning contexts (Fu et al., 2025; Zhao et al., 2025).

Overall, accessibility and multimodality were conceptualized not as peripheral interface enhancements, but as foundational mechanisms through which Gen-AI systems can support inclusive participation, communication, learner agency, and educational access across diverse SEND populations (Fu et al., 2025; Wu & Zhang, 2025; Zhao et al., 2025).

Limits of Automation and the Central Role of Human Oversight and Participatory Collaboration

The findings indicate that engineers perceive strong ethical and practical limits to automation in special education contexts. Participants emphasized that Gen-AI systems should support educational processes without replacing human judgment, professional expertise, contextual interpretation, or relational aspects of teaching and care (García-López et al., 2025; Rasool et al., 2025; Salih et al., 2025; Tan, 2025).

This finding aligns with literature emphasizing teacher agency, human-centered AI governance, and collaborative implementation approaches within educational environments (Rasool et al., 2025; Salih et al., 2025; Tan, 2025). Through interviews, participants rejected the use of Gen-AI for autonomous diagnosis, educational placement, behavioral interpretation, emotional surveillance, disciplinary action, or unsupported mental-health intervention. This resistance to automation may reflect recognition that many decisions within special education involve complex contextual, ethical, and relational considerations that cannot be fully captured through algorithmic processes. Decisions regarding support provision, behavioral interpretation, educational placement, or learner well-being often require professional judgment, knowledge of the learner's broader circumstances, and sensitivity to evolving educational contexts. Participants therefore appeared to view limits on automation not as technological weaknesses, but as safeguards for preserving human responsibility and accountability in educational decision-making.

Automation was viewed as ethically problematic when it affects learner rights, educational opportunity, support allocation, identity formation, or access to services. Consequently, participants advocated human-in-the-loop models in which Gen-AI functions as a bounded assistive system operating under educator and specialist supervision. AI systems were conceptualized as tools capable of generating, adapting, scaffolding, or summarizing educational content, while humans remain responsible for interpretation, approval, contextual judgment, safeguarding, and accountability (Rasool et al., 2025; Salih et al., 2025; Tan, 2025).

Participatory design and interdisciplinary collaboration also emerged as essential. Participants emphasized that SEND-oriented Gen-AI systems cannot be responsibly developed through isolated technical processes detached from classroom realities. Instead, engineers advocated collaborative development involving teachers, therapists, learners, families, accessibility specialists, and support professionals throughout the design and implementation process. These findings support previous literature emphasizing the importance of collaborative implementation and teacher involvement in educational AI development (Rasool et al., 2025; Tan, 2025).

Classroom feasibility was highlighted as a critical but often underestimated challenge. Educational environments were described as highly variable, resource-constrained, noisy, and technologically inconsistent settings requiring stable interfaces, assistive technology compatibility, manageable latency, low-bandwidth functionality, and teacher-facing controls. Responsible deployment therefore depends not only on model capability, but also on contextual adaptability and compatibility with real educational infrastructures (Bencsik et al., 2026; Maleki, 2026; Rasool et al., 2025; Tan, 2025). This finding may reflect the fact that engineers with experience in educational settings recognize that many AI systems fail not because of insufficient technical performance, but because they are designed without adequate consideration of classroom realities, resource limitations, and everyday teaching practices

Long-term accountability and institutional governance were also central. Participants emphasized the importance of accessibility testing, bias auditing, procurement standards, incident reporting procedures, professional development, and ongoing oversight mechanisms. These findings align with broader discussions regarding responsible AI governance and institutional accountability in educational technology implementation (García-López et al., 2025; Salih et al., 2025).

Overall, engineers conceptualized responsible Gen-AI implementation in special education as a collaborative socio-technical process grounded in human oversight, participatory design, accessibility-centered development, institutional accountability, and long-term ethical responsibility rather than purely technical innovation (Al-Emran et al., 2025; García-López et al., 2025; Rasool et al., 2025; Salih et al., 2025; Tan, 2025).

IMPLICATIONS

Implications for Special Education Practice

The findings of the present study have several important implications for special education practice. First, Gen-AI systems may be most beneficial when implemented as assistive and adaptive educational supports rather than as autonomous instructional authorities. Gen-AI can strengthen accessibility, participation, communication, and differentiated instruction, if educators retain pedagogical control and professional oversight. Special education implementation models should therefore prioritize teacher-governed adaptation rather than unrestricted automation.

Second, personalization in SEND-oriented Gen-AI systems should be grounded in functional learning needs rather than simplistic diagnostic categories. This has important implications for individualized educational planning and differentiated instruction. Teachers and support professionals may increasingly require tools that allow them to configure pacing, modality, scaffolding level, communication supports, sensory adaptations, and feedback style according to learner participation needs rather than relying exclusively on SEND labels.

Third, the study highlights the importance of multimodal accessibility and flexible participation pathways. Educational institutions implementing Gen-AI systems should ensure compatibility with assistive technologies, AAC systems, captioning, text-to-speech, speech-to-text, symbol-supported communication, keyboard navigation, and alternative response formats. Accessibility should be treated as a baseline requirement for educational AI procurement and deployment rather than as an optional enhancement.

Fourth, educators will require substantial professional development regarding the capabilities, limitations, risks, and governance requirements of Gen-AI systems. Teachers need to understand how to inspect AI outputs, identify hallucinations or inappropriate adaptations, maintain data privacy, and prevent overreliance on automated supports. This implication aligns with recent literature emphasizing teacher preparedness and AI literacy as central conditions for responsible educational AI integration (Rasool et al., 2025; Tan, 2025).

Fifth, schools and educational systems should adopt stronger governance mechanisms before deploying Gen-AI tools in SEND contexts. Such mechanisms may include accessibility audits, data protection procedures, procurement standards, incident reporting systems, bias evaluation protocols, and clear human-oversight responsibilities. SEND-oriented AI systems should be treated as high-responsibility educational technologies because of their potential influence on learner participation, support provision, educational opportunity, and well-being.

Finally, educational practice should avoid framing Gen-AI as a replacement for human relationships, mentorship, or pedagogical expertise. Instead, the role of Gen-AI in special education should be understood as supporting learner agency, reducing barriers to participation, and strengthening inclusive educational practices while preserving the relational and contextual dimensions of teaching and support.

Implications for AI Engineers and System Developers

The study also carries important implications for engineers, AI developers, and technology designers involved in educational and accessibility-oriented Gen-AI systems.

First, SEND-oriented Gen-AI systems require design priorities that differ from those of many mainstream educational AI products. Optimization for engagement, speed, or conversational fluency alone is insufficient. Engineers must prioritize accessibility, stability, explainability, safety, configurability, and teacher governance from the earliest stages of system design.

Second, modular and layered system architectures are particularly important. Participants rejected the idea that a single unconstrained foundation model can adequately address the complexity of SEND learning contexts. Instead, engineers advocated hybrid systems combining retrieval-augmented generation, accessibility transformation layers, pedagogical orchestration systems, rule-based constraints, multimodal interfaces, and teacher-facing review mechanisms. Future educational AI systems for SEND contexts should therefore prioritize constrained and inspectable adaptation rather than unrestricted generative autonomy.

Third, accessibility must be embedded directly into the engineering process. It cannot be retrofitted after deployment. Engineers should integrate compatibility with screen readers, AAC systems, switch access, captioning, keyboard navigation, alternative input devices, and multimodal interaction pathways as core architectural requirements. Accessibility testing should also involve real users with diverse SEND profiles rather than relying solely on automated compliance checks.

Fourth, explainability and transparent adaptation logic should be treated as central design requirements. Teachers must be able to understand why the system generated a particular scaffold, simplified content, altered pacing, or modified interaction style. Engineers should therefore prioritize inspectable learner-support layers, transparent recommendation systems, and editable adaptation pipelines rather than opaque personalization mechanisms.

Fifth, privacy-preserving infrastructure should become a central engineering priority in SEND-oriented AI systems. Participants advocated data minimization, encryption, pseudonymization, short retention periods, role-based access control, local or private deployment where feasible, and restrictions on training models using identifiable educational data. Developers should treat SEND-oriented educational AI as a high-governance domain requiring stronger safeguards than many general-purpose consumer AI applications.

Sixth, fairness auditing and bias evaluation must extend beyond traditional benchmark testing. Engineers should evaluate accessibility failures, reading-level mismatches, inappropriate simplification, speech-recognition disparities, culturally biased outputs, and subgroup-specific performance differences across diverse learner populations. Fairness auditing should also involve collaboration with educators, therapists, accessibility experts, learners, and families.

Finally, the findings support participatory and interdisciplinary development processes. Engineers should collaborate with special educators, therapists, learners, families, and accessibility specialists from the earliest stages of design rather than treating them as late-stage evaluators. Such collaboration may improve not only usability and accessibility, but also classroom feasibility, pedagogical relevance, and long-term trustworthiness.

LIMITATIONS

Several limitations of the present study should be acknowledged. First, the study involved a relatively small purposive sample of ten expert participants. Although the sample provided substantial depth and technical richness, the findings cannot be generalized to all engineers, developers, or AI practitioners working in educational or accessibility-related domains.

Second, although the interviews were transcribed and systematically analyzed, the transcription process was conducted by the researchers rather than through external verbatim transcription services. While this approach facilitated close familiarity with the dataset and supported in-depth thematic interpretation, some nuances of spoken interaction may not have been captured fully.

Third, the study focused on professional conceptualizations and expert perspectives rather than on direct implementation outcomes in real educational settings. Consequently, the findings reflect anticipated design priorities, concerns, and governance perspectives rather than empirically observed classroom effectiveness.

Fourth, although participants represented substantial expertise in AI systems, accessibility, and educational technologies, the sample did not equally represent all professional roles involved in SEND-oriented Gen-AI development. Perspectives from additional stakeholders, including therapists, students with disabilities, families, policymakers, and school administrators, may reveal further implementation concerns and priorities.

Fifth, the rapidly evolving nature of Gen-AI technologies represents an additional limitation. Technical capabilities, governance frameworks, regulatory environments, and educational implementation models continue to change rapidly. As a result, some concerns, risks, and design approaches identified in the present study may evolve alongside future developments in AI systems and educational policies.

Finally, the study focused primarily on conceptual, ethical, technical, and accessibility-oriented dimensions of Gen-AI design rather than on quantitative evaluation of learning outcomes or system effectiveness. Future research may therefore benefit from classroom-based implementation studies, participatory co-design projects, accessibility evaluations, and longitudinal investigations examining how Gen-AI systems influence learner participation, teacher workload, educational inclusion, and student autonomy over time.

CONCLUSION

The present study explored how engineers and Gen-AI developers conceptualize the technical, pedagogical, and ethical dimensions involved in designing Gen-AI systems intended to support students with SEND. The findings show that technical experts understand Gen-AI not as an autonomous educational authority, but as a human-governed assistive infrastructure designed to support accessibility, participation, communication, and adaptive learning.

Across interviews, responsible SEND-oriented Gen-AI systems were associated with bounded automation, strong teacher oversight, multimodal accessibility, privacy-preserving architectures, explainable adaptation processes, and ongoing human accountability. Engineers rejected one-size-fits-all approaches and advocated personalization grounded in functional learner needs rather than simplistic diagnostic categorization. Accessibility and multimodality were conceptualized as foundational architectural requirements rather than optional interface enhancements, while participatory collaboration between engineers, educators, therapists, learners, and families was viewed as essential for responsible implementation.

The study also highlights significant concerns regarding bias, surveillance, data governance, institutional misuse, and over-automation in educational AI systems. Participants emphasized that SEND-oriented Gen-AI tools should not independently diagnose, classify, discipline, or make consequential educational decisions affecting vulnerable learners. Instead, Gen-AI was framed as a bounded support system operating under meaningful human oversight and aligned with pedagogical and ethical principles.

Overall, the future of Gen-AI in special education depends not only on advances in model capability, but also on the development of transparent, accessible, accountable, and educator-governed socio-technical systems. The central challenge is therefore not simply how to make educational AI more powerful, but how to ensure that it supports learner dignity, educational inclusion, meaningful participation, and human-centered special education practice.

REFERENCES

Abulibdeh, A. (2025). A systematic and bibliometric review of artificial intelligence in sustainable education: Current trends and future research directions. *Sustainable Futures : An Applied Journal of Technology, Environment and Society*, *10*, 101033. DOI: 10.1016/j.sftr.2025.101033

Al-Emran, M., Al-Qaysi, N., Al-Sharafi, M. A., Khoshkam, M., Foroughi, B., & Ghobakhloo, M. (2025). Role of perceived threats and knowledge management in shaping generative AI use in education and its impact on social sustainability. *International Journal of Management Education*, *23*(1), 101105. DOI: 10.1016/j.ijme.2024.101105

Bencsik, A., Jenei, S., & Szalai, S. M. (2026). Who gets to use ChatGPT? A global study on digital access and inequality in higher education. *Social Sciences & Humanities Open*, *13*, 102479. DOI: 10.1016/j.ssaho.2026.102479

Bhuiyan, M. A., Rahman, M. K., Basile, V., Ping, H., & Mainul Bari, A. B. M. (2025). Adoption of ChatGPT for students' learning effectiveness. *International Journal of Management Education*, *23*(3), 101255. DOI: 10.1016/j.ijme.2025.101255

Boulhrir, T., & Hamash, M. (2025). Unpacking artificial intelligence in elementary education: A comprehensive thematic analysis systematic review. *Computers and Education: Artificial Intelligence*, *9*, 100442. DOI: 10.1016/j.caeai.2025.100442

Braun, V., & Clarke, V. (2006). Using thematic analysis in psychology. *Qualitative Research in Psychology*, *3*(2), 77–101. DOI: 10.1191/1478088706qp063oa

Braun, V., & Clarke, V. (2022). Thematic analysis: A practical guide. *Sage (Atlanta, Ga.)*.

Fu, B., Hadid, A., & Damer, N. (2025). Generative AI in the context of assistive technologies: Trends, limitations and future directions. *Image and Vision Computing*, *154*, 105347. DOI: 10.1016/j.imavis.2024.105347

Funa, A. A., & Gabay, R. A. E. (2025). Policy guidelines and recommendations on AI use in teaching and learning: A meta-synthesis study. *Social Sciences & Humanities Open*, *11*, 101221. DOI: 10.1016/j.ssaho.2024.101221

García-López, I. M., González González, C. S., Ramírez-Montoya, M.-S., & Molina-Espinosa, J.-M. (2025). Challenges of implementing ChatGPT on education: Systematic literature review. *International Journal of Educational Research Open*, *8*, 100401. DOI: 10.1016/j.ijedro.2024.100401

Maleki, A. (2026). "We cannot incorporate them because …": Challenges of integrating generative AI into online formative assessments in EFL contexts. *Computers in Human Behavior Reports*, *21*, 100934. DOI: 10.1016/j.chbr.2026.100934

Nussbaum, M., & Bekerman, Z. (2025). Advancing holistic educational goals through generative language-based technologies. *Learning and Individual Differences*, *117*, 102600. DOI: 10.1016/j.lindif.2024.102600

Rasool, U., Li, J., & Liu, M. (2025). Perceptions of generative AI in teaching and learning: UTAUT and TPACK model-based study of teachers and students. *Acta Psychologica*, *261*, 105827. DOI: 10.1016/j.actpsy.2025.105827 PMID: 41166843

Salih, S., Husain, O., Hamdan, M., Abdelsalam, S., Elshafie, H., & Motwakel, A. (2025). Transforming education with AI: A systematic review of ChatGPT's role in learning, academic practices, and institutional adoption. *Results in Engineering*, *25*, 103837. DOI: 10.1016/j.rineng.2024.103837

Shneiderman, B. (2020). Human-centered artificial intelligence: Reliable, safe & trustworthy. *International Journal of Human-Computer Interaction*, *36*(6), 495–504. DOI: 10.1080/10447318.2020.1741118

Tan, Q. (2025). Reimagining teacher development in the era of generative AI: A scoping review. *Teaching and Teacher Education*, *168*, 105236. DOI: 10.1016/j.tate.2025.105236

Wu, D., & Zhang, J. (2025). Generative artificial intelligence in secondary education: Applications and effects on students' innovation skills and digital literacy. *PLoS One*, *20*(5), e0323349. DOI: 10.1371/journal.pone.0323349 PMID: 40344078

Zhao, X., Cox, A., & Chen, X. (2025). The use of generative AI by students with disabilities in higher education. *The Internet and Higher Education*, *66*, 101014. DOI: 10.1016/j.iheduc.2025.101014

APPENDIX

(1) Semi-Structured Interview Protocol

Demographics

1. **Gender:** Female Male Other Prefer not to say
2. **Age group:** 25–34 35–44 45–54 55+
3. **Highest level of education:** Bachelor's degree Master's degree Doctorate
4. **Marital status:** Single Married In a civil partnership Divorced Widowed Prefer not to say
5. **Number of children:** None 1 2 3 or more Prefer not to say
6. **Primary field of expertise:**
   Computer Engineering
   Computer Science
   Artificial Intelligence / Machine Learning
   Other (please specify)
7. **Years of professional experience in computing/AI:**
   1–5 6–10 11–15 16+
8. **Current professional setting:**
   University / Research
   Private sector
   Public sector
   Start-up / Spin-off
   Other
9. **Experience in projects or applications related to education:** Yes No

If yes, please briefly describe your experience:

10. **Experience in applications for special education or vulnerable populations:** Yes No

If yes, please briefly describe your experience:

(2) Semi-Structured Interview Guide

Opening Question

1. How do you perceive the role of Artificial Intelligence (AI) in education, particularly in applications involving vulnerable student populations?

Warm-Up Question

2. Could you briefly tell us about your professional background and how you became involved in AI?

Section A: General Approach & Perceptions

3. How do you view the role of Gen-AI in the education of students with SEND?
4. In which forms of support do you believe it can offer the greatest added value?

Section B: Personalization & Pedagogical Functionality

5. What core features do you believe a Gen-AI system should include to support personalized and adaptive learning for students with SEND?
6. From a technical perspective, how can a Gen-AI system respond to diverse learning needs and student profiles without applying a "one-size-fits-all" approach? Why?

Section C: Data, Privacy & Bias

7. What are the main challenges in using and training Gen-AI models with data related to special education, particularly regarding data protection and privacy?
8. In your opinion, how can the risk of bias in Gen-AI models designed for special education be reduced? Why?

Section D: Interfaces & Technical Challenges

9. What technical challenges arise when developing dynamic or real-time adaptive interfaces for SEND students?
10. How can interface design account for users' cognitive, sensory, or communication limitations?

Section E: Gen-AI Frameworks & Multimodality

11. Which existing Gen-AI frameworks or architectures do you consider most suitable for SEND applications, and why?
12. How do you think multimodal Gen-AI (e.g., text, image, speech, symbols) can enhance accessibility and participation for students with SEND?

Section F: Limits, Responsibilities & Collaboration with Educators

13. What do you consider to be the limits of automation in the use of Gen-AI in special education?
14. How do you envision collaboration between computer engineers and special education teachers in designing such systems?

Synthesis Question

15. If you could influence the future design of Gen-AI in special education, what element would you consider essential to include?

Closing Question

16. Is there anything else you would like to add that you consider critical for the design or use of Gen-AI systems in special education that has not yet been discussed?

Thank you very much for your time!

Chapter 6

Artificial Intelligence in Inclusive Education: Supporting Students With Learning Difficulties in the Contemporary Greek School

Chrysanthi Koza
http://orcid.org/0000-0002-8486-3166
University of the Aegean, Greece

Georgia Lazakidou
http://orcid.org/0009-0004-2455-8866
Hellenic Open University, Greece

ABSTRACT

This chapter examines the role of Artificial Intelligence (AI) in special and inclusive education from a pedagogical, sociocultural, and ethical perspective. It explores how AI technologies, particularly Generative AI, can support personalized learning, differentiated instruction, accessibility, and learner participation while also introducing new challenges related to algorithmic bias, data privacy, equity, and learner agency. Drawing on recent international literature and policy developments, the chapter discusses the implications of AI for teaching, professional competence, and educational inclusion, with particular attention to the Greek educational context. Rather than presenting AI as a technological solution to educational challenges, the chapter argues that its educational value depends on pedagogically informed implementation, critical teacher mediation, and ethical governance. It concludes that AI can contribute to more inclusive and responsive educational environments only when its use is guided by principles of equity, transparency, human oversight, and social justice.

DOI: 10.4018/979-8-3373-9169-4.ch006

1. INTRODUCTION

The growing integration of Artificial Intelligence (AI) into educational settings is reshaping how teaching and learning are conceptualized and enacted. In special education, these developments carry particular weight, as they intersect directly with longstanding efforts to support inclusion and address learner diversity. However, as Selwyn (2016) cautions, technological innovation in education often reproduces existing inequalities, raising critical questions about who benefits from AI-driven practices and under what conditions.

Within inclusive education, which seeks to remove barriers to participation and learning for all students (UNESCO, 2017), AI acquires particular significance. Students with learning difficulties frequently encounter challenges that stem not only from individual cognitive characteristics but also from the structure and organization of educational systems (Florian, 2014). Recent advances in AI, particularly Generative AI, offer new opportunities to support these learners through personalized content, multimodal representations, and adaptive feedback.

Yet the growing use of AI in education cannot be viewed simply as a technological innovation. Its implementation is embedded within broader pedagogical, social, and political contexts that shape how educational opportunities are distributed. The shift from the medical to the social model of disability (Oliver, 1996), together with the increasing emphasis on differentiated instruction (Tomlinson, 2014), provides an important conceptual framework for understanding AI as a technology that can either promote inclusion or reinforce existing inequalities.

Although international research on AI in education has expanded considerably, there is still a need for context-sensitive and critically informed analyses that examine how these technologies operate within particular educational systems. This need is especially relevant in Greece, where structural inequalities, uneven technological infrastructure, and the limited systematic integration of digital innovation continue to shape educational practice.

This chapter critically examines the role of Artificial Intelligence, with particular emphasis on Generative AI, in supporting students with learning difficulties within inclusive education. It explores the pedagogical opportunities offered by AI alongside the practical and ethical challenges associated with its use, drawing on sociocultural theory and contemporary approaches to differentiated instruction.

More specifically, the chapter contributes to the field by:

(a) synthesizing theoretical perspectives on inclusive education, sociocultural learning, and AI;
(b) analyzing the pedagogical affordances and limitations of AI applications in special education; and

(c) proposing a critical framework for the equitable and pedagogically grounded integration of AI within the Greek educational context.

The remainder of the chapter is organized as follows. Section 2 outlines the theoretical framework underpinning inclusive education and examines AI as a pedagogical mediator. Section 3 reviews key applications of AI in special education. Section 4 discusses the Greek educational context, while Sections 5 and 6 examine the pedagogical potential of AI and the evolving role of teachers. Section 7 addresses the main ethical and social challenges associated with AI, and the final section summarizes the principal conclusions and implications for educational policy and practice.

2. THEORETICAL FRAMEWORK

2.1 Inclusive Education as a Framework of Social Justice

Inclusive education has become a central concept in contemporary educational theory and policy. Rather than focusing solely on the placement of students with diverse educational needs in mainstream classrooms, it calls for the transformation of educational systems so that all learners can participate meaningfully and achieve their potential (Ainscow et al., 2006; Florian, 2014). From this perspective, education is viewed not simply as a process of knowledge transmission but as a social institution that can either reproduce or challenge existing inequalities.

The principles of inclusive education are reflected in international policy documents, including the Salamanca Statement (UNESCO, 1994) and the Convention on the Rights of Persons with Disabilities (United Nations, 2006), both of which recognise education as a universal right grounded in equity, participation, and respect for diversity. At the same time, contemporary scholarship emphasizes that inclusion extends well beyond access to mainstream schooling. It also concerns the conditions that enable learners to participate meaningfully and benefit from educational opportunities.

Sen's (1992) capabilities approach provides a valuable framework for understanding inclusion as the expansion of individuals' real opportunities to achieve outcomes they value. Equality, from this perspective, cannot be reduced to equal access alone; it also requires attention to learners' differing capabilities and the support they need to engage successfully in learning. Rawls' (1971) difference principle offers a complementary perspective by arguing that educational inequalities are justifiable only when they improve the opportunities available to the least advantaged. This provides a strong philosophical foundation for differentiated pedagogical practices that respond to learner diversity.

A more critical perspective is offered by Bourdieu and Passeron (1977), who argue that education often reproduces existing social hierarchies by privileging dominant forms of cultural capital. Their analysis remains highly relevant in discussions of AI-supported education. Although AI technologies are frequently presented as objective or neutral, they may unintentionally reinforce existing inequalities if they reflect the assumptions and biases embedded in the data and systems on which they rely.

In Greece, inclusive education has been progressively strengthened through legislation and support structures such as integration units and parallel support services. Nevertheless, implementation remains uneven. Limited resources, insufficient teacher preparation, and persistent structural inequalities continue to restrict the consistent application of inclusive practices across schools (Kaltsouni, 2021; Zoniou-Sideri, 2011). Consequently, inclusion often functions more as a policy aspiration than as an established educational reality.

These considerations provide an important foundation for understanding the role of Artificial Intelligence in education. AI, including Generative AI, should not be regarded as a neutral technological innovation. Its educational impact depends on the social, institutional, and pedagogical contexts in which it is implemented. As a result, AI can either expand opportunities for participation and learning or contribute to the reproduction of existing educational inequalities. Its integration into inclusive education therefore needs to be guided by principles of equity, social justice, and critical pedagogical reflection.

2.2 Sociocultural theory and Artificial Intelligence as a pedagogical mediator

Sociocultural theory, developed primarily through the work of Vygotsky (1978), views learning as a fundamentally social and culturally mediated process. Knowledge is constructed through interaction with others and through engagement with cultural tools rather than acquired in isolation. Central to this perspective is the concept of the Zone of Proximal Development (ZPD), which describes the distance between what learners can accomplish independently and what they are able to achieve with appropriate guidance.

Bruner's (1983) notion of scaffolding extends this perspective by highlighting the importance of temporary and adaptive support that gradually enables learners to become more independent. In contemporary educational settings, digital technologies increasingly function as mediating tools that contribute to this process by expanding the ways learners interact with knowledge and with others.

AI introduces new possibilities for educational mediation. AI systems can analyse learner responses, provide personalized feedback, adjust task difficulty, and present information through multiple modes of representation. These capabilities allow AI to support learning processes within each learner's Zone of Proximal Development by offering assistance that is responsive to individual needs.

Generative AI further extends this mediating role. Unlike conventional educational software, generative systems can engage learners in natural-language dialogue, produce tailored explanations, and support problem-solving through continuous interaction. Rather than serving simply as instructional resources, these systems can participate in the co-construction of knowledge by providing context-sensitive guidance throughout the learning process.

The growing role of AI as a learning mediator also raises important pedagogical questions. Continuous algorithmic support may influence learner autonomy, alter patterns of cognitive engagement, and encourage excessive reliance on AI-generated assistance. As Selwyn (2016) reminds us, educational technologies do more than facilitate learning; they shape educational practices, influence patterns of thinking, and redefine relationships between learners, teachers, and knowledge.

Within the Greek educational context, digital platforms such as e-me and e-class provide initial infrastructure for technology-enhanced learning. Nevertheless, the pedagogical integration of such tools remains limited without systematic instructional redesign and teacher training (Komis, 2014). From this perspective, AI should be understood as a complementary pedagogical mediator that enriches, rather than replaces, human interaction and professional judgement.

2.3 Differentiated instruction and Artificial Intelligence

Differentiated instruction is widely recognised as a cornerstone of inclusive education, reflecting the understanding that learners vary in their abilities, interests, prior knowledge, and preferred ways of learning (Tomlinson, 2014). Rather than relying on a single instructional approach, differentiation encourages teachers to adapt content, learning activities, and expected outcomes in ways that respond to learner diversity while maintaining high educational expectations.

Artificial Intelligence considerably expands the possibilities for implementing differentiated instruction. By analysing patterns in learner performance and interaction, AI systems can personalize instructional content, adjust the pace of learning, and generate timely feedback that responds to individual learning needs. These capabilities allow teachers to provide more flexible forms of support than are typically feasible in traditional classroom settings.

Such affordances are particularly relevant in special education. Students with learning difficulties, including dyslexia and dyscalculia, may benefit from text simplification, multimodal representations, scaffolded activities, and continuous formative feedback that adapts to their progress. These applications are closely aligned with the principles of Universal Design for Learning (CAST, 2018), which advocate the proactive design of flexible learning environments capable of accommodating learner variability from the outset rather than through subsequent adaptation.

Generative AI further enhances differentiation by enabling the creation of customized learning materials, adaptive explanations, and interactive learning scenarios. Learners can engage in dialogue with AI systems, receive personalized support, and develop metacognitive awareness through immediate feedback. Such interactions may also encourage the development of self-regulated learning by prompting learners to monitor their progress, reflect on their thinking, and adjust their learning strategies accordingly (Zimmerman, 2002).

Despite these possibilities, differentiated instruction cannot be fully automated. Effective pedagogical differentiation requires professional judgement, contextual understanding, and sensitivity to learners' needs. AI may generate recommendations or adapt instructional materials, but teachers remain responsible for interpreting these outputs, deciding when they are pedagogically appropriate, and ensuring that technological support serves broader educational goals rather than simply improving efficiency.

These considerations are particularly relevant in the Greek educational system, where differentiated instruction continues to face practical challenges associated with large class sizes, limited resources, and uneven preparation in inclusive pedagogy. Under these conditions, AI should be viewed as a resource that can strengthen teachers' capacity to differentiate instruction, provided that its use is accompanied by sustained professional learning and thoughtful pedagogical integration.

2.4 Conceptualizing Artificial Intelligence in Inclusive Education

Building on the theoretical perspectives discussed above, this chapter examines AI in inclusive education as a socio-technical phenomenon shaped by the interaction of pedagogy, social justice, and technological innovation. From a sociocultural perspective, AI functions as a cognitive and cultural tool that mediates learning by influencing how students engage with tasks, respond to feedback, and construct knowledge. At the same time, perspectives grounded in social justice remind us that access to AI technologies, as well as the benefits they offer, remains uneven, raising important questions about equity, participation, and inclusion.

The emergence of Generative AI further expands these possibilities by supporting real-time dialogue, collaborative knowledge construction, and more adaptive forms of scaffolding. Its educational contribution, however, depends less on the technology itself than on the ways it is integrated into teaching practices and embedded within specific institutional and educational contexts.

Rather than viewing AI as a stand-alone solution to educational challenges, this chapter approaches it as one component of a broader pedagogical ecosystem that includes learners, teachers, policy frameworks, and the social and cultural conditions in which learning takes place. From this perspective, AI has the potential both to widen educational opportunities and to reinforce existing inequalities if its design and implementation are not guided by inclusive pedagogical principles.

This conceptual perspective provides the foundation for the chapters that follow, which examine the educational applications of AI, its pedagogical implications, and the ethical challenges associated with its use in special and inclusive education, with particular attention to the Greek educational context.

3. APPLICATIONS OF ARTIFICIAL INTELLIGENCE IN SPECIAL EDUCATION

3.1 Adaptive Learning Systems

Adaptive learning systems are among the most established applications of Artificial Intelligence in education. Drawing on machine learning algorithms, they analyze learner performance and adjust instructional content, pacing, and feedback in response to individual learning needs (Holmes et al., 2019; Luckin et al., 2016). Unlike conventional instructional approaches, adaptive systems are designed around the premise that learning does not follow a uniform or linear trajectory. Instead, they acknowledge that students develop at different rates and often require different pathways to achieve similar learning outcomes.

In special education, these systems have considerable potential to support students with learning difficulties, including dyslexia and dyscalculia, by offering personalized learning trajectories (Holmes et al., 2019; Mitchell, 2014). A learner experiencing reading difficulties, for example, may benefit from scaffolded phonological activities, simplified texts, and multimodal representations. Similarly, students with mathematical learning difficulties can be supported through visual representations, step-by-step guidance, and progressively structured problem-solving tasks.

Viewed through a sociocultural lens, adaptive learning systems can be interpreted as mediating tools that operate within the learner's Zone of Proximal Development by providing timely and responsive scaffolding (Vygotsky, 1978). Their capacity to personalize instruction is one of their greatest strengths, but it also raises important pedagogical questions. Most adaptive systems rely on pattern recognition and predictive modelling to determine appropriate learning pathways. As a result, they may reinforce learners' existing performance profiles instead of encouraging movement towards more challenging forms of learning. In some circumstances, students may remain within relatively low levels of task difficulty because the system prioritises predicted success over opportunities for cognitive growth (Selwyn, 2016; Williamson & Eynon, 2020).

Another important consideration concerns the limited transparency of algorithmic decision-making. Because many adaptive systems provide little insight into how recommendations are generated, teachers may find it difficult to evaluate, question, or modify the instructional decisions made by the technology (Williamson & Eynon, 2020). For this reason, adaptive learning systems should be regarded as tools that complement, rather than replace, professional pedagogical judgement. Their educational value ultimately depends on thoughtful teacher mediation and their integration into well-designed instructional practices.

3.2 AI for Language and Communication Support

Artificial Intelligence has substantially expanded the range of tools available to support students with language-related learning difficulties. Technologies such as speech-to-text, text-to-speech, and natural language processing applications enable learners to access educational content and communicate their ideas in ways that are less constrained by decoding difficulties, spelling challenges, or limitations in written expression (Davou & Misailidis, 2018; Holmes, Bialik, & Fadel, 2019).

Recent research has also highlighted that language models do not always respond equally well to the communication patterns of neurodivergent learners. Variations in language use, discourse structure, or communication style may lead to less accurate or less appropriate AI-generated responses, underlining the importance of teacher mediation and careful evaluation of AI-supported language tools (Kasneci et al., 2023; UNESCO, 2023).

For students with dyslexia, text-to-speech applications can improve access to written material by presenting information through an auditory channel, while speech-to-text technologies facilitate more fluent written production by reducing the mechanical demands of writing (Mitchell, 2014). AI-based translation and language simplification tools also play an increasingly important role in multilingual classrooms, where they can help learners from diverse linguistic backgrounds participate more confidently in classroom activities (UNESCO, 2019).

Beyond improving accessibility, these technologies can reduce unnecessary cognitive demands and allow students to focus more effectively on comprehension, communication, and higher-order learning tasks. In this respect, they align closely with the principles of Universal Design for Learning, which advocate providing multiple means of representation and expression to accommodate learner variability (CAST, 2018).

The educational benefits of language-support technologies, however, should not be taken for granted. If assistive tools are used without appropriate instructional planning, students may become overly dependent on technological support, limiting opportunities to develop core literacy skills independently (Selwyn, 2016). Teachers therefore need to make informed decisions about when AI should provide temporary scaffolding and when learners should be encouraged to perform tasks without technological assistance.

A further challenge concerns the limitations of natural language processing itself. Because language models are trained on large datasets that may underrepresent linguistic diversity, their outputs are not always equally accurate across languages, dialects, or communication styles. Recent research has also highlighted that these limitations may affect neurodivergent learners, whose language use or communication patterns are often underrepresented in training data. As a result, AI-generated responses may not always align with learners' individual communication needs, reinforcing the importance of careful pedagogical evaluation and human oversight (Kasneci et al., 2023; UNESCO, 2023). Ongoing teacher oversight is therefore essential to ensure that these technologies promote inclusion rather than unintentionally creating new barriers to participation.

3.3 Generative Artificial Intelligence as a Transformative Learning Tool

Generative Artificial Intelligence marks a significant development in the educational use of AI. Built on large language models, these systems can generate explanations, summaries, instructional materials, and dialogue in real time while adapting their responses to learners' questions and levels of understanding (Holmes et al., 2019; UNESCO, 2021).

These capabilities are particularly promising in special education. Generative AI can simplify complex concepts, produce alternative explanations, guide students through problem-solving processes, and provide immediate feedback tailored to individual learning needs (Holmes et al., 2019; Kasneci et al., 2023; Luckin et al., 2016; Tlili et al., 2023). Unlike conventional educational software, it also supports sustained interaction, allowing learners to revisit misconceptions, refine their understanding, and receive continuous guidance throughout the learning process.

Viewed from a sociocultural perspective, Generative AI extends established notions of mediated learning by creating opportunities for dialogue that support the co-construction of knowledge (Vygotsky, 1978). This interactive dimension is particularly valuable for students who benefit from ongoing scaffolding, as it offers flexible support that is available beyond the temporal constraints of classroom instruction.

Despite these advantages, the educational implications of Generative AI remain far from straightforward. Questions concerning the accuracy of generated information, the possibility of misinformation, and the tendency to encourage superficial engagement with learning continue to attract considerable attention (UNESCO, 2021; Williamson & Eynon, 2020). Easy access to AI-generated responses may also reduce learners' willingness to engage in sustained reasoning or independent problem solving, with potential consequences for the development of critical thinking skills (Selwyn, 2016).

Generative AI also challenges established understandings of authorship and academic integrity. As students increasingly incorporate AI-generated content into their work, distinguishing between legitimate educational support and the substitution of learners' own intellectual effort becomes more difficult. This issue is especially important in special education, where the goal is simultaneously to remove barriers to participation and to foster genuine learning and increasing independence.

For these reasons, the educational value of Generative AI cannot be separated from the pedagogical choices that shape its use. Its greatest contribution lies not in replacing teaching or learning, but in supporting carefully designed learning activities in which teachers retain responsibility for guidance, critical evaluation, and instructional decision-making.

3.4 Pedagogical Evaluation of AI Applications in Special Education

The use of Artificial Intelligence in special education presents both significant opportunities and important pedagogical challenges. AI technologies can enhance inclusion by supporting personalised learning, improving accessibility, and facilitating differentiated instruction. At the same time, they may reinforce existing educational inequalities if their implementation is driven primarily by technological efficiency rather than pedagogical considerations (Selwyn, 2016; Williamson & Eynon, 2020; UNESCO, 2023).

The educational value of AI depends on several interrelated conditions. First, its integration should be guided by the principles of inclusive education, ensuring that technology broadens rather than constrains learners' opportunities to participate and succeed. Second, AI needs to remain embedded within teacher-led instructional design, as professional judgement is essential for interpreting AI-generated recommendations, adapting them to learners' needs, and responding to the complexities of classroom practice (Fullan, 2007). Finally, AI-supported learning should encourage active participation, self-regulation, and metacognitive reflection instead of promoting passive reliance on automatically generated content (Zimmerman, 2002; Kasneci et al., 2023).

These considerations are particularly relevant in the Greek educational context. Structural constraints, unequal access to digital infrastructure, and limited opportunities for systematic professional development continue to influence the adoption of AI in schools (Komis, 2014; OECD, 2019). Consequently, AI is often introduced as a collection of isolated technological tools rather than as part of a coherent pedagogical strategy that supports inclusive teaching and learning.

Recent international research also emphasises that successful AI integration depends not only on technological innovation but equally on teachers' AI literacy, ethical awareness, and capacity to critically evaluate AI-generated outputs (OECD, 2024; UNESCO, 2023; Varsik & Vosberg, 2024). Without these conditions, AI applications risk becoming instruments of automation rather than meaningful resources for inclusive pedagogy.

Ultimately, the contribution of Artificial Intelligence to special education should be evaluated not by its technical capabilities alone, but by the extent to which it promotes educational equity, learner agency, meaningful participation, and high-quality learning experiences. From this perspective, AI is best understood as a pedagogical resource that complements professional expertise and supports, rather than replaces, inclusive educational practice.

4. ARTIFICIAL INTELLIGENCE IN THE GREEK EDUCATIONAL CONTEXT

The integration of Artificial Intelligence (AI) into the Greek educational system is currently at an early and transitional stage. While significant progress has been made in terms of digital infrastructure and the adoption of online learning platforms, the systematic incorporation of AI remains limited and uneven (European Commission, 2020; OECD, 2019).

The rapid digital transformation that took place during the COVID-19 pandemic accelerated the adoption of platforms such as e-me and e-class, supported by the Institute of Educational Policy (IEP). These platforms established an important digital foundation for Greek schools, although they continue to function primarily as learning management and communication environments rather than AI-enabled educational systems capable of adaptive learning or learning analytics.

A key structural limitation concerns the absence of a coherent national strategy for Artificial Intelligence in education. Greek educational policy has primarily focused on the development of basic digital skills, with limited emphasis on advanced technologies such as AI, machine learning, or data-driven pedagogical practices

(European Commission, 2020). As a result, the integration of AI remains fragmented and dependent on individual initiatives rather than systemic implementation.

Recent European policy developments place increasing emphasis on Artificial Intelligence literacy, responsible AI, and the ethical governance of educational technologies (European Union, 2024; OECD, 2024; UNESCO, 2023). Although these priorities are gradually influencing educational policy across Europe, their systematic translation into classroom practice remains limited in Greece. This highlights the need for a more coherent national framework that combines technological innovation with pedagogical development and teacher professional learning.

In the context of special education, these limitations become even more pronounced. Although institutional frameworks for inclusive education exist such as integration units and parallel support services (Law 3699/2008) their effectiveness is often constrained by insufficient resources, uneven distribution of support structures, and lack of specialized training for educators (Kaltsouni, 2021; Sakelariou, 2022; Zoniou-Sideri, 2011). Consequently, the potential of AI to support differentiated instruction and personalized learning is not fully realized in practice.

Another critical issue is the digital divide, which significantly affects the equitable implementation of AI-based educational tools. According to Van Dijk (2020), digital inequality extends beyond access to technology to include differences in digital skills, usage patterns, and the ability to critically engage with digital environments. In Greece, disparities between urban and rural areas, as well as between socio-economic groups, continue to influence students' access to digital tools and infrastructure (OECD, 2019). The experience of remote education during the pandemic highlighted these inequalities, particularly for students with learning difficulties who often require specialized assistive technologies. Recent OECD analyses further suggest that inequalities in AI readiness are increasingly associated not only with access to digital infrastructure but also with differences in teachers' digital competence and students' opportunities to develop AI literacy (OECD, 2024).

Furthermore, teacher preparedness constitutes a central challenge. Research indicates that many Greek educators have limited training in the pedagogical use of digital technologies, and even less exposure to Artificial Intelligence applications in education (Komis, 2014; European Commission, 2020). Professional development initiatives often focus on technical skills rather than on pedagogical integration, critical use, or ethical considerations of emerging technologies. This creates a gap between the potential of AI and its effective classroom implementation. Emerging research also indicates that many teachers report uncertainty regarding the educational use of Generative AI, particularly in relation to assessment, academic integrity, and the ethical use of AI-generated content (OECD, 2024; UNESCO, 2023).

From a critical perspective, the introduction of AI into the Greek educational system must also be examined in relation to broader issues of educational inequality and institutional capacity. As Selwyn (2016) argues, educational technologies are embedded within existing social and political structures and may reproduce inequalities if not critically implemented. In this context, the adoption of AI without a clear pedagogical framework risks reinforcing existing disparities rather than addressing them.

At the same time, the Greek educational context presents important opportunities for the meaningful integration of AI. The increasing availability of digital platforms, combined with ongoing curriculum reforms and European policy initiatives, creates a foundation for the development of more inclusive and technologically enriched learning environments (European Commission, 2020). AI has the potential to support differentiated instruction, enhance formative assessment, and provide personalized learning pathways, particularly in heterogeneous classrooms.

Realizing this potential will require coordinated action at multiple levels. A coherent national strategy for AI in education, sustained investment in digital infrastructure, systematic professional development for teachers, and clear ethical and pedagogical guidelines are all essential if AI is to become a meaningful component of inclusive educational practice rather than a collection of isolated technological initiatives.

The evolving European regulatory landscape also has important implications for the educational use of Artificial Intelligence. The European Union's Artificial Intelligence Act establishes a common legal framework for the development and deployment of trustworthy AI, placing particular emphasis on transparency, human oversight, accountability, risk management, and the protection of fundamental rights (European Union, 2024). Although the Act is not education-specific, its principles provide an important regulatory foundation for the responsible use of AI in schools, particularly when AI systems are used to support teaching, assessment, or decision-making involving children and other potentially vulnerable groups.

In conclusion, the Greek educational system illustrates the broader challenges of integrating Artificial Intelligence into education. While technological developments create new opportunities for inclusion and personalization, their impact is mediated by institutional structures, policy frameworks, and social inequalities. Therefore, the integration of AI in Greece should not be approached as a purely technological innovation, but as a complex educational reform that requires alignment between policy, pedagogy, and social justice.

5. PEDAGOGICAL POTENTIAL OF ARTIFICIAL INTELLIGENCE IN INCLUSIVE EDUCATION

The integration of Artificial Intelligence (AI) in education extends beyond technical innovation, introducing significant transformations in pedagogical practices, learning processes, and the roles of both learners and educators. Within inclusive education, AI offers new opportunities to create learning environments that are more personalized, flexible, and responsive to learner diversity. At the same time, its growing presence in educational settings raises important questions about knowledge construction, learner agency, and the role of technology in teaching and learning (UNESCO, 2023; Kasneci et al., 2023).

5.1 Personalized and Adaptive Learning

One of the most widely recognized pedagogical affordances of AI is its ability to facilitate personalized learning. By analyzing learner data and interaction patterns, AI systems can adapt content, pacing, and feedback to individual needs, thereby supporting differentiated instruction (Holmes, Bialik, & Fadel, 2019; Luckin et al., 2016). This is particularly important in inclusive classrooms, where learners present diverse cognitive profiles, learning styles, and educational needs.

From a pedagogical perspective, personalized learning reflects the principles of learner-centred education and differentiated instruction (Tomlinson, 2014). AI can support the implementation of these principles by enabling continuous adaptation of learning experiences. Recent research, however, suggests that effective personalization depends not only on algorithmic accuracy but also on teachers' ability to interpret, evaluate, and appropriately integrate AI-generated recommendations into classroom practice (Kasneci et al., 2023; OECD, 2024).

At the same time, the concept of personalization warrants critical examination. As Williamson (2017) argues, data-driven approaches may reduce learners to algorithmically constructed profiles, potentially narrowing rather than expanding learning opportunities. Similar concerns have been raised in recent discussions of Generative AI, where personalized recommendations may unintentionally reinforce existing learning patterns or biases if they are not critically monitored (UNESCO, 2023).

For these reasons, personalized learning should be understood not simply as algorithmic adaptation but as a pedagogical process in which AI complements professional judgement. Teachers remain responsible for ensuring that technological support is aligned with broader educational goals and the diverse needs of learners.

5.2 AI as a Tool for Scaffolding and Metacognitive Development

Artificial Intelligence can act as a form of instructional scaffolding, supporting learners as they build understanding and move gradually toward greater autonomy. Through immediate feedback, guided explanations, and interactive dialogue, AI systems can support learners in working through complex tasks and concepts (Luckin et al., 2016).

The emergence of Generative AI has further expanded these possibilities by enabling more dynamic and dialogic forms of support. Learners can engage in iterative conversations with AI systems, request clarification, explore alternative explanations, and receive immediate feedback tailored to their current level of understanding. Viewed through a sociocultural perspective, these interactions can extend mediated learning by encouraging dialogue, reflection, and the co-construction of knowledge (Vygotsky, 1978). Recent empirical research also suggests that AI-supported tutoring environments can enhance knowledge acquisition, critical thinking, and reflective learning when embedded within well-designed instructional activities rather than used as stand-alone technological tools (Melanou & Beege, 2026).

AI also has considerable potential to promote metacognitive development. By encouraging learners to monitor their understanding, evaluate alternative solutions, and regulate their learning strategies, AI can strengthen processes of self-regulated learning (Zimmerman, 2002). Empirical evidence (Michalsky, 2024) indicates that appropriately designed metacognitive scaffolding improves learners' ability to plan, monitor, and evaluate their own learning, while fostering greater autonomy and reflective thinking.

These benefits, however, are not automatic. Recent studies (Yan et al., 2024) emphasize that the educational impact of Generative AI depends less on the technology itself than on the pedagogical conditions under which it is used. When learners rely uncritically on AI-generated responses, opportunities for reasoning, productive struggle, and independent problem-solving may be diminished. Conversely, when teachers design learning activities that require students to question, evaluate, and justify AI-generated outputs, Generative AI can become a catalyst for deeper learning and metacognitive engagement rather than a substitute for thinking.

5.3 Enhancing Accessibility and Participation

A central pedagogical contribution of AI in inclusive education lies in its ability to enhance accessibility and participation. Through assistive technologies, multimodal content, and adaptive interfaces, AI can reduce barriers to learning and enable students with diverse needs to engage more fully in educational activities (CAST, 2018; UNESCO, 2017).

Students with reading difficulties, for example, may benefit from text-to-speech applications that improve access to written information, while speech-to-text technologies can facilitate written expression for learners experiencing difficulties with writing or motor coordination. More recently, Generative AI has expanded these possibilities by adapting the complexity of texts, generating personalized explanations, summarizing information, and providing alternative representations of concepts according to learners' individual needs. Emerging empirical evidence suggests that these adaptive features can improve learner engagement and perceived accessibility, particularly when AI tools are integrated into structured instructional activities rather than used independently (Evmenova et al., 2024; Tlili et al., 2023).

These developments are consistent with the principles of Universal Design for Learning (UDL), which advocate providing multiple means of engagement, representation, and expression to accommodate learner variability (CAST, 2018). Nevertheless, accessibility should not be interpreted simply as making learning tasks easier. Instead, inclusive pedagogy seeks to remove unnecessary barriers while maintaining high expectations and providing appropriate support for all learners.

Recent research also highlights that accessibility depends not only on the availability of AI tools but also on their design and implementation. AI systems that are insufficiently sensitive to learner diversity or that rely on biased training data may unintentionally disadvantage some groups of learners, including neurodivergent students or those with diverse linguistic and cultural backgrounds (UNESCO, 2023; Varsik & Vosberg, 2024). These findings underline the importance of combining technological innovation with inclusive design principles and ongoing teacher mediation.

From this perspective, AI should be viewed not as a mechanism for reducing cognitive challenge but as a means of expanding opportunities for participation, engagement, and meaningful learning. Its educational value ultimately depends on how effectively technological affordances are aligned with inclusive pedagogical practices and learners' individual strengths.

5.4 Reconfiguring the Role of the Learner

The integration of Artificial Intelligence in education introduces a significant reconfiguration of the learner's role, shifting from traditional models of passive knowledge reception toward more active, interactive, and self-regulated forms of learning. AI-supported environments enable learners to engage with content dynamically, explore alternative pathways of understanding, and receive continuous feedback, thereby fostering greater autonomy and agency (Holmes et al., 2019).

Generative AI has further expanded these possibilities by making interaction with educational content more conversational and iterative. Instead of following predetermined learning pathways, students can refine questions, request clarification, and revisit concepts from different perspectives. Recent empirical studies indicate that this type of dialogue can support conceptual understanding and learner engagement, provided that AI is integrated into pedagogical activities that require active participation rather than simple answer retrieval (Kasneci et al., 2023; Lo, 2023).

This shift aligns with constructivist and sociocultural approaches to learning, which emphasize active participation and the co-construction of knowledge (Vygotsky, 1978). For students with learning difficulties, such environments can reduce barriers to participation and provide opportunities for engagement that might not be possible in traditional instructional settings. The ability to receive immediate, personalized responses can enhance confidence, persistence, and motivation.

At the same time, greater access to AI-generated content also changes the demands placed on learners. The immediate availability of explanations, summaries, and completed responses may reduce the effort invested in analyzing information or solving problems independently. Recent research has highlighted this phenomenon as a potential challenge for learning, suggesting that excessive reliance on AI may weaken opportunities for sustained reasoning and knowledge construction if learners are not encouraged to question and evaluate AI-generated outputs (Selwyn, 2016; Yan et al., 2024;).

Furthermore, the role of the learner becomes more complex in relation to authorship and epistemic responsibility. When learners interact with Generative AI, the boundaries between their own thinking and externally generated content become blurred. This raises important questions about what it means to "know," "understand," or "produce" knowledge in AI-mediated environments. For students with learning difficulties, this tension is particularly significant, as AI can simultaneously support participation and risk substituting genuine learning processes.

Another important dimension concerns the development of critical AI literacy. As learners increasingly interact with AI systems, they must develop the ability to evaluate the accuracy, reliability, and bias of generated content (UNESCO, 2021). This extends beyond technical competence and includes critical judgement, source evaluation, and awareness that AI-generated responses may contain inaccuracies or reflect biases present in training data (UNESCO, 2023; European Union, 2024).

Taken together, these developments suggest that AI does not simply make learners more autonomous. Instead, it reshapes the ways in which they participate in learning by introducing new responsibilities related to judgement, reflection, and decision-making. The educational challenge is therefore not to maximize interaction with AI, but to design learning experiences in which technology supports inquiry, critical thinking, and meaningful participation without replacing learners' own intellectual engagement.

5.5 Conditions for Effective Pedagogical Integration

The pedagogical potential of Artificial Intelligence is not inherent in the technology itself, but emerges through its integration into educational practice. Three key conditions are essential for the effective use of AI in inclusive education.

First, AI must be aligned with inclusive pedagogical principles, ensuring that it supports equity, participation, and learner diversity (UNESCO, 2017). Second, its use must be mediated by educators, who play a central role in designing learning experiences, interpreting AI outputs, and supporting students' engagement. Third, AI should be embedded within pedagogical frameworks that promote critical thinking, metacognition, and active learning.

Without these conditions, there is a risk that AI will be used in a superficial or instrumental manner, focusing on efficiency rather than meaningful learning. As Selwyn (2016) emphasizes, educational technologies must be critically examined in relation to their pedagogical and social implications.

In conclusion, the pedagogical potential of AI in inclusive education lies in its capacity to transform learning environments, enhance accessibility, and support personalized learning. However, its impact depends on how it is used, by whom, and within which educational and social contexts.

6. THE ROLE OF THE TEACHER AND PROFESSIONAL DEVELOPMENT

The integration of Artificial Intelligence (AI) into education is reshaping teachers' work in ways that extend far beyond the adoption of new digital tools. As AI becomes increasingly embedded in teaching and learning, educators are expected to make informed pedagogical decisions about when, how, and why these technologies should be used. In inclusive education, these responsibilities are particularly demanding because teachers must ensure that AI supports learner diversity, promotes equitable participation, and remains consistent with broader educational goals rather than simply increasing efficiency (OECD, 2024; UNESCO, 2023).

6.1 Reconfiguring the Role of the Teacher

Traditionally, the teacher has been positioned as the primary source of knowledge and authority in the classroom. However, AI-supported learning environments challenge this model by providing learners with direct access to information, feedback, and instructional support. As a result, the teacher's role shifts from knowledge transmission to the facilitation and orchestration of learning processes (Holmes, Bialik, & Fadel, 2019).

As AI becomes part of everyday educational practice, teachers increasingly assume the role of learning designers. Their work involves selecting appropriate AI tools, adapting them to learners' needs, and integrating them into instructional activities that encourage participation, collaboration, and critical thinking rather than passive consumption of AI-generated information (Kasneci et al., 2023).

These developments also reshape teachers' professional identity. Rather than being valued primarily for transmitting knowledge, teachers are increasingly recognized for their ability to exercise professional judgement, interpret AI-generated information critically, and create learning environments in which technology complements, rather than replaces, human interaction. Recent studies indicate that many educators view these new responsibilities as opportunities for professional growth, while also expressing uncertainty about their preparedness to use AI effectively in everyday teaching (OECD, 2024; Villar-Onrubia et al., 2025).

6.2 Teacher as Pedagogical Mediator of AI

Despite the increasing sophistication of Artificial Intelligence systems, the role of the teacher as a pedagogical mediator becomes more critical in AI-supported learning environments. While AI can generate content, provide feedback, and suggest learning pathways, it lacks the contextual, relational, and ethical awareness required for meaningful educational practice.

The concept of mediation, grounded in sociocultural theory, highlights the role of the teacher in shaping how learners interact with knowledge, tools, and learning processes (Vygotsky, 1978). In the context of AI, this mediating function extends to the interpretation and regulation of algorithmically generated outputs. Teachers are required to evaluate the relevance, accuracy, and pedagogical appropriateness of AI-generated content, ensuring that it aligns with curricular goals and learners' needs.

This mediating role requires teachers to develop what recent research describes as AI literacy and professional judgement. Beyond operating AI tools, educators need to understand how AI systems generate responses, recognise their limitations, identify potential biases, and evaluate whether AI-generated content is appropriate for specific learning objectives and learner characteristics (OECD, 2024; UNESCO, 2023).

Recent empirical research consistently identifies teacher preparedness as one of the strongest predictors of successful AI integration in education. Although many educators recognise the potential of AI to support teaching and learning, they also report limited confidence in selecting appropriate AI tools, designing AI-supported learning activities, and addressing ethical issues such as privacy, transparency, and academic integrity (Villar-Onrubia et al., 2025). These findings suggest that professional development should focus not only on technical competence but also on pedagogical decision-making and responsible AI use.

Furthermore, the teacher's mediating role includes orchestrating the interaction between learners and AI. This involves designing learning activities that guide how students engage with AI systems, framing questions, structuring tasks, and encouraging critical reflection. In this sense, the teacher becomes a designer of AI-mediated learning experiences, ensuring that interaction with technology promotes understanding rather than superficial engagement.

In inclusive education settings, this role is even more complex. Teachers must ensure that AI tools are used in ways that support diverse learners without reinforcing inequalities or lowering expectations. This requires sensitivity to individual differences, as well as the ability to adapt AI-generated content to specific learning profiles.

6.3 AI Literacy and Professional Competence

The integration of Artificial Intelligence in education necessitates a redefinition of professional competence, extending beyond traditional digital literacy toward what is increasingly conceptualized as AI literacy. This form of literacy encompasses not only technical understanding, but also critical, pedagogical, and ethical dimensions (Long & Magerko, 2020; Ng et al., 2021).

At a foundational level, AI literacy involves an understanding of how AI systems function, including basic principles of data processing, machine learning, and algorithmic decision-making. However, such technical knowledge alone is insufficient for educational practice. Recent studies indicate that teachers frequently report uncertainty when interpreting AI-generated outputs, particularly with regard to accuracy, transparency, and reliability. Consequently, professional competence increasingly involves the ability to evaluate AI recommendations critically rather than accepting them at face value (OECD, 2024; Villar-Onrubia et al., 2025).

More importantly, AI literacy should be understood as a form of critical professional competence. Teachers are required to engage with AI not as neutral technology, but as a socio-technical system shaped by specific assumptions, data structures, and power relations (Selwyn, 2016). This involves questioning how such systems represent knowledge, whose perspectives are included or excluded, and how their use may impact different groups of learners.

In pedagogical terms, AI literacy includes the capacity to design learning experiences that integrate AI in ways that promote active engagement, critical thinking, and metacognitive awareness. Teachers must be able to guide students in interacting with AI systems, helping them to evaluate outputs, identify inaccuracies, and reflect on their own learning processes. In this sense, AI literacy is closely linked to the development of students' critical AI literacy, positioning teachers as facilitators of informed and reflective technology use.

Ethical competence has become an integral component of AI literacy. Beyond concerns about privacy and data protection, teachers are increasingly expected to recognise issues related to algorithmic bias, transparency, fairness, and accountability when selecting or using AI-supported educational applications (European Union, 2024; UNESCO, 2023).

Finally, AI literacy should not be viewed as a static set of skills, but as an evolving competence that develops through ongoing professional learning and reflective practice. As these technologies continue to evolve, teachers must continuously update their knowledge, adapt their pedagogical approaches, and critically engage with new developments.

In this context, professional competence in the age of AI is defined not by mastery of technology alone, but by the ability to integrate technological, pedagogical, and ethical knowledge into coherent and context-sensitive educational practice.

6.4 Professional Development and Systemic Challenges

The successful integration of Artificial Intelligence into educational practice depends largely on teachers' opportunities to develop the knowledge and confidence required to use these technologies effectively. Although interest in AI has grown rapidly, recent studies consistently report that many teachers feel insufficiently prepared to integrate AI into their everyday teaching. The greatest challenges concern not the technical use of AI tools, but their pedagogical application, the evaluation of AI-generated content, and the ethical issues associated with their use (OECD, 2024; Villar-Onrubia et al., 2025).

Professional development therefore needs to move beyond short-term training focused on digital skills. Recent research suggests that effective AI-related professional learning should combine technical understanding with opportunities to design AI-supported learning activities, discuss authentic classroom experiences, and reflect on issues such as assessment, inclusion, academic integrity, and algorithmic bias (Ng et al., 2021; UNESCO, 2023).

These challenges are particularly relevant in the Greek educational context. Although considerable progress has been made in strengthening digital infrastructure, opportunities for systematic professional development in Artificial Intelligence remain limited. Existing training initiatives have traditionally emphasized the use of digital technologies rather than the pedagogical integration of AI into teaching and learning (Komis, 2014; OECD, 2024). As a result, many teachers continue to rely on individual experimentation rather than structured institutional support.

Strengthening teachers' professional competence therefore requires more than expanding access to these technologies. It also depends on coherent educational policies, sustained professional learning, and school cultures that encourage collaboration, reflection, and the responsible use of Artificial Intelligence in support of inclusive education

6.5 Toward a Reflective and Critical Teaching Profession

The integration of Artificial Intelligence in education necessitates a fundamental rethinking of teaching as a reflective, critical, and ethically grounded profession. In AI-supported learning environments, teachers are not merely implementers of technological tools, but active agents who shape how these technologies are interpreted, applied, and experienced in practice.

Reflective practice has become increasingly important in AI-supported learning environments, as teachers are expected to evaluate not only how AI tools are used in the classroom, but also how they influence learning, inclusion, and pedagogical decision-making. This requires continuous reflection on the educational value of AI applications, their limitations, and their implications for different groups of learners.

Yet, the increasing presence of algorithmic systems in education raises important questions about professional autonomy. AI technologies can influence instructional decisions through recommendations, analytics, and automated feedback, potentially shaping teaching practices in subtle but significant ways. This creates a tension between teacher agency and what may be described as algorithmic governance, where decision-making is partially guided by technological systems (Selwyn, 2016; Williamson & Eynon, 2020).

In this context, maintaining professional autonomy requires the capacity to critically evaluate and, when necessary, resist or adapt AI-driven suggestions. Teachers must retain control over pedagogical decisions, ensuring that technology serves educational goals rather than defining them. This is particularly important in inclusive education, where sensitivity to individual learner needs cannot be fully captured by algorithmic models.

A critical teaching profession also involves ethical responsibility. The use of AI raises complex issues related to data privacy, bias, surveillance, and equity. Teachers must be able to navigate these challenges, making informed decisions that prioritize the well-being, dignity, and rights of learners (UNESCO, 2021). Ethical awareness is therefore not an optional dimension of professional practice, but a core component of teaching in AI-mediated environments.

A reflective approach to teaching also requires educators to consider the broader social consequences of AI. Recent discussions emphasise that educational technologies may unintentionally reproduce existing inequalities unless their use is guided by principles of inclusion, equity, and social justice (OECD, 2024; UNESCO, 2023). From this perspective, teachers contribute not only by adapting instruction to individual learners but also by questioning how AI influences participation, opportunity, and educational decision-making.

Rather than reducing the importance of teachers, the increasing use of Artificial Intelligence highlights the value of professional judgement, ethical responsibility, and reflective practice. Technology can support teaching in important ways, but decisions about learning, inclusion, and assessment continue to depend on educators who are able to interpret AI critically and respond to the needs of diverse learners.

7. ETHICAL AND SOCIAL CHALLENGES OF ARTIFICIAL INTELLIGENCE IN EDUCATION

The growing use of Artificial Intelligence (AI) in education has intensified discussions about its ethical and social implications. While AI offers important opportunities for supporting inclusion, personalised learning, and accessibility, it also raises concerns about fairness, transparency, accountability, and the protection of learners' rights. These issues are particularly significant in special and inclusive education, where educational decisions can have long-term consequences for learners who are already at greater risk of exclusion (European Union, 2024; UNESCO, 2023).

7.1 Algorithmic Bias and Inequality

One of the most critical ethical challenges associated with Artificial Intelligence in education is the presence of algorithmic bias, which refers to systematic distortions in AI outputs resulting from the data, assumptions, and design choices embedded within these systems. Rather than operating as neutral technologies, AI systems reflect the characteristics of the data on which they are trained, the assumptions embedded in their design, and the educational contexts in which they are deployed. Consequently, existing social inequalities may be reproduced or amplified through algorithmic decision-making (O'Neil, 2016; UNESCO, 2023; Williamson & Eynon, 2020).

Algorithmic bias emerges through multiple mechanisms. First, training datasets may lack adequate representation of diverse learner populations, particularly students with disabilities or atypical learning profiles. As a result, such systems may be calibrated to "average" learners, leading to inaccuracies or misinterpretations when applied to students who deviate from these norms. For example, natural language processing systems may misinterpret non-standard language use associated with learning difficulties, while adaptive learning systems may inaccurately assess learner performance due to atypical response patterns.

Second, bias can be embedded in the design of algorithms themselves, which often rely on predefined categories, performance metrics, and normative assumptions about learning. These models tend to prioritize measurable outcomes, such as speed or accuracy, potentially overlooking alternative forms of understanding and expression that are common among learners with special educational needs (Selwyn, 2016). In this sense, AI systems may implicitly define what counts as "successful learning," thereby marginalizing learners who do not conform to these criteria.

In educational assessment, the implications of algorithmic bias are particularly significant. AI-driven assessment tools may produce evaluations that do not accurately reflect learners' abilities, especially when those abilities are expressed in non-traditional ways. This raises concerns about fairness, validity, and the potential for misclassification, which can have long-term consequences for students' educational trajectories.

Recent research has drawn particular attention to the implications of algorithmic bias for neurodivergent learners. Because many AI systems are developed using datasets that primarily represent neurotypical patterns of behaviour and communication, they may not accurately recognise the ways in which autistic learners or students with other neurodevelopmental differences engage with learning activities. This may result in inappropriate recommendations, inaccurate performance evaluations, or reduced access to personalised support, highlighting the importance of inclusive dataset design and human oversight (UNESCO, 2023; Varsik & Vosberg, 2024).

From an inclusion perspective, algorithmic bias intersects with issues of disability, language, and socio-economic background, creating compounded forms of disadvantage. Learners who are already marginalized may be further excluded if AI systems fail to recognize or appropriately respond to their needs. This highlights the risk that AI, rather than reducing inequality, may reinforce and legitimize existing disparities.

Addressing algorithmic bias requires more than technical adjustments; it necessitates a critical re-examination of the assumptions underlying AI systems and their role in education. Teachers, researchers, and policymakers must engage with questions about whose knowledge is represented, whose learning is valued, and how technological systems shape educational opportunities.

Ultimately, the ethical challenge is not simply to make AI systems more accurate, but to ensure that they are aligned with the principles of inclusive and equitable education. This involves recognizing bias as an inherent feature of socio-technical systems and developing pedagogical and policy frameworks that actively work to mitigate its impact.

7.2 Data Protection, Privacy, and Ethical Governance

The use of AI in education is closely linked to processes of datafication, where learners' activities, behaviors, and performances are continuously recorded, analyzed, and transformed into data (Williamson, 2017). While such data can support personalized learning and informed decision-making, it also raises significant concerns regarding privacy and surveillance.

AI systems often require large amounts of data to function effectively, including sensitive information about learners' performance, behavior, and, in some cases, personal characteristics. In special education, this data may include information about disabilities or learning difficulties, making privacy concerns even more critical. The widespread adoption of Generative AI has further expanded these concerns because user prompts and interactions may be stored, analysed, or incorporated into the further development of AI systems. Consequently, schools and teachers need to consider carefully which AI applications are appropriate for educational use and under what conditions learners' data can be processed safely (European Union, 2024).

The continuous monitoring of learners can create environments of surveillance, where students' actions are constantly tracked and evaluated. This may affect learners' sense of autonomy, increase anxiety, and influence how they engage with learning tasks. Moreover, questions arise regarding who has access to this data, how it is used, and how it is protected (UNESCO, 2021).

Addressing these challenges requires more than compliance with data protection regulations. Recent policy frameworks emphasise the importance of transparency, human oversight, informed consent where appropriate, and clear governance mechanisms that ensure AI systems remain accountable to educational values rather than solely to technical performance (European Union, 2024; UNESCO, 2023).

7.3 Dependency, Agency, and Cognitive Implications

The increasing reliance on AI tools in education raises important questions about learner dependency and cognitive engagement. While AI can provide valuable support, there is a risk that learners may become overly dependent on technological systems for answers, explanations, and problem-solving.

Recent studies have renewed interest in the concept of cognitive offloading in the context of Generative AI. Because intelligent systems can generate explanations, solve problems, and produce written responses almost instantaneously, learners may increasingly rely on these systems to perform cognitive tasks that would otherwise require sustained reasoning and reflection. Although such support can reduce cognitive load and facilitate task completion, excessive dependence may limit opportunities for critical thinking, problem-solving, and knowledge construction (Kasneci et al., 2023; Yan et al., 2024).

At the same time, empirical evidence suggests that the impact of AI on learner agency depends largely on instructional design. When AI is incorporated into activities that encourage questioning, explanation, and reflection, it can strengthen self-regulated learning and learner autonomy. In contrast, when AI is used primarily to generate ready-made answers, learners are more likely to adopt passive strategies that reduce meaningful engagement with learning tasks (Lo, 2023; Tlili et al., 2023)

7.4 Inclusion vs. Exclusion: A Critical Tension

Artificial Intelligence is frequently framed as a transformative tool for promoting inclusion in education, particularly through its capacity to support personalization, accessibility, and differentiated instruction (Holmes, Bialik, & Fadel, 2019; UNESCO, 2023). However, the relationship between AI and inclusion is neither straightforward nor inherently positive. Rather, it reflects a fundamental tension between the potential to expand educational opportunities and the risk of reproducing or even intensifying existing forms of exclusion (Selwyn, 2016; Williamson & Eynon, 2020).

Inclusion should not be understood merely as access to technological tools, but as a broader pedagogical and social project aimed at ensuring meaningful participation, equity, and recognition of learner diversity (UNESCO, 2017). From this perspective, the use of AI does not automatically lead to inclusive outcomes. Instead, its impact depends on how technologies are designed, implemented, and integrated within specific educational contexts (Holmes, Bialik, & Fadel, 2019).

AI systems can enhance inclusion by providing adaptive learning pathways, assistive technologies, and multimodal forms of engagement that respond to diverse learner needs (Luckin et al., 2016). For students with disabilities or learning difficulties, such tools can reduce barriers and support participation in ways that traditional instructional models may not (Mitchell, 2014). Generative AI, in particular, can offer alternative explanations, simplify complex content, and facilitate access to knowledge through interactive dialogue (UNESCO, 2021).

However, these benefits are unevenly distributed. Structural inequalities such as disparities in access to technology, differences in digital literacy, and variations in institutional support significantly influence who is able to benefit from AI-based educational tools (Van Dijk, 2020). In contexts such as the Greek educational system, where infrastructural and training limitations persist, the integration of AI may reinforce existing gaps between learners rather than bridge them (European Commission, 2020; OECD, 2019).

Moreover, inclusion is not only a question of access, but also of representation and recognition. AI systems are often designed around dominant linguistic, cultural, and cognitive norms, which may not adequately reflect the diversity of learners in inclusive classrooms (Williamson & Eynon, 2020). As a result, certain learners may be implicitly marginalized if their ways of learning, communicating, or expressing knowledge are not supported by these systems. Recent analyses also suggest that these challenges may be particularly relevant for neurodiverse learners, whose communication styles and learning profiles are often underrepresented in the datasets used to develop such systems (Varsik & Vosberg, 2024).

There is also a risk that AI-driven personalization may lead to forms of educational segregation. By tailoring content to individual performance levels, adaptive systems may inadvertently limit learners' exposure to more complex or challenging material, thereby reinforcing existing achievement gaps (Selwyn, 2016). In inclusive education, where the goal is to promote both participation and high expectations, such outcomes are particularly problematic.

From a critical perspective, Artificial Intelligence should be understood as a socio-technical system whose effects are shaped by pedagogical practices, institutional structures, and broader socio-economic conditions (Williamson & Eynon, 2020). Addressing the tension between inclusion and exclusion therefore requires a shift from a purely technology-centered approach to one grounded in pedagogy and policy.

In practical terms, inclusion must be actively designed and supported through intentional instructional strategies, teacher mediation, and equitable policy frameworks (UNESCO, 2017). Without such efforts, the integration of AI risks reinforcing the very inequalities it seeks to address.

Ultimately, the question is not whether AI can support inclusion, but under what conditions it does so, for whom, and to what extent (Selwyn, 2016). A critical and context-sensitive approach is therefore essential to ensure that Artificial Intelligence contributes to inclusive and socially just educational practices.

7.5 Toward Ethical and Responsible AI in Education

The increasing integration of Artificial Intelligence in education has led to a growing recognition of the need for ethical and responsible frameworks to guide its development and use. While AI technologies offer significant opportunities for enhancing teaching and learning, their implementation must be aligned with fundamental educational values, including equity, inclusion, transparency, and respect for human rights (European Commission, 2020; UNESCO, 2023).

A key principle in this context is transparency. AI systems often operate as "black boxes," making it difficult for educators and learners to understand how decisions are made or how outputs are generated. This lack of transparency can undermine trust and limit the capacity of teachers to exercise informed pedagogical judgement (Williamson & Eynon, 2020). Recent European policy developments emphasize that transparency should be accompanied by meaningful human oversight, ensuring that educational decisions remain under the responsibility of educators rather than automated systems (European Union, 2024). Thus, promoting transparency involves not only technical explainability, but also the development of practices that enable educators to critically interpret and contextualize AI outputs.

Fairness and equity constitute another central dimension of ethical AI. As discussed in previous sections, algorithmic systems may reproduce existing inequalities if they are trained on biased datasets or designed around narrow definitions of learning (O'Neil, 2016; Selwyn, 2016). Ethical AI requires deliberate efforts to identify, monitor, and mitigate such biases, ensuring that technologies support rather than undermine inclusive educational goals.

Accountability is also essential. Questions regarding who is responsible for AI-generated decisions (developers, institutions, or educators) remain complex and often unresolved. In educational contexts, accountability must be shared, but clearly defined, ensuring that the use of AI does not obscure responsibility for pedagogical decisions and learner outcomes (UNESCO, 2021).

In addition, ethical AI in education must address issues of data protection and privacy. The extensive data collection required for AI systems raises concerns about how learner information is stored, used, and shared. These concerns are particularly acute in special education, where sensitive data related to learning difficulties or disabilities may be involved. Safeguarding this data is essential for protecting learners' rights and maintaining trust in educational systems (European Commission, 2020; UNESCO, 2021).

From a pedagogical perspective, ethical AI is not limited to compliance with regulations, but involves the intentional design of learning environments that promote critical engagement, learner agency, and meaningful participation. Teachers play a central role in this process, as they mediate the use of AI and ensure that it aligns with educational objectives and ethical principles (Luckin et al., 2016).

At the policy level, the development of coherent national and institutional strategies is crucial for the responsible integration of AI. Such strategies should include guidelines for ethical use, investment in teacher training, and measures to ensure equitable access to technological resources (European Commission, 2020; OECD, 2019). Without coordinated policy frameworks, the implementation of AI is likely to remain fragmented and inconsistent.

The responsible use of Artificial Intelligence in education depends not only on technological innovation but also on educational judgement, ethical governance, and inclusive pedagogical practice. AI can contribute meaningfully to teaching and learning only when its use is guided by clear educational purposes, supported by appropriate policies, and critically mediated by teachers. Under these conditions, AI has the potential to strengthen rather than undermine inclusive and socially just education.

8. CONCLUSIONS

The discussion presented in this chapter demonstrates that the integration of Artificial Intelligence into special and inclusive education is far more than a technological development. It represents a broader educational transformation that influences how teaching is organized, how learning is supported, and how educational decisions are made. Although AI offers important opportunities to personalize learning, improve accessibility, and facilitate participation, these benefits are neither automatic nor equally distributed across educational contexts.

A central argument of this chapter is that AI should be understood as a socio-technical system whose educational impact depends on the interaction between technology, pedagogy, institutional conditions, and social values. Its contribution to inclusive education is therefore shaped not only by technical capabilities, but also by the ways educators, schools, and policymakers interpret and integrate AI into everyday practice.

The analysis also highlights the dual nature of AI applications in special education. Adaptive and generative AI technologies can enrich learning by providing personalised support, immediate feedback, and flexible forms of interaction. At the same time, they raise important concerns regarding learner dependency, algorithmic bias, unequal access, data privacy, and the transparency of automated decision-making. These challenges reinforce the need for continuous human oversight and pedagogical judgement rather than unquestioned reliance on technological systems.

The Greek educational context illustrates many of these opportunities and challenges. While recent digital developments and European policy initiatives create favorable conditions for the wider adoption of AI, important barriers remain, including uneven infrastructure, limited teacher preparation, and the absence of a comprehensive national strategy for AI in education. Addressing these issues requires sustained investment in professional learning, institutional capacity, and educational policies that place inclusion and equity at the centre of technological innovation.

The chapter further argues that the successful use of AI depends on strengthening teachers' professional competence and learners' critical engagement with AI technologies. AI literacy, ethical awareness, and reflective pedagogical practice are no longer optional skills but increasingly important components of educational professionalism. At the same time, learners need opportunities to develop the critical capacity to question, evaluate, and use AI-generated information responsibly rather than relying on it uncritically.

Recent international policy frameworks increasingly emphasise that trustworthy AI requires transparency, human oversight, accountability, and respect for fundamental rights (European Union, 2024; OECD, 2024; UNESCO, 2023). These principles are particularly relevant in inclusive education, where technological decisions may have profound consequences for learners who already face educational disadvantage.

Future research should move beyond discussions of AI's potential and examine how these technologies are implemented in authentic educational settings. Greater attention is needed to the experiences of teachers and learners, the impact of AI on students with special educational needs, and the long-term effects of AI-supported learning on participation, achievement, and educational equity.

Ultimately, the educational significance of Artificial Intelligence will not be determined by technological innovation alone. Its value will depend on whether it is implemented in ways that strengthen inclusion, support meaningful learning, and respect the diversity, dignity, and rights of all learners. Under these conditions, AI can become an important resource for developing more equitable and responsive educational systems rather than simply another technological innovation.

REFERENCES

Ainscow, M., Booth, T., & Dyson, A. (2006). *Improving schools, developing inclusion*. Routledge. DOI: 10.4324/9780203967157

Bourdieu, P., & Passeron, J.-C. (1977). *Reproduction in education, society and culture*. Sage. https://monoskop.org/images/8/82/Bourdieu_Pierre_Passeron_Jean_Claude_Reproduction_in_Education_Society_and_Culture_1990.pdf

Bruner, J. (1983). *Child's talk: Learning to use language*. Oxford University Press.

CAST. (2018). *Universal Design for Learning guidelines version 2.2*. http://udlguidelines.cast.org

Davou, V., & Misailidis, P. (2018). *Technologies supporting learning and learning difficulties*. Ellinika Grammata. [in Greek]

European Commission. (2020). *Digital education action plan 2021–2027: Resetting education and training for the digital age*. Publications Office of the European Union. https://ec.europa.eu

European Union. (2024). Regulation (EU) 2024/1689 of the European Parliament and of the Council of 13 June 2024 laying down harmonised rules on artificial intelligence (Artificial Intelligence Act). Official Journal of the European Union, L 2024/1689. https://eur-lex.europa.eu/eli/reg/2024/1689/oj

Evmenova, A. S., Borup, J., & Shin, J. K. (2024). Harnessing the Power of Generative AI to Support ALL Learners. *TechTrends*, *68*(4), 820–831. DOI: 10.1007/s11528-024-00966-x

Florian, L. (2014). Reimagining special education: Why new approaches are needed. In Florian, L. (Ed.), *The Sage Handbook of Special Education* (2nd ed., pp. 9–19). Sage. DOI: 10.4135/9781446282236.n3

Fullan, M. (2007). *The new meaning of educational change* (4th ed.). Teachers College Press. https://shorturl.at/K0Pel

Holmes, W., Bialik, M., & Fadel, C. (2019). *Artificial intelligence in education: Promises and implications for teaching and learning*. Center for Curriculum Redesign. Retrieved May 12, 2026, from https://curriculumredesign.org/wp-content/uploads/AIED-Book-Excerpt-CCR.pdf

Kaltsouni, P. (2021). Inclusive education in GREECE. *Social Work Education*, *8*(3), 385–394. DOI: 10.25128/2520-6230.21.3.7

Kasneci, E., Seßler, K., Küchemann, S., Bannert, M., Dementieva, D., Fischer, F., Gasser, U., Groh, G., Günnemann, S., Hüllermeier, E., Krusche, S., Kutyniok, G., Michaeli, T., Nerdel, C., Pfeffer, J., Poquet, O., Sailer, M., Schmidt, A., Seidel, T., & Kasneci, G. (2023). ChatGPT for Good? On Opportunities and Challenges of Large Language Models for Education. *Learning and Individual Differences, 103*, 102274. DOI: 10.1016/j.lindif.2023.102274

Komis, V. (2014). *Didactics of Informatics and ICT.* Klidarithmos. (in Greek)

Lo, C. K. (2023). What Is the Impact of ChatGPT on Education? A Rapid Review of the Literature. *Education Sciences, 13*(4), 410. DOI: 10.3390/educsci13040410

Long, D., & Magerko, B. (2020). What Is AI Literacy? Competencies and Design Considerations. In Proceedings of the 2020 CHI *Conference on Human Factors in Computing Systems* (pp. 1-16). Association for Computing Machinery. DOI: 10.1145/3313831.3376727

Luckin, R., Holmes, W., Griffiths, M., & Forcier, L. B. (2016). *Intelligence unleashed: An argument for AI in education.* Pearson Education.

Melanou, C., & Beege, M. (2026). Scaffolding Generative AI as a Tutor: A Quasi-Experimental Study of Learning Outcomes and Motivational, Cognitive and Metacognitive Processes. *Education Sciences, 16*(4), 651. DOI: 10.3390/educsci16040651

Michalsky, T. (2024). Metacognitive scaffolding for preservice teachers' self-regulated design of higher order thinking tasks. *Heliyon, 10*(2), e24280. DOI: 10.1016/j.heliyon.2024.e24280 PMID: 38293459

Mitchell, D. (2014). *What really works in special and inclusive education: Using evidence-based teaching strategies* (2nd ed.). Routledge. DOI: 10.4324/9780203105313

Ng, D. T. K., Leung, J. K. L., Chu, K. W. S., & Qiao, M. S. (2021). AI Literacy: Definition, Teaching, Evaluation and Ethical Issues. *Proceedings of the Association for Information Science and Technology, 58*(1), 504–509. DOI: 10.1002/pra2.487

O'Neil, C. (2016). *Weapons of math destruction: How big data increases inequality and threatens democracy.* Crown Publishing Group.

OECD. (2019). *Equity in education: Breaking down barriers to social mobility.* OECD Publishing. DOI: 10.1787/9789264073234-

OECD. (2024). *Education Policy Outlook 2024: Reshaping Teaching into a Thriving Profession from ABCs to AI.* OECD Publishing. DOI: 10.1787/dd5140e4-

Oliver, M. (1996). *Understanding disability: From theory to practice*. Macmillan. DOI: 10.1007/978-1-349-24269-6

Rawls, J. (1971). *A theory of justice*. Harvard University Press. DOI: 10.4159/9780674042605

Sakelariou, M. (2022). *Synchronous and Asynchronous Distance Teaching and Learning*. Pedio. (in Greek)

Selwyn, N. (2016). *Education and technology: Key issues and debates*. Bloomsbury Publishing.

Sen, A. (1992). *Inequality reexamined*. Oxford University Press.

Tlili, A., Shehata, B., Adarkwah, M., Bozkurt, A., Hickey, D., Huang, R., & Agyemang, B. (2023). What if the devil is my guardian angel: ChatGPT as a case study of using chatbots in education. *Smart Learning Environments*, *10*(1), 15. DOI: 10.1186/s40561-023-00237-x

Tomlinson, C. A. (2014). *The differentiated classroom: Responding to the needs of all learners* (2nd ed.). ASCD. https://rutamaestra.santillana.com.co/wp-content/uploads/2020/01/The-Differentiated-Classroom-Responding-to-the-Needs.pdf

UNESCO. (1994). *The Salamanca statement and framework for action on special needs education*. UNESCO. https://unesdoc.unesco.org/

UNESCO. (2017). *A guide for ensuring inclusion and equity in education*. UNESCO. https://www.unesco.org/en/articles/guide-ensuring-inclusion-and-equity-education-0

UNESCO. (2019). *Artificial intelligence in education: Challenges and opportunities for sustainable development*. UNESCO. https://unesdoc.unesco.org/ark:/48223/pf0000366994

UNESCO. (2021). *AI and education: Guidance for policy-makers. UNESCO*. https://unesdoc.unesco.org/ark:/48223/pf0000376709

UNESCO. (2023). *Guidance for generative AI in education and research*. UNESCO. https://unesdoc.unesco.org/ark:/48223/pf0000386693

United Nations. (2006). *Convention on the rights of persons with disabilities*. https://www.un.org/disabilities/documents/convention/convoptprot-e.pdf

Van Dijk, J. (2020). *The digital divide*. Polity Press., DOI: 10.1002/asi.24355

Varsik, S., & Vosberg, L. (2024). *The potential impact of Artificial Intelligence on equity and inclusion in education* (OECD Artificial Intelligence Papers, No. 23). OECD Publishing. https://doi.org/DOI: 10.1787/dee339a8-en

Villar-Onrubia, D., Cachia, R., Rietz, C., Feltrero, R., Niemi, H., Hallissy, M., Reuter, R., Sánchez-Prieto, J. C., Vuorikari, R., & Punie, Y. (2025). *Generative artificial intelligence in secondary education: Uses and perceptions from the perspective of early adopters across five European countries*. Publications Office of the European Union., DOI: 10.2760/8636621

Vygotsky, L. S. (1978). *Mind in society: The development of higher psychological processes*. Harvard University Press., DOI: 10.2307/j.ctvjf9vz4

Williamson, B. (2017). *Big data in education: The digital future of learning, policy and practice*. SAGE Publications. DOI: 10.4135/9781529714920

Williamson, B., & Eynon, R. (2020). Historical threads, missing links, and future directions in AI in education. *Learning, Media and Technology*, *45*(3), 223–235. DOI: 10.1080/17439884.2020.1798995

Yan, L., Greiff, S., Teuber, Z., & Gašević, D. (2024). Promises and challenges of generative artificial intelligence for human learning. *Nature Human Behaviour*, *8*(10), 1839–1850. DOI: 10.1038/s41562-024-02004-5 PMID: 39438686

Zimmerman, B. J. (2002). Becoming a self-regulated learner: An overview. *Theory into Practice*, *41*(2), 64–70. DOI: 10.1207/s15430421tip4102_2

Zoniou-Sideri, A. (2011). *Education and inclusion: Theory and practice*. Pedio. (in Greek)

KEY TERMS AND DEFINITIONS

AI Literacy: AI literacy is the knowledge, skills, and critical understanding required to use, evaluate, and make informed decisions about Artificial Intelligence in educational contexts.

Algorithmic Bias: Algorithmic bias refers to systematic and unfair outcomes produced by AI systems as a result of biased data, design assumptions, or computational processes that disadvantage particular individuals or groups.

Artificial Intelligence: Artificial Intelligence refers to computational systems that analyze data, recognize patterns, and generate predictions or content in ways that support educational decision-making and learning processes.

Generative Artificial Intelligence: Generative Artificial Intelligence refers to AI systems capable of producing original text, images, or other content through large language models and related machine learning techniques, enabling interactive and personalised educational support.

Inclusive Education: Inclusive education is an educational approach that seeks to ensure equitable participation and meaningful learning opportunities for all learners by recognizing and responding to learner diversity.

Chapter 7

Educational Change in AI–Supported Practices for Specific Learning Disorders in Primary Education:

From Assistive Tools to Generative AI

Çiğdem Cesur
http://orcid.org/0000-0002-0793-2340
Çanakkale Onsekiz Mart University, Turkey

Mustafa Yunus Eryaman
http://orcid.org/0000-0002-4214-1202
Çanakkale Onsekiz Mart University, Turkey

ABSTRACT

While considering the use of artificial intelligence (AI) to help students with specific learning difficulties in primary education, this chapter further discusses the various forms of SLDs, such as dyslexia, dyscalculia and dysgraphia, the evolution of AI from assistive technology to machine learning-based adaptive systems and finally, to recent generative AI (GenAI) tools. The narrative literature review in this chapter examines how advancements in technology have influenced teaching methodologies, the role of teachers and how students experience learning. This chapter also places emphasis on AI's impact on accessibility, customisation, and changes to instructional methods. Other ethical concerns regarding AI are discussed, such as privacy of data,

DOI: 10.4018/979-8-3373-9169-4.ch007

bias and fairness of access. A structure for understanding the opportunities and barriers associated with the implementation of AI into inclusive primary education has been developed through the idea of AI as a means for educational change.

1. INTRODUCTION

Why SLD in Primary Education Matters

The primary school years are a major period of growth in terms of both cognitive and academic skills and should focus on developing critical literacy and numeracy skills (Winarno et al., 2024). Fast intervention is critical to providing children who experience learning disorders, including dyslexia, dyscalculia, etc. (Grigorenko et al., 2019). If children with learning disorders have reading, writing and/or math difficulties with their learning, and these issues are not treated as soon as they manifest, it may create significant barriers to their long-term academic success. Research confirms that early support in primary education is necessary to close the learning gap, improve student performance, and create a strong foundation of self-esteem and motivation to learn (Bailey et al., 2018). Recent systematic review evidence suggests that AI-based interventions may support academic and cognitive outcomes for students with learning disorders, but the evidence remains preliminary and requires more rigorous, long-term, classroom-based validation (Paglialunga & Melogno, 2025). Therefore, during this period, it is important to ensure that we are providing effective support for all students who require it to ensure all students have equal opportunities to access an equitable and inclusive education.

Why AI is an Educational Change Driver in Special Education

Traditionally, education has always been an evolving field that is currently experiencing a dramatic shift due to the advent of Artificial Intelligence (AI). One of the key differences between AI-enabled instructional resources and those used traditionally (such as printed textbooks/audio-visuals) is that AI-enabled instructional resources are created in real-time with immediate and highly adaptive feedback based on how each student interacts with them (Hariyanto et al., 2025).

This capability to understand and modify content instantaneously has given teachers the ability to interpret data on their students' achievement and then immediately adjust instructional materials to fit the needs of each individual student, as well as providing instant feedback on students' learning (Christodoulou & Angeli, 2022). Therefore, when teachers use AI to modify instruction, they are providing a significant benefit to students with specific learning disorders (SLDs) by addressing many of the barriers these students will experience (Daher, 2025). AI is a very powerful disruptive innovation, and thus it will also be an agent of change within the field of education. For instance, the introduction of AI into classrooms will radically alter the way that instruction is delivered to students, how student learning is assessed, and how teachers' interactions with students are structured. In addition, by providing students with individualized instruction, enhancing access for all students, and providing students with opportunities for participation in special education across the board; AI will build momentum for the systematic use of inclusive and learner-centered approaches to education.

Scope of the Review

This chapter examines the use of AI in primary education for students with SLDs, with a particular focus on dyslexia, dyscalculia, and dysgraphia. These three SLDs create persistent difficulties in reading, writing, and mathematical processing, and they require early and sustained support within inclusive education systems (American Psychiatric Association, 2013). The primary school years are especially important because foundational literacy and numeracy skills are developed during this period. Although research on AI and SLDs is still limited, the field is gradually expanding. Current studies appear to be more concentrated on dyslexia, particularly in relation to early screening and detection. For example, AI-based dyslexia research has examined eye-tracking data, reading patterns, and linguistic features as possible indicators of dyslexia (Rello & Ballesteros, 2015). In dysgraphia, researchers have explored handwriting analysis and machine learning (ML) algorithms to identify fine motor and writing-related difficulties, although school-based and non-experimental research remains relatively limited (Drotár & Dobeš, 2020). Compared with dyslexia, research on AI-supported practices for dyscalculia appears less extensive, suggesting an imbalance in the current evidence base between literacy-related and numeracy-related SLDs.

Across these areas, AI-supported practices can be grouped into several overlapping functions: screening and identification, intervention and tutoring, accessibility and accommodation, assessment and feedback, and teacher support. Earlier technologies, such as text-to-speech and speech-to-text tools, mainly focused on improving access to learning materials, while newer AI systems offer more advanced forms of personalization and support (Holmes et al., 2019; Luckin et al., 2016). More recently, generative AI (GenAI) and large language models (LLMs) have attracted attention because they can generate explanations, support writing, simplify texts, and provide interactive scaffolding through chat-like interfaces. These tools may offer flexible language-based support for students with SLDs, but empirical evidence on their use in authentic primary classrooms is still developing (Kasneci et al., 2023).

The existing literature also points to important methodological, pedagogical, and ethical limitations. Many studies have been conducted in controlled or experimental settings rather than in real primary classrooms, and sample sizes are often small. There is also a lack of longitudinal research examining the sustained effects of AI-supported interventions over time. In addition, the growing use of AI in education raises concerns about data privacy, algorithmic bias, transparency, equity, and access, especially in policy-oriented discussions (UNESCO, 2023). Therefore, while AI-supported practices hold promise for students with SLDs, their effectiveness, scalability, and ethical use in inclusive primary education require further critical examination.

Review Orientation and Analytical Lens

This chapter is designed as a narrative literature review that synthesizes selected studies, reviews, and policy-oriented sources on AI-supported practices for students with SLDs in primary education. Rather than treating AI tools as isolated technological products, the review interprets them through an educational change lens. This lens focuses on three interrelated dimensions: the historical evolution of AI-supported practices, the pedagogical functions of AI across dyslexia, dyscalculia, and dysgraphia, and the implications of these practices for classroom routines, teacher roles, inclusion, professional development, and ethical governance. Accordingly, the chapter does not aim to provide a systematic review or meta-analysis; instead, it offers a critical and integrative discussion of how AI-supported practices have shifted from access-oriented assistive technologies to adaptive and generative systems that may reshape teaching and learning in inclusive primary education.

The chapter's main contribution lies in bringing together the three major SLD areas—dyslexia, dyscalculia, and dysgraphia—within a single change-oriented synthesis, showing not only what AI tools are used for, but also how their educational purposes, risks, and implications have changed over time.

2. EVOLUTION OVER TIME: FROM ASSISTIVE TOOLS TO GENAI/LLMS

Assistive Technology Phase (Access and Accommodation Focus)

The first stage of AI incorporation into special education has been characterized by the development of assistive technology solutions to expand access to learning resources (Torres et al., 2023). Examples of these types of tools include text-to-speech and speech-to-text programs, along with basic spell-checking and grammar assistance software. All of these tools were initially developed with the purpose of lessening the barriers experienced by the student populations with SLD by providing different means of gaining and producing information through non-standard means (Yenduri et al., 2023). In this period, technology primarily served as supporting rather than instructive technologies; therefore, these tools did not provide specific support to the learner to meet their individual needs in terms of providing them with personalized guidance (Coflan & Kaye, 2020). Instead, the function of these tools, at this point in time, served only to provide a means for these students to access traditional educational programmes through accommodation. While such technologies increased access to learning opportunities, the extent to which they actually contributed to the development of higher-order cognitive processes was very limited.

Machine Learning and Adaptive Systems Phase

Phase two is a major development in the use of ML and adaptive learning systems (Animashaun et al., 2024). Unlike previous assistive technology tools, ML and adaptive systems can use large volumes of learner data and process it for patterns, prediction of potential learner difficulties and adjustment of the instruction (Schmucker, 2024). In this phase, AI was beginning to be used to help screen and diagnose educational conditions, such as dyslexia and dyscalculia for example (Adams et al., 2022). At the same time, intelligent tutoring systems were being developed to provide individualised and personalised learning paths as well as real-time feedback (Meenakshi, 2024). These systems could adjust the amount of difficulty for tasks, provide support for targeted practice and support the learning path of each student (Fitas, 2025). This movement indicates a move from passive assistance to active instruction. AI systems are now more interactive as well as a predominant part in the learning process versus simply providing an avenue for access.

Generative AI and Large Language Models Phase

The recent phase can be referred to as 'the development and implementation of GenAI and LLMs for enhanced ways to provide language-based learning support.' These systems can produce text; provide explanations or descriptions of various concepts; help facilitate the completion of a writing activity; and provide interactive communication between the learner and the system. GenAI also enables a more robust form of scaffolding (Jin et al., 2024) than what was previously available for SLD when compared to earlier technologies (Yan et al., 2024) through its ability to simplify complex written material, offer step-by-step explanations, and assist students with organizing the structure of their writing. By providing this ability for interaction to students, GenAI provides a much greater degree of flexibility and responsiveness than earlier technology solutions. While this phase also presents new challenges; it has created an awareness of additional concerns surrounding data security and privacy; algorithmic bias; the accuracy of generated content, and the age-appropriate use of GenAI (Melzer et al., 2025). Therefore, when determining the use of GenAI within an educational context, it is essential to not only consider the educational advantages of using GenAI, but also to adhere to the principles of ethical and governance requirements.

Key Transformation Across Phases

Throughout the three phases of development for AI within an educational context, a gradual change in terms of the integration of AI can be seen. Initially, AI served only as a supplemental layer to help individuals in learning experience success; specifically, it provided them with increased access to educational content by assisting with doing so (Almulla & Ali, 2024). These forms of technology supported the ability to learn through accommodation but did not change the core structure of an instructional experience or what was being taught or learned (Amado-Salvatierra et al., 2023). As a result, the relationship between technology and pedagogy was primarily outside each other because technology was acting as a support mechanism instead of transforming existing pedagogical practices. The introduction of ML and adaptive learning systems changed the way that this function was performed as well as how it affects people through learning experiences (Hariyanto et al., 2025). AI also began to shift from static assistance toward dynamic, data-informed support that could improve performance, reduce errors, and tailor instructional content to individual student needs (Hariyanto et al., 2025). Thus, in this phase of AI's evolution within education, it transitioned from using accommodation methods to personalization methods because the goal was more than just providing access but also optimizing learning paths (Wu & Yu, 2024). In this phase of AI's development within education, it began to have an independent role in how instructional delivery occurred as well as how instructional content was sequenced and reinforced (Arya & Verma, 2024). There has been another revolution in the development of GenAI with the introduction of interactivity, flexibility, and response capabilities (Tu et al., 2025). Generative tools differ from previous systems by having the ability to create conversations, provide explanations, and carry out higher-order cognitive processing (e.g., writing, summarizing, solving problems) (Leon, 2026). In the case of students with SLDs, new forms of scaffolding have emerged that allow learning support to be fluid and adaptive to the learner and instruction in a constantly changing environment (Tonga, 2025). This will result in increasing alignment between the needs of learners and the instructional response to those needs (Nickl et al., 2024).

These changes also represent a shift in how technology and pedagogy are thought of together (Anaroua et al., 2025). Technology is no longer an "add-on" to support learning; rather, it is now viewed as part of the learning process, integrated into the learning environment (Creely & Carabott, 2025). This has significant implications regarding how teaching and learning are viewed within an inclusive education context (Melo-López et al., 2025). The redesigned learning experience provided by AI-enhanced environments is aimed at promoting participation, independence, and meaningful engagement of all learners, rather than solely providing compensation for deficits (Porayska-Pomsta, 2023).

3. AI FUNCTIONS ACROSS DYSLEXIA, DYSCALCULIA AND DYSGRAPHIA

Dyslexia

Yuzaidey et al. (2018) describe dyslexia as 'a neurobiological impairment that primarily affects reading ability' (p. 311). According to Jan and Khan (2023), EEG (electroencephalogram) signals used in brain-based studies can detect brain activity and connectivity associated with dyslexia. Accordingly, dyslexia is a type of SLD, and reported prevalence estimates generally range between 5% and 10%, depending on assessments and studies conducted (Knight, 2018; Siegel, 2006). It has been stated that the inclusion of AI tools in education effectively supports dyslexic students pedagogically. Accordingly, from this section onwards, under the main headings of dyslexia, dyscalculia, and dysgraphia learning disorders, the roles of AI in screening and identification processes and its effectiveness in intervention and special education are discussed. Furthermore, it evaluates how AI tools facilitate adaptation and accessibility, transform assessment and feedback mechanisms, and influence educators in a supportive role through special teacher support systems.

The rapid changes and advancements in technology, and consequently in AI, have led to a rapid increase in applications for students with SLDs, such as dyslexia. Moreover as stated by Yap et al. (2025), it is particularly difficult for teachers to identify students struggling with these neurobiological issues, and providing them with customized lesson content and materials to achieve learning outcomes will not be very effective in a traditional teaching environment that demands a curriculum that needs to be kept up with in this rapidly evolving age of AI.

Considering the identification function, it is stated that if diagnosis is delayed, adverse effects may be observed, but early diagnosis can protect students from these adverse effects, improve their quality of life, and prevent problems such as low self-esteem (Wajuihian & Naidoo, 2012). A method called convolutional neural networks

(CNNs) is very useful in early diagnosis of this SLD and in personalized education processes. CNNs are frequently used to extract features from medical images. These models are more useful for early diagnosis and identifying specific patterns than for treatment purposes. As this study by Alkhurayyif and Sait (2024) shows, it can be said that this is an AI-assisted technique used to analyze data such as MRI scans and EEG signals in the detection of dyslexia. According to Usman et al. (2021), in a recent and comprehensive review of the applications of AI to identify dyslexia, it was also mentioned that these detections were made not only with neurological data but also with different data types used to train AI algorithms, such as facial videos or images, reading test errors, test scores, and eye-tracking.

After dyslexia identification, appropriate AI functions can be used to intervene and provide specific tutoring. Dabaghi et al. (2026) noted that recent developments in AI, ML, natural language processing, and intelligent tutoring systems have increasingly shaped teaching and learning through adaptive feedback, personalized content, and data-informed instructional support. Prior to 2018, AI used for dyslexia was limited to text-to-speech or speech-to-text systems, which offered valuable contributions to reading comprehension and writing skills (MacArthur, 2009). However, recent developments, particularly after 2024, have shifted the focus to 'personalized tutoring systems' and have begun to assist in creating personalized learning materials. Botchu et al. (2024) discuss several ways in which ChatGPT may support individuals with dyslexia, particularly in reading and writing-related tasks. The tool may provide individualized language support, assist with idea generation, reduce fear of criticism through a non-judgmental interaction space, and offer flexible support beyond the limits of time and place. These affordances suggest that GenAI may contribute not only to academic support but also to confidence, participation, and perceived autonomy. However, such claims should be interpreted cautiously, as the practical use of GenAI with primary-aged dyslexic learners still requires stronger empirical validation and careful adult supervision.

Beyond direct intervention and special instruction for dyslexic individuals, AI also possesses adaptation and accessibility functions. It provides accessibility and adaptation to students by minimizing or eliminating difficulties or limitations in learning environments. For example, in the 'Let AI Read First' study by Zhao et al. (2025), having the AI tool read the text first relieved the cognitive load on the dyslexic student and increased their participation. Another study by Goodman et al. (2024) that reduces cognitive load is 'LaMPOST (prototype email writing interface)', where AI performs complex tasks. It is a study on the accessibility function of AI, designed to make drafting, organizing ideas, and ultimately writing emails more helpful for dyslexic individuals.

As indicated in a recent study, when considering the feedback and evaluation function, AI can provide comprehensive assessments for dyslexic students, going beyond relying solely on verbal or written data, by analyzing the student's symptoms both individually and in combination (Rokade et al., 2024). Alternatively, in studies conducted for university students, it allows them to break free from the limitations of the traditional lecture and examination environment (Aremu et al., 2025). Regardless of concerns about AI replacing teachers in schools, AI-based tools, models, or methods are proving very useful for teachers, especially in the case of SLDs requiring special attention, as they help in identification, monitoring student progress, saving time, simplifying learning, and individualizing (Yap et al., 2025).

Overall, the dyslexia literature suggests that AI-supported practices have moved from basic reading and writing accommodations toward more sophisticated screening, text-processing, and generative language support. However, much of the evidence remains concentrated on detection accuracy, tool potential, and adult or controlled-use contexts rather than sustained implementation in primary classrooms. This indicates that dyslexia is the most visible SLD area in AI research, but the field still needs stronger classroom-based evidence on how these tools affect reading development, learner autonomy, and teacher decision-making.

Dyscalculia

As Giri et al. (2020) define, dyscalculia is a type of SLD where an individual has difficulty understanding mathematical concepts. Approximately 6% of people with learning disorders have dyscalculia. This learning disability, also known as numerical dyslexia or numerical blindness, is difficult to diagnose despite affecting only 6-7 percent of the population (Berch & Mazzocco, 2007). Neurodevelopmental disorders such as dyslexia, autism, ADHD, and dyscalculia are classified as a wide variety of childhood and adolescent mental disorders in the Diagnostic and Statistical Manual of Mental Disorders (DSM) and have received significant scientific attention over the past fifty years (Bhushan et al., 2024). The weaknesses caused by dyscalculia affect children's school performance first, then their career management and emotional state, as adequately functioning mathematical skills lead to academic success, easier daily life and well-being (El-Sabagh, 2021). In traditional learning environments, the abstract nature of mathematics instruction and the pressure to adhere to and keep up with the curriculum can create difficulties for students with dyscalculia. Recently, there has been an increase in studies aiming to bridge the gap and alleviate these challenges through AI.

As with dyslexia, early diagnosis is known to be a good step towards reducing the severity of dyscalculia. Using AI-driven applications that familiarize children with mathematical concepts has also been shown to be a good example of reducing the severity of this SLD in diagnosed children (Ferraz et al., 2016). A review study found that 6 out of 24 tests used external AI-based appearances. The majority of studies analyzed also used them to diagnose and screen for learning disorders.

The study, which indicates that dyscalculia can affect a student's academic progress and self-confidence, is an example of an application that uses an intelligent tutoring system targeting individualized learning for children aged 6-10. As a result of the evaluation of these students, they developed a web-based learning tool called Early Detection and Intervention for Insufficient Number Sense (Jadhav et al., 2025). It is clear that this is a valuable example of a study in terms of intervention and special education. Similarly, another study focusing on the function of tutoring and intervention targeted not only dyscalculia but also autism and other SLDs, examining how ChatGPT could help them. The CHAT (Child Helper and Assistant Tool) system was introduced to the GPT, and its interaction with children was simulated accordingly. The results showed that ChatGPT's approach to children was therapeutic and educational (Angeli, 2024).

One of the challenges for students with dyscalculia is the accessibility of abstract concepts like numbers or complex structures. Applications involving AI-assisted learning show that various studies have been conducted to overcome these challenges. By providing interactive support, offering encouraging feedback, and simplifying challenging stages for students with helpful tips, ChatGPT maximizes accessibility. Alternatively, using tools like CHAT enables students to understand abstract concepts in smaller groups and perform mathematical operations comfortably without feeling pressured.

Another study focuses on how AI can be used to accelerate the detection and assessment of SLDs such as dyslexia, ADHD, dyscalculia, and dyspraxia (motor coordination), and how reliable the results will be. Indeed, ML has been shown to provide much faster and more consistent results compared to classical manual assessments. Particularly in dyscalculia, the study focuses on assessments of processing, arithmetic, and numerical reasoning abilities (Dhar et al., 2025). Regarding the feedback function, Jadhav et al. (2025) in the same study, found that AI has been process- and development-oriented in overcoming the difficulties in number sense in dyscalculia patients, rather than focusing directly on the outcome. This is a very valuable step from a developmental perspective.

Compared with dyslexia, the dyscalculia literature appears more limited and more fragmented. Existing studies show promise in early screening, adaptive mathematics support, and number-sense interventions, but the evidence base is still developing. The educational significance of AI in dyscalculia lies less in replacing mathematics instruction and more in supporting diagnostic teaching, step-by-step feedback, and the concretization of abstract numerical concepts. Future studies need to examine whether these benefits are sustained in real primary classrooms and how teachers interpret AI-generated learning data.

Dysgraphia

Dysgraphia, (Kunhoth et al., 2024; Rangasrinivasan et al., 2025) is one of the least diagnosed disorders compared to other SLDs. It significantly impacts a child's academic performance and severely damages their self-confidence and self-esteem (McCloskey & Rapp, 2017). It is estimated that between 5 and 20 percent of school-aged children show signs of dysgraphia (Zolna et al., 2019). And as with other SLDs, children with dysgraphia experience impacts on their academic performance and emotional well-being (Prasanthi & Sushma, 2025).

The traditional method of detecting dysgraphia using various screening tests remains. However, this method has limitations because the meticulous work of those performing the assessment is extremely time-consuming. Early diagnosis and interventions are crucial for the child's development (Asselborn et al., 2018). Weraduwa et al. (2024) further demonstrated that ML models provide a solid foundation for the early detection of dysgraphia learning disability compared to other classical methods. Additionally, another scope review study noted the accuracy and speed of detections made using AI models, specifically CNNs and Support Vector Machines (SVMs), compared to traditional results (Fallah et al., 2025). In another study, a prototype AI-powered application was developed and designed specifically to assist students with dyscalculia and dysgraphia. This application helped these students by detecting and correcting errors in real time. It provided immediate feedback on both spelling and grammar, assisting children within the scope of intervention and special education functions (Prasanthi & Sushma, 2025). In another study, an experimental approach was taken to help dysgraphia children aged 8-10 years old achieve 'coherence' in their writing and improve their writing skills using ChatGPT, and the potential it can offer to their individual learning was clearly demonstrated (Gharaibeh et al., 2025).

For students to continue with the curriculum without being hindered by writing difficulties, the accessibility function of AI is crucial. Just as with other SLDs, features like spelling correction and grammar error detection are useful in reducing the cognitive burden on students with writing difficulties. Beyond primary and secondary education, studies conducted at the aforementioned universities also demonstrate that AI-powered tools for spelling error detection and accessibility are very beneficial for individuals with dysgraphia (Aremu et al., 2025). Another review study noted that technology-assisted dysgraphia assessment and feedback is a promising, accessible, and skills-developing method for the future (Han & Wang, 2025). Another review study examined how current methods for screening for dysgraphia and dyslexia could use AI to detect handwriting while using digital tablets and smart pens, thereby creating early warning signs for these conditions (Rangasrinivasan et al., 2025). In terms of the benefits it provides to teachers, AI fills a significant gap in detection, intervention, curriculum regulation, and process management. When the cause of a student's dysgraphia is identified, AI technology provides clarity and ease of understanding for the family, school administration, and teacher. This, in turn, largely supports the teacher's decision-making process.

The dysgraphia literature highlights the value of AI for handwriting analysis, spelling support, writing feedback, and composition assistance. Nevertheless, a distinction should be made between tools that detect dysgraphia-related features and tools that directly improve students' writing development. While ML models may show promising accuracy in controlled settings, their classroom value depends on whether they help teachers provide timely support and whether they strengthen students' written expression without creating overdependence on automated assistance.

4. OUTCOMES REPORTED AND EVIDENCE STRENGTH

Achievement Outcomes

When examining three types of SLDs dyslexia, dyscalculia, and dysgraphia and considering them from a holistic perspective, particularly targeting children aged 6-10, AI-supported education has emerged as crucial for cognitive, affective, and psychomotor development. Studies show that it acts as an early warning or early diagnosis system, preventing students from feeling deficient or behind, thus providing affective benefits (Alkhurayyif & Sait, 2024; Wajuihian & Naidoo, 2012). Early diagnosis also supports students who might otherwise experience academic deficiencies or fall behind, and its accessibility helps prevent them from falling further behind. This also benefits cognitive development (Bailey et al., 2018; Grigorenko et al., 2019). Finally, especially in tasks requiring psychomotor skills such as writing and calculation, it helps reduce the cognitive load on students with SLDs by breaking down tasks into smaller parts, making them easier to perform (Goodman et al., 2024; Zhao et al., 2025). As a result, improvements in abilities, increased motivation, and enhanced self-esteem and self-confidence have been observed in students' achievement outcomes (Botchu et al., 2024; Jadhav et al., 2025).

Access and Participation

In the context of independence and interaction, considering the access and participation of students with dyslexia, dyscalculia, and dysgraphia in AI-assisted learning, the aforementioned studies aim to enable students to individualize and autonomously manage their academic processes. These studies encompass both primary, secondary, and university students. For example, in a university study in

Nigeria, AI was used as a tool to help students improve their writing skills so that they would not struggle when taking institutional exams (Aremu et al., 2025). This contributed to their academic progress without assistance despite their learning disorders. Similarly, in preschool and primary school students, systems and applications like Let AI Read First or disMAT allow children with dyslexia and dyscalculia to overcome their reading difficulties and experience a sense of accomplishment in understanding mathematical concepts (Jadhav et al., 2025; Zhao et al., 2025). In terms of participation, gamification in AI-assisted applications increases the participation of young students, and this increase is parallel to their motivation. The personalization option, due to its inclusive nature, provides the learner with a unique journey, connecting them to the learning process.

Motivation and Affective Outcomes

This section synthesizes the student's motivation, emotional state, anxiety, and self-confidence. Studies show that when divided by age groups, individuals with dyslexia, dyscalculia, and dysgraphia have different expectations from AI-based learning. For example, elementary school students have mentioned that AI-supported gamified learning creates fun and excitement for them emotionally (Ouherrou et al., 2018). Problems such as hesitations while reading in class, mixing up letters while writing, or inability to concretize numbers while performing calculations have decreased with AI, and the fear of being judged has disappeared.

Among adolescent students using the CHAT system, expectations were primarily focused on being understood and accepted. In line with their age-appropriate expectations, these students were able to reduce their learning difficulties through this method. Furthermore, these children also showed increased success and a reduced sense of inadequacy. In young adults, this can be described as a solution to intellectual inadequacy, a subcategory within feelings of inadequacy. This support system, which increases their self-confidence, also contributes to their easier integration into professional environments. Regarding anxiety, since students with learning disorders experience increased anxiety levels in critical environments, the AI system's non-judgmental and safe environment helps reduce their fears (Botchu et al., 2024).

Strength of Evidence

Finally, this section also includes a synthesis on evidentiary strength and reliability. It addresses the methods and systems used in all these studies, their reliability and generalizability, and finally, their limitations and reliability issues. Regarding general design and methods, it is clear that the studies show diversity. Instead of focusing on a single test, they concentrate on technical and various details such as eye tracking, demographic data, handwriting duration, and waiting time. There is also diversity in terms of the models and algorithms of the AI systems used. For example, in addition to ML such as Support Vector Machines (SVM), image, signal-to-sensor (EEG), and CNNs models have also been used. Some ML and deep learning studies report high classification accuracy in controlled datasets, especially in dyslexia and dysgraphia screening studies using eye-tracking, handwriting, EEG, or related performance indicators. However, high accuracy in controlled or technical datasets should not be interpreted as direct evidence of classroom effectiveness. For educational purposes, the more important question is whether these systems improve identification, intervention planning, student participation, and long-term learning outcomes in authentic primary education settings (Rello & Ballesteros, 2015; Rangasrinivasan et al., 2025). In terms of evolving findings, whether models examining data in different languages demonstrate the same consistency is still under development. The high cost and difficulty in using brain-based detection devices like fMRI and EEG hinder their widespread adoption. Finally, regarding limitations and reliability issues in studies, the imbalance in the ratio between students without learning disorders and those coping with them can cause AI to ignore students with disorders during data input. Large sample sizes are necessary for generalizability; the small size of these groups in some studies makes this difficult. As mentioned, the high cost of materials used for tracking and diagnosis is also a limitation. And finally, it is ethically and morally important that data collected from students, especially younger age groups, is stored and shared using pseudonyms or similar methods.

5. EDUCATIONAL CHANGE IMPLICATIONS

The integration of AI into special education should be understood as a multidimensional process of educational change rather than as the simple adoption of digital tools. At the classroom level, AI may reshape feedback cycles, scaffolding practices, differentiated instruction, and opportunities for independent practice. At the teacher level, it may change professional responsibilities by requiring teachers to select appropriate tools, interpret AI-generated data, verify AI outputs, and make ethical decisions about use. At the system level, AI integration requires attention to infrastructure, data privacy, child protection, age-appropriate access, institutional readiness, and equity. These three levels—classroom practice, teacher professionalism, and system governance—provide the basis for discussing the practical implications of AI-supported practices for students with SLDs.

Changes in Teaching Routines and Inclusion Practices

In the course of time, the use of assistive and supportive tools in the education of students with SLDs has become more common thanks to the developments in the everyday technological tools, making this process more natural and not requiring specially designed equipment. Additional to these, with the appearance of AI and later GenAI, the shift from the classical perspective of assistive technologies to personalized, enhanced, and dynamic learning opportunities make it possible to create ways for empowering students with disorders and supporting their teachers (Harkins-Brown et al., 2025). Implementation of AI in education differs depending on the instructional goals. According to review paper by Hopcan et al. (2023), it provides personalized learning environments, benefits for special education students, and assistance in administrative tasks and assessment of students. In terms of students with special needs, personalized learning opportunities improve quality of instruction and thus, more effective learning can be achieved. Similarly, in the systematic review written by Ulaş et al. (2025), regarding dyslexia, dysgraphia, dyscalculia, and other learning disorders, the types of applications are classified based on the studies conducted in 2015 – 2025, noting that the use AI and digital technologies could potentially provide individualized and attainable learning environments for students with LD. Acar et al. (2024) conducted a study on the barriers leading to language learning failure, specifically overcrowded classrooms and outdated teaching practices are mentioned. In these cases, with the help of AI and GenAI tools, Intelligent Tutoring Systems and personalized learning environments can be utilized.

Furthermore, students with SLDs encounter some problems throughout their education in academic and socio-emotional domains, which can be low academic performance and levels of motivation, unfair treatment, and low confidence and interest in their classes as another systematic review reveals (Papalexandratou et al., 2024). On the other hand, their study demonstrates that with the implementation of AI and appropriate tools in the students' instructional routines could improve these students' educational experiences, assisting with their learning and academic performance; AI use could reduce difficulties and inequalities students confront while contributing to their success via providing equal circumstances. In line with Sustainable Development Goal 4, inclusive education requires equal access to education and training opportunities for vulnerable groups, including persons with disabilities and children in vulnerable situations (United Nations, 2020). In these diverse classes it is significant to have positive attitudes towards differences, knowing how to display care, and teachers possessing self-efficacy beliefs when teaching to their students creates appropriate learning environment and respect in differences (Kırcalı & Cesur, 2024).

Teacher Roles and Professional Development Needs

Roles of teachers have undergone changes over time, especially with the emergence and development of digital technologies, AI, and GenAI. While these abovementioned technologies modify and support teaching routines, they also bring some new challenges and responsibilities to teachers' job descriptions. In the education of students with SLDs, there are different steps than general education. The diagnosis of disability and creating personalized teaching routines, as well as other instructional responsibilities, could be demanding for teachers; however, especially AI has found to be transformational and, it offers solutions to mentioned challenges (Harkins-Brown et al., 2025; Yap et al., 2025).

Furthermore, acknowledging the technologies and AI are evolving day by day, professional development of teachers and schools plays a vital role in applying special education related instructional strategies. The elements limiting AI applications include AI knowledge of teachers is mainly defined as intermediate, infrastructural insufficiency, and the use of software, emphasizing the need for teacher training to improve their competencies, technical assistance, and transformation in systems (Ulaş et al., 2025). To fulfill the professional development needs of the teachers, MOOCs can be beneficial due to their accessibility regardless of the sources of the region they are working in (Uygun et al., 2026).

Governance/Ethics

While implementing these technologies and AI, it is crucial to focus on governance and ethical considerations to ensure the safety of learners. It is important to take care of their privacy, use age-appropriate content and unbiased tools, and provide equal opportunities for all of the students in the educational environments. Firstly, in special education contexts students' personal data can be utilized containing information regarding disabilities, assessment outcomes, and behaviors; accordingly, the data should be anonymized, and parents should be informed before the process (Harkins-Brown et al., 2025). Secondly, *Guidance for Generative AI in Education and Research* published by UNESCO (2023) informs about Regulations on GenAI. In the policy document it is stated that most GenAI tools are chiefly designed for grown-ups, meaning that they may have the risk of including inappropriate and manipulative content for children. For this reason, regulations require age thresholds (e.g., 13 or 16 years of age) and parental monitoring for independent use in primary education.

Thirdly, the LLMs used in the training of AI may include biases, stereotypes, and under-representation of population's characteristics; therefore, using biased tools may result in affecting students' path of learning adversely (Harkins-Brown et al., 2025).

Moreover, competent teachers not only in AI but also in interculturality strengthen their teaching practices enabling them to recognize their biases and stereotypical knowledge (Mikhailova & Cesur, 2025). Last but not least, equal access to these AI and GenAI tools should be mentioned in this section. As stated earlier, the data is required to train the models, and most of them are accessible to the companies managed by a few countries located in the Global North which brings them wealth in terms of data, and thus positioning the Global South countries in a "data poverty" condition (Marwala, 2023).

Responsible implementation should follow a human-centred approach in which AI supports, rather than replaces, teacher judgement and inclusive pedagogical decision-making. In primary special education, this requires teacher supervision, parental awareness, careful data protection, and explicit safeguards against overreliance on automated recommendations.

6. GAPS AND FUTURE RESEARCH PRIORITIES

The gaps identified in the literature are not merely technical; they are pedagogical, methodological, and ethical. They concern not only whether AI systems can detect or support SLDs, but also whether these systems can be implemented safely, equitably, and meaningfully in real primary classrooms. Future research therefore needs to move beyond tool performance and examine classroom integration, teacher decision-making, learner autonomy, long-term outcomes, and the ethical conditions under which AI-supported practices can enhance inclusive education. Therefore, a research agenda needs to be prepared to ensure that these mentioned instructional practices could be implemented safely, efficiently, and equally in primary education settings. They can be grouped into four categories: under-researched groups and contexts, need for longitudinal and classroom-embedded studies, comparative effectiveness and cost/equity considerations, and responsible GenAI use.

The proposed research agenda should also move beyond the current dominance of dyslexia-related studies and more equitably address dyscalculia and dysgraphia, as these areas remain comparatively under-represented in the literature. Future studies should prioritize empirical research with primary school-aged children in authentic classroom settings rather than relying mainly on studies conducted with young adults in higher education contexts. Such a shift is necessary to generate ecologically valid evidence about how AI-supported tools function in real instructional environments. In addition, future research should examine the practical conditions required for responsible implementation, including infrastructural readiness, teachers' AI literacy, and the need for sustained professional development. Ethical research agendas should also give stronger attention to age-appropriate GenAI use in primary education, including clear regulations, strict age thresholds, parental monitoring, data protection, and teacher supervision. Future research should also examine how teachers' and preservice teachers' ethical AI literacy develops over time, since recent evidence suggests that functional AI competence does not necessarily translate into ethical awareness or responsible decision-making (Uygun, 2026). Finally, researchers should critically investigate the biases, stereotypes, and under-representation embedded in LLMs, since these limitations may adversely affect the learning pathways of vulnerable students with SLDs.

Under-Researched Groups and Contexts

When reviewing the existing literature related to using AI in educational context, the studies including students without learning disorders outnumber the studies including students with learning disorders. Additionally, the studies conducted with students with LDs generally take place in higher education contexts with young adults rather than primary school aged students. Another point in the current literature, dyslexia, is largely the topic of research related to learning disorders, meaning the other learning disorders should be emphasized more with respect to students having other comorbidities of LDs. Lastly, learners speaking multiple languages need to be incorporated in the newly conducted studies, as well.

Need For Longitudinal and Classroom-Embedded Studies

The need for classroom-embedded empirical studies with students with learning disorders in primary education is mentioned above. Furthermore, research focusing on real classroom settings with more students is essential for this area to develop due to small sample groups can be detected in the existing literature. On the other hand, this is significant not only because of the reflection of the atmosphere in the classroom, but also because of the generalizability of the studies.

Comparative Effectiveness and Cost/Equity Considerations

It is significant to consider the comparative effect of AI intervention and human based teaching practices and routines while examining the learning experiences of students with learning disorders. Whether AI tools or human interaction would be more effective in the classroom conditions should be delved into. Likewise, the cost of using latest technology in classroom settings could be higher than it is expected. Therefore, the cost-benefit ratio of these applications should be calculated by researchers and stakeholders of the educational systems.

Responsible GenAI Use Research Agendas

Technological advancements in this area encourage the use of GenAI with the students having learning disorders. However, this may lead to some ethical concerns detailed in the previous parts in the paper. Due to algorithmic bias against students with LDs and issues regarding privacy and security of these students, it is especially important to examine the responsible use of GenAI.

7. CONCLUSION

Summary of Evolution, Functions, Outcomes, and Change Implications

This chapter analyzed AI-supported practices for students with SLDs in primary education through an educational change lens. The review showed a shift from assistive tools that mainly provide access and accommodation, to ML systems that support screening and personalization, and finally to GenAI and LLMs that offer interactive scaffolding, writing support, and new ethical challenges.

Key Takeaways for Special Educators, Researchers, and Policy Stakeholders

On one hand, this transition brings various opportunities to students, teachers, and other stakeholders in its wake. On the other hand, some challenges can be faced while adopting these developments in the classrooms or other learning environments. Special educators and teachers need to be aware of the innovations and to be competent to apply these novelties. As the current literature in special education highlights, gaps remain in primary education, meaning it demonstrates the requirement of longitudinal, and classroom-embedded research. As for policy stakeholders, parents, teachers, and researchers, it is critical to work collaboratively in order to address ethical issues regarding the use of AI/ GenAI tools. As a conclusion, if these applications are implemented responsibly and securely by stakeholders in the educational environments, AI has the potential to ensure a good quality of education and applications to primary education students with learning disorders. The central issue, therefore, is not whether AI should enter primary special education, but under what pedagogical, ethical, and institutional conditions it can genuinely enhance access, participation, and learning for students with SLDs. Therefore, the future integration of AI and GenAI in primary special education should be guided not only by technological innovation but also by balanced research across dyslexia, dyscalculia, and dysgraphia, classroom-based empirical evidence, teacher professional development, infrastructural readiness, and strict ethical safeguards for young learners.

REFERENCES

Acar, S. C., Cesur, K., Mikhailova, T., & Akshulakova, B. (2024). A netnographic study on the reasons why people fail to learn English. *Participatory Educational Research, 11*(6), 134–151. DOI: 10.17275/per.24.83.11.6

Adams, C., Pente, P., Lemermeyer, G., Turville, J., & Rockwell, G. (2022). Artificial intelligence and teachers' new ethical obligations. *International Journal of Information Ethics, 31*(1). Advance online publication. DOI: 10.29173/irie483

Alkhurayyif, Y., & Sait, A. R. W. (2024). A review of artificial intelligence-based dyslexia detection techniques. *Diagnostics (Basel), 14*(21), 2362. Advance online publication. DOI: 10.3390/diagnostics14212362 PMID: 39518334

Almulla, M., & Ali, S. I. (2024). The changing educational landscape for sustainable online experiences: Implications of ChatGPT in Arab students' learning experience. *International Journal of Learning. Teaching and Educational Research, 23*(9), 285–302. DOI: 10.26803/ijlter.23.9.15

Amado-Salvatierra, H. R., Morales, M., & Hernández-Rizzardini, R. (2023). Combining human creativity and AI-based tools in the instructional design of MOOCs: Benefits and limitations. *2023 IEEE Learning with MOOCS (LWMOOCS)*, 1–5. DOI: 10.1109/LWMOOCS58322.2023.10306023

American Psychiatric Association. (2013). *Diagnostic and statistical manual of mental disorders* (5th ed.)., DOI: 10.1176/appi.books.9780890425596

Anaroua, F. I., Li, Q., Tang, Y., & Liu, H. P. (2025). AI-driven formative assessment and adaptive learning in data-science education: Evaluating an LLM-powered virtual teaching assistant. DOI: 10.48550/arxiv.2509.20369

Angeli, F. (2024). CHAT (Child Helper and Assistant Tool): An AI-based educational tool for supporting neurodiverse children with autism, dyscalculia, and DSA. *CEUR Workshop Proceedings, 3880*, Paper 18.

Animashaun, E. S., Familoni, B. T., & Onyebuchi, N. C.Enitan Shukurat AnimashaunBabajide Tolulope FamiloniNneamaka Chisom Onyebuchi. (2024). Advanced machine learning techniques for personalising technology education. *Computer Science & IT Research Journal, 5*(6), 1300–1315. DOI: 10.51594/csitrj.v5i6.1198

Aremu, E. S., Ojo, A., & Useghan, N. O. (2025). The role of artificial intelligence in managing handwriting and spelling difficulties among university students with perceived specific learning disabilities (PSLDs). *The Exceptional Child: Journal of National Association for Exceptional Children (NAEC), 25*(1), 12–21. https://naechildren.org

Arya, R., & Verma, A. (2024). Role of artificial intelligence in education. *International Journal of Advanced Research in Science. Tongxin Jishu, 4*(2), 589–594. DOI: 10.48175/IJARSCT-19461

Asselborn, T., Gargot, T., Kidziński, Ł., Johal, W., Cohen, D., Jolly, C., & Dillenbourg, P. (2018). Automated human-level diagnosis of dysgraphia using a consumer tablet. *npj. Digital Medicine, 1*(1), 42. DOI: 10.1038/s41746-018-0049-x PMID: 31304322

Bailey, D. H., Fuchs, L. S., Gilbert, J. K., Geary, D. C., & Fuchs, D. (2018). Prevention: Necessary but insufficient? A 2-year follow-up of an effective first-grade mathematics intervention. *Child Development, 91*(2), 382–396. DOI: 10.1111/cdev.13175 PMID: 30358181

Berch, D. B., & Mazzocco, M. M. M. (Eds.). (2007). *Why is math so hard? A view of mathematical learning disabilities from multiple perspectives*. Paul H. Brookes Publishing Co.

Bhushan, S., Arunkumar, S., Eisa, T. A. E., Nasser, M., Singh, A. K., & Kumar, P. (2024). AI-enhanced dyscalculia screening: A survey of methods and applications for children. *Diagnostics (Basel), 14*(13), 1441. DOI: 10.3390/diagnostics14131441 PMID: 39001330

Botchu, B., Iyengar, K. P., & Botchu, R. (2024). Can ChatGPT empower people with dyslexia? *Disability and Rehabilitation. Assistive Technology, 19*(5), 2131–2132. DOI: 10.1080/17483107.2023.2256805 PMID: 37697967

Christodoulou, A., & Angeli, C. (2022). Adaptive learning techniques for personalized educational software in developing teachers' technological pedagogical content knowledge. *Frontiers in Education, 7*, 789397. DOI: 10.3389/feduc.2022.789397

Coflan, C. M., & Kaye, T. (2020). *Using education technology to support learners with special educational needs and disabilities in low- and middle-income countries*. EdTech Hub. DOI: 10.53832/edtechhub.0021

Creely, E., & Carabott, K. (2025). Teaching and learning with AI: An integrated AI-oriented pedagogical model. *Australian Educational Researcher, 52*(6), 4633–4655. DOI: 10.1007/s13384-025-00913-6

Dabaghi, K., D'Urso, S., & Sciarrone, F. (2026). Artificial intelligence to help people with dyslexia in education: An interdisciplinary literature review. *International Journal of Artificial Intelligence in Education, 36*(1–2), 100012. Advance online publication. DOI: 10.1016/j.ijaied.2026.100012

Daher, R. F. (2025). Integrating AI literacy into teacher education: A critical perspective paper. *Discover Artificial Intelligence, 5*(1), 217. DOI: 10.1007/s44163-025-00475-7

Dhar, D., Rahman, A., Chowdhury, M., & Dipto, A. S. (2025). Dyslexia, ADHD, dyscalculia, and dyspraxia prediction in children using machine learning and explainable AI. *Proceedings of the 9th International Conference on Computational System and Information Technology for Sustainable Solutions (CSITSS)*, 1–6. DOI: 10.1109/CSITSS67709.2025.11294091

Drotár, P., & Dobeš, M. (2020). Dysgraphia detection through machine learning. *Scientific Reports, 10*(1), 21541. Advance online publication. DOI: 10.1038/s41598-020-78611-9 PMID: 33299092

El-Sabagh, H. (2021). Adaptive e-learning environment based on learning styles and its impact on development students' engagement. *International Journal of Educational Technology in Higher Education, 18*(1), 53. Advance online publication. DOI: 10.1186/s41239-021-00289-4

Fallah, A., ZandiyeVakili, Y., & Sajedi, H. (2025). AI-driven approaches for dysgraphia diagnosis using online and offline handwriting data: A comprehensive scoping review. *PLoS One, 20*(12), e0328722. Advance online publication. DOI: 10.1371/journal.pone.0328722 PMID: 41474692

Ferraz, F., Neves, J., Costa, A., & Vicente, H. (2016). An artificial intelligence approach to dyscalculia. In Kim, K., Wattanapongsakorn, N., & Joukov, N. (Eds.), *Mobile and wireless technologies 2016* (Vol. 391, pp. 221–230). Springer., DOI: 10.1007/978-981-10-1409-3_23

Fitas, R. (2025). Inclusive education with AI: Supporting special needs and tackling language barriers. *AI and Ethics, 5*(6), 5729–5757. Advance online publication. DOI: 10.1007/s43681-025-00824-3

Gharaibeh, M., Ayasrah, M. N., & Almulla, A. A. (2025). Supplemental role of ChatGPT in enhancing writing ability for children with dysgraphia in the Arabic language. *Education and Information Technologies, 30*(15), 21019–21039. DOI: 10.1007/s10639-025-13605-6

Giri, N., Saini, T., Bhole, K., Bhosale, A., Shetty, T., Subramanyam, A., & Shelke, S. (2020). Detection of dyscalculia using machine learning. In *2020 5th International Conference on Communication and Electronics Systems (ICCES)* (pp. 1–6). IEEE. DOI: 10.1109/ICCES48766.2020.9137871

Goodman, S. M., Buehler, E., Clary, P., Coenen, A., Donsbach, A., Horne, T. N., Lahav, M., MacDonald, R., Michaels, R. B., Narayanan, A., Pushkarna, M., Riley, J., Santana, A., Shi, L., Sweeney, R., Weaver, P., Yuan, A., & Morris, M. R. (2024). LaMPost: AI writing assistance for adults with dyslexia using large language models. *Communications of the ACM*, *67*(9), 80–89. DOI: 10.1145/3626952

Grigorenko, E. L., Compton, D. L., Fuchs, L. S., Wagner, R. K., Willcutt, E. G., & Fletcher, J. M. (2019). Understanding, educating, and supporting children with specific learning disabilities: 50 years of science and practice. *The American Psychologist*, *75*(1), 37–51. DOI: 10.1037/amp0000452 PMID: 31081650

Han, W., & Wang, T. (2025). From motor skills to digital solutions: Developmental dysgraphia interventions over two decades. *Children (Basel, Switzerland)*, *12*(5), 542. Advance online publication. DOI: 10.3390/children12050542 PMID: 40426721

Hariyanto, H., Kristianingsih, F. X. D., & Maharani, R. (2025). Artificial intelligence in adaptive education: A systematic review of techniques for personalized learning. *Discover Education*, *4*(1), 458. Advance online publication. DOI: 10.1007/s44217-025-00908-6

Harkins-Brown, A. R., Carling, L. Z., & Peloff, D. C. (2025). Artificial intelligence in special education. *Encyclopedia*, *5*(1), 11. Advance online publication. DOI: 10.3390/encyclopedia5010011

Holmes, W., Bialik, M., & Fadel, C. (2019). *Artificial intelligence in education: Promises and implications for teaching and learning*. Center for Curriculum Redesign.

Hopcan, S., Polat, E., Ozturk, M. E., & Ozturk, L. (2023). Artificial intelligence in special education: A systematic review. *Interactive Learning Environments*, *31*(10), 7335–7353. DOI: 10.1080/10494820.2022.2067186

Jadhav, D., Chettri, S. K., Tripathy, A. K., & Saikia, M. J. (2025). A technology-driven assistive learning tool and framework for personalized dyscalculia interventions. *European Journal of Investigation in Health, Psychology and Education*, *15*(5), 85. Advance online publication. DOI: 10.3390/ejihpe15050085 PMID: 40422314

Jan, T. G., & Khan, S. M. (2023). A systematic review of research dimensions towards dyslexia screening using machine learning. *Journal of The Institution of Engineers (India): Series B*, *104*(2), 465–478. DOI: 10.1007/s40031-023-00853-8

Jin, Y., Yang, K., Yan, L., Echeverría, V., Zhao, L., Milesi, M., Fan, J., Li, X., Gašević, D., & Martínez-Maldonado, R. (2024). Chatting with a learning analytics dashboard: The role of generative AI literacy on learner interaction. DOI: 10.48550/arxiv.2411.15597

Kasneci, E., Sessler, K., Küchemann, S., Bannert, M., Dementieva, D., Fischer, F., Gasser, U., Groh, G., Günnemann, S., Hüllermeier, E., Krusche, S., Kutyniok, G., Michaeli, T., Nerdel, C., Pfeffer, J., Poquet, O., Sailer, M., Schmidt, A., Seidel, T., & Kasneci, G. (2023). ChatGPT for good? On opportunities and challenges of large language models for education. *Learning and Individual Differences*, *103*, 102274. Advance online publication. DOI: 10.1016/j.lindif.2023.102274

Kırcalı, M., & Cesur, K. (2024). Development and validation of a cultural and linguistic diversity scale to measure pre-service EFL teachers' self-efficacy beliefs. *SAGE Open*, *14*(1), 21582440241236589. Advance online publication. DOI: 10.1177/21582440241236589

Knight, C. (2018). What is dyslexia? An exploration of the relationship between teachers' understandings of dyslexia and their training experiences. *Dyslexia (Chichester, England)*, *24*(3), 207–219. DOI: 10.1002/dys.1593 PMID: 30019501

Kunhoth, J., Al-Maadeed, S., Kunhoth, S., Akbari, Y., & Saleh, M. (2024). Automated systems for diagnosis of dysgraphia in children: A survey and novel framework. *International Journal on Document Analysis and Recognition*, *27*(3), 707–735. DOI: 10.1007/s10032-024-00464-z

Leon, M. (2026). Generative AI as a general-purpose technology: Foundations, applications, and labor market implications. *Big Data and Cognitive Computing*, *10*(3), 69. Advance online publication. DOI: 10.3390/bdcc10030069

Luckin, R., Holmes, W., Griffiths, M., & Forcier, L. B. (2016). *Intelligence unleashed: An argument for AI in education*. Pearson.

MacArthur, C. A. (2009). Reflections on research on writing and technology for struggling writers. *Learning Disabilities Research & Practice*, *24*(2), 93–103. DOI: 10.1111/j.1540-5826.2009.00283.x

Marwala, T. (2023, June 22). *Algorithm bias: Synthetic data should be an option of last resort when training AI systems*. United Nations University. https://unu.edu/article/algorithm-bias-synthetic-data-should-be-option-last-resort-when-training-ai-systems

McCloskey, M., & Rapp, B. (2017). *Developmental dysgraphia: Theoretical and clinical advances*. Routledge.

Meenakshi, M. (2024). Leveraging AI technologies for personalized learning support in dyslexic students. *International Journal for Research in Applied Science and Engineering Technology, 12*(12), 2192–2198. DOI: 10.22214/ijraset.2024.65734

Melo-López, V.-A., Basantes-Andrade, A., Gudiño-Mejía, C.-B., & Hernández-Martínez, E. (2025). The impact of artificial intelligence on inclusive education: A systematic review. *Education Sciences, 15*(5), 539. Advance online publication. DOI: 10.3390/educsci15050539

Melzer, S., Asselborn, T., & Möller, R. (2025). Generative AI for interactive learning in education. *Datenbank-Spektrum: Zeitschrift fur Datenbanktechnologie: Organ der Fachgruppe Datenbanken der Gesellschaft fur Informatik e.V, 25*(2), 87–93. Advance online publication. DOI: 10.1007/s13222-025-00507-7

Mikhailova, T., & Cesur, K. (2025). Enhancing global awareness and intercultural competence in English language teacher education. In Bafralı, G. (Ed.), *Challenges in teacher education* (pp. 235–266). IGI Global. DOI: 10.4018/979-8-3693-7342-2.ch008

Nickl, M., Sommerhoff, D., Radkowitsch, A., Huber, S., Bauer, E., Ufer, S., Plass, J. L., & Seidel, T. (2024). Effects of real-time adaptivity of scaffolding. *Learning and Instruction, 94*, 101994. DOI: 10.1016/j.learninstruc.2024.101994

Ouherrou, N., Benmarrakchi, F., Elhammoumi, O., & El Kafi, J. (2018). A heuristic evaluation of an educational game for children with dyslexia. *2018 5th International Federation of Computer Science (CIST)*, 386–391. DOI: 10.1109/CIST.2018.8596393

Paglialunga, A., & Melogno, S. (2025). The effectiveness of artificial intelligence-based interventions for students with learning disabilities: A systematic review. *Brain Sciences, 15*(8), 806. Advance online publication. DOI: 10.3390/brainsci15080806 PMID: 40867139

Papalexandratou, P., Stathopoulou, A., & Skanavis, C. (2024). The use of artificial intelligence in the education of students with learning disabilities. *Global Journal of Engineering and Technology Advances, 21*(3), 229–240. DOI: 10.30574/gjeta.2024.21.3.0223

Porayska-Pomsta, K. (2023). A manifesto for a proactively responsible AI in education. *International Journal of Artificial Intelligence in Education, 34*(1), 73–86. DOI: 10.1007/s40593-023-00346-1

Prasanthi, C. L., & Sushma, G. (2025). AI-based assistive system for correcting dysgraphia and dyscalculia in children. *2025 International Conference on Electrical, Communication and Computer Engineering (ICECCE)*, 1–6. DOI: 10.1109/ICECCE67514.2025.11257986

Rangasrinivasan, S., Sumi Suresh, M. S., Olszewski, A., Setlur, S., Jayaraman, B., & Govindaraju, V. (2025). AI-enhanced child handwriting analysis: A framework for the early screening of dyslexia and dysgraphia. *SN Computer Science*, *6*(5), 399. Advance online publication. DOI: 10.1007/s42979-025-03927-0

Rello, L., & Ballesteros, M. (2015). Detecting readers with dyslexia using machine learning with eye tracking measures. *Proceedings of the 12th Web for All Conference*. DOI: 10.1145/2745555.2746644

Rokade, D., Jabde, M. K., & Patil, C. H. (2024). Screening application of dyslexia and dysgraphia using cognitive AI. *2024 10th International Conference on Smart Computing and Communication (ICSCC)*, 182–186. DOI: 10.1109/ICSCC62041.2024.10690576

Schmucker, R. (2024). Harnessing machine learning and generative AI in tutoring systems. *XRDS: Crossroads. The ACM Magazine for Students*, *31*(1), 40–45. DOI: 10.1145/3688086

Siegel, L. S. (2006). Perspectives on dyslexia. *Paediatrics & Child Health*, *11*(9), 581–587. DOI: 10.1093/pch/11.9.581 PMID: 19030329

Tonga, A. (2025). *The ascendant role of artificial intelligence in contemporary tertiary education*. SSRN Electronic Journal. DOI: 10.2139/ssrn.5126867

Torres, E. R., Rodríguez, R. C., & Briñez, E. T. (2023). Use of AI to improve teaching-learning process in children with special abilities. *LatIA*, *1*, 21–30. DOI: 10.62486/latia202321

Tu, Y., Chen, J., & Huang, C. (2025). Empowering personalized learning with generative AI. *Frontiers of Digital Education*, *2*(2), 56. Advance online publication. DOI: 10.1007/s44366-025-0056-9

Ulaş, R., Adcı, B., & İlker, Ö. (2025). Artificial intelligence and innovative educational technologies in students with learning disabilities: A systematic review. *Journal of Teacher Education and Lifelong Learning*, *7*(2), 248–262. DOI: 10.51535/tell.1725012

UNESCO. (2023). *Guidance for generative AI in education and research*. https://unesdoc.unesco.org/ark:/48223/pf0000386693

United Nations. (2020). Sustainable development goals: Goal 4: Quality Education. Retrieved April 22, 2026, from https://www.un.org/sustainabledevelopment/education/

Usman, L., Muniyandi, R. C., Omar, K., & Mohamad, M. (2021). Advance machine learning methods for dyslexia biomarker detection: A review of implementation details and challenges. *IEEE Access : Practical Innovations, Open Solutions*, *9*, 36879–36897. DOI: 10.1109/ACCESS.2021.3062709

Uygun, E. (2026). Clashing AIs: Artificial intelligence literacy and academic integrity in an EFL context. *Journal of Academic Ethics*, *24*(1), 7. DOI: 10.1007/s10805-025-09676-2

Uygun, E., Cesur, K., Karahan, P., & Mikhailova, T. (2026). Participant perspectives on dropout factors and course enhancement needs in a general English MOOC. *Discover Education*, *5*(1), 1126. Advance online publication. DOI: 10.1007/s44217-026-01126-4

Wajuihian, S. O., & Naidoo, K. S. (2012). Dyslexia: An overview. *Optometry and Vision Development*, *43*(1), 24–33.

Weraduwa, S., Asanka, P. P. G. D., & Mahanama, T. V. (2024). Advanced computational techniques for dysgraphia prediction through handwriting recognition using machine learning and deep learning methods. *The Journal of Desk Research Review and Analysis*, *2*(1), 216–234. DOI: 10.4038/jdrra.v2i1.56

Winarno, W., Muchtarom, M., & Fauziyah, H. (2024). Readiness of teachers in developing literacy and numeracy skills. *Journal of Education and Learning*, *18*(4), 1209–1218. DOI: 10.11591/edulearn.v18i4.21425

Wu, R., & Yu, Z. (2024). Do AI chatbots improve students learning outcomes? Evidence from a meta-analysis. *British Journal of Educational Technology*, *55*(1), 10–33. DOI: 10.1111/bjet.13334

Yan, L., Greiff, S., Teuber, Z., & Gašević, D. (2024). Promises and challenges of generative artificial intelligence for human learning. *Nature Human Behaviour*, *8*(10), 1839–1850. DOI: 10.1038/s41562-024-02004-5 PMID: 39438686

Yap, J. R., Aruthanan, T., & Chin, M. (2025). Artificial intelligence in dyslexia research and education: A scoping review. *IEEE Access : Practical Innovations, Open Solutions*, *13*, 7130–7145. DOI: 10.1109/ACCESS.2025.3526189

Yenduri, G., Kaluri, R., Rajput, D. S., Lakshmanna, K., Gadekallu, T. R., Mahmud, M., & Brown, D. J. (2023). From assistive technologies to metaverse in inclusive education. *arXiv*. /arxiv.2305.11057DOI: 10.48550

Yuzaidey, N. A. M., Din, N. C., Ahmad, M., Ibrahim, N., Razak, R. A., & Harun, D. (2018). Interventions for children with dyslexia: A review on current intervention methods. *The Medical Journal of Malaysia*, *73*(5), 311–320. PMID: 30350811

Zhao, S., Xiong, S. C., Pang, B., Tang, X., & He, P. (2025). Let AI read first: Enhancing reading abilities for individuals with dyslexia through artificial intelligence. *CHI EA '25: Extended Abstracts of the CHI Conference on Human Factors in Computing Systems*. DOI: 10.1145/3706599.3720113

Zolna, K., Asselborn, T., Jolly, C., Casteran, L., Nguyen-Morel, M.-A., Johal, W., & Dillenbourg, P. (2019). *The dynamics of handwriting improves the automated diagnosis of dysgraphia*. DOI: 10.48550/arXiv.1906.07576

KEY TERMS AND DEFINITIONS

Adaptive Learning Systems: Adaptive Learning Systems are computer based educational platforms designed to deliver personalized, real-time learning experiences.

Assistive Technology: Assistive Technology encompasses tools that give children with a disability alternative way to obtain and create information without necessarily changing the core method of instruction; examples include text to speech and spell/grammar checkers.

Educational Change: Educational change is an ongoing process wherein advances in technology create changes in the way educators perform their regular instructional tasks, how students in classroom interact with each other and their teacher, and how educators' professional roles evolve over time.

Generative AI (GenAI): GenAI is a specific type of AI technology designed to generate new content (e.g., written descriptions or interactive explanations), helping students with a disability by providing flexible scaffolding within their respective learning environments.

Inclusive Education: Inclusive Education is an approach to teaching that aims to provide all students the same opportunities to access and participate in general education regardless of their specific needs/desires.

Large Language Models (LLMs): Large Language Models are highly advanced AI systems that have been trained on large volumes of text data to automatically produce human-like written responses from a large corpus of text data to assist teachers in guiding students through complex texts and providing tutoring using chat-based applications.

Specific Learning Disorders (SLD): Neurodevelopmental conditions, including dyslexia, dyscalculia, and dysgraphia, which help create challenges in acquiring foundational literacy and numeracy skills despite average intellectual ability.

Chapter 8
AI-Assisted Design of Differentiated Assessment Tools:
A Comparative Study of Teacher-Created vs. AI-Enhanced Rubrics for Students With Special Educational Needs

Emmanouil Skordialos
http://orcid.org/0009-0007-4518-5618
National and Kapodistrian University of Athens, Greece

ABSTRACT

Assessment of students with Special Educational Needs and Disabilities (SEND) remains one of the most challenging aspects of inclusive education, as traditional tools often fail to capture diverse learning trajectories. The emergence of Generative Artificial Intelligence (Gen-AI) tools such as ChatGPT and Claude offers unprecedented opportunities to support educators in designing differentiated assessment instruments. This chapter addresses this gap by presenting findings from a quasi-experimental study conducted in Greece, comparing rubrics created with Gen-AI assistance versus rubrics created through conventional means, focusing on accommodations for students with SEND. Findings inform professional development and contribute evidence-based recommendations for responsible Gen-AI integration in special education assessment.

DOI: 10.4018/979-8-3373-9169-4.ch008

INTRODUCTION

The assessment of students with Special Educational Needs and Disabilities (SEND) represents one of the most persistent and consequential challenges in inclusive education. Conventional assessment tools—rubrics, rating scales, checklists, and standardized tests—are predominantly constructed around normative expectations, frequently failing to capture the distinctive learning trajectories, cognitive profiles, and communicative strengths of learners with dyslexia, dyscalculia, Attention Deficit Hyperactivity Disorder (ADHD), Autism Spectrum Disorder (ASD), and mild intellectual disabilities. Teachers working in inclusive primary classrooms are routinely required to design differentiated assessment instruments capable of meaningfully capturing each student's progress—a task demanding substantial time, specialized pedagogical expertise, and detailed familiarity with specific disability characteristics (Black & Wiliam, 2018; Tomlinson & Imbeau, 2010). Yet systematic professional preparation for this task remains uneven across Greek and international educational contexts.

The rapid proliferation of Generative Artificial Intelligence (Gen-AI) tools—including ChatGPT (OpenAI) and Claude (Anthropic)—has introduced new and largely unexplored possibilities for educational professional practice. These tools can generate differentiated content at scale, propose assessment criteria tailored to specific learner profiles, suggest inclusive language formulations, and help educators articulate performance descriptors in accessible, student-oriented terms. Despite growing scholarly interest in Gen-AI applications in education (Kasneci et al., 2023; Mollick & Mollick, 2023; Zhai et al., 2021), empirical investigation into the practical value of AI-assisted rubric design for SEND populations remains markedly scarce. Most existing research focuses on student-facing applications of Gen-AI or on generic instructional content generation, leaving the domain of inclusive assessment design substantially underexplored.

This chapter addresses this gap by presenting findings from a small-scale, seminar-based pilot study conducted in Greece during the 2025–2026 academic year. The study examined whether primary school teachers who used Gen-AI tools during rubric design produced assessment instruments of significantly higher quality—and with better-developed SEND accommodations—compared to teachers who created rubrics through conventional methods. The study additionally investigated differences in time efficiency and explored teacher perceptions regarding the professional value of Gen-AI as a collaborative tool. A key methodological concern was the observed imbalance in prior AI experience between groups, which was addressed through covariate analysis to ensure that observed differences were attributable to the intervention rather than pre-existing familiarity with AI tools.

BACKGROUND

Generative AI in Educational Contexts

Generative Artificial Intelligence refers to a class of machine learning models capable of producing coherent, contextually appropriate text, images, code, or other outputs in response to natural language prompts (Brown et al., 2020). In educational settings, tools such as ChatGPT, Claude, and Google Gemini have attracted considerable scholarly attention, with researchers exploring their potential for content generation, formative feedback, lesson planning, personalized learning, and professional development support (Baidoo-Anu & Owusu Ansah, 2023; Mollick & Mollick, 2023; Zhai et al., 2021). These tools represent a qualitative shift in the availability of on-demand, context-sensitive professional support for educators.

Several studies have documented the capacity of Gen-AI to produce educationally valuable content. Kasneci et al. (2023) examined the implications of large language models for higher education, identifying both transformative potential and significant risks including hallucination, bias, and over-reliance. Crompton and Burke (2023) conducted a systematic review of AI in higher education, documenting the rapid expansion of AI applications across educational contexts. While their focus was not exclusively on special education, their findings regarding the concentration of AI applications in specific domains are relevant to understanding the broader landscape within which SEND-focused AI research is emerging. Similarly, Su and Yang (2023) reviewed AI-assisted learning environments, noting that inclusive assessment remained an underserved area despite its clear theoretical fit with AI capabilities.

Concerns about uncritical adoption of Gen-AI in education are well-documented. Researchers have highlighted the risk of producing generic, culturally insensitive, or pedagogically inappropriate content (Lund & Wang, 2023; Zawacki-Richter et al., 2019). Selwyn (2022) urges caution against technological solutionism in education, arguing that AI tools are frequently introduced without adequate attention to their pedagogical implications or the professional judgments they displace. In the context of SEND, these risks are compounded by the need for nuanced, individually tailored assessment instruments that reflect specific disability profiles and comply with legal frameworks such as Individualized Education Programs (IEPs). The potential for AI-generated accommodations to appear comprehensive yet remain superficial or contextually inappropriate is a critical concern that this study sought to investigate empirically.

Recent work by Nazaretsky et al. (2022) on teacher trust in AI-powered educational technology provides a valuable theoretical anchor for understanding how educators engage with AI-generated professional content. Their findings suggest that trust is built incrementally through direct experience rather than through abstract endorsement, a pattern reflected in the present study's finding that hands-on AI use during the intervention generated substantially stronger adoption intentions than prior theoretical knowledge alone.

Differentiated Assessment and Students with SEND

Assessment in inclusive education must fulfill a dual purpose: it must document student achievement in relation to curriculum goals while simultaneously accommodating diverse learning profiles (Florian & Black-Hawkins, 2011; Tomlinson, 2014). Differentiated assessment—the systematic adaptation of assessment tasks, criteria, and formats to reflect individual learning needs—is considered best practice in inclusive education, yet its implementation remains inconsistent and frequently superficial across mainstream classrooms (Subban, 2006). Cross-national comparisons of teacher preparation for special and inclusive education reveal persistent gaps in professional readiness across European contexts, including Greece (Tsibidaki, 2020), underscoring the urgency of scalable professional development approaches such as those examined in the present study. Research in Greek primary education contexts has consistently documented limited teacher preparedness for differentiated assessment, with many educators reporting insufficient training in special education assessment principles (Zoniou-Sideri & Vlachou, 2006). Recent work by Tsibidaki (2026) further confirms that meaningful participation for students with learning difficulties in Greek primary schools depends critically on teacher responsiveness to individual profiles, reinforcing the need for assessment tools that genuinely reflect diverse learning trajectories.

Rubrics, as structured scoring guides defining performance levels across multiple criteria, are among the most widely used differentiated assessment tools in primary education (Brookhart, 2013). Well-designed rubrics serve multiple functions: they communicate expectations transparently to students and families, provide structured feedback that informs subsequent instruction, and support consistent evaluation across different educators. For students with SEND, rubric design requires particular attention to language accessibility, the inclusion of alternative demonstration modes, and the articulation of criteria that reflect genuine learning progress rather than normalized performance expectations (Andrade, 2013; Mertler, 2001).

Research on rubric design as a professional competency reveals that many teachers lack systematic training in this area (Jonsson & Svingby, 2007). Of particular significance for the present study is the documented tendency for teachers designing rubrics for SEND students to concentrate accommodations within the most familiar disability categories—primarily dyslexia and ADHD—while leaving less commonly encountered profiles such as ASD and mild intellectual disabilities substantially underserved. This clustering phenomenon, first described by Florian (2014) in the context of inclusive pedagogy more broadly, has direct implications for equitable assessment practice and represents one of the most practically significant findings of the present study.

Vygotsky's (1978) concept of the Zone of Proximal Development provides a theoretical bridge between assessment design and disability accommodation: effective rubrics for SEND students should not simply document current performance but should scaffold progression toward the next developmental level, a function that requires sophisticated understanding of each disability profile. This theoretical requirement helps explain why AI-generated rubrics—drawing on extensive training data encompassing special education literature—may provide accommodations of greater breadth and specificity than those produced from individual teacher knowledge alone.

Early empirical work in the Greek context further substantiates the challenges of supporting students with learning difficulties in primary mathematics. Skordialos and Baralis (2017) demonstrated that mediated learning experience—structured adult intervention that scaffolds students' cognitive processes—significantly supported fraction comprehension among primary school students with learning difficulties, highlighting the critical role of tailored pedagogical mediation in mathematics education for SEND learners. This finding underscores a key premise of the present study: that effective support for students with SEND in mathematics requires not only specialized knowledge of disability profiles but also deliberate, structured instructional and assessment design—precisely the type of professional task that Gen-AI tools may be positioned to support.

Gen-AI as a Professional Support Tool for Teachers

Beyond its student-facing applications, Gen-AI is increasingly explored as a professional support tool for educators. Researchers have examined AI assistance in lesson planning (Mollick & Mollick, 2023), feedback generation (Ding & Zou, 2024), material design (Pavlik, 2023), and professional reflection (Schiff, 2021). A particularly promising application area is the use of Gen-AI for generating differentiated instructional and assessment materials, a task that traditionally demands substantial time and expertise, and that represents a significant source of professional burden in inclusive classrooms.

Prompt engineering—the practice of crafting structured natural language instructions to elicit high-quality AI outputs—has emerged as a key professional competency for educators seeking to leverage Gen-AI effectively (White et al., 2023). Research suggests that structured, context-rich prompts significantly improve the quality and relevance of AI-generated educational content (Liu et al., 2022). Training educators in prompt engineering has been proposed as a scalable professional development strategy, with the potential to democratize access to high-quality differentiated assessment design across resource-constrained school contexts. The present study provides empirical evidence on the effectiveness of brief prompt engineering training in the specific context of SEND assessment design.

Studies on teacher attitudes toward AI tools reveal a complex picture. While many educators express interest in AI-assisted workflows, concerns about accuracy, depersonalization, and professional autonomy are frequently cited (Nazaretsky et al., 2022; Schiff, 2021). In the Greek higher education context, Kostas et al. (2025) documented a dual perspective among university students toward AI tools, recognizing their potential for enhancing efficiency while simultaneously raising concerns about ethical considerations and content reliability—a tension that mirrors the findings of the present study regarding the Perceived-Actual Quality Gap. Teo (2011) and Scherer et al. (2019) demonstrate through large-scale TAM applications that perceived usefulness is the strongest predictor of sustained technology adoption among teachers—a finding that underscores the importance of providing educators with genuine functional benefits rather than technologically impressive but practically cumbersome tools.

ICT integration in primary mathematics education in Greece has been examined by Skordialos (2024a), who documented the role of interactive technologies in enhancing teacher competencies and student engagement in inclusive classrooms. Similarly, Skordialos (2024b) explored the integration of the Van Hiele model with ICT support in geometry education, demonstrating how technology-assisted frameworks can scaffold complex pedagogical tasks that individual teachers find challenging to implement independently. Zaranis et al. (2015) further demonstrated the effectiveness of ICT-based approaches grounded in Realistic Mathematics Education for first-grade students, including those with diverse learning needs. These findings collectively inform the present study's premise that technology-assisted professional practice can yield measurable quality improvements when appropriately supported and contextually grounded.

The intersection of Gen-AI, inclusive assessment, and teacher professional development represents fertile but largely unexplored research territory. The present study responds to this gap by providing quasi-experimental evidence on whether AI assistance produces demonstrably superior differentiated assessment tools for students with SEND, and by examining the conditions under which such benefits are most reliably realized. Crucially, the study attends to the gap between teachers' subjective perceptions of AI utility and the objective quality judgments of expert raters—a distinction rarely addressed in existing literature—to provide a more nuanced and practically actionable account of Gen-AI's professional value.

Theoretical Framework

The study is grounded in three complementary theoretical perspectives that together provide a comprehensive lens for examining AI-assisted assessment design in inclusive education: Universal Design for Learning (UDL), the Technology Acceptance Model (TAM), and the principles of Differentiated Instruction (DI). These frameworks were selected because they address distinct but interrelated dimensions of the research problem: UDL speaks to the quality criteria for inclusive assessment tools; TAM addresses teacher adoption of technological aids; and DI articulates the pedagogical principles that should guide rubric construction in heterogeneous classrooms. Figure 1 illustrates the relationships between these frameworks and the key outcome measures of the study.

Figure 1. Conceptual framework showing the three theoretical bases, the research design, and the outcome measures of the study

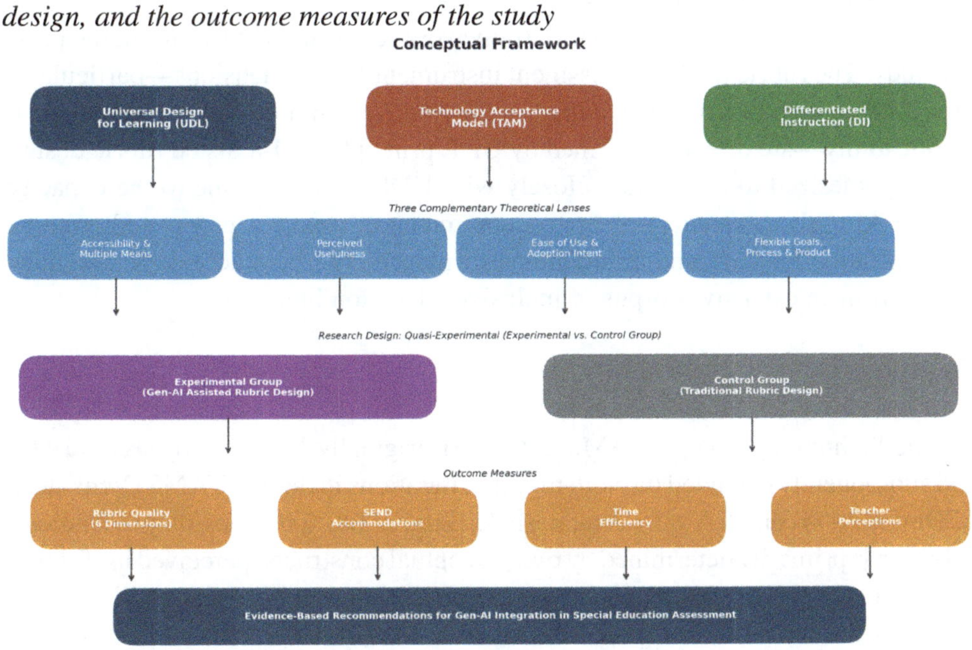

Universal Design for Learning

Universal Design for Learning (UDL) is an educational framework developed by the Center for Applied Special Technology (CAST) that proposes designing learning environments, instructional materials, and assessment tools to accommodate the widest possible range of learner variability from the outset, rather than retrofitting accommodations after the fact (CAST, 2018; Meyer et al., 2014). UDL operates through three core principles aligned with three networks of the brain involved in learning: providing multiple means of representation (recognizing networks), multiple means of action and expression (strategic networks), and multiple means of engagement (affective networks).

In the context of assessment design, UDL principles translate into rubrics that offer multiple ways for students to demonstrate competence, use clear and universally accessible language, minimize construct-irrelevant barriers to performance, and acknowledge diverse pathways to mastery. Rose and Meyer (2002) articulate the principle that assessment barriers can be distinguished from the construct being assessed—a distinction with direct implications for rubric design. A rubric that penalizes a dyslexic student for written fluency when assessing mathematical reasoning, for example, violates UDL principles by conflating construct-relevant and construct-irrelevant demands.

UDL provides the primary quality framework for evaluating rubrics in the present study. The rubric quality assessment instrument's six dimensions—particularly Student-Friendly Language, Quality of SEND Accommodations, and Practical Applicability—are directly informed by UDL principles. AI-assisted rubric design was hypothesized to align more closely with UDL principles due to the capacity of Gen-AI tools to generate diverse accommodation options, propose alternative demonstration formats, and articulate performance criteria in accessible language drawn from an extensive corpus of inclusive education literature.

Technology Acceptance Model

The Technology Acceptance Model (TAM), originally developed by Davis (1989) and subsequently extended through multiple iterations including TAM2 (Venkatesh & Davis, 2000) and TAM3 (Venkatesh & Bala, 2008), proposes that technology adoption is primarily determined by two perceptual constructs: perceived usefulness (the degree to which a person believes that using a particular system will enhance their job performance) and perceived ease of use (the degree to which a person believes that using the system will be free of effort). TAM has been extensively applied in educational technology research to understand factors influencing teachers' adoption of digital tools across diverse contexts (Teo, 2011; Scherer et al., 2019).

TAM is particularly relevant to the present study because it helps explain the pattern of perceptions documented in the post-task questionnaire data. The high rates of perceived usefulness (89%) and adoption intention (81%) among experimental group participants are consistent with TAM's prediction that directly experiencing a tool's functional benefits powerfully shapes adoption attitudes—a mechanism

TAM terms 'subjective norm mediated by behavioral intention.' At the same time, TAM's distinction between perceived usefulness and perceived ease of use helps interpret the finding that participants who engaged in iterative dialogue with AI tools—investing cognitive effort in refinement—achieved higher rubric quality than those who accepted initial AI outputs with minimal modification.

In the present study, TAM informs the investigation of teacher perceptions through post-task questionnaire items operationalizing perceived usefulness, ease of use, and intention for future use. The study extends standard TAM applications by examining whether pre-existing AI experience (a known antecedent of ease-of-use perceptions in TAM3) moderated the relationship between AI assistance and rubric quality outcomes—a methodologically important consideration given the imbalance in prior AI experience between groups. It is important to note that this pilot study does not aim to test a structural equation model or validate the full TAM paths; rather, TAM constructs are employed as a descriptive evaluative framework to capture teachers' immediate post-task attitudes.

Differentiated Instruction

Differentiated Instruction (DI), as articulated by Tomlinson (2014) and Tomlinson and Imbeau (2010), is a pedagogical philosophy rooted in the recognition that learners differ meaningfully in their readiness, interests, and learning profiles, and that effective teaching responds to these differences through systematic variation in content, process, product, and learning environment. DI positions the teacher as a responsive professional who continually adjusts instructional and assessment strategies in light of ongoing learner data—an orientation that makes substantial cognitive and professional demands on educators.

Assessment within a DI framework is inherently formative and growth-oriented, emphasizing what students can do and supporting progression toward clearly articulated goals. Tomlinson (2014) explicitly distinguishes between differentiated assessment—which adapts task format, criteria, and demonstrations of learning to individual profiles—and merely modified assessment, which simply reduces demands without repositioning expectations toward each student's zone of proximal development. This distinction is operationalized in the present study's rubric quality instrument, which evaluates the specificity and developmental appropriateness of SEND accommodations rather than simply their presence or absence.

DI principles also inform the interpretation of the study's most striking finding: that AI-assisted rubrics were not merely quantitatively superior in the number of accommodations included, but qualitatively different in their coverage of SEND profiles. Control group rubrics displayed the clustering phenomenon documented by Florian (2014), concentrating accommodations within familiar categories (dyslexia, ADHD) while inadequately addressing ASD and mild intellectual disabilities. Experimental group rubrics, by contrast, reflected the broader ecological awareness of diverse disability profiles that DI principles require but that individual teacher knowledge often cannot provide without systematic support.

MAIN FOCUS OF THE CHAPTER

Research Design

This study employed a quasi-experimental between-subjects design with two conditions: an experimental group in which participants used Gen-AI assistance during rubric creation, and a control group in which participants created rubrics through conventional methods. The quasi-experimental rather than true experimental designation reflects the practical realities of teacher professional development research: participants were recruited from existing professional development seminars, and while purposive stratified assignment was used to equate groups on key variables, the constraints of naturalistic recruitment precluded fully random assignment in the statistical sense. Participants were therefore purposively assigned to conditions based on stratification variables rather than through unrestricted randomization, rendering the design quasi-experimental as defined by Shadish et al. (2002). Given the pilot nature of the study and the practical constraints of seminar-based recruitment, findings should be interpreted with appropriate caution rather than as definitive proof of AI effectiveness. Figure 2 provides a step-by-step overview of the research procedure.

Figure 2. Research design flowchart illustrating the six procedural steps, from participant recruitment through to statistical analysis

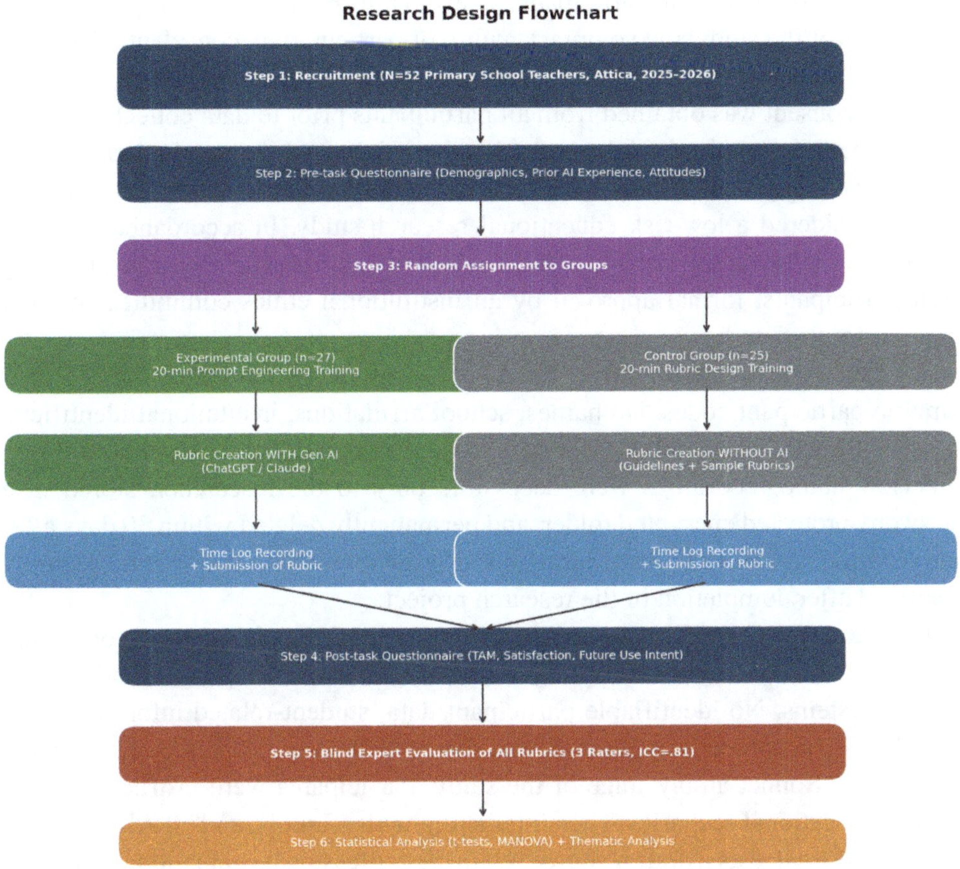

Participants

Ethical Considerations and Data Protection

The study involved 52 primary school teachers who participated voluntarily through online Greek teacher communities and professional social media groups during the 2025–2026 academic year. The research followed the ethical principles of responsible research conduct and complied with the requirements of the General

Data Protection Regulation (GDPR) and applicable Greek legislation on personal data protection (Law 4624/2019).

Before participation, all participants received information about the purpose and procedures of the study, the voluntary nature of participation, confidentiality measures, and their right to withdraw at any stage without any consequences. Written informed consent was obtained from all participants prior to data collection.

As the study involved adult professional participants, did not include minors or vulnerable populations, and did not involve intervention within school settings, it was considered a low-risk educational research study. In accordance with the applicable Greek research ethics framework for non-invasive research involving adult participants, formal approval by an institutional ethics committee was not required for this study.

All data were anonymised from the point of collection through the use of alphanumeric participant codes. No names, school affiliations, institutional identifiers, or other directly identifiable information were retained in the research dataset. Interview audio recordings were accessible only to the researcher, stored in a password-protected encrypted folder, and permanently deleted within 30 days after transcription. Transcripts were anonymised prior to analysis and will be securely destroyed after completion of the research project.

Regarding the use of Generative AI tools, participants were instructed not to enter any identifiable information related to students, schools, colleagues, or individuals into AI systems. No identifiable participant data, student-related information, or school-specific content was entered into, shared with, or processed by ChatGPT-4 or Claude 3 Sonnet at any stage of the study. Participants were instructed to use generic educational scenarios when interacting with AI tools, and all AI-generated content was treated as a draft resource requiring professional evaluation and refinement by the participants.

Group Assignment

Participants were purposively assigned to the experimental group (n = 27) or the control group (n = 25) using a stratified assignment procedure designed to ensure comparable distributions of teacher type (general vs. special education) and years of teaching experience across conditions. Table 1 presents the full demographic profile of participants by group.

Table 1. Participant demographic characteristics by group

Characteristic	Experimental Group (n = 27)	Control Group (n = 25)
Gender: Female	16 (59.3%)	15 (60.0%)
Gender: Male	11 (40.7%)	10 (40.0%)
General education teachers	18 (66.7%)	16 (64.0%)
Special education teachers	9 (33.3%)	9 (36.0%)
Teaching experience, M (SD)	11.7 (5.6) years	11.1 (6.1) years
Teaching experience, range	3–24 years	3–23 years
Prior AI experience: Yes	14 (51.9%)	7 (28.0%)
Prior AI experience: No	13 (48.1%)	18 (72.0%)

Note. Percentages may not sum to 100 due to rounding. Groups were equated on teacher type and teaching experience through purposive stratified assignment.

As shown in Table 1, the two groups were well-matched in terms of gender distribution (approximately 60% female in both groups), teacher type (approximately two-thirds general education), and teaching experience (overall M = 11.4 years, SD = 5.8). One notable imbalance emerged despite stratified assignment: 51.9% of experimental group participants reported prior experience using AI tools, compared to 28.0% of control group participants. This imbalance was not anticipated at the design stage and represents a potential confound requiring careful analytical attention. As detailed in the Data Analysis section, prior AI experience was consequently entered as a covariate in all primary analyses to ensure that observed group differences in rubric quality were attributable to the experimental manipulation rather than pre-existing familiarity with AI tools.

Instruments

Rubric Creation Task

All participants were asked to design an analytic assessment rubric for evaluating Grade 5 mathematical problem-solving performance. The task specifications, provided in identical written form to all participants, required: (a) four assessment criteria; (b) four performance levels per criterion (labeled Beginning, Developing, Proficient, and Advanced); (c) specific accommodations for students with learning disabilities (dyslexia and dyscalculia), ADHD, and mild intellectual disabilities; and (d) student-friendly language throughout. The mathematical domain was selected because it is central to Greek primary curriculum requirements and because problem-solving rubrics involve a range of complex criteria that are expected to challenge participants in both conditions.

Rubric Quality Assessment Instrument

A purpose-designed rubric quality assessment instrument was developed to evaluate the rubrics produced by participants. Drawing on established frameworks for rubric evaluation (Brookhart, 2013; Jonsson & Svingby, 2007) and UDL principles (CAST, 2018), the instrument comprises six dimensions rated on a 4-point scale (1 = Inadequate, 2 = Developing, 3 = Proficient, 4 = Exemplary):

(a) Clarity of Criteria: the degree to which each criterion is unambiguously defined and operationally distinct from others; (b) Differentiation between Performance Levels: the extent to which consecutive performance levels are meaningfully distinguished rather than nominally varied; (c) Alignment with Learning Objectives: the correspondence between rubric criteria and the mathematical problem-solving objectives specified in the Greek primary curriculum; (d) Quality of SEND Accommodations: the specificity, appropriateness, and breadth of adaptations provided for identified disability profiles; (e) Student-Friendly Language: the accessibility and comprehensibility of performance descriptors for primary-age students; and (f) Practical Applicability: the feasibility of using the rubric in everyday classroom assessment practice. The instrument was reviewed for content validity by three external experts in special education assessment prior to use in the study.

Prior to use, the instrument underwent expert review by three specialists in special education and assessment who evaluated content validity and provided feedback on scoring anchors. Raters participated in a calibration session using five practice rubrics before independently evaluating the study rubrics. Pre-consensus ICC was .74, rising to .81 following discussion of discrepancies. The six dimensions were not empirically validated through factor analysis but were used as a purpose-designed evaluative framework informed by UDL principles and established rubric evaluation literature.

Post-Task Questionnaire

A 20-item post-task questionnaire assessed participants' perceptions of the rubric design process. Items were adapted from validated scales including the TAM questionnaire (Davis, 1989; Venkatesh & Bala, 2008) and the Perceived Usefulness Scale. The questionnaire used a 5-point Likert scale (1 = Strongly Disagree to 5 = Strongly Agree) and addressed perceived usefulness of Gen-AI (experimental group only), ease of use of the process, satisfaction with the created rubric, and intention to use Gen-AI tools in future professional practice. Internal consistency across all items was acceptable (Cronbach's $\alpha = .86$).

Semi-Structured Interviews

A purposive subsample of 14 participants (8 from the experimental group, 6 from the control group) completed individual semi-structured interviews of approximately 20 minutes each. Participants were selected to represent variation in teacher type, years of experience, and prior AI familiarity. Interview protocols explored experiences with the rubric creation task, perceptions of AI assistance quality, concerns about the professional implications of AI-generated content, and views on training and support needs. Interviews were audio-recorded with participants' consent and transcribed verbatim by the researcher.

Procedure

Data collection took place asynchronously via Google Classroom between November 2025 and February 2026. The researcher, holding a doctorate in ICT integration in education, designed and delivered all training materials independently through the online platform. Participants submitted their rubrics within 15 days of receiving the task. All sessions followed an identical procedural structure to ensure consistency of task conditions. In the first session (approximately 120 minutes total), participants completed a pre-task questionnaire gathering demographic information, prior AI experience, and baseline attitudes toward technology in professional practice.

Following the pre-task questionnaire, participants received group-specific training. Experimental group participants received a 20-minute structured introduction to prompt engineering for educational content creation, covering core strategies for eliciting differentiated rubric criteria, SEND-specific accommodation suggestions, and accessible language formulations. The training included three worked examples demonstrating iterative prompt refinement and output evaluation. Control group participants received an equivalent 20-minute introduction to rubric design principles and documented best practices for SEND accommodations, drawing on published guidelines and sample rubrics. Neither group received information about the other group's training content.

Following training, all participants completed the rubric creation task with a 45-minute time limit. Experimental group participants had access to ChatGPT-4 and Claude 3 Sonnet through their personal devices and were explicitly encouraged to engage in iterative dialogue with the AI tools—asking follow-up questions, requesting revisions, and incorporating their own professional modifications into AI-generated content. A sample prompt template provided during training is included in the Appendix. Control group participants had access to three sample rubrics (for different subject areas and grade levels) and the one-page reference guide provided during training, but no digital AI tools. All participants self-recorded their actual task completion time using a standardized time log sheet.

Post-task questionnaires were administered immediately following rubric submission. Semi-structured interviews were conducted individually via video call within two weeks of rubric submission. Interview recordings were transcribed and returned to participants for member checking, with any requested amendments incorporated before analysis.

Data Analysis

Rubrics were anonymized and assigned random identification codes prior to evaluation. Three independent expert raters—two with research specializations in special education assessment and one with expertise in primary mathematics assessment—evaluated all 52 rubrics using the quality assessment instrument. Raters were blind to participants' group assignment and to the purpose of the study. Inter-rater reliability was calculated using the two-way mixed intraclass correlation coefficient (ICC) for absolute agreement, yielding a value of .81, indicating good reliability consistent with established benchmarks (Koo & Mae, 2016). Any initial discrepancies in ratings exceeding one scale point were resolved through discussion to consensus.

Quantitative data were analyzed using IBM SPSS Statistics 29. Given the observed imbalance in prior AI experience between groups (51.9% experimental vs. 28.0% control), prior AI experience (binary: yes/no) was entered as a covariate in all primary analyses. The primary analytical approach was therefore Multivariate Analysis of Covariance (MANCOVA) examining group differences across the six rubric quality dimensions simultaneously, with prior AI experience as covariate. Univariate follow-up ANCOVAs were conducted for each quality dimension. For the time efficiency analysis, a one-way ANCOVA was conducted with prior AI experience as covariate. All F statistics for MANCOVA and ANCOVA reflect adjusted means controlling for the covariate. Effect sizes were calculated using partial eta-squared (ηp^2) for omnibus tests and Cohen's d for pairwise comparisons. Statistical significance was set at $\alpha = .05$, with Bonferroni correction applied for multiple univariate comparisons. A post-hoc power analysis was conducted using G*Power 3.1 to assess the statistical power of the primary MANCOVA analysis. The achieved power was estimated at .82 ($\alpha = .05$), indicating adequate statistical power for detecting the observed multivariate effect. However, given the relatively small sample size and the non-randomised nature of the study design, these findings should be interpreted cautiously. Further studies with larger and more diverse samples are needed to confirm the robustness and generalisability of the results.

Interview transcripts were analyzed using reflexive thematic analysis following the six-phase procedure described by Braun and Clarke (2006): familiarization with data, generating initial codes, searching for themes, reviewing themes, defining and naming themes, and producing the report. Two researchers independently coded the data before meeting to reconcile codes and develop themes through discussion. Member checking was conducted with a subsample of five interview participants, none of whom requested substantive amendments to the researcher's thematic account.

Prior to analysis, data were screened for normality using Shapiro-Wilk tests and visual inspection of Q-Q plots. Minor deviations from normality were observed but deemed acceptable given the robustness of MANCOVA to moderate violations with samples above 20 per group. Homogeneity of regression slopes was confirmed for all dependent variables. No significant outliers were identified using boxplot inspection and standardized residual analysis. Missing data were minimal ($n = 2$ incomplete time logs) and handled through listwise deletion. It should be noted that a non-significant covariate effect does not eliminate the possibility of confounding; the binary operationalisation of prior AI experience represents a limitation, as frequency, quality, and type of previous AI use may have differentially influenced outcomes.

Results

Preliminary Analysis: Covariate Effects

Before presenting primary results, the effect of the covariate (prior AI experience) on rubric quality outcomes is reported. ANCOVA results indicated that prior AI experience did not significantly predict overall rubric quality, $F(1, 49) = 2.14$, $p = .150$, $\eta p^2 = .04$, confirming that the observed imbalance in prior AI experience between groups did not substantively confound rubric quality outcomes. The covariate was similarly non-significant for time efficiency, $F(1, 49) = 1.87$, $p = .177$. These findings suggest that the binary measure of prior AI experience did not account for a statistically significant linear portion of variance in rubric quality outcomes. However, a non-significant covariate does not eliminate the possibility of residual confounding: frequency, quality, and type of prior AI use were not assessed, and their potential influence on outcomes cannot be ruled out. Observed group differences should therefore be interpreted as consistent with, rather than definitively caused by, the experimental manipulation.

Rubric Quality

MANCOVA results indicated a significant multivariate effect of group on rubric quality dimensions after controlling for prior AI experience, Wilks' $\Lambda = .55$, F(6,

44) = 6.02, $p < .001$, partial $\eta^2 = .45$. Table 2 presents adjusted means, standard errors, and univariate ANCOVA results for each quality dimension.

Table 2. Adjusted rubric quality scores by group, with prior AI experience as covariate

Quality Dimension	Exp. Adj. M (SE)	Ctrl. Adj. M (SE)	F(1, 49)	p	ηp^2	d
Clarity of criteria	3.35 (.09)	2.74 (.10)	21.84	< .001	.31	1.19
Differentiation between levels	3.02 (.10)	2.51 (.11)	13.79	< .001	.22	0.95
Alignment with objectives	3.16 (.10)	2.72 (.11)	11.35	.001	.19	0.87
Quality of SEND accommodations	3.41 (.08)	2.35 (.09)	50.42	< .001	.51	1.84
Student-friendly language	3.25 (.10)	2.63 (.11)	19.71	< .001	.29	1.13
Practical applicability	2.91 (.11)	2.69 (.12)	1.79	.187	.04	0.38
Overall quality score	3.18 (.09)	2.61 (.10)	17.76	< .001	.27	1.09

Note. Adj. M = adjusted mean; SE = standard error. Scale: 1 = Inadequate, 2 = Developing, 3 = Proficient, 4 = Exemplary. ηp^2 = partial eta-squared. d = Cohen's d based on adjusted means. All F tests have df = (1, 49). Bonferroni-corrected significance threshold: $p < .008$.

As shown in Table 2, the experimental group produced rubrics of significantly higher overall quality (adjusted M = 3.18, SE = 0.09) compared to the control group (adjusted M = 2.61, SE = 0.10), $F(1, 49) = 17.76$, $p < .001$, $\eta p^2 = .27$, d = 1.09. Five of six individual quality dimensions reached statistical significance after Bonferroni correction. The largest effect was observed for Quality of SEND Accommodations ($\eta p^2 = .51$, d = 1.84), underscoring that AI assistance exerted its strongest influence precisely on the dimension most critical to inclusive assessment practice. Significant differences were also found for Clarity of Criteria ($\eta p^2 = .31$), Student-Friendly Language ($\eta p^2 = .29$), Differentiation between Levels ($\eta p^2 = .22$), and Alignment with Objectives ($\eta p^2 = .19$). Practical Applicability was the only dimension that did not reach statistical significance after Bonferroni correction ($p = .187$), a finding interpreted further in the Discussion section.

Figure 3 provides a visual comparison of adjusted mean rubric quality scores across all six dimensions.

Figure 3. Adjusted mean rubric quality scores by group across six dimensions

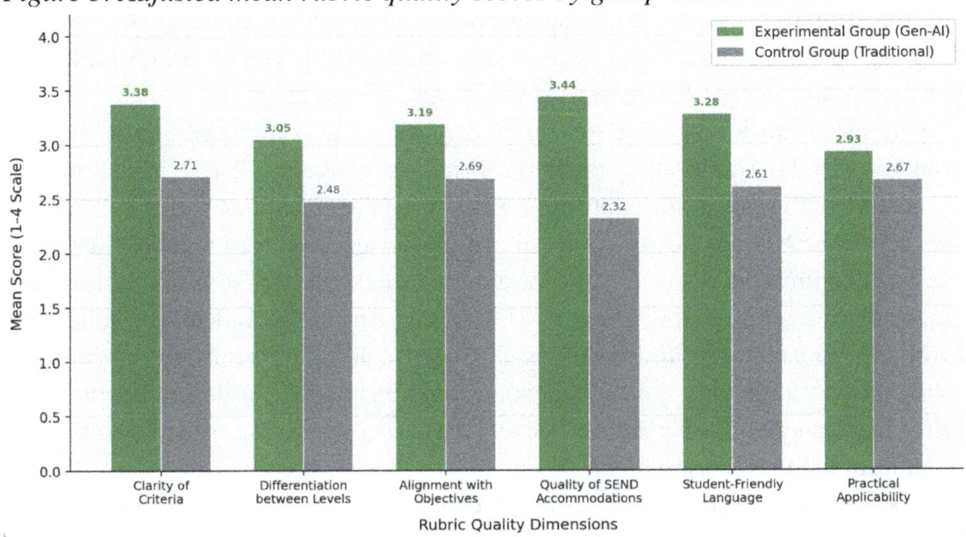

SEND Accommodations

A more granular analysis of SEND accommodations revealed meaningful differences not only in the quantity but in the specificity, diversity, and cross-category coverage of adaptations included. Table 3 presents the mean number of specific, actionable accommodations per rubric by SEND category.

Table 3. Mean number of specific SEND accommodations per rubric by category and group

SEND Category	Experimental Group M	Control Group M
Learning disabilities (dyslexia/dyscalculia)	3.2	1.8
ADHD	2.4	1.1
Mild intellectual disabilities	1.9	0.9
Autism spectrum disorder	1.2	0.4
Total accommodations per rubric	8.7	4.2

Note. Accommodations were counted as discrete, actionable adaptations.

Accommodations were operationally defined as discrete, actionable adaptations (e.g., 'provide extended time,' 'allow oral response,' 'use visual task-segmentation supports') distinguished from generic statements (e.g., 'adapt as needed'). Double coding was applied to 20% of rubrics by a second researcher, yielding agreement of 87%. Decision rules specified that accommodations were classified by the primary SEND category they addressed; where an accommodation addressed multiple categories, it was assigned to the most specific applicable category.

AI-assisted rubrics included a mean of 8.7 specific accommodations per rubric, compared to 4.2 in traditionally created rubrics—a difference of 107.1%. However, the most theoretically significant finding concerns the distribution of accommodations across SEND categories. Control group rubrics displayed a clear clustering pattern: accommodations were concentrated within the two most familiar disability categories (learning disabilities and ADHD), leaving ASD and mild intellectual disabilities substantially underaddressed. Specifically, control group participants included on average only 0.4 ASD accommodations and 0.9 mild intellectual disability accommodations per rubric—levels that expert raters rated as inadequate for meaningful inclusive assessment.

Experimental group rubrics, by contrast, distributed accommodations significantly more equitably across all four SEND categories. Raters noted that AI-assisted rubrics more frequently incorporated concrete, evidence-based adaptations including visual supports, chunked task descriptions, extended time provisions, alternative response formats, and scaffolded criterion descriptors. This broader ecological coverage of SEND profiles represents arguably the most practically significant contribution of Gen-AI assistance in this domain, directly addressing the professional knowledge gap documented in the existing literature (Florian, 2014; Zoniou-Sideri & Vlachou, 2006).

Time Efficiency

A one-way ANCOVA controlling for prior AI experience indicated that participants in the experimental group required significantly less time to complete the rubric design task (adjusted $M = 22.6$ minutes, $SE = 1.5$) compared to the control group (adjusted $M = 41.5$ minutes, $SE = 1.6$), $F(1, 49) = 54.89$, $p < .001$, $\eta p^2 = .53$, $d = 1.92$. This represents a time saving of approximately 46% in favor of the experimental group—a finding with substantial practical implications given that teacher workload is consistently cited as a primary barrier to differentiated assessment implementation. Figure 4 illustrates the between-group difference in adjusted mean rubric creation time.

Figure 4. Adjusted mean rubric creation time in minutes by group, with error bars representing one standard error

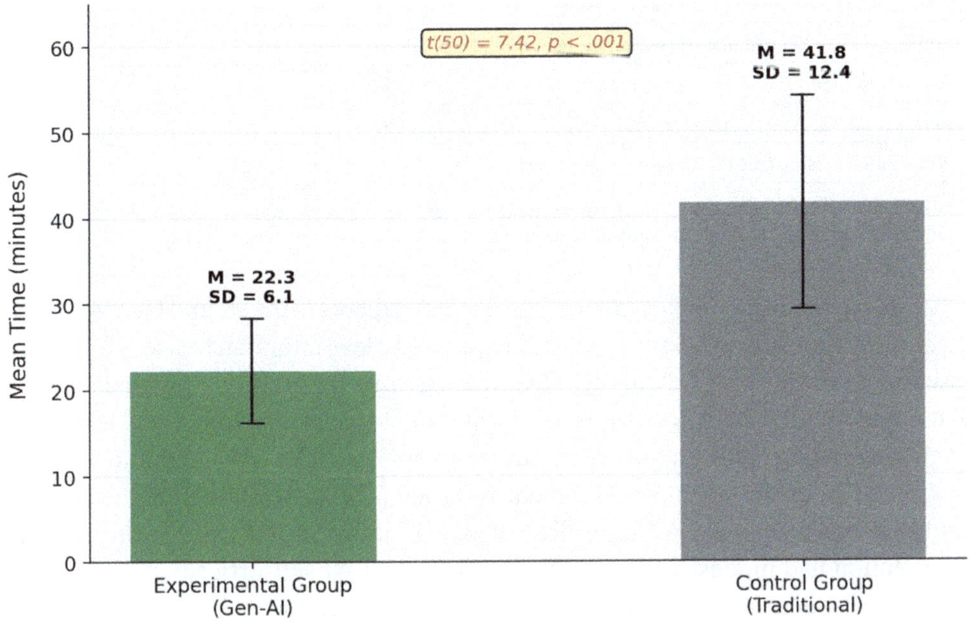

Supplementary analyses confirmed the robustness of this finding. Among participants with no prior AI experience, the experimental group still completed the task significantly faster (adjusted M = 24.1 min) than their control group counterparts (adjusted M = 42.8 min), suggesting that the 20-minute prompt engineering training was sufficient to enable productive AI-assisted work even for AI novices. The standard deviation of completion times was notably lower in the experimental group (SD = 6.1 vs. SD = 12.4), indicating that Gen-AI assistance also reduced variability in task completion—a professional development benefit in its own right.

Teacher Perceptions

Table 4 presents the distribution of responses to key questionnaire items assessing experimental group participants' perceptions of Gen-AI assistance in rubric design.

Table 4. Experimental group teacher perceptions of Gen-AI assistance (n = 27)

Item	Agree (%)	Neutral (%)	Disagree (%)
Gen-AI assistance was useful for rubric design	89	7	4
I would use Gen-AI again for assessment design	81	11	8
Gen-AI improved the quality of my rubric	78	15	7
Human review of AI output is essential	96	4	0
I feel confident using Gen-AI for professional tasks	67	22	11

Note. Items used a 5-point Likert scale. Agree combines Agree and Strongly Agree responses; Disagree combines Disagree and Strongly Disagree responses.

A strong majority of experimental group participants (89%) found Gen-AI assistance useful for rubric design, and 81% expressed clear intention to use it for future assessment design tasks. Notably, 96% of experimental group participants agreed that human review of AI output is essential—the highest agreement rate across all items—a finding with important implications for how Gen-AI integration should be framed in professional development programs. Sixty-seven percent expressed confidence in using Gen-AI for professional tasks more broadly, suggesting that the intervention had modest spillover effects on general AI self-efficacy.

Thematic analysis of interview data identified three primary themes that illuminate the quantitative findings and introduce important nuances. The first theme, AI as a Cognitive Scaffold, captured participants' descriptions of Gen-AI output as a generative starting structure rather than a finished product. Participants consistently described a pattern of receiving an AI-generated draft and then engaging in substantive professional evaluation and modification. As one experienced special educator noted, 'The AI gave me a skeleton I could actually work from. It knew things about ASD accommodations I genuinely didn't have at my fingertips.' This theme reinforces the theoretical framing of Gen-AI as a Vygotskian scaffold that amplifies rather than supplants professional knowledge.

The second theme, The Imperative of Human Refinement, reflected widespread recognition—shared by virtually all experimental group participants—that AI-generated content required active professional judgment to contextualize, validate, and adapt. One participant noted: "The AI gave me five accommodations for ASD that looked impressive, but two of them would never work in a real Greek classroom — I had to think carefully about what actually makes sense for my students".

Several participants noted that initial AI outputs occasionally included accommodations that were technically sound but culturally or contextually mismatched to the Greek primary school environment. This finding aligns with Lund and Wang's (2023) documentation of cultural specificity limitations in large language models and underscores the non-negotiable role of teacher agency in AI-assisted professional workflows.

The third theme, The Perceived-Actual Quality Gap, emerged as a theoretically significant finding not anticipated in the original study design. Interview data revealed that experimental group participants who expressed high satisfaction with their AI-assisted rubrics (78% reported improved quality) had often not subjected their rubrics to the same critical scrutiny applied by expert raters. In several cases, participants expressed confidence in the comprehensiveness of their SEND accommodations precisely because the AI had generated a larger number of adaptations—without necessarily evaluating whether those adaptations were optimally specific or practically implementable. As one teacher reflected: "I thought my rubric was perfect because it had so many accommodations. But when I read it again the next day, I realised some parts were too complicated to actually use during a lesson". This gap between perceived usefulness (TAM construct) and objective quality (expert rating) represents a subtle but important finding: Gen-AI can create an impression of comprehensiveness that exceeds the actual pedagogical value of the generated content, particularly for educators who lack the deep domain knowledge needed to critically evaluate AI-generated accommodations.

SOLUTIONS AND RECOMMENDATIONS

The findings of this study provide meaningful empirical support for the professional value of Gen-AI assistance in differentiated assessment design for students with SEND. Experimental group participants produced rubrics of significantly higher overall quality, with the largest advantages in Quality of SEND Accommodations, Clarity of Criteria, and Student-Friendly Language. These findings are consistent with theoretical predictions derived from UDL principles and suggest that Gen-AI tools can serve as powerful cognitive scaffolds for generating diverse, evidence-informed accommodation strategies that individual teachers may not produce independently from their existing professional knowledge base.

The finding that Quality of SEND Accommodations showed the largest effect size ($\eta p^2 = .51$, $d = 1.84$) is particularly noteworthy and represents the study's most practically consequential contribution. This dimension captures precisely the aspect of differentiated assessment that demands the deepest specialist knowledge—specific, actionable adaptations for diverse disability profiles—and it is here that the gap between AI-assisted and conventionally created rubrics was most dramatic. The clustering pattern observed in control group rubrics, concentrating accommodations within familiar categories (dyslexia, ADHD) while leaving ASD and mild intellectual disabilities substantially underaddressed, confirms the professional knowledge gap documented by Florian (2014) and Zoniou-Sideri and Vlachou (2006). AI-assisted rubrics broke this clustering pattern consistently, suggesting that Gen-AI's extensive training on special education literature provides a breadth of disability-specific knowledge that compensates for gaps in individual teacher expertise.

The non-significant result for Practical Applicability ($p = .187$) deserves careful interpretation and cannot be dismissed as a mere technical anomaly. Expert raters noted that several AI-assisted rubrics, while theoretically comprehensive, included accommodation lists of such length and specificity that they appeared unwieldy for routine classroom use. This finding reveals a fundamental tension at the heart of AI-assisted professional content generation: the same capacity to generate comprehensive, multi-category accommodation lists that produces superior ratings on SEND Accommodation Quality can simultaneously create instruments that feel overwhelming in practice. Critically, this tension was largely invisible to the teachers themselves—a finding that directly addresses the Perceived-Actual Quality Gap theme identified in the qualitative analysis. Teachers rated their AI-assisted rubrics as improved in quality (78% agreement) precisely because they contained more content, without necessarily evaluating whether that content was optimally calibrated for implementation. This gap between teacher perception and expert judgment is not unique to AI-assisted work—it mirrors the well-documented overconfidence effect in novice assessment design (Jonsson & Svingby, 2007)—but the AI context amplifies it by producing superficially impressive output that may discourage critical scrutiny.

The time efficiency finding (46% reduction, $\eta p^2 = .53$) is among the most practically significant results of the study. Teacher workload is a consistently documented barrier to differentiated assessment implementation (Subban, 2006; Tomlinson, 2014), and demonstrating that Gen-AI can substantially reduce rubric design time while simultaneously improving quality addresses this barrier directly. The additional finding that time variability was lower in the experimental group ($SD = 6.1$ vs. 12.4) suggests that AI assistance also provides a degree of professional scaffolding that reduces the impact of individual knowledge differences on task performance—a democratizing benefit with particular relevance in contexts where access to specialist knowledge is unevenly distributed.

The TAM framework helps contextualize the perceptual findings. High rates of perceived usefulness (89%) and adoption intention (81%) among experimental group participants confirm TAM's central prediction that direct functional benefit is the primary driver of technology adoption. However, the near-universal endorsement of the necessity of human oversight (96%) indicates that these positive perceptions were not naive: participants valued Gen-AI as a professional tool precisely because they experienced it as amplifying rather than replacing their own professional agency. This finding aligns with Nazaretsky et al.'s (2022) documentation of the conditions under which teacher trust in AI-powered tools develops—gradual, experience-based, and contingent on perceived professional control.

These findings extend and enrich the existing literature on ICT integration in Greek primary education (Skordialos, 2024a; Zaranis et al., 2015) by demonstrating that technology-assisted professional practice yields measurable quality improvements in assessment design as well as in direct instructional applications. They also add nuance to the broader literature on Gen-AI in education by providing the first empirical comparison of AI-assisted and conventional approaches to SEND assessment design—a domain whose high stakes and specialist demands make it both particularly promising and particularly risk-laden as a site for AI integration.

FUTURE RESEARCH DIRECTIONS

Several important avenues for future research emerge from this study. First, longitudinal studies examining whether AI-assisted rubric design translates into improved monitoring of student progress and improved outcomes for students with SEND in authentic classroom contexts are needed to establish ecological validity beyond structured professional development settings. Second, experimental research examining how specific prompt engineering strategies influence the quality and cross-category coverage of SEND accommodations could provide more granular guidance for professional development design. Third, replication studies in different national educational systems, subject areas, and age groups would contribute to the generalizability of these findings.

Fourth, the Perceived-Actual Quality Gap identified in this study warrants dedicated investigation. Research examining the conditions under which teachers accurately evaluate AI-generated professional content—and the training approaches that best develop this metacognitive competency—would make a significant contribution to the emerging literature on AI-assisted professional practice. Fifth, studies addressing the ethical dimensions of AI integration in SEND assessment—including data privacy, algorithmic bias in AI-generated accommodations, and the risk that AI assistance masks rather than addresses professional knowledge gaps—represent a critical priority as Gen-AI adoption accelerates. Finally, the development and validation of standardized quality frameworks for evaluating AI-assisted assessment tools, building on the instrument developed in this study, would support more systematic cross-context comparison and provide educators with practical self-evaluation resources.

CONCLUSION

This small-scale pilot study provides preliminary quasi-experimental evidence suggesting that Gen-AI assistance may improve the quality, comprehensiveness, and efficiency of differentiated rubric design for students with SEND. Teachers who used ChatGPT and Claude during the rubric creation process produced assessment instruments with substantially stronger SEND accommodations—particularly for ASD and mild intellectual disabilities, which are typically underaddressed in conventionally created rubrics—while completing the task in approximately half the time required by conventionally working peers.

The most theoretically significant finding is the documented pattern of accommodation clustering in control group rubrics and its disruption in AI-assisted rubrics. Control group teachers, working from their individual professional knowledge, systematically concentrated accommodations within familiar disability categories while neglecting less commonly encountered profiles. AI-assisted rubrics broke this pattern by drawing on the breadth of disability-specific knowledge embedded in Gen-AI training data. This finding suggests that Gen-AI's most valuable professional contribution in SEND assessment design may lie not in replacing teacher expertise but in extending its reach—ensuring that assessment tools genuinely serve all students with SEND rather than only those whose profiles teachers most readily recognize.

Equally important is the identification of the Perceived-Actual Quality Gap: the tendency for teachers to overestimate the practical quality of AI-generated content based on its apparent comprehensiveness, without subjecting it to the critical professional scrutiny that expert evaluation reveals as necessary. This finding carries a direct implication for professional development design: training teachers to use Gen-AI effectively must include explicit instruction in critical evaluation and contextual refinement of AI output, not merely in the technical mechanics of prompt engineering.

At the policy level, these findings suggest that Gen-AI tools represent a meaningful opportunity to advance educational equity for students with SEND by enabling teachers to design assessment instruments that reflect a broader ecology of disability profiles. Realizing this potential, however, requires deliberate institutional investment in targeted professional development, ethical guidelines for AI use in assessment, and ongoing empirical monitoring of AI integration outcomes.

REFERENCES

Andrade, H. L. (2013). Classroom assessment in the context of learning theory and research. In McMillan, J. H. (Ed.), *Sage handbook of research on classroom assessment* (pp. 17–34). SAGE. DOI: 10.4135/9781452218649.n2

Baidoo-Anu, D., & Owusu Ansah, L. (2023). Education in the era of generative artificial intelligence (AI): Understanding the potential benefits of ChatGPT in promoting teaching and learning. *Journal of AI*, *7*(1), 52–62. DOI: 10.61969/jai.1337500

Black, P., & Wiliam, D. (2018). Classroom assessment and pedagogy. *Assessment in Education: Principles, Policy & Practice*, *25*(6), 551–575. DOI: 10.1080/0969594X.2018.1441807

Braun, V., & Clarke, V. (2006). Using thematic analysis in psychology. *Qualitative Research in Psychology*, *3*(2), 77–101. DOI: 10.1191/1478088706qp063oa

Brookhart, S. M. (2013). *How to create and use rubrics for formative assessment and grading*. ASCD.

Brown, T. B., Mann, B., Ryder, N., Subbiah, M., Kaplan, J., Dhariwal, P., & Amodei, D. (2020). Language models are few-shot learners. *Advances in Neural Information Processing Systems*, *33*, 1877–1901.

CAST. (2018). *Universal design for learning guidelines version 2.2*. CAST. http://udlguidelines.cast.org

Crompton, H., & Burke, D. (2023). Artificial intelligence in higher education: The state of the field. *International Journal of Educational Technology in Higher Education*, *20*(1), 1–22. DOI: 10.1186/s41239-023-00392-8

Davis, F. D. (1989). Perceived usefulness, perceived ease of use, and user acceptance of information technology. *Management Information Systems Quarterly*, *13*(3), 319–340. DOI: 10.2307/249008

Ding, L., & Zou, D. (2024). Automated writing evaluation systems: A systematic review of Grammarly, Pigai, and Criterion with a perspective on future directions in the age of generative artificial intelligence. *Education and Information Technologies*, *29*(11), 14151–14203. DOI: 10.1007/s10639-023-12402-3

Florian, L. (2014). What counts as evidence of inclusive education? *European Journal of Special Needs Education*, *29*(3), 286–294. DOI: 10.1080/08856257.2014.933551

Florian, L., & Black-Hawkins, K. (2011). Exploring inclusive pedagogy. *British Educational Research Journal*, *37*(5), 813–828. DOI: 10.1080/01411926.2010.501096

Jonsson, A., & Svingby, G. (2007). The use of scoring rubrics: Reliability, validity and educational consequences. *Educational Research Review*, *2*(2), 130–144. DOI: 10.1016/j.edurev.2007.05.002

Kasneci, E., Sessler, K., Küchemann, S., Bannert, M., Dementieva, D., Fischer, F., & Kasneci, G. (2023). ChatGPT for good? On opportunities and challenges of large language models for education. *Learning and Individual Differences*, *103*, 102274. DOI: 10.1016/j.lindif.2023.102274

Koo, T. K., & Mae, M. Y. (2016). A guideline of selecting and reporting intraclass correlation coefficients for reliability research. *Journal of Chiropractic Medicine*, *15*(2), 155–163. DOI: 10.1016/j.jcm.2016.02.012 PMID: 27330520

Kostas, A., Paraschou, V., Spanos, D., Tzortzoglou, F., & Sofos, A. (2025). AI and ChatGPT in higher education: Greek students' perceived practices, benefits, and challenges. *Education Sciences*, *15*(5), 605. DOI: 10.3390/educsci15050605

Liu, P., Yuan, W., Fu, J., Jiang, Z., Hayashi, H., & Neubig, G. (2022). Pre-train, prompt, and predict: A systematic survey of prompting methods in natural language processing. *ACM Computing Surveys*, *55*(9), 1–35. DOI: 10.1145/3560815

Lund, B. D., & Wang, T. (2023). Chatting about ChatGPT: How may AI and GPT impact academia and libraries? *Library Hi Tech News*, *40*(3), 26–29. DOI: 10.1108/LHTN-01-2023-0009

Mertler, C. A. (2001). Designing scoring rubrics for your classroom. *Practical Assessment, Research & Evaluation*, *7*(25). Advance online publication. DOI: 10.7275/gcy8-0w24

Meyer, A., Rose, D. H., & Gordon, D. (2014). *Universal design for learning: Theory and practice*. CAST Professional Publishing.

Mollick, E. R., & Mollick, L. (2023). *Assigning AI: Seven approaches for students, with prompts. SSRN*. DOI: 10.2139/ssrn.4475995

Nazaretsky, T., Ariely, M., Cukurova, M., & Alexandron, G. (2022). Teachers' trust in AI-powered educational technology and a professional development program to improve it. *British Journal of Educational Technology*, *53*(4), 914–931. DOI: 10.1111/bjet.13232

Pavlik, J. V. (2023). Collaborating with ChatGPT: Considering the implications of generative artificial intelligence for journalism and media education. *Journalism & Mass Communication Educator*, *78*(1), 84–93. DOI: 10.1177/10776958221149577

Rose, D. H., & Meyer, A. (2002). *Teaching every student in the digital age: Universal design for learning*. ASCD.

Scherer, R., Siddiq, F., & Tondeur, J. (2019). The technology acceptance model (TAM): A meta-analytic structural equation modeling approach to explaining teachers' adoption of digital technology in education. *Computers & Education*, *128*, 13–35. DOI: 10.1016/j.compedu.2018.09.009

Schiff, D. (2021). Out of the laboratory and into the classroom: The future of artificial intelligence in education. *AI & Society*, *36*(1), 331–348. DOI: 10.1007/s00146-020-01033-8 PMID: 32836908

Selwyn, N. (2022). The future of AI and education: Some cautionary notes. *European Journal of Education*, *57*(4), 620–631. DOI: 10.1111/ejed.12532

Shadish, W. R., Cook, T. D., & Campbell, D. T. (2002). *Experimental and quasi-experimental designs for generalized causal inference*. Houghton Mifflin.

Skordialos, E. (2024a). Empowering mathematics education in Greek primary schools: Bridging the divide through ICT integration and interactive boards for enhanced teacher ICT literacy. *European Journal of Education and Pedagogy*, *5*(2), 59–63. DOI: 10.24018/ejedu.2024.5.2.779

Skordialos, E. (2024b). Enhancing primary school geometry education: A comprehensive exploration of the Van Hiele model and ICT integration. *Science and Technology*, *8*(2), 1655–1659.

Skordialos, E., & Baralis, G. (2017). Mediated learning experience and its role in teaching fractions to pupils with learning difficulties. *International Journal of Learning and Teaching*, *10*(2), 158–165. DOI: 10.18844/ijlt.v10i2.3410

Su, J., & Yang, W. (2023). Artificial intelligence in early childhood education: A scoping review. *Computers and Education: Artificial Intelligence*, *5*, 100049. DOI: 10.1016/j.caeai.2022.100049

Subban, P. (2006). Differentiated instruction: A research basis. *International Education Journal*, *7*(7), 935–947.

Teo, T. (2011). Factors influencing teachers' intention to use technology: Model development and test. *Computers & Education*, *57*(4), 2432–2440. DOI: 10.1016/j.compedu.2011.06.008

Tomlinson, C. A. (2014). *The differentiated classroom: Responding to the needs of all learners* (2nd ed.). ASCD.

Tomlinson, C. A., & Imbeau, M. B. (2010). *Leading and managing a differentiated classroom*. ASCD.

Tsibidaki, A. (2026). Listening to students with learning difficulties: Student voice, participation, and recommendations for inclusive practice in primary education. *Education Sciences*, *16*(4), 655. DOI: 10.3390/educsci16040655

Tsibidaki, A., Kogiami, A., Flagkou, A., Vagianou, S., & Trecha, S. (2020). Introducing teacher training for special and inclusive education in Cyprus, Germany, Great Britain, Greece, and Italy. *Journal of Education and Human Development*, *9*(2), 91–103. DOI: 10.15640/jehd.v9n2a10

Venkatesh, V., & Bala, H. (2008). Technology acceptance model 3 and a research agenda on interventions. *Decision Sciences*, *39*(2), 273–315. DOI: 10.1111/j.1540-5915.2008.00192.x

Venkatesh, V., & Davis, F. D. (2000). A theoretical extension of the technology acceptance model: Four longitudinal field studies. *Management Science*, *46*(2), 186–204. DOI: 10.1287/mnsc.46.2.186.11926

Vygotsky, L. S. (1978). *Mind in society: The development of higher psychological processes*. Harvard University Press.

White, J., Fu, Q., Hays, S., Sandborn, M., Olea, C., Gilbert, H., Elnashar, A., Spencer-Smith, J., & Schmidt, D. C. (2023). *A prompt pattern catalog to enhance prompt engineering with ChatGPT*. DOI: 10.48550/arXiv.2302.11382

Zaranis, N., Baralis, G., & Skordialos, E. (2015). Comparing the effectiveness of using ICT for teaching addition in the first grade students based on Realistic Mathematics Education. *International Journal of Information Technology & Computer Science*, *19*(1), 127–138.

Zawacki-Richter, O., Marín, V. I., Bond, M., & Gouverneur, F. (2019). Systematic review of research on artificial intelligence applications in higher education – where are the educators? *International Journal of Educational Technology in Higher Education*, *16*(1), 39. DOI: 10.1186/s41239-019-0171-0

Zhai, X., Chu, X., Chai, C. S., Jong, M. S. Y., Istenic, A., Spector, M., & Li, Y. (2021). A review of artificial intelligence (AI) in education from 2010 to 2020. *Complexity*, *8812542*(1), 8812542. DOI: 10.1155/2021/8812542

Zoniou-Sideri, A., & Vlachou, A. (2006). Greek teachers' belief systems about disability and inclusive education. *International Journal of Inclusive Education*, *10*(4–5), 379–394. DOI: 10.1080/13603110500430690

ADDITIONAL READING

Ainscow, M., & Miles, S. (2008). Making education for all inclusive: Where next? *Prospects*, *38*(1), 15–34. DOI: 10.1007/s11125-008-9055-0

Fernández-Sánchez, A., Lorenzo-Castiñeiras, J. J., & Sánchez-Bello, A. (2025). Navigating the future of pedagogy: The integration of AI tools in developing educational assessment rubrics. *European Journal of Education*, *60*(1), e12826. DOI: 10.1111/ejed.12826

Gebremariam, H. T., & Gedamu, A. D. (2023). Primary school teachers' assessment for learning practice for students' learning improvement. *Frontiers in Education*, *8*, 1145195. DOI: 10.3389/feduc.2023.1145195

Hopcan, S., Polat, E., Ozturk, M. E., & Ozturk, L. (2023). Artificial intelligence in special education: A systematic review. *Interactive Learning Environments*, *31*(10), 7335–7353. DOI: 10.1080/10494820.2022.2067186

Marino, M. T., Vasquez, E., Dieker, L., Basham, J., & Blackorby, J. (2023). The future of artificial intelligence in special education technology. *Journal of Special Education Technology*, *38*(3), 404–416. DOI: 10.1177/01626434231165977

Nieminen, J. H., Moriña, A., & Biagiotti, G. (2024). Assessment as a matter of inclusion: A meta-ethnographic review of the assessment experiences of students with disabilities in higher education. *Educational Research Review*, *42*, 100582. DOI: 10.1016/j.edurev.2023.100582

Paglialunga, A., & Melogno, S. (2025). The effectiveness of artificial intelligence-based interventions for students with learning disabilities: A systematic review. *Brain Sciences*, *15*(8), 806. DOI: 10.3390/brainsci15080806 PMID: 40867139

Zdravkova, K., Krasniqi, V., Dalipi, F., & Ferati, M. (2022). Cutting-edge communication and learning assistive technologies for disabled children: An artificial intelligence perspective. *Frontiers in Artificial Intelligence*, *5*, 970430. DOI: 10.3389/frai.2022.970430 PMID: 36388402

Zhang, L., Carter, R. A., Liu, Y., & Peng, P. (2024). Let's CHAT about artificial intelligence for students with disabilities: A systematic literature review and meta-analysis. *Review of Educational Research*. Advance online publication. DOI: 10.3102/00346543241293424

KEY TERMS AND DEFINITIONS

Analytic Rubric: An assessment tool that evaluates student performance across multiple distinct criteria, each with defined performance levels and descriptors, enabling detailed diagnostic feedback that supports both grading and instructional planning.

Differentiated Assessment: A systematic approach to evaluating student learning that adapts task formats, criteria, and evaluation methods to accommodate individual differences in learning needs, abilities, and profiles, ensuring that assessment instruments measure intended constructs rather than disability-related barriers.

Generative Artificial Intelligence (Gen-AI): A class of machine learning systems capable of producing original, contextually appropriate content—including text, images, and structured documents—in response to natural language instructions, drawing on large-scale training corpora.

MANCOVA (Multivariate Analysis of Covariance): A statistical procedure that simultaneously examines group differences across multiple dependent variables while controlling for the influence of one or more covariates, enabling more precise estimation of treatment effects in quasi-experimental designs.

Perceived-Actual Quality Gap: A discrepancy between a practitioner's subjective evaluation of professionally created content and its objective quality as assessed by independent expert raters; identified in this study as a specific risk associated with AI-assisted professional content generation.

Prompt Engineering: The practice of designing and iteratively refining natural language instructions provided to AI systems to elicit high-quality, relevant, and contextually appropriate outputs aligned with specific professional or educational goals.

Special Educational Needs and Disabilities (SEND): A range of conditions that affect a learner's ability to access the curriculum or participate in educational activities without appropriate support, including learning disabilities, ADHD, autism spectrum disorder, sensory impairments, and intellectual disabilities.

Technology Acceptance Model (TAM): A theoretical framework explaining individual technology adoption behavior through the constructs of perceived usefulness and perceived ease of use, widely applied in educational technology research to understand teachers' decisions regarding the adoption of digital tools.

Universal Design for Learning (UDL): An educational framework that proposes designing learning materials and assessment instruments to accommodate the widest possible range of learner variability by providing multiple means of representation, action and expression, and engagement, minimizing barriers from the design stage rather than retrofitting accommodations.

APPENDIX

Appendix A: Experimental Group Materials

A1. Asynchronous Training Content

The asynchronous training module delivered via Google Classroom consisted of five sequential steps completed at the participant's own pace prior to the rubric creation task. The module was designed and delivered by the researcher following the study objectives and intervention protocol. Table 5 outlines the content of each step.

Table 5. Experimental group asynchronous training content delivered through Google Classroom

Step	Topic	Content
1	Introduction to Gen-AI tools	Overview of ChatGPT-4 and Claude 3 Sonnet; key capabilities and limitations for educational use
2	Principles of effective prompting	Role assignment, specificity, structured output requests, avoiding vague instructions
3	Worked examples	Three annotated examples of rubric prompts with AI outputs: generic prompt, structured prompt, and iterative refinement prompt for SEND accommodations
4	Critical evaluation of AI output	How to identify generic, incomplete, or contextually inappropriate accommodations; guidelines for professional refinement
5	Task briefing	Distribution of rubric creation task specifications and submission instructions via Google Classroom

Note. Total estimated completion time was approximately 20 minutes. All materials were delivered asynchronously via Google Classroom.

A2. Prompt Template

Following the training module, participants used the prompt template presented in Table 6 as their starting point for the rubric creation task. Participants were explicitly encouraged to engage in iterative dialogue with the AI tools, asking follow-up questions, requesting revisions, and incorporating their own professional judgment into the final rubric.

Table 6. Prompt template provided to the experimental group

Element	Content
Initial prompt	Act as a special education expert and experienced primary school teacher. Create an analytic assessment rubric for evaluating Grade 5 mathematical problem-solving performance. The rubric must include: (a) four assessment criteria; (b) four performance levels per criterion (Beginning, Developing, Proficient, Advanced); (c) specific, actionable accommodations for students with dyslexia/dyscalculia, ADHD, mild intellectual disabilities, and autism spectrum disorder; and (d) student-friendly language throughout.
Follow-up refinement prompt	Please revise the accommodations for [specific SEND category] to be more specific and actionable. Ensure they reflect Universal Design for Learning principles and are distinct from the other categories.

Note. The template was provided as a starting point rather than a fixed script. Participants were free to modify, extend, or replace any element based on their professional judgment.

A3. Sample AI Output

Table 7 presents a representative AI-generated output produced in response to the prompt template above, together with the corresponding expert rater evaluation. This example illustrates the type and specificity of content generated by the AI tools during the study.

Table 7. Sample AI-generated accommodation and expert rater evaluation

Element	Content
AI model	ChatGPT-4
Criterion addressed	Criterion 2 — Strategy planning
SEND category	ADHD
AI-generated accommodation	Provide the problem in three sequential sub-questions, each presented on a separate line with a checkbox (Step 1: Read the problem carefully. Step 2: Choose your operation. Step 3: Write your answer). Allow the student to complete one sub-question before proceeding to the next, and permit a short movement break between steps if needed.
Expert rater evaluation	Rated as specific and actionable by all three expert raters (4/4 on the Quality of SEND Accommodations dimension). Raters noted that it operationalises the chunking principle precisely and is directly implementable in a primary classroom context.

Note. This excerpt is provided for illustrative purposes. Participants were encouraged to critically evaluate and modify all AI-generated content before finalising their rubrics.

Appendix B: Control Group Materials

Control group participants received the materials summarised in Table 8 via Google Classroom, simultaneously with the task briefing. No AI tools were accessible to this group at any point during the task.

Table 8. Reference materials provided to the control group

Material	Description
Sample Rubric A	Analytic rubric for a primary school science inquiry task (three criteria, four levels) with no SEND accommodations
Sample Rubric B	Holistic rubric for a primary school writing task (Grades 4–6) with generic differentiation notes
Sample Rubric C	Analytic rubric for mathematics problem-solving at a different grade level, with two SEND accommodation examples
Reference Guide	One-page written guide covering the definition and components of analytic rubrics, principles of differentiated assessment, and a brief overview of SEND categories relevant to the task

Note. All materials were provided in PDF format via Google Classroom. No AI tools or internet search assistance were permitted during the task.

Appendix C: Contamination Prevention Procedures

To minimise the risk of contamination between groups, participants were assigned to conditions prior to receiving any materials and were instructed not to discuss the task with colleagues until after the submission deadline, 15 days from task distribution. Group assignment was not disclosed to participants; each participant received only the materials relevant to their own condition, delivered through separate Google Classroom streams. No participant indicated awareness of the other group's training approach in the post-task questionnaire or in the interview data.

Chapter 9
Arts-Based Interventions for Skill Development in Special Education Through Artificial Intelligence:
A Systematic Literature Review (2020-2025)

Maria Kladaki
http://orcid.org/0000-0003-3146-6914
University of the Aegean, Greece

Panagiotis Alexopoulos
http://orcid.org/0009-0000-3768-5136
University of the Aegean, Greece

Konstantinos Mastrothanasis
http://orcid.org/0000-0002-8703-9607
Open University of Cyprus, Cyprus

ABSTRACT

This systematic literature review examines arts-based interventions supported by Artificial Intelligence (AI) for skill development in students with Special Educational Needs and/or Disabilities (SEND). The review focuses on English-language studies published between January 2020 and April 2025 and indexed in Scopus. Thirty-seven studies met the inclusion criteria, while eight incorporated arts-based elements,

DOI: 10.4018/979-8-3373-9169-4.ch009

mainly creative writing, storytelling, visual arts, music, theater, and dance. The findings indicate growing research activity after 2022, with most interventions focusing on primary education and students with autism spectrum disorder. Literature-based practices, especially creative writing and storytelling, were the most frequent arts-based forms. Most studies reported improvements in social, communication, learning-related, cognitive, emotional, and creative skills. The review identifies the need for stronger integration of arts-based pedagogy, broader SEND representation, and greater attention to ethical, accessibility, and pedagogical issues.

INTRODUCTION

The use of technology in Special Education can be an effective factor in supporting students with Special Educational Needs and/or Disabilities (SEND), contributing to skill development, the promotion of autonomy, and equal participation in the learning process (Drossinou Korea & Alexopoulos, 2022; Olakanmi et al., 2020). For instance, the meta-analysis by Wang et al. (2025) found that the use of robots in interventions with students with Autism Spectrum Disorder (ASD) has significant positive effects, especially in language and social skills, particularly when teachers are actively involved in the process. Furthermore, studies by Cheng and Lai (2019) and Mohamed Mokmin and Rassy (2024) highlight the positive impact of technologies such as tablets and augmented reality on improving motor skills, participation, and school performance in students with disabilities. Digital applications, serious educational games, and other interactive technologies provide multiple forms of support in Special Education by enhancing key soft skills such as collaboration and communication, as well as student engagement. Additionally, when technology is used in a multisensory manner and tailored to the needs of students with SEND, it can foster innovative learning experiences, improving skills such as reading comprehension, answering questions, social interaction, and self-motivation. A playful approach, in particular, appears to boost students' interest and motivation, creating an engaging and flexible learning environment. Moreover, supportive technologies, including Web 2.0 tools, software, and mobile devices, promote autonomy and social inclusion, enhancing students' participation in school life (Dumitru, 2025; Fernández-Batanero et al., 2022; Gallud et al., 2023; Kaimara, 2026; Shaaban & Mohamed, 2024).

The above-mentioned benefits can be further enhanced with the advent of emerging Artificial Intelligence (AI) technologies, such as Large Language Models (Drossinou Korea & Alexopoulos, 2024a, 2025b; Kladaki et al., 2025; Mastrothanasis et al., 2026). Within this broader field, Generative Artificial Intelligence (GenAI) occupies a distinct position, since it can produce text, images, audio, and multimodal learning materials that may be adapted to students' profiles, communication needs, and learning goals. As technological progress enables the creation of intelligent systems with natural language processing, computer vision, machine learning, and real-time interaction capabilities, the literature increasingly turns to the pedagogical applications of these technologies to support students with Special Educational Needs and/or Disabilities (SEND). According to Drossinou Korea and Alexopoulos (2024a), generative AI applications, such as ChatGPT, can be utilized in Special Education, as they can provide differentiated support to both students and teachers. Zhai's (2023) study showed that ChatGPT can adapt science teaching for students with dyslexia, while Rakap (2024) found that novice teachers designed more effective programs for students with ASD with the help of such tools. Furthermore, these applications can enhance the language and communication skills of students with Specific Learning Difficulties (SpLDs), ASD, intellectual, or multiple disabilities by facilitating the understanding of complex concepts and the expression of emotions (Bertacchini et al., 2023; Choi, 2023; Dumitru et al., 2024; Karakose & Tülübaş, 2023; Rane, 2023). Additionally, their use is associated with increased interest and active participation in learning, as shown in the research by Jauhiainen and Guerra (2023).

However, despite the pedagogical possibilities associated with such technologies in Special Education, issues related to accessibility, inadequate teacher training, and lack of targeted use remain. In this context, targeted, practice-oriented professional development programs have been shown to significantly enhance teachers' self-efficacy and readiness to integrate AI technologies into their pedagogical practices (Alexopoulos et al., 2025). Furthermore, since each case of a student with SEND is unique, there is a risk that large-scale technological solutions used in education may not align with the principles of Special Education, which emphasize individualization and differentiation (Aljedaani et al., 2023; Bong & Chen, 2024; Cheng & Lai, 2020; Javed et al., 2024; Kumm et al., 2022; Prado et al., 2023; Zhang et al., 2020). In the case of Artificial Intelligence in particular, the literature expresses reservations regarding the actual personalization of content, as it often produces standardized, mechanistic responses that contradict the principles of differentiated instruction (Alenezi et al., 2023; Bertacchini et al., 2023; Rakap, 2024). Tools such as TISIPfSENDs, which require hetero-observation, understanding of the student's individual profile, and targeted differentiation, something that can only emerge through teacher-student interaction, highlight the limitations of AI (Drossinou Korea & Alexopoulos, 2024a). Furthermore, the lack of emotional intelligence, the possibility of incorrect or misleading answers, the risk of copying, and the possibility of overreliance or excessive use, particularly among students who may require structured routines and guided digital engagement, should be carefully considered (AlZu'bi et al., 2023; Choi, 2023; Mastrothanasis et al., 2025a, 2025b). Therefore, the effective use of AI in the education of students with SEND requires continuous pedagogical awareness, sensitivity, and deliberate, targeted implementation within individualized intervention programs, with the teacher maintaining a central role so that technology serves as a supportive tool (Mastrothanasis et al., 2025a).

Arts-based interventions in Special Education have been associated with multiple dimensions of skill development, including communication, emotional expression, social interaction, motor coordination, and creative engagement. Specifically, as Mastrothanasis et al. (2025a) point out, every form of art can contribute in different ways to the development of skills in students with SEND. Music, for instance, may strengthen memory and auditory processing skills, as well as enhance emotional regulation and communication, especially in students who experience difficulties with language expression (Mastrothanasis, 2025; Yan, 2024). Theater and theatrical play activities, on the other hand, provide a safe space for social experimentation, helping students understand roles and social consequences (Boal, 2002; Dumitru et al., 2026; Giagazoglou et al., 2026; Koltsida & Lenakakis, 2017; Mastrothanasis et al., 2024; Şimşek et al., 2019). Additionally, the visual arts allow for nonverbal expression, enhance fine motor skills, and help transform emotions into visual forms (Round et al., 2017). Finally, dance not only improves physical fitness but also supports emotional expression, stress management, and the regulation of hyperactivity (Bresler Nardi et al., 2022; Shuper Engelhard, 2024). The combination of arts-based pedagogy and AI-supported tools therefore forms an emerging area of inquiry in Special Education, particularly in relation to skill development, participation, and individualized support.

In this chapter, arts-based interventions are understood as intentionally designed educational activities that use artistic forms and aesthetic experience as part of the learning process. These interventions include narrative, visual, musical, theatrical, dance-based, performative, and multimodal practices through which students make meaning, communicate, participate, and express emotions or ideas. This definition draws on arts-based learning theory, which treats artistic making as a form of inquiry and meaning-making (Barone & Eisner, 2012; Eisner, 2002), aesthetic education, which emphasizes perception, interpretation, and qualitative judgment through artistic experience (Dewey, 1934), multimodal pedagogy, which recognizes meaning as distributed across language, image, sound, gesture, movement, space, and material forms (Kress, 2010), and embodied learning, which views bodily action, rhythm, voice, movement, and sensory participation as integral to cognition and learning (Shapiro & Stolz, 2019). In Special Education, this framing is particularly important because students with SEND may engage with learning and demonstrate understanding through multiple expressive modes.

Although research on technology, AI, and Special Education has expanded in recent years, the intersection between AI-supported interventions and arts-based pedagogical practices remains insufficiently synthesized. Existing reviews tend to examine assistive technologies, robotics, digital tools, or AI applications in Special Education more broadly, while limited attention has been given to the ways in which artistic forms such as storytelling, creative writing, visual arts, music, theater, and dance are incorporated into AI-supported interventions for students with SEND. This gap is important because arts-based approaches are closely linked to communication, social participation, emotional expression, creativity, and embodied learning, which are central dimensions of skill development in Special Education. The present systematic literature review addresses this gap by examining AI-supported interventions for students with SEND and by identifying the extent, forms, and reported outcomes of arts-based elements within these interventions.

Scope, Research Questions, and Contribution

Considering the above, this systematic literature review examines interventions for students with SEND, in which Artificial Intelligence technologies are used to enhance students' skills, with particular attention to the extent to which arts-based elements are incorporated into these interventions. Therefore, the research questions are framed as follows:

1) What is the trend in Special Education interventions that use AI to enhance the skills of students with SEND? To answer this question, the type and year of publication, the countries where the research was conducted, the research methodology followed, and the participants' educational level are examined.
2) Which SEND, and which AI technologies, are most frequently addressed in the interventions?
3) What is the role of the arts in these interventions?
4) What skills can be enhanced through these interventions?

This systematic literature review attempts to fill an important research gap by focusing on interventions in Special Education that utilize Artificial Intelligence to enhance the skills of students with SEND. Its particular contribution lies in the systematic examination of the intersection between Artificial Intelligence and the arts, highlighting their role in Special Education interventions.

METHODOLOGY

The design and implementation of educational research require a systematic approach, involving stages such as topic selection, literature review, and the careful selection of research tools. The present review was conducted in accordance with the Preferred Reporting Items for Systematic Reviews and Meta-Analyses 2020 statement (PRISMA 2020), which supports transparent and reproducible reporting in systematic reviews (Page et al., 2021). The review process was carried out in four successive stages: identification, screening, eligibility, and inclusion. These stages ensured a comprehensive and methodologically sound approach to literature selection and evaluation. The PRISMA 2020 framework was used to organize the search, screening, eligibility assessment, and final inclusion of studies.

Identification and Pre-Screening

The scope of this review included studies published in English between January 2020 and April 2025. This period was selected because it coincides with major developments in the field of Generative Artificial Intelligence. Extending the time-frame further back could have resulted in inconsistencies with current technological developments and emerging research trends, particularly in light of the advances that followed 2022 and the introduction of ChatGPT. In addition, the search was restricted to the Scopus database, using a complex query that yielded 1,043 results; TITLE-ABS-KEY ((“special education” OR “inclusive education” OR “special needs education” OR “special educational needs” OR “learning disabilities” OR “learning difficulties” OR dyslexia OR dysgraphia OR autism OR “autism spectrum disorder” OR asd OR “developmental disorders” OR neurodivergent OR neurodiversity OR adhd OR “attention deficit hyperactivity disorder”) AND (“Generative AI” OR “Artificial Intelligence” OR ai OR “Large Language Model*” OR llm* OR gpt OR chatgpt OR gemini OR “image generation” OR “text-to-image” OR “text-to-video” OR “text-to-music” OR “music generation” OR “video generation” OR “multimodal AI” OR “creative AI” OR “generative model*” OR “transformer model*”) AND (app* OR application* OR tool* OR platform* OR chatbot* OR “assistive technology” OR “educational technology” OR edtech)) AND PUBYEAR > 2019 AND PUBYEAR < 2026 AND (LIMIT-TO (DOCTYPE, “ar”) OR LIMIT-TO (DOCTYPE, “cp”)) AND (LIMIT-TO (LANGUAGE, “English”)) AND (LIMIT-TO (PUBSTAGE, “final”)). The search was conducted in April 2025. Although arts-related terms were not included as separate search terms, the role of the arts was examined during data extraction and synthesis, in line with the third research question. This broader search strategy was adopted in order to avoid excluding AI-supported interventions in which arts-based elements were embedded in the intervention design but were not explicitly indexed in the title, abstract, or keywords.

Inclusion and Exclusion Criteria

The selection of studies was determined by inclusion and exclusion criteria related to (a) the type of publication, (b) the language of the text, (c) the research design, and (d) the quality of the study. More specifically, regarding the type of publication, eligible studies included journal articles and conference proceedings, provided they were written in English. As for the research design, priority was given to qualitative, quantitative, or mixed-method studies involving interventions targeting students with SEND, in which Artificial Intelligence was used in vivo and resulted in measurable changes in students' skills after the intervention. The presence of arts-based elements was not used as an initial eligibility criterion; rather, it was treated as an analytical category during data extraction. Arts-based elements were coded when the intervention included practices such as storytelling, creative writing, visual arts, music, theater, dance, animation, comics, or other creative modalities connected to skill development. The studies identified were assessed by two independent reviewers, who approved those that met the inclusion criteria based on the quality assessment framework developed by Kmet et al. (2004). Inter-rater agreement was calculated using Cohen's kappa coefficient, indicating an acceptable level of agreement ($\kappa \geq 0.60$).

In addition to the inclusion and exclusion criteria, the methodological quality of the included studies was considered during synthesis. Given the heterogeneity of study designs, the Kmet et al. (2004) framework was used as a structured quality-appraisal tool. The synthesis treated the findings with different evidentiary weight. Studies with clear sampling procedures, defined intervention protocols, comparison or control conditions, validated outcome measures, and transparent statistical or qualitative analysis were interpreted as stronger evidence. Studies with small samples, limited procedural detail, weak outcome measurement, or short intervention duration were treated as lower-weight evidence. This approach functioned as a risk-of-bias sensitivity check and helped prevent the synthesis from assigning equal evidentiary strength to all reported improvements.

RESULTS

Following the above procedure and after a thorough review of 91 studies based on the inclusion and exclusion criteria, a total of 37 studies were ultimately selected. These studies involved in vivo use of Artificial Intelligence in Special Education interventions, where an impact on the skills of students with SEND was observed. The selection process that led to the final inclusion of 37 studies is illustrated with quantitative data in the PRISMA 2020 flow diagram (Figure 1).

Figure 1. PRISMA 2020 flow diagram for the study selection process

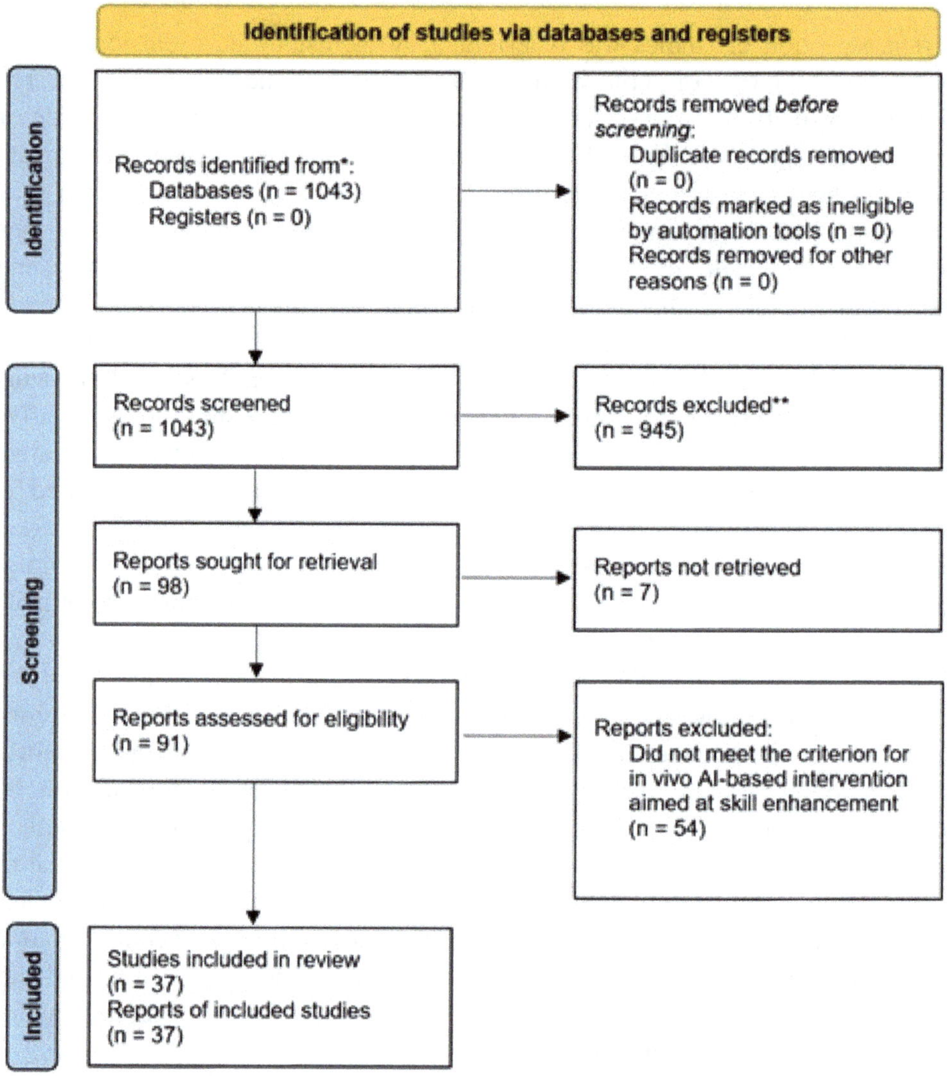

Trends in AI-Supported Special Education Interventions

Regarding the type of publication, among the 37 studies, most of them (n = 27, 72.97%) were published in scientific journals. The remaining 10 studies (27.03%) were published in conference proceedings (see Table 1).

Table 1. Publication type of studies

Publication type	n	%
Article in scientific journals	27	72.97
Article in conference proceedings	10	27.03
Total	37	100

Focusing on the publication year of the selected studies between January 2020 and April 2025, the largest number of studies was published in 2024 (n = 13, 35.14%). An equal number of studies was published in 2023 and in the first four months of 2025 (n = 7, 18.92% in each case). In addition, five studies were published in 2022 (13.51%), four in 2021 (10.81%), and one in 2020 (2.70%) (see Table 2).

Table 2. Publication date of studies

Year of publication	n	%
2024	13	35.14
2025	7	18.92
2023	7	18.92
2022	5	13.51
2021	4	10.81
2020	1	2.70
Total	37	100

Examining the country where the studies were conducted, it is observed (Figure 2) that the majority of country mentions referred to India (n = 6, 14.63%) and China (n = 5, 12.20%), followed by Spain (n = 4, 9.76%) and Saudi Arabia (n = 4, 9.76%). In addition, 3 country mentions (7.32%) referred to the USA, while 2 country mentions (4.88%) referred to Brazil, the United Arab Emirates, Kazakhstan, and Taiwan. Finally, 1 country mention (2.44%) referred to Kuwait, Iran, Ecuador, Japan, Slovenia, Jordan, Italy, Russia, Greece, the Netherlands, and Thailand. It should be noted that the total number of countries mentioned was 41 because some studies referred to more than one country.

Figure 2. Countries where the interventions were implemented

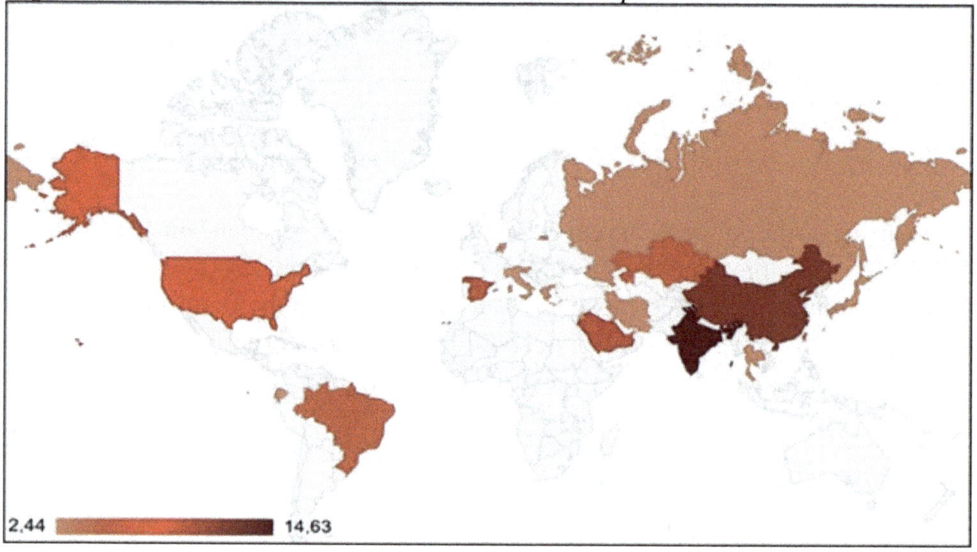

In terms of the research methodology, the majority used quantitative methodology (n = 26, 70.27%), indicating a clear preference for research designs based on numerical data and statistical analysis. On the other hand, 7 studies (18.92%) adopted a mixed methodology, combining quantitative and qualitative data, while only 4 (10.81%) were based entirely on a qualitative approach (see Table 3).

Table 3. Research methodology of the included studies

Methodology	n	%
Quantitative	26	70.27
Mixed	7	18.92
Qualitative	4	10.81
Total	37	100

Finally, focusing on the age group and level of education in which the interventions were implemented, it is found that the majority of studies involved children aged 6-12, which represents primary education (n = 26, 72.22%). Eleven studies (30.56%) included preschool-age children, six studies (16.67%) included higher education students or adults, and five studies (13.89%) included participants in secondary education. It is worth noting that in 1 study (Tozadore et al., 2022), the participants' age was not explicitly mentioned (Table 4, percentages exceed 100% because some studies included multiple educational levels).

Table 4. Participants' age - educational level

Study	Age group – participants' educational level			
	Pre-school age (ages 2-5)	**Primary education (ages 6–12)**	**Secondary education (ages 13-17)**	**Higher education - adults (≥ ages 18)**
Ahuja et al. (2022)		✓		
Aldakhil (2024)		✓		
Alnafjan et al. (2025)	✓	✓		
Alsolami (2025)		✓		
Ayasrah et al. (2024)		✓		
Berrezueta-Guzman et al. (2021)		✓		
Fan et al. (2025)	✓	✓		
Fang et al. (2024)				✓
Jafarian & Kramer (2025)				✓
Katsarou et al. (2025)		✓		
Lorenzo & Lorenzo-Lledó (2024)		✓		
Mao et al. (2025)				✓
Marrauwi et al. (2023)		✓	✓	
Medina et al. (2021)		✓		
Morciano et al. (2024)				✓
Mutawa et al. (2023)	✓	✓		
Panda et al. (2024)	✓	✓		
Podpečan (2023)	✓	✓	✓	✓
Poobrasert & Satsutthi (2020)		✓		
Renjith & Jeeva (2025)			✓	
Rodríguez-Quevedo et al. (2023)		✓		
Safi et al. (2021)	✓	✓		
Serpa-Andrade et al. (2022)	✓			
Singh et al. (2024)		✓		
Su et al. (2024)		✓		

continued on following page

Table 4. Continued

Study	Age group – participants' educational level			
	Pre-school age (ages 2-5)	**Primary education (ages 6–12)**	**Secondary education (ages 13-17)**	**Higher education - adults (≥ ages 18)**
Taheri et al. (2021)	✓	✓		
Thomas et al. (2024)		✓		
Toyokawa et al. (2023)		✓		
Tozadore et al. (2022)	*Not mentioned*			
Utepbayeva et al. (2024)	✓			
Valentim et al. (2023)	✓			
Ventura (2024)			✓	
Wang (2023)		✓		
Wang et al. (2022)			✓	✓
Wang et al. (2024)	✓	✓		
Xu (2024)		✓		
Zhao et al. (2022)		✓		
Total n	11	26	5	6
Total %	30.56	72.22	13.89	16.67

SEND Categories and AI Technologies Addressed in the Interventions

Regarding the type of Special Educational Need and/or Disability targeted by the interventions, it was found that the majority of studies (n = 20, 54.05%) focused on ASD. In addition, several studies addressed specific learning difficulties, such as dyslexia and dysorthographia (n = 10, 27.03%), as well as ADHD (n = 9, 24.32%). By contrast, only two studies (5.41%) involved students with intellectual disabilities, while one study (2.70%) targeted individuals with sensory disabilities (hearing impairments), speech disorders (e.g., stuttering), or emotional difficulties, respectively (Table 5).

Table 5. Study classification by type of SEND

Type of SEND	Study	n	%
Autism Spectrum Disorder (ASD)	Alnafjan et al. (2025), Fan et al. (2025), Fang et al. (2024), Lorenzo & Lorenzo-Lledó (2024), Marrauwi et al. (2023), Mutawa et al. (2023), Panda et al. (2024), Podpečan (2023), Rodríguez-Quevedo et al. (2023), Safi et al. (2021), Singh et al. (2024), Su et al. (2024), Taheri et al. (2021), Toyokawa et al. (2023), Tozadore et al. (2022), Valentim et al. (2023), Wang (2023), Wang et al. (2024), Xu (2024), Zhao et al. (2022)	20	54.05
Specific learning difficulties (dyslexia, dysgraphia, etc.)	Ahuja et al. (2022), Ayasrah et al. (2024), Fang et al. (2024), Katsarou et al. (2025), Morciano et al. (2024), Poobrasert & Satsutthi (2020), Renjith & Jeeva (2025), Thomas et al. (2024), Ventura (2024), Wang et al. (2022)	10	27.03
Attention Deficit Disorder and/or Hyperactivity Disorder (ADHD)	Aldakhil (2024), Berrezueta-Guzman et al. (2021), Fang et al. (2024), Jafarian & Kramer (2025), Katsarou et al. (2025), Medina et al. (2021), Podpečan (2023), Serpa-Andrade et al. (2022), Su et al. (2024)	9	24.32
Intellectual disability	Alsolami (2025), Renjith & Jeeva (2025)	2	5.41
Sensory disabilities (hearing problems)	Mao et al. (2025)	1	2.70
Speech disorders (stuttering, etc.)	Utepbayeva et al. (2024)	1	2.70
Emotional difficulties	Su et al. (2024)	1	2.70

Focusing on the AI technologies used in the interventions, adaptive learning systems, speech recognition, and Intelligent Tutoring Systems (ITS) were the most frequent category, appearing in 17 studies (45.95%). These are followed by computer vision systems, which were used in 14 studies (37.84%), while large language models, chatbots, and natural language processing were identified in 11 studies (29.73%). Social robotics was combined with AI in 9 interventions (24.32%), while virtual/augmented reality (VR/AR) and digital games were used in 7 (18.92%). Finally, 5 interventions (13.51%) utilized perception systems through sensors and neurofeedback, while 4 (10.81%) focused on multimedia production through Generative AI, such as sound and image (see Table 6).

Table 6. AI technologies used in the included studies

AI Technology	Study	n	%
Adaptive Learning Systems, Speech Recognition & Intelligent Tutoring Systems (ITS)	Ahuja et al. (2022), Aldakhil (2024), Alsolami (2025), Katsarou et al. (2025), Medina et al. (2021), Morciano et al. (2024), Mutawa et al. (2023), Panda et al. (2024), Safi et al. (2021), Serpa-Andrade et al. (2022), Thomas et al. (2024), Toyokawa et al. (2023), Utepbayeva et al. (2024), Valentim et al. (2023), Ventura (2024), Wang et al. (2022), Zhao et al. (2022)	17	45.95
Computer Vision Systems	Aldakhil (2024), Alnafjan et al. (2025), Ayasrah et al. (2024), Fan et al. (2025), Lorenzo & Lorenzo-Lledó (2024), Mutawa et al. (2023), Panda et al. (2024), Podpečan (2023), Renjith & Jeeva (2025), Rodríguez-Quevedo et al. (2023), Taheri et al. (2021), Tozadore et al. (2022), Valentim et al. (2023), Xu (2024)	14	37.84
Large Language Models, Chatbots & Natural Language Processing	Aldakhil (2024), Fang et al. (2024), Jafarian & Kramer (2025), Katsarou et al. (2025), Podpečan (2023), Poobrasert & Satsutthi (2020), Safi et al. (2021), Singh et al. (2024), Su et al. (2024), Wang (2023), Zhao et al. (2022)	11	29.73
Social robotics	Alnafjan et al. (2025), Berrezueta-Guzman et al. (2021), Lorenzo & Lorenzo-Lledó (2024), Mutawa et al. (2023), Podpečan (2023), Rodríguez-Quevedo et al. (2023), Serpa-Andrade et al. (2022), Taheri et al. (2021), Wang (2023)	9	24.32
Virtual Reality & digital games	Ahuja et al. (2022), Aldakhil (2024), Ayasrah et al. (2024), Medina et al. (2021), Serpa-Andrade et al. (2022), Utepbayeva et al. (2024), Zhao et al. (2022)	7	18.92
Sensor-based AI & Neurofeedback	Aldakhil (2024), Berrezueta-Guzman et al. (2021), Marrauwi et al. (2023), Taheri et al. (2021), Wang et al. (2024)	5	13.51
Multimedia production through Generative AI	Jafarian & Kramer (2025), Mao et al. (2025), Su et al. (2024), Ventura (2024)	4	10.81

Arts-Based Elements in AI-Supported Interventions

In order to examine the role of the arts, the 37 selected studies were coded according to the presence and type of arts-based elements within the AI-supported interventions. Eight studies (21.62%) included arts-based elements (Table 7). Specifically, it was found that literature was used most frequently, through activities such as creative writing and storytelling (n = 5, 13.51%).

In particular, in Aldakhil's (2024) research, the intervention focused on improving the quality of life of children with ADHD through playful activities supported by Artificial Intelligence. One of the 12 thematic axes of the intervention was the "Emotion-Driven Storytelling" activity, which employed literary expression and creative writing to enhance children's emotional expression and creativity. Through this activity, children created stories with the help of AI. Tools such as ChatGPT and Quill AI were used to generate narratives. The intervention was implemented over four weeks and consisted of twelve 45-minute sessions, held three times a week in schools in Saudi Arabia. The program included 61 boys aged 8–12 years with diagnosed ADHD (30 in the experimental group and 31 in the control group). The results of the study showed a statistically significant improvement in all dimensions of quality of life (physical, social, academic, and emotional functioning) for the experimental group, while the level of satisfaction with the intervention was high.

Similarly, the intervention by Fan et al. (2025) aimed to improve the emotional development of children with ASD through the use of literature in storytelling animation and creative writing, combined with multi-level games and emotion recognition technology supported by Artificial Intelligence. A total of 12 children with ASD, aged 4 to 7, participated in the program, along with five special education teachers with 5–8 years of experience. The intervention lasted for three weeks, and each child attended three to seven 30-minute sessions, held two or three times per week. The intervention focused on narrative stories inspired by the social stories technique, which were presented through animation. The results showed a statistically significant improvement in both the recognition and production of facial expressions. Notably, educators observed increased levels of interest and enthusiasm in the children while they watched the stories and engaged in artistic activities.

Furthermore, in the intervention presented in Poobrasert & Satsutthi's (2020) study, literature, and specifically creative writing, was used in order to improve writing skills in students with SpLDs. The intervention was based on the development of the digital AI system "Kid Can Write," which asked children to observe images and describe their details in 12 steps. The aim was to enhance imagination, vocabulary, and narrative skills, strengthening students' creative expression through story writing. The intervention was conducted with 16 students diagnosed with learning difficulties in writing (mainly dysorthography and dyslexia) who were enrolled in the 4th, 5th, and 6th grades of elementary schools in Bangkok. The results showed significant improvement in both language skills and creative expression.

In Serpa-Andrade et al.'s (2022) intervention for students with ADHD, AI and literature were utilized. Specifically, the participants were preschool and early school-age students. The intervention was implemented in school contexts and involved child–family–school interaction supported by robot-based educational and therapeutic tools, games, and AI-enabled computers. Particular emphasis was placed on the use of narratives, stories, comics, incomplete sentences, and creative activities, that is, forms of creative literary expression that enabled children to express themselves through play and storytelling. The stories were used to identify children's thoughts and feelings, develop alternative scenarios, and enhance problem-solving and creative thinking skills. The results of the intervention showed that the children developed better self-control, greater creativity, and increased adaptability.

Finally, Su et al. (2024) attempted an intervention that utilized AI, along with literature (creative writing) and visual arts (illustration and comic book creation), in the context of supporting elementary school students with emotional difficulties, ADHD, and ASD. A total of 22 5th and 6th grade elementary school students from a school in Taiwan participated, and the intervention lasted 3 months. The students were asked to write down their experiences and feelings, and with the help of AI technologies, the writings were turned into illustrated comics. Through this artistic and literary process, students expressed themselves freely and engaged in dialogical activities. The results showed that the experimental group made significant progress in all social-emotional skills, self-awareness, self-regulation, social awareness, relationship skills, and responsible decision-making.

Table 7. Studies involving the arts

Type of Art	Study	SEND	n	%
Literature (creative writing - storytelling)	Aldakhil (2024), Fan et al. (2025), Poobrasert & Satsutthi (2020), Serpa-Andrade et al. (2022), Su et al. (2024)	ADHD, ASD, Emotional difficulties, SpLDs	5	13.51
Painting - Visual Arts	Fan et al. (2025), Mao et al. (2025), Su et al. (2024)	ADHD, ASD, Sensory disabilities (hearing problems)	3	8.11
Music	Ventura (2024)	SpLDs	1	2.70
Theater - Dance	Podpečan (2023)	ADHD, ASD	1	2.70
Total studies involving arts			8	21.62

Besides literature, as shown in Table 7 and already mentioned in the above research, 3 studies (8.11%) used visual arts. For instance, Mao et al. (2025) designed an intervention to enhance art skills in students with hearing disability through the use of visual arts, specifically painting and drawing, with the help of AI. A total of 32 students participated, 16 of whom had hearing impairments, and they were randomly divided into four groups (experimental and control). The main AI tool used was "Midjourney AI," which enables image generation. The intervention lasted 3 weeks, and the results showed that the use of AI tools significantly reduced creation time, improved the aesthetics and completeness of the works, and helped students with hearing impairments overcome difficulties, without, however, being a substitute for human creativity, an area in which no significant differences were observed.

Finally, in 1 study (2.70%), music was utilized (Ventura, 2024), and in 1 study (2.70%), theater and dance were utilized (Podpečan, 2023). In particular, the intervention presented by Ventura (2024) aimed to support students with dyslexia in studying music. The innovation of the intervention was based on an AI algorithm, which acted as a "virtual teacher." The algorithm did not provide ready-made solutions, but provided visual cues for the music. The study was applied to a group of 12 students aged 15-16, 6 of whom had dyslexia, and the intervention lasted 4 months (January–April 2023). As it turned out, after the introduction of the algorithm, the majority of students were able to successfully complete the harmony exercises. Although the intervention focuses on music education and art is not used as a supplementary tool, it offers important insights into the use of AI in combination with music in the context of Special Education. Students with dyslexia showed clear improvement, with some completing up to 90% of the exercise. In addition, there was an increase in their motivation, performance, and self-esteem, as they learned to continue the exercise even when the algorithm did not provide assistance. Also, Podpečan's (2023) intervention used theater and dance, along with AI tech, for students with disorders such as ADHD and ASD. Specifically, a NAO robot was used to perform simple and complex choreographies, and the children watched and spontaneously stood up and copied the robot's movements. Theatrical performances were also presented, in which the robot played leading roles. During these performances, children actively participated, coming into contact with NAO. Results showed intense enthusiasm, long-lasting concentration, increased willingness to participate, and positive emotional responses.

Skill Domains Reported in the Interventions

Furthermore, in order to answer the last research question, the selected studies were examined according to their reported outcomes in relation to participants' skills. As found, in 36 of the 37 studies (97.30%), skill improvement was reported, except for that of Taheri et al. (2021) (n = 1, 2.70%), in which no significant improvements were observed (Table 8). In more detail, as found, in most studies (n = 18, 48.65%), the social and communication skills of the participants were increased, such as cooperation, imitation, social interaction, eye contact, and dialogue. These studies focused on individuals with ADHD, ASD, emotional difficulties, and speech disorders.

Furthermore, in 12 studies (32.43%), learning-related skills such as reading, writing, arithmetic, spelling, and language expression were observed. These studies focused on individuals with ADHD, ASD, intellectual disability, and SpLDs. An almost equal number of interventions in which AI was used in vivo (n = 10, 27.03%) increased cognitive and problem-solving skills, such as memory, critical thinking, and independent work in individuals with ADHD, ASD, emotional difficulties, intellectual disability, sensory disabilities (hearing problems), and SpLDs.

Additionally, in 8 studies (21.62%), improvements were observed in emotional regulation and expression skills, such as self-regulation, self-confidence, and emotional expression, among students with ADHD, ASD, emotional difficulties, and SpLDs. In an equal number of studies (n = 8, 21.62%), enhancements were reported in visual-motor and sensory skills, including attention span, fine motor coordination, and visuospatial memory, in students with ADHD, ASD, and SpLDs. In 5 of the 37 studies (13.51%), improvements were noted in creative and artistic expression skills, such as imagination, originality, and creativity. These interventions involved students with ADHD, ASD, sensory disabilities (hearing impairments), and SpLDs. Finally, in 2 studies (5.41%), adaptive and daily functioning skills, such as following rules and moving around independently, were enhanced in participants with ADHD and ASD.

Table 8. Skill domains reported in AI-supported Special Education interventions

Skill	Study	SEND	n	%
Social skills & communication (cooperation, imitation, social interaction, eye contact, dialogue, etc.)	Aldakhil (2024), Alnafjan et al. (2025), Fan et al. (2025), Lorenzo & Lorenzo-Lledó (2024), Mutawa et al. (2023), Panda et al. (2024), Podpečan (2023), Rodríguez-Quevedo et al. (2023), Safi et al. (2021), Serpa-Andrade et al. (2022), Singh et al. (2024), Su et al. (2024), Utepbayeva et al. (2024), Valentim et al. (2023), Wang (2023), Wang et al. (2024), Xu (2024), Zhao et al. (2022)	ADHD, ASD, Emotional Difficulties, Speech Disorders	18	48.65
Learning-related skills (reading, writing, numeracy, spelling, language expression, etc.)	Ahuja et al. (2022), Aldakhil (2024), Alsolami (2025), Jafarian & Kramer (2025), Katsarou et al. (2025), Morciano et al. (2024), Poobrasert & Satsutthi (2020), Renjith & Jeeva (2025), Thomas et al. (2024), Toyokawa et al. (2023), Tozadore et al. (2022), Wang et al. (2022)	ADHD, ASD, Intellectual Disability, SpLDs	12	32.43
Cognitive and problem-solving skills (memory, critical thinking, independent work, etc.)	Ahuja et al. (2022), Ayasrah et al. (2024), Berrezueta-Guzman et al. (2021), Katsarou et al. (2025), Mao et al. (2025), Medina et al. (2021), Renjith & Jeeva (2025), Su et al. (2024), Ventura (2024), Wang (2023)	ADHD, ASD, Emotional difficulties, Intellectual Disability, Sensory Disabilities (hearing problems), SpLDs	10	27.03
Emotional regulation and expression skills (reducing impulsiveness, self-regulation, self-confidence, expressing emotions, etc.)	Aldakhil (2024), Berrezueta-Guzman et al. (2021), Fan et al. (2025), Lorenzo & Lorenzo-Lledó (2024), Medina et al. (2021), Renjith & Jeeva (2025), Su et al. (2024), Ventura (2024)	ADHD, ASD, Emotional Difficulties, SpLDs	8	21.62
Visual-motor and sensory skills (attention span, fine motor skills, motor coordination, visual-spatial memory, etc.)	Ahuja et al. (2022), Aldakhil (2024), Ayasrah et al. (2024), Berrezueta-Guzman et al. (2021), Medina et al. (2021), Valentim et al. (2023), Wang et al. (2024), Zhao et al. (2022)	ADHD, ASD, SpLDs	8	21.62
Creative and artistic expression skills (creativity, originality, etc.)	Fang et al. (2024), Mao et al. (2025), Poobrasert & Satsutthi (2020), Serpa-Andrade et al. (2022), Ventura (2024)	ADHD, ASD, Sensory disabilities (hearing problems), SpLDs	5	13.51
Adaptive and daily functioning skills (following rules, getting from place to place, etc.)	Marrauwi et al. (2023), Serpa-Andrade et al. (2022)	ADHD, ASD	2	5.41
No improvement in skills observed	Taheri et al. (2021)	ASD	1	2.70

DISCUSSION

The aim of this systematic literature review was to examine AI-supported in vivo interventions and their reported outcomes for skill development among students with SEND. The findings show a clear increase in relevant studies after 2022, which can be associated with the rapid development of AI technologies and the growing educational interest in GenAI applications. This trend is consistent with recent reviews showing that AI in education and inclusive education has gained increasing attention during the same period (Matos et al., 2025; Melo-López et al., 2025). The predominance of journal publications also indicates that this field is gradually acquiring a more stable research presence.

The geographical distribution of the studies suggests broad international interest in AI-supported Special Education. The presence of countries with different levels of digital maturity indicates that AI-supported interventions are being explored across diverse educational systems. At the same time, this distribution should be interpreted cautiously, since technological infrastructure, teacher training, digital literacy, and policy priorities differ across national contexts. In the Greek context, recent studies have also shown the need for targeted teacher preparation in the pedagogical use of GenAI and AI-supported instruction for students with SEND (Drossinou Korea & Alexopoulos, 2024b; Kladaki et al., 2025).

The methodological profile of the included studies shows a strong preference for quantitative designs. This tendency is understandable, since AI-supported interventions are often evaluated through measurable outcomes, standardized tasks, and comparable indicators of effectiveness. The limited presence of qualitative and mixed-method research restricts the field's understanding of students' lived experience, emotional engagement, classroom participation, and teacher mediation. In Special Education, such dimensions are important because each student may respond differently to the same technological or artistic activity (Drossinou Korea, 2020).

The emphasis on primary education may reflect the importance of early support for communication, social participation, and learning-related skills. The limited number of studies in preschool, secondary, adult, and higher education settings indicates that AI-supported interventions for SEND remain unevenly distributed across educational levels. This pattern differs from parts of the broader AI-in-education literature, where higher education has received considerable attention (Dimeli & Kostas, 2025). In Special Education, the stronger focus on younger students may be connected to the priority given to early intervention, although the present findings are insufficient to establish greater effectiveness at these ages.

The second research question concerned the SEND categories and AI technologies addressed in the interventions. The findings show that most studies focused on students with ASD, followed by studies involving students with specific learning difficulties and ADHD. This emphasis is partly expected, since ASD has often been linked with AI-supported tools such as social robots, emotion recognition systems, adaptive environments, and virtual interaction spaces. The use of technology for students with ASD is also well established in prior Special Education research (Drossinou Korea & Alexopoulos, 2022).

At the same time, the evidence base remains uneven. Students with intellectual disabilities, sensory disabilities, speech disorders, emotional difficulties, physical disabilities, multiple disabilities, complex communication needs, and high access needs were limited or absent in the included studies. This imbalance is important because these learners may require different forms of AI-supported and arts-based participation, including accessible interfaces, alternative input systems, multimodal communication, assistive devices, and intensive human support. Future intervention studies should include these groups more systematically and report how accessibility adaptations shape participation, engagement, and skill development.

Regarding AI technologies, adaptive learning systems, speech recognition systems, and Intelligent Tutoring Systems were the most common categories. This finding aligns with the broader expectation that AI can support personalization, feedback, and differentiated learning pathways (Abbes et al., 2024; Adiguzel et al., 2023; Baidoo-Anu & Owusu Ansah, 2023; Holmes et al., 2019; Kasneci et al., 2023; Rane, 2023; Sunmboye et al., 2025; Tu et al., 2025). Large Language Models, chatbots, natural language processing, social robotics, computer vision, and GenAI-based multimedia production also appeared in the corpus, showing that AI-supported Special Education is becoming technologically diverse.

This technological expansion needs a human-centered framework. In SEND contexts, AI-supported interventions should be evaluated in relation to student agency, teacher oversight, transparency, accessibility, data privacy, and the interpretability of system outputs (Miao & Holmes, 2023; Shneiderman, 2022). Explainable AI is particularly relevant because teachers need to understand why a system suggests a prompt, feedback item, activity sequence, or learner classification before using it within individualized support. Participatory design is also important, since students with SEND, teachers, families, therapists, and accessibility specialists can help define suitable interaction modes, including text, speech, image, gesture, haptic feedback, captioning, audio description, visual supports, and alternative input systems. In this sense, AI should remain a pedagogically mediated tool that strengthens human judgment, creative participation, and individualized support.

The third research question examined the role of the arts within AI-supported interventions. Only a small number of studies incorporated arts-based elements, with literature-based practices, especially creative writing and storytelling, appearing most frequently. This pattern may be related to the growing use of Large Language Models and chatbot-based tools, which can support narrative prompts, story generation, character-based scenarios, and differentiated written expression. In Special Education, storytelling and creative writing can function as structured forms of symbolic expression, emotional organization, perspective-taking, and social meaning-making.

Visual arts were also present, mainly through drawing, painting, illustration, and comic creation. These activities are relevant for students who benefit from nonverbal or multimodal forms of expression. AI-generated images and visual design tools may support students who need alternative ways to externalize emotions, ideas, or experiences, especially when verbal communication is limited. Such tools require careful teacher mediation, since artistic participation should support meaning-making and personal expression rather than simple production of visually appealing outputs.

The limited presence of music, theater, and dance is a central finding. Existing literature has shown that these art forms can support communication, social interaction, emotional expression, embodied participation, and inclusive engagement (Bololia et al., 2022; Drill & Bellini, 2022; Hautala et al., 2022; Mastrothanasis et al., 2023; Mastrothanasis, Gkontelos, et al., 2025; Zakopoulos et al., 2023, 2026). Theater-based techniques, in particular, have been examined in relation to students with ASD, ADHD, and intellectual disabilities (Geiger et al., 2020; Karaolis, 2023; Kejani & Raeisi, 2022; Layachi et al., 2024; Lee & Wang, 2025; Mohamadi Dolatabad et al., 2023; Mojahed et al., 2021; Mpella & Evaggelinou, 2018; Mpella et al., 2019; Robinson & Crane, 2025; Wu et al., 2020). Their limited integration into AI-supported interventions indicates that the field still privileges text-based, screen-based, and easily measurable activities, while embodied, performative, and relational arts remain underexplored.

This point is important for creative and embodied learning. In arts-based pedagogy, learning emerges through voice, gesture, movement, rhythm, image, material interaction, role-taking, and shared interpretation. AI can support these processes by generating prompts, visual stimuli, adaptive narratives, soundscapes, or feedback cues. The educational value of the activity depends on human mediation. Teacher guidance remains necessary in order to connect AI-generated material with students' lived experience, sensory participation, emotional safety, peer interaction, and reflective meaning-making.

The fourth research question concerned the skills reported in the included interventions. Most studies reported improvements, especially in social and communication skills, followed by learning-related, cognitive, emotional, visual-motor, sensory, adaptive, creative, and artistic skills. These findings should be interpreted cautiously, since the included studies differed in design, duration, sample characteristics, intervention content, and outcome measures. The predominance of communication and social outcomes is also related to the strong representation of ASD-focused studies in the corpus.

The limited focus on creative and artistic outcomes is important for the present review. Although arts-based pedagogy is closely connected with creativity, imagination, emotional expression, embodied participation, and expressive agency, these dimensions were measured less frequently than communication, social interaction, or school performance. This suggests that AI-supported arts-based interventions in Special Education need assessment tools that capture creative process, expressive agency, participation, and interaction quality, rather than focusing only on easily quantifiable skill gains.

More specifically, the assessment of effectiveness should include both product and process criteria. Product-oriented criteria may concern originality, elaboration, expressive clarity, aesthetic coherence, narrative quality, musical or visual organization, and task completion. Process-oriented criteria may concern engagement, persistence, risk-taking, collaboration, embodied participation, multimodal communication, expressive agency, and the quality of interaction with peers, teachers, and digital tools. For students with SEND, assessment should also include accessibility indicators, such as the suitability of input and output modes, the availability of visual or auditory scaffolds, the student's capacity to participate without excessive cognitive load, and the extent to which the activity supports meaningful expression. This broader assessment logic is aligned with creative thinking frameworks that examine the generation, evaluation, and improvement of ideas, as well as arts education frameworks that emphasize habits of mind, reflection, expression, and persistence (Hetland et al., 2013; OECD, 2023).

CONCLUSIONS

The present systematic review highlighted the growing role of AI-supported interventions in enhancing the skills of students with SEND. The results showed that the majority of studies published from 2022 onward, coinciding with the emergence of Generative AI applications, reported positive outcomes in students' skills, particularly in the development of social and communication skills, with a strong emphasis on students with ASD. In addition, a research shift towards preschool and school-age children was observed, while notable research gaps were also identified. Specifically, there was limited focus on higher education, as well as on individuals with intellectual disabilities, sensory or motor disabilities, and speech disorders. This highlights the need to broaden the scope of research to better address these underrepresented groups.

Furthermore, the limited use of the arts in AI-based interventions should be taken into account. The underutilization of theater, music, and dance represents a significant gap, especially considering that international literature confirms their contribution to the development of key soft skills. Therefore, integrating AI with the arts in Special Education emerges as an underexplored field of research and practice that deserves greater attention in future interventions. Future work should examine how AI can support arts-based pedagogical processes, such as storytelling, role-taking, movement, rhythm, visual expression, improvisation, and creative collaboration, while preserving the central role of teacher mediation and human interaction. Finally, the findings should be interpreted within the methodological boundaries of the review. The search was limited to Scopus, English-language publications, journal articles, and conference proceedings, while grey literature, dissertations, technical reports, policy documents, preprints, and unpublished intervention evaluations were outside the corpus. The focus on the period from January 2020 to April 2025 supported attention to recent AI and GenAI developments, although a wider timeframe could yield a broader historical view of technology-supported arts-based interventions in Special Education. The absence of arts-related terms from the initial search query may also have influenced the corpus, although arts-based elements were examined during data extraction. Future reviews should expand database coverage, compare indexed and non-indexed evidence, include grey literature where appropriate, and apply more detailed risk-of-bias reporting across different study designs. Future empirical studies should also include students with physical disabilities, multiple disabilities, complex communication needs, and high access needs, with stronger attention to accessibility, multimodal participation, human-centered AI, explainability, and teacher-guided creative learning.

REFERENCES

Abbes, F., Bennani, S., & Maalel, A. (2024). Generative AI and gamification for personalized learning: Literature review and future challenges. *SN Computer Science*, *5*(8), 1154. DOI: 10.1007/s42979-024-03491-z

Adiguzel, T., Kaya, M. H., & Cansu, F. K. (2023). Revolutionizing education with AI: Exploring the transformative potential of CHATGPT. *Contemporary Educational Technology*, *15*(3), ep429. DOI: 10.30935/cedtech/13152

Ahuja, N. J., Dutt, S., Choudhary, S. I., & Kumar, M. (2022). Intelligent tutoring system in education for disabled learners using human–computer interaction and augmented reality. *International Journal of Human-Computer Interaction*. DOI: 10.1080/10447318.2022.2124359

Aldakhil, A. F. (2024). Investigating the impact of an AI-based play activities intervention on the quality of life of school-aged children with ADHD. *Research in Developmental Disabilities*, *154*, 104858. DOI: 10.1016/j.ridd.2024.104858 PMID: 39413561

Alenezi, M. A. K., Mohamed, A. M., & Shaaban, T. S. (2023). Revolutionizing EFL special education: How ChatGPT is transforming the way teachers approach language learning. *Innoeduca. International Journal of Technology and Educational Innovation*, *9*(2), 5–23. DOI: 10.24310/innoeduca.2023.v9i2.16774

Alexopoulos, P., Mastrothanasis, K., Andreadakis, N., Kladaki, M., & Kostas, A. (2025). Training interventions for teachers' self-efficacy enhancement in the use of Artificial Intelligence: A systematic literature review in the five-year period 2020–2025. *Παιδαγωγικά Ρεύματα στο Αιγαίο*, *14*(1), 45–55. https://doi.org/DOI: 10.12681/revmata.43576

Aljedaani, W., Krasniqi, R., Aljedaani, S., Mkaouer, M. W., Ludi, S., & Al-Raddah, K. (2023). If online learning works for you, what about deaf students? Emerging challenges of online learning for deaf and hearing-impaired students during COVID-19: A literature review. *Universal Access in the Information Society*, *22*(3), 1027–1046. DOI: 10.1007/s10209-022-00897-5 PMID: 35910240

Alnafjan, A., Alghamdi, M., Alhakbani, N., & Al-Ohali, Y. (2025). Improving imitation skills in children with autism spectrum disorder using the NAO robot and a human action recognition. *Diagnostics (Basel)*, *15*(1), 60. DOI: 10.3390/diagnostics15010060 PMID: 39795588

Alsolami, A. S. (2025). The effectiveness of using artificial intelligence in improving academic skills of school-aged students with mild intellectual disabilities in Saudi Arabia. *Research in Developmental Disabilities, 156*, 104884. DOI: 10.1016/j.ridd.2024.104884 PMID: 39631141

AlZu'bi, S., Mughaid, A., Quiam, F., & Hendawi, S. (2023). Exploring the Capabilities and Limitations of ChatGPT and Alternative Big Language Models. *Artificial Intelligence and Applications (Commerce, Calif.), 2*(1), 28–37. DOI: 10.47852/bonviewAIA3202820

Ayasrah, S., Hanandeh, A., Abu Ghazal, H., & AlEid, W. (2024). Utilizing PROKET Technology Program: An evaluation of assistive tools in enhancing developmental skills for students with specific learning disorders. *International Journal of Information and Education Technology (IJIET), 14*(7), 988–995. DOI: 10.18178/ijiet.2024.14.7.2126

Baidoo-Anu, D., & Owusu Ansah, L. (2023). Education in the era of Generative Artificial Intelligence (AI): Understanding the potential benefits of CHATGPT in promoting teaching and learning. SSRN *Electronic Journal.* DOI: 10.2139/ssrn.4337484

Barone, T., & Eisner, E. W. (2012). *Arts based research.* SAGE Publications., DOI: 10.4135/9781452230627

Berrezueta-Guzman, J., Pau, I., Martín-Ruiz, M.-L., & Máximo-Bocanegra, N. (2021). Assessment of a robotic assistant for supporting homework activities of children with ADHD. *IEEE Access : Practical Innovations, Open Solutions, 9*, 93450–93465. DOI: 10.1109/ACCESS.2021.3093233

Bertacchini, F., Demarco, F., Scuro, C., Pantano, P., & Bilotta, E. (2023). A social robot connected with chatGPT to improve cognitive functioning in ASD subjects. *Frontiers in Psychology, 14*, 1232177. DOI: 10.3389/fpsyg.2023.1232177 PMID: 37868599

Boal, A. (2002). *Games for actors and non-actors* (2nd ed.). Routledge.

Bololia, L., Williams, J., Macmahon, K., & Goodall, K. (2022). Dramatherapy for children and adolescents with autism spectrum disorder: A systematic integrative review. *The Arts in Psychotherapy, 80*, 101918. DOI: 10.1016/j.aip.2022.101918

Bong, W. K., & Chen, W. (2024). Increasing faculty's competence in digital accessibility for inclusive education: A systematic literature review. *International Journal of Inclusive Education, 28*(2), 197–213. DOI: 10.1080/13603116.2021.1937344

Bresler Nardi, A., Bat Or, M., & Shuper Engelhard, E. (2022). Dance movement therapy processes and interventions in the treatment of children with anxiety disorders derived from therapy logs. *The Arts in Psychotherapy*, *80*, 101951. DOI: 10.1016/j.aip.2022.101951

Cheng, S. C., & Lai, C. L. (2019). Facilitating learning for students with special needs: A review of technology-supported special education studies. *Journal of Computers in Education*, *7*(8), 131–153. DOI: 10.1007/s40692-019-00150-8

Choi, E. (2023). A Comprehensive Inquiry into the Use of ChatGPT Examining General, Educational, and Disability-Focused Perspectives. *International Journal of Arts, Humanities &. Social Science*, *04*(11), 1–7. DOI: 10.56734/ijahss.v4n11a1

Dewey, J. (1934). *Art as experience*. Minton, Balch & Company.

Dimeli, M., & Kostas, A. (2025). The role of ChatGPT in education: Applications, challenges: Insights from a systematic review. *Journal of Information Technology Education*, *24*, 2. DOI: 10.28945/5422

Drill, R. B., & Bellini, S. (2022). Combining Readers Theater, Story Mapping and Video Self-Modeling Interventions to Improve Narrative Reading Comprehension in Children with Autism Spectrum Disorder. *Journal of Autism and Developmental Disorders*, *52*(1), 1–15. DOI: 10.1007/s10803-021-04908-x PMID: 33590425

Drossinou Korea, M. (2020). *Handbook of special education and educational narratives*. Opportuna. (in Greek)

Drossinou Korea, M., & Alexopoulos, P. (2022). Teaching social skills interventions with digital cognitive and language machines to a student with autism. *International Journal of Social Science and Human Research*, *05*(11), 5234–5241. DOI: 10.47191/ijsshr/v5-i11-55

Drossinou Korea, M., & Alexopoulos, P. (2024a). Factors arising from the utilization of Artificial Intelligence and Large Language Models in Special Education. *European Journal of Special Education Research*, *10*(2), 1–16. DOI: 10.46827/ejse.v10i2.5209

Drossinou Korea, M., & Alexopoulos, P. (2024b). Higher Education Students' Views on the Use of Artificial Intelligence for Teaching Students with Specific Learning Difficulties. *European Journal of Open Education and E-Learning Studies*, *9*(1). DOI: 10.46827/ejoe.v9i1.5518

Dumitru, C. (2025). Assistive Technology and Alternative and Augmentative Communication Options in the Language Skills Development of Students with Specific Learning Disorders. *Education Sciences*, *15*(2), 170. DOI: 10.3390/educsci15020170

Dumitru, C., Koulianou, M., & Mastrothanasis, K. (2024). Inclusion of students with specific learning disorders in higher education: a systematic literature review. *Journal of Educational Sciences & Psychology, 15 (76)*(2), 46–64. DOI: 10.51865/JESP.2024.2.06

Dumitru, C., Mastrothanasis, K., Pikoulis, E., Kladaki, M., Zervoudakis, K., Dogan, C. D., Gonullu, I., Stan, M. M., Karamagioli, E., Ledaki, M., Alexopoulos, P., Papantoniou, D., Pikouli, A., Papantoniou, S., & Erden, S. (2026). Drama-based simulations in first aid education: Psychometric validation of a student assessment tool in school settings. *Frontiers in Public Health, 14*, 1710189. DOI: 10.3389/fpubh.2026.1710189 PMID: 41846832

Eisner, E. W. (2002). *The arts and the creation of mind*. Yale University Press.

Fan, M., Jin, S., Fan, J., Guo, W., & Chen, X. (2025). EmoLand: Utilizing narrative animations, multilevel games, and affective computing to foster emotional development in children with autism spectrum disorder. *International Journal of Human-Computer Studies, 199*, 103486. DOI: 10.1016/j.ijhcs.2025.103486

Fang, M., Abdallah, A. K., & Vorfolomeyeva, O. (2024). Collaborative AI-enhanced digital mind-mapping as a tool for stimulating creative thinking in inclusive education for students with neurodevelopmental disorders. *BMC Psychology, 12*(1), 488. DOI: 10.1186/s40359-024-01975-4 PMID: 39289718

Fernández-Batanero, J. M., Montenegro-Rueda, M., Fernández-Cerero, J., & García-Martínez, I. (2022). Assistive technology for the inclusion of students with disabilities: A systematic review. *Educational Technology Research and Development, 70*(5), 1911–1930. DOI: 10.1007/s11423-022-10127-7

Gallud, J. A., Carreño, M., Tesoriero, R., Sandoval, A., Lozano, M. D., Durán, I., Penichet, V. M. R., & Cosio, R. (2023). Technology-enhanced and game based learning for children with special needs: A systematic mapping study. *Universal Access in the Information Society, 22*(1), 227–240. DOI: 10.1007/s10209-021-00824-0 PMID: 34248457

Geiger, A., Shpigelman, C.-N., & Feniger-Schaal, R. (2020). The socio-emotional world of adolescents with intellectual disability: A drama therapy-based participatory action research. *The Arts in Psychotherapy, 70*, 101679. DOI: 10.1016/j.aip.2020.101679

Giagazoglou, P., Dampa, A., Alexiadis, A., Lenakakis, A., Dimitropoulou, D., & Magos, K. (2026). From Fairy Tales to Real-Life Safety: An Educational Drama-Based Intervention for Children's Self-Protection Skills. *International Journal of Education & the Arts, 27*(4). DOI: 10.26209/ijea27n4

Hautala, J., Ronimus, M., & Junttila, E. (2022). Readers' Theater Projects for Special Education: A Randomized Controlled Study. *Scandinavian Journal of Educational Research, 67*(5), 663–678. DOI: 10.1080/00313831.2022.2042846

Hetland, L., Winner, E., Veenema, S., & Sheridan, K. M. (2013). *Studio thinking 2: The real benefits of visual arts education* (2nd ed.). Teachers College Press.

Holmes, W., Bialik, M., & Fadel, C. (2019). *Artificial intelligence in education: Promises and implications for teaching and learning*. Centre for Curriculum Redesign.

Jafarian, N. R., & Kramer, A.-W. (2025). AI-assisted audio-learning improves academic achievement through motivation and reading engagement. *Computers and Education: Artificial Intelligence, 8*, 100357. DOI: 10.1016/j.caeai.2024.100357

Jauhiainen, J. S., & Guerra, A. G. (2023). Generative AI and ChatGPT in School Children's Education: Evidence from a School Lesson. *Sustainability (Basel), 15*(18), 14025. DOI: 10.3390/su151814025

Javed, S., Muniandy, M., Lee, C. K., & Husni, H. (2024). Enhancing teaching and learning for pupils with dyslexia: A comprehensive review of technological and non-technological interventions. *Education and Information Technologies, 29*(8), 9607–9643. DOI: 10.1007/s10639-023-12195-5

Kaimara, P. (2026). Digital Transformation Stands Alongside Inclusive Education: Lessons Learned from a Project Called "Waking Up in the Morning". *Technology. Knowledge and Learning, 31*(1), 51–77. DOI: 10.1007/s10758-023-09667-5

Karakose, T., & Tülübaş, T. (2023). How Can ChatGPT Facilitate Teaching and Learning: Implications for Contemporary Education. *Educational Process International Journal, 12*(4). DOI: 10.22521/edupij.2023.124.1

Karaolis, O. (2023). Not just a toy: Puppets for autistic teenagers. *Youth, 3*(4), 1174–1182. DOI: 10.3390/youth3040074

Kasneci, E., Sessler, K., Küchemann, S., Bannert, M., Dementieva, D., Fischer, F., Gasser, U., Groh, G., Günnemann, S., Hüllermeier, E., Krusche, S., Kutyniok, G., Michaeli, T., Nerdel, C., Pfeffer, J., Poquet, O., Sailer, M., Schmidt, A., Seidel, T., & Kasneci, G. (2023). Chatgpt for good? on opportunities and challenges of large language models for Education. *Learning and Individual Differences, 103*, 102274. DOI: 10.1016/j.lindif.2023.102274

Katsarou, D. V., Mantsos, E., Papadopoulou, S., Sofologi, M., Efthymiou, E., Vasileiou, I., Megari, K., Theodoratou, M., & Kougioumtzis, G. A. (2025). Exploring AI technology in grammar performance testing for children with learning disabilities. *Education Sciences, 15*(3), 351. DOI: 10.3390/educsci15030351

Kejani, M., & Raeisi, Z. (2022). The effect of drama therapy on working memory and its components in primary school children with ADHD. *Current Psychology (New Brunswick, N.J.)*, *41*(1), 417–426. DOI: 10.1007/s12144-019-00564-8

Kladaki, M., Kostas, A., & Alexopoulos, P. (2025). Exploring teachers' beliefs about ChatGPT in arts education. *Education Sciences*, *15*(7), 795. DOI: 10.3390/educsci15070795

Kmet, L. M., Cook, L. S., & Lee, R. C. (2004). *Standard quality assessment criteria for evaluating primary research papers from a variety of fields*. Alberta Heritage Foundation for Medical Research. https://doi.org/DOI: 10.7939/R37M04F16

Koltsida, M., & Lenakakis, A. (2017). Contemporary performance by and for those with disabilities: The case of Greece. *Research in Drama Education*, *22*(3), 339–344. DOI: 10.1080/13569783.2017.1326809

Kress, G. (2010). *Multimodality: A social semiotic approach to contemporary communication*. Routledge.

Kumm, A. J., Viljoen, M., & de Vries, P. J. (2022). The digital divide in technologies for autism: Feasibility considerations for low- and middle-income countries. *Journal of Autism and Developmental Disorders*, *52*(6), 2300–2313. DOI: 10.1007/s10803-021-05084-8 PMID: 34121159

Layachi, A., Douglas, G., & Reraki, M. (2024). Drama-based intervention to support social inclusion: Evaluation of an approach to include students with ADHD in Algeria. *Educational Psychology in Practice*, *40*(1), 36–58. DOI: 10.1080/02667363.2023.2258780

Lee, I.-J., & Wang, W.-Z. (2025). Applying theatre-based role-playing combined with AR and VR game strategies to enhance imagination and symbolic play skills in children with autism spectrum disorder. *Universal Access in the Information Society*, *24*(3), 2531–2552. DOI: 10.1007/s10209-025-01206-6

Lorenzo, G., & Lorenzo-Lledó, A. (2024). The use of artificial intelligence for detecting the duration of autistic students' emotions in social interaction with the NAO robot: A case study. *International Journal of Information Technology : an Official Journal of Bharati Vidyapeeth's Institute of Computer Applications and Management*, *16*(2), 625–631. DOI: 10.1007/s41870-023-01682-0

Mao, Y., Ying, F., & Liu, K. (2025). Exploring the impact of AI painting tools on graphic design education for hearing-impaired students. In Figueroa, P., Di Iorio, A., Guzman del Rio, D., Gonzalez Clua, E. W., & Cuevas Rodriguez, L. (Eds.), Lecture Notes in Computer Science: Vol. 15192. *Entertainment computing – ICEC 2024*. Springer., DOI: 10.1007/978-3-031-74353-5_34

Marrauwi, M., Sajak, A. A. B., & Yafi, E. (2023). Behavior analysis of people with autism using Internet of Things - A conceptual study. *Journal of Engineering Science and Technology, ICIST2022, 18*(1), 90-102.

Mastrothanasis, K., Gkontelos, A., Kladaki, M., & Papouli, E. (2025). Examining puppetry's contribution to the learning, social and therapeutic support of students with complex educational and psychosocial needs in special school settings: A phenomenological study. *Disabilities, 5*(3), 67. DOI: 10.3390/disabilities5030067

Mastrothanasis, K., Kladaki, M., & Alexopoulos, P. (2025a). *ChatGPT and the digital transformation of arts-based general and special education*. Symmetria Publications. [in Greek]

Mastrothanasis, K., Kladaki, M., & Alexopoulos, P. (2025b). *Developing soft skills in arts education through artificial intelligence*. Grigoris Publications. [in Greek]

Mastrothanasis, K., Kladaki, M., & Alexopoulos, P. (2026). Artificial Intelligence and Rhetorical Art: Argumentative Debate with ChatGPT. [IJMECS]. *International Journal of Modern Education and Computer Science, 18*(1), 48–60. DOI: 10.5815/ijmecs.2026.01.03

Mastrothanasis, K., Kladaki, M., & Andreou, A. (2023). A systematic review and meta-analysis of the Readers' Theatre impact on the development of reading skills. *International Journal of Educational Research Open, 4*, 100243. DOI: 10.1016/j.ijedro.2023.100243

Mastrothanasis, K., Zervoudakis, K., & Kladaki, M. (2024). An application of Computational Intelligence in group formation for digital drama education. *Iran Journal of Computer Science, 7*(3), 551–563. DOI: 10.1007/s42044-024-00186-9

Matos, T., Santos, W., Zdravevski, E., Coelho, P. J., Pires, I. M., & Madeira, F. (2025). A systematic review of artificial intelligence applications in education: Emerging trends and challenges. *Decision Analytics Journal, 15*, 100571. DOI: 10.1016/j.dajour.2025.100571

Medina, R., Bouhaben, J., de Ramón, I., Cuesta, P., Antón-Toro, L., Pacios, J., Quintero, J., Ramos-Quiroga, J. A., & Maestú, F. (2021). Electrophysiological brain changes associated with cognitive improvement in a pediatric attention deficit hyperactivity disorder digital artificial intelligence-driven intervention: Randomized controlled trial. *Journal of Medical Internet Research*, *23*(11), e25466. DOI: 10.2196/25466 PMID: 34842533

Melo-López, V.-A., Basantes-Andrade, A., Gudiño-Mejía, C.-B., & Hernández-Martínez, E. (2025). The impact of artificial intelligence on inclusive education: A systematic review. *Education Sciences*, *15*(5), 539. DOI: 10.3390/educsci15050539

Miao, F., & Holmes, W. (2023). *Guidance for generative AI in education and research*. UNESCO.

Mohamadi Dolatabad, M., Rezapour Mirsaleh, Y., & Choobforoushzadeh, A. (2023). The effectiveness of dramatherapy on the aggression of children with ADHD diagnosis. *Journal of Psychology of Exceptional Individuals*, *13*(50), 101–128. DOI: 10.22054/JPE.2023.68260.2461

Mohamed Mokmin, N. A., & Rassy, R. P. (2024). Review of the trends in the use of augmented reality technology for students with disabilities when learning physical education. *Education and Information Technologies*, *29*(2), 1251–1277. DOI: 10.1007/s10639-022-11550-2

Mojahed, A., Zaheri, Y., & Firoozkoohi Moqaddam, M. (2021). Effectiveness of group psychodrama on aggression and social anxiety of children with attention-deficit/hyperactivity disorder: A randomized clinical trial. *The Arts in Psychotherapy*, *73*, 101756. DOI: 10.1016/j.aip.2021.101756

Morciano, G., Alcalde Llergo, J. M., Zingoni, A., Yeguas Bolívar, E., Taborri, J., & Calabrò, G. (2024). Use of recommendation models to provide support to dyslexic students. *Expert Systems with Applications*, *249*, 123738. DOI: 10.1016/j.eswa.2024.123738

Mpella, M., & Evaggelinou, C. (2018). Does theatrical play promote social skills development in students with autism? A systematic review of the methods and measures employed in the literature. *Preschool and Primary Education*, *6*(2), 96–118. DOI: 10.12681/ppej.16135

Mpella, M., Evaggelinou, C., Koidou, E., & Tsigilis, N. (2019). The Effects of a Theatrical Play Programme on Social Skills Development for Young Children with Autism Spectrum Disorders. *International Journal of Special Education*, *33*(4), 828–845.

Mutawa, A. M., Al Mudhahkah, H. M., Al-Huwais, A., Al-Khaldi, N., Al-Otaibi, R., & Al-Ansari, A. (2023). Augmenting mobile app with NAO robot for autism education. *Machines (Basel), 11*(8), 833. DOI: 10.3390/machines11080833

OECD. (2023). *PISA 2022 assessment and analytical framework*. OECD Publishing., DOI: 10.1787/dfe0bf9c-

Olakanmi, O. A., Akcayir, G., Ishola, O. M., & Demmans Epp, C. (2020). Using technology in special education: Current practices and trends. *Educational Technology Research and Development, 68*(4), 1711–1738. DOI: 10.1007/s11423-020-09795-0

Page, M. J., McKenzie, J. E., Bossuyt, P. M., Boutron, I., Hoffmann, T. C., Mulrow, C. D., Shamseer, L., Tetzlaff, J. M., Akl, E. A., Brennan, S. E., Chou, R., Glanville, J., Grimshaw, J. M., Hróbjartsson, A., Lalu, M. M., Li, T., Loder, E. W., Mayo-Wilson, E., McDonald, S., & Moher, D. (2021). The PRISMA 2020 statement: An updated guideline for reporting systematic reviews. *BMJ (Clinical Research Ed.), 372*, 71. DOI: 10.1136/bmj.n71 PMID: 33782057

Panda, P. K., Elwadhi, A., Gupta, D., Palayullakandi, A., Tomar, A., Singh, M., Vyas, A., Kumar, D., & Sharawat, I. K. (2024). Effectiveness of IMPUTE ADT-1 mobile application in children with autism spectrum disorder: An interim analysis of an ongoing randomized controlled trial. *Journal of Neurosciences in Rural Practice, 15*(2), 262–269. DOI: 10.25259/JNRP_599_2023 PMID: 38746516

Podpečan, V. (2023). Can you dance? A study of child–robot interaction and emotional response using the NAO robot. *Multimodal Technologies and Interaction, 7*(9), 85. DOI: 10.3390/mti7090085

Poobrasert, O., & Satsutthi, N. (2020). Developing of Kid Can Write as assistive technology for students with learning disabilities. In Miesenberger, K., Manduchi, R., Covarrubias Rodriguez, M., & Peňáz, P. (Eds.), Lecture notes in computer science: Vol. 12377. *Computers helping people with special needs. ICCHP 2020* (pp. 73–80). Springer., DOI: 10.1007/978-3-030-58805-2_9

Prado, B. B., Gobbo, J. A.Junior, & Bezerra, B. S. (2023). Emerging themes for digital accessibility in education. *Sustainability (Basel), 15*(14), 11392. DOI: 10.3390/su151411392

Rakap, S. (2024). Chatting with GPT: Enhancing Individualized Education Program Goal Development for Novice Special Education Teachers. *Journal of Special Education Technology, 39*(3), 339–348. DOI: 10.1177/01626434231211295

Rane, N. (2023). Chatbot-Enhanced Teaching and Learning: Implementation Strategies, Challenges, and the Role of ChatGPT in Education. SSRN *Electronic Journal*. DOI: 10.2139/ssrn.4603204

Renjith, P. R., & Jeeva, J. (2025). An intuitive number conversion system employing gestural recognition for students with special educational needs in Computer Science. *IJERI: International Journal of Educational Research and Innovation*, (23), 1–16. DOI: 10.46661/ijeri.10880

Robinson, E., & Crane, L. (2025). Examining the impact of drama-based sessions on the social emotional well-being of Autistic pupils in a special school: A multi-informant qualitative study. *British Journal of Special Education*, *52*(2), 157–170. DOI: 10.1111/1467-8578.70000

Rodríguez-Quevedo, Á., Lledó, G. L., Carreres, A. L., & Pérez-Vázquez, E. (2023). Emotion recognition in ASD students with social robotics: Case study. In *Proceedings of the 2023 XIII International Conference on Virtual Campus (JICV)* (pp. 1–4). IEEE. DOI: 10.1109/JICV59748.2023.10565661

Round, A., Baker, W. J., & Rayner, C. (2017). Using visual arts to encourage children with autism spectrum disorder to communicate their feelings and emotions. *Open Journal of Social Sciences*, *5*, 90–108. DOI: 10.4236/jss.2017.510009

Safi, M. F., Al Sadrani, B., & Mustafa, A. (2021). Virtual voice assistant applications improved expressive verbal abilities and social interactions in children with autism spectrum disorder: A Single-Subject experimental study. *International Journal of Developmental Disabilities*, *69*(4), 555–567. DOI: 10.1080/20473869.2021.1977596 PMID: 37346256

Serpa-Andrade, L., Vélez, R. G., & Serpa-Andrade, G. (2022). Iteration of children with attention deficit disorder, impulsivity and hyperactivity, cognitive behavioral therapy, and artificial intelligence. In Ahram, T., & Taiar, R. (Eds.), *Human interaction, emerging technologies and future systems V* (Vol. 319, pp. 91–99). Springer., DOI: 10.1007/978-3-030-85540-6_12

Shaaban, T. S., & Mohamed, A. M. (2024). Exploring the effectiveness of augmented reality technology on reading comprehension skills among early childhood pupils with learning disabilities. *Journal of Computers in Education*, *11*(2), 423–444. DOI: 10.1007/s40692-023-00269-9

Shapiro, L., & Stolz, S. A. (2019). Embodied cognition and its significance for education. *Theory and Research in Education*, *17*(1), 19–39. DOI: 10.1177/1477878518822149

Shneiderman, B. (2022). *Human-centered AI*. Oxford University Press. DOI: 10.1093/oso/9780192845290.001.0001

Shuper Engelhard, E. (2024). Working with unrepresented states in dance/movement therapy for children. *Body, Movement and Dance in Psychotherapy, 19*(4), 369–380. DOI: 10.1080/17432979.2024.2326010

Şimşek, Ç., Küçük, L., & Akgün Yıldırım, E. (2019). Psychodrama practices in adolescents. *Journal of Academic Research in Nursing*. DOI: 10.5222/jaren.2019.48030

Singh, A. A., Jadon, J. S., Nayak, S. R., & Kumar, R. (2024). Conversation AI for verbal children with ASD to facilitate social interaction. In Pattnaik, P. K. (Eds.), *Proceedings of 3rd International Conference on Smart Computing and Cyber Security* (pp. 295–303). Springer. DOI: 10.1007/978-981-97-0573-3_24

Su, S.-W., Hung, C.-H., Chen, L.-X., & Yuan, S.-M. (2024). Development of an AI-based system to enhance school counseling models for Asian elementary students with emotional disorders. *IEEE Access : Practical Innovations, Open Solutions, 12*, 159121–159135. DOI: 10.1109/ACCESS.2024.3483456

Sunmboye, K., Strafford, H., Noorestani, S., & Wilison-Pirie, M. (2025). Exploring the influence of artificial intelligence integration on personalized learning: A cross-sectional study of undergraduate medical students in the United Kingdom. *BMC Medical Education, 25*(1), 570. DOI: 10.1186/s12909-025-07084-z PMID: 40247306

Taheri, A., Meghdari, A., & Mahoor, M. H. (2021). A close look at the imitation performance of children with autism and typically developing children using a robotic system. *International Journal of Social Robotics, 13*(5), 1125–1147. DOI: 10.1007/s12369-020-00704-2

Thomas, D. R., Gatz, E., Gupta, S., Aleven, V., & Koedinger, K. R. (2024). The neglected 15%: Positive effects of hybrid human-AI tutoring among students with disabilities. In Olney, A. M., Chounta, I. A., Liu, Z., Santos, O. C., & Bittencourt, I. I. (Eds.), Lecture Notes in Computer Science: Vol. 14829. *Artificial intelligence in education. AIED 2024* (pp. 409–423). Springer. DOI: 10.1007/978-3-031-64302-6_29

Toyokawa, Y., Horikoshi, I., Majumdar, R., & Ogata, H. (2023). Challenges and opportunities of AI in inclusive education: A case study of data-enhanced active reading in Japan. *Smart Learning Environments, 10*(1), 67. DOI: 10.1186/s40561-023-00286-2

Tozadore, D. C., Tozadore, M. C., & de Alcantara Gil, M. S. C. (2022). Supporting therapists' assessment in parent-mediated training through autonomous data collection. In Rodrigo, M. M., Matsuda, N., Cristea, A. I., & Dimitrova, V. (Eds.), *Artificial intelligence in education: Posters and late breaking results, workshops and tutorials, industry and innovation tracks, practitioners' and doctoral consortium* (Vol. 13356, pp. 560–563). Springer. DOI: 10.1007/978-3-031-11647-6_115

Tu, Y., Chen, J., & Huang, C. (2025). Empowering personalized learning with generative artificial intelligence: Mechanisms, challenges and pathways. *Frontiers of Digital Education*, *2*(2), 19. DOI: 10.1007/s44366-025-0056-9

Utepbayeva, A., Zhiyenbayeva, N., Assylbekova, L., & Tapalova, O. (2024). Artificial intelligence applications (Fluency SIS, Articulation Station Pro, and Apraxia Farm) in the psycholinguistic development of preschool children with speech disorders. *International Journal of Information and Education Technology (IJIET)*, *14*(7), 927–935. DOI: 10.18178/ijiet.2024.14.7.2119

Valentim, N. A., Dorça, F. A., Asnis, V. P., & Elias, N. C. (2023). The artificial intelligence as a technological resource in the application of tasks for the development of joint attention in children with autism. In M. C. Naldi & R. A. C. Bianchi (Eds.), *BRACIS 2023: Lecture notes in artificial intelligence:* Vol. 14195. *Proceedings of the 12th Brazilian conference on intelligent systems* (pp. 306–320). Springer. DOI: 10.1007/978-3-031-45368-7_20

Ventura, M. D. (2024). Self-adaptive learning algorithm as a tool for the development and strengthening of the dyslexic student's skills in the study of musical composition. In Fortino, G., Kumar, A., Swaroop, A., & Shukla, P. (Eds.), *Proceedings of Third International Conference on Computing and Communication Networks. ICCCN 2023. Lecture Notes in Networks and Systems* (Vol. 917, pp. 415–426). Springer. DOI: 10.1007/978-981-97-0892-5_33

Wang, C.-P. (2023). Training children with autism spectrum disorder, and children in general with AI robots related to the automatic organization of sentence menus and interaction design evaluation. *Expert Systems with Applications*, *229*, 120527. DOI: 10.1016/j.eswa.2023.120527

Wang, M., Muthu, B., & Sivaparthipan, C. B. (2022). Smart assistance to dyslexia students using artificial intelligence based augmentative alternative communication. *International Journal of Speech Technology*, *25*(2), 343–353. DOI: 10.1007/s10772-021-09921-0

Wang, W., Xiao, J., & Diao, L. (2025). The effects of robots on children with autism spectrum disorder: A meta-analysis. *Journal of Autism and Developmental Disorders*. DOI: 10.1007/s10803-025-06883-z PMID: 40397050

Wang, X., Zhang, T., Han, B., Luo, W., Liu, W., Yang, Z., Disi, A., Sun, Y., & Yang, J. (2024). Wearable EEG neurofeedback based on machine learning algorithms for children with autism: A randomized, placebo-controlled study. *Current Medical Science*, *44*(6), 1141–1147. DOI: 10.1007/s11596-024-2938-3 PMID: 39565505

Wu, J., Chen, K., Ma, Y., & Vomočilová, J. (2020). Early intervention for children with intellectual and developmental disability using drama therapy techniques. *Children and Youth Services Review*, *109*, 104689. DOI: 10.1016/j.childyouth.2019.104689

Xu, C. (2024). Exploring AI-based reciprocal eye engagement training to enhance dyadic behavior in individuals with alexithymia. In *Proceedings of the 2024 IEEE 3rd International Conference on Computing and Machine Intelligence (ICMI)* (pp. 1–7). IEEE. DOI: 10.1109/ICMI60790.2024.10586064

Yan, P. (2024). Study of the Effect of Music on the Perceptual Abilities of Children with Autism. *International Journal of Education and Humanities*, *16*(1), 296–298. DOI: 10.54097/hv3h0517

Zakopoulos, V., Makri, A., Ntanos, S., & Tampakis, S. (2023). Drama/Theatre Performance in Education through the Use of Digital Technologies for Enhancing Students' Sustainability Awareness: A Literature Review. *Sustainability (Basel)*, *15*(18), 13387. DOI: 10.3390/su151813387

Zakopoulos, V., Xanthopoulou, P., & Makri, A. (2026). Integrating Digital Technologies in Theatre/Drama Education: A Systematic Literature Review. *Arts*, *15*(4), 72. DOI: 10.3390/arts15040072

Zhai, X. (2023). ChatGPT User Experience: Implications for Education. SSRN *Electronic Journal*, 1–18. DOI: 10.2139/ssrn.4312418

Zhang, X., Tlili, A., Nascimbeni, F., Burgos, D., Huang, R., Chang, T.-W., Jemni, M., & Khribi, M. K. (2020). Accessibility within open educational resources and practices for disabled learners: A systematic literature review. *Smart Learning Environments*, *7*(1), 1–19. DOI: 10.1186/s40561-019-0113-2

Zhao, H., Amat, A. Z., Migovich, M., Swanson, A., Weitlauf, A. S., Warren, Z., & Sarkar, N. (2022). INC-Hg: An intelligent collaborative haptic-gripper virtual reality system. *ACM Transactions on Accessible Computing*, *15*(1), 1–23. DOI: 10.1145/3487606

ADDITIONAL READINGS

Guidi, A., Di Geronimo, V., Giretti, A., & Ripa di Meana, F. (2026). Enhancing artistic education through artificial intelligence: Tracking creative behavior in higher arts education. In Sampson, D. G., Isaías, P., & Ifenthaler, D. (Eds.), *Teaching and learning in the generative artificial intelligence age* (pp. 27–56). Springer. DOI: 10.1007/978-3-032-05817-1_2

Hutson, J. (2025). Multimodal GAI in arts-based multiliteracies: Fostering interdisciplinary creativity. In Peters, B. (Ed.), *Arts-based multiliteracies for teaching and learning*. IGI Global Scientific Publishing. DOI: 10.4018/979-8-3693-3184-2.ch008

Panjwani-Charania, S., & Zhai, X. (2024). AI for students with learning disabilities: A systematic review. In Zhai, X., & Krajcik, J. (Eds.), *Uses of artificial intelligence in STEM education* (pp. 469–493). Oxford University Press. DOI: 10.1093/oso/9780198882077.003.0021

Walters, A. G. (Ed.). (2024). *Transforming special education through artificial intelligence*. IGI Global Scientific Publishing. DOI: 10.4018/979-8-3693-5538-1

KEY TERMS AND DEFINITIONS

Artificial Intelligence (AI): Computational systems that support tasks such as language processing, image recognition, adaptation, prediction, and feedback in educational settings.

Arts-Based Interventions: Structured educational activities that use artistic forms, such as storytelling, visual arts, music, theater, dance, comics, animation, and performance, to support learning and participation.

Creative Expression: The use of artistic, narrative, visual, musical, or performative means to communicate ideas, emotions, experiences, and meanings.

Drama Pedagogy: A pedagogical approach that uses dramatic play, role-taking, improvisation, embodied action, and reflection to support learning and social development.

Embodied Learning: Learning that takes place through movement, gesture, voice, rhythm, spatial interaction, and bodily participation.

Generative Artificial Intelligence (GenAI): AI systems that generate new text, images, audio, video, or multimodal material for learning, communication, and creative work.

Human-AI Collaboration: The use of AI as a supportive tool while teachers retain responsibility for interpretation, guidance, ethical judgment, and pedagogical decisions.

Skill Development: The strengthening of social, communication, learning-related, cognitive, emotional, creative, sensory-motor, and adaptive skills.

Special Educational Needs and/or Disabilities (SEND): Learning, developmental, sensory, motor, emotional, or communication-related needs that require adapted educational support.

Theater-Based Techniques: Applied theater practices, such as role-play, tableaux, dramatization, forum theater, puppetry, and readers' theater, used for educational or psychosocial purposes.

Chapter 10
Teaching With Generative AI in Special Education: Educators' Perspectives on Practice, Personalization, and Safeguarding

Assimina Tsibidaki
http://orcid.org/0000-0001-6430-2436
University of the Aegean, Greece

Vana Chiou
http://orcid.org/0000-0003-1594-4496
University of the Aegean, Greece

Charalampos Politis
http://orcid.org/0009-0009-0713-6609
Independent Researcher, UK

Michail Terezakis
University of Patras, Greece

ABSTRACT

Generative Artificial Intelligence (Gen-AI) raises important questions for special education and inclusive schooling. This study explores the views of ten Greek primary-level special education teachers on its potential, challenges, and ethical implications. Using semi-structured interviews and thematic analysis, the findings show that teachers viewed Gen-AI as a supportive tool for personalized learning, differentiated instruction, accessible multimodal materials, communication, and emotional regulation. However, they emphasized the need for professional oversight,

DOI: 10.4018/979-8-3373-9169-4.ch010

data privacy, cultural sensitivity, content accuracy, and safeguards against overreliance. Overall, Gen-AI was framed as a tool that can support, but not replace, teacher expertise within human-centered and ethically grounded pedagogy.

INTRODUCTION

The rapid development of Generative Artificial Intelligence (Gen-AI) is reshaping educational discussions, with important implications for special education and inclusive schooling (Hu, 2025; Liu et al., 2025). As schools seek more responsive and flexible ways to support learners with diverse needs, Gen-AI is emerging as a technology that may enhance personalization, accessibility, and instructional innovation (Liu et al., 2025; Tan, 2025). The perspectives of special education teachers are particularly important, as these professionals are responsible for translating technological possibilities into meaningful classroom practices that respond to individualized learning, communication, and social-emotional needs (Ng et al., 2025; Prilop et al., 2025).

Teachers frequently identify personalized learning as one of the most promising areas of Gen-AI application. Advanced models capable of generating adaptable content may support the development of individualized learning materials that respond to diverse cognitive, linguistic, and social-emotional profiles. Multimodal resources, including simplified texts, text-to-speech support, visual scaffolds, and alternative representations of content, may reduce learning barriers and promote equitable participation (Hu, 2025; Liu et al., 2025). Gen-AI is also associated with timely feedback, adaptive pacing, and structured repetition, features that may be especially valuable for students who benefit from predictable support and individualized scaffolding (Brunton et al., 2025; Li et al., 2025; Lo et al., 2025; Yang, 2025).

Beyond student-focused applications, Gen-AI may support teachers' professional work by assisting with curriculum design, lesson planning, assessment, instructional adaptation, and the creation of differentiated materials (Al-Emran et al., 2025; Liu et al., 2025; Matos et al., 2025; Ng et al., 2025; Rasool et al., 2025). In classrooms where students present diverse and complex needs, such tools may reduce preparation time and make interactive, scenario-based, and flexible teaching approaches more feasible (Liu et al., 2025; Tan, 2025). In this sense, Gen-AI is not only viewed as a content-generation tool but also as a potential catalyst for pedagogical innovation, provided that its use remains aligned with curriculum goals, inclusive educational values, and teacher expertise (Abu Eideh, 2026; Savolainen et al., 2026; Stewart et al., 2026; Zaim et al., 2024).

However, effective implementation requires more than access to technology. Educators emphasize the need for professional development, AI literacy, clear guidelines, and reliable institutional support (Gamlem et al., 2026; Liu et al., 2025; Matos et al., 2025; Ng et al., 2025; Prilop et al., 2025). Training should address not only technical skills but also critical evaluation of AI-generated content, ethical decision-making, and strategies for adapting AI outputs to individual learners and classroom contexts. Collaborative curriculum design, shared experimentation, and school-level policies may further reduce uncertainty and support the responsible integration of Gen-AI into practice (Padovano & Cardamone, 2024; Yuwono et al., 2024).

In special education contexts, teacher-guided use is especially important to ensure that learners with special educational needs and disabilities can engage safely and productively with AI-supported environments (Liu et al., 2025). Although Gen-AI may help address barriers related to communication, anxiety, accessibility, and participation, its effectiveness depends on contextual factors such as institutional readiness, technological infrastructure, policy support, and cultural relevance. These factors indicate that successful implementation depends not only on technical capacity but also on supportive organizational and policy environments (Altakhaineh et al., 2026; Hu, 2025; Liu et al., 2025).

Alongside these opportunities, teachers consistently raise concerns related to safeguarding, ethics, and responsible use. Data privacy, accuracy of AI-generated content, algorithmic bias, cultural sensitivity, and the protection of vulnerable learners remain central issues in the use of Gen-AI in education (Altakhaineh et al., 2026; Gamlem et al., 2026; Liu et al., 2025; Ng et al., 2025; Rasool et al., 2025). Educators also stress the importance of maintaining a balance between technology and human interaction, ensuring that AI complements rather than replaces the relational, ethical, and professional dimensions of teaching (Altakhaineh et al., 2026; Gamlem et al., 2026; Tan, 2025). Concerns about over-reliance on AI further highlight the need to protect students' independent thinking, creativity, and social interaction skills (Waluyo & Kusumastuti, 2024; Zaim et al., 2024). A balanced model of human-AI collaboration is therefore essential for preserving the human-centered core of special education (Gidiotis, 2026; Padovano & Cardamone, 2024; Savolainen et al., 2026).

Overall, educators recognize that Gen-AI represents a significant shift in educational practice, offering opportunities for innovation, personalization, and efficiency while also presenting complex ethical, technical, and pedagogical challenges (Gupta et al., 2024; Stewart et al., 2026). They stress the need for transparent, inclusive, and strategically guided integration, where technological capabilities are continuously negotiated in relation to educational values and safeguarding principles (Rasool et al., 2025; Savolainen et al., 2026).

Within the Greek educational context, the integration of digital technologies in special and inclusive education is shaped by both policy aspirations and structural challenges. Although inclusive education has been increasingly promoted at the legislative and policy levels, schools often operate with limited specialized resources, uneven access to support services, and varying levels of digital infrastructure (European Agency for Special Needs and Inclusive Education, 2026; OECD, 2026). Teachers frequently balance high expectations for individualized support with large caseloads and administrative demands, which can constrain the consistent implementation of differentiated and inclusive practices (OECD, 2026). In this environment, emerging technologies such as Gen-AI are viewed with both interest and caution. On one hand, Gen-AI is seen as a potential tool for easing workload and enhancing personalization. On the other hand, its effective use depends on professional support, contextual adaptation, and clear ethical guidance. Exploring teachers' perspectives within this national context therefore provides valuable insight into how Gen-AI may be realistically integrated into special education settings where inclusion is both a guiding principle and an ongoing practical challenge (European Agency for Special Needs and Inclusive Education, 2026).

The Present Study

Despite the rapidly expanding interest in Gen-AI in educational contexts, research has only begun to address how these technologies are perceived by special education teachers who work daily with learners with diverse and complex needs (Hu, 2025; Liu et al., 2025). Much of the existing literature emphasizes technological capabilities, system performance, or general classroom applications, while the lived experiences and professional judgments of special education practitioners remain comparatively underrepresented (Ng et al., 2025; Prilop et al., 2025).

This gap is important because the effective use of Gen-AI in special education depends not only on technical functionality but also on contextualized classroom knowledge, teacher mediation, and sensitivity to students' diverse profiles (Liu et al., 2025; Tan, 2025). Without incorporating teachers' perspectives, AI tools may be misaligned with instructional needs, cultural contexts, and the relational dimensions of teaching that are central to special education practice (Gamlem et al., 2026; Ng et al., 2025).

Moreover, the integration of Gen-AI in special education raises important safeguarding and ethical considerations, including data privacy, algorithmic bias, and the protection of vulnerable learners (Altakhaineh et al., 2026; Rasool et al., 2025). Teachers often serve as the primary mediators between technology and students, particularly in inclusive and special education settings where individualized support and professional judgment are essential (Gamlem et al., 2026). Empirical research that systematically explores how educators understand these responsibilities and negotiate the balance between technological innovation and human-centered pedagogy therefore remains necessary.

Conceptually, the study is informed by inclusive pedagogy, teacher professional agency, and human-centered AI integration. Within this lens, Gen-AI is understood not as an autonomous pedagogical agent but as a mediating resource whose educational value depends on responsiveness to learner variability, professional judgment, relational responsibility, and ethical human oversight. This framing guides the interpretation of teachers' perspectives on personalization, safeguarding, and implementation (Gamlem et al., 2026; Ng et al., 2025; Tan, 2025).

The present study aims to explore how special education teachers perceive the role of Gen-AI in supporting teaching, learning, and inclusion in everyday educational practice. It seeks to connect technological possibilities with classroom realities by examining how teachers interpret the potential, limitations, and ethical implications of Gen-AI within inclusive and special education contexts.

This study is guided by the following research questions:

1. How do special education teachers perceive the potential role of Gen-AI in addressing current educational challenges and student needs?
2. In what ways do teachers believe Gen-AI can support personalized learning and differentiated instruction in inclusive classrooms?
3. How do teachers view the role of Gen-AI in supporting students' communication, emotional regulation, and participation?
4. What concerns do teachers raise regarding cultural sensitivity, safeguarding, ethical use, and human oversight of Gen-AI in classroom practice?
5. What limitations do teachers identify in existing AI tools, and what improvements do they expect from future Gen-AI systems?

METHOD

Participants

The study involved ten special education teachers working in primary education in inclusive and special school settings. Participants were selected using purposive sampling to include educators with direct experience in supporting students with diverse and complex learning needs. All participants had professional experience in special education, and several had prior exposure to digital tools in teaching. Table 1 presents the demographic characteristics of the sample.

Table 1. Demographic characteristics of participants (N = 10)

Variable	Category	n
Gender	Female	6
	Male	4
	Other / Prefer not to say	0
Age group	25–34	2
	35–44	4
	45–54	3
	55+	1
Years of teaching experience	1–5	2
	6–10	3
	11–15	3
	16+	2
Professional role	Special education teacher	6
	Parallel support teacher	2
	Inclusion class teacher	2
	Other	0
School setting	Mainstream (inclusive) school	6
	Special school	4
Familiarity with digital tools	Low	1
	Moderate	5
	High	4
Experience with AI / Gen-AI	Yes	6
	No	4

Note. All participants were special education teachers working in primary education within the Greek educational context.

Data Collection

Data were collected through semi-structured interviews, a method well suited for exploring participants' experiences, perceptions, and professional judgments in depth (Kallio et al., 2016; Patton, 2015). A semi-structured interview guide was developed to allow consistency across interviews while providing flexibility for participants to elaborate on issues they considered significant.

The interview guide focused on teachers' views regarding the potential of Gen-AI to support personalized learning and differentiated instruction, communication and emotional regulation, as well as perceived limitations, ethical concerns, and safeguarding considerations. It further examined the potential role of Gen-AI in addressing current educational challenges and students' needs. Indicative questions included: *"How do you perceive the role of Gen-AI in supporting students with diverse learning needs?"* and *"What improvements would you consider necessary in future Gen-AI tools to better respond to the needs of special education?"*. The full interview protocol is provided in Appendix A.

Interviews were conducted individually, lasted approximately 35 to 55 minutes, and were audio-recorded with participants' informed consent.

Data Analysis

Interview data were analyzed using thematic analysis, following an inductive and interpretive approach (Braun & Clarke, 2006, 2022). This method was selected because it allows for the systematic identification of patterns of meaning across qualitative data while remaining sensitive to participants' perspectives and contextual nuances.

The analysis followed a multi-stage process. First, transcripts were read multiple times to ensure familiarization with the data. During this phase, preliminary notes were made regarding recurring ideas and significant statements. Next, initial codes were generated across the dataset to capture meaningful features related to teachers' perceptions of Gen-AI in special education contexts. Coding was conducted at a semantic level, focusing on explicit meanings expressed by participants, while also allowing for interpretive reflection on underlying pedagogical and ethical concerns.

Subsequently, codes were reviewed, refined, and grouped into broader conceptual categories. These categories were then organized into overarching themes that reflect shared patterns across participants' accounts. The progression from initial codes to refined categories and final themes is presented in Table 2. This table illustrates how specific teacher statements, such as references to workload reduction, content adaptation, or concerns about data privacy, were systematically clustered into higher-level themes including perceived pedagogical benefits, personalization and differentiation, limitations of existing AI tools, communication and emotional support, ethical and safeguarding considerations, and the need for professional and institutional support.

To enhance the trustworthiness of the analysis, a second researcher independently reviewed a subset of transcripts and the preliminary coding framework. Percentage agreement between the two researchers reached 96%, indicating a high level of consistency in the coding process. Discrepancies were discussed and resolved through dialogue, leading to refinement of code definitions and theme boundaries. This collaborative process strengthened the credibility and dependability of the findings.

Throughout the process, attention was paid to maintaining a strong link between the themes and participants' own language, while also situating interpretations within the broader context of AI integration in special and inclusive education. This approach enabled a nuanced understanding of how teachers interpret the role of Gen-AI in relation to classroom realities, student needs, and professional responsibilities.

Table 2. Overview of coding framework and theme development

Initial Codes	Refined Categories	Final Themes
"Saves preparation time"	Reduction of teacher workload	Perceived Benefits of Gen-AI for Teaching Practice
"Helps me simplify texts"	Support for content adaptation	Perceived Benefits of Gen-AI for Teaching Practice
"Can create different levels of activities"	Differentiated material generation	Personalization and Differentiation
"Useful for students who need visuals"	Multimodal accessibility support	Personalization and Differentiation
"Sometimes gives wrong information"	Concerns about accuracy	Limitations of Existing AI Tools
"Not always suitable for Greek context"	Cultural and linguistic mismatch	Limitations of Existing AI Tools
"Could help with social stories"	Support for communication	Communication and Emotional Support
"Might help with anxiety during transitions"	Emotional regulation assistance	Communication and Emotional Support
"I worry about student data"	Data privacy concerns	Ethical and Safeguarding Considerations
"Teachers must check everything"	Need for human oversight	Ethical and Safeguarding Considerations
"We need training before using it"	Professional development needs	Implementation and Professional Support
"School policy is unclear"	Institutional guidance gaps	Implementation and Professional Support

Ethical Considerations

The study was conducted in accordance with institutional research guidelines and ethical standards for research involving human participants and was guided by the principles of the Declaration of Helsinki. Participation was voluntary, and informed consent was obtained from all participants prior to data collection. Anonymity and confidentiality were ensured using pseudonyms and the removal of identifying details from transcripts and reports. Participants were informed of their right to withdraw from the study at any time without consequence. All data were securely stored and handled in accordance with applicable data protection regulations.

RESULTS

Gen-AI as a Support Tool for Addressing Diverse Educational Needs

Teachers largely perceived Gen-AI as a supportive pedagogical tool that could help them respond more effectively to the complex and diverse needs present in special and inclusive classrooms. Most participants (8 out of 10) emphasized that contemporary special education contexts are characterized by increasing heterogeneity, with students presenting cognitive, communication, emotional, and behavioral differences that require continuous adaptation of teaching strategies. Within this demanding environment, Gen-AI was seen as a potential resource for easing instructional planning and enabling more flexible responses to students' needs.

Several teachers (7/10) described Gen-AI as supporting, rather than replacing, the work of the educator. As one participant noted, *"AI could help us find ideas faster and adapt materials, but it cannot understand the child the way a teacher does."* Another teacher explained that *"in a classroom with many different needs, having a tool that suggests alternatives could save time and help us respond more quickly."* These comments reflect a shared view that Gen-AI may serve as a practical aid in situations when differentiating instruction under time and resource constraints.

Half of the participants (5/10) also connected Gen-AI to the possibility of generating adapted materials and alternative explanations for students who struggle with conventional forms of instruction. One teacher remarked, *"Sometimes a student does not understand the way the book explains something. If AI can offer another version or a simpler explanation, that could be very helpful."* Others highlighted that such support could be especially valuable for students who need repeated clarification, visual cues, or step-by-step breakdowns of tasks.

At the same time, most participants (9/10) consistently framed Gen-AI as a tool that requires active teacher mediation and pedagogical judgement. They stressed that the educator must remain responsible for selecting, adapting, and evaluating AI-generated content. As one participant stated, *"AI can propose ideas, but the teacher has to decide what fits the student and the moment."* Another added, *"It should always be used under the teacher's supervision, because only we know the student's emotional state and learning history."*

Overall, teachers perceived Gen-AI as a potentially valuable support mechanism for addressing the everyday challenges of special education, particularly in terms of flexibility and responsiveness. However, they clearly positioned its role as complementary to professional expertise, emphasizing that meaningful use depends on teacher judgment, contextual awareness, and a strong understanding of individual student needs.

Gen-AI, Personalized, and Differentiated Learning

Personalized and differentiated instruction emerged as one of the most strongly emphasized perceived benefits of Gen-AI. Almost all participants (9/10) associated Gen-AI with the possibility of adapting learning materials and activities to better match individual students' profiles, particularly in classrooms where learners with diverse abilities and needs are educated together.

Teachers described Gen-AI as a tool that could help them adjust the complexity, language level, and format. Several participants noted that this could be especially useful for students who require simplified language, visual scaffolding, or structured step-by-step instructions. One teacher explained, *"It could help us take the same topic and present it in different ways, depending on what each child can manage."* Another added, *"Sometimes I spend hours adapting worksheets. If AI can give me a starting point, that would make differentiation more realistic."*

Some participants (6/10) also highlighted the importance of multimodal accessibility, suggesting that Gen-AI could facilitate the creation of materials that combine text, images, and audio. This was seen as particularly beneficial for students with language difficulties, attention challenges, or processing differences. As one participant stated, *"If a text can also become audio or be supported with pictures, more students can access the same content."* Teachers linked this potential to greater participation of students who might otherwise be excluded from whole-class activities due to language or comprehension barriers.

In addition, several teachers emphasized the relevance of Gen-AI for supporting learning aligned with Individualized Education Plans (IEPs). Half of the participants (5/10) noted that AI tools could assist in generating activities tailored to specific goals, such as developing communication skills, strengthening basic academic abilities, or practicing social scenarios. One teacher remarked, *"If it can suggest exercises that match the goals we set in the IEP, it could save time and give us more ideas."*

Despite this optimism, teachers consistently stressed that effective personalization requires professional interpretation and adjustment. All participants underlined that AI-generated materials must be reviewed to ensure that they are developmentally appropriate, emotionally sensitive, and aligned with each student's current learning level. As one participant cautioned, *"AI does not really know the child. We must make sure what it produces truly fits the student."*

Overall, Gen-AI was perceived as a promising resource for enhancing personalized and differentiated instruction, particularly by making adaptation more feasible within the time constraints of everyday teaching. However, teachers clearly positioned these tools as supporting, rather than automating, pedagogical decision-making, reinforcing the central role of human judgment in inclusive and special education practice.

Gen-AI and Support for Communication, Emotional Regulation, and Participation

Teachers identified communication and emotional regulation as areas in which Gen-AI could offer meaningful support, particularly for students who experience difficulties in expressing themselves, understanding social situations, or managing emotional responses in the classroom. Most participants (8/10) described scenarios in which Gen-AI could assist in creating structured materials to support social understanding and communication.

Several teachers (7/10) suggested that Gen-AI could be used to generate social stories, visual scripts, or step-by-step guides to help students prepare for specific situations, such as transitions, group work, or unfamiliar school events. One participant noted, *"It could help us create social stories more quickly, especially for situations that make a child anxious."* Another teacher explained, *"If we can generate simple dialogues or examples of how to respond in social situations, that might support children who struggle with communication."*

Half of the participants (5/10) also connected Gen-AI to the potential to support emotional regulation, particularly through the creation of calming narratives, visual supports, or structured routines. Teachers described how AI-generated materials might help students anticipate what will happen next or reflect on their feelings. As one participant stated, *"If it can help us design materials that explain emotions or daily routines in a clear way, that could reduce anxiety."*

In addition, some teachers (6/10) emphasized that Gen-AI might contribute to greater classroom participation, especially for students who find it difficult to engage through traditional verbal or written tasks. For example, AI-supported multimodal materials could allow students to access content through audio or visual formats, thereby supporting their inclusion in whole-class activities. One teacher commented, *"If a child cannot read a long text but can listen to it or see it in pictures, they can still be part of the lesson."*

Despite recognizing these possibilities, participants consistently stressed that Gen-AI should be used as a supporting structure rather than an independent interaction partner. Most teachers (9/10) underlined that emotional and social learning depend heavily on human relationships and that AI cannot replace the role of the teacher in modeling, guiding, and responding to students' emotional needs. As one participant explained, *"Technology can help prepare materials, but emotional support comes from real human interaction."*

Overall, teachers viewed Gen-AI as a potentially useful tool for enhancing communication, emotional understanding, and participation, particularly through structured and multimodal supports. However, they clearly emphasized that its role should remain complementary, with the teacher maintaining primary responsibility for social-emotional guidance and classroom interaction.

Ethical Concerns, Safeguarding, Cultural Sensitivity, and the Need for Human Oversight

Across interviews, ethical considerations and safeguarding emerged as central conditions for the acceptable use of Gen-AI in special and inclusive education. Almost all participants (9 /10) stressed that the use of Gen-AI in the classroom must be guided by clear pedagogical, ethical, and professional boundaries.

A primary concern raised by teachers related to data privacy and the protection of vulnerable learners. Several participants (7/10) expressed uncertainty about how student information might be used or stored when interacting with AI systems. One teacher noted, *"We work with sensitive information about children. We need to be very careful about what data is shared."* Another added, *"Before using these tools widely, we should know exactly how student data is protected."* These comments highlight a perceived need for transparency and institutional guidance regarding data governance.

Teachers also raised concerns about the accuracy and appropriateness of Gen-AI outputs. Many participants (7/10) emphasized that AI-generated content cannot be accepted uncritically, especially when working with students who require carefully adapted and emotionally sensitive materials. As one participant stated, *"We cannot assume that what AI gives us is correct or suitable for our students. It always needs checking."* This reflects a broader perception that Gen-AI should function as a resource that supports teacher work, rather than as an authoritative source of information.

Cultural sensitivity was another issue frequently mentioned. Some teachers (6/10) pointed out that examples, scenarios, or language produced by Gen-AI may not always align with local educational contexts or students' cultural backgrounds. One participant explained, *"Sometimes the examples feel distant from our students' reality, so we have to adapt them."* This underscores the importance of contextual filtering and teacher mediation to ensure that materials remain meaningful and respectful.

Most importantly, all teachers strongly emphasized the necessity of continuous human oversight. All participants described the teacher as the final decision-maker regarding when and how Gen-AI should be used. One teacher stated, *"AI can suggest, but the teacher must decide what is appropriate."* Another commented, *"It should never replace the teacher's role. We are responsible for the child, not the tool."* These views position professional judgment, relational understanding, and ethical responsibility as essential safeguards in any AI-supported learning environment.

Overall, teachers framed ethical use, safeguarding, cultural sensitivity, and human oversight not as obstacles to Gen-AI integration, but as foundational requirements.

Their perspectives suggest that meaningful adoption of Gen-AI in special education depends on clear ethical frameworks, institutional support, and the continued central role of the teacher as mediator, evaluator, and protector of student well-being.

Limitations of Existing AI Tools and Expectations for Future Gen-AI

While teachers acknowledged the potential of Gen-AI, they also identified several limitations in current AI tools and expressed clear expectations for how future Gen-AI systems should evolve to better support special and inclusive education. Most participants (8/10) reported that existing tools often produce content that is too generic, linguistically complex, or insufficiently aligned with the developmental and emotional needs of their students.

Teachers emphasized that many AI-generated materials require significant modification before they can be used in the classroom (8/10). One participant explained, *"Often the language is still too difficult, so I have to simplify it again myself."* Another noted, *"The ideas can be useful, but they are not always realistic for the level of my students."* These comments suggest that while Gen-AI may provide a helpful starting point, it does not yet fully address the nuanced requirements of special education contexts.

Half of the participants (5/10) also raised concerns regarding cultural and contextual relevance. Some teachers observed that AI-generated examples or scenarios do not always reflect the cultural, linguistic, or school realities familiar to their students. As one participant stated, *"Sometimes the examples feel distant from our everyday classroom life, so I need to adapt them."* This highlights the importance of locally meaningful content in ensuring that Gen-AI outputs are pedagogically appropriate and engaging.

Another recurring limitation involved accuracy and appropriateness. Several teachers (7/10) expressed concern that Gen-AI may produce information or suggestions that are not fully correct or educationally suitable. One teacher remarked, *"We cannot just trust what it gives us. We must check everything."* This reinforces the idea that teacher oversight remains essential when integrating Gen-AI into instructional practice.

Regarding future expectations, most participants (9/10) expressed a desire for Gen-AI tools that are more sensitive to developmental levels, special educational needs, and inclusive classroom realities. Teachers envisioned systems capable of generating materials that are already adapted for different ability levels, communication profiles, and learning paces. As one participant put it, *"It would be helpful if the tool understood that we work with children who learn in very different ways."*

Overall, teachers viewed current limitations not as reasons to reject Gen-AI, but as indicators that these technologies require further development to become truly responsive to special education practice. Their reflections underline the need for future Gen-AI systems to be more context-aware, adaptable, and aligned with the pedagogical and cultural realities of inclusive classrooms.

DISCUSSION

Gen-AI as a Response to Contemporary Challenges in Special Education

The findings indicate that teachers perceive Gen-AI primarily as a supportive tool for addressing persistent challenges in special education, particularly the need for individualized instruction, time constraints, and the diversity of student profiles. Participants consistently described Gen-AI as a means of making instruction more flexible and responsive, aligning with research that highlights generative systems as tools that can enhance personalization, adaptive learning, and instructional efficiency, while also supporting teachers' productivity and curriculum innovation (Hu, 2025; Liu et al., 2025; Rasool et al., 2025; Savolainen et al., 2026).

However, teachers did not frame Gen-AI as a replacement for professional expertise. Instead, they emphasized its role as a complementary aid that can assist with preparation and material adaptation, while pedagogical decision-making remains firmly grounded in teacher judgment. This perspective supports earlier arguments that technological innovation in inclusive education must be mediated through professional knowledge and contextual awareness (Ng et al., 2025; Tan, 2025).

Supporting Personalization and Differentiated Instruction

A central theme in the data concerns the perceived capacity of Gen-AI to facilitate personalized learning and differentiated instruction. Teachers described how AI-generated materials could be adapted in terms of language complexity, task structure, and modality, making learning content more accessible to students with diverse cognitive and communicative needs. These perceptions closely reflect the literature on Gen-AI's potential to produce multimodal and adaptable learning resources that reduce barriers to participation and provide individualized feedback, particularly for learners with diverse or complex educational needs (Brunton et al., 2025; Hu, 2025; Li et al., 2025; Liu et al., 2025).

At the same time, participants stressed that personalization requires careful pedagogical filtering. Gen-AI outputs were viewed as drafts or starting points rather than finished instructional materials. This reinforces the idea that AI-supported differentiation is most effective when embedded in teacher-guided scaffolding processes, especially in special education contexts (Liu et al., 2025; Prilop et al., 2025).

Communication, Emotional Regulation, and Participation

Another key finding relates to the role of Gen-AI in supporting students' communication and emotional regulation. Teachers described potential uses in preparing visual support, social stories, simplified explanations, and structured prompts that could assist students during transitions or socially demanding situations. These uses resonate with emerging views of Gen-AI as a supplementary learning companion that can provide structured prompts, repeated explanations, and multimodal supports, particularly valuable for learners who benefit from predictable and scaffolded interaction (Li et al., 2025; Liu et al., 2025; Yang, 2025).

Importantly, participants emphasized that such tools should be used under close teacher supervision. Emotional and social support were seen as deeply relational processes that cannot be automated, reinforcing the need to balance technological assistance with human presence and professional care (Gamlem et al., 2026; Ng et al., 2025).

Cultural Sensitivity, Safeguarding, and Human Oversight

Ethical and safeguarding considerations emerged as a dominant theme across interviews. Teachers expressed concerns about data privacy, the potential for biased or culturally inappropriate outputs, and the need to protect vulnerable learners. These concerns strongly mirror those reported in international research on AI ethics in education, particularly regarding data protection, algorithmic bias, academic integrity, and the risks of over-reliance on automated systems (Altakhaineh et al., 2026; Rasool et al., 2025; Savolainen et al., 2026; Zaim et al., 2024).

Participants clearly positioned teachers as the final decision-makers regarding the use of Gen-AI in the classroom. Human oversight was viewed as essential for ensuring that AI-generated content is pedagogically appropriate, culturally sensitive, and aligned with students' individual profiles. This finding reinforces the broader literature arguing that responsible AI integration in education depends on strong professional agency and ethical governance rather than technological autonomy (Gamlem et al., 2026; Ng et al., 2025).

Limitations of Existing AI Tools and Expectations for Improvement

Teachers were also highly aware of the current limitations of AI tools. Concerns included inaccuracies in generated content, limited alignment with specific curricular or cultural contexts, and insufficient sensitivity to the complexity of special educational needs. These findings echo prior studies noting that AI systems often lack contextual awareness and may produce outputs that require substantial human revision (Gamlem et al., 2026; Ng et al., 2025).

Participants expressed a strong desire for future Gen-AI tools that are more adaptable, culturally responsive, and designed with special education in mind. Their expectations highlight the importance of involving educators in the co-design of AI tools to ensure that technological development is informed by classroom realities and pedagogical values, a need that has been increasingly emphasized in recent discussions on responsible AI integration in education (Padovano & Cardamone, 2024; Prilop et al., 2025; Tan, 2025).

Overall Interpretation

The findings portray Gen-AI as a promising but carefully bounded innovation in special education. Teachers recognize its potential to enhance personalization, accessibility, and instructional efficiency, consistent with emerging research on AI-supported inclusive practices (Hu, 2025; Liu et al., 2025). However, they also situate its use within a framework of professional responsibility, ethical vigilance, and human-centered pedagogy (Gamlem et al., 2026; Ng et al., 2025).

Rather than embracing Gen-AI uncritically, participants advocate for a balanced model in which technology extends but does not replace teacher expertise. This perspective highlights the importance of professional development, clear guidelines, and participatory design processes to ensure that Gen-AI serves educational rather than purely technological agendas (Alammari, 2024; Ng et al., 2025; Prilop et al., 2025; Yang, 2025).

Gen-AI in the Greek Special Education Context

The findings should also be interpreted within the specific context of the Greek educational system. Participants generally viewed Gen-AI as a promising resource for supporting personalized learning, differentiated instruction, accessibility, and teacher workload management. However, their reflections suggest that the successful integration of Gen-AI in Greek special education depends on several contextual factors, including teachers' digital readiness, access to technological infrastructure, and the availability of institutional support (European Agency for Special Needs and Inclusive Education, 2026; OECD, 2026).

The emphasis participants placed on professional guidance, training, and human oversight may reflect broader challenges within the Greek educational context, where teachers often work under demanding conditions characterized by limited resources, increasing administrative responsibilities, and uneven access to specialized support services (European Agency for Special Needs and Inclusive Education, 2026; OECD, 2026). These conditions may explain why participants consistently framed Gen-AI as a supportive tool rather than a replacement for professional expertise.

Furthermore, the findings highlight the importance of strengthening AI literacy and providing clear ethical and pedagogical guidance for educators. Ensuring equitable access to digital tools, reducing disparities in technological infrastructure, and establishing coherent national guidelines may be particularly important for supporting responsible and inclusive implementation of Gen-AI within Greek special education (Gamlem et al., 2026; Ng et al., 2025; Prilop et al., 2025).

IMPLICATIONS FOR PRACTICE

The findings of this study offer several important implications for educational practice in special and inclusive education contexts where Gen-AI is beginning to enter classroom environments.

A central implication concerns the need for structured and ongoing professional development focused on pedagogical uses of Gen-AI. Teachers in this study expressed interest in using Gen-AI to support planning, material adaptation, and differentiation, but also highlighted uncertainty regarding effective and responsible implementation. Professional development initiatives should therefore move beyond technical training and focus on pedagogical integration, critical evaluation of AI-generated content, and strategies for adapting outputs to individual learner profiles. Such training can strengthen teachers' professional agency and ensure that Gen-AI is used as a tool that supports, rather than directs, instructional decision-making.

Teachers consistently framed Gen-AI as a complementary resource rather than a replacement for professional expertise. This suggests that school policies and professional guidelines should explicitly position Gen-AI as an assistive and preparatory tool that supports teachers in designing inclusive learning experiences. Emphasizing teacher oversight and professional judgment helps maintain the relational and ethical dimensions of special education practice, ensuring that technology enhances, rather than diminishes, the human elements of teaching.

The study highlights the practical potential of Gen-AI to assist with the creation of differentiated and accessible materials. However, effective personalization depends on careful teacher mediation. Educators should be supported in developing routines for reviewing, adapting, and contextualizing AI-generated materials to align with Individualized Education Programs and classroom goals. Schools can promote collaborative practices in which teachers share adapted prompts, materials, and strategies, fostering collective expertise in the responsible use of Gen-AI for inclusive instruction.

Teachers identified meaningful opportunities for Gen-AI to support communication, social understanding, and emotional regulation, particularly through visual support, simplified explanations, and structured scenarios. In practice, these tools should be embedded within broader pedagogical and relational frameworks, where teachers guide students in using AI-generated supports while maintaining direct interpersonal interaction. This approach ensures that Gen-AI contributes to participation and well-being without replacing human relationships that are central to special education.

Ethical use and safeguarding emerged as critical areas for practice. Schools and educational authorities should develop clear policies regarding data protection, responsible use, and the review of AI-generated content. Teachers need practical guidance on how to identify biased, inaccurate, or culturally inappropriate outputs, and how to address these issues before materials reach students. Establishing transparent procedures for human oversight reinforces trust and protects vulnerable learners, particularly in special education contexts.

Finally, the findings suggest that effective integration of Gen-AI requires a whole-school perspective. Leadership plays a key role in creating supportive conditions, including access to reliable infrastructure, time for professional collaboration, and opportunities for shared reflection on practice. By fostering a culture of critical and ethical engagement with AI, schools can ensure that technological innovation aligns with inclusive values and educational goals rather than being adopted in fragmented or purely technical ways.

LIMITATIONS

Several limitations should be considered when interpreting the findings of this study.

First, the study involved a relatively small sample of ten special education teachers, all working in primary education contexts. While this allowed for in-depth exploration of participants' perspectives, it limits the generalizability of the findings to other educational levels or national contexts. Future research could include larger and more diverse samples, incorporating teachers from preschool, secondary education and vocational education.

Second, the data are based on self-reported perceptions rather than direct classroom observations of Gen-AI use. As a result, the findings reflect teachers' expectations, beliefs, and professional judgments, which may differ from actual implementation practices. Observational or intervention-based studies could provide further insight into how Gen-AI is enacted in school environments.

Third, participants' levels of prior experience with AI technologies varied, and for some, familiarity with Gen-AI was limited. Their perspectives may therefore reflect emerging understandings rather than well-established practices. In addition, previous experience with AI tools may have influenced participants' perceptions regarding the usefulness, limitations, and risks of Gen-AI, potentially shaping the degree of optimism or caution expressed during the interviews (Prilop et al., 2025; Rasool et al., 2025). Longitudinal studies could explore how teachers' views evolve as Gen-AI becomes more embedded in everyday educational work.

The study did not examine teachers' perceptions separately according to disability or support-need category. Although participants referred to cognitive, communication, emotional, and behavioral differences, the potential benefits and risks of Gen-AI may vary considerably across learners with different educational and support profiles. The findings should therefore not be interpreted as applying uniformly across all SEND groups. Future research should investigate category- and context-specific applications of Gen-AI while avoiding deficit-based generalizations.

Finally, the study was conducted within a specific cultural and educational context. Issues such as curriculum structure, inclusion policies, and technological infrastructure may shape how Gen-AI is perceived and used. Comparative international research would help clarify how contextual factors influence the integration of Gen-AI in special education.

CONCLUSION

This study explored special education teachers' perspectives on the role of Gen-AI in supporting teaching, learning, and inclusion in everyday educational practice. The findings present Gen-AI as a promising but carefully bounded innovation, valued for its potential to enhance personalization, accessibility, and instructional flexibility, yet consistently framed as requiring strong professional mediation.

Teachers recognized the usefulness of Gen-AI for generating adaptable materials, supporting differentiated instruction, and facilitating communication and emotional regulation. At the same time, they emphasized that effective use depends on teacher expertise, contextual knowledge, and ethical awareness. Gen-AI was not perceived as a substitute for professional judgment or relational pedagogy, but as a tool whose educational value emerges through thoughtful and responsible integration.

Concerns about safeguarding, data privacy, cultural sensitivity, and the risk of over-reliance on technology highlight the importance of clear guidelines, professional development, and institutional support. These findings reinforce the view that the future of Gen-AI in special education lies not in automation, but in human-AI collaboration grounded in inclusive values and pedagogical care.

By centering teachers' voices, this study contributes to a more context-sensitive understanding of Gen-AI in special education and underscores the need for research, policy, and practice to evolve together. The integration of Gen-AI in inclusive educational settings should therefore be guided by professional expertise, ethical responsibility, and a commitment to supporting the diverse needs of learners.

REFERENCES

Abu Eideh, B. (2026). Reimagining instructional design: ChatGPT, Bloom's taxonomy, and the role of teacher expertise. *Social Sciences & Humanities Open, 13*, 102325. DOI: 10.1016/j.ssaho.2025.102325

Al-Emran, M., Al-Qaysi, N., Al-Sharafi, M. A., Khoshkam, M., Foroughi, B., & Ghobakhloo, M. (2025). Role of perceived threats and knowledge management in shaping generative AI use in education and its impact on social sustainability. *International Journal of Management Education*, *23*(1), 101105. DOI: 10.1016/j.ijme.2024.101105

Alammari, A. (2024). Evaluating generative AI integration in Saudi Arabian education: A mixed-methods study. *PeerJ. Computer Science*, *10*, e1879. DOI: 10.7717/peerj-cs.1879 PMID: 38435558

Altakhaineh, A. R. M., Alkhatib, R. N., & Awad, T. (2026). Integrating artificial intelligence to enhance inclusive education for students with special needs in Jordan and the UAE: Perspectives of teachers and parents. *Acta Psychologica*, *263*, 106252. DOI: 10.1016/j.actpsy.2026.106252 PMID: 41558316

Braun, V., & Clarke, V. (2006). Using thematic analysis in psychology. *Qualitative Research in Psychology*, *3*(2), 77–101. DOI: 10.1191/1478088706qp063oa

Braun, V., & Clarke, V. (2022). *Thematic analysis: A practical guide. Sage (Atlanta, Ga.).*

Brunton, R. J., Rhazzafe, S., Moodley, R., Kuhn, S., Caraffini, F., Wilford, S., Higginbottom, R., Colreavy-Donnelly, S., & Gongora, M. (2025). Using generative artificial intelligence to enhance the performance of disadvantaged students in secondary education. *Social Sciences & Humanities Open*, *12*, 102110. DOI: 10.1016/j.ssaho.2025.102110

European Agency for Special Needs and Inclusive Education. (2026). *Country Information for Greece.* https://www.european-agency.org/country-information/greece

Gamlem, S. M., Johnston, S.-K., Moltudal, S., McGrane, J., & Hopfenbeck, T. N. (2026). Generative AI in initial teacher education: Exploring the alignment of perceptions and experiences of pre-service teachers and their teacher educators. *Teaching and Teacher Education*, *172*, 105382. DOI: 10.1016/j.tate.2026.105382

Gidiotis, I. (2026). Speculative futures of artificial intelligence in education: A causal layered analysis of education fiction. *Futures*, *176*, 103762. DOI: 10.1016/j.futures.2026.103762

Gupta, P., Mahajan, R., Badhera, U., & Kushwaha, P. S. (2024). Integrating generative AI in management education: A mixed-methods study using social construction of technology theory. *International Journal of Management Education*, *22*(3), 101017. DOI: 10.1016/j.ijme.2024.101017

Hu, Z. (2025). A method for generating personalized learning content based on AIGC. *Sustainable Futures : An Applied Journal of Technology, Environment and Society*, *10*, 101331. DOI: 10.1016/j.sftr.2025.101331

Kallio, H., Pietilä, A.-M., Johnson, M., & Kangasniemi, M. (2016). Systematic methodological review: Developing a framework for a qualitative semi-structured interview guide. *Journal of Advanced Nursing*, *72*(12), 2954–2965. DOI: 10.1111/jan.13031 PMID: 27221824

Li, H.-J., Huang, Q.-R., Wen, L.-P., Chen, W., & Xu, Z.-Z. (2025). Generative artificial intelligence supported programming learning: Learning effectiveness and core competence. *SAGE Open*, *15*(3), 21582440251377986. DOI: 10.1177/21582440251377986

Liu, L., Liu, W., Luo, Z., & Yue, L. (2025). Scaffolds, screens, and readiness: How teacher-guided AI lifts special-education students into conversational agents. *Acta Psychologica*, *261*, 105889. DOI: 10.1016/j.actpsy.2025.105889 PMID: 41192401

Lo, N., Wong, A., & Chan, S. (2025). The impact of generative AI on essay revisions and student engagement. *Computers and Education Open*, *9*, 100249. DOI: 10.1016/j.caeo.2025.100249

Matos, T., Santos, W., Zdravevski, E., Coelho, P. J., Pires, I. M., & Madeira, F. (2025). A systematic review of artificial intelligence applications in education: Emerging trends and challenges. *Decision Analytics Journal*, *15*, 100571. DOI: 10.1016/j.dajour.2025.100571

Ng, D. T. K., Chan, E. K. C., & Lo, C. K. (2025). Opportunities, challenges and school strategies for integrating generative AI in education. *Computers and Education: Artificial Intelligence*, *8*, 100373. DOI: 10.1016/j.caeai.2025.100373

OECD. (2026). *OECD Education GPS.* https://gpseducation.oecd.org/

Padovano, A., & Cardamone, M. (2024). Towards human-AI collaboration in the competency-based curriculum development process: The case of industrial engineering and management education. *Computers and Education: Artificial Intelligence*, *7*, 100256. DOI: 10.1016/j.caeai.2024.100256

Patton, M. Q. (2015). *Qualitative research & evaluation methods* (4th ed.). Sage.

Prilop, C. N., Mah, D.-K., Jacobsen, L. J., Hansen, R. R., Weber, K. E., & Hoya, F. (2025). Generative AI in teacher education: Educators' perceptions of transformative potentials and the triadic nature of AI literacy explored through AI-enhanced methods. *Computers and Education: Artificial Intelligence*, *9*, 100471. DOI: 10.1016/j.caeai.2025.100471

Rasool, U., Li, J., & Liu, M. (2025). Perceptions of generative AI in teaching and learning: UTAUT and TPACK model-based study of teachers and students. *Acta Psychologica*, *261*, 105827. DOI: 10.1016/j.actpsy.2025.105827 PMID: 41166843

Savolainen, I., Ylinen, L., Grönroos, R., & Oksanen, A. (2026). AI transformation in working life: A systematic review of usage and attitudes towards AI among workers. *Digital Business*, *6*(1), 100162. DOI: 10.1016/j.digbus.2025.100162

Stewart, C. M., Nugent, P., Williams Newman, R., Burns, M., Jeremiah, J., & Barrio, G.Jr. (2026). Preparing educational leaders for the age of AI: Lessons from a graduate course combining curriculum innovation and institutional inquiry. *International Journal of Management Education*, *24*(1), 101313. DOI: 10.1016/j.ijme.2025.101313

Tan, Q. (2025). Reimagining teacher development in the era of generative AI: A scoping review. *Teaching and Teacher Education*, *168*, 105236. DOI: 10.1016/j.tate.2025.105236

Waluyo, B., & Kusumastuti, S. (2024). Generative AI in student English learning in Thai higher education: More engagement, better outcomes? *Social Sciences & Humanities Open*, *10*, 101146. DOI: 10.1016/j.ssaho.2024.101146

Yang, H. (2025). Harnessing generative AI: Exploring its impact on cognitive engagement, emotional engagement, learning retention, reward sensitivity, and motivation through reinforcement theory. *Learning and Motivation*, *90*, 102136. DOI: 10.1016/j.lmot.2025.102136

Yuwono, E. I., Tjondronegoro, D., Riverola, C., & Loy, J. (2024). Co-creation in action: Bridging the knowledge gap in artificial intelligence among innovation champions. *Computers and Education: Artificial Intelligence*, *7*, 100272. DOI: 10.1016/j.caeai.2024.100272

Zaim, M., Arsyad, S., Waluyo, B., Ardi, H., Al Hafizh, M., Zakiyah, M., Syafitri, W., Nusi, A., & Hardiah, M. (2024). AI-powered EFL pedagogy: Integrating generative AI into university teaching preparation through UTAUT and activity theory. *Computers and Education: Artificial Intelligence*, *7*, 100335. DOI: 10.1016/j.caeai.2024.100335

APPENDIX

Semi-Structured Interview Protocol

(1) Demographic Information

The following information is collected solely for research purposes. Participation is anonymous and voluntary.

1. **Gender:** Female Male Other Prefer not to answer
2. **Age group:** 25-34 35-44 45-54 55+
3. **Years of teaching experience:** 1-5 6-10 11-15 16+
4. **Marital status:** Single Married In a civil partnership Divorced Widowed Prefer not to answer
5. **Number of children:** None 1 2 3 or more Prefer not to answer
6. **Educational role:**
   Special school teacher
   Parallel support teacher
   Inclusion class teacher
   Other (please specify): ___________________
7. **Educational level:**
   Preschool Primary Secondary Post-secondary
8. **Type of school setting:**
   General education school (mainstream school)
   Special education school
   Other: ___________________
9. **Level of familiarity with digital tools in teaching:**
   Low Moderate High
10. **Experience using AI or Gen-AI tools in education:**
    Yes No

If yes, please provide a brief description:

(2) Semi-Structured Interview Guide

Opening Question

How would you describe the current reality of special education and inclusion in schools based on your own experience?

Main questions

Which needs in special education do you believe most urgently require support through Gen-AI tools in daily teaching? For example, cognitive, communication, emotional, or organizational needs. Why?

In what ways do you think Gen-AI could support the creation or adaptation of individualized learning activities aligned with students' IEPs?

How do you think Gen-AI could contribute to differentiated instruction within an inclusive classroom setting?

What potential problems, limitations, or concerns do you foresee in using Gen-AI for both personalized and differentiated instruction?

In which school situations do you think Gen-AI could support communication or emotional regulation for students in special education? For example, transitions, anxiety, or social interactions. Why?

How do you think Gen-AI responses should be monitored or supervised to ensure cultural sensitivity and pedagogical appropriateness, particularly within the Greek educational context?

Who do you believe should have the final responsibility for the use of Gen-AI and its outputs in the classroom?

Have you noticed any limitations or difficulties in existing AI tools used with students in special education? For example, accuracy, flexibility, linguistic or cultural adaptation.

What improvements would you consider necessary in future Gen-AI tools to better respond to the needs of special education?

Closing Question

Is there anything else you consider important regarding the use of Gen-AI in special education that we have not discussed?

Thank you very much for your time!

Chapter 11
A Never-Ending Transmedia and AI Framework for Inclusive and Special Education:
Empowering Teachers Through Human-Centered Design

Polyxeni Kaimara
http://orcid.org/0000-0002-7053-8186
Institute for Games Research (IGR), Ionian University, Greece

Ioannis Arvanitakis
http://orcid.org/0000-0002-3024-6007
School of Social Sciences and Humanities, University of Western Macedonia, Greece

Emmanuel Fokides
http://orcid.org/0000-0003-3962-0314
School of Humanities, University of the Aegean, Greece

ABSTRACT

The chapter proposes a transmedia and AI-supported framework for inclusive and special education, grounded in the pedagogical narrative of activities of daily living, with emphasis on the morning routine. Addressing the fragmentation of educational technologies in special education, learning is conceptualized as a "never ending" transmedia ecosystem in which a stable instructional narrative is preserved while its representation evolves across tactile, visual, immersive, auditory, and AI-supported

DOI: 10.4018/979-8-3373-9169-4.ch011

modalities. The framework builds on the WUIM project, a multisensory learning environment informed by inclusive design principles. Within this context, SuDoCapp is presented as a student designed, early stage proof-of-concept rather than a deployed assistive application. Its contribution lies in collaborative design and the use of LLM simulated stakeholder personas for preliminary, low risk evaluation. Overall, the chapter positions Generative AI as a human supervised methodological layer supporting ethical design and teacher professional development in inclusive education.

INTRODUCTION

Inclusive and special education continue to evolve as we increasingly recognize that learners with diverse cognitive, sensory, emotional, and communicative profiles require educational environments that are both equitable and meaningfully accessible. While international frameworks consistently underscore the right of all learners to participate fully in education (UNESCO, 2020; United Nations, 2016), translating these principles into everyday pedagogical practice remains uneven. A major obstacle is the fragmented way in which educational technologies are typically introduced. Tools such as mobile applications, digital games, virtual reality environments, and isolated augmentative communication supports often operate independently. Without forming a coherent system, they struggle to sustain long-term learning for students with Special Educational Needs and Disabilities (SEND) (Ainscow, 2020; Florian, 2014).

This fragmentation concerns not only technological implementation but also deeper pedagogical challenges related to coherence, continuity, and alignment between instructional design and learner needs. In SEND contexts, the absence of structured and interconnected learning environments can increase cognitive load, reduce predictability, and limit opportunities for skill generalization across settings. As a result, there is an increasing need for frameworks that integrate technological tools within stable pedagogical narratives, ensuring that learning remains consistent, accessible, and adaptable across different modalities and contexts.

To address this fragmentation, this chapter introduces an integrated, transmedia, and AI-supported ecosystem grounded in a stable pedagogical narrative: activities of daily living (ADLs), specifically the morning routine. This narrative acts as a pedagogical spine that remains constant even as its representation shifts across different media. The foundation of this framework is the Waking Up in the Morning (WUIM) project, a transdisciplinary, multisensory learning environment. WUIM incorporated tactile materials (such as flashcards and Montessori-based wooden blocks), art-based production, Augmented Reality (AR), Virtual Reality (VR), and

360° videos (Kaimara, 2026; Kaimara et al., 2021). Through iterative formative evaluation, WUIM established a set of evidence-informed design guidelines rooted in Universal Design for Learning (UDL) (CAST, 2018), differentiated instruction (DI) (Tomlinson et al., 2003), Augmentative and Alternative Communication (AAC) (Calculator, 2009), and the Cognitive Theory of Multimedia Learning (CTML) (Mayer, 2009). These principles create a coherent instructional structure that supports learners with autism, Attention Deficit/Hyperactivity Disorder (ADHD), dyslexia, intellectual disability (ID), and complex communication needs. The pedagogical backbone developed in WUIM demonstrated that narrative continuity, symbolic stability, scaffolding, and multimodal cues can be preserved across platforms. It highlighted the power of a transmedia approach that does not simply replicate content, but reimagines it to respect learners' diverse cognitive and sensory preferences.

Importantly, this approach shifts the focus from individual technologies to the relationships between them, emphasizing how learning experiences can be structured around continuity, progression, and meaningful variation. In this sense, transmedia design operates not as a collection of tools but as a pedagogical strategy that supports coherence across different sensory channels while maintaining stable learning objectives. Such an approach is particularly valuable in inclusive education, where learners benefit from predictable structures combined with flexible pathways for engagement.

This transmedia ecosystem can also be extended conceptually through SuDoCapp, a related student-led design case inspired by the WUIM narrative. Developed as an early-stage proof-of-concept rather than a finalized application, SuDoCapp explored how a daily routine could be translated into a speech-based App Inventor prototype with verbal prompts, confirmations, and simple branching logic. Its relevance to the present framework is therefore primarily methodological: it offers a concrete case for examining how early prototypes in SEND contexts can be reviewed through AI-supported, human-supervised stakeholder simulation before any direct involvement of vulnerable learners. Prior research on immersive technologies has highlighted the risks of overstimulation, cognitive overload, and emotional dysregulation among children and adolescents (Kaimara et al., 2022). Consequently, testing early-stage or incomplete prototypes directly in SEND contexts presents significant ethical challenges. To mitigate this, the SuDoCapp evaluation case utilized Large Language Models (LLMs) such as ChatGPT to simulate diverse stakeholder personas, including autistic learners, students with ADHD, caregivers, teachers, and therapists. Although synthetic, these simulations functioned as an ethically safer extension of participatory design, allowing designers to reflect on cognitive load, emotional tone, accessibility, and error recovery before engaging vulnerable learners. This responsible innovation aligns with parallel developments in educational AI governance, underscoring the need for systems that are trustworthy, explainable, and aligned with pedagogical values (Holmes et al., 2019; UNESCO, 2023).

Thus, Generative AI can be understood not as a standalone technological solution, but as an additional layer in the transmedia ecosystem, extending existing pedagogical practices into new forms of simulation and evaluation. Its role is therefore relational rather than autonomous, supporting designers and educators in anticipating user needs and refining instructional design decisions in a controlled and ethically sensitive manner. Rather than treating WUIM, the SuDoCapp proof-of-concept, and AI-supported persona simulations as equivalent or separate initiatives, this chapter uses them as related moments in a broader discussion of how stable pedagogical narratives can inform design, prototyping, and evaluation at different levels of maturity. Each case extends the same concern for narrative stability, scaffolding, and sensitivity to learner diversity into a new technological or methodological context. By bridging research, policy, and practice, the chapter advances a cumulative argument linking theoretical foundations, empirical evidence, and methodological innovation.

The chapter is structured to advance a cumulative argument that links theoretical foundations, empirical evidence, and methodological innovation. It begins by establishing the conceptual basis of the transmedia learning ecosystem and then examines WUIM as the originating locus of its pedagogical architecture. The analysis subsequently traces how this architecture informed a student-designed speech-based proof-of-concept through SuDoCapp and how this design case was used to explore AI-supported stakeholder simulations, which introduce both methodological and ethical considerations. The final sections synthesize these developments into an integrated framework that outlines implications for inclusive design, professional practice, and future research trajectories, positioning the chapter as both a theoretical contribution and a practical roadmap for responsible innovation in SEND education.

THE NEVER-ENDING TRANSMEDIA LEARNING ECOSYSTEM

The concept of a "transmedia learning ecosystem" has gained significant traction in educational research, illustrating how knowledge can be constructed across multiple representational forms while maintaining deep conceptual coherence. Meaning emerges when learners engage with a unified narrative expressed through varied media that enrich, rather than fragment, the learning experience (Fleming, 2013; Scolari, 2009). This approach is especially critical in inclusive and special education, where structural stability, symbolic predictability, and emotional safety are essential for supporting attention, comprehension, and self-regulation.

Transmedia learning environments can be conceptualized as systems that distribute cognitive and sensory demands across multiple channels while preserving conceptual coherence. Instead of concentrating all information in a single modality, the ecosystem allows complementary representations to reinforce each other, supporting learners with different sensory preferences and processing profiles. This distribution reduces overload and increases accessibility without disrupting the continuity of the learning experience. Recent applied examples further illustrate this approach. In particular, studies on AR-enhanced museum-based learning environments demonstrate how the integration of physical artefacts with digital storytelling and interactive tasks can support bilingual language development among learners with diverse needs (Geng & Yamada, 2025; Kaimara et al., 2026; Poulimenou et al., 2023). In such contexts, learners engage with content through multimodal pathways, including visual, auditory, and kinaesthetic interactions, which enhance comprehension, reduce cognitive load, and support active participation. The never-ending ecosystem proposed in this chapter is anchored in a single, stable pedagogical narrative: ADLs, specifically the morning routine. ADLs hold developmental significance for learners with SEND because they directly connect to functional independence, the acquisition of adaptive behavior, and the strengthening of self-determination skills (Kaimara et al., 2019; Wehmeyer, 2006). When this familiar content is delivered across different media formats, the narrative continuity provides cognitive and emotional predictability, helping learners generalize these vital skills to everyday real-world contexts (Alwell & Cobb, 2009; American Association on Intellectual and Developmental Disabilities, 2010).

The selection of ADLs as a narrative foundation strengthens ecological validity, as the learning content directly reflects everyday routines and practical outcomes. This connection supports transfer of learning, enabling learners to move from structured instructional environments to real-life situations with greater confidence and independence. The stability of the narrative, therefore, functions both as a cognitive anchor and as a bridge between guided learning and autonomous action. What makes this ecosystem truly "never-ending" is its balance of adaptability with pedagogical stability. Stability is maintained through a consistent narrative spine, shared symbolic vocabulary, and uniform scaffolding. Adaptability lies in the narrative's capacity to migrate across media as learners mature or their sensory needs change. A learner might initially engage with concrete tactile materials for sensory grounding, move to AR to enhance visual attention (Billinghurst & Duenser, 2012), transition to VR for low-pressure immersion (Newbutt et al., 2020), or. Research has confirmed that learners can benefit when consistent conceptual structures reinforce one another across multiple modalities in this way (Kaimara, 2026; Mayer, 2009). This progression is not fixed or identical for all learners. It reflects a flexible trajectory, where individuals may move between modalities depending on their developmental level, sensory profile, and situational context. Such flexibility is essential for SEND populations, where variability is inherent. The ecosystem, therefore, supports both progression and personalization, maintaining coherence while allowing adaptation in how learning is accessed.

Finally, this ecosystem is never-ending in a sociocultural sense. It creates a shared ecological continuity where learners, teachers, therapists, and caregivers collectively construct meaning as they encounter the same narrative across different environments. This reflects a sociocultural understanding of learning, where knowledge is socially mediated and embedded in collective activity systems (Engeström, 2009; Kaimara et al., 2021; Vygotsky, 1978). For learners with SEND, this shared framework not only strengthens communication between stakeholders but also dramatically reduces the cognitive cost of transitioning between different tools and learning settings. The presence of a shared narrative and symbolic system also facilitates alignment across stakeholders. Educators, caregivers, and therapists can coordinate their practices more effectively, using common references and routines that reduce fragmentation in both instruction and support. This alignment contributes to a more stable and predictable learning experience, reinforcing continuity across contexts and reducing the demands associated with transitions between environments.

WUIM AS A RESEARCH-DRIVEN CONTENT DESIGN ENGINE

The WUIM project constitutes the pedagogical and methodological core of the broader transmedia ecosystem. Its true contribution lies not in the individual technologies it employs, but in its systematic, research-driven design logic. Through this logic, content, scaffolding, symbolic representation, and multimodal learning pathways are constructed cohesively. Developed through a sustained research program grounded in inclusive education theory, educational psychology, multimedia learning, and transdisciplinary design practice, WUIM operated as a reproducible "content design engine." Its principles remain stable even as the ecosystem expands into new modalities tailored to the learning needs of students with SEND.

This design logic can be understood as a structured framework that organizes not only what is learned, but also how learning unfolds across modalities and contexts. It establishes a clear relationship between pedagogical intention, representation, and interaction, ensuring that each component of the learning environment contributes to a coherent instructional experience. In this sense, WUIM does not function simply as a project, but as a transferable model for designing inclusive learning environments that maintain consistency while allowing adaptation. As previously noted, WUIM was organized around ADLs, emphasizing the morning routine. This narrative was selected for its ecological validity and suitability for hierarchical task analysis, allowing learning content to be decomposed into discrete, meaningful steps. The resulting instructional structure was preserved across tactile materials, AR environments, VR experiences, and 360° videos. This allowed learners to encounter the same cognitive sequence through different media while maintaining strict coherence and predictability. Such structural stability is critical for learners who rely on clear sequencing, repetition, and consistent symbolic cues to internalize routines (Kaimara, 2026; Kaimara et al., 2021). The breakdown of the narrative into structured steps also supports instructional clarity, enabling learners to process complex activities as manageable units. This step-by-step organization aligns with principles of task analysis commonly used in special education, where breaking down routines into smaller components facilitates comprehension, reduces cognitive load, and supports gradual mastery. As a result, learners are able to build confidence through repeated exposure to clearly defined sequences that remain stable across different representations. Throughout its development, WUIM was continuously refined via iterative formative evaluation. This involved a transdisciplinary team including educators, therapists, learners with SEND, an educational psychologist, special educators, instructional designers, multimedia designers, and technical developers. Feedback gathered through observation-based protocols and validated evaluation instruments informed crucial decisions related to pacing, content segmentation, visual clarity, auditory cues, and degrees of user agency (Fokides et al., 2019; Kaimara et al., 2021). This iterative process demonstrated how a stable pedagogical structure can be flexibly realized across media without compromising accessibility, emotional safety, or learner participation. This continuous cycle of design, evaluation, and refinement highlights the importance of responsiveness in inclusive learning environments. Rather than assuming that initial design decisions are sufficient, the WUIM approach emphasizes adaptation based on observed learner interaction and feedback. This responsiveness ensures that the learning environment evolves in relation to learner needs, while still maintaining its underlying pedagogical coherence.

The pedagogical design of WUIM draws extensively on complementary strands of inclusive education and multimedia learning research. These frameworks shape access to learning content, allow variation in learning pathways without fracturing the narrative core, stabilize meaning through symbolic mediation, and regulate cognitive load through explicit design constraints (Calculator, 2009; CAST, 2018; Mayer, 2009; Tomlinson et al., 2003). The practical realization of these design logics in the transmedia learning environment is examined below. The integration of these theoretical perspectives is not additive but synergistic, as each framework contributes to a different dimension of the learning experience. UDL ensures accessibility, DI supports variability, AAC stabilizes communication and meaning, and CTML regulates cognitive demands. Together, they form a coordinated design system that balances flexibility with structure, enabling inclusive learning to be implemented consistently across contexts and technologies.

Structuring Access via Universal Design for Learning

In WUIM, access to learning content was embedded as a core design property of the environment rather than treated as an individualized accommodation. The morning routine was engineered so that the same instructional content can be accessed through diverse representational and sensory formats, without altering the underlying learning objectives or fragmenting the narrative. This reflects a Universal Design for Learning (UDL) approach, where learner variability is anticipated and addressed through the initial structuring of the learning environment (CAST, 2018). Consequently, learners engage with the same routine through modalities aligning with their specific sensory and cognitive profiles, preserving instructional consistency throughout. This approach fundamentally shifts accessibility from a reactive adaptation to a proactive design principle. Instead of modifying content after identifying learner difficulties, the learning environment is intentionally constructed to accommodate variability from the outset. This proactive structuring reduces the need for individualized adjustments and supports a more inclusive learning experience where all learners engage with the same content through different pathways. Practically, this means that learners can access the same instructional sequence through tactile, visual, or auditory representations depending on their needs, without experiencing a disruption in the narrative structure. Such consistency is particularly important in SEND contexts, where changes in content representation can lead to confusion or increased cognitive demands. By maintaining a stable narrative across modalities, learners are able to focus on the meaning of the task rather than adapting to new instructional formats. This perspective also invites a critical reconsideration of traditional support structures commonly implemented within inclusive education systems. While resource rooms and parallel support models represented important historical advances toward educational access, their implementation may at times unintentionally reinforce perceptions of difference by spatially or functionally separating learners from the shared classroom experience. Such arrangements, although pedagogically valuable, can position support as an individualized corrective intervention rather than as a collective property of the learning environment. WUIM extends beyond this compensatory logic by reconceptualizing support as distributed orchestration within the shared classroom ecology. In this framework, the classroom teacher assumes the role of pedagogical conductor, while parallel support educators, transmedia resources, and AI-enhanced multimodal tools operate as coordinated co-mediators of learning. Rather than delivering isolated interventions to selected learners, these interconnected supports create multiple simultaneous pathways through which all students can access, interpret, and engage with the same instructional narrative. This distributed co-presence reduces the visibility of differentiation as an exception and reframes inclusion as a naturally embedded feature of the collective learning experience. At the same time, UDL in this context supports not only access but also engagement. Providing multiple means of representation allows learners to select or respond to modalities that align with their preferences and strengths, increasing motivation and participation. This alignment between accessibility and engagement reinforces the effectiveness of the learning experience, particularly for learners who may otherwise disengage in more rigid instructional environments.

Differentiating Learning Pathways

While UDL frames access at the environmental level, Differentiated Instruction (DI) allows for dynamic variation in learning pathways while maintaining the shared instructional narrative. In WUIM, all learners engage with the same ADLs content and learning goals, but differentiation is achieved by modulating modality, pacing, levels of instructional support, and forms of participation. In this way, differentiation operates without the creation of parallel content tracks or the segmentation of learners into distinct instructional groups (Tomlinson et al., 2003). The morning routine functions as a common pedagogical backbone that remains stable across contexts, while learners may interact with it through tactile materials, immersive or non-immersive digital environments, or guided observational formats depending on readiness, sensory tolerance, and situational needs. Design features such as task decomposition, graded prompts, and adjustable sequencing enable learners to progress through the same routine with varying degrees of scaffolding, ensuring both flexibility and coherence. This relationship between DI and UDL is illustrated in Figure 1, where the two approaches are presented as complementary components of inclusive learning design. While UDL ensures equitable access at the level of the learning environment, DI operates by adapting content engagement, learning processes, learner outputs, and the learning environment itself (CAST, 2018; Tomlinson et al., 2003). In WUIM, differentiation is therefore not applied in isolation, but builds on a shared design foundation that secures access before instructional pathways are adjusted.

Figure 1. Relationship between UDL and DI in inclusive learning environments

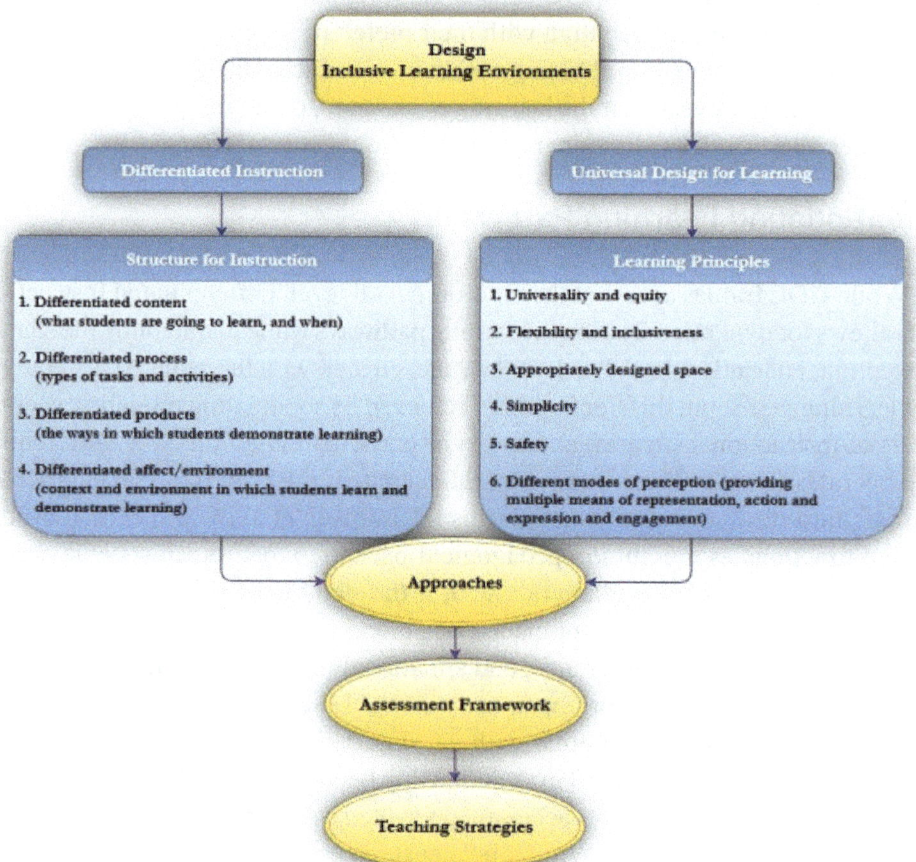

In this ecosystem, differentiation does not imply the creation of separate instructional trajectories, but rather the flexible adaptation of how the same content is experienced. All learners remain engaged with the same narrative structure, while the pathways through which they access and process that structure are adjusted. This approach preserves inclusion by avoiding fragmentation and supports a shared learning experience with individualized entry points. For example, one learner may engage with the morning routine through hands-on manipulation of tangible materials, while another may follow the same sequence through guided observation or auditory prompts. Both learners encounter identical conceptual content, but through different modes aligned with their cognitive and sensory profiles. In addition, the modulation of pacing and instructional support plays a central role in differentiation. Some learners may require slower sequencing, repetition, or additional prompts, while others may progress more independently or at a faster rate. By embedding these variations in the design, WUIM supports sustained engagement while minimizing frustration and cognitive overload. This balance between support and autonomy is essential for facilitating participation and gradual progression toward independence. As shown in Table 1, DI can be enacted across multiple instructional dimensions, including content, process, products, and the learning environment. In WUIM, these dimensions are operationalized through concrete design choices that regulate modality, pacing, and forms of engagement while preserving shared learning objectives.

Table 1. Differentiated instruction practices applied in inclusive learning environments

Differentiated Instruction Practices	
Content	**Simultaneous presentation of information using both visual and auditory modes**
Process	Providing additional time for a learner to complete a task, or encouraging a more advanced learner to explore a topic in greater depth
Products	Offering multiple options for expression (e.g., creating a puppet show, writing a letter, producing drawings)
Learning environment	Designing spaces where learners can work independently and quietly, or engage collaboratively without interruption

Differentiation is therefore realized through variation in how learners access and engage with the same routine, rather than through modification of instructional content or expectations. This approach is particularly relevant in SEND contexts, where learner needs may fluctuate across time, settings, and activities. By embedding differentiation into the design of the learning environment, WUIM allows flexibility while safeguarding predictability, inclusivity, and instructional coherence, ensuring that all learners remain connected to a shared learning experience.

Symbolic Mediation Through Augmentative and Alternative Communication

In the WUIM ecosystem, Augmentative and Alternative Communication (AAC) operated not merely as a supplementary aid, but as a fundamental symbolic and organizational infrastructure. Symbolic systems were embedded throughout the learning environment, offering stable reference points that support meaning-making, orientation, sequencing, and participation within the ADL narrative (Calculator, 2009)(Figure 2).

Figure 2. Morning routine using PCS® (used with permission of Tobii Dynavox)

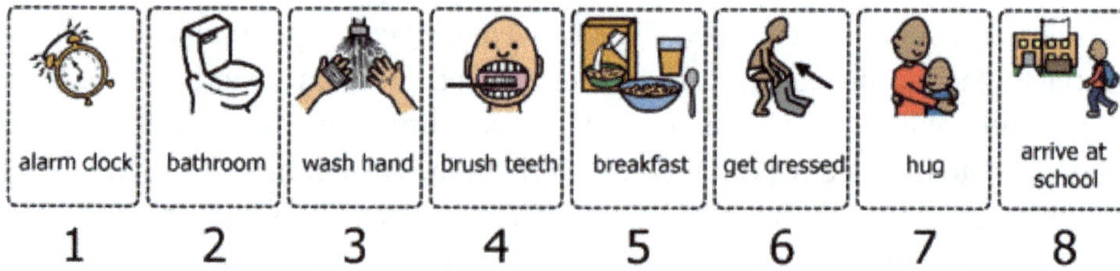

AAC functions as a shared symbolic language bridging various modalities. The exact symbols utilized in tactile materials reappear in digital and immersive environments. This cross-modal continuity drastically reduced the cognitive demands typically associated with transitions. By stabilizing meaning and providing visual anchors, AAC supports expressive communication, comprehension, procedural learning, and independent engagement. Rather than relying primarily on verbal instruction, WUIM used these symbols as a complementary channel, enabling learners to anticipate and rehearse steps smoothly. AAC thus became a foundational element of WUIM's inclusive design, reinforcing continuity and agency. The role of AAC in this context extends beyond communication support, functioning as a core mechanism for structuring learning experiences. By providing consistent symbolic representations across modalities, AAC reduces the need for learners to reinterpret information when transitioning between different formats. This stability is particularly important for learners who rely on visual supports to organize understanding and predict upcoming actions, as it minimizes uncertainty and supports continuity of meaning. At the same time, the repeated use of the same symbols across tactile, visual, and immersive environments strengthens associative learning. Learners begin to link symbols with specific actions, sequences, and outcomes, gradually internalizing the structure of the routine. This process supports not only comprehension but also procedural memory, allowing learners to reproduce steps more independently over time. The integration of AAC also contributes to reducing cognitive load by externalizing key elements of the task structure. Instead of requiring learners to retain all steps in working memory, symbolic cues act as external supports that guide attention and action. This is particularly beneficial for learners with attention or memory difficulties, as it allows them to focus on task execution rather than information retention. Furthermore, AAC enhances learner agency by enabling participation through alternative communication pathways. Learners who may have limited verbal abilities can still engage with the routine, make choices, and demonstrate understanding using symbolic systems. This inclusive functionality ensures that participation is not dependent on a single mode of communication, but is supported through multiple accessible channels aligned with learner needs.

Regulating Cognitive Load Through the Cognitive Theory of Multimedia Learning

Instructional design decisions in WUIM, such as modality use, pacing, and sequencing, were firmly guided by the Cognitive Theory of Multimedia Learning (CTML) (Mayer, 2009). Rather than abstract concepts, these principles acted as concrete design constraints governing how information was presented and processed. A concern was regulating cognitive load, particularly for learners sensitive to overstimulation, unpredictability, or excessive simultaneous input. In this context, cognitive load is not treated as a secondary consideration but as a central design parameter that shapes how learning experiences are constructed. For learners with SEND, limitations in working memory, attentional control, and sensory processing require instructional environments where information is carefully structured and presented in manageable units. Managing cognitive load, therefore, becomes essential for maintaining engagement and supporting successful task completion. CTML conceptualizes learning as the coordinated processing across sensory memory, working memory, and long-term memory via dual-channel processing of verbal and pictorial information. Applying this framework, WUIM segmented instructional input, coordinated verbal guidance with visual representations, and prevented unnecessary competition between sensory channels. Each step of the ADL narrative was delivered in a controlled, predictable manner, isolating essential elements and eliminating decorative stimuli. This segmentation strategy plays a critical role in supporting learners who may experience limitations in working memory and attentional control. By presenting information in discrete, manageable units, the instructional design reduces cognitive overload and allows learners to focus on one element of the task at a time. This is particularly important for learners with SEND, who may find the simultaneous processing of multiple inputs challenging and benefit from clearly defined, sequential instructional structures. In addition, the coordination between verbal and visual elements ensures that information is reinforced rather than duplicated or competing for attention. When modalities are aligned in this way, learners can form stronger associative links between representations, thereby supporting deeper processing and facilitating transfer to long-term memory. This coherence across channels contributes to a more efficient use of cognitive resources and enhances overall comprehension of the learning sequence. This CTML-informed logic also informed the interpretation of SuDoCapp as a speech-based prototype. Rather than providing evidence of an implemented auditory intervention, the case illustrates how the same cognitive-load constraints can guide early design decisions: linear verbal scaffolding, predictable turn-taking, and reduced visual load. By treating cognitive load regulation as foundational, WUIM's design logic can inform multimodal and transmedia expansion in ways that remain supportive, predictable, and cognitively sustainable for diverse learners. The move toward speech-based prototyping further highlights the importance of temporal structuring in instructional design. In the absence of rich visual cues, learners rely more heavily on the sequential organization of verbal information, making pacing and clarity especially critical. This reinforces the relevance of CTML principles in guiding design decisions, as the same constraints related to segmentation, coherence, and cognitive load management must be considered even when the modality changes. At the same time, the SuDoCapp case demonstrates that cognitive design principles can be used to evaluate early prototypes before they are treated as learner-facing interventions. Even as the ecosystem evolves, the underlying logic of reducing extraneous load, structuring information sequentially, and aligning instructional elements remains stable.

SUDOCAPP AS A STUDENT-DESIGNED PROOF-OF-CONCEPT AND EVALUATION CASE

SuDoCapp should be understood as an exploratory, student-designed proof-of-concept inspired by the WUIM architecture rather than as a completed or deployed application. While WUIM expressed the morning routine narrative across tactile, visual, immersive, and 360° videos, the SuDoCapp project asked how a similar daily-routine support scenario might be represented through speech-based interaction. The project, therefore, constitutes a tentative cross-modal design exploration: the narrative logic and task sequencing of the morning routine were translated into verbal prompts, confirmations, and simple branching paths in MIT App Inventor. This framing is important because the application was not completed as a professional assistive technology nor evaluated with real end users. Its value within this chapter lies in the design questions it raised and in the subsequent AI-supported preliminary evaluation.

Translating the ADL Narrative Into a Prototype Interaction Flow

SuDoCapp was developed by four 13-year-old lower-secondary students in a school-based maker lab as part of a national student technology competition, under the guidance of educators, technical mentors, and a psychologist. Their contribution extended beyond coding. The students analyzed the daily-routine scenario, decomposed it into micro-steps, discussed potential user challenges, and worked with the psychologist to create a basic decision tree for how a speech-based support application could respond to different user answers (Figure 3).

Figure 3. Student-led task decomposition and decision-tree design

In this sense, the project functioned as a design-learning experience as much as a technical exercise. It enabled students to engage with inclusive design, routine support, and user-centered thinking, while remaining within the realistic constraints of a school-based prototype developed in MIT App Inventor. This transformation should therefore be understood as a design intention rather than as evidence of an implemented intervention. The students attempted to translate spatial and visual representations into temporally structured verbal sequences, where meaning unfolds step by step rather than being simultaneously available. Each step of the routine had to be rephrased in a way that was concise, explicit, and easy to follow, so that a future learner could process information sequentially without ambiguity. Although the prototype remained unfinished, this translation highlights the importance of linguistic clarity and structured phrasing in speech-based support systems, particularly when addressing learners who rely on predictable and repetitive instructional patterns.

Speech-Based Scaffolding as a Design Intention

At the core of SuDoCapp's concept was the proposed transformation of WUIM's visual and immersive scaffolding into a linear, verbal progression. The students designed each step of the morning routine to be conveyed through predictable pacing, clear articulation, confirmation requests, and adaptive repetition. This modality was hypothesized to be supportive for autistic students and learners with ADHD or dyslexia, who may benefit from consistent verbal patterns and reduced visual complexity. However, this remains a design hypothesis generated through prototyping and simulated evaluation, not a validated claim based on real-user testing. Practically, the scaffolding was planned in the form of step-by-step prompts, confirmation requests, and repeated or simplified instructions when the user hesitated or responded negatively. For example, the system might prompt the learner to complete a specific action ("Have you brushed your teeth?"), wait for a response, and adjust its next instruction accordingly. This responsive pattern was intended to support both guidance and autonomy while keeping the learner within a structured routine.

At the same time, this proposed scaffolding reflects a shift from spatially distributed support to temporally organized guidance. Instead of relying on simultaneous visual cues, learners would process information sequentially, which could reduce attentional competition and support sustained focus. This sequential organization is particularly relevant for learners who experience overload in multimodal environments, as it simplifies interaction while preserving the coherence of the instructional sequence. In the SuDoCapp case, this remained a design direction to be further developed and tested.

Auditory Mediation and the Pedagogical-Agent Concept

In the SuDoCapp concept, the pedagogical agent was imagined as a consistent auditory guide. In WUIM, the pedagogical agent's presence was distributed across multimodal cues, visual prompts, and verbal feedback. In the SuDoCapp prototype, this idea was reinterpreted through a single speech-based presence that would provide prompts, feedback, and emotional reassurance through structured phrasing and predictable tone patterns. The planned interaction flow relied on turn-taking sequences, where a learner's response and the corresponding system feedback would follow each prompt. Such predictability was intended to reduce uncertainty and support engagement throughout the routine. However, because the prototype was not completed or tested with learners, these statements should be read as design aims and evaluation criteria rather than as demonstrated learning outcomes. The audio-focused modality was considered promising for reducing sensory demands among learners who may find visually rich environments overwhelming, but this potential requires future real-user testing. SuDoCapp was intended to offer an alternative entry point into familiar daily routine content through a less visually demanding modality. The design team explored whether auditory rehearsal could help represent the routine as a linguistic script supporting real-world application. Because the ADL narrative is stable across modalities, a learner might, in principle, begin with tactile sequencing in WUIM, move to immersive VR practice, and later use a speech-based tool for rehearsal. In the present case, however, SuDoCapp should be treated as an unfinished prototype that allowed the design team to explore this possibility, not as evidence that learners had already internalized the routine through the application.

AI-Supported Interaction Under Human Supervision

SuDoCapp provided a practical context for experimenting with AI-supported evaluation in the ecosystem's subsequent methodological stage. Its planned reliance on structured verbal scaffolding mirrors the conversational patterns utilized by LLM-generated personas. Because both the prototype and the simulated personas operate through prompt-response sequences, it became possible to examine how instructions might be interpreted, where communication could break down, and how the interaction flow might be refined before any real-user testing. This alignment allowed the evaluation process to follow the same structural logic as the intended learning interaction, while keeping the claims explicitly limited to early-stage design reflection. In the SuDoCapp case, AI was employed primarily during the design, simulation, and evaluation phases; it did not function as an autonomous instructional authority or as a learner-facing component of a completed application. Human supervision, pedagogical judgment, and ethical caution remained central to all AI-mediated interactions. From a methodological perspective, this approach introduces a controlled layer of formative evaluation, where interaction scenarios can be explored without the risks associated with early-stage testing in SEND contexts. Simulated personas provide indicative response patterns related to comprehension, pacing, and cognitive load, supporting iterative refinement of the design. Importantly, AI use remains explicitly bounded by human oversight. Educators and designers interpret generated outputs, validate their relevance, and make all instructional decisions, ensuring that AI functions as a supportive evaluative tool rather than an autonomous system. This maintains alignment with ethical principles and reinforces a human-centered approach to inclusive educational design.

GENERATIVE AI AS A NEW TRANSMEDIA LAYER: LLM-SIMULATED STAKEHOLDER EVALUATION

The integration of Large Language Models (LLMs) represents a methodological advancement that can extend participatory and cross-modal design practices into the evaluative stages of development. In the SuDoCapp case, Generative AI did not add a new learner-facing function to a finished product. Instead, it introduced an additional reflective layer that supported the student team in reviewing an early-stage prototype through simulated perspectives while keeping the underlying pedagogical structure open to revision. Early-stage testing with autistic students or other learners with SEND raises significant ethical, emotional, and practical concerns, particularly when prototypes have not yet reached sufficient stability. These concerns include heightened cognitive load, sensitivity to interface unpredictability, difficulty interpreting incomplete interactions, and the risk of frustration or emotional overwhelm. To address these challenges, the development team employed LLM-based simulations to approximate diverse stakeholder perspectives and gather preliminary feedback before engaging real users. This anticipatory evaluation aligns with broader movements toward inclusive and low-risk design practices in special education. These simulations allowed the team to explore how different user profiles might interpret prompts, respond to structured guidance, and navigate task sequences. By reproducing prompt-response interaction patterns similar to those planned in SuDoCapp, the evaluation process maintained consistency with the intended learning interaction. At the same time, the use of simulated personas did not aim to replicate authentic user behavior, but to provide indicative scenarios that support early-stage reflection. The insights generated from these interactions helped identify potential issues related to clarity, pacing, and cognitive load, guiding iterative refinement before any real-user engagement.

Crafting Simulated Personas

The simulated personas were carefully crafted to represent a wide range of stakeholders: autistic students, students with ADHD or dyslexia, individuals with intellectual disabilities, caregivers with differing levels of digital literacy, classroom teachers, special educators, therapists, and assistive technology specialists. Each persona was prompted to respond to the system as a plausible user with a unique cognitive, emotional, or contextual profile. These personas were not designed to replicate specific individuals but to represent indicative patterns of interaction and variability commonly observed in SEND populations. Their construction was informed by pedagogical knowledge, prior research, and practical experience with diverse learner needs, ensuring that simulated responses remained grounded in realistic educational contexts. This method provided useful preliminary insight into diverse experiential pathways, allowing the design team to detect potential obstacles related to pacing, comprehension, sensory load, and linguistic clarity. The simulations generated feedback on instructional tone, transition predictability, error recovery, and user comfort, offering early refinements that could inform later live user testing. In practice, each persona engaged with the system through structured prompt-response exchanges, allowing the design team to observe how variations in comprehension, response timing, and behavioral consistency might affect the flow of interaction. These simulated responses functioned as heuristic indicators of possible design issues, highlighting areas where instructions could be simplified, pacing adjusted, or scaffolding strengthened. At the same time, the use of multiple personas enabled comparative analysis across different user profiles. By examining how diverse stakeholders might interact with the same instructional sequence, the design team was able to identify elements that seemed stable across users, as well as components that required adaptation. This process supported a more inclusive design approach, ensuring that variability was addressed proactively rather than retrospectively.

The Ethical Bridge and Multidimensional Feedback

In the SuDoCapp evaluation case, LLM-simulated personas served as an "ethical bridge" between design intent and human-centered evaluation, rather than a replacement for authentic learner participation. By enabling the exploration of diverse cognitive, emotional, and contextual perspectives in a controlled, low-risk environment, these AI-supported simulations allowed designers and educators to anticipate usability challenges and accessibility constraints before exposing vulnerable learners to early-stage prototypes. This anticipatory evaluation is particularly valuable in SEND contexts, where emotional dysregulation or sensory stress can arise quickly if interactions are not carefully calibrated. Recent empirical work similarly used LLMs as auxiliary, human-supervised mechanisms that support reflective design while minimizing ethical risks and cognitive disruption (Daniela, 2026). What is important is that the use of LLMs supported multidimensional evaluation across the prototype:

- Autistic student personas provided insight into sensory sensitivities, preferences for predictable phrasing, and potential areas of confusion in verbal instruction.
- ADHD student personas generated useful feedback regarding pacing, sustained engagement, and the need for concise, structured cues.
- Dyslexia student personas offered perspectives on linguistic clarity and phonological load.
- Caregiver personas revealed expectations regarding autonomy, safety, and communication with educators.
- Educator and therapist personas pointed to alignment with curricular goals, the appropriateness of scaffolding, and the perceived utility of the tool in learning environments.

This feedback allowed the prototype to be examined not only as a technical artifact, but also as a possible educational support situated within real learning ecologies. The multidimensional feedback structure extended the evaluative capacity of the design process by integrating perspectives that would typically require extensive field testing. By consolidating diverse viewpoints within the simulation phase, the design process became more anticipatory, allowing potential issues to be identified and addressed before implementation. At the same time, the concept of an "ethical bridge" highlights the transitional role of AI-supported evaluation. Rather than replacing user participation, it creates a preparatory layer that may enhance safety and methodological rigor. This is particularly critical in SEND contexts, where premature or poorly calibrated interactions may have disproportionate cognitive or emotional impact. Furthermore, the integration of multiple stakeholder perspectives contributed to a more ecologically informed evaluation process. By incorporating simulated insights from learners, caregivers, and professionals, the prototype was assessed not only in terms of usability but also in relation to its potential practical relevance and applicability across real-world educational settings.

Methodological continuity and structural alignment

Equally significant is the alignment between the simulated personas and the structure of the SuDoCapp prototype. Because SuDoCapp was designed as a verbal decision tree with prompts, confirmations, and adaptive responses, it offered a natural foundation for conversational testing through AI simulation. The predictable turn-taking, verbal scaffolding, and task decomposition planned in the prototype map directly onto the dialogic structure required by LLM-driven interactions. This structural compatibility ensured that LLM simulations operated in relation to a coherent design concept rather than generating responses in isolation. Rather than introducing a separate evaluation layer, LLM-based simulation extended the existing design logic into a new methodological context, preserving continuity between prototyping and evaluation. Despite its benefits, the use of simulated personas was strictly framed as a preparatory stage. It preserved the integrity of participatory design by ensuring that human stakeholders could later interact with a more refined, conceptually coherent, and emotionally safer prototype. In this sense, LLM-supported simulations extend, rather than replace, the collaborative foundations of the design process. This positioning is particularly important in safeguarding the role of authentic user participation, ensuring that simulated interaction serves as a support mechanism rather than a substitute. By preparing and stabilizing the design in advance, the approach can enhance the quality and safety of subsequent real-world engagement. Finally, the integration of LLM simulations underscores the adaptability of the broader transmedia framework. Just as the ADL narrative can migrate across sensory modalities, the evaluative framework can also evolve into new methodological territories. In the SuDoCapp case, GenAI is best understood as an embedded methodological layer, aligned with the foundational principles of inclusive, predictable, and learner-centered design. In this way, the integration of AI-supported evaluation does not disrupt the framework's structure but reinforces its capacity for responsible expansion. The same principles that guide content delivery, i.e., stability, predictability, and accessibility, are extended to the evaluation process, ensuring that innovation remains pedagogically grounded.

ETHICAL INTEGRATION OF AI IN SEND CONTEXTS

Recent discussions on sustainable and responsible technology-enhanced learning noted that pedagogical coherence, ethical transparency, and cognitive well-being must precede technological adoption, particularly in contexts involving vulnerable learners (Daniela, 2026; Holmes et al., 2019; UNESCO, 2023). The incorporation of GenAI into learning environments for autistic students and other learners with SEND introduces ethical responsibilities that extend far beyond conventional considerations of data privacy or technical reliability. These responsibilities encompass emotional safety, cognitive load, agency, trust, and the potential shaping of learner behavior through interactions with intelligent systems. In this context, ethical integration is not treated as an external constraint but as an intrinsic design requirement that informs all stages of the ecosystem, from content structuring to interaction modeling and evaluation. This positioning ensures that technological innovation remains aligned with pedagogical intent rather than driving it.

Foundational to this framework is the recognition that SEND populations present diverse sensory, cognitive, and emotional profiles that heighten their vulnerability. Prior research on immersive environments extensively documented the risks of sensory overstimulation, emotional dysregulation, heightened anxiety, and cognitive overload when stimuli are unpredictable or insufficiently scaffolded (Kaimara et al., 2022). Therefore, the WUIM-SuDoCapp ecosystem requires a framework that firmly aligns technological innovation with the principles of inclusive education, human dignity, and learner-centered design. This alignment reinforces the need for environments that not only provide access but also actively safeguard learner well-being through controlled interaction, predictable structures, and carefully calibrated sensory input. Transparency and predictability are central ethical requirements for AI systems operating in SEND contexts, as learners rely on consistent patterns to feel secure and maintain cognitive focus. For this reason, the conversational structures of SuDoCapp and the LLM-simulated personas were deliberately designed to follow predictable turn-taking, explicit causal sequencing, and controlled linguistic complexity. This design directly aligns with established principles of cognitive load theory and UDL (CAST, 2018; Mayer, 2009). The ethical imperative is to ensure that AI interactions consistently support, rather than destabilize, the learner's cognitive and emotional equilibrium. By embedding these constraints directly into system design, the ecosystem minimizes variability that could otherwise lead to confusion or distress, ensuring that interaction patterns remain stable and interpretable across different contexts.

A critical ethical consideration concerns the risk of over-attribution of competence to AI systems. AI-generated personas or conversational agents may appear confident, coherent, or authoritative, but they possess no genuine understanding and cannot genuinely perceive a learner's emotional state. Ethical practice dictates that educators, designers, and caregivers must interpret AI outputs critically and maintain strict human oversight in all decisions relating to learning, safety, and well-being. This is consistent with international guidelines calling for human-centric governance in educational AI (Holmes et al., 2019; UNESCO, 2023). In this ecosystem, AI serves explicitly as a support mechanism, never a replacement for human judgment. This distinction is critical in maintaining trust, as it prevents the misinterpretation of AI-generated responses as authoritative knowledge and reinforces the central role of human expertise in educational decision-making. Furthermore, mitigating bias is essential. LLMs are trained on data that may contain inaccuracies, stereotypes, or incomplete representations of disability, which could inadvertently reinforce misconceptions. To address this, the design team curated prompt structures and interaction constraints that drastically reduced opportunities for speculative or ambiguous responses. AI-simulations were rigorously used to interrogate system behavior and correct potential misalignments before human engagement. Such controlled use of AI supports a more responsible and critically informed deployment, where outputs are continuously examined against pedagogical expectations and ethical standards. Technologies that fully automate guidance, feedback, or decision-making can limit learners' autonomy. In contrast, the pedagogical agent embedded in WUIM and conceptualized in SuDoCapp was designed to model, support, and scaffold, never to direct or constrain. Extended into the AI-supported evaluation layer, this principle ensured that the design process remained oriented toward learner empowerment rather than dependency. The emotional dimension is equally critical. Autistic students and other learners with SEND may interpret tone, pacing, or phrasing in highly individualized ways. Ethical AI integration requires careful attention to linguistic calibration, affective neutralization, and the avoidance of metaphors or ambiguous speech patterns that could confuse. In the SuDoCapp evaluation case, the planned verbal scaffolding provided a useful basis for constraining AI simulations toward safe, predictable linguistic structures. This emphasis on linguistic precision and affective neutrality further ensures that interaction remains accessible and interpretable, reducing the risk of misunderstanding and supporting consistent engagement.

Ethical AI is not a single design choice but an ongoing, iterative process demanding observance, collaboration, and transparency. As AI systems evolve and learners' needs inevitably change, the ecosystem must remain responsive. By embedding AI into a pedagogical architecture already grounded in inclusive design, symbolic stability, and structured scaffolding, the WUIM-SuDoCapp framework suggests how emerging technologies can be introduced responsibly. This dynamic approach ensures that ethical considerations are continuously revisited and refined, allowing the system to adapt without compromising its foundational principles. The ethical dimensions discussed above are synthesized in Table 2, which consolidates the core principles embedded in the WUIM framework and the SuDoCapp evaluation case and illustrates how ethical considerations can be translated into concrete design decisions.

Table 2. Core ethical principles for integrating GenAI in the WUIM framework and SuDoCapp evaluation

Ethical principle	Description in SEND contexts	Operationalization within the WUIM framework and the SuDoCapp evaluation case
Emotional safety	Learners with SEND may experience anxiety or emotional dysregulation in unpredictable digital environments.	Stable narrative sequencing, emotionally neutral language, and predictable interaction patterns across WUIM, the SuDoCapp prototype, and AI-supported dialogue.
Cognitive load regulation	Ethical AI design minimizes extraneous cognitive demands for learners with limited working memory or attentional control.	Linear verbal scaffolding, segmented instructions, and constrained AI responses that mirror low-cognitive-load design principles at the prototype-evaluation stage.
Predictability and transparency	Predictable system behavior supports trust and cognitive security for learners with SEND.	Explicit turn-taking, causal sequencing, and consistent interaction logic across modalities and simulated evaluation scenarios.
Human oversight and accountability	AI systems must not replace human pedagogical judgment or care.	AI-supported simulations used as preparatory design tools under continuous human supervision.
Bias awareness and mitigation	LLMs may reflect stereotypes or incomplete representations of disability.	Prompt constraints and simulated personas used to identify and correct potentially biased or misleading responses before any learner-facing use.
Learner agency	Ethical systems protect autonomy and avoid learner dependency on automation.	Pedagogical agents are designed or conceptualized to scaffold and gradually withdraw support, reinforcing independence rather than dependency.

continued on following page

Table 2. Continued

Ethical principle	Description in SEND contexts	Operationalization within the WUIM framework and the SuDoCapp evaluation case
Linguistic clarity and affective calibration	Individualized interpretation of tone and language requires careful linguistic design.	AI interactions constrained to literal, clear, and emotionally neutral language structures.
Iterative responsibility	Ethical AI integration requires continuous monitoring and refinement.	AI embedded in iterative evaluation cycles aligned with inclusive design principles, with real-user testing reserved for ethically approved later stages.

IMPLICATIONS FOR TEACHER PROFESSIONAL DEVELOPMENT AND INCLUSIVE PRACTICE

The unified transmedia and cross-modal framework illustrated through WUIM, the SuDoCapp proof-of-concept, and AI-supported simulations offers not only a coherent pedagogical architecture but also a substantive contribution to teacher professional development (TPD). As educators increasingly navigate the complexities of diverse classrooms, including autistic students and learners with ADHD, dyslexia, and intellectual disabilities, they require frameworks that move beyond isolated digital tools, providing instead integrated methodologies for accessible and adaptive instruction. This shift reflects a broader transformation in the professional role of educators, who are increasingly expected to integrate pedagogical, technological, and design-oriented competencies to respond effectively to diverse learner needs.

Traditional teacher professional development in inclusive education often emphasizes theoretical knowledge without providing concrete design practices that teachers can immediately transfer to their classrooms. The ecosystem presented in this chapter bridges this gap by grounding abstract pedagogical principles in tangible, cross-media examples. The symbolic stability, narrative continuity, and scaffolded pacing embedded in the WUIM architecture act as visible demonstrations of how UDL,

DI, AAC, and multimedia learning theories can be practically enacted. Teachers are thus able to see not only why these principles matter but how they can be applied, expanded, or adapted in their own curricular contexts. This connection between theory and practice enhances the applicability of professional learning, allowing educators to translate conceptual knowledge into structured instructional decisions that can be implemented across different learning environments.

Educators frequently express hesitation regarding the adoption of emerging technologies like AR, VR, or AI-driven tools. This hesitation is well-documented and often stems from concerns over cognitive overload, classroom management demands, and the fear that such technologies may replace rather than support teacher expertise (Fokides & Daskalou, 2026; Kaimara et al., 2021, 2022). The structured, predictable, and pedagogically transparent design logic illustrated by WUIM and explored through the SuDoCapp evaluation case can help counter these barriers. By positioning technology as a structured extension of pedagogy, guided by narrative coherence and sensory predictability, teachers gain confidence in adopting these tools without compromising learner safety or relinquishing pedagogical control. In this way, the ecosystem supports a reconceptualization of technology as a pedagogically governed resource rather than an external or disruptive element in instructional practice.

The integration of AI-supported simulations offers an additional, highly practical layer of professional insight. By engaging with simulated personas that reflect a variety of learner profiles, teachers can explore how different students might respond to pacing, instructional tone, or linguistic complexity before real learners interact with the tool. These simulations serve as low-risk opportunities for "professional rehearsal," allowing educators to reflect on their instructional decisions, anticipate potential misunderstandings, and practice strategies to support students requiring different types of scaffolding. This form of simulated engagement supports reflective practice by enabling educators to examine instructional choices in a controlled environment, reducing uncertainty and strengthening pedagogical decision-making.

Finally, the ecosystem supports TPD by fostering reflective, transdisciplinary collaborative practice. Its use naturally encourages educators to collaborate with psychologists, therapists, caregivers, and technical specialists, mirroring the design processes that produced WUIM and informed the SuDoCapp proof-of-concept. Such ecosystem-level approaches resonate deeply with broader frameworks of inclusive digital education that emphasize coherence across pedagogy, practice, teacher development, and systemic support. Teachers who engage with this stable yet flexible ecosystem acquire a replicable framework for future innovation. They learn how to construct narrative spines, design symbolic systems, scaffold sequences, and calibrate sensory load in ways that can be sustainably applied to any content domain, empowering them to navigate the rapidly changing landscape of inclusive education. This sustained engagement with design principles contributes to the development of adaptive expertise, enabling educators to respond flexibly to emerging technologies and evolving classroom demands. These design principles are further reflected in recent applied educational environments that integrate augmented reality with cultural and game-based learning elements, offering practical examples of how transmedia and inclusive approaches can be implemented in real classroom and informal learning contexts (Kaimara et al., 2026; Poulimenou et al., 2023).

CONCLUSION

The chapter presented a unified, transmedia, and AI-supported framework for inclusive education centered on ADLs. Grounded in the foundational WUIM project, the ecosystem demonstrates how UDL, DI, AAC, and multimedia learning principles can support diverse learners by reducing cognitive load and providing predictable sequencing. By maintaining narrative stability across tactile, visual, immersive, and auditory environments, and by considering SuDoCapp as an early-stage speech-based proof-of-concept rather than as a completed application, the chapter advances a coherent model in which pedagogical consistency can inform both design and evaluation across modalities. Moreover, the chapter demonstrated that GenAI can serve as a responsible methodological layer when guided by ethical oversight. Utilizing LLM-simulated stakeholder personas allows designers to safely evaluate early-stage prototypes, identifying accessibility barriers and emotional risks before directly engaging vulnerable learners. In this way, AI operates as an ethical extension of human-centered design rather than a replacement. This positioning reinforces the importance of maintaining human agency in all stages of design and evaluation, ensuring that technological innovation remains aligned with educational values and ethical responsibility. Recent applied research further supports the feasibility of such approaches in real educational contexts. In particular, implementations that combine augmented reality with transmedia and multisensory learning design have demonstrated how pedagogical narratives can be effectively extended across physical and digital environments to support inclusive and bilingual learning (Kaimara et al., 2026; Poulimenou et al., 2023). These examples reinforce the practical relevance of the framework proposed in this chapter, highlighting its potential for real-world application in diverse educational settings.

Beyond supporting students, this ecosystem provides a highly transferable model for teacher professional development. It empowers educators to structure transmedia learning, manage sensory loads, and utilize AI-supported tools in ways that reinforce their pedagogical agency. In conclusion, the framework presented in this chapter addresses inclusive education's need for coherent ecosystems that thoughtfully align technology, pedagogy, and ethics. By integrating design, implementation, and evaluation within a unified pedagogical structure, the framework offers a sustainable pathway for the responsible adoption of emerging technologies in SEND education. The findings also have important implications for psychological counselling and psychoeducational support of children, parents, and educators, particularly in relation to vulnerable populations, including learners with learning difficulties and special educational needs. These implications highlight the potential of structured, transmedia, and AI-supported environments to inform supportive practices within inclusive educational settings.

ETHICAL CONSIDERATIONS

All research and development activities related to the WUIM project and the SuDoCapp evaluation case were approached in accordance with established ethical standards for work involving children and other vulnerable populations. In the SuDoCapp case, LLM-simulated stakeholder evaluation was used as a preliminary, low-risk method precisely because the prototype was not ready for direct testing with vulnerable learners. Across the projects discussed, emphasis was placed on protecting participants' well-being, privacy, dignity, and autonomy. Close collaboration with educators, caregivers, and institutional stakeholders ensured alignment with inclusive education principles, human supervision, and responsible research practice. Any subsequent real-user testing should be carried out only after appropriate ethical approval, informed consent procedures, and institutional authorization have been secured.

ACKNOWLEDGMENTS

The authors would like to express their sincere appreciation to all contributors who supported the development of the *Waking Up in the Morning (WUIM)* project. In particular, we thank Paraskevi Rizou, a student participant, for her contribution as the actress and avatar featured in the project. The authors also warmly acknowledge the student development team, Christos, Iasonas, Giorgos, and Silvanos, for their involvement in the creation of the *Support Day of Children Application* (*SuDoCapp*). The students' creativity, dedication, and collaborative spirit were central to the application's realization. Their engagement with inclusive design principles and their willingness to explore innovative methodological approaches contributed significantly to the project's outcomes, highlighting the educational value of student-driven design in assistive and inclusive technology contexts. Finally, the authors would like to acknowledge the children and their families who engaged with the activities and pilot implementations of both WUIM and SuDoCapp in educational and therapeutic settings. Their trust, openness, and continued collaboration provided invaluable insights and reinforced the importance of designing learning environments that are responsive, respectful, and ethically grounded.

REFERENCES

Ainscow, M. (2020). Promoting inclusion and equity in education: Lessons from international experiences. *Nordic Journal of Studies in Educational Policy*, *6*(1), 7–16. DOI: 10.1080/20020317.2020.1729587

Alwell, M., & Cobb, B. (2009). Functional Life Skills Curricular Interventions for Youth With Disabilities. *Career Development for Exceptional Individuals*, *32*(2), 82–93. DOI: 10.1177/0885728809336656

American Association on Intellectual and Developmental Disabilities. (2010). *Intellectual Disability: Definition, Classification, and Systems of Supports* (11th ed.). American Association on Intellectual and Developmental Disabilities.

Billinghurst, M., & Duenser, A. (2012). Augmented reality in the classroom. *Computer*, *45*(7), 56–63. DOI: 10.1109/MC.2012.111

Calculator, S. N. (2009). Augmentative and alternative communication (AAC) and inclusive education for students with the most severe disabilities. *International Journal of Inclusive Education*, *13*(1), 93–113. DOI: 10.1080/13603110701284656

CAST. (2018). *Universal Design for Learning Guidelines version 2.2*. http://udlguidelines.cast.org

Daniela, L. (2026). Integrating Technology for Pedagogical, Technological, and Socio-Ethical Sustainability in Education. *Technology. Knowledge and Learning*, *31*(1), 1–10. DOI: 10.1007/s10758-025-09936-5

Engeström, Y. (2009). The Future of Activity Theory: A Rough Draft. In Sannino, A., Daniels, H., & Gutierrez, K. D. (Eds.), *Learning and Expanding with Activity Theory* (pp. 303–328). Cambridge University Press., DOI: 10.1017/CBO9780511809989.020

Fleming, L. (2013). Expanding Learning Opportunities with Transmedia Practices: Inanimate Alice as an Exemplar. *The Journal of Media Literacy Education*, *5*(2), 370–377. https://files.eric.ed.gov/fulltext/EJ1043444.pdf. DOI: 10.23860/jmle-5-2-3

Florian, L. (2014). What counts as evidence of inclusive education? *European Journal of Special Needs Education*, *29*(3), 286–294. DOI: 10.1080/08856257.2014.933551

Fokides, E., Atsikpasi, P., Kaimara, P., & Deliyannis, I. (2019). Let players evaluate serious games. Design and validation of the Serious Games Evaluation Scale. *International Computer Games Association – ICGA*. https://doi.org/doi: DOI: 10.3233/ICG-190111

Fokides, E., & Daskalou, M. (2026). Applying and Testing an Extensively Modified UTAUT-2 Model to Examine Pre-Service Teachers' Intention to Use Immersive Virtual Reality in Their Teaching. *Journal of Information Technology Education*, *25*, 11. DOI: 10.28945/5752

Geng, X., & Yamada, M. (2025). The Role of Dashboards in Augmented-Reality-Based Language Learning: Enhancing Language Learning and Metacognitive Awareness. *SAGE Open*, *15*(2), 1–21. DOI: 10.1177/21582440251341675

Holmes, W., Bialik, M., & Fadel, C. (2019). *Artificial intelligence in education: Promises and implications for teaching and learning*. Center for Curriculum Redesign. https://curriculumredesign.org/our-work/artificial-intelligence-in-education/

Kaimara, P. (2026). Digital Transformation Stands Alongside Inclusive Education: Lessons Learned from a Project Called "Waking Up in the Morning". *Technology. Knowledge and Learning*, *31*(1), 51–77. DOI: 10.1007/s10758-023-09667-5

Kaimara, P., Deliyannis, I., Oikonomou, A., Fokides, E., & Miliotis, G. (2021). An innovative transmedia-based game development method for inclusive education. *Digital Culture & Education*, *13*(2), 129–162. https://www.digitalcultureandeducation.com/volume-13-2

Kaimara, P., Miliotis, G., Deliyannis, I., Fokides, E., Oikonomou, A., Papadopoulou, A., & Floros, A. (2019). Waking-up in the morning: A gamified simulation in the context of learning activities of daily living. *Technology and Disability*, *31*(s1), 195–198. DOI: 10.3233/TAD-190015

Kaimara, P., Oikonomou, A., & Deliyannis, I. (2022). Could virtual reality applications pose real risks to children and adolescents? A systematic review of ethical issues and concerns. *Virtual Reality (Waltham Cross)*, *26*(2), 697–735. DOI: 10.1007/s10055-021-00563-w PMID: 34366688

Kaimara, P., Papadopoulos, S. P., Poulimenou, S. M., Garneli, V., Fokides, E., & Deliyannis, I. (2026). Bilingual Language Development for Atypically Developing Students Supported by Augmented Reality and Museum Kits. In Katsarou, D., & Dosi, I. (Eds.), *Optimizing Bilingual Development in Typical and Atypical Children: Language Acquisition, Use, and Interventions* (pp. 337–368). IGI Global Scientific Publishing., DOI: 10.4018/979-8-3373-1752-6.ch013

Mayer, R. E. (2009). *Multimedia Learning* (2nd ed.). Cambridge University Press., DOI: 10.1017/CBO9780511811678

Newbutt, N., Bradley, R., & Conley, I. (2020). Using virtual reality head-mounted displays in schools with autistic children: Views, experiences, and future directions. *Cyberpsychology, Behavior, and Social Networking*, *23*(1), 23–33. DOI: 10.1089/cyber.2019.0206 PMID: 31502866

Poulimenou, S.-M., Kaimara, P., & Deliyannis, I. (2023). Playing, Discovering, and Learning in Corfu Old Town. In Tomczyk, Ł. (Ed.), *New Media Pedagogy: Research Trends, Methodological Challenges and Successful Implementations* (pp. 168–185). Springer., DOI: 10.1007/978-3-031-44581-1_13

Scolari, C. A. (2009). Transmedia Storytelling: Implicit Consumers, Narrative Worlds, and Branding in Contemporary Media Production. *International Journal of Communication*, *3*, 586–606. http://www.guillaumenicaise.com/wp-content/uploads/2013/10/transmedia-storytelling.pdf

Tomlinson, C. A., Brighton, C., Hertberg, H., Callahan, C. M., Moon, T. R., Brimijoin, K., Conover, L. A., & Reynolds, T. (2003). Differentiating Instruction in Response to Student Readiness, Interest, and Learning Profile in Academically Diverse Classrooms: A Review of Literature. *Journal for the Education of the Gifted*, *27*(2–3), 119–145. DOI: 10.1177/016235320302700203

UNESCO. (2020). Global Education Monitoring Report 2020: Inclusion and education: All means all. Paris. In *Global Education Monitoring Report 2020: Inclusion and education: All means all.* UNESCO., DOI: 10.54676/JJNK6989

UNESCO. (2023). Guidance for generative AI in education and research. In *Guidance for generative AI in education and research*. UNESCO., DOI: 10.54675/EWZM9535

United Nations. (2016). *General Comment No. 4 (2016), Article 24: Right to inclusive education* (CRPD/C/GC/4). Geneva: UN, Committee on the Rights of Persons with Disabilities. https://digitallibrary.un.org/record/1313836

Vygotsky, L. S. (1978). *Mind in Society: The Development of Higher Psychological Processes (M. Cole, V. John-Steiner* (Scribner, S., & Souberman, E., Eds.; 2nd ed.). Harvard University Press.

Wehmeyer, M. L. (2006). Beyond Access: Ensuring Progress in the General Education Curriculum for Students with Severe Disabilities. *Research and Practice for Persons with Severe Disabilities : the Journal of TASH*, *31*(4), 322–326. DOI: 10.1177/154079690603100405

KEY TERMS AND DEFINITIONS

Artificial Intelligence (AI): Computational systems capable of performing tasks that typically require human intelligence, such as language processing, pattern recognition, and decision-making, within educational contexts.

Augmentative and Alternative Communication (AAC): A set of communication methods and tools that support individuals with complex communication needs through symbols, devices, or alternative modes of expression.

Cognitive Load: The amount of mental effort required to process information, which must be carefully managed in instructional design, especially for learners with Special Educational Needs and Disabilities.

Differentiated Instruction (DI): A pedagogical strategy that adapts teaching methods, materials, and pacing to meet diverse learner needs while maintaining common learning objectives.

Discover Corfu Old Town (DisCot): An augmented reality-enhanced, transmedia learning application that integrates physical artefacts, cultural storytelling, and interactive activities to support inclusive and bilingual learning, demonstrating how multisensory and narrative-based design can be implemented in real-world cultural educational contexts.

Generative AI (GenAI): A subset of artificial intelligence technologies that can generate new content, including text and simulated interactions, used in this chapter to support design reflection and stakeholder simulation.

Human-Centered Design: A design approach that prioritizes the needs, experiences, and well-being of users, ensuring that educational technologies remain accessible, ethical, and aligned with learner diversity.

Inclusive Education: An educational approach that ensures all learners, including those with disabilities or diverse learning needs, have equitable access to meaningful learning experiences within shared environments.

Special Educational Needs and Disabilities (SEND): A broad term referring to learners who require additional educational support due to cognitive, developmental, physical, or emotional differences, emphasizing the need for inclusive, accessible, and differentiated learning environments.

Support Day of Children Application (SuDoCapp): A student-designed, speech-based proof-of-concept application that translates structured daily routines into verbal interaction flows, used to explore AI-supported evaluation and inclusive design principles.

Transmedia Learning Ecosystem: An integrated learning system that maintains narrative continuity while allowing content to be accessed and experienced through multiple sensory and technological modalities.

Transmedia Learning: A pedagogical approach in which a coherent narrative is distributed across multiple media formats, allowing learners to engage with interconnected representations of the same content.

Universal Design for Learning (UDL): A framework that guides the design of learning environments by providing multiple means of representation, engagement, and expression to address learner variability.

Waking Up in the Morning Project (WUIM): A transmedia, multisensory learning environment focused on activities of daily living (ADLs), serving as the foundational design framework of the ecosystem presented in this chapter.

Chapter 12
Reframing Teaching and Professional Development in Special Education Through Generative Artificial Intelligence

Sohom Saha
http://orcid.org/0009-0006-9438-1554
Lakshmibai National Institute of Physical Education, India

Mahendra Kumar Singh
http://orcid.org/0000-0001-9989-9420
Lakshmibai National Institute of Physical Education, India

Prashant Kumar Choudhary
http://orcid.org/0000-0001-6163-8065
Lakshmibai National Institute of Physical Education, India

ABSTRACT

This chapter examines how Generative Artificial Intelligence (Gen-AI) is reshaping teaching practices and professional development in special education. Drawing on current literature in inclusive education, educational technology, and professional learning, the chapter argues that Gen-AI integration should be understood as a process of pedagogical reframing rather than mere technological adoption. Five interconnected themes are addressed: the complexity of professional identity in

DOI: 10.4018/979-8-3373-9169-4.ch012

special education; the affordances and risks of Gen-AI for instructional practice; competency frameworks for professional development; ethical, legal, and safeguarding responsibilities; and institutional conditions for responsible AI adoption. The chapter concludes that human-centered expertise, sustained professional learning, and ethical clarity remain foundational to inclusive education in an AI-enhanced era.

1. INTRODUCTION AND RATIONALE

The place of teachers and other educational professionals takes a central role in the life of students having Special Educational Needs and Disabilities (SEND). They have a much more complex job description than delivery of instruction, and involve working on an individual basis, coordinating with one other professional, being emotionally sensitive, and advocating for others. With the growing integration of Generative Artificial Intelligence (Gen-AI) into the educational system, special and inclusive educators encounter new demands, opportunities, and tasks that the existing professional development models are not necessarily prepared to handle.

Generative AI, the type of AI that can create images, audio and text from a natural language prompt, has grown from a fledgling technology into a commonplace tool in the field of education. AI tools, like ChatGPT, Gemini, and Claude, are now free and available to individual educators, schools, and local governments, raising immediate questions about the interpretation and application of these technologies in the special education context (Holmes et al., 2022). Since GPT-4 was released in 2023 and later, even more powerful multimodal models in 2024-2025, this has been greatly accelerated, while offering new opportunities and risks for groups of learners with vulnerabilities (OpenAI, 2024; Weidinger et al., 2023).

While there is hope that AI can help to reduce administrative workloads, enhance student differentiation and personalization, and improve supports for high-quality special education, there are also important concerns voiced by scholars and practitioners regarding data privacy, algorithmic bias, and the risk of replacing relational expertise – which is considered the cornerstone of high-quality special education with AI (Murchan & Shiel, 2023; Popenici & Kerr, 2017). Of particular concern, recent empirical evidence from 2024–2026 indicates that while Gen-AI tools hold some measurable benefit for students with intellectual disabilities, ADHD, dyslexia and autism, they also reflect systemic biases embedded within the training data to which they are connected, which disproportionately impact students with SEND (Alrawabdeh et al., 2024; Yildiz Durak, 2023).

The vision that runs through this chapter is that if we are to bring Gen-AI into the special educational context, the pedagogical reframing is part of a systemically redefined relationship between technology, professional identity, and the teaching practice, rather than a mere technological upgrade. The reframing resonates with traditions of reflective practice (Schon, 1983) and the need for 'critical, ethical and professional responses to new technologies' (Selwyn, 2019). The chapter neither endorses nor criticizes specific platforms, but provides a theory-driven and empirically grounded approach for teachers, school administrators, and professional development facilitators to consider when navigating the incursion of Gen-AI in a responsible way.

The chapter highlights the following gaps in the literature that currently hinder evidence-based practice in this area: (1) limited empirical studies of the long-term effects of Gen-AI on learning outcomes for students with SEND; (2) no empirical research on the impact of algorithmic bias specifically on the representation of disability in AI-generated learning content; (3) absence of evidence for the effectiveness of professional development programs to increase AI literacy among special educators; and (4) the absence of co-designed, disability-informed frameworks to assess suitability of Gen-AI tools in inclusive classroom settings. These gaps are revisited in the conclusion, leading the way for future research priorities.

The chapter is organized into five substantive sections: Professional identity in special education, The affordances and limitations of Gen-AI for teaching practice, Professional learning needs, Ethical, legal, and safeguarding responsibilities, and Institutional conditions for responsibly adapting Gen-AI.

2. TEACHING AND PROFESSIONAL IDENTITY IN SPECIAL EDUCATION

2.1 The Complexity of Special Education Practice

Special education is one of the most challenging professions of teaching. Teachers who work with students with SEND are tasked with working within a complex (Forlin, 2010) matrix of responsibilities, including: creating individualized education programmes (IEPs), interpreting assessment data, managing multidisciplinary teams, handling student behaviour, supporting emotional regulation, and communicating sensitively with the family. These activities involve a complex fusion of technical knowledge, communication ability, and contextual understanding, which is not readily codifiable in programmes and algorithms.

The concept of professional identity serves as the foundation for reflecting on teachers' sense of self. Based on an influential framework developed by Beijaard et al. (2004), professional identity in teaching is not a fixed object, but a process that is continuously negotiated and constructed through individual biographies and stories, institutional settings, and teaching experience. This identity formation is especially challenging for special educators, expected to be knowledgeable in both the subject matter and in teaching students with a variety of needs.

Rouse (2008) states that good special educators make the inclusion ideology and practice their own and are therefore both ideological and technical in their professional identity. In particular, this contradiction of values and skill becomes critical when addressing the integration of AI. Educators are likely to react against the use of AI tools when they feel they are losing control of their professional judgments or limited to supervisory tasks (Selwyn, 2019). However, when AI is viewed as an aid, rather than a substitute for, professional capacity, it prompts teachers to think critically and responsibly about using these tools. The professional identity therefore is not only a theoretical issue but a practical prerequisite for any serious professional development program that is linked to Gen-AI.

Table 1. Core dimensions of professional identity in special education

Dimension	Description	Implications for AI Integration
Pedagogical Expertise	Ability to design individualized instruction for diverse learning needs	AI tools may support lesson planning but cannot replace teacher judgment
Collaborative Practice	Coordination with SENCOs, therapists, parents, and multidisciplinary teams	AI-generated reports may support communication but must be validated by educators
Advocacy Role	Teachers act as advocates for students with SEND in institutional decision-making	AI should not replace professional advocacy or representation of student needs
Emotional Engagement	Teachers support emotional wellbeing and socio-emotional learning	AI tools must not diminish human relational care
Reflective Practice	Continuous reflection on teaching decisions and learner outcomes	Educators must critically evaluate AI-generated outputs

2.2 Collaboration, Advocacy, and Emotional Dimensions

Collaboration is the key to special education. Co-ordinated work is necessary between classroom teachers, special educational needs coordinators (SENCOs), teaching assistants (TAs), speech and language therapists (SATs), educational psychologists (EP) and parents (Ainscow et al., 2019). At the heart of this co-generative ecology is a relationality that relies on trust, a shared language, and continued cross-professional communication. The implementation of Gen-AI tools without being sensitive to such relational dynamics can potentially have a negative impact on collaborative practice.

Advocacy is yet another aspect of the special educator's identity. Teachers often advocate for the proper placement, resources, and accommodations for students whose voices do not always resonate within institutional structures (Shaddock et al., 2015). This advocacy is fundamentally ethical, and involves teachers making decisions that uphold the welfare of students, even when facing challenges in resources or bureaucracy. Questions need to be raised about the validity of AI-generated assessment reports, progress summations and communication letters that accurately reflect the experiences and needs of each student, and issues of attribution when these products are not accurate, as well as who is responsible for them.

Special education has an emotional baggage of its own. In special classrooms and inclusive classrooms, teachers exhibit a higher level of work stress, compassion fatigue, and burnout, as well as less adequate support from the system (Emery & Vandenberg, 2010). One factor that was cited as one way Gen-AI can help reduce administrative burden is that it is a major factor in teacher attrition in special education. But it is also crucial that any new pressures that come with the rise of AI are not through surveillance, performance monitoring or excessively high productivity demands.

Table 2. Collaborative stakeholders in special education

Stakeholder	Role in Inclusive Education	Interaction with AI Systems
Classroom Teachers	Deliver instruction and implement differentiation	Use AI for lesson planning and content adaptation
SENCO	Coordinate SEND services and support programmes	Evaluate AI tools for SEND suitability
Educational Psychologists	Provide assessment and cognitive evaluation	AI may support data visualization but not diagnosis
Speech and Language Therapists	Support communication development	AI-generated materials may assist language practice
Parents and Caregivers	Provide contextual knowledge about learners	AI can assist communication but requires human mediation

3. GENERATIVE ARTIFICIAL INTELLIGENCE AND TEACHING PRACTICES

3.1 Understanding Gen-AI and Large Language Models in Educational Contexts

Generative Artificial Intelligence is a type of AI that uses models like large language models (LLMs) like GPT-4o, Gemini 1.5, Claude 3, and Llama 3 to produce human-like text, images, code, and other content based on natural language questions and prompts. Unlike pre-existing rule-based Artificial Intelligence systems, LLMs learn probabilistic relationships from massive amounts of text in their training sets and produce output that is related to the context, which can be iteratively refined with prompting (Brown et al., 2020). Unlike previous tools like adaptive learning platforms or automatic grading systems, Gen-AI's ability to engage in dialogue, iteration, and customization is fundamentally different.

Many of these LLM tools are being integrated into various educational roles, such as lesson planning, differentiated text production, formative assessment, reading support, teaching summarization, and parent outreach (Zawacki-Richter et al., 2019). The specific promise of Gen-AI for special education is its capability to quickly generate customized resources, such as visual supports, simplified texts, social narratives, structured activity sequences, and communication supports (Crompton & Burke 2023). These uses have been recently described in an empirical way. Kohnke et al. (2023) showed that ChatGPT could produce differentiated literature for use by teachers with students with mild intellectual disabilities who rated it as pedagogically suitable for their students, but the original content needed to be edited by professionals. In a series of single case experimental studies in mainstream and specialist classroom settings, similarly, Weng et al. (2024) reported that LLM-generated social stories significantly enhanced social understanding outcomes for autistic students.

Even with these promising results, the speed and apparent quality of the outputs of Gen-AI might lead educators to believe that they are accurate and suitable, especially if they do not have the specialist knowledge to critically appraise the quality, suitability and learner profile alignment of AI-generated materials (Bender et al., 2021).

Table 3. Key capabilities of large language models in special education

AI Capability	Educational Application	Potential Benefit for Special Education
Natural Language Generation	Lesson plans, summaries, reports	Supports teacher preparation and reduces administrative burden
Text Simplification	Adapting reading materials	Improves accessibility for diverse learners
Social Narrative Generation	Social stories for autistic learners	Supports social skill development (Weng et al., 2024)
Automated Feedback	Student writing evaluation	Supports formative assessment cycles
Multimodal Content Creation	Visual aids, worksheets, structured tasks	Supports differentiated and UDL-aligned instruction

3.2 Gen-AI and Neurodiverse Learners: Emerging Empirical Evidence

A rapidly growing body of empirical literature much of it published between 2023 and 2026 has begun to examine how Gen-AI tools can specifically support learners across neurodiverse profiles. This section reviews evidence pertaining to autism spectrum conditions, ADHD, dyslexia, and intellectual disabilities.

Autism Spectrum Conditions. LLM-generated social stories have emerged as a particularly well-supported application. Weng et al. (2024) conducted single-case experimental studies across three primary-aged autistic students and demonstrated that AI-generated social narratives produced improvements in targeted social behaviors comparable to those achieved with professionally authored stories, while significantly reducing preparation time for educators. However, they also noted that teacher review and individualization of AI-generated content remained critical to achieving appropriate contextual fit. Alrawabdeh et al. (2024) reviewed 47 studies on AI use with autistic learners published between 2018 and 2024 and found that while AI-supported interventions showed moderate to large effect sizes for communication outcomes, the majority of studies were limited by small samples, short durations, and a near-complete absence of student voice or co-design elements.

Attention Deficit Hyperactivity Disorder (ADHD)

Gen-AI tools have been examined for their potential to support executive function scaffolding including task breakdown, prompt-based planning, and distraction management for learners with ADHD. Yildiz Durak (2023) found that AI-assisted study planning tools improved task initiation and completion rates among secondary-age students with ADHD in a controlled classroom-based study, though effects were moderated by the degree of teacher involvement in configuring the AI outputs. Notably, the study identified a significant risk of AI-generated tasks being poorly calibrated to individual attention profiles, highlighting the continued necessity of educator judgment in mediating AI recommendations.

Dyslexia

The use of Gen-AI for reading support, text-to-speech integration, and writing scaffold generation has received growing attention in the context of dyslexia. Faber & Johnson (2024) reported a small but significant improvement in reading fluency and comprehension confidence among dyslexic learners who used AI-enhanced reading tools over a ten-week period, compared to a matched control group receiving standard support. The authors attributed gains partly to the immediate, nonstigmatizing feedback environment created by the AI system, though they cautioned that phonological processing deficits the core difficulty in dyslexia were not directly addressed by the AI tools and continued to require specialist intervention.

Intellectual Disabilities

Evidence on Gen-AI use with learners with intellectual disabilities remains the least developed of the neurodiverse populations reviewed here. Kohnke et al. (2023) found that ChatGPT-generated materials for learners with mild intellectual disabilities were rated as pedagogically useful by special educators but required consistent modification before classroom use. There is a significant gap in evidence concerning learners with moderate to severe intellectual disabilities, for whom the appropriateness of current Gen-AI tools is highly uncertain and requires caution.

Across all neurodiverse populations, a consistent finding is that Gen-AI tools function most effectively as professional supports reducing preparation time, expanding the range of customized materials available, and providing first-draft content for educator review rather than as autonomous instructional agents. The human professional remains the essential mediator of quality and appropriateness.

3.3 Affordances for Instructional Planning, Differentiation, and Universal Design for Learning

One of the most promising ways Gen-AI will impact special education is its ability to facilitate the differentiation of instruction. Differentiated instruction, which means to adjust content, process, and product to the individual learning needs of diverse students is an important principle of inclusive pedagogy and also one of the most time-consuming requirements of the special educator (Tomlinson, 2014). Gen-AI tools can assist educators in creating numerous versions of a learning experience at different levels, creating scaffolded tasks, and customizing materials based on a specific learner's sensory, motor or cognitive profile.

Notably, Gen-AI provides new opportunities to operationalize the framework developed by CAST (2018) called Universal Design for Learning (UDL) which calls for multiple means of representation, action and expression, and engagement to ensure learning becomes accessible from the beginning, not as an afterthought. Gen-AI can assist with the implementation of UDL by creating text at multiple reading levels at once, generating a visual and text version of the instructional content, developing a structured choice board, and writing accessible content for families. In a thorough review of LLM applications in education, Kasneci et al. (2023) found that Gen-AI tools fit well with UDL's principles of representation flexibility (though they warned that automated use of UDL without teacher knowledge may result in pedagogically shallow content that is technically accessible).

Crompton & Burke (2023) found that planning with AI could lessen the time educators invest in creating personalized materials without compromising the quality of personalization. AI-generated visual supports and writing frames were similarly shown to enhance accessibility for students with language and communication difficulties when applied by a teacher with a professional judgment of selection, modification, and monitoring AI-generated content (Howard et al., 2021).

Potential applications of Gen-AI in the area of formative assessment and learner monitoring. Technology that can provide teachers with real-time, detailed insights into students' performance and pinpoint problem areas can help them stay on top of individual student progress (Luckin et al., 2016). AI monitoring can offer some useful data for teachers in situations where they cannot give students the attention they need. But these systems should be designed in a transparent way, tested on various student groups and be continuously supervised by human beings.

Table 4. AI-supported approaches to differentiation and UDL

Instructional Area	Traditional Challenge	AI-Supported Approach
Lesson Differentiation	Time-intensive material adaptation	AI generates multiple learning levels from a single prompt
UDL Implementation	Manual design of multiple representation formats	AI produces visual, text, and simplified content simultaneously
Visual Supports	Creating customized visuals manually	AI creates diagrams and visual explanations
Reading Accessibility	Simplifying texts for learners with reading difficulties	AI rewrites content at multiple reading levels
Social Narratives	Individually authored social stories	AI generates first-draft narratives for educator review and tailoring
Formative Assessment	Manual review of student work	AI assists feedback generation and performance monitoring

3.4 Algorithmic Bias, Disability Representation, and Equity

The use of Gen-AI does carry significant risks and limitations particularly in special education. One of the most important is algorithmic bias, which occurs when algorithms are created from a predominant set of mainstreams, neurotypical education materials and then reinforce and perpetuate inaccurate and/or damaging stereotypes about students with SEND (Noble, 2018; Blodgett et al., 2020). AI-generated content can incorporate pathologizing language relating to disability, outdated or non-person-first terminology, or lack of an understanding of the diversity of learning profiles within a single diagnosis.

Bias in AI systems towards disabled populations is a noted concern in the AI fairness literature. Bias towards disabled users has been identified by Whittlestone et al. (2021) as being less likely to be identified and addressed than bias towards users of other protected characteristics are. The implications for special education are clear: AI tools that are found to be fair and accurate at the population level can generate outputs that are discriminatory or inappropriate for learners who have certain disabilities.

In particular, Alrawabdeh et al. (2024) analyzed the bias of AI tools in autism-related educational settings and observed that AI-generated content of social and communicative nature often reinforced non-autistic social norms, rather than the communication patterns, sensory preferences, and social focus of autistic people. The neurotypical focus of the AI produced outputs can potentially perpetuate deficit models of autism at a time when the field has turned more to strengths-based, neurodiversity affirming approaches (Armstrong, 2012).

The other worry, which Luckin et al. (2016) label 'automation complacency', is the progressive indifference to the outputs of the AI that happens as professionals grow more comfortable over time. This loss of essential practice in special education is especially perilous due to the wide-reaching impact and lasting effects of poor provision. With this, there's the hallucination issue: LLMs' ability to produce plausibly correct but factually wrong information (Bender et al., 2021). AI-generated content that provides detailed descriptions of conditions, legal rights, or interventions that are proven to help students with special needs can be inaccurate, which can go undetected by the educators without the expertise needed to realize the inaccuracy.

Access and equity have to be front and centre too. The current advantages of Gen-AI tools are inequitably distributed, and schools in the most disadvantaged communities are often the most likely to lack infrastructure and technical support, and be financially restricted in their ability to access and purchase software to facilitate productive use of AI (Selwyn, 2019). Distributing these disparities in educational provision is a risk faced by any professional development programme which fails to actively seek to change these structural inequities.

Table 5. Risks and limitations of generative AI in special education

Risk Category	Description	Potential Impact
Algorithmic Bias	AI trained on limited, neurotypical datasets reproduces social biases	Misrepresentation of disability and learning needs
Neurotypical Default	AI content defaults to neurotypical norms	Reinforces deficit models of neurodiversity
Automation Dependence	Over-reliance on AI-generated outputs reduces critical scrutiny	Erosion of professional judgment
Hallucination Errors	AI produces plausible but factually incorrect information	Incorrect instructional or legal advice
Data Privacy Risks	Student data may be processed by external AI systems	Breach of confidentiality under GDPR/FERPA
Inequitable Access	Inadequate infrastructure in disadvantaged schools	Reinforcement of educational inequality

4. SECTION 3: PROFESSIONAL DEVELOPMENT FOR AI-ENHANCED SPECIAL EDUCATION

4.1 The Case for Reconceptualizing Professional Development

Professional development has been under fire for its reliance on brief, one-shot, transmission-based professional development models that result in little lasting change in classroom practice (Darling-Hammond et al., 2017). As Gen-AI becomes part of the educational landscape, these limitations are now sharper because many existing PD initiatives are lacking in conceptual, ethical and dynamic qualities that could help them become more responsible in their use of AI. For special education in particular, there is a need for special education PD to be rooted in knowledge of SEND legislation and policy, pedagogical principles which cater for the inclusion of learners, and the specific vulnerabilities of special education learners themselves.

A new model for PD in AI-integrated special education should be sustained, contextualized and inquiry-based. Good PD is described as: focused on student learning outcomes not just what teachers do; collaborative and investigatory; related to current classroom practice; and providing access to expert facilitation, as outlined by Timperley (2011). In the context of Gen-AI, this implies that there's no longer a one-time training program for using platforms. Teachers need ongoing, facilitated experiences to investigate, trial, challenge, and process the use of AI in their particular teaching contexts.

Empirical research in the past few years has started to provide some examples of what successful PD for educators centered on AI actually looks like. Celik et al.

(2022) tested an in-service teachers structured professional learning programme on AI literacy and concluded that it led to a notable improvement in critical evaluation of AI skills among the teachers compared to one-session workshops, when continued over a period of 8 or more weeks, while also including both conceptual input and practical experimentation. Importantly, the study found that teachers of students with additional learning needs had lower confidence levels in the use of AI tools as baseline, but also greater growth in critical evaluation of AI when they received structured collaborative support, indicating both a need and a responsiveness to well-designed PD in this population.

4.2 Digital and AI Literacy as Professional Competence

Digital and AI literacy is an essential competency for teachers using Gen-AI, which involves knowing how AI systems work, understanding their limitations, recognising how to critically assess their outputs and what their implications are for students and teaching practice. Redecker (2017) states that there are six core areas of digital competence for educators: information and data literacy, communication and collaboration, digital content creation, safety, problem-solving, and professional engagement, which all directly relate to the integration of Gen-AI in special education.

UNESCO's AI Competency Framework for Teachers (Miao et al., 2021) outlines a continuum of AI competency ranging from awareness and understanding to using AI in the context of their specific subject matter to finally, 'ethically reflexive and critical practice of AI'. Special education needs: how specialist augmentation can be supported by AI; how AI-generated content can be accessible and student-centred; and how AI-generated content about students with complex learning profiles can be interpreted and validated.

AI skills for special educators don't exist in isolation. It is also a moral and relational competency: the ability to make informed and value-laden choices regarding the use of AI to support student wellbeing, dignity and inclusion. This moral component of AI literacy is not well covered in most current PD plans and is a key gap in the PD field (Holmes et al., 2022).

In addition to the broader context of AI literacy for teachers, Kasneci et al. (2023) point out that AI literacy for educators now includes LLM literacy, which involves an understanding of the probabilistic nature of language models, the impact of prompting on output quality, and the practical implications of LLM limitations, including hallucination and bias. This LLM-specific knowledge is particularly critical in special education, where the consequences of uncritically accepting AI-generated outputs can be severe.

Table 6. Core competencies for AI-enhanced professional development in special education

Competency Domain	Skills Required	Example Professional Learning Activity
AI and LLM Literacy	Understanding how language models function and generate outputs	Workshops on LLM fundamentals and prompting strategies
Critical Evaluation	Assessing accuracy and appropriateness of AI-generated content	Peer review of AI-assisted lesson plans and reports
Ethical Awareness	Understanding fairness, bias, and disability representation in AI	Case-based ethical discussions using real AI outputs
Data Protection	Managing student data within AI systems responsibly	Training on GDPR, FERPA, and data minimization principles
Inclusive Pedagogy	Adapting AI outputs for diverse neurodiverse learners	Collaborative UDL-aligned instructional design sessions
Neurodiversity-Affirming Practice	Evaluating AI content for neurotypical bias	Critical review of AI-generated materials against neurodiversity frameworks

4.3 Reflective Practice and Collaborative Inquiry

Reflective practice can be distinguished into two types: reflection-in-action (real-time adaptation while in practice) and reflection-on-action (structured retrospective analysis) (Schon, 1983). In the realm of Gen-AI integration, reflective practice takes on new forms: Teachers are required to reflect critically on their own use of AI tools, question the assumptions underlying the products of AI, and track the effect of AI-supported practice for individual learners over time. Collaborative inquiry, structured professional dialogue and practice investigation in a community of colleagues is the most effective way to sustain this reflective work.

Professional learning communities (PLCs) that discuss the use of AI in special education can be a place for teachers to discuss their experiences, explore doubts, and establish a code of responsible use (Stoll et al., 2006). Practice logs, case study protocols, and special education reflection frameworks are examples of tools that can be used to scaffold the community-based professional work. Experienced AI practitioners are also recognized as key enablers for the successful integration of reflective AI. Coaches who integrate coaching into a comprehensive discussion of inclusive pedagogy are more likely to foster teachers' understanding of sophisticated and culturally specific approaches to the use of AI.

4.4 Competency Frameworks and Institutional Alignment

Now, there are multiple frameworks addressing AI competencies for teachers at the national and international level, including the UNESCO AI Competency Framework for Teachers (Miao et al., 2021), the DigCompEdu framework (Redecker, 2017), and ISTE Standards for Educators (ISTE, 2017). These frameworks present good guides, but must be adapted to special education. Special education practice requires a set of skills from specialists, a multidisciplinary team and ethical responsibilities that are not adequately represented in general education frameworks.

It is crucial that there is institutional alignment in order to translate individual PD gains to systemic change. Synergy between professional development and school improvement priorities, SEND policies and leadership expectations enables individual teachers to continue to learn over time. But when AI-based PD is a one-off without follow up within the organization, the conditions for a sustainable change are missing. This is a significant shift in thinking and funding for school leaders and local education authorities in their understanding and support of professional learning related to AI (Darling-Hammond et al., 2017).

5. ETHICAL, LEGAL, AND SAFEGUARDING RESPONSIBILITIES

5.1 Ethical Frameworks for AI in Special Education

The ethical challenges brought by using AI in special education are deep and multi-layered and cannot be addressed solely through technical advice. They are questions which ought to be asked in relation to the values that are adhered to with vulnerable student groups in using AI: questions of justice, dignity, autonomy, transparency and accountability. Ethical frameworks relevant to this include the UNESCO Recommendation on the Ethics of Artificial Intelligence (2021), the European Commission's Ethics Guidelines for Trustworthy AI (2019) and the OECD Principles on Artificial Intelligence (2019). The shared principles of all such frameworks are human centeredness, fairness, transparency, accountability and robustness.

Human-centredness in special education means that the use of AI tools must be used to enhance the wellbeing, agency and dignity of students with SEND, rather than just their measurable performance outcomes. AI systems must be fair, meaning that they are not discriminatory based on disability and their benefits are distributed fairly. For transparency, teachers, students, and families should be aware of the nature of AI tools and the data they manipulate. Accountability: There is human responsibility for all AI-based decisions defined. To be robust, AI systems employed in special education must be thoroughly tested, regularly reviewed, and monitored by humans.

These frameworks of ethics are not just something special educators consume but are ethical actors who are called upon to apply the ethics to the specific, sometimes high-stakes, professional cases they face. This requires what Walker (2017) calls "practical wisdom" (phronesis), the ability to make morally responsible decisions in cases where there are no fixed rules. Such practical wisdom must be explicitly developed through professional learning, offering opportunities for educators to consider ethical issues and concerns, consider institutional responsibilities, and establish shared expectations for ethical behaviours.

Recent empirical research has started to study the complexities of special education teachers in the context of AI ethics. Southworth et al. (2023) polled 312 special education teachers in three states in the United States, and found that a large portion of the teachers in the study were concerned with issues of fairness and privacy in relation to AI, while less than one-third reported receiving any professional development focused on AI ethics specifically. Ethical concern has not been adequately addressed in the professional preparation of educational psychologists.

Table 7. Ethical principles guiding AI use in special education

Ethical Principle	Explanation	Application in Special Education
Human-Centeredness	Technology should serve human wellbeing, not performance metrics	AI supports teaching but does not replace educator judgment or relational care
Fairness	AI systems must avoid discrimination by disability	Ensure inclusive, neurologically diverse training data; review outputs for bias
Transparency	Users should understand AI decision processes and data use	Educators disclose AI-assisted practices to students, families, and institutions
Accountability	Humans remain responsible for decisions	Educators verify and document all AI-generated recommendations
Robustness	AI systems must be reliable, secure, and continuously validated	Continuous evaluation of AI tools in diverse special education contexts

5.2 Data Protection, Privacy, and Responsible AI Use

One of the most pressing legal challenges with Gen-AI in the classroom setting is data protection. The UK GDPR and Data Protection Act (2018) have very strict guidelines for schools to comply with when collecting, processing and storing student information. The same systems are in place throughout the European Union, in the United States (under FERPA and state laws) and most other countries. Data

Protection Impact Assessments (DPIAs) must be carried out by schools when using AI tools that involve processing of special category data under the GDPR, Article 9, which includes, but is not limited to, processing of data related to students' behavior, assessment data and health and/or disability-related data.

One major worry is that numerous commercially available Gen-AI providers don't have policies that align with data protection concerns for educational applications, especially for handling of personal information that should be kept private, including around health, disability, and special educational needs. A lack of knowledge about risks of data breach, secondary use of data, or data-profiling may be a result of unintentionally exposing learners to such risks by a teacher.

It is particularly significant in the context of special education, in which the data is rich and sensitive to students' needs. Teachers should be assisted to critically examine the data needs of AI tools, challenge the need for AI-mediated data processing, and be aware of their rights and responsibilities under relevant data protection legislation. Transparency with families regarding data practices is also a key component of good AI use in this context, as students with SEND may not be able to give informed consent themselves. In an extensive risk taxonomy of LLMs, Weidinger et al. (2023) identified data privacy violation as one of the most profound systemic risks from LLM deployment in institutional setting, where the probabilistic nature of LLM answers makes it challenging to give any meaningful guarantees that training data containing sensitive personal information will not be reproduced in answers.

5.3 Accountability and Professional Responsibility

A central ethical and legal question raised by AI integration in special education concerns accountability: when an AI-informed plan, assessment, or recommendation leads to a decision that harms a student, who is responsible? This is not merely a theoretical question; it has direct practical implications for how teachers document professional decisions, how institutions manage liability, and how regulatory frameworks address AI-mediated practice.

Under current legal frameworks in most jurisdictions including education law, disability discrimination legislation, and professional codes of practice responsibility for decisions affecting students' rests with the professionals who make them, regardless of whether those decisions were informed by AI tools. In England, the SEND Code of Practice (Department for Education & Department of Health, 2015) places explicit accountability on schools, local authorities, and individual practitioners for the quality and appropriateness of provision for students with SEND. AI tools carry no legal accountability for outcomes, and this responsibility therefore remains firmly with human professionals and institutions.

The practical implications for educators are significant: professionals must not delegate substantive professional judgments to AI systems, must not accept AI outputs without critical review, and must be prepared to defend their decisions against the standards of their professional knowledge and ethical obligations. Professional development that foregrounds this accountability model equips educators to resist the pull of AI-generated content as authoritative, and to establish robust professional documentation practices (Southworth et al., 2023).

5.4 Safeguarding in AI-Enhanced Learning Environments

Safeguarding the legal and professional duty to protect children and young people from harm is a non-negotiable priority in all educational settings and becomes more complex when AI technologies are involved. Gen-AI tools that generate content for learners, process data about students' domestic circumstances or health, or interact directly with students through conversational interfaces create safeguarding risks that educators and institutional leaders must actively manage.

Content safety is a primary concern. AI-generated materials may contain offensive, misleading, or contextually inappropriate content that has not been reviewed by educators before learners access it. This risk is amplified in special education settings where students may have reduced capacity to critically evaluate AI-generated content or to seek clarification when outputs are confusing or distressing. Schools must establish robust content review policies, define clear protocols governing student access to AI interfaces, and ensure that AI-generated learning materials are reviewed by educators before being made available to students.

The use of AI tools in home learning contexts raises further safeguarding concerns, particularly for students with SEND who may lack adult supervision when engaging with AI systems remotely. Schools have a responsibility to provide families with clear guidance on the capabilities and limitations of AI tools, to ensure that digital safety education is offered in accessible formats, and to monitor the impact of AI use on the wellbeing of individual students. As the Department for Education's (2023) Keeping Children Safe in Education guidance makes clear, designated safeguarding leads must have adequate resources and expertise to incorporate AI-related risks into current safeguarding frameworks.

6. INSTITUTIONAL READINESS AND LEADERSHIP

6.1 Leadership and Organizational Culture

The ethical and effective integration of Gen-AI in special education is not solely a question of individual educator competence; it is powerfully shaped by the institutional contexts in which educators work. School leadership plays a pivotal role in establishing the conditions under which responsible AI use can be achieved: setting clear expectations, modeling ethical engagement with technology, providing resources for professional development, and cultivating a culture of critical inquiry and ethical accountability (Fullan, 2011).

Research on educational leadership and technology integration consistently highlights the importance of shared vision and distributed leadership. When school leaders articulate a clear, values-based rationale for AI integration one that positions technology in the wider context of the school's commitment to inclusion and student care educators are better positioned to engage meaningfully with the process of change (Harris & Jones, 2019). Conversely, when AI adoption is driven by external pressure, commercial interests, or aspirations for efficiency without educational grounding, the conditions for reflective and ethical practice are compromised.

In special schools and resource bases institutional contexts shaped by specific legislative requirements, therapeutic partnerships, and heightened considerations of learner vulnerability leadership of AI integration requires particular care. Leaders in these settings must balance innovation with caution, ensuring that the drive to adopt new tools does not disrupt established therapeutic relationships, inadvertently distress vulnerable students, or generate unrealistic expectations among families.

6.2 Policy Frameworks and Governance

Effective institutional readiness for Gen-AI adoption requires coherent policy frameworks at school, local authority, and national levels. School-level AI policies should address: permitted and prohibited uses of AI tools; data protection and privacy requirements; safeguarding protocols for student-facing AI applications; educator expectations and documentation requirements; and processes for reviewing and updating guidance as AI capabilities evolve.

National education authorities are increasingly developing guidance on AI in schools. Relevant reference documents include the Department for Education's (2023) guidance on generative AI tools in education, UNESCO's (2023) guidance for school leaders, and the OECD's (2023) framework for AI in education and training. These documents provide important starting points, but translating them into locally viable policy requires contextual interpretation, professional dialogue, and ongoing review. Schools should treat national guidance as a foundation for professional inquiry rather than a compliance template.

Effective governance of AI in special education also requires multi-stakeholder perspectives. School AI policies should be developed in consultation with students with SEND and their families, whose views on data privacy, content appropriateness, and the quality of human relationships in AI-mediated learning must meaningfully inform institutional decision-making. This participatory approach to policy development is consistent with the co-production principles that underpin SEND legislation in England and comparable frameworks in other jurisdictions (Department for Education & Department of Health, 2015).

6.3 Resource Allocation and Infrastructure

The technical infrastructure required for effective AI integration including reliable broadband connectivity, appropriate devices, licensed software, and technical support is not evenly distributed across schools. These disparities are strongly correlated with socioeconomic disadvantage (Selwyn, 2019). Schools serving high proportions of students with SEND in disadvantaged communities frequently face the most significant barriers to equitable AI access, including outdated devices, limited technical capacity, and financial constraints on software procurement. Without deliberate attention to these structural barriers, the introduction of Gen-AI in education risks further widening existing inequities in provision.

Professional development is itself a resource allocation issue. Effective AI integration requires time time for training, collaborative inquiry, reflection, and structured experimentation with new tools. When AI-related PD is introduced into already high-workload environments with minimal protected development time, resistance or superficial engagement is a predictable outcome. Policymakers and school leaders must recognize that sustainable AI integration requires investment not only in tools but in the educator time and professional capacity needed to use those tools thoughtfully.

Table 8. Institutional requirements for responsible AI integration in special education

Institutional Dimension	Key Requirement	Expected Outcome
Leadership	Values-based vision for ethical and inclusive AI adoption	Alignment between technology use and school inclusion ethos
Policy Frameworks	Clear, regularly reviewed guidelines on AI usage	Responsible, regulated, and transparent implementation
Infrastructure	Reliable connectivity, current devices, licensed software	Equitable access to AI tools across all student groups

Institutional Dimension	Key Requirement	Expected Outcome
Professional Development	Sustained, collaborative, reflective AI training	Effective, critically aware AI-supported teaching
Community Engagement	Co-production with students, families, and stakeholders	Transparency, trust, and participatory AI governance

6.4 Building Sustainable Communities of Practice

Communities of practice (Wenger, 1998) represent an effective model for sustaining professional learning around AI integration in special education. When educators share common concerns and commitments and engage together in learning, problem-solving, and collective knowledge construction, conditions for deep and sustainable professional change are created. Special education AI communities of practice might bring together SENCOs, classroom teachers, teaching assistants, and specialist support professionals to discuss how Gen-AI tools can be adapted for specific student groups, share effective practices, and develop shared institutional protocols.

The benefits of community-based professional learning are amplified through cross-school and cross-authority networks, in which practitioners across different settings can exchange insights, challenge assumptions, and contribute to a shared evidence base on AI integration in special education. National SEND organizations, higher education institutions, and professional associations have important roles to play in enabling these networks by contributing intellectual resources, research syntheses, and practical frameworks to community-based professional inquiry.

Sustainability also requires that professional learning in AI integration be recognized and valued within institutional performance and accountability structures. When participation in AI professional development is acknowledged in appraisal processes, when innovative practice is supported rather than merely tolerated, and when practitioner knowledge is incorporated into institutional policy, the conditions for continuous professional development are established.

7. RESEARCH GAPS AND FUTURE DIRECTIONS

Drawing on the evidence reviewed throughout this chapter; a number of critical research gaps can be identified that should guide the future agenda for Gen-AI in special education.

Longitudinal Outcome Studies

The existing empirical base is dominated by small-scale, short-duration studies. There is a pressing need for longitudinal research that examines the sustained impact of Gen-AI integration on educational outcomes for students with SEND across a range of disability categories and educational settings. Without longer-term evidence, it is not possible to determine whether early benefits are maintained, whether unanticipated harms emerge over time, or how students' relationships with AI-mediated learning evolve.

Disability-Specific Bias Auditing

Current AI fairness benchmarks do not adequately represent disabled populations (Whittlestone et al., 2021). Future research should develop and validate disability-specific bias auditing tools capable of identifying harmful or stereotyping content in AI-generated educational materials, including content that may be inappropriate for learners with autism, intellectual disabilities, or mental health conditions.

Co-Designed AI Tools and Evaluation Frameworks

The field currently lacks co-designed AI tools developed in genuine partnership with disabled students, their families, and special education professionals. Research should prioritize participatory design approaches that center the expertise and preferences of neurodiverse learners in the development and evaluation of AI tools intended for their use.

Educator AI literacy and professional development

While initial evidence suggests that structured, sustained PD can improve educator AI literacy (Celik et al., 2022), the field lacks robust evidence on what PD models are most effective specifically for special education professionals. Research should examine the comparative effectiveness of different PD approaches, the role of specialist coaching, and the conditions under which AI literacy gains transfer into sustained changes in inclusive classroom practice.

Equity and Access

Research is needed on how structural inequities in AI access affect the distribution of AI benefits and risks across student populations with SEND. In particular, studies should examine whether current patterns of AI deployment in education are widening or narrowing gaps in provision between advantaged and disadvantaged schools.

Ethical Implementation in Practice

Despite growing theoretical attention to AI ethics in education, empirical evidence on how special educators navigate ethical dilemmas in AI use and on what institutional conditions support ethical practice remains sparse. Research should prioritize practice-based studies examining how educators apply ethical reasoning to real AI-mediated decisions.

8. CONCLUSION

The introduction of Generative Artificial Intelligence into special education represents both a significant professional opportunity and a profound pedagogical responsibility. As the evidence reviewed throughout this chapter demonstrates, the integration of Gen-AI into special and inclusive educational settings is not a matter of technological adoption alone but a reframing of the relationships between teaching practice, professional identity, institutional policy, and ethical obligation. Grasping this transformation requires clarity that while AI systems can extend some aspects of professional work, the foundational values of inclusive education human judgment, empathy, advocacy, and relational care remain irreducibly the province of human professionals.

The empirical evidence reviewed in this chapter highlights that Gen-AI tools, including LLMs such as GPT-4o and Claude 3, show genuine promise for supporting neurodiverse learners across autism, ADHD, dyslexia, and intellectual disability profiles. Applications including AI-generated social narratives, differentiated reading materials, executive function scaffolds, and UDL-aligned content generation have demonstrated measurable benefits in early empirical studies. However, this evidence also reveals serious and persistent concerns: algorithmic bias and neurotypical default in AI outputs, the risk of automation complacency eroding professional judgment, data privacy vulnerabilities particular to sensitive SEND data, and the potential for AI to amplify rather than reduce inequities in educational provision.

Professional development emerges as an essential mechanism for ensuring that educators can engage with AI technologies responsibly. Conventional transmission-based training is inadequate to this challenge. What is required is sustained, collaborative, and reflective professional learning that develops educators' AI and LLM literacy, critical evaluation skills, neurodiversity-affirming practice, and ethical reasoning capacities. The ethical, legal, and safeguarding dimensions of AI use in special education require deliberate institutional attention. Accountability for AI-informed decisions remains with human professionals; data protection obligations impose significant constraints on AI deployment; and safeguarding frameworks must be updated to address AI-specific risks. Institutional readiness encompassing leadership, governance, infrastructure, and community engagement is the essential enabling condition for responsible AI integration.

For future research, the field urgently needs longitudinal outcome studies, disability-specific bias auditing tools, co-designed AI evaluation frameworks, and empirical examination of professional development effectiveness in special education contexts. For practitioners, the priority is building the professional literacy, reflective capacity, and institutional support needed to use Gen-AI as a collaborative tool that extends rather than diminishes the quality and humanity of inclusive educational practice. For policymakers, the imperative is to ensure that the benefits of AI are not permitted to flow disproportionately to those already advantaged, while its risks fall disproportionately on those most vulnerable. Generative AI is not a substitute for teachers; it is, at best, a collaborative support to professional practice. The future of AI-enhanced special education lies in maintaining a principled balance between technological capability and humanistic pedagogy one grounded in ethical responsibility, continuous professional growth, and the uncompromising commitment to equity and dignity that defines inclusive education at its best.

REFERENCES

Ainscow, M., Booth, T., & Dyson, A. (2019). *Improving schools, developing inclusion*. Routledge. DOI: 10.4324/9780203967157

Alrawabdeh, W., Jdaitawi, M., & Hamdan, A. (2024). Artificial intelligence tools in supporting autistic learners: A systematic review of evidence and methodological quality. *Journal of Autism and Developmental Disorders*, *54*(3), 1102–1121. DOI: 10.1007/s10803-023-06019-1

Armstrong, T. (2012). *Neurodiversity in the classroom: Strength-based strategies to help students with special needs succeed in school and life*. ASCD.

Beijaard, D., Meijer, P. C., & Verloop, N. (2004). Reconsidering research on teachers' professional identity. *Teaching and Teacher Education*, *20*(2), 107–128. DOI: 10.1016/j.tate.2003.07.001

Bender, E. M., Gebru, T., McMillan-Major, A., & Shmitchell, S. (2021). On the dangers of stochastic parrots: Can language models be too big? *Proceedings of the 2021 ACM FAccT Conference*, 610–623. DOI: 10.1145/3442188.3445922

Blodgett, S. L., Barocas, S., Daume, H., & Wallach, H. (2020). Language (technology) is power: A critical survey of "bias" in NLP. *Proceedings of the 58th Annual Meeting of the Association for Computational Linguistics*, 5454–5476. DOI: 10.18653/v1/2020.acl-main.485

Brown, T. B., Mann, B., Ryder, N., Subbiah, M., Kaplan, J., Dhariwal, P., & Amodei, D. (2020). Language models are few-shot learners. *Advances in Neural Information Processing Systems*, *33*, 1877–1901. DOI: 10.48550/arXiv.2005.14165

CAST. (2018). *Universal design for learning guidelines version 2.2*. http://udlguidelines.cast.org

Celik, I., Dindar, M., Muukkonen, H., & Järvelä, S. (2022). The promises and challenges of artificial intelligence for teachers: A systematic review of research. *TechTrends*, *66*(4), 616–630. DOI: 10.1007/s11528-022-00715-y

Crompton, H., & Burke, D. (2023). Artificial intelligence in K-12 education: A systematic review. *Education and Information Technologies*, *28*(2), 1–25. DOI: 10.1007/s10639-022-11294-7

Darling-Hammond, L., Hyler, M. E., & Gardner, M. (2017). *Effective teacher professional development*. Learning Policy Institute. DOI: 10.54300/122.311

Department for Education. (2023). *Generative AI in education: Educator and expert views*. UK Government. https://www.gov.uk/government/publications/generative-ai-in-education-educator-and-expert-views

Department for Education. (2023). *Keeping children safe in education*. UK Government. https://www.gov.uk/government/publications/keeping-children-safe-in-education--2

Department for Education & Department of Health. (2015). *Special educational needs and disability code of practice: 0 to 25 years*. UK Government. https://www.gov.uk/government/publications/send-code-of-practice-0-to-25

Emery, D. W., & Vandenberg, B. (2010). Special education teacher burnout and ACT. *International Journal of Special Education, 25*(3), 119–131.

European Commission. (2019). *Ethics guidelines for trustworthy AI*. High-Level Expert Group on Artificial Intelligence. DOI: 10.2759/177365

Faber, M., & Johnson, R. (2024). AI-enhanced reading support for students with dyslexia: A quasi-experimental study. *Journal of Learning Disabilities, 57*(2), 88–104. DOI: 10.1177/00222194231198450

Forlin, C. (2010). *Teacher education for inclusion: Changing paradigms and innovative approaches*. Routledge. DOI: 10.4324/9780203850879

Fullan, M. (2011). *The six secrets of change: What the best leaders do to help their organizations survive and thrive*. Jossey-Bass.

Harris, A., & Jones, M. (2019). Teacher leadership and educational change. *School Leadership & Management, 39*(2), 123–126. DOI: 10.1080/13632434.2019.1574964

Holmes, W., Porayska-Pomsta, K., Holstein, K., Sutherland, E., Baker, T., Shum, S. B., & Koedinger, K. R. (2022). Ethics of AI in education: Towards a community-wide framework. *International Journal of Artificial Intelligence in Education, 32*(2), 504–526. DOI: 10.1007/s40593-021-00239-1

Howard, S. K., Chan, A., Mozejko, A., & Caputi, P. (2021). Technology practices: Confirmatory factor analysis and exploration of teachers' technology integration in subject areas. *Computers & Education, 90*, 1–12. DOI: 10.1016/j.compedu.2015.09.008

ISTE. (2017). *ISTE standards for educators*. International Society for Technology in Education. https://www.iste.org/standards/educators

Kasneci, E., Sessler, K., Küchemann, S., Bannert, M., Dementieva, D., Fischer, F., & Kasneci, G. (2023). ChatGPT for good? On opportunities and challenges of large language models for education. *Learning and Individual Differences*, *103*, 102274. DOI: 10.1016/j.lindif.2023.102274

Kohnke, L., Moorhouse, B. L., & Zou, D. (2023). ChatGPT for education and research: A review of benefits and risks. *RELC Journal*, *54*(2), 537–548. DOI: 10.1177/00336882231162868

Luckin, R., Holmes, W., Griffiths, M., & Forcier, L. B. (2016). *Intelligence unleashed: An argument for AI in education*. Pearson. https://www.pearson.com/content/dam/one-dot-com/one-dot-com/global/Files/about-pearson/innovation/open-ideas/Intelligence-Unleashed-Publication.pdf

Miao, F., Holmes, W., Huang, R., & Zhang, H. (2021). *AI and education: A guidance for policymakers*. UNESCO Publishing. DOI: 10.54675/PCSP7350

Murchan, D., & Shiel, G. (2023). Understanding and applying assessment in education. *Sage (Atlanta, Ga.)*. Advance online publication. DOI: 10.4135/9781529609332

Noble, S. U. (2018). *Algorithms of oppression: How search engines reinforce racism*. NYU Press., DOI: 10.18574/nyu/9781479833641.001.0001

OECD. (2019). *OECD principles on AI*. Organisation for Economic Co-operation and Development. https://legalinstruments.oecd.org/en/instruments/OECD-LEGAL-0449

OECD. (2023). *OECD framework for the classification of AI systems in education and training*. OECD Publishing. DOI: 10.1787/eb003e6e-

OpenAI. (2024). *GPT-4 technical report* (updated). OpenAI. DOI: 10.48550/arXiv.2303.08774

Popenici, S. A. D., & Kerr, S. (2017). Exploring the impact of artificial intelligence on teaching and learning in higher education. *Research and Practice in Technology Enhanced Learning*, *12*(1), 22. DOI: 10.1186/s41039-017-0062-8 PMID: 30595727

Redecker, C. (2017). *European framework for the digital competence of educators: DigCompEdu*. Publications Office of the European Union. DOI: 10.2760/159770

Rouse, M. (2008). Developing inclusive practice: A role for teachers and teacher education? *Education in the North*, *16*(1), 6–13.

Schon, D. A. (1983). *The reflective practitioner: How professionals think in action*. Basic Books.

Selwyn, N. (2019). *Should robots replace teachers? AI and the future of education*. Polity Press.

Shaddock, A., O'Neill, S., Spinks, A., & van den Berg, H. (2015). *Students with disability in mainstream schools*. Australian Institute for Teaching and School Leadership.

Southworth, J., Migliaccio, K., Glover, J., Glover, J., Reed, D., Sullivan, C., & Audiso, M. (2023). Developing a model for AI across the curriculum: Transforming the higher education landscape via innovation in AI literacy. *Computers and Education: Artificial Intelligence*, *4*, 100127. DOI: 10.1016/j.caeai.2023.100127

Stoll, L., Bolam, R., McMahon, A., Wallace, M., & Thomas, S. (2006). Professional learning communities: A review of the literature. *Journal of Educational Change*, *7*(4), 221–258. DOI: 10.1007/s10833-006-0001-8

Timperley, H. (2011). *Realizing the power of professional learning*. Open University Press.

Tomlinson, C. A. (2014). *The differentiated classroom: Responding to the needs of all learners* (2nd ed.). ASCD.

UNESCO. (2021). *Recommendation on the ethics of artificial intelligence*. United Nations Educational, Scientific and Cultural Organization. https://unesdoc.unesco.org/ark:/48223/pf0000381137

UNESCO. (2023). *ChatGPT and artificial intelligence in higher education: Quick start guide*. UNESCO. https://www.iesalc.unesco.org/en/2023/04/14/chatgpt-and-artificial-intelligence-in-higher-education-quick-start-guide/

Walker, J. (2017). Practical wisdom in professional education. In Peters, M. A. (Ed.), *Encyclopedia of educational philosophy and theory* (pp. 1836–1841). Springer., DOI: 10.1007/978-981-287-588-4_44

Weidinger, L., Uesato, J., Rauh, M., Griffin, C., Huang, P. S., Mellor, J., & Gabriel, I. (2023). Taxonomy of risks posed by language models. *Proceedings of the 2022 ACM FAccT Conference*, 214–229. DOI: 10.1145/3531146.3533088

Weng, Z., Guo, Y., & Chen, X. (2024). Using large language models to generate social stories for autistic students: A single-case experimental study. *Journal of Special Education Technology*, *39*(1), 45–61. DOI: 10.1177/01626434231195870

Wenger, E. (1998). *Communities of practice: Learning, meaning, and identity*. Cambridge University Press. DOI: 10.1017/CBO9780511803932

Whittlestone, J., Nyrup, R., Alexandrova, A., & Cave, S. (2021). The role and limits of principles in AI ethics: Towards a focus on tensions. *Proceedings of the 2019 AAAI/ACM AIES Conference*, 195–200. DOI: 10.1145/3306618.3314289

Yildiz Durak, H. (2023). Examining the effects of AI-based adaptive tools on self-regulation in students with ADHD. *Journal of Computer Assisted Learning*, *39*(4), 1143–1158. DOI: 10.1111/jcal.12809

Zawacki-Richter, O., Marin, V. I., Bond, M., & Gouverneur, F. (2019). Systematic review of research on artificial intelligence applications in higher education — Where are the educators? *International Journal of Educational Technology in Higher Education*, *16*(1), 39. DOI: 10.1186/s41239-019-0171-0

Compilation of References

Abbes, F., Bennani, S., & Maalel, A. (2024). Generative AI and gamification for personalized learning: Literature review and future challenges. *SN Computer Science*, *5*(8), 1154. DOI: 10.1007/s42979-024-03491-z

Abu Eideh, B. (2026). Reimagining instructional design: ChatGPT, Bloom's taxonomy, and the role of teacher expertise. *Social Sciences & Humanities Open*, *13*, 102325. DOI: 10.1016/j.ssaho.2025.102325

Abulibdeh, A. (2025). A systematic and bibliometric review of artificial intelligence in sustainable education: Current trends and future research directions. *Sustainable Futures : An Applied Journal of Technology, Environment and Society*, *10*, 101033. DOI: 10.1016/j.sftr.2025.101033

Acar, S. C., Cesur, K., Mikhailova, T., & Akshulakova, B. (2024). A netnographic study on the reasons why people fail to learn English. *Participatory Educational Research*, *11*(6), 134–151. DOI: 10.17275/per.24.83.11.6

Adams, C., Pente, P., Lemermeyer, G., Turville, J., & Rockwell, G. (2022). Artificial intelligence and teachers' new ethical obligations. *International Journal of Information Ethics*, *31*(1). Advance online publication. DOI: 10.29173/irie483

Adiguzel, T., Kaya, M. H., & Cansu, F. K. (2023). Revolutionizing education with AI: Exploring the transformative potential of CHATGPT. *Contemporary Educational Technology*, *15*(3), ep429. DOI: 10.30935/cedtech/13152

Ahuja, N. J., Dutt, S., Choudhary, S. I., & Kumar, M. (2022). Intelligent tutoring system in education for disabled learners using human–computer interaction and augmented reality. *International Journal of Human-Computer Interaction*. DOI: 10.1080/10447318.2022.2124359

Ai, J., Zhang, X., & Chen, Q. (2025, September). The Application of Generative Artificial Intelligence in Individualized Education Program for Exceptional Children: Value Connotation, Realistic Challenge and Practical Path. In *2025 5th International Conference on Educational Technology (ICET)* (pp. 654-657). IEEE. https://doi.org/ DOI: 10.1109/ICET67421.2025.11380433

Ainscow, M. (2020). Promoting inclusion and equity in education: Lessons from international experiences. *Nordic Journal of Studies in Educational Policy*, *6*(1), 7–16. DOI: 10.1080/20020317.2020.1729587

Ainscow, M., Booth, T., & Dyson, A. (2006). *Improving schools, developing inclusion*. Routledge. DOI: 10.4324/9780203967157

Alam, A. (2023). Possibilities and challenges of GenAI in education. *International Journal of Advanced Educational Research*, *8*(4), 15–22.

Alammari, A. (2024). Evaluating generative AI integration in Saudi Arabian education: A mixed-methods study. *PeerJ. Computer Science*, *10*, e1879. DOI: 10.7717/peerj-cs.1879 PMID: 38435558

Aldakhil, A. F. (2024). Investigating the impact of an AI-based play activities intervention on the quality of life of school-aged children with ADHD. *Research in Developmental Disabilities*, *154*, 104858. DOI: 10.1016/j.ridd.2024.104858 PMID: 39413561

Al-Emran, M., Al-Qaysi, N., Al-Sharafi, M. A., Khoshkam, M., Foroughi, B., & Ghobakhloo, M. (2025). Role of perceived threats and knowledge management in shaping generative AI use in education and its impact on social sustainability. *International Journal of Management Education*, *23*(1), 101105. DOI: 10.1016/j.ijme.2024.101105

Alenezi, M. A. K., Mohamed, A. M., & Shaaban, T. S. (2023). Revolutionizing EFL special education: How ChatGPT is transforming the way teachers approach language learning. *Innoeduca. International Journal of Technology and Educational Innovation*, *9*(2), 5–23. DOI: 10.24310/innoeduca.2023.v9i2.16774

Aleven, V., McLaughlin, E. A., Glenn, R. A., & Koedinger, K. R. (2017). Instruction based on adaptive learning technologies. In Mayer, R. E., & Alexander, P. A. (Eds.), *Handbook of research on learning and instruction* (2nd ed., pp. 522–560). Routledge.

Alexopoulos, P., Mastrothanasis, K., Andreadakis, N., Kladaki, M., & Kostas, A. (2025). Training interventions for teachers' self-efficacy enhancement in the use of Artificial Intelligence: A systematic literature review in the five-year period 2020–2025. *Παιδαγωγικά Ρεύματα στο Αιγαίο, 14*(1), 45–55. https://doi.org/DOI: 10.12681/revmata.43576

Alfarwan, A. (2025, September). Generative AI use in K-12 education: A systematic review. In *Frontiers in Education* (Vol. 10, p. 1647573). Frontiers Media SA. https://doi.org/DOI: 10.3389/feduc.2025.1647573

Alharbi, A., & Stevenson, M. (2020). Refining Boolean queries to identify relevant studies for systematic review updates. *Journal of the American Medical Informatics Association : JAMIA, 27*(11), 1658–1666. DOI: 10.1093/jamia/ocaa148 PMID: 33067630

Aljedaani, W., Krasniqi, R., Aljedaani, S., Mkaouer, M. W., Ludi, S., & Al-Raddah, K. (2023). If online learning works for you, what about deaf students? Emerging challenges of online learning for deaf and hearing-impaired students during COVID-19: A literature review. *Universal Access in the Information Society, 22*(3), 1027–1046. DOI: 10.1007/s10209-022-00897-5 PMID: 35910240

Alkhurayyif, Y., & Sait, A. R. W. (2024). A review of artificial intelligence-based dyslexia detection techniques. *Diagnostics (Basel), 14*(21), 2362. Advance online publication. DOI: 10.3390/diagnostics14212362 PMID: 39518334

Allison, J., Hwang, G. J., Mayer, R. E., Pellas, N., Karnalim, O., de Freitas, S., Ng, O.-L., Huang, Y.-M., Hooshyar, D., Seidman, R. H., Al-Emran, M., Mikropoulos, T. A., Schroeder, N. L., Roscoe, R. D., & Sanusi, I. (2025). From generative AI to extended reality: Multidisciplinary perspectives on the challenges, opportunities, and future of educational computing. *Journal of Educational Computing Research, 63*(6), 1327–1363. DOI: 10.1177/07356331251359964

Almulla, M., & Ali, S. I. (2024). The changing educational landscape for sustainable online experiences: Implications of ChatGPT in Arab students' learning experience. *International Journal of Learning. Teaching and Educational Research, 23*(9), 285–302. DOI: 10.26803/ijlter.23.9.15

Alnafjan, A., Alghamdi, M., Alhakbani, N., & Al-Ohali, Y. (2025). Improving imitation skills in children with autism spectrum disorder using the NAO robot and a human action recognition. *Diagnostics (Basel), 15*(1), 60. DOI: 10.3390/diagnostics15010060 PMID: 39795588

Alqarni, T. M. (2026). Teachers' perceptions of generative AI in inclusive classrooms: Enhancing engagement for students with learning disabilities. *Universal Access in the Information Society*, *25*(1), 22. DOI: 10.1007/s10209-025-01301-8

Alrawabdeh, W., Jdaitawi, M., & Hamdan, A. (2024). Artificial intelligence tools in supporting autistic learners: A systematic review of evidence and methodological quality. *Journal of Autism and Developmental Disorders*, *54*(3), 1102–1121. DOI: 10.1007/s10803-023-06019-1

Alsahli, M., Alanezi, F. Sh., Basri, W., Attar, R. W., Alghamdi, A., Alyahya, N. M., Albagmi, S., Almutairi, S. A., Alsedrah, I. T., Arif, W. M., Alsadhan, A. A., AlShammary, M. H., Bakhshwain, A. M., Almuhanna, A. F., Alnaim, N., & Alhazmi, A. H. (2025). Effectiveness of ChatGPT in facilitating learning for students with special educational needs: An empirical study in Saudi Arabia. *Nutrition and Health (Berkhamsted, Hertfordshire)*, *31*(4), 1579–1589. DOI: 10.1177/02601060241307770 PMID: 39819330

Alsolami, A. S. (2025). The effectiveness of using artificial intelligence in improving academic skills of school-aged students with mild intellectual disabilities in Saudi Arabia. *Research in Developmental Disabilities*, *156*, 104884. DOI: 10.1016/j.ridd.2024.104884 PMID: 39631141

Altakhaineh, A. R. M., Alkhatib, R. N., & Awad, T. (2026). Integrating artificial intelligence to enhance inclusive education for students with special needs in Jordan and the UAE: Perspectives of teachers and parents. *Acta Psychologica*, *263*, 106252. DOI: 10.1016/j.actpsy.2026.106252 PMID: 41558316

Alwell, M., & Cobb, B. (2009). Functional Life Skills Curricular Interventions for Youth With Disabilities. *Career Development for Exceptional Individuals*, *32*(2), 82–93. DOI: 10.1177/0885728809336656

AlZu'bi, S., Mughaid, A., Quiam, F., & Hendawi, S. (2023). Exploring the Capabilities and Limitations of ChatGPT and Alternative Big Language Models. *Artificial Intelligence and Applications (Commerce, Calif.)*, *2*(1), 28–37. DOI: 10.47852/bonviewAIA3202820

Amado-Salvatierra, H. R., Morales, M., & Hernández-Rizzardini, R. (2023). Combining human creativity and AI-based tools in the instructional design of MOOCs: Benefits and limitations. *2023 IEEE Learning with MOOCS (LWMOOCS)*, 1–5. DOI: 10.1109/LWMOOCS58322.2023.10306023

American Association on Intellectual and Developmental Disabilities. (2010). *Intellectual Disability: Definition, Classification, and Systems of Supports* (11th ed.). American Association on Intellectual and Developmental Disabilities.

American Psychiatric Association. (2013). *Diagnostic and statistical manual of mental disorders* (5th ed.)., DOI: 10.1176/appi.books.9780890425596

Amershi, S., Weld, D. S., Vorvoreanu, M., Fourney, A., Nushi, B., Collisson, P., Suh, J., Iqbal, S. T., Bennett, P. N., Inkpen, K., Teevan, J., Kikin-Gil, R., & Horvitz, E. (2019). Guidelines for human-AI interaction. *Proceedings of the 2019 CHI Conference on Human Factors in Computing Systems*, Article 3, 1–13. ACM. DOI: 10.1145/3290605.3300233

Anaroua, F. I., Li, Q., Tang, Y., & Liu, H. P. (2025). AI-driven formative assessment and adaptive learning in data-science education: Evaluating an LLM-powered virtual teaching assistant. DOI: 10.48550/arxiv.2509.20369

Andrade, H. L. (2013). Classroom assessment in the context of learning theory and research. In McMillan, J. H. (Ed.), *Sage handbook of research on classroom assessment* (pp. 17–34). SAGE. DOI: 10.4135/9781452218649.n2

Angeli, F. (2024). CHAT (Child Helper and Assistant Tool): An AI-based educational tool for supporting neurodiverse children with autism, dyscalculia, and DSA. *CEUR Workshop Proceedings, 3880*, Paper 18.

Animashaun, E. S., Familoni, B. T., & Onyebuchi, N. C.Enitan Shukurat AnimashaunBabajide Tolulope FamiloniNneamaka Chisom Onyebuchi. (2024). Advanced machine learning techniques for personalising technology education. *Computer Science & IT Research Journal*, *5*(6), 1300–1315. DOI: 10.51594/csitrj.v5i6.1198

Anselimus, S. M. (2026). Generative AI for university students with disabilities: Challenges and opportunities. *Educational Research*, *68*(2), 1–19. DOI: 10.1080/00131881.2026.2632852

Aremu, E. S., Ojo, A., & Useghan, N. O. (2025). The role of artificial intelligence in managing handwriting and spelling difficulties among university students with perceived specific learning disabilities (PSLDs). *The Exceptional Child: Journal of National Association for Exceptional Children (NAEC), 25*(1), 12–21. https://naechildren.org

Arinushkina, A. A. (Ed.). (2024). *Integration strategies of generative AI in higher education*. IGI Global., DOI: 10.4018/979-8-3693-5518-3

Arksey, H., & O'Malley, L. (2005). Scoping studies: Towards a methodological framework. *International Journal of Social Research Methodology*, *8*(1), 19–32. DOI: 10.1080/1364557032000119616

Armstrong, T. (2012). *Neurodiversity in the classroom: Strength-based strategies to help students with special needs succeed in school and life*. ASCD.

Arslan, B., Lehman, B., Tenison, C., Sparks, J. R., López, A. A., Gu, L., & Zapata-Rivera, D. (2024). Opportunities and challenges of using generative AI to personalize educational assessment. *Frontiers in Artificial Intelligence*, *7*, 1460651. DOI: 10.3389/frai.2024.1460651 PMID: 39434872

Arya, R., & Verma, A. (2024). Role of artificial intelligence in education. *International Journal of Advanced Research in Science. Tongxin Jishu*, *4*(2), 589–594. DOI: 10.48175/IJARSCT-19461

Asselborn, T., Gargot, T., Kidziński, Ł., Johal, W., Cohen, D., Jolly, C., & Dillenbourg, P. (2018). Automated human-level diagnosis of dysgraphia using a consumer tablet. *npj. Digital Medicine*, *1*(1), 42. DOI: 10.1038/s41746-018-0049-x PMID: 31304322

Ayasrah, S., Hanandeh, A., Abu Ghazal, H., & AlEid, W. (2024). Utilizing PROKET Technology Program: An evaluation of assistive tools in enhancing developmental skills for students with specific learning disorders. *International Journal of Information and Education Technology (IJIET)*, *14*(7), 988–995. DOI: 10.18178/ijiet.2024.14.7.2126

Bae, H., & Bozkurt, A. (2024). The untold story of training students with generative AI: Are we preparing students for true learning or just personalization. *Online Learning : the Official Journal of the Online Learning Consortium*, *28*(3), 1–9. DOI: 10.24059/olj.v28i3.4689

Baglieri, S., & Shapiro, A. (2012). *Disability studies and the inclusive classroom: Critical practices for creating least restrictive attitudes*. Routledge. DOI: 10.4324/9780203837399

Bahja, M., Hammad, R., Alkazemi, A., & Alhabsi, Z. (2025). The Potential of Generative AI in Special Education: A Review of Applications and Impact. *Unleashing User Innovation*, 192-213. https://doi.org/DOI: 10.1201/9781003485698-14

Baidoo-Anu, D., & Owusu Ansah, L. (2023). Education in the era of Generative Artificial Intelligence (AI): Understanding the potential benefits of CHATGPT in promoting teaching and learning. SSRN *Electronic Journal*. DOI: 10.2139/ssrn.4337484

Baidoo-Anu, D., & Owusu Ansah, L. (2023). Education in the era of generative artificial intelligence (AI): Understanding the potential benefits of ChatGPT in promoting teaching and learning. *Journal of AI*, *7*(1), 52–62. DOI: 10.61969/jai.1337500

Bailey, D. H., Fuchs, L. S., Gilbert, J. K., Geary, D. C., & Fuchs, D. (2018). Prevention: Necessary but insufficient? A 2-year follow-up of an effective first-grade mathematics intervention. *Child Development, 91*(2), 382–396. DOI: 10.1111/cdev.13175 PMID: 30358181

Balikci, S., Terzioglu, N. K., & Rakap, S. (2026). ChatGPT-assisted task analysis for special education teachers: An exploratory study of alignment, readability, efficiency, and acceptability. *Future Internet, 18*(3), 158. DOI: 10.3390/fi18030158

Barbu, M., Iordache, D.-D., Petre, I., Barbu, D.-C., & Băjenaru, L. (2025). Framework design for reinforcing the potential of XR technologies in transforming inclusive education. *Applied Sciences (Basel, Switzerland), 15*(3), 1484. DOI: 10.3390/app15031484

Barone, T., & Eisner, E. W. (2012). *Arts based research.* SAGE Publications., DOI: 10.4135/9781452230627

Barua, P. D., Vicnesh, J., Gururajan, R., Oh, S. L., Palmer, E., Azizan, M. M., Kadri, N. A., & Acharya, U. R. (2022). Artificial intelligence enabled personalised assistive tools to enhance education of children with neurodevelopmental disorders—A review. *International Journal of Environmental Research and Public Health, 19*(3), 1192. DOI: 10.3390/ijerph19031192 PMID: 35162220

Batta, A. (2024). Transforming higher education through generative AI: Opportunity and challenges. *Paradigm, 28*(2), 241–243. DOI: 10.1177/09718907241286221

Beijaard, D., Meijer, P. C., & Verloop, N. (2004). Reconsidering research on teachers' professional identity. *Teaching and Teacher Education, 20*(2), 107–128. DOI: 10.1016/j.tate.2003.07.001

Bencsik, A., Jenei, S., & Szalai, S. M. (2026). Who gets to use ChatGPT? A global study on digital access and inequality in higher education. *Social Sciences & Humanities Open, 13*, 102479. DOI: 10.1016/j.ssaho.2026.102479

Bender, E. M., Gebru, T., McMillan-Major, A., & Shmitchell, S. (2021). On the dangers of stochastic parrots: Can language models be too big? *Proceedings of the 2021 ACM Conference on Fairness, Accountability, and Transparency* (pp. 610–623). ACM. DOI: 10.1145/3442188.3445922

Benz, C., Scott-Jeffs, W., McKercher, K. A., Welsh, M., Norman, R., Hendrie, D., Locantro, M., & Robinson, S. (2024). Community-based participatory-research through co-design: Supporting collaboration from all sides of disability. *Research Involvement and Engagement, 10*(1), 47. Advance online publication. DOI: 10.1186/s40900-024-00573-3 PMID: 38730283

Berch, D. B., & Mazzocco, M. M. M. (Eds.). (2007). *Why is math so hard? A view of mathematical learning disabilities from multiple perspectives*. Paul H. Brookes Publishing Co.

Berrezueta-Guzman, J., Pau, I., Martín-Ruiz, M.-L., & Máximo-Bocanegra, N. (2021). Assessment of a robotic assistant for supporting homework activities of children with ADHD. *IEEE Access : Practical Innovations, Open Solutions*, *9*, 93450–93465. DOI: 10.1109/ACCESS.2021.3093233

Bertacchini, F., Demarco, F., Scuro, C., Pantano, P., & Bilotta, E. (2023). A social robot connected with chatGPT to improve cognitive functioning in ASD subjects. *Frontiers in Psychology*, *14*, 1232177. DOI: 10.3389/fpsyg.2023.1232177 PMID: 37868599

Beukelman, D. R., & Light, J. C. (2020). *Augmentative and alternative communication: Supporting children and adults with complex communication needs* (5th ed.). Paul H. Brookes Publishing.

Bhaskaru, O., & Lalitha, K. (2026). Empowering Special Education Through Generative AI With Opportunities, Challenges, and Case Studies. In *Shaping Inclusive Educational Policies and Practices With Generative AI* (pp. 171–204). IGI Global Scientific Publishing., DOI: 10.4018/979-8-3373-3745-6.ch007

Bhuiyan, M. A., Rahman, M. K., Basile, V., Ping, H., & Mainul Bari, A. B. M. (2025). Adoption of ChatGPT for students' learning effectiveness. *International Journal of Management Education*, *23*(3), 101255. DOI: 10.1016/j.ijme.2025.101255

Bhushan, S., Arunkumar, S., Eisa, T. A. E., Nasser, M., Singh, A. K., & Kumar, P. (2024). AI-enhanced dyscalculia screening: A survey of methods and applications for children. *Diagnostics (Basel)*, *14*(13), 1441. DOI: 10.3390/diagnostics14131441 PMID: 39001330

Billinghurst, M., & Duenser, A. (2012). Augmented reality in the classroom. *Computer*, *45*(7), 56–63. DOI: 10.1109/MC.2012.111

Black, P., & Wiliam, D. (2018). Classroom assessment and pedagogy. *Assessment in Education: Principles, Policy & Practice*, *25*(6), 551–575. DOI: 10.1080/0969594X.2018.1441807

Blodgett, S. L., Barocas, S., Daume, H., & Wallach, H. (2020). Language (technology) is power: A critical survey of "bias" in NLP. *Proceedings of the 58th Annual Meeting of the Association for Computational Linguistics*, 5454–5476. DOI: 10.18653/v1/2020.acl-main.485

Boal, A. (2002). *Games for actors and non-actors* (2nd ed.). Routledge.

Bololia, L., Williams, J., Macmahon, K., & Goodall, K. (2022). Dramatherapy for children and adolescents with autism spectrum disorder: A systematic integrative review. *The Arts in Psychotherapy*, *80*, 101918. DOI: 10.1016/j.aip.2022.101918

Bommasani, R., Hudson, D. A., Adeli, E., Altman, R., Arora, S., von Arx, S., Bernstein, M. S., Bohg, J., Bosselut, A., Brunskill, E., & Liang, P. (2021). On the opportunities and risks of foundation models. arXiv. https://arxiv.org/abs/2108.07258

Bong, W. K., & Chen, W. (2024). Increasing faculty's competence in digital accessibility for inclusive education: A systematic literature review. *International Journal of Inclusive Education*, *28*(2), 197–213. DOI: 10.1080/13603116.2021.1937344

Botchu, B., Iyengar, K. P., & Botchu, R. (2024). Can ChatGPT empower people with dyslexia? *Disability and Rehabilitation. Assistive Technology*, *19*(5), 2131–2132. DOI: 10.1080/17483107.2023.2256805 PMID: 37697967

Bougdira, A., & Al Murshidi, G. (2025). Generative AI as a tool for personalized STEAM K-12 education. In *Prompt engineering and generative AI applications for teaching and learning* (pp. 387–410). IGI Global Scientific Publishing., DOI: 10.4018/979-8-3693-7332-3.ch023

Bouguettaya, S., Pupo, F., Chen, M., & Fortino, G. (2025). A Meta-survey of generative AI in education: Trends, challenges, and research directions. *Big Data and Cognitive Computing*, *9*(9), 237. DOI: 10.3390/bdcc9090237

Boulhrir, T., & Hamash, M. (2025). Unpacking artificial intelligence in elementary education: A comprehensive thematic analysis systematic review. *Computers and Education: Artificial Intelligence*, *9*, 100442. DOI: 10.1016/j.caeai.2025.100442

Bourdieu, P., & Passeron, J.-C. (1977). *Reproduction in education, society and culture*. Sage. https://monoskop.org/images/8/82/Bourdieu_Pierre_Passeron_Jean_Claude_Reproduction_in_Education_Society_and_Culture_1990.pdf

Bozkurt, A., Xiao, J., Lambert, S. R., Pazurek, A., Crompton, H., Koseoglu, S., Farrow, R., Bond, M., Nerantzi, C., Honeychurch, S., Bali, M., Dron, J., Mir, K., Stewart, B., & Jandrić, P. (2023). Speculative futures on ChatGPT and GenAI(AI): A collective reflection from the educational landscape. *Asian Journal of Distance Education*, *18*(1), 53–130. DOI: 10.5281/zenodo.7636568

Braun, V., & Clarke, V. (2006). Using thematic analysis in psychology. *Qualitative Research in Psychology*, *3*(2), 77–101. DOI: 10.1191/1478088706qp063oa

Braun, V., & Clarke, V. (2022). Thematic analysis: A practical guide. *Sage (Atlanta, Ga.)*.

Bresler Nardi, A., Bat Or, M., & Shuper Engelhard, E. (2022). Dance movement therapy processes and interventions in the treatment of children with anxiety disorders derived from therapy logs. *The Arts in Psychotherapy*, *80*, 101951. DOI: 10.1016/j.aip.2022.101951

Brookhart, S. M. (2013). *How to create and use rubrics for formative assessment and grading*. ASCD.

Brown, T. B., Mann, B., Ryder, N., Subbiah, M., Kaplan, J., Dhariwal, P., & Amodei, D. (2020). Language models are few-shot learners. *Advances in Neural Information Processing Systems*, *33*, 1877–1901.

Bruner, J. (1983). *Child's talk: Learning to use language*. Oxford University Press.

Brunton, R. J., Rhazzafe, S., Moodley, R., Kuhn, S., Caraffini, F., Wilford, S., Higginbottom, R., Colreavy-Donnelly, S., & Gongora, M. (2025). Using generative artificial intelligence to enhance the performance of disadvantaged students in secondary education. *Social Sciences & Humanities Open*, *12*, 102110. DOI: 10.1016/j.ssaho.2025.102110

Calculator, S. N. (2009). Augmentative and alternative communication (AAC) and inclusive education for students with the most severe disabilities. *International Journal of Inclusive Education*, *13*(1), 93–113. DOI: 10.1080/13603110701284656

CAST. (2018). *Universal design for learning guidelines version 2.2*. CAST. http://udlguidelines.cast.org

CAST. (2018). *Universal design for learning guidelines version 2.2*. http://udlguidelines.cast.org

CAST. (2018). *Universal Design for Learning guidelines version 2.2*. http://udlguidelines.cast.org

CAST. (2018). *Universal Design for Learning Guidelines version 2.2*. http://udlguidelines.cast.org

CAST. (2024). *Universal design for learning guidelines version 3.0*. CAST. http://udlguidelines.cast.org

CAST. (2024). *Universal Design for Learning Guidelines version 3.0*. CAST. https://udlguidelines.cast.org

Castleman, B. V. Western New England University, Jarvinen, L. Z., Westfield State University, Jarvinen, M. K., & Western New England University. (2024). Neurodiversity in the minds of students: From perception to campus programming. *Journal of Undergraduate Neuroscience Education, 22*(3), A217–A223. DOI: 10.59390/QCWZ6366

Çela, E., Vedishchev, A., Fonkam, M., Eappen, P., Potluri, R. M., & Vajjhala, N. R. (2025). Integrating generative AI in education: Themes, challenges, and future directions. In *Generative Artificial Intelligence (AI) approaches for industrial applications* (pp. 149–167). Springer Nature Switzerland., DOI: 10.1007/978-3-031-76710-4_8

Celik, I., Dindar, M., Muukkonen, H., & Järvelä, S. (2022). The promises and challenges of artificial intelligence for teachers: A systematic review of research. *TechTrends*, *66*(4), 616–630. DOI: 10.1007/s11528-022-00715-y

Cheng, S. C., & Lai, C. L. (2019). Facilitating learning for students with special needs: A review of technology-supported special education studies. *Journal of Computers in Education*, *7*(8), 131–153. DOI: 10.1007/s40692-019-00150-8

Chen, L., Chen, P., & Lin, Z. (2020). Artificial intelligence in education: A Review. *IEEE Access : Practical Innovations, Open Solutions*, *8*, 75264–75278. DOI: 10.1109/ACCESS.2020.2988510

Ching, Y. H., Hsu, Y. C., & Hung, A. (2024). Introduction to the special section on integrating generative AI in education. *TechTrends*, *68*(4), 771–772. DOI: 10.1007/s11528-024-00990-x

Chiu, T. K. F., Xia, Q., Zhou, X., Chai, C. S., & Cheng, M. (2023). Systematic literature review on opportunities, challenges, and future research recommendations of artificial intelligence in education. *Computers and Education: Artificial Intelligence*, *4*, 100118. DOI: 10.1016/j.caeai.2022.100118

Choi, E. (2023). A Comprehensive Inquiry into the Use of ChatGPT Examining General, Educational, and Disability-Focused Perspectives. *International Journal of Arts, Humanities &. Social Science*, *04*(11), 1–7. DOI: 10.56734/ijahss.v4n11a1

Chopra, K. (2025). Motivating older adults with special needs for learning using generative artificial intelligence. *Educational Gerontology*, •••, 1–20. DOI: 10.1080/03601277.2025.2538205

Christodoulou, A., & Angeli, C. (2022). Adaptive learning techniques for personalized educational software in developing teachers' technological pedagogical content knowledge. *Frontiers in Education*, *7*, 789397. DOI: 10.3389/feduc.2022.789397

Coflan, C. M., & Kaye, T. (2020). *Using education technology to support learners with special educational needs and disabilities in low- and middle-income countries*. EdTech Hub. DOI: 10.53832/edtechhub.0021

Creely, E., & Blannin, J. (2025). Creative partnerships with generative AI. Possibilities for education and beyond. *Thinking Skills and Creativity*, *56*, 101727. DOI: 10.1016/j.tsc.2024.101727

Creely, E., & Carabott, K. (2025). Teaching and learning with AI: An integrated AI-oriented pedagogical model. *Australian Educational Researcher*, *52*(6), 4633–4655. DOI: 10.1007/s13384-025-00913-6

Crompton, H., & Burke, D. (2023). Artificial intelligence in higher education: The state of the field. *International Journal of Educational Technology in Higher Education*, *20*(1), 22. Advance online publication. DOI: 10.1186/s41239-023-00392-8

Crompton, H., & Burke, D. (2023). Artificial intelligence in K-12 education: A systematic review. *Education and Information Technologies*, *28*(2), 1–25. DOI: 10.1007/s10639-022-11294-7

Dabaghi, K., D'Urso, S., & Sciarrone, F. (2026). Artificial intelligence to help people with dyslexia in education: An interdisciplinary literature review. *International Journal of Artificial Intelligence in Education*, *36*(1–2), 100012. Advance online publication. DOI: 10.1016/j.ijaied.2026.100012

Daher, R. F. (2025). Integrating AI literacy into teacher education: A critical perspective paper. *Discover Artificial Intelligence*, *5*(1), 217. DOI: 10.1007/s44163-025-00475-7

Daniela, L. (2026). Integrating Technology for Pedagogical, Technological, and Socio-Ethical Sustainability in Education. *Technology. Knowledge and Learning*, *31*(1), 1–10. DOI: 10.1007/s10758-025-09936-5

Darling-Hammond, L., Hyler, M. E., & Gardner, M. (2017). *Effective teacher professional development*. Learning Policy Institute. DOI: 10.54300/122.311

Davis, F. D. (1989). Perceived usefulness, perceived ease of use, and user acceptance of information technology. *Management Information Systems Quarterly*, *13*(3), 319–340. DOI: 10.2307/249008

Davou, V., & Misailidis, P. (2018). *Technologies supporting learning and learning difficulties*. Ellinika Grammata. [in Greek]

De Marco, V., Sciarrone, F., & Temperini, M. (2024, July). TutorChat: a Chatbot for the Support to Dyslexic Learner's activity through Generative AI. In *2024 IEEE International Conference on Advanced Learning Technologies (ICALT)* (pp. 155-157). IEEE. https://doi.org/DOI: 10.1109/ICALT61570.2024.00051

Department for Education & Department of Health. (2015). *Special educational needs and disability code of practice: 0 to 25 years*. UK Government. https://www.gov.uk/government/publications/send-code-of-practice-0-to-25

Department for Education. (2023). *Generative AI in education: Educator and expert views*. UK Government. https://www.gov.uk/government/publications/generative-ai-in-education-educator-and-expert-views

Department for Education. (2023). *Keeping children safe in education*. UK Government. https://www.gov.uk/government/publications/keeping-children-safe-in-education--2

Dewey, J. (1934). *Art as experience*. Minton, Balch & Company.

Dey, A. K., Chauhan, V. K., Singh, P. K., & Sarkar, A. (2024, December). Exploring the integration of generative ai in modern education systems: A comprehensive analysis. In *2024 International Conference on Artificial Intelligence and Quantum Computation-Based Sensor Application (ICAIQSA)* (pp. 1-8). IEEE. https://doi.org/DOI: 10.1109/ICAIQSA64000.2024.10882259

Dhar, D., Rahman, A., Chowdhury, M., & Dipto, A. S. (2025). Dyslexia, ADHD, dyscalculia, and dyspraxia prediction in children using machine learning and explainable AI. *Proceedings of the 9th International Conference on Computational System and Information Technology for Sustainable Solutions (CSITSS)*, 1–6. DOI: 10.1109/CSITSS67709.2025.11294091

Dimeli, M., & Kostas, A. (2025). The role of ChatGPT in education: Applications, challenges: Insights from a systematic review. *Journal of Information Technology Education, 24*, 2. DOI: 10.28945/5422

Ding, L., & Zou, D. (2024). Automated writing evaluation systems: A systematic review of Grammarly, Pigai, and Criterion with a perspective on future directions in the age of generative artificial intelligence. *Education and Information Technologies, 29*(11), 14151–14203. DOI: 10.1007/s10639-023-12402-3

Dong, W., Pan, D., & Kim, S. (2024). Exploring the integration of IoT and Generative AI in English language education: Smart tools for personalized learning experiences. *Journal of Computational Science, 82*, 102397. DOI: 10.1016/j.jocs.2024.102397

Drelick, A. M., Woodfield, C., & Freedman, J. E. (2026). Designing and using custom Chatbots to support students with disabilities: An educator's guide. *Journal of Special Education Technology, 01626434261420392*, 01626434261420392. DOI: 10.1177/01626434261420392

Drill, R. B., & Bellini, S. (2022). Combining Readers Theater, Story Mapping and Video Self-Modeling Interventions to Improve Narrative Reading Comprehension in Children with Autism Spectrum Disorder. *Journal of Autism and Developmental Disorders*, *52*(1), 1–15. DOI: 10.1007/s10803-021-04908-x PMID: 33590425

Drossinou Korea, M. (2020). *Handbook of special education and educational narratives*. Opportuna. (in Greek)

Drossinou Korea, M., & Alexopoulos, P. (2022). Teaching social skills interventions with digital cognitive and language machines to a student with autism. *International Journal of Social Science and Human Research*, *05*(11), 5234–5241. DOI: 10.47191/ijsshr/v5-i11-55

Drossinou Korea, M., & Alexopoulos, P. (2024a). Factors arising from the utilization of Artificial Intelligence and Large Language Models in Special Education. *European Journal of Special Education Research*, *10*(2), 1–16. DOI: 10.46827/ejse.v10i2.5209

Drossinou Korea, M., & Alexopoulos, P. (2024b). Higher Education Students' Views on the Use of Artificial Intelligence for Teaching Students with Specific Learning Difficulties. *European Journal of Open Education and E-Learning Studies*, *9*(1). DOI: 10.46827/ejoe.v9i1.5518

Drotár, P., & Dobeš, M. (2020). Dysgraphia detection through machine learning. *Scientific Reports*, *10*(1), 21541. Advance online publication. DOI: 10.1038/s41598-020-78611-9 PMID: 33299092

Dumitru, C., Koulianou, M., & Mastrothanasis, K. (2024). Inclusion of students with specific learning disorders in higher education: a systematic literature review. *Journal of Educational Sciences & Psychology, 15 (76)*(2), 46–64. DOI: 10.51865/JESP.2024.2.06

Dumitru, C. (2025). Assistive Technology and Alternative and Augmentative Communication Options in the Language Skills Development of Students with Specific Learning Disorders. *Education Sciences*, *15*(2), 170. DOI: 10.3390/educsci15020170

Dumitru, C., Mastrothanasis, K., Pikoulis, E., Kladaki, M., Zervoudakis, K., Dogan, C. D., Gonullu, I., Stan, M. M., Karamagioli, E., Ledaki, M., Alexopoulos, P., Papantoniou, D., Pikouli, A., Papantoniou, S., & Erden, S. (2026). Drama-based simulations in first aid education: Psychometric validation of a student assessment tool in school settings. *Frontiers in Public Health*, *14*, 1710189. DOI: 10.3389/fpubh.2026.1710189 PMID: 41846832

Dwivedi, Y. K., Kshetri, N., Hughes, L., Slade, E. L., Jeyaraj, A., Kar, A. K., Baabdullah, A. M., Koohang, A., Raghavan, V., Ahuja, M., Albanna, H., Albashrawi, M. A., Al-Busaidi, A. S., Balakrishnan, J., Barlette, Y., Basu, S., Bose, I., Brooks, L., Buhalis, D., & Wright, R. (2023). Opinion Paper: "So what if ChatGPT wrote it?" Multidisciplinary perspectives on opportunities, challenges and implications of generative conversational AI for research, practice and policy. *International Journal of Information Management*, *71*, 102642. DOI: 10.1016/j.ijinfomgt.2023.102642

Eisner, E. W. (2002). *The arts and the creation of mind*. Yale University Press.

Elkot, M. A., Youssif, E., & Elmahdi, O. E. H. (2025). Generative Conversational AI: Active Practices for Fostering Students with Mild Intellectual Disabilities to Improve English Communication Skills. *Contemporary Educational Technology*, *17*(1), ep549. Advance online publication. DOI: 10.30935/cedtech/15688

El-Sabagh, H. (2021). Adaptive e-learning environment based on learning styles and its impact on development students' engagement. *International Journal of Educational Technology in Higher Education*, *18*(1), 53. Advance online publication. DOI: 10.1186/s41239-021-00289-4

Emery, D. W., & Vandenberg, B. (2010). Special education teacher burnout and ACT. *International Journal of Special Education*, *25*(3), 119–131.

Engeström, Y. (2009). The Future of Activity Theory: A Rough Draft. In Sannino, A., Daniels, H., & Gutierrez, K. D. (Eds.), *Learning and Expanding with Activity Theory* (pp. 303–328). Cambridge University Press., DOI: 10.1017/CBO9780511809989.020

Eradze, M., Manna, M., Sunar, A., Dovigo, F., & Ianes, D. (2025). Harnessing generative AI for inclusive education: opportunities and challenges. In *Frontiers in Education* (Vol. 10, p. 1765687). Frontiers Media SA. https://doi.org/DOI: 10.3389/feduc.2025.1765687

Ertel, W. (2017). Introduction. In W. Ertel, *Introduction to Artificial Intelligence* (pp. 1–21). Springer International Publishing. DOI: 10.1007/978-3-319-58487-4_1

European Agency for Special Needs and Inclusive Education. (2026). *Country Information for Greece*. https://www.european-agency.org/country-information/greece

European Commission, Directorate-General for Education, Youth, Sport and Culture. (2022). *Ethical guidelines on the use of artificial intelligence and data in teaching and learning for educators*. Publications Office of the European Union., DOI: 10.2766/153756

European Commission. (2019). *Ethics guidelines for trustworthy AI*. High-Level Expert Group on Artificial Intelligence. DOI: 10.2759/177365

European Commission. (2020). *Digital education action plan 2021–2027: Resetting education and training for the digital age*. Publications Office of the European Union. https://ec.europa.eu

European Union. (2024). Regulation (EU) 2024/1689 of the European Parliament and of the Council of 13 June 2024 laying down harmonised rules on artificial intelligence (Artificial Intelligence Act). Official Journal of the European Union, L 2024/1689. https://eur-lex.europa.eu/eli/reg/2024/1689/oj

Evmenova, A. S., Borup, J., & Shin, J. K. (2024). Harnessing the power of generative AI to support all learners. *TechTrends*, *68*(4), 820–831. DOI: 10.1007/s11528-024-00966-x

Evmenova, A. S., Regan, K., Mergen, R., & Hrisseh, R. (2024). Improving writing feedback for struggling writers: Generative AI to the rescue? *TechTrends*, *68*(4), 790–802. DOI: 10.1007/s11528-024-00965-y

Evmenova, A. S., Regan, K., Mergen, R., & Hrisseh, R. (2025). Educational games and the potential of AI to transform writing across the curriculum. *Education Sciences*, *15*(5), 567. DOI: 10.3390/educsci15050567

Ewoldt, K. B., & Flanagan, S. M. (2025). Generative artificial intelligence as an educational collaborator: A next-generation resource. *Teaching Exceptional Children*, *00400599251340611*. DOI: 10.1177/00400599251340611

Faber, M., & Johnson, R. (2024). AI-enhanced reading support for students with dyslexia: A quasi-experimental study. *Journal of Learning Disabilities*, *57*(2), 88–104. DOI: 10.1177/00222194231198450

Fallah, A., ZandiyeVakili, Y., & Sajedi, H. (2025). AI-driven approaches for dysgraphia diagnosis using online and offline handwriting data: A comprehensive scoping review. *PLoS One*, *20*(12), e0328722. Advance online publication. DOI: 10.1371/journal.pone.0328722 PMID: 41474692

Fang, M., Abdallah, A. K., & Vorfolomeyeva, O. (2024). Collaborative AI-enhanced digital mind-mapping as a tool for stimulating creative thinking in inclusive education for students with neurodevelopmental disorders. *BMC Psychology*, *12*(1), 488. DOI: 10.1186/s40359-024-01975-4 PMID: 39289718

Fan, M., Jin, S., Fan, J., Guo, W., & Chen, X. (2025). EmoLand: Utilizing narrative animations, multilevel games, and affective computing to foster emotional development in children with autism spectrum disorder. *International Journal of Human-Computer Studies*, *199*, 103486. DOI: 10.1016/j.ijhcs.2025.103486

Farhah, N. S., Wadood, A., Alqarni, A. A., Uddin, M. I., & Aldhyani, T. H. (2025). Enhancing adaptive learning with generative ai for tailored educational support for students with disabilities. *Journal of Disability Research*, *4*(3), 20250012. DOI: 10.57197/JDR-2025-0012

Farrelly, T., & Baker, N. (2023). Generative artificial intelligence: Implications and considerations for higher education practice. *Education Sciences*, *13*(11), 1109. DOI: 10.3390/educsci13111109

Fenta, A. A. (2025). A review on enhancing education with AI: Exploring the potential of ChatGPT, Bard, and generative AI. *Discover Education*, *4*(1), 38. DOI: 10.1007/s44217-025-00426-5

Fernández-Batanero, J. M., Montenegro-Rueda, M., Fernández-Cerero, J., & García-Martínez, I. (2022). Assistive technology for the inclusion of students with disabilities: A systematic review. *Educational Technology Research and Development*, *70*(5), 1911–1930. DOI: 10.1007/s11423-022-10127-7

Ferraz, F., Neves, J., Costa, A., & Vicente, H. (2016). An artificial intelligence approach to dyscalculia. In Kim, K., Wattanapongsakorn, N., & Joukov, N. (Eds.), *Mobile and wireless technologies 2016* (Vol. 391, pp. 221–230). Springer., DOI: 10.1007/978-981-10-1409-3_23

Fitas, R. (2025). Inclusive education with AI: Supporting special needs and tackling language barriers. *AI and Ethics*, *5*(6), 5729–5757. Advance online publication. DOI: 10.1007/s43681-025-00824-3

Fleming, L. (2013). Expanding Learning Opportunities with Transmedia Practices: Inanimate Alice as an Exemplar. *The Journal of Media Literacy Education*, *5*(2), 370–377. https://files.eric.ed.gov/fulltext/EJ1043444.pdf. DOI: 10.23860/jmle-5-2-3

Fletcher-Watson, S., Adams, J., Brook, K., Charman, T., Crane, L., Cusack, J., Leekam, S., Milton, D., Parr, J. R., & Pellicano, E. (2019). Making the future together: Shaping autism research through meaningful participation. *Autism, 23*(4), 943–953. DOI: 10.1177/1362361318786721 PMID: 30095277

Florian, L. (2014). Reimagining special education: Why new approaches are needed. In Florian, L. (Ed.), *The Sage Handbook of Special Education* (2nd ed., pp. 9–19). Sage. DOI: 10.4135/9781446282236.n3

Florian, L. (2014). What counts as evidence of inclusive education? *European Journal of Special Needs Education, 29*(3), 286–294. DOI: 10.1080/08856257.2014.933551

Florian, L., & Black-Hawkins, K. (2011). Exploring inclusive pedagogy. *British Educational Research Journal, 37*(5), 813–828. DOI: 10.1080/01411926.2010.501096

Florian, L., & Spratt, J. (2013). Enacting inclusion: A framework for interrogating inclusive practice. *European Journal of Special Needs Education, 28*(2), 119–135. DOI: 10.1080/08856257.2013.778111

Fokides, E., Atsikpasi, P., Kaimara, P., & Deliyannis, I. (2019). Let players evaluate serious games. Design and validation of the Serious Games Evaluation Scale. *International Computer Games Association – ICGA*. https://doi.org/doi: DOI: 10.3233/ICG-190111

Fokides, E., & Daskalou, M. (2026). Applying and Testing an Extensively Modified UTAUT-2 Model to Examine Pre-Service Teachers' Intention to Use Immersive Virtual Reality in Their Teaching. *Journal of Information Technology Education, 25*, 11. DOI: 10.28945/5752

Forlin, C. (2010). *Teacher education for inclusion: Changing paradigms and innovative approaches*. Routledge. DOI: 10.4324/9780203850879

Fu, B., Hadid, A., & Damer, N. (2025). Generative AI in the context of assistive technologies: Trends, limitations and future directions. *Image and Vision Computing, 154*, 105347. DOI: 10.1016/j.imavis.2024.105347

Fullan, M. (2007). *The new meaning of educational change* (4th ed.). Teachers College Press. https://shorturl.at/K0Pel

Fullan, M. (2011). *The six secrets of change: What the best leaders do to help their organizations survive and thrive*. Jossey-Bass.

Funa, A. A., & Gabay, R. A. E. (2025). Policy guidelines and recommendations on AI use in teaching and learning: A meta-synthesis study. *Social Sciences & Humanities Open, 11*, 101221. DOI: 10.1016/j.ssaho.2024.101221

Gallud, J. A., Carreño, M., Tesoriero, R., Sandoval, A., Lozano, M. D., Durán, I., Penichet, V. M. R., & Cosio, R. (2023). Technology-enhanced and game based learning for children with special needs: A systematic mapping study. *Universal Access in the Information Society*, *22*(1), 227–240. DOI: 10.1007/s10209-021-00824-0 PMID: 34248457

Gamlem, S. M., Johnston, S.-K., Moltudal, S., McGrane, J., & Hopfenbeck, T. N. (2026). Generative AI in initial teacher education: Exploring the alignment of perceptions and experiences of pre-service teachers and their teacher educators. *Teaching and Teacher Education*, *172*, 105382. DOI: 10.1016/j.tate.2026.105382

García-López, I. M., & Trujillo-Liñán, L. (2025, June). Ethical and regulatory challenges of Generative AI in education: a systematic review. In *Frontiers in Education* (Vol. 10, p. 1565938). Frontiers Media SA. https://doi.org/DOI: 10.3389/feduc.2025.1565938

García-López, I. M., González González, C. S., Ramírez-Montoya, M.-S., & Molina-Espinosa, J.-M. (2025). Challenges of implementing ChatGPT on education: Systematic literature review. *International Journal of Educational Research Open*, *8*, 100401. DOI: 10.1016/j.ijedro.2024.100401

Geiger, A., Shpigelman, C.-N., & Feniger-Schaal, R. (2020). The socio-emotional world of adolescents with intellectual disability: A drama therapy-based participatory action research. *The Arts in Psychotherapy*, *70*, 101679. DOI: 10.1016/j.aip.2020.101679

Geng, X., & Yamada, M. (2025). The Role of Dashboards in Augmented-Reality-Based Language Learning: Enhancing Language Learning and Metacognitive Awareness. *SAGE Open*, *15*(2), 1–21. DOI: 10.1177/21582440251341675

Gharaibeh, M., Ayasrah, M. N., & Almulla, A. A. (2025). Supplemental role of ChatGPT in enhancing writing ability for children with dysgraphia in the Arabic language. *Education and Information Technologies*, *30*(15), 21019–21039. DOI: 10.1007/s10639-025-13605-6

Giagazoglou, P., Dampa, A., Alexiadis, A., Lenakakis, A., Dimitropoulou, D., & Magos, K. (2026). From Fairy Tales to Real-Life Safety: An Educational Drama-Based Intervention for Children's Self-Protection Skills. *International Journal of Education & the Arts*, *27*(4). DOI: 10.26209/ijea27n4

Giannakos, M., Azevedo, R., Brusilovsky, P., Cukurova, M., Dimitriadis, Y., Hernandez-Leo, D., Järvelä, S., Mavrikis, M., & Rienties, B. (2025). The promise and challenges of generative AI in education. *Behaviour & Information Technology*, *44*(11), 2518–2544. DOI: 10.1080/0144929X.2024.2394886

Gidiotis, I. (2026). Speculative futures of artificial intelligence in education: A causal layered analysis of education fiction. *Futures, 176*, 103762. DOI: 10.1016/j.futures.2026.103762

Gilbert, T. K. (2024). Generative AI and generative education. *Annals of the New York Academy of Sciences, 1534*(1), 11–14. DOI: 10.1111/nyas.15129 PMID: 38512308

Giri, N., Saini, T., Bhole, K., Bhosale, A., Shetty, T., Subramanyam, A., & Shelke, S. (2020). Detection of dyscalculia using machine learning. In *2020 5th International Conference on Communication and Electronics Systems (ICCES)* (pp. 1–6). IEEE. DOI: 10.1109/ICCES48766.2020.9137871

Goldman, S. R., Carreon, A., & Smith, S. J. (2026). Teaching students with learning disabilities to be prompt engineers. *Intervention in School and Clinic, 61*(3), 142–150. DOI: 10.1177/10534512251387080

Goldman, S. R., Taylor, J., Carreon, A., & Smith, S. J. (2024). Using AI to support special education teacher workload. *Journal of Special Education Technology, 39*(3), 434–447. DOI: 10.1177/01626434241257240

González-Eras, A., Pérez, J., Puerto, E., González, W. E. P., & Aguilar, J. (2025, October). A Reference Framework for the Use of Generative AI in Higher Education. In *2025 LI Latin American Computer Conference (CLEI)* (pp. 1-10). IEEE. https://doi.org/DOI: 10.1109/CLEI67442.2025.11420309

Goodman, S. M., Buehler, E., Clary, P., Coenen, A., Donsbach, A., Horne, T. N., Lahav, M., MacDonald, R., Michaels, R. B., Narayanan, A., Pushkarna, M., Riley, J., Santana, A., Shi, L., Sweeney, R., Weaver, P., Yuan, A., & Morris, M. R. (2024). LaMPost: AI writing assistance for adults with dyslexia using large language models. *Communications of the ACM, 67*(9), 80–89. DOI: 10.1145/3626952

Grandbastien, M., Horbach, A., Jansen, T., & Linden, T. (2026). Special issue editorial: Initial studies on the applications of generative AI in education. *Education and Information Technologies, 1-5*(6), 1787–1791. Advance online publication. DOI: 10.1007/s10639-025-13875-0

Grigorenko, E. L., Compton, D. L., Fuchs, L. S., Wagner, R. K., Willcutt, E. G., & Fletcher, J. M. (2019). Understanding, educating, and supporting children with specific learning disabilities: 50 years of science and practice. *The American Psychologist, 75*(1), 37–51. DOI: 10.1037/amp0000452 PMID: 31081650

Gu, P., Xu, F., Chen, L., Ma, Z., Zhang, M., & Zhang, Y. (2025). Technological affordances and applications of chatbots for conversational skill interventions in autism: A scoping review. *Education and Information Technologies*, *30*(7), 9311–9340. DOI: 10.1007/s10639-024-13191-z

Gupta, P., Mahajan, R., Badhera, U., & Kushwaha, P. S. (2024). Integrating generative AI in management education: A mixed-methods study using social construction of technology theory. *International Journal of Management Education*, *22*(3), 101017. DOI: 10.1016/j.ijme.2024.101017

Han, A., Zhou, X., Cai, Z., Han, S., Ko, R., Corrigan, S., & Peppler, K. A. (2024, May). Teachers, parents, and students' perspectives on integrating generative AI into elementary literacy education. In *Proceedings of the 2024 CHI Conference on Human Factors in Computing Systems* (pp. 1-17). https://doi.org/DOI: 10.1145/3613904.3642438

Han, W., & Wang, T. (2025). From motor skills to digital solutions: Developmental dysgraphia interventions over two decades. *Children (Basel, Switzerland)*, *12*(5), 542. Advance online publication. DOI: 10.3390/children12050542 PMID: 40426721

Hariyanto, H., Kristianingsih, F. X. D., & Maharani, R. (2025). Artificial intelligence in adaptive education: A systematic review of techniques for personalized learning. *Discover Education*, *4*(1), 458. Advance online publication. DOI: 10.1007/s44217-025-00908-6

Harkins-Brown, A. R., Carling, L. Z., & Peloff, D. C. (2025). Artificial intelligence in special education. *Encyclopedia*, *5*(1), 11. Advance online publication. DOI: 10.3390/encyclopedia5010011

Haroud, S., & Saqri, N. (2025). Generative AI in higher education: Teachers' and students' perspectives on support, replacement, and digital literacy. *Education Sciences*, *15*(4), 396. DOI: 10.3390/educsci15040396

Harris, A., & Jones, M. (2019). Teacher leadership and educational change. *School Leadership & Management*, *39*(2), 123–126. DOI: 10.1080/13632434.2019.1574964

Hattie, J., & Timperley, H. (2007). The power of feedback. *Review of Educational Research*, *77*(1), 81–112. DOI: 10.3102/003465430298487

Hautala, J., Ronimus, M., & Junttila, E. (2022). Readers' Theater Projects for Special Education: A Randomized Controlled Study. *Scandinavian Journal of Educational Research*, *67*(5), 663–678. DOI: 10.1080/00313831.2022.2042846

Hellenic Republic. (2008). *Law 3699/2008: Special education and training of people with disabilities or special educational needs and other provisions* (Government Gazette A 199/02-10-2008).Holmes, W., & Tuomi, I. (2022). State of the art and practice in AI in education. *European Journal of Education, 57*(4), 542–570. DOI: 10.1111/ejed.12533

Hetland, L., Winner, E., Veenema, S., & Sheridan, K. M. (2013). *Studio thinking 2: The real benefits of visual arts education* (2nd ed.). Teachers College Press.

Hınız, G. (2026). A year of generative AI in English language teaching and learning- A case study. *Journal of Research on Technology in Education, 58*(2), 291–311. DOI: 10.1080/15391523.2024.2404132

Holmes, W., Bialik, M., & Fadel, C. (2019). *Artificial intelligence in education: Promises and implications for teaching and learning.* Center for Curriculum Redesign. https://curriculumredesign.org/our-work/artificial-intelligence-in-education/

Holmes, W., Bialik, M., & Fadel, C. (2019). *Artificial intelligence in education: Promises and implications for teaching and learning.* Center for Curriculum Redesign. Retrieved May 12, 2026, from https://curriculumredesign.org/wp-content/uploads/AIED-Book-Excerpt-CCR.pdf

Holmes, W., Bialik, M., & Fadel, C. (2019). *Artificial intelligence in education: Promises and implications for teaching and learning.* Center for Curriculum Redesign.

Holmes, W., Bialik, M., & Fadel, C. (2023). Artificial intelligence in education. In Stückelberger, C., & Duggal, P. (Eds.), *Data ethics: Building trust: How digital technologies can serve humanity* (pp. 621–653). Globethics Publications., DOI: 10.58863/20.500.12424/4276068

Holmes, W., Porayska-Pomsta, K., Holstein, K., Sutherland, E., Baker, T., Buckingham Shum, S., Santos, O. C., Rodrigo, M. T., Cukurova, M., Bittencourt, I. I., & Koedinger, K. R. (2019). Ethics of AI in education: Towards a community-wide agenda. *International Journal of Artificial Intelligence in Education, 32*(3), 504–526. DOI: 10.1007/s40593-021-00239-1

Hopcan, S., Polat, E., Ozturk, M. E., & Ozturk, L. (2023). Artificial intelligence in special education: A systematic review. *Interactive Learning Environments, 31*(10), 7335–7353. DOI: 10.1080/10494820.2022.2067186

Howard, S. K., Chan, A., Mozejko, A., & Caputi, P. (2021). Technology practices: Confirmatory factor analysis and exploration of teachers' technology integration in subject areas. *Computers & Education, 90*, 1–12. DOI: 10.1016/j.compedu.2015.09.008

Hu, Z. (2025). A method for generating personalized learning content based on AIGC. *Sustainable Futures : An Applied Journal of Technology, Environment and Society, 10*, 101331. DOI: 10.1016/j.sftr.2025.101331

Întorsureanu, I., Oprea, S. V., Bâra, A., & Vespan, D. (2025). Generative AI in education: Perspectives through an academic lens. *Electronics (Basel), 14*(5), 1053. DOI: 10.3390/electronics14051053

ISTE. (2017). *ISTE standards for educators*. International Society for Technology in Education. https://www.iste.org/standards/educators

Jadhav, D., Chettri, S. K., Tripathy, A. K., & Saikia, M. J. (2025). A technology-driven assistive learning tool and framework for personalized dyscalculia interventions. *European Journal of Investigation in Health, Psychology and Education, 15*(5), 85. Advance online publication. DOI: 10.3390/ejihpe15050085 PMID: 40422314

Jafarian, N. R., & Kramer, A.-W. (2025). AI-assisted audio-learning improves academic achievement through motivation and reading engagement. *Computers and Education: Artificial Intelligence, 8*, 100357. DOI: 10.1016/j.caeai.2024.100357

Jamal Eddine, R., Gide, E., & Al-Sabbagh, A. (2026). Systematised evidence mapping of generative artificial intelligence (GenAI) and digital divide phenomena in higher education. *Discover Computing, 29*(1), 157. DOI: 10.1007/s10791-026-10044-w

Jambunathan, S. (2025). Integrating artificial intelligence into early childhood teacher education. *Contemporary Issues in Early Childhood, 14639491251340141*, 14639491251340141. DOI: 10.1177/14639491251340141

Jan, T. G., & Khan, S. M. (2023). A systematic review of research dimensions towards dyslexia screening using machine learning. *Journal of The Institution of Engineers (India): Series B, 104*(2), 465–478. DOI: 10.1007/s40031-023-00853-8

Jauhiainen, J. S., & Garagorry Guerra, A. (2024, November). Generative AI and education: dynamic personalization of pupils' school learning material with ChatGPT. In *Frontiers in Education* (Vol. 9, p. 1288723). Frontiers Media SA. https://doi.org/ DOI: 10.3389/feduc.2024.1288723

Jauhiainen, J. S., & Guerra, A. G. (2023). Generative AI and ChatGPT in school children's education: Evidence from a school lesson. *Sustainability (Basel), 15*(18), 14025. DOI: 10.3390/su151814025

Javed, S., Muniandy, M., Lee, C. K., & Husni, H. (2024). Enhancing teaching and learning for pupils with dyslexia: A comprehensive review of technological and non-technological interventions. *Education and Information Technologies, 29*(8), 9607–9643. DOI: 10.1007/s10639-023-12195-5

Jin, Y., Yang, K., Yan, L., Echeverría, V., Zhao, L., Milesi, M., Fan, J., Li, X., Gašević, D., & Martínez-Maldonado, R. (2024). Chatting with a learning analytics dashboard: The role of generative AI literacy on learner interaction. DOI: 10.48550/arxiv.2411.15597

Jonsson, A., & Svingby, G. (2007). The use of scoring rubrics: Reliability, validity and educational consequences. *Educational Research Review*, *2*(2), 130–144. DOI: 10.1016/j.edurev.2007.05.002

Jukiewicz, M. (2025, August). How generative artificial intelligence transforms teaching and influences student wellbeing in future education. In *Frontiers in education* (Vol. 10, p. 1594572). Frontiers., DOI: 10.3389/feduc.2025.1594572

Kaimara, P. (2026). Digital Transformation Stands Alongside Inclusive Education: Lessons Learned from a Project Called "Waking Up in the Morning". *Technology. Knowledge and Learning*, *31*(1), 51–77. DOI: 10.1007/s10758-023-09667-5

Kaimara, P., Deliyannis, I., Oikonomou, A., Fokides, E., & Miliotis, G. (2021). An innovative transmedia-based game development method for inclusive education. *Digital Culture & Education*, *13*(2), 129–162. https://www.digitalcultureandeducation.com/volume-13-2

Kaimara, P., Miliotis, G., Deliyannis, I., Fokides, E., Oikonomou, A., Papadopoulou, A., & Floros, A. (2019). Waking-up in the morning: A gamified simulation in the context of learning activities of daily living. *Technology and Disability*, *31*(s1), 195–198. DOI: 10.3233/TAD-190015

Kaimara, P., Oikonomou, A., & Deliyannis, I. (2022). Could virtual reality applications pose real risks to children and adolescents? A systematic review of ethical issues and concerns. *Virtual Reality (Waltham Cross)*, *26*(2), 697–735. DOI: 10.1007/s10055-021-00563-w PMID: 34366688

Kaimara, P., Papadopoulos, S. P., Poulimenou, S. M., Garneli, V., Fokides, E., & Deliyannis, I. (2026). Bilingual Language Development for Atypically Developing Students Supported by Augmented Reality and Museum Kits. In Katsarou, D., & Dosi, I. (Eds.), *Optimizing Bilingual Development in Typical and Atypical Children: Language Acquisition, Use, and Interventions* (pp. 337–368). IGI Global Scientific Publishing., DOI: 10.4018/979-8-3373-1752-6.ch013

Kallio, H., Pietilä, A.-M., Johnson, M., & Kangasniemi, M. (2016). Systematic methodological review: Developing a framework for a qualitative semi-structured interview guide. *Journal of Advanced Nursing*, *72*(12), 2954–2965. DOI: 10.1111/jan.13031 PMID: 27221824

Kaltsouni, P. (2021). Inclusive education in GREECE. *Social Work Education, 8*(3), 385–394. DOI: 10.25128/2520-6230.21.3.7

Karakose, T., & Tülübaş, T. (2023). How Can ChatGPT Facilitate Teaching and Learning: Implications for Contemporary Education. *Educational Process International Journal, 12*(4). DOI: 10.22521/edupij.2023.124.1

Karaolis, O. (2023). Not just a toy: Puppets for autistic teenagers. *Youth, 3*(4), 1174–1182. DOI: 10.3390/youth3040074

Kasneci, E., Sessler, K., Küchemann, S., Bannert, M., Dementieva, D., Fischer, F., Gasser, U., Groh, G., Günnemann, S., Hüllermeier, E., Krusche, S., Kutyniok, G., Michaeli, T., Nerdel, C., Pfeffer, J., Poquet, O., Sailer, M., Schmidt, A., Seidel, T., & Kasneci, G. (2023). ChatGPT for good? On opportunities and challenges of large language models for education. *Learning and Individual Differences, 103*, 102274. DOI: 10.1016/j.lindif.2023.102274

Katsarou, D. V., Mantsos, E., Papadopoulou, S., Sofologi, M., Efthymiou, E., Vasileiou, I., Megari, K., Theodoratou, M., & Kougioumtzis, G. A. (2025). Exploring AI technology in grammar performance testing for children with learning disabilities. *Education Sciences, 15*(3), 351. DOI: 10.3390/educsci15030351

Kayyali, M. (2025). Generative AI and Education: Transforming Teaching and Learning Through Collaborative Intelligence. In *Humans and Generative AI Tools for Collaborative Intelligence* (pp. 25-52). IGI Global Scientific Publishing. https://doi.org/DOI: 10.4018/979-8-3693-8332-2.ch002

Kejani, M., & Raeisi, Z. (2022). The effect of drama therapy on working memory and its components in primary school children with ADHD. *Current Psychology (New Brunswick, N.J.), 41*(1), 417–426. DOI: 10.1007/s12144-019-00564-8

Khlaif, Z. N., Alshakhshir, R., Hamamra, B., & Joma, A. (2025). Reimagining inclusive education: The assistive power of generative AI in promoting accessibility and equity. *British Journal of Visual Impairment, 02646196251382469*, 02646196251382469. DOI: 10.1177/02646196251382469

Kim, J. H., Moldavan, A. M., Terry, R., & Massey, C. C. (2025). Enhancing Student Engagement with Generative AI. In *Transformative AI Practices for Personalized Learning Strategies* (pp. 69–106). IGI Global Scientific Publishing., DOI: 10.4018/979-8-3693-8744-3.ch004

Kırcalı, M., & Cesur, K. (2024). Development and validation of a cultural and linguistic diversity scale to measure pre-service EFL teachers' self-efficacy beliefs. *SAGE Open*, *14*(1), 21582440241236589. Advance online publication. DOI: 10.1177/21582440241236589

Kladaki, M., Kostas, A., & Alexopoulos, P. (2025). Exploring teachers' beliefs about ChatGPT in arts education. *Education Sciences*, *15*(7), 795. DOI: 10.3390/educsci15070795

Kloos, C. D., Alario-Hoyos, C., Estévez-Ayres, I., Callejo-Pinardo, P., Hombrados-Herrera, M. A., Muñoz-Merino, P. J., & Ibáñez, M. B. (2024, May). How can Generative AI support education? In *2024 IEEE Global Engineering Education Conference (EDUCON)* (pp. 1-7). IEEE. https://doi.org/DOI: 10.1109/EDUCON60312.2024.10578716

Kmet, L. M., Cook, L. S., & Lee, R. C. (2004). *Standard quality assessment criteria for evaluating primary research papers from a variety of fields*. Alberta Heritage Foundation for Medical Research. https://doi.org/DOI: 10.7939/R37M04F16

Knight, C. (2018). What is dyslexia? An exploration of the relationship between teachers' understandings of dyslexia and their training experiences. *Dyslexia (Chichester, England)*, *24*(3), 207–219. DOI: 10.1002/dys.1593 PMID: 30019501

Kohnke, L., Moorhouse, B. L., & Zou, D. (2023). ChatGPT for education and research: A review of benefits and risks. *RELC Journal*, *54*(2), 537–548. DOI: 10.1177/00336882231162868

Koltsida, M., & Lenakakis, A. (2017). Contemporary performance by and for those with disabilities: The case of Greece. *Research in Drama Education*, *22*(3), 339–344. DOI: 10.1080/13569783.2017.1326809

Komis, V. (2014). *Didactics of Informatics and ICT*. Klidarithmos. (in Greek)

Koo, T. K., & Mae, M. Y. (2016). A guideline of selecting and reporting intraclass correlation coefficients for reliability research. *Journal of Chiropractic Medicine*, *15*(2), 155–163. DOI: 10.1016/j.jcm.2016.02.012 PMID: 27330520

Kostas, A., Paraschou, V., Spanos, D., Tzortzoglou, F., & Sofos, A. (2025). AI and ChatGPT in higher education: Greek students' perceived practices, benefits, and challenges. *Education Sciences*, *15*(5), 605. DOI: 10.3390/educsci15050605

Kouo, J., Feng, J. H., & Jiao, E. (2025, June). Creating a Dataset of Autistic Individuals to Recommend Evidence-Based Practices through Generative Artificial Intelligence. In *2025 IEEE 13th International Conference on Healthcare Informatics (ICHI)* (pp. 126-136). IEEE. https://doi.org/DOI: 10.1109/ICHI64645.2025.00023

Kress, G. (2010). *Multimodality: A social semiotic approach to contemporary communication*. Routledge.

Krishnan, U. C. A., Lathabai, H. H., Kanjilal, R., Raman, R., & Nedungadi, P. (2026). Generative AI in disability-inclusive learning: A bibliometric and systematic literature analysis. *Disability and Rehabilitation. Assistive Technology*, •••, 1–30. DOI: 10.1080/17483107.2026.2653073 PMID: 41973863

Kumar, T., & Kait, R., Ankita, & Malik, A. (2023, September). The role of generative artificial intelligence (GAI) in Education: a detailed review for enhanced learning experiences. In *International conference on entrepreneurship, innovation, and leadership* (pp. 195-207). Singapore: Springer Nature Singapore. https://doi.org/DOI: 10.1007/978-981-97-1682-1_17

Kumm, A. J., Viljoen, M., & de Vries, P. J. (2022). The digital divide in technologies for autism: Feasibility considerations for low- and middle-income countries. *Journal of Autism and Developmental Disorders*, *52*(6), 2300–2313. DOI: 10.1007/s10803-021-05084-8 PMID: 34121159

Kunhoth, J., Al-Maadeed, S., Kunhoth, S., Akbari, Y., & Saleh, M. (2024). Automated systems for diagnosis of dysgraphia in children: A survey and novel framework. *International Journal on Document Analysis and Recognition*, *27*(3), 707–735. DOI: 10.1007/s10032-024-00464-z

Kusumaningsih, D., Wicaksana, M. F., Rustinar, E., Saputra, A. D., Maalikih, M. D., Nurhana, M., & Naimah, M. (2026). AI applications in education: Technological innovations for overcoming dyslexia and dysgraphia challenges in students. *Multidisciplinary Reviews*, *9*(8), 2026340. DOI: 10.31893/multirev.2026340

Lalar, S., Kumar, T., Kumar, R., & Kumar, S. (2025). Unlocking Potential: The Role of Artificial Intelligence in Revolutionizing Special Education for Inclusive Learning. In *Impacts of Generative AI on the Future of Research and Education* (pp. 201-232). IGI Global Scientific Publishing. https://doi.org/DOI: 10.4018/979-8-3693-0884-4.ch009

Lang, R., McLay, L., & Rispoli, M. (2023). Advanced language models: Potential to improve augmentative and alternative communication for individuals with intellectual and developmental disabilities. *Advances in Neurodevelopmental Disorders*, *7*(3), 481–484. DOI: 10.1007/s41252-023-00350-5

Lan, L., Li, K., & Li, D. (2025). Exploring the application of AI in the education of children with autism: A public health perspective. *Frontiers in Psychiatry*, *15*, 1521926. DOI: 10.3389/fpsyt.2024.1521926 PMID: 39935626

Layachi, A., Douglas, G., & Reraki, M. (2024). Drama-based intervention to support social inclusion: Evaluation of an approach to include students with ADHD in Algeria. *Educational Psychology in Practice*, *40*(1), 36–58. DOI: 10.1080/02667363.2023.2258780

Lee, I.-J., & Wang, W.-Z. (2025). Applying theatre-based role-playing combined with AR and VR game strategies to enhance imagination and symbolic play skills in children with autism spectrum disorder. *Universal Access in the Information Society*, *24*(3), 2531–2552. DOI: 10.1007/s10209-025-01206-6

Leon, M. (2026). Generative AI as a general-purpose technology: Foundations, applications, and labor market implications. *Big Data and Cognitive Computing*, *10*(3), 69. Advance online publication. DOI: 10.3390/bdcc10030069

Levac, D., Colquhoun, H., & O'Brien, K. K. (2010). Scoping studies: Advancing the methodology. *Implementation Science : IS*, *5*(1), 69. DOI: 10.1186/1748-5908-5-69 PMID: 20854677

Lewis, K. D. (2025). Preparing gifted educators for generative AI: The essential role of educator preparation programs. *Journal of Advanced Academics*, *36*(4), 852–878. DOI: 10.1177/1932202X251356322

Li, D., & Samah, N. A. (2025). Generative AI in inclusive classrooms: Enhancing social interactions, personalized learning, and metacognitive skills. *Sodobna Pedagogika*, *76*(2), 155–176. DOI: 10.63384/spB52z813a

Li, H.-J., Huang, Q.-R., Wen, L.-P., Chen, W., & Xu, Z.-Z. (2025). Generative artificial intelligence supported programming learning: Learning effectiveness and core competence. *SAGE Open*, *15*(3), 21582440251377986. DOI: 10.1177/21582440251377986

Lin, X., Cui, H., & Zhu, X. (2026). Chinese special education teachers' experiences with generative AI: Differences in perceptions, use, and tam pathways for IEP writing and lesson planning. *Journal of Special Education Technology*, *01626434261435251*, 01626434261435251. DOI: 10.1177/01626434261435251

Lin, X., Han, X., & Qiu, J. (2025, April). Generative AI in Special Education: Teachers' Insights on Instructional Enrichment vs. Accommodations. In *Proceedings of the Extended Abstracts of the CHI Conference on Human Factors in Computing Systems* (pp. 1-6). https://doi.org/DOI: 10.1145/3706599.3719972

Liu, J., Wang, C., Liu, Z., Gao, M., Xu, Y., Chen, J., & Cheng, Y. (2024). A bibliometric analysis of generative AI in education: Current status and development. *Asia Pacific Journal of Education*, *44*(1), 156–175. DOI: 10.1080/02188791.2024.2305170

Liu, L., Liu, W., Luo, Z., & Yue, L. (2025). Scaffolds, screens, and readiness: How teacher-guided AI lifts special-education students into conversational agents. *Acta Psychologica, 261*, 105889. DOI: 10.1016/j.actpsy.2025.105889 PMID: 41192401

Liu, P., Yuan, W., Fu, J., Jiang, Z., Hayashi, H., & Neubig, G. (2022). Pre-train, prompt, and predict: A systematic survey of prompting methods in natural language processing. *ACM Computing Surveys, 55*(9), 1–35. DOI: 10.1145/3560815

Liu, X., Yang, J., Zhao, W., & Wang, T. (2026). Generative Artificial Intelligence Self-Efficacy and Learning Engagement Among Special Education Teacher Trainees: A Moderated Mediation Model. *Behavioral Sciences (Basel, Switzerland), 16*(4), 488. DOI: 10.3390/bs16040488 PMID: 42073851

Lo, C. K. (2023). What Is the Impact of ChatGPT on Education? A Rapid Review of the Literature. *Education Sciences, 13*(4), 410. DOI: 10.3390/educsci13040410

Lo, N., Wong, A., & Chan, S. (2025). The impact of generative AI on essay revisions and student engagement. *Computers and Education Open, 9*, 100249. DOI: 10.1016/j.caeo.2025.100249

Long, D., & Magerko, B. (2020). What Is AI Literacy? Competencies and Design Considerations. In Proceedings of the 2020 CHI *Conference on Human Factors in Computing Systems* (pp. 1-16). Association for Computing Machinery._DOI: 10.1145/3313831.3376727

Lopez-Gazpio, I. (2025). Integrating large language models into accessible and inclusive education: Access democratization and individualized learning enhancement supported by generative artificial intelligence. *Information (Basel), 16*(6), 473. DOI: 10.3390/info16060473

Lorenzo, G., & Lorenzo-Lledó, A. (2024). The use of artificial intelligence for detecting the duration of autistic students' emotions in social interaction with the NAO robot: A case study. *International Journal of Information Technology : an Official Journal of Bharati Vidyapeeth's Institute of Computer Applications and Management, 16*(2), 625–631. DOI: 10.1007/s41870-023-01682-0

Luckin, R., Holmes, W., Griffiths, M., & Forcier, L. B. (2016). *Intelligence unleashed: An argument for AI in education.* Pearson. https://static.googleusercontent.com/media/edu.google.com/en//pdfs/Intelligence-Unleashed-Publication.pdf

Luckin, R., Holmes, W., Griffiths, M., & Forcier, L. B. (2016). *Intelligence unleashed: An argument for AI in education.* Pearson. https://www.pearson.com/content/dam/one-dot-com/one-dot-com/global/Files/about-pearson/innovation/open-ideas/Intelligence-Unleashed-Publication.pdf

Luckin, R. (2018). *Machine learning and human intelligence: The future of education for the 21st century*. UCL Institute of Education Press.

Luckin, R., Holmes, W., Griffiths, M., & Forcier, L. B. (2016). *Intelligence unleashed: An argument for AI in education*. Pearson Education.

Lund, B. D., & Wang, T. (2023). Chatting about ChatGPT: How may AI and GPT impact academia and libraries? *Library Hi Tech News*, *40*(3), 26–29. DOI: 10.1108/LHTN-01-2023-0009

MacArthur, C. A. (2009). Reflections on research on writing and technology for struggling writers. *Learning Disabilities Research & Practice*, *24*(2), 93–103. DOI: 10.1111/j.1540-5826.2009.00283.x

Maleki, A. (2026). "We cannot incorporate them because ...": Challenges of integrating generative AI into online formative assessments in EFL contexts. *Computers in Human Behavior Reports*, *21*, 100934. DOI: 10.1016/j.chbr.2026.100934

Mao, Y., Ying, F., & Liu, K. (2025). Exploring the impact of AI painting tools on graphic design education for hearing-impaired students. In Figueroa, P., Di Iorio, A., Guzman del Rio, D., Gonzalez Clua, E. W., & Cuevas Rodriguez, L. (Eds.), Lecture Notes in Computer Science: Vol. 15192. *Entertainment computing – ICEC 2024*. Springer., DOI: 10.1007/978-3-031-74353-5_34

Marino, M. T., Vasquez, E., Dieker, L., Basham, J., & Blackorby, J. (2023). The future of artificial intelligence in special education technology. *Journal of Special Education Technology*, *38*(3), 404–416. DOI: 10.1177/01626434231165977

Marrauwi, M., Sajak, A. A. B., & Yafi, E. (2023). Behavior analysis of people with autism using Internet of Things - A conceptual study. *Journal of Engineering Science and Technology, ICIST2022, 18*(1), 90-102.

Martínez, P., Ramos, A., & Moreno, L. (2024). Exploring large language models to generate easy to read content. *Frontiers of Computer Science*, *6*, 1394705. Advance online publication. DOI: 10.3389/fcomp.2024.1394705

Marwala, T. (2023, June 22). *Algorithm bias: Synthetic data should be an option of last resort when training AI systems*. United Nations University. https://unu.edu/article/algorithm-bias-synthetic-data-should-be-option-last-resort-when-training-ai-systems

Marzano, D. (2025). Generative Artificial Intelligence (GAI) in Teaching and Learning Processes at the K-12 Level: A Systematic Review: D. Marzano. *Technology, Knowledge and Learning*, 1-41. https://doi.org/DOI: 10.1007/s10758-025-09853-7

Mastrothanasis, K., Kladaki, M., & Alexopoulos, P. (2025a). *ChatGPT and the digital transformation of arts-based general and special education*. Symmetria Publications. [in Greek]

Mastrothanasis, K., Kladaki, M., & Alexopoulos, P. (2025b). *Developing soft skills in arts education through artificial intelligence*. Grigoris Publications. [in Greek]

Mastrothanasis, K., Gkontelos, A., Kladaki, M., & Papouli, E. (2025). Examining puppetry's contribution to the learning, social and therapeutic support of students with complex educational and psychosocial needs in special school settings: A phenomenological study. *Disabilities*, *5*(3), 67. DOI: 10.3390/disabilities5030067

Mastrothanasis, K., Kladaki, M., & Alexopoulos, P. (2026). Artificial Intelligence and Rhetorical Art: Argumentative Debate with ChatGPT. [IJMECS]. *International Journal of Modern Education and Computer Science*, *18*(1), 48–60. DOI: 10.5815/ijmecs.2026.01.03

Mastrothanasis, K., Kladaki, M., & Andreou, A. (2023). A systematic review and meta-analysis of the Readers' Theatre impact on the development of reading skills. *International Journal of Educational Research Open*, *4*, 100243. DOI: 10.1016/j.ijedro.2023.100243

Mastrothanasis, K., Zervoudakis, K., & Kladaki, M. (2024). An application of Computational Intelligence in group formation for digital drama education. *Iran Journal of Computer Science*, *7*(3), 551–563. DOI: 10.1007/s42044-024-00186-9

Matos, T., Santos, W., Zdravevski, E., Coelho, P. J., Pires, I. M., & Madeira, F. (2025). A systematic review of artificial intelligence applications in education: Emerging trends and challenges. *Decision Analytics Journal*, *15*, 100571. DOI: 10.1016/j.dajour.2025.100571

Mayer, R. E. (2009). *Multimedia Learning* (2nd ed.). Cambridge University Press., DOI: 10.1017/CBO9780511811678

McCloskey, M., & Rapp, B. (2017). *Developmental dysgraphia: Theoretical and clinical advances*. Routledge.

McGrew, J., Ruble, L., Cormier, C. J., & Dueber, D. (2023). Special educators' mental health and burnout: A comparison of general and teacher specific risk factors. *Teaching and Teacher Education*, *132*, 104209. DOI: 10.1016/j.tate.2023.104209

McLennan, H., Aberdein, R., Saggers, B., & Gillett-Swan, J. (2025). Neurodiversity: A scoping review of empirical research. *Neurodiversity*, *3*, 27546330251337874. DOI: 10.1177/27546330251337874

Medina, R., Bouhaben, J., de Ramón, I., Cuesta, P., Antón-Toro, L., Pacios, J., Quintero, J., Ramos-Quiroga, J. A., & Maestú, F. (2021). Electrophysiological brain changes associated with cognitive improvement in a pediatric attention deficit hyperactivity disorder digital artificial intelligence-driven intervention: Randomized controlled trial. *Journal of Medical Internet Research, 23*(11), e25466. DOI: 10.2196/25466 PMID: 34842533

Meenakshi, M. (2024). Leveraging AI technologies for personalized learning support in dyslexic students. *International Journal for Research in Applied Science and Engineering Technology, 12*(12), 2192–2198. DOI: 10.22214/ijraset.2024.65734

Melanou, C., & Beege, M. (2026). Scaffolding Generative AI as a Tutor: A Quasi-Experimental Study of Learning Outcomes and Motivational, Cognitive and Metacognitive Processes. *Education Sciences, 16*(4), 651. DOI: 10.3390/educsci16040651

Melo-López, V.-A., Basantes-Andrade, A., Gudiño-Mejía, C.-B., & Hernández-Martínez, E. (2025). The impact of artificial intelligence on inclusive education: A systematic review. *Education Sciences, 15*(5), 539. Advance online publication. DOI: 10.3390/educsci15050539

Melzer, S., Asselborn, T., & Möller, R. (2025). Generative AI for interactive learning in education. *Datenbank-Spektrum: Zeitschrift fur Datenbanktechnologie: Organ der Fachgruppe Datenbanken der Gesellschaft fur Informatik e.V, 25*(2), 87–93. Advance online publication. DOI: 10.1007/s13222-025-00507-7

Mertler, C. A. (2001). Designing scoring rubrics for your classroom. *Practical Assessment, Research & Evaluation, 7*(25). Advance online publication. DOI: 10.7275/gcy8-0w24

Meyer, A., Rose, D. H., & Gordon, D. (2014). *Universal design for learning: Theory and practice*. CAST Professional Publishing.

Miao, F., & Cukurova, M. (2023). *AI competency framework for educators*. Publications UNESCO., DOI: 10.54675/ZJTE2084

Miao, F., Holmes, W., Huang, R., & Zhang, H. (2021). *AI and education: A guidance for policymakers*. UNESCO Publishing. DOI: 10.54675/PCSP7350

Michalsky, T. (2024). Metacognitive scaffolding for preservice teachers' self-regulated design of higher order thinking tasks. *Heliyon, 10*(2), e24280. DOI: 10.1016/j.heliyon.2024.e24280 PMID: 38293459

Michel-Villarreal, R., Vilalta-Perdomo, E., Salinas-Navarro, D. E., Thierry-Aguilera, R., & Gerardou, F. S. (2023). Challenges and opportunities of generative AI for higher education as explained by ChatGPT. *Education Sciences, 13*(9), 856. DOI: 10.3390/educsci13090856

Mikhailova, T., & Cesur, K. (2025). Enhancing global awareness and intercultural competence in English language teacher education. In Bafralı, G. (Ed.), *Challenges in teacher education* (pp. 235–266). IGI Global. DOI: 10.4018/979-8-3693-7342-2.ch008

Mirea, C. M., Bologa, R., Toma, A., Clim, A., Plăcintă, D. D., & Bobocea, A. (2025). Transforming learning with generative AI: From student perceptions to the design of an educational solution. *Applied Sciences (Basel, Switzerland), 15*(10), 5785. DOI: 10.3390/app15105785

Mishra, P., Margerum-Leys, J., Trainin, G., Hill-Jackson, V., Bobley, L., Bedesem, P. L., Williams, J. A.III, & Craig, C. J. (2025). Teacher education in the age of generative artificial intelligence: Introducing the special issue. *Journal of Teacher Education, 76*(3), 225–229. DOI: 10.1177/00224871251324713

Mitchell, D. (2014). *What really works in special and inclusive education: Using evidence-based teaching strategies* (2nd ed.). Routledge. DOI: 10.4324/9780203105313

Mitchell, M., Wu, S., Zaldivar, A., Barnes, P., Vasserman, L., Hutchinson, B., Spitzer, E., Raji, I. D., & Gebru, T. (2019). Model cards for model reporting. *Proceedings of the Conference on Fairness, Accountability, and Transparency (FAT* '19)* (pp. 220–229). ACM. DOI: 10.1145/3287560.3287596

Mittal, U., Sai, S., Chamola, V., & Sangwan, D. (2024). A comprehensive review on generative AI for education. *IEEE Access : Practical Innovations, Open Solutions, 12*, 142733–142759. DOI: 10.1109/ACCESS.2024.3468368

Mohamadi Dolatabad, M., Rezapour Mirsaleh, Y., & Choobforoushzadeh, A. (2023). The effectiveness of dramatherapy on the aggression of children with ADHD diagnosis. *Journal of Psychology of Exceptional Individuals, 13*(50), 101–128. DOI: 10.22054/JPE.2023.68260.2461

Mohamed Mokmin, N. A., & Rassy, R. P. (2024). Review of the trends in the use of augmented reality technology for students with disabilities when learning physical education. *Education and Information Technologies, 29*(2), 1251–1277. DOI: 10.1007/s10639-022-11550-2

Mojahed, A., Zaheri, Y., & Firoozkoohi Moqaddam, M. (2021). Effectiveness of group psychodrama on aggression and social anxiety of children with attention-deficit/hyperactivity disorder: A randomized clinical trial. *The Arts in Psychotherapy*, *73*, 101756. DOI: 10.1016/j.aip.2021.101756

Mollick, E. R., & Mollick, L. (2023). *Assigning AI: Seven approaches for students, with prompts. SSRN*. DOI: 10.2139/ssrn.4475995

Morciano, G., Alcalde Llergo, J. M., Zingoni, A., Yeguas Bolívar, E., Taborri, J., & Calabrò, G. (2024). Use of recommendation models to provide support to dyslexic students. *Expert Systems with Applications*, *249*, 123738. DOI: 10.1016/j.eswa.2024.123738

Mpella, M., & Evaggelinou, C. (2018). Does theatrical play promote social skills development in students with autism? A systematic review of the methods and measures employed in the literature. *Preschool and Primary Education*, *6*(2), 96–118. DOI: 10.12681/ppej.16135

Mpella, M., Evaggelinou, C., Koidou, E., & Tsigilis, N. (2019). The Effects of a Theatrical Play Programme on Social Skills Development for Young Children with Autism Spectrum Disorders. *International Journal of Special Education*, *33*(4), 828–845.

Murchan, D., & Shiel, G. (2023). Understanding and applying assessment in education. *Sage (Atlanta, Ga.)*. Advance online publication. DOI: 10.4135/9781529609332

Mutawa, A. M., Al Mudhahkah, H. M., Al-Huwais, A., Al-Khaldi, N., Al-Otaibi, R., & Al-Ansari, A. (2023). Augmenting mobile app with NAO robot for autism education. *Machines (Basel)*, *11*(8), 833. DOI: 10.3390/machines11080833

Myrie, D. N., Dowd, N. T., & Latiker, M. D. (2024). Addressing the shortage of special education teachers of color: Implications for teacher education programs and K-12 systems. *Social Sciences (Basel, Switzerland)*, *13*(11), 622. DOI: 10.3390/socsci13110622

Naatz, A. J., & Ruppar, A. (2026). Special education teachers' use of generative artificial intelligence (AI): An exploratory survey of frequency and factors influencing adoption. *Journal of Special Education Technology*, *41*(2), 227–239. DOI: 10.1177/01626434251379800

Najeeb, P., & Quadt, L. (2024). Autistic well-being: A scoping review of scientific studies from a neurodiversity-affirmative perspective. *Neurodiversity*, *2*, 27546330241233088. DOI: 10.1177/27546330241233088

Nazaretsky, T., Ariely, M., Cukurova, M., & Alexandron, G. (2022). Teachers' trust in AI-powered educational technology and a professional development program to improve it. *British Journal of Educational Technology*, *53*(4), 914–931. DOI: 10.1111/bjet.13232

Nedungadi, P., Tang, K. Y., & Raman, R. (2024). The transformative power of generative artificial intelligence for achieving the sustainable development goal of quality education. *Sustainability (Basel)*, *16*(22), 9779. DOI: 10.3390/su16229779

Newbutt, N., Bradley, R., & Conley, I. (2020). Using virtual reality head-mounted displays in schools with autistic children: Views, experiences, and future directions. *Cyberpsychology, Behavior, and Social Networking*, *23*(1), 23–33. DOI: 10.1089/cyber.2019.0206 PMID: 31502866

Ng, D. T. K., Chan, E. K. C., & Lo, C. K. (2025). Opportunities, challenges and school strategies for integrating generative AI in education. *Computers and Education: Artificial Intelligence*, *8*, 100373. DOI: 10.1016/j.caeai.2025.100373

Ng, D. T. K., Leung, J. K. L., Chu, K. W. S., & Qiao, M. S. (2021). AI Literacy: Definition, Teaching, Evaluation and Ethical Issues. *Proceedings of the Association for Information Science and Technology*, *58*(1), 504–509. DOI: 10.1002/pra2.487

Nickl, M., Sommerhoff, D., Radkowitsch, A., Huber, S., Bauer, E., Ufer, S., Plass, J. L., & Seidel, T. (2024). Effects of real-time adaptivity of scaffolding. *Learning and Instruction*, *94*, 101994. DOI: 10.1016/j.learninstruc.2024.101994

Nikolopoulou, K. (2025). Child-centered integration of generative AI in early learning: Balancing promises and challenges. *AI. Brain and Child*, *1*(1), 21. DOI: 10.1007/s44436-025-00023-1

Noble, S. U. (2018). *Algorithms of oppression: How search engines reinforce racism*. NYU Press., DOI: 10.18574/nyu/9781479833641.001.0001

Noroozi, O., Soleimani, S., Farrokhnia, M., & Banihashem, S. K. (2024). Generative AI in Education: Pedagogical, Theoretical, and Methodological Perspectives. *International Journal of Technology in Education*, *7*(3), 373–385. DOI: 10.46328/ijte.845

Nussbaum, M., & Bekerman, Z. (2025). Advancing holistic educational goals through generative language-based technologies. *Learning and Individual Differences*, *117*, 102600. DOI: 10.1016/j.lindif.2024.102600

O'Dea, X. (2024). Generative AI: Is it a paradigm shift for higher education? *Studies in Higher Education*, *49*(5), 811–816. DOI: 10.1080/03075079.2024.2332944

O'Neil, C. (2016). *Weapons of math destruction: How big data increases inequality and threatens democracy*. Crown Publishing Group.

OECD. (2019). *Equity in education: Breaking down barriers to social mobility*. OECD Publishing. DOI: 10.1787/9789264073234-

OECD. (2019). *OECD principles on AI*. Organisation for Economic Co-operation and Development. https://legalinstruments.oecd.org/en/instruments/OECD-LEGAL-0449

OECD. (2021). *Digital education outlook 2021: Pushing the frontiers with artificial intelligence, blockchain and robots*. OECD Publishing., DOI: 10.1787/589b283f-

OECD. (2022). *"OECD Framework for the Classification of AI systems", OECD Digital Economy Papers, No. 323*. OECD Publishing. DOI: 10.1787/cb6d9eca-

OECD. (2023). *OECD digital education Outlook 2023: Towards an effective digital education ecosystem*. OECD Publishing. DOI: 10.1787/c74f03de-

OECD. (2023). *OECD framework for the classification of AI systems in education and training*. OECD Publishing. DOI: 10.1787/eb003e6e-

OECD. (2023). *PISA 2022 assessment and analytical framework*. OECD Publishing., DOI: 10.1787/dfe0bf9c-

OECD. (2024). *Education policy outlook 2024: Reshaping teaching into a thriving profession from ABCs to AI*. OECD Publishing., DOI: 10.1787/dd5140e4-

OECD. (2026). *OECD Education GPS*. https://gpseducation.oecd.org/

Ogunleye, B., Zakariyyah, K. I., Ajao, O., Olayinka, O., & Sharma, H. (2024). A systematic review of generative AI for teaching and learning practice. *Education Sciences*, *14*(6), 636. DOI: 10.3390/educsci14060636

Olakanmi, O. A., Akcayir, G., Ishola, O. M., & Demmans Epp, C. (2020). Using technology in special education: Current practices and trends. *Educational Technology Research and Development*, *68*(4), 1711–1738. DOI: 10.1007/s11423-020-09795-0

Oleribe, O. O. (2025, August). Leveraging and harnessing generative artificial intelligence to mitigate the burden of neurodevelopmental disorders (NDDs) in children. In *Healthcare* (Vol. 13, No. 15, p. 1898). MDPI. https://doi.org/DOI: 10.3390/healthcare13151898

Oliver, M. (1990). *The politics of disablement*. Red Globe Press., DOI: 10.1007/978-1-349-20895-1

Oliver, M. (1996). *Understanding disability: From theory to practice*. Macmillan. DOI: 10.1007/978-1-349-24269-6

OpenAI. (2023). *GPT-4 technical report* (arXiv:2303.08774). arXiv. /arXiv.2303.08774DOI: 10.48550

OpenAI. (2024). *GPT-4 technical report* (updated). OpenAI. DOI: 10.48550/arXiv.2303.08774

Ouherrou, N., Benmarrakchi, F., Elhammoumi, O., & El Kafi, J. (2018). A heuristic evaluation of an educational game for children with dyslexia. *2018 5th International Federation of Computer Science (CIST)*, 386–391. DOI: 10.1109/CIST.2018.8596393

Ouzzani, M., Hammady, H., Fedorowicz, Z., & Elmagarmid, A. (2016). Rayyan—A web and mobile app for systematic reviews. *Systematic Reviews*, *5*(1), 210. DOI: 10.1186/s13643-016-0384-4 PMID: 27919275

Oyebode, O., Fowles, J., Steeves, D., & Orji, R. (2023). Machine learning techniques in adaptive and personalized systems for health and wellness. *International Journal of Human-Computer Interaction*, *39*(9), 1938–1962. DOI: 10.1080/10447318.2022.2089085

Öztürk, H., & Aksoy, S. (2026). Tailored Learning at Scale: Leveraging Generative AI for Dynamic Content Creation in Special Education. In *Rethinking Education and Agency in the Age of Human-Generative AI Interaction* (pp. 95-116). IGI Global Scientific Publishing. https://doi.org/DOI: 10.4018/979-8-3373-1195-1.ch003

Padovano, A., & Cardamone, M. (2024). Towards human-AI collaboration in the competency-based curriculum development process: The case of industrial engineering and management education. *Computers and Education: Artificial Intelligence*, *7*, 100256. DOI: 10.1016/j.caeai.2024.100256

Page, M. J., McKenzie, J. E., Bossuyt, P. M., Boutron, I., Hoffmann, T. C., Mulrow, C. D., Shamseer, L., Tetzlaff, J. M., Akl, E. A., Brennan, S. E., Chou, R., Glanville, J., Grimshaw, J. M., Hróbjartsson, A., Lalu, M. M., Li, T., Loder, E. W., Mayo-Wilson, E., McDonald, S., & Moher, D. (2021). The PRISMA 2020 statement: An updated guideline for reporting systematic reviews. *BMJ (Clinical Research Ed.)*, *372*, 71. DOI: 10.1136/bmj.n71 PMID: 33782057

Paglialunga, A., & Melogno, S. (2025). The effectiveness of artificial intelligence-based interventions for students with learning disabilities: A systematic review. *Brain Sciences*, *15*(8), 806. Advance online publication. DOI: 10.3390/brainsci15080806 PMID: 40867139

Panda, P. K., Elwadhi, A., Gupta, D., Palayullakandi, A., Tomar, A., Singh, M., Vyas, A., Kumar, D., & Sharawat, I. K. (2024). Effectiveness of IMPUTE ADT-1 mobile application in children with autism spectrum disorder: An interim analysis of an ongoing randomized controlled trial. *Journal of Neurosciences in Rural Practice*, *15*(2), 262–269. DOI: 10.25259/JNRP_599_2023 PMID: 38746516

Papalexandratou, P., Stathopoulou, A., & Skanavis, C. (2024). The use of artificial intelligence in the education of students with learning disabilities. *Global Journal of Engineering and Technology Advances*, *21*(3), 229–240. DOI: 10.30574/gjeta.2024.21.3.0223

Park, E.-Y., & Shin, M. (2020). A meta-analysis of special education teachers' burnout. *SAGE Open*, *10*(2), 2158244020918297. DOI: 10.1177/2158244020918297

Park, J., & Choo, S. (2025). Generative AI prompt engineering for educators: Practical strategies. *Journal of Special Education Technology*, *40*(3), 411–417. DOI: 10.1177/01626434241298954

Patton, M. Q. (2015). *Qualitative research & evaluation methods* (4th ed.). Sage.

Pavlik, J. V. (2023). Collaborating with ChatGPT: Considering the implications of generative artificial intelligence for journalism and media education. *Journalism & Mass Communication Educator*, *78*(1), 84–93. DOI: 10.1177/10776958221149577

Pellegrino, J. W., & Hilton, M. L. (Eds.). (2012). *Education for life and work: Developing transferable knowledge and skills in the 21st century*. National Academies Press. DOI: 10.17226/13398

Pesovski, I., Santos, R., Henriques, R., & Trajkovik, V. (2024). Generative AI for customizable learning experiences. *Sustainability (Basel)*, *16*(7), 3034. DOI: 10.3390/su16073034

Peters, M. D. J., Godfrey, C., McInerney, P., Munn, Z., Tricco, A. C., Khalil, H., & Parker, D. (2020). Chapter 11: Scoping reviews. In Joanna Briggs Institute (Ed.), *JBI manual for evidence synthesis*. DOI: 10.46658/JBIMES-20-12

Pierrès, O., Darvishy, A., & Christen, M. (2025). Exploring the role of generative AI in higher education: Semi-structured interviews with students with disabilities. *Education and Information Technologies*, *30*(7), 8923–8952. DOI: 10.1007/s10639-024-13134-8

Podpečan, V. (2023). Can you dance? A study of child–robot interaction and emotional response using the NAO robot. *Multimodal Technologies and Interaction*, *7*(9), 85. DOI: 10.3390/mti7090085

Poobrasert, O., & Satsutthi, N. (2020). Developing of Kid Can Write as assistive technology for students with learning disabilities. In Miesenberger, K., Manduchi, R., Covarrubias Rodriguez, M., & Peňáz, P. (Eds.), Lecture notes in computer science: Vol. 12377. *Computers helping people with special needs. ICCHP 2020* (pp. 73–80). Springer., DOI: 10.1007/978-3-030-58805 2_9

Popenici, S. A. D., & Kerr, S. (2017). Exploring the impact of artificial intelligence on teaching and learning in higher education. *Research and Practice in Technology Enhanced Learning*, *12*(1), 22. DOI: 10.1186/s41039-017-0062-8 PMID: 30595727

Porayska-Pomsta, K. (2016). AI as a methodology for supporting educational praxis and teacher metacognition. *International Journal of Artificial Intelligence in Education*, *26*(2), 679–700. DOI: 10.1007/s40593-016-0101-4

Porayska-Pomsta, K. (2023). A manifesto for a proactively responsible AI in education. *International Journal of Artificial Intelligence in Education*, *34*(1), 73–86. DOI: 10.1007/s40593-023-00346-1

Porayska-Pomsta, K., Alcorn, A. M., Avramides, K., Beale, S., Bernardini, S., Foster, M. E., Frauenberger, C., Good, J., Guldberg, K., Keay-Bright, W., Kossyvaki, L., Lemon, O., Mademtzi, M., Menzies, R., Pain, H., Rajendran, G., Waller, A., Wass, S., & Smith, T. J. (2018). Blending human and artificial intelligence to support autistic children's social communication skills. *ACM Transactions on Computer-Human Interaction*, *25*(6), 1–35. DOI: 10.1145/3271484

Poulimenou, S.-M., Kaimara, P., & Deliyannis, I. (2023). Playing, Discovering, and Learning in Corfu Old Town. In Tomczyk, Ł. (Ed.), *New Media Pedagogy: Research Trends, Methodological Challenges and Successful Implementations* (pp. 168–185). Springer., DOI: 10.1007/978-3-031-44581-1_13

Prabagar, S., Mothkur, R., Swetha, C. B., Kurian, A., Pavithra, K., & Aarthi, S. (2026). Generative AI for Inclusive Special Education: Case Studies in Accessibility, Personalization, and Ethical Design. In *Shaping Inclusive Educational Policies and Practices With Generative AI* (pp. 205-236). IGI Global Scientific Publishing. https://doi.org/DOI: 10.4018/979-8-3373-3745-6.ch008

Prado, B. B., Gobbo, J. A.Junior, & Bezerra, B. S. (2023). Emerging themes for digital accessibility in education. *Sustainability (Basel)*, *15*(14), 11392. DOI: 10.3390/su151411392

Prasanthi, C. L., & Sushma, G. (2025). AI-based assistive system for correcting dysgraphia and dyscalculia in children. *2025 International Conference on Electrical, Communication and Computer Engineering (ICECCE)*, 1–6. DOI: 10.1109/ICECCE67514.2025.11257986

Pratschke, B. M. (2024). *Generative AI and education: Digital pedagogies, teaching innovation and learning design*. Springer Nature., DOI: 10.1007/978-3-031-67991-9

Preiksaitis, C., & Rose, C. (2023). Opportunities, challenges, and future directions of generative artificial intelligence in medical education: Scoping review. *JMIR Medical Education*, *9*(1), e48785. DOI: 10.2196/48785 PMID: 37862079

Prilop, C. N., Mah, D.-K., Jacobsen, L. J., Hansen, R. R., Weber, K. E., & Hoya, F. (2025). Generative AI in teacher education: Educators' perceptions of transformative potentials and the triadic nature of AI literacy explored through AI-enhanced methods. *Computers and Education: Artificial Intelligence*, *9*, 100471. DOI: 10.1016/j.caeai.2025.100471

Rahim, S., Sahar, G., Jabeen, G., Khatoon, S., & Angaiz, D. (2025). Harnessing generative AI: Reviewing applications, challenges, and solutions for out-of-school children in developing regions. *Sustainable Futures : An Applied Journal of Technology, Environment and Society*, *10*, 101206. DOI: 10.1016/j.sftr.2025.101206

Rakap, S. (2024). Chatting with GPT: Enhancing individualized education program goal development for novice special education teachers. *Journal of Special Education Technology*, *39*(3), 339–348. DOI: 10.1177/01626434231211295

Rane, N. (2023). Chatbot-Enhanced Teaching and Learning: Implementation Strategies, Challenges, and the Role of ChatGPT in Education. SSRN *Electronic Journal*. DOI: 10.2139/ssrn.4603204

Rangasrinivasan, S., Sumi Suresh, M. S., Olszewski, A., Setlur, S., Jayaraman, B., & Govindaraju, V. (2025). AI-enhanced child handwriting analysis: A framework for the early screening of dyslexia and dysgraphia. *SN Computer Science*, *6*(5), 399. Advance online publication. DOI: 10.1007/s42979-025-03927-0

Rappa, N. A., Nonis, K. P., Tang, K. S., Cooper, G., Cooper, M., & Sims, C. (2026). Can Generative AI support the learning agency of students with disability? A case study of an Australian secondary school. *British Journal of Educational Technology*, *57*(4), 924–942. Advance online publication. DOI: 10.1111/bjet.70048

Rasool, U., Li, J., & Liu, M. (2025). Perceptions of generative AI in teaching and learning: UTAUT and TPACK model-based study of teachers and students. *Acta Psychologica*, *261*, 105827. DOI: 10.1016/j.actpsy.2025.105827 PMID: 41166843

Rawls, J. (1971). *A theory of justice*. Harvard University Press. DOI: 10.4159/9780674042605

Redecker, C. (2017). *European framework for the digital competence of educators: DigCompEdu*. Publications Office of the European Union. DOI: 10.2760/159770

Rello, L., & Ballesteros, M. (2015). Detecting readers with dyslexia using machine learning with eye tracking measures. *Proceedings of the 12th Web for All Conference*. DOI: 10.1145/2745555.2746644

Renjith, P. R., & Jeeva, J. (2025). An intuitive number conversion system employing gestural recognition for students with special educational needs in Computer Science. *IJERI: International Journal of Educational Research and Innovation*, (23), 1–16. DOI: 10.46661/ijeri.10880

Rice, M., DePascal, N., Argüello de Jesús, J. T., McFeely, H., Traylor, A., & Heaviland, L. (2025). What is the machine? Teachers' professional learning about generative artificial intelligence as tutors for children. *Professional Development in Education*, *51*(3), 418–433. DOI: 10.1080/19415257.2024.2407413

Rizos, I., Foykas, E., & Georgakopoulos, S. V. (2024). Enhancing Mathematics Education for Students with Special Educational Needs through Generative AI: A Case Study in Greece. *Contemporary Educational Technology*, *16*(4), ep535. Advance online publication. DOI: 10.30935/cedtech/15487

Robinson, E., & Crane, L. (2025). Examining the impact of drama-based sessions on the social emotional well-being of Autistic pupils in a special school: A multi-informant qualitative study. *British Journal of Special Education*, *52*(2), 157–170. DOI: 10.1111/1467-8578.70000

Rodríguez-Ortiz, M. Á., Santana-Mancilla, P. C., & Anido-Rifón, L. E. (2025). Machine learning and generative AI in learning analytics for higher education: A systematic review of models, trends, and challenges. *Applied Sciences (Basel, Switzerland)*, *15*(15), 8679. DOI: 10.3390/app15158679

Rodríguez-Quevedo, Á., Lledó, G. L., Carreres, A. L., & Pérez-Vázquez, E. (2023). Emotion recognition in ASD students with social robotics: Case study. In *Proceedings of the 2023 XIII International Conference on Virtual Campus (JICV)* (pp. 1–4). IEEE. DOI: 10.1109/JICV59748.2023.10565661

Rokade, D., Jabde, M. K., & Patil, C. H. (2024). Screening application of dyslexia and dysgraphia using cognitive AI. *2024 10th International Conference on Smart Computing and Communication (ICSCC)*, 182–186. DOI: 10.1109/ICSCC62041.2024.10690576

Ronksley-Pavia, M., Nguyen, L., Wheeley, E., Rose, J., Neumann, M. M., Bigum, C., & Neumann, D. L. (2025). A scoping literature review of generative artificial intelligence for supporting neurodivergent school students. *Computers and Education: Artificial Intelligence*, *9*, 100437. DOI: 10.1016/j.caeai.2025.100437

Ronksley-Pavia, M., Ronksley-Pavia, S., & Bigum, C. (2025). Experimenting with generative ai to create personalized learning experiences for twice-exceptional and multi-exceptional neurodivergent students. *Journal of Advanced Academics, 36*(4), 601–639. DOI: 10.1177/1932202X251346349

Rose, D. H., & Meyer, A. (2002). *Teaching every student in the digital age: Universal design for learning*. ASCD.

Round, A., Baker, W. J., & Rayner, C. (2017). Using visual arts to encourage children with autism spectrum disorder to communicate their feelings and emotions. *Open Journal of Social Sciences, 5*, 90–108. DOI: 10.4236/jss.2017.510009

Rouse, M. (2008). Developing inclusive practice: A role for teachers and teacher education? *Education in the North, 16*(1), 6–13.

Ruiz-Rojas, L. I., Acosta-Vargas, P., De-Moreta-Llovet, J., & Gonzalez-Rodriguez, M. (2023). Empowering education with generative artificial intelligence tools: Approach with an instructional design matrix. *Sustainability (Basel), 15*(15), 11524. DOI: 10.3390/su151511524

Safi, M. F., Al Sadrani, B., & Mustafa, A. (2021). Virtual voice assistant applications improved expressive verbal abilities and social interactions in children with autism spectrum disorder: A Single-Subject experimental study. *International Journal of Developmental Disabilities, 69*(4), 555–567. DOI: 10.1080/20473869.2021.1977596 PMID: 37346256

Sağdıç, A., Elumar-Efe, E., & Sani-Bozkurt, S. (2024). GenAI, robots, and inclusive special education: autism spectrum disorder in the age of generative AI. In *Transforming education with generative AI: Prompt engineering and synthetic content creation* (pp. 309–326). IGI Global Scientific Publishing., DOI: 10.4018/979-8-3693-1351-0.ch015

Sakelariou, M. (2022). *Synchronous and Asynchronous Distance Teaching and Learning*. Pedio. (in Greek)

Sakowicz, M., & Hamidi, F. (2025). Exploring the role of generative AI in supporting students with disabilities, through the lens of universal design for learning. *American Journal of STEM Education, 15*, 1–22. DOI: 10.32674/yeyaaq64

Salih, S., Husain, O., Hamdan, M., Abdelsalam, S., Elshafie, H., & Motwakel, A. (2025). Transforming education with AI: A systematic review of ChatGPT's role in learning, academic practices, and institutional adoption. *Results in Engineering, 25*, 103837. DOI: 10.1016/j.rineng.2024.103837

Sandhu, R., Channi, H. K., Ghai, D., Cheema, G. S., & Kaur, M. (2024). An introduction to generative AI tools for education 2030. *Integrating generative AI in education to achieve sustainable development goals*, 1-28. https://doi.org/DOI: 10.4018/979-8-3693-2440-0.ch001

Savolainen, I., Ylinen, L., Grönroos, R., & Oksanen, A. (2026). AI transformation in working life: A systematic review of usage and attitudes towards AI among workers. *Digital Business*, *6*(1), 100162. DOI: 10.1016/j.digbus.2025.100162

Scherer, R., Siddiq, F., & Tondeur, J. (2019). The technology acceptance model (TAM): A meta-analytic structural equation modeling approach to explaining teachers' adoption of digital technology in education. *Computers & Education*, *128*, 13–35. DOI: 10.1016/j.compedu.2018.09.009

Schiff, D. (2021). Out of the laboratory and into the classroom: The future of artificial intelligence in education. *AI & Society*, *36*(1), 331–348. DOI: 10.1007/s00146-020-01033-8 PMID: 32836908

Schmucker, R. (2024). Harnessing machine learning and generative AI in tutoring systems. *XRDS: Crossroads. The ACM Magazine for Students*, *31*(1), 40–45. DOI: 10.1145/3688086

Schon, D. A. (1983). *The reflective practitioner: How professionals think in action*. Basic Books.

Scolari, C. A. (2009). Transmedia Storytelling: Implicit Consumers, Narrative Worlds, and Branding in Contemporary Media Production. *International Journal of Communication*, *3*, 586–606. http://www.guillaumenicaise.com/wp-content/uploads/2013/10/transmedia-storytelling.pdf

Selwyn, N. (2016). *Education and technology: Key issues and debates*. Bloomsbury Publishing.

Selwyn, N. (2019). *Should robots replace teachers? AI and the future of education*. Polity Press.

Selwyn, N. (2022). The future of AI and education: Some cautionary notes. *European Journal of Education*, *57*(4), 620–631. DOI: 10.1111/ejed.12532

Sen, A. (1992). *Inequality reexamined*. Oxford University Press.

Serpa-Andrade, L., Vélez, R. G., & Serpa-Andrade, G. (2022). Iteration of children with attention deficit disorder, impulsivity and hyperactivity, cognitive behavioral therapy, and artificial intelligence. In Ahram, T., & Taiar, R. (Eds.), *Human interaction, emerging technologies and future systems V* (Vol. 319, pp. 91–99). Springer., DOI: 10.1007/978-3-030-85540-6_12

Shaaban, T. S., & Mohamed, A. M. (2024). Exploring the effectiveness of augmented reality technology on reading comprehension skills among early childhood pupils with learning disabilities. *Journal of Computers in Education, 11*(2), 423–444. DOI: 10.1007/s40692-023-00269-9

Shaddock, A., O'Neill, S., Spinks, A., & van den Berg, H. (2015). *Students with disability in mainstream schools*. Australian Institute for Teaching and School Leadership.

Shadish, W. R., Cook, T. D., & Campbell, D. T. (2002). *Experimental and quasi-experimental designs for generalized causal inference*. Houghton Mifflin.

Shafik, W., Aslam, M. M., Namoun, A., & Tufail, A. (2025). Innovative Strategies for Educating Learners with Disabilities Using Generative Artificial Intelligence. In *AI Roles and Responsibilities in Education* (pp. 447–474). Springer Nature Switzerland., DOI: 10.1007/978-3-031-96855-6_19

Shapiro, L., & Stolz, S. A. (2019). Embodied cognition and its significance for education. *Theory and Research in Education, 17*(1), 19–39. DOI: 10.1177/1477878518822149

Shneiderman, B. (2020). Human-centered artificial intelligence: Reliable, safe & trustworthy. *International Journal of Human-Computer Interaction, 36*(6), 495–504. DOI: 10.1080/10447318.2020.1741118

Shneiderman, B. (2022). *Human-centered AI*. Oxford University Press. DOI: 10.1093/oso/9780192845290.001.0001

Shuper Engelhard, E. (2024). Working with unrepresented states in dance/movement therapy for children. *Body, Movement and Dance in Psychotherapy, 19*(4), 369–380. DOI: 10.1080/17432979.2024.2326010

Siegel, L. S. (2006). Perspectives on dyslexia. *Paediatrics & Child Health, 11*(9), 581–587. DOI: 10.1093/pch/11.9.581 PMID: 19030329

Şimşek, Ç., Küçük, L., & Akgün Yıldırım, E. (2019). Psychodrama practices in adolescents. *Journal of Academic Research in Nursing*. DOI: 10.5222/jaren.2019.48030

Singh, A. A., Jadon, J. S., Nayak, S. R., & Kumar, R. (2024). Conversation AI for verbal children with ASD to facilitate social interaction. In Pattnaik, P. K. (Eds.), *Proceedings of 3rd International Conference on Smart Computing and Cyber Security* (pp. 295–303). Springer. DOI: 10.1007/978-981-97-0573-3_24

Skordialos, E. (2024a). Empowering mathematics education in Greek primary schools: Bridging the divide through ICT integration and interactive boards for enhanced teacher ICT literacy. *European Journal of Education and Pedagogy*, *5*(2), 59–63. DOI: 10.24018/ejedu.2024.5.2.779

Skordialos, E. (2024b). Enhancing primary school geometry education: A comprehensive exploration of the Van Hiele model and ICT integration. *Science and Technology*, *8*(2), 1655–1659.

Skordialos, E., & Baralis, G. (2017). Mediated learning experience and its role in teaching fractions to pupils with learning difficulties. *International Journal of Learning and Teaching*, *10*(2), 158–165. DOI: 10.18844/ijlt.v10i2.3410

Slee, R. (2011). *The irregular school: Exclusion, schooling and inclusive education*. Routledge., DOI: 10.4324/9780203831564

Sohn, J. S., Lee, E., Kim, J. J., Oh, H. K., & Kim, E. (2025). Implementation of generative AI for the assessment and treatment of autism spectrum disorders: A scoping review. *Frontiers in Psychiatry*, *16*, 1628216. DOI: 10.3389/fpsyt.2025.1628216 PMID: 40766925

Sousa, A. E., & Cardoso, P. (2025). Use of generative AI by higher education students. *Electronics (Basel)*, *14*(7), 1258. DOI: 10.3390/electronics14071258

Southworth, J., Migliaccio, K., Glover, J., Glover, J., Reed, D., Sullivan, C., & Audiso, M. (2023). Developing a model for AI across the curriculum: Transforming the higher education landscape via innovation in AI literacy. *Computers and Education: Artificial Intelligence*, *4*, 100127. DOI: 10.1016/j.caeai.2023.100127

Stewart, C. M., Nugent, P., Williams Newman, R., Burns, M., Jeremiah, J., & Barrio, G.Jr. (2026). Preparing educational leaders for the age of AI: Lessons from a graduate course combining curriculum innovation and institutional inquiry. *International Journal of Management Education*, *24*(1), 101313. DOI: 10.1016/j.ijme.2025.101313

Stoll, L., Bolam, R., McMahon, A., Wallace, M., & Thomas, S. (2006). Professional learning communities: A review of the literature. *Journal of Educational Change*, *7*(4), 221–258. DOI: 10.1007/s10833-006-0001-8

Subban, P. (2006). Differentiated instruction: A research basis. *International Education Journal*, *7*(7), 935–947.

Su, J., & Yang, W. (2023). Artificial intelligence in early childhood education: A scoping review. *Computers and Education: Artificial Intelligence*, *5*, 100049. DOI: 10.1016/j.caeai.2022.100049

Su, J., & Yang, W. (2023). Unlocking the power of ChatGPT: A framework for applying generative AI in education. *ECNU Review of Education*, *6*(3), 355–366. DOI: 10.1177/20965311231168423

Sunmboye, K., Strafford, H., Noorestani, S., & Wilison-Pirie, M. (2025). Exploring the influence of artificial intelligence integration on personalized learning: A cross-sectional study of undergraduate medical students in the United Kingdom. *BMC Medical Education*, *25*(1), 570. DOI: 10.1186/s12909-025-07084-z PMID: 40247306

Su, S.-W., Hung, C.-H., Chen, L.-X., & Yuan, S.-M. (2024). Development of an AI-based system to enhance school counseling models for Asian elementary students with emotional disorders. *IEEE Access : Practical Innovations, Open Solutions*, *12*, 159121–159135. DOI: 10.1109/ACCESS.2024.3483456

Swaminathan, M., & Naik, T. (2025, October). Generative AI for Teachers with Vision Impairments in the Global South: A Bridge Too Far? In *Proceedings of the 27th International ACM SIGACCESS Conference on Computers and Accessibility* (pp. 1-18). https://doi.org/DOI: 10.1145/3663547.3746392

Taheri, A., Meghdari, A., & Mahoor, M. H. (2021). A close look at the imitation performance of children with autism and typically developing children using a robotic system. *International Journal of Social Robotics*, *13*(5), 1125–1147. DOI: 10.1007/s12369-020-00704-2

Tang, Q., Deng, W., Huang, Y., Wang, S., & Zhang, H. (2025). Can generative artificial intelligence be a good teaching assistant?—An empirical analysis based on generative ai-assisted teaching. *Journal of Computer Assisted Learning*, *41*(3), e70027. DOI: 10.1111/jcal.70027

Tang, Y., Chen, L., Chen, Z., Chen, W., Cai, Y., Du, Y., & Sun, L. (2024, May). Emoeden: Applying generative artificial intelligence to emotional learning for children with high-function autism. In *Proceedings of the 2024 CHI Conference on Human Factors in Computing Systems* (pp. 1-20). https://doi.org/DOI: 10.1145/3613904.3642899

Tan, Q. (2025). Reimagining teacher development in the era of generative AI: A scoping review. *Teaching and Teacher Education*, *168*, 105236. DOI: 10.1016/j.tate.2025.105236

Teo, T. (2011). Factors influencing teachers' intention to use technology: Model development and test. *Computers & Education*, *57*(4), 2432–2440. DOI: 10.1016/j.compedu.2011.06.008

Thomas, D. R., Gatz, E., Gupta, S., Aleven, V., & Koedinger, K. R. (2024). The neglected 15%: Positive effects of hybrid human-AI tutoring among students with disabilities. In Olney, A. M., Chounta, I. A., Liu, Z., Santos, O. C., & Bittencourt, I. I. (Eds.), Lecture Notes in Computer Science: Vol. 14829. *Artificial intelligence in education. AIED 2024* (pp. 409–423). Springer. DOI: 10.1007/978-3-031-64302-6_29

Timperley, H. (2011). *Realizing the power of professional learning*. Open University Press.

Tlili, A., Shehata, B., Adarkwah, M., Bozkurt, A., Hickey, D., Huang, R., & Agyemang, B. (2023). What if the devil is my guardian angel: ChatGPT as a case study of using chatbots in education. *Smart Learning Environments*, *10*(1), 15. DOI: 10.1186/s40561-023-00237-x

Tomczyk, Ł., & Majkut, A. (2025). Integrating AI in education: An analysis of factors influencing the acceptance, concerns, attitudes, competencies and use of generative artificial intelligence among Polish teachers. *Human Behavior and Emerging Technologies*, *2025*(1), 5599169. DOI: 10.1155/hbe2/5599169

Tomlinson, C. A. (2014). *The differentiated classroom: Responding to the needs of all learners* (2nd ed.). ASCD. https://rutamaestra.santillana.com.co/wp-content/uploads/2020/01/The-Differentiated-Classroom-Responding-to-the-Needs.pdf

Tomlinson, C. A. (2014). *The differentiated classroom: Responding to the needs of all learners* (2nd ed.). ASCD.

Tomlinson, C. A., Brighton, C., Hertberg, H., Callahan, C. M., Moon, T. R., Brimijoin, K., Conover, L. A., & Reynolds, T. (2003). Differentiating Instruction in Response to Student Readiness, Interest, and Learning Profile in Academically Diverse Classrooms: A Review of Literature. *Journal for the Education of the Gifted*, *27*(2–3), 119–145. DOI: 10.1177/016235320302700203

Tomlinson, C. A., & Imbeau, M. B. (2010). *Leading and managing a differentiated classroom*. ASCD.

Tonga, A. (2025). *The ascendant role of artificial intelligence in contemporary tertiary education*. SSRN Electronic Journal. DOI: 10.2139/ssrn.5126867

Torres, E. R., Rodríguez, R. C., & Briñez, E. T. (2023). Use of AI to improve teaching-learning process in children with special abilities. *LatIA*, *1*, 21–30. DOI: 10.62486/latia202321

Toyokawa, Y., Horikoshi, I., Majumdar, R., & Ogata, H. (2023). Challenges and opportunities of AI in inclusive education: A case study of data-enhanced active reading in Japan. *Smart Learning Environments*, *10*(1), 67. DOI: 10.1186/s40561-023-00286-2

Tozadore, D. C., Tozadore, M. C., & de Alcantara Gil, M. S. C. (2022). Supporting therapists' assessment in parent-mediated training through autonomous data collection. In Rodrigo, M. M., Matsuda, N., Cristea, A. I., & Dimitrova, V. (Eds.), *Artificial intelligence in education: Posters and late breaking results, workshops and tutorials, industry and innovation tracks, practitioners' and doctoral consortium* (Vol. 13356, pp. 560–563). Springer. DOI: 10.1007/978-3-031-11647-6_115

Triantafyllou, S. A., Georgiadis, C., & Sapounidis, T. (2025). Gamification in education and training: A literature review. *International Review of Education*, *71*(3), 483–517. DOI: 10.1007/s11159-024-10111-8

Tricco, A. C., Lillie, E., Zarin, W., O'Brien, K. K., Colquhoun, H., Levac, D., Moher, D., Peters, M. D. J., Horsley, T., Weeks, L., Hempel, S., Akl, E. A., Chang, C., McGowan, J., Stewart, L., Hartling, L., Aldcroft, A., Wilson, M. G., Garritty, C., & Straus, S. E. (2018). PRISMA extension for scoping reviews (PRISMA-ScR): Checklist and explanation. *Annals of Internal Medicine*, *169*(7), 467–473. DOI: 10.7326/M18-0850 PMID: 30178033

Tsibidaki, A. (2026). Listening to students with learning difficulties: Student voice, participation, and recommendations for inclusive practice in primary education. *Education Sciences*, *16*(4), 655. DOI: 10.3390/educsci16040655

Tsibidaki, A., Kogiami, A., Flagkou, A., Vagianou, S., & Trecha, S. (2020). Introducing teacher training for special and inclusive education in Cyprus, Germany, Great Britain, Greece, and Italy. *Journal of Education and Human Development*, *9*(2), 91–103. DOI: 10.15640/jehd.v9n2a10

Tsimpidaki, A. (2013). *Child with special needs, family and school. A relationship in interaction* (2nd ed.). Papazisis.

Turner, C. (2025, December 3). *50 years after the birth of special education, some fear for its future under Trump. NPR.* https://www.npr.org/2025/12/03/nx-s1-5591152/trump-special-education-disabilties-schools

Tu, Y., Chen, J., & Huang, C. (2025). Empowering personalized learning with generative AI. *Frontiers of Digital Education*, *2*(2), 56. Advance online publication. DOI: 10.1007/s44366-025-0056-9

Ulaş, R., Adcı, B., & İlker, Ö. (2025). Artificial intelligence and innovative educational technologies in students with learning disabilities: A systematic review. *Journal of Teacher Education and Lifelong Learning*, *7*(2), 248–262. DOI: 10.51535/tell.1725012

UNESCO. (1994). *The Salamanca statement and framework for action on special needs education*. UNESCO.

UNESCO. (1994). *The Salamanca statement and framework for action on special needs education*. UNESCO. https://unesdoc.unesco.org/

UNESCO. (2017). *A guide for ensuring inclusion and equity in education*. UNESCO. https://www.unesco.org/en/articles/guide-ensuring-inclusion-and-equity-education-0

UNESCO. (2019). *Artificial intelligence in education: Challenges and opportunities for sustainable development*. UNESCO. https://unesdoc.unesco.org/ark:/48223/pf0000366994

UNESCO. (2020). Global Education Monitoring Report 2020: Inclusion and education: All means all. Paris. In *Global Education Monitoring Report 2020: Inclusion and education: All means all*. UNESCO., DOI: 10.54676/JJNK6989

UNESCO. (2021). *AI and education: Guidance for policy-makers*. UNESCO Publishing.

UNESCO. (2021). *AI and education: Guidance for policy-makers. UNESCO*. https://unesdoc.unesco.org/ark:/48223/pf0000376709

UNESCO. (2021). *Recommendation on the ethics of artificial intelligence*. United Nations Educational, Scientific and Cultural Organization. https://unesdoc.unesco.org/ark:/48223/pf0000381137

UNESCO. (2021). *Reimagining our futures together: A new social contract for education*. UNESCO Publishing. https://unesdoc.unesco.org/ark:/48223/pf0000379707

UNESCO. (2023). *ChatGPT and artificial intelligence in higher education: Quick start guide*. UNESCO. https://www.iesalc.unesco.org/en/2023/04/14/chatgpt-and-artificial-intelligence-in-higher-education-quick-start-guide/

UNESCO. (2023). *Guidance for generative AI in education and research*. https://unesdoc.unesco.org/ark:/48223/pf0000386693

UNESCO. (2023). *Guidance for generative AI in education and research*. UNESCO Publishing.

UNESCO. (2023). *Guidance for Generative AI in Education and Research*. UNESCO.

UNESCO. (2023). *Guidance for generative AI in education and research*. UNESCO. https://unesdoc.unesco.org/ark:/48223/pf0000386693

UNESCO. (2024). *Global report on teachers: Addressing teacher shortages and transforming the profession*. https://www.unesco.org/en/articles/global-report-teachers-addressing-teacher-shortages-and-transforming-profession

United Nations Children's Fund. (2022). *Pulse check on digital learning*. https://www.unicef.org/reports/pulse-check-digital-learning

United Nations Educational, Scientific and Cultural Organization. (2021). *Recommendation on the ethics of artificial intelligence*. https://unesdoc.unesco.org/ark:/48223/pf0000381137

United Nations Educational, Scientific and Cultural Organization. (2023). *Guidance for generative AI in education and research*. https://unesdoc.unesco.org/ark:/48223/pf0000386693

United Nations. (2006). *Convention on the rights of persons with disabilities*. https://www.un.org/disabilities/documents/convention/convention_accessible_pdf.pdf

United Nations. (2006). *Convention on the Rights of Persons with Disabilities*. https://www.un.org/disabilities/documents/convention/convention_accessible_pdf.pdf

United Nations. (2006). *Convention on the rights of persons with disabilities*. https://www.un.org/disabilities/documents/convention/convoptprot-e.pdf

United Nations. (2006). *Convention on the rights of persons with disabilities*. United Nations. https://www.un.org/disabilities/documents/convention/convoptprot-e.pdf

United Nations. (2016). *General Comment No. 4 (2016), Article 24: Right to inclusive education* (CRPD/C/GC/4). Geneva: UN, Committee on the Rights of Persons with Disabilities. https://digitallibrary.un.org/record/1313836

United Nations. (2020). Sustainable development goals: Goal 4: Quality Education. Retrieved April 22, 2026, from https://www.un.org/sustainabledevelopment/education/

United Nations. (2022). *Artificial intelligence and the rights of persons with disabilities: Report of the Special Rapporteur on the rights of persons with disabilities*. United Nations Human Rights Council. https://documents.un.org/doc/undoc/gen/n22/683/45/pdf/n2268345.pdf

Upadhyay, A. K. (2024). Generative AI and training employees with special needs. *Strategic HR Review, 23*(6), 221–224. DOI: 10.1108/SHR-05-2024-0039

Usman, L., Muniyandi, R. C., Omar, K., & Mohamad, M. (2021). Advance machine learning methods for dyslexia biomarker detection: A review of implementation details and challenges. *IEEE Access : Practical Innovations, Open Solutions, 9*, 36879–36897. DOI: 10.1109/ACCESS.2021.3062709

Utepbayeva, A., Zhiyenbayeva, N., Assylbekova, L., & Tapalova, O. (2024). Artificial intelligence applications (Fluency SIS, Articulation Station Pro, and Apraxia Farm) in the psycholinguistic development of preschool children with speech disorders. *International Journal of Information and Education Technology (IJIET), 14*(7), 927–935. DOI: 10.18178/ijiet.2024.14.7.2119

Uygun, E. (2026). Clashing AIs: Artificial intelligence literacy and academic integrity in an EFL context. *Journal of Academic Ethics, 24*(1), 7. DOI: 10.1007/s10805-025-09676-2

Uygun, E., Cesur, K., Karahan, P., & Mikhailova, T. (2026). Participant perspectives on dropout factors and course enhancement needs in a general English MOOC. *Discover Education, 5*(1), 1126. Advance online publication. DOI: 10.1007/s44217-026-01126-4

Valencia, S., Cave, R., Kallarackal, K., Seaver, K., Terry, M., & Kane, S. K. (2023). "The less I type, the better": How AI language models can enhance or impede communication for AAC users. *Proceedings of the 2023 CHI Conference on Human Factors in Computing Systems*, Article 830, 1–14. DOI: 10.1145/3544548.3581560

Valentim, N. A., Dorça, F. A., Asnis, V. P., & Elias, N. C. (2023). The artificial intelligence as a technological resource in the application of tasks for the development of joint attention in children with autism. In M. C. Naldi & R. A. C. Bianchi (Eds.), *BRACIS 2023: Lecture notes in artificial intelligence:* Vol. 14195. *Proceedings of the 12th Brazilian conference on intelligent systems* (pp. 306–320). Springer. DOI: 10.1007/978-3-031-45368-7_20

Van Dijk, J. (2020). *The digital divide*. Polity Press., DOI: 10.1002/asi.24355

van Garderen, D., Lannin, J., Rodrigues, J., Smith, C. M., & Shahale, F. V. (2025). Using generative ai to create scaffolded instructional resources for students with disabilities. *Journal of Special Education Technology, 01626434251408056*, 01626434251408056. DOI: 10.1177/01626434251408056 PMID: 41953893

Varsik, S., & Vosberg, L. (2024). *The potential impact of Artificial Intelligence on equity and inclusion in education* (OECD Artificial Intelligence Papers, No. 23). OECD Publishing. https://doi.org/DOI: 10.1787/dee339a8-en

Venkatesh, V., & Bala, H. (2008). Technology acceptance model 3 and a research agenda on interventions. *Decision Sciences, 39*(2), 273–315. DOI: 10.1111/j.1540-5915.2008.00192.x

Venkatesh, V., & Davis, F. D. (2000). A theoretical extension of the technology acceptance model: Four longitudinal field studies. *Management Science, 46*(2), 186–204. DOI: 10.1287/mnsc.46.2.186.11926

Ventura, M. D. (2024). Self-adaptive learning algorithm as a tool for the development and strengthening of the dyslexic student's skills in the study of musical composition. In Fortino, G., Kumar, A., Swaroop, A., & Shukla, P. (Eds.), *Proceedings of Third International Conference on Computing and Communication Networks. ICCCN 2023. Lecture Notes in Networks and Systems* (Vol. 917, pp. 415–426). Springer. DOI: 10.1007/978-981-97-0892-5_33

Vhatkar, A., Pawar, V., & Chavan, P. (2024, August). Generative AI in education: a bibliometric and thematic analysis. In *2024 8th International Conference on Computing, Communication, Control and Automation (ICCUBEA)* (pp. 1-6). IEEE. https://doi.org/DOI: 10.1109/ICCUBEA61740.2024.10774819

Villar-Onrubia, D., Cachia, R., Rietz, C., Feltrero, R., Niemi, H., Hallissy, M., Reuter, R., Sánchez-Prieto, J. C., Vuorikari, R., & Punie, Y. (2025). *Generative artificial intelligence in secondary education: Uses and perceptions from the perspective of early adopters across five European countries*. Publications Office of the European Union., DOI: 10.2760/8636621

Vygotsky, L. S. (1978). *Mind in Society: The Development of Higher Psychological Processes (M. Cole, V. John-Steiner* (Scribner, S., & Souberman, E., Eds.; 2nd ed.). Harvard University Press.

Vygotsky, L. S. (1978). *Mind in society: The development of higher psychological processes*. Harvard University Press.

Wajuihian, S. O., & Naidoo, K. S. (2012). Dyslexia: An overview. *Optometry and Vision Development, 43*(1), 24–33.

Walker, J. (2017). Practical wisdom in professional education. In Peters, M. A. (Ed.), *Encyclopedia of educational philosophy and theory* (pp. 1836–1841). Springer., DOI: 10.1007/978-981-287-588-4_44

Waluyo, B., & Kusumastuti, S. (2024). Generative AI in student English learning in Thai higher education: More engagement, better outcomes? *Social Sciences & Humanities Open*, *10*, 101146. DOI: 10.1016/j.ssaho.2024.101146

Wang, C.-P. (2023). Training children with autism spectrum disorder, and children in general with AI robots related to the automatic organization of sentence menus and interaction design evaluation. *Expert Systems with Applications*, *229*, 120527. DOI: 10.1016/j.eswa.2023.120527

Wang, M., Muthu, B., & Sivaparthipan, C. B. (2022). Smart assistance to dyslexia students using artificial intelligence based augmentative alternative communication. *International Journal of Speech Technology*, *25*(2), 343–353. DOI: 10.1007/s10772-021-09921-0

Wang, M., Tlili, A., Khribi, M. K., Lo, C. K., & Huang, R. (2025). Generative artificial intelligence in special education: A systematic review through the lens of the mediated-action model. *Information Development*, *02666669251335655*, 02666669251335655. Advance online publication. DOI: 10.1177/02666669251335655

Wang, W., Xiao, J., & Diao, L. (2025). The effects of robots on children with autism spectrum disorder: A meta-analysis. *Journal of Autism and Developmental Disorders*. DOI: 10.1007/s10803-025-06883-z PMID: 40397050

Wang, X., Zhang, T., Han, B., Luo, W., Liu, W., Yang, Z., Disi, A., Sun, Y., & Yang, J. (2024). Wearable EEG neurofeedback based on machine learning algorithms for children with autism: A randomized, placebo-controlled study. *Current Medical Science*, *44*(6), 1141–1147. DOI: 10.1007/s11596-024-2938-3 PMID: 39565505

Warschauer, M., & Matuchniak, T. (2010). New technology and digital worlds: Analyzing evidence of equity in access, use, and outcomes. *Review of Research in Education*, *34*(1), 179–225. DOI: 10.3102/0091732X09349791

Waterfield, D. A., Coleman, O. F., Welker, N. P., Kennedy, M. J., Mcdonald, S. D., & Cook, B. G. (2026). IEPs in the age of AI: Examining IEP goals written with and without ChatGPT. *Journal of Special Education Technology*, *41*(1), 57–71. DOI: 10.1177/01626434251324592

Wehmeyer, M. L. (2006). Beyond Access: Ensuring Progress in the General Education Curriculum for Students with Severe Disabilities. *Research and Practice for Persons with Severe Disabilities : the Journal of TASH*, *31*(4), 322–326. DOI: 10.1177/154079690603100405

Weidinger, L., Uesato, J., Rauh, M., Griffin, C., Huang, P. S., Mellor, J., & Gabriel, I. (2023). Taxonomy of risks posed by language models. *Proceedings of the 2022 ACM FAccT Conference*, 214–229. DOI: 10.1145/3531146.3533088

Wenger, E. (1998). *Communities of practice: Learning, meaning, and identity*. Cambridge University Press. DOI: 10.1017/CBO9780511803932

Weng, Z., & Fu, Y. (2025). Generative AI in language education: Bridging divide and fostering inclusivity. *International Journal of Technology in Education*, *8*(2), 395–420. DOI: 10.46328/ijte.1056

Weng, Z., Guo, Y., & Chen, X. (2024). Using large language models to generate social stories for autistic students: A single-case experimental study. *Journal of Special Education Technology*, *39*(1), 45–61. DOI: 10.1177/01626434231195870

Weraduwa, S., Asanka, P. P. G. D., & Mahanama, T. V. (2024). Advanced computational techniques for dysgraphia prediction through handwriting recognition using machine learning and deep learning methods. *The Journal of Desk Research Review and Analysis*, *2*(1), 216–234. DOI: 10.4038/jdrra.v2i1.56

White, J., Fu, Q., Hays, S., Sandborn, M., Olea, C., Gilbert, H., Elnashar, A., Spencer-Smith, J., & Schmidt, D. C. (2023). *A prompt pattern catalog to enhance prompt engineering with ChatGPT*. DOI: 10.48550/arXiv.2302.11382

Whittlestone, J., Nyrup, R., Alexandrova, A., & Cave, S. (2021). The role and limits of principles in AI ethics: Towards a focus on tensions. *Proceedings of the 2019 AAAI/ACM AIES Conference*, 195–200. DOI: 10.1145/3306618.3314289

Williamson, B. (2017). *Big data in education: The digital future of learning, policy and practice*. SAGE Publications. DOI: 10.4135/9781529714920

Williamson, B., & Eynon, R. (2020). Historical threads, missing links, and future directions in AI in education. *Learning, Media and Technology*, *45*(3), 223–235. DOI: 10.1080/17439884.2020.1798995

Winarno, W., Muchtarom, M., & Fauziyah, H. (2024). Readiness of teachers in developing literacy and numeracy skills. *Journal of Education and Learning*, *18*(4), 1209–1218. DOI: 10.11591/edulearn.v18i4.21425

World Health Organization. (2022). *Global report on health equity for persons with disabilities*. https://www.who.int/publications/i/item/9789240063600

Wu, D., & Zhang, J. (2025). Generative artificial intelligence in secondary education: Applications and effects on students' innovation skills and digital literacy. *PLoS One*, *20*(5), e0323349. DOI: 10.1371/journal.pone.0323349 PMID: 40344078

Wu, J., Chen, K., Ma, Y., & Vomočilová, J. (2020). Early intervention for children with intellectual and developmental disability using drama therapy techniques. *Children and Youth Services Review, 109*, 104689. DOI: 10.1016/j.childyouth.2019.104689

Wu, R., & Yu, Z. (2024). Do AI chatbots improve students learning outcomes? Evidence from a meta-analysis. *British Journal of Educational Technology, 55*(1), 10–33. DOI: 10.1111/bjet.13334

Wu, T. F., Lo, H. S., Huang, T. C., & Hong, J. C. (2025, July). Developing a Generative AI Interview Skills Training System for Individuals with Disabilities. In *Proceedings of the 2025 9th International Conference on Education and Multimedia Technology* (pp. 343-349). https://doi.org/DOI: 10.1145/3761843.3761923

Xiaoyu, W., Zainuddin, Z., & Hai Leng, C. (2025). Generative artificial intelligence in pedagogical practices: A systematic review of empirical studies (2022–2024). *Cogent Education, 12*(1), 2485499. DOI: 10.1080/2331186X.2025.2485499

Xu, C. (2024). Exploring AI-based reciprocal eye engagement training to enhance dyadic behavior in individuals with alexithymia. In *Proceedings of the 2024 IEEE 3rd International Conference on Computing and Machine Intelligence (ICMI)* (pp. 1–7). IEEE. DOI: 10.1109/ICMI60790.2024.10586064

Xu, H., Binti Hussain, D. D. Y., Li, X., & Wang, L. (2025). Study on factors influencing primary and secondary school teachers' acceptance of ai tools based on the UTAUT model: A case study of Tianchang City, Anhui Province. *Journal of Education and Educational Research, 12*(3), 106–110. DOI: 10.54097/6kmfe396

Xu, X., Zhang, X., Khan, M., Dou, W., Xue, S., & Yu, S. (2020). A balanced virtual machine scheduling method for energy-performance trade-offs in cyber-physical cloud systems. *Future Generation Computer Systems, 105*, 789–799. DOI: 10.1016/j.future.2017.08.057

Yang, H. (2025). Harnessing generative AI: Exploring its impact on cognitive engagement, emotional engagement, learning retention, reward sensitivity, and motivation through reinforcement theory. *Learning and Motivation, 90*, 102136. DOI: 10.1016/j.lmot.2025.102136

Yan, L., Greiff, S., Teuber, Z., & Gašević, D. (2024). Promises and challenges of generative artificial intelligence for human learning. *Nature Human Behaviour, 8*(10), 1839–1850. DOI: 10.1038/s41562-024-02004-5 PMID: 39438686

Yan, P. (2024). Study of the Effect of Music on the Perceptual Abilities of Children with Autism. *International Journal of Education and Humanities, 16*(1), 296–298. DOI: 10.54097/hv3h0517

Yap, J. R., Aruthanan, T., & Chin, M. (2025). Artificial intelligence in dyslexia research and education: A scoping review. *IEEE Access : Practical Innovations, Open Solutions*, *13*, 7130–7145. DOI: 10.1109/ACCESS.2025.3526189

Yildiz Durak, H. (2023). Examining the effects of AI-based adaptive tools on self-regulation in students with ADHD. *Journal of Computer Assisted Learning*, *39*(4), 1143–1158. DOI: 10.1111/jcal.12809

Yu, H., & Guo, Y. (2023, June). Generative artificial intelligence empowers educational reform: current status, issues, and prospects. In *Frontiers in education* (Vol. 8, p. 1183162). Frontiers Media SA. https://doi.org/DOI: 10.3389/feduc.2023.1183162

Yu, H., Liu, Z., & Guo, Y. (2023, April). application Status, Problems and Future Prospects of Generative ai in education. In *2023 5th International Conference on Computer Science and Technologies in Education (CSTE)* (pp. 1-7). IEEE. https://doi.org/DOI: 10.1109/CSTE59648.2023.00065

Yuwono, E. I., Tjondronegoro, D., Riverola, C., & Loy, J. (2024). Co-creation in action: Bridging the knowledge gap in artificial intelligence among innovation champions. *Computers and Education: Artificial Intelligence*, *7*, 100272. DOI: 10.1016/j.caeai.2024.100272

Yuzaidey, N. A. M., Din, N. C., Ahmad, M., Ibrahim, N., Razak, R. A., & Harun, D. (2018). Interventions for children with dyslexia: A review on current intervention methods. *The Medical Journal of Malaysia*, *73*(5), 311–320. PMID: 30350811

Zaim, M., Arsyad, S., Waluyo, B., Ardi, H., Al Hafizh, M., Zakiyah, M., Syafitri, W., Nusi, A., & Hardiah, M. (2024). AI-powered EFL pedagogy: Integrating generative AI into university teaching preparation through UTAUT and activity theory. *Computers and Education: Artificial Intelligence*, *7*, 100335. DOI: 10.1016/j.caeai.2024.100335

Zakopoulos, V., Makri, A., Ntanos, S., & Tampakis, S. (2023). Drama/Theatre Performance in Education through the Use of Digital Technologies for Enhancing Students' Sustainability Awareness: A Literature Review. *Sustainability (Basel)*, *15*(18), 13387. DOI: 10.3390/su151813387

Zakopoulos, V., Xanthopoulou, P., & Makri, A. (2026). Integrating Digital Technologies in Theatre/Drama Education: A Systematic Literature Review. *Arts*, *15*(4), 72. DOI: 10.3390/arts15040072

Zallio, M., Ike, C. B., & Chivăran, C. (2025). Designing artificial intelligence: Exploring inclusion, diversity, equity, accessibility, and safety in human-centric emerging technologies. *AI*, *6*(7), 143. DOI: 10.3390/ai6070143

Zaranis, N., Baralis, G., & Skordialos, E. (2015). Comparing the effectiveness of using ICT for teaching addition in the first grade students based on Realistic Mathematics Education. *International Journal of Information Technology & Computer Science*, *19*(1), 127–138.

Zawacki-Richter, O., Marín, V. I., Bond, M., & Gouverneur, F. (2019). Systematic review of research on artificial intelligence applications in higher education: Where are the educators? *International Journal of Educational Technology in Higher Education*, *16*(39), 1–27. DOI: 10.1186/s41239-019-0171-0

Zhai, X. (2023). ChatGPT User Experience: Implications for Education. SSRN *Electronic Journal*, 1–18. DOI: 10.2139/ssrn.4312418

Zhai, X., Chu, X., Chai, C. S., Jong, M. S. Y., Istenic, A., Spector, M., Liu, J.-B., Yuan, J., & Li, Y. (2021). A review of artificial intelligence (AI) in education from 2010 to 2020. *Complexity*, *2021*(1), 8812542. DOI: 10.1155/2021/8812542

Zhang, X., Tlili, A., Nascimbeni, F., Burgos, D., Huang, R., Chang, T.-W., Jemni, M., & Khribi, M. K. (2020). Accessibility within open educational resources and practices for disabled learners: A systematic literature review. *Smart Learning Environments*, *7*(1), 1–19. DOI: 10.1186/s40561-019-0113-2

Zhao, S., Xiong, S. C., Pang, B., Tang, X., & He, P. (2025). Let AI read first: Enhancing reading abilities for individuals with dyslexia through artificial intelligence. *CHI EA '25: Extended Abstracts of the CHI Conference on Human Factors in Computing Systems*. DOI: 10.1145/3706599.3720113

Zhao, H., Amat, A. Z., Migovich, M., Swanson, A., Weitlauf, A. S., Warren, Z., & Sarkar, N. (2022). INC-Hg: An intelligent collaborative haptic-gripper virtual reality system. *ACM Transactions on Accessible Computing*, *15*(1), 1–23. DOI: 10.1145/3487606

Zhao, X., Chen, X., & Cox, A. (2026). Exploring the affordances of generative AI in academic writing for students with disabilities: A bottom-up approach to inform GenAI policies. *Policy Futures in Education*, *24*(1), 59–81. DOI: 10.1177/14782103251395436

Zhao, X., Cox, A., & Chen, X. (2025). The use of generative AI by students with disabilities in higher education. *The Internet and Higher Education*, *66*, 101014. DOI: 10.1016/j.iheduc.2025.101014

Zimmerman, B. J. (2002). Becoming a self-regulated learner: An overview. *Theory into Practice*, *41*(2), 64–70. DOI: 10.1207/s15430421tip4102_2

Zolna, K., Asselborn, T., Jolly, C., Casteran, L., Nguyen-Morel, M.-A., Johal, W., & Dillenbourg, P. (2019). *The dynamics of handwriting improves the automated diagnosis of dysgraphia*. DOI: 10.48550/arXiv.1906.07576

Zombron, A., Zaini, R., & Alnajashi, A. (2024). Beyond visual limits: Systems thinking for the visually impaired using generative AI. *International Journal on Responsibility*, *7*(1), 5. DOI: 10.62365/2576-0955.1123

Zoniou-Sideri, A. (2011). *Education and inclusion: Theory and practice*. Pedio. (in Greek)

Zoniou-Sideri, A., & Vlachou, A. (2006). Greek teachers' belief systems about disability and inclusive education. *International Journal of Inclusive Education*, *10*(4–5), 379–394. DOI: 10.1080/13603110500430690

About the Contributors

Assimina Tsibidaki is an Associate Professor of Special Education in the Department of Primary Education at the University of the Aegean (Greece). She specializes in the psychopedagogical aspects of special and inclusive education. Her research interests include learners with special educational needs and disabilities (SEND), family support, home-school collaboration, social support networks, disability and technology, and representations of disability in children's literature and cinema. She holds academic degrees from the Universities of Crete, the University of Manchester, and the University of the Aegean, and collaborates with international research institutions, such as UCL's Sleep Education and Research Laboratory. Her academic output includes authored books, edited volumes, and numerous national and international journal articles, as well as regular participation in scientific conferences. She also serves on several scientific and editorial committees. In addition to her academic role, she serves as Academic Lead of the Psychological and Counselling Support Center (Rhodes branch) of the University of the Aegean, Coordinator of the Center for Teaching and Learning Support (KEDIMA) of the University of the Aegean, and Chair of the Academic Coordination Committee of KEDIMA. Her work in these roles focuses on academic well-being, student support, and the enhancement of teaching and learning practices in higher education.

ApostolosKostas is an Assistant Professor in the Department of Primary Education, University of the Aegean, Greece. He teaches various undergraduate and postgraduate courses on "Digital Environments for Learning and Teaching". Since May 2018, he serves as Director of the Center for Lifelong Learning, University of the Aegean, while since 2020 he served as Tutor at the Hellenic Open University in the thematic "Open and Distance Education". He has participated in many national and EU-funded programs, and his research interests include e-Learning, Online Distance Education/Training, AI in Education, Lifelong Learning and Teacher Professional Development.

Charalampos Politis holds a BSc in Computer Science from the University of London and an MSc in Advanced Computing from Imperial College London, with a specialization in Logic and Artificial Intelligence. After completing his academic training, he worked as a software engineer before transitioning into product management in healthcare advertising and later in medical communications. For the past 13 years, he has led digital product teams focused on the design and development of digital products and platforms for healthcare professionals and patients. His professional interests focus on the application of AI to optimize medical education, with particular emphasis on personalized and adaptive learning, intelligent simulators, and data-driven insights that enhance engagement, efficiency, and educational outcomes.

Michail Terezakis is a PhD Candidate in the Department of Computer Engineering and Informatics at the University of Patras, Greece. He holds an Integrated Master's degree in Computer Engineering and Informatics from the same department. He works as a Lead Software Engineer at Yodiwo S.A. in Patras and contributes to the design and administration of the department's IT infrastructure through its Computer Center. His research and professional interests include large-scale data architectures, Internet of Things (IoT) systems, software engineering, and robotics. He has co-authored several peer-reviewed conference papers focusing on inclusive STEAM interventions, serious games, and digital platforms for young adults with intellectual disabilities. In addition, he co-manages the University of Patras Robotics Club, with a focus on the development of small autonomous robots.

***

Ashraf Alam is currently serving as an Assistant Professor in the Department of Education at NIT Calicut, Kerala, India. He has been recognised among the World's Top 2% Scientists by Stanford University and Elsevier. He earned his Ph.D. from IIT Kharagpur, where his research engaged with foundational concerns in educational policy, curriculum design, educational technology, philosophy of education, innovation in education, educational administration, governance, and pedagogical transformation. His academic contributions include more than 95 Scopus-indexed publications and over 100 conference presentations delivered at national and international academic forums. His work has appeared in reputed research publication platforms including Elsevier, Springer, Taylor & Francis, CRC Press, Routledge, Atlantis Press, Springer Nature, Palgrave Macmillan, and IEEE. His work is grounded in a transdisciplinary orientation that draws from educational sciences, digital pedagogy, curriculum theory, learning analytics, sustainability education, instructional design, artificial intelligence, ethics of technology, and socio-technical studies. Dr. Ashraf's scholarship strives to interrogate and expand the boundaries of educational thought by examining the epistemological, ethical, and social dimensions of digital and post-digital pedagogies. His work critically engages with the changing nature of knowledge production, learner agency, pedagogical mediation, and institutional transformation in technologically saturated educational environments. He is particularly invested in advancing inclusive digital learning, gamified instructional strategies, AI-mediated educational ecosystems, and ethically governed technology integration in education. His research agenda is animated by the pursuit of design-oriented, ethically attuned, and contextually responsive frameworks that can support meaningful educational reform. Through his work, he seeks to contribute to the development of pedagogical models that are not only technologically innovative but also socially just, epistemically inclusive, developmentally sensitive, and aligned with the broader goals of sustainable and human-centred education.

Panagiotis Alexopoulos is affiliated with the Department of Primary Education at the University of the Aegean, Greece.

Theoxaris Anastasiadis is a PhD Candidate at the Ionian University, with a research focus on algorithmic techniques of Data Science and their applications in Marketing. He holds two postgraduate degrees, in New Media and Digital Marketing, as well as in Science Teaching, while he holds a degree in Computer Science. His professional experience includes adult education, IT teaching and digital skills development. He specializes in Artificial Intelligence, Machine Learning, NLP, Digital Marketing and Python application development. It combines academic knowledge with practical technological orientation.

Ioannis Arvanitakis has been teaching Computer Science in primary and secondary education since 2004. Since 2013, he has been working at the Experimental Primary School of Florina, teaching computer science and educational robotics. He holds a Bachelor's degree in Applied Informatics from the University of Macedonia and a Master's degree in Pedagogy, with a specialization in School Pedagogy (Teaching Methodology and Curricula) and New Technologies. He is currently a PhD candidate in the Department of Primary Education at the University of Western Macedonia. In parallel, he is the founder and pedagogical mentor of the award-winning student group "Young Hackers," active since the 2016–2017 academic year, which engages upper-grade primary school students from across the region in computing, programming, and educational robotics. The group has received multiple national and international distinctions and maintains close collaboration with the Florina Educational Innovation Hub.

Ioannis Avlogiaris is an undergraduate student in the Department of Psychology at Democritus University of Thrace, Greece. His academic interests include personality psychology, mental health, emotional regulation, and interpersonal relationships.

Çiğdem Cesur received her BA degree in English Language Education from Hacettepe University in 2005. She later completed her MA degree in English Language Education at Çanakkale Onsekiz Mart University in 2009. She has been working at Çanakkale Onsekiz Mart University School of Foreign Languages since 2006 as an instructor/lecturer of English. She currently serves as a lecturer in the Department of Foreign Languages and has also held administrative roles, including Unit Coordinator since 2020 and Deputy Head of Department in Modern Languages since 2024. Her academic background also includes an undergraduate degree in Child Development from Istanbul University. Her areas of teaching include foreign language teaching, early childhood language education, inclusive language teaching, and teaching English through games.

Vana Chiou is member of the Laboratory Teaching Staff at the Department of Geography, University of the Aegean (Greece) in Educational Psychology. Her research interests include contemporary methods of teaching, didactics in teaching geography, teacher training, and inclusion in education. She is co-editor of the book series "Voices from the Classroom" (Waxman publications). Her published work includes editing books, chapters in books, and articles in Greek and international journals. She is a participant in and co-coordinator of different European projects.

Prashant Kumar Choudhary is an Assistant Professor at the Lakshmibai National Institute of Physical Education, Gwalior, India.

Mustafa Yunus Eryaman is a leading figure in education policy and research, with a distinguished career spanning diverse academic institutions and leadership roles. He currently serves as Professor of Curriculum and Instruction at Canakkale Onsekiz Mart University, Turkey, and has held prestigious appointments such as President of the World Education Research Association and Research Expert at the European Commission. Dr. Eryaman's academic journey reflects his commitment to international collaboration and intellectual exchange. He was a DAAD-TUBITAK Professor at the University of Hamburg, Germany, and a Visiting Professor and Honorary Research Fellow at the Institute for Policy Studies in Education at London Metropolitan University, UK. His research interests encompass educational policy, philosophy of education, curriculum theory and research, qualitative inquiry, and progressive education, as evidenced by his publications like "Teaching as Practical Philosophy" and his editorship of renowned book series like "Evidence, Science and

Public Good in Education" with Springer and "Global perspectives on Education Research" with Routledge. He received his MEd from the University of Missouri-Columbia and his PhD from the University of Illinois at Urbana-Champaign, USA. He currently serves as the regional editor of the "Bloomsbury Education and Childhood Studies" series of Bloomsbury Publishing and editor of the SAGE Special Collection entitled "The Evolving Landscape of Qualitative Research: Embracing the Potential and Navigating the Challenges of Artificial Intelligence." Dr. Eryaman's dedication to advancing knowledge extends beyond his own scholarship. He serves as the managing editor of the "Educational Policy Analysis and Strategic Research," and has curated impactful edited volumes like "Evidence and Public Good in Educational Policy, Research and Practice" and "International Handbook of Progressive Education."

Emmanuel Fokides is an Associate Professor in the Department of Primary School Education, University of the Aegean, Greece. His courses focus on the educational uses of emerging technologies, virtual reality, digital storytelling, augmented reality, and serious games. Since 1994, he is involved in a number of research projects regarding distance and lifelong learning and the educational uses of virtual and augmented reality. His work is published in several conference proceedings, chapters in edited books, and journals. He is also the co-author of two books.

Polyxeni Kaimara is a post-doctoral researcher at the Department of Audio and Visual Arts of the Ionian University and a member of the Institute for Games Research (IGR) and the Interactive Arts Laboratory InArts.eu. She holds a PhD in Psychoeducational Approaches and Digital Transformation in Inclusive Education, focusing on the design and development of interactive and gamified educational applications for both typically developing students and learners with special educational needs within inclusive learning environments. She also holds three postgraduate qualifications: an MSc in School–Developmental Psychology, an MSc in Public Health with a specialization in Human Behavior, and a Diploma in Counseling. She has extensive teaching experience in higher education, contributing to undergraduate and postgraduate programs in psychology, educational technology, and inclusive education. She serves as an assessor in adult certification examinations and supervises psychology students during their practicum. Her research interests include the design and evaluation of educational systems for special and inclusive education, emerging technologies, transmedia storytelling for learning, and the development of digital educational games. Professionally, she works as a Licensed BSc Psychologist within the 3rd Regional Health Authority of Macedonia, serving at the General Hospital of Florina and at the Center for Physical Medicine and

Rehabilitation. She has also worked at the Psychiatric Clinic of the Corfu General Hospital. She has authored and co-authored numerous research papers published in high IF international journals, edited volumes, and conference proceedings.

Maria Kladaki is an Associate Professor in the Department of Primary Education, University of the Aegean (Rhodes-Greece). She has a postgraduate degree M.A. in Education specializing in Theatre and Dramatic Play and a Ph.D in Theatre Studies (Panteion University of Athens, Greece). Her field of research includes drama in education, theory/ history of theatre, gender issues in theatrical works for children, theatre for young audiences, theatre education, and educational drama.

Chrysanthi Koza is a Special Education Advisor in the Dodecanese. She holds a PhD from the University of the Aegean and a Master's degree in Educational Sciences with a focus on the use of New Technologies. Her research interests focus on the pedagogical use of folk tales in combination with Information and Communication Technologies (ICT) and literate orality. She has participated in conferences with presentations on educational topics and has published articles in academic journals and edited volumes.

Christina Krystamtsi is a PhD Candidate in the Department of Primary Education at the University of the Aegean, Greece. Her research interests focus on family functioning, special education, and preschool education within inclusive learning environments. She holds a bachelor's degree in Preschool Education from the University of Ioannina and a master's degree with distinction from the University of the Peloponnese. She has also received training in special education, intercultural education, Braille, and digital skills.

Georgia Lazakidou is an experienced educator with a strong background in educational administration and professional development. She currently serves as an Education Advisor for Primary Education in the South Aegean Region and has worked as an Adjunct Tutor at the Hellenic Open University since 2020. Her professional expertise includes e-learning, human resources consulting, coaching, lecturing, and organizational development. She holds a PhD in Information Technology and a master's degree in Economics Education from the University of Piraeus.

Konstantinos Mastrothanasis holds a PhD from the Department of Primary Education at the University of the Aegean and is currently a postdoctoral researcher at the Medical School of the National and Kapodistrian University of Athens. His research interests include applied theater for education, health, and psychosocial well-being with a particular focus on children and young people, especially during times of crises, pandemics, and disasters. His work also emphasizes education, integrating innovative approaches to teaching and learning, and it explores how art can be utilized as a tool for psychosocial development. He also teaches at multiple academic institutions, including the Open University of Cyprus, the University of the Aegean, and ASPETE.

Saurabh Pandey is working as Assistant Professor in United college of Engineering and Research, Prayagraj. He has over 16 years of experience in academics. He has published papers in the field of Electrical and Electronics Engineering. His area of interest is application of Electrical and Electronics Engineering.

Sohom Saha is affiliated with the Lakshmibai National Institute of Physical Education, Gwalior, India.

Mahendra Kumar Singh is a Senior Professor at the Lakshmibai National Institute of Physical Education, Gwalior, India.

Emmanouil Skordialos holds a PhD in Educational Sciences from the National and Kapodistrian University of Athens, Greece, specializing in Realistic Mathematics Education (RME), mobile learning, and ICT integration in primary mathematics education. His academic background includes degrees from the University of Athens (Department of Primary Education, the Faculty of Philosophy, the Department of Psychology, and the Faculty of Theology), as well as master's degrees in Special Education, ICT in Education, and New Technologies, Innovation and Didactics in Educational Sciences. He is a permanent primary school teacher in Greek public education and a Lecturer at the School of Pedagogical and Technological Education (ASPETE), where he teaches Educational Methodology and Educational Technology. His research focuses on technology-enhanced mathematics education, Generative AI in education, ICT integration, educational innovation, teacher professional development, and the cognitive and affective dimensions of early mathematical learning. He has published in national and international peer-reviewed journals and conference proceedings on mathematics education, educational technology, and innovative teaching approaches. His work integrates teaching, research, and teacher education, contributing to the development of evidence-informed practices that support meaningful and inclusive learning in contemporary educational settings.

Kyriaki Stavrou, PhD, AFBPsS, CPsychol, is a Postdoctoral Researcher at the Medical School of the National and Kapodistrian University of Athens in collaboration with Portland State University, USA, and a Scientific Collaborator at Aiginiteio Hospital. She teaches psychology courses at Greek universities.

Her research focuses on developmental and clinical psychology, developmental psychopathology, neurodevelopmental disorders, child and adolescent mental health, and special and inclusive education.

Ilias Vasileiadis is a School Psychologist, Psychotherapist and Group Encourager. He completed his undergraduate and postgraduate studies at the Aristotle University of Thessaloniki. He completed his doctoral research in Special Education at the Department of Pedagogy of the Aristotle University of Thessaloniki. He has a rich scientific literature, as well as experience in the coordination of seminars and actively participates in scientific conferences. His research interests focus on the inclusion of students with disabilities, emotional and social empowerment in the school context.

Index

A

C

D

E

G

H

I

L

M

N

P

R

S

T

U

V

W

www.ingramcontent.com/pod-product-compliance
Lightning Source LLC
LaVergne TN
LVHW081248011026
849162LV00004BA/659
* 9 7 9 8 3 3 7 3 9 1 6 9 4 *